GO!
with Microsoft®

Outlook 2007
Comprehensive
First Edition

Shelley Gaskin and Carol L. Martin

D1307539

PEARSON

Upper Saddle River, New Jersey

Library of Congress Cataloging-in-Publication Data

Gaskin, Shelley.
Go! with Outlook comprehensive / Shelley Gaskin and Carol L. Martin.—1st ed.
    p. cm.
  Includes index.
  ISBN 0-13-500124-2
  1. Microsoft Outlook. 2. Time management—Computer programs. 3. Personal information management—Computer
programs. 4. Electronic mail systems—Computer programs. I. Martin, Carol L., 1949- II. Title.

HF5548.4.M5255G374 2009
005.5'7—dc22

2008029552

Vice President/Publisher: Natalie E. Anderson	**Manager of Rights & Permissions:** Charles Morris
Editor in Chief: Michael Payne	**Senior Operations Specialist:** Nick Sklitsis
AVP/Executive Acquisitions Editor, Print: Stephanie Wall	**Operations Specialist:** Natacha St. Hill Moore
	Senior Art Director: Jonathan Boylan
Director, Product Development: Pamela Hersperger	**Art Director:** Anthony Gemmellaro
Product Development Manager: Eileen Bien Calabro	**AV Project Manager:** Rhonda Aversa
Editorial Project Manager: Terenia McHenry	**Cover Design:** Anthony Gemmellaro
Development Editor: Harrison Ridge Services, LLC	**Cover Illustration/Photo:** Courtesy of Getty Images, Inc./Marvin Mattelson
AVP/Executive Editor, Media: Richard Keaveny	
AVP/Executive Producer: Lisa Strite	**Director, Image Resource Center:** Melinda Patelli
Content Development Manager: Cathi Profitko	**Manager, Rights and Permissions:** Zina Arabia
Editorial Media Project Manager: Alana Coles	**Manager: Visual Research:** Beth Brenzel
Production Media Project Manager: Lorena Cerisano	**Manager, Cover Visual Research & Permissions:** Karen Sanatar
Senior Marketing Manager: Tori Olsen-Alves	
Marketing Assistant: Angela Frey	**Composition:** GGS Book Services
Senior Sales Associate: Rebecca Scott	**Full-Service Project Management:** GGS Book Services
Senior Managing Editor: Cynthia Zonneveld	**Printer/Binder:** RR Donnelly/Willard
Associate Managing Editor: Camille Trentacoste	**Cover Printer:** Phoenix Color
Production Project Manager: Mike Lackey	**Typeface:** 10/12 Times

Credits and acknowledgments borrowed from other sources and reproduced, with permission, in this textbook are as
follows: page 2: © Guy Cali/PAL Operation Team; page 90: © Jeffrey Lepore/Photo Researchers, Inc.; page 180: Nelson
Hancock © Rough Guides; page 256: © Greg Stott/Masterfile; page 340: © Linda Whitwam © Dorling Kindersley; page 438:
© Peter R. Skinner/Mira.com.

Microsoft, Windows, Word, PowerPoint, Outlook, FrontPage, Visual Basic, MSN, The Microsoft Network, and/or other
Microsoft products referenced herein are either trademarks or registered trademarks of the Microsoft Corporation in the
U.S.A. and other countries. Screen shots and icons reprinted with permission from the Microsoft Corporation. This book is
not sponsored or endorsed by or affiliated with the Microsoft Corporation.

Pearson Education Ltd., London	Pearson Education North Asia Ltd., Hong Kong
Pearson Education Singapore, Pte. Ltd	Pearson Educación de Mexico, S.A. de C.V.
Pearson Education, Canada, Inc.	Pearson Education Malaysia, Pte. Ltd.
Pearson Education¬Japan	Pearson Education, Upper Saddle River, New Jersey
Pearson Education Australia PTY, Limited	

Prentice Hall
is an imprint of

www.pearsonhighered.com

10 9 8 7 6 5 4 3 2 1
ISBN-13: 978-0-13-500124-0
ISBN-10: 0-13-500124-2

Contents in Brief

Table of Contents

Letter from the Editor

Dear Instructors and Students,

The primary goal of the *GO!* Series is two-fold. The first goal is to help instructors teach the course they want in less time. The second goal is to provide students with the skills to solve business problems using the computer as a tool, for both themselves and the organization for which they might be employed.

The *GO!* Series was originally created by Series Editor Shelley Gaskin and published with the release of Microsoft Office 2003. Her ideas came from years of using textbooks that didn't meet all the needs of today's diverse classroom and that were too confusing for students. Shelley continues to enhance the series by ensuring we stay true to our vision of developing quality instruction and useful classroom tools.

But we also need your input and ideas.

Over time, the *GO!* Series has evolved based on direct feedback from instructors and students using the series. *We are the publisher that listens.* To publish a textbook that works for you, it's critical that we continue to listen to this feedback. It's important to me to talk with you and hear your stories about using *GO!* Your voice can make a difference.

My hope is that this letter will inspire you to write me an e-mail and share your thoughts on using the *GO!* Series.

Stephanie Wall
Executive Editor, *GO!* Series
stephanie.wall@pearson.com

GO! System Contributors

We thank the following people for their hard work and support in making the *GO!* System all that it is!

Additional Author Support

Coyle, Diane	Montgomery County Community College
Fry, Susan	Boise State
Townsend, Kris	Spokane Falls Community College
Stroup, Tracey	

Instructor Resource Authors

Amer, Beverly	Northern Arizona University	Paterson, Jim	Paradise Valley Community College
Boito, Nancy	Harrisburg Area Community College	Prince, Lisa	Missouri State
Coyle, Diane	Montgomery County Community College	Rodgers, Gwen	Southern Nazarene University
		Ruymann, Amy	Burlington Community College
Dawson, Tamara	Southern Nazarene University	Ryan, Bob	Montgomery County Community College
Driskel, Loretta	Niagara County Community College		
Elliott, Melissa	Odessa College	Smith, Diane	Henry Ford College
Fry, Susan	Boise State	Spangler, Candice	Columbus State Community College
Geoghan, Debra	Bucks County Community College	Thompson, Joyce	Lehigh Carbon Community College
Hearn, Barbara	Community College of Philadelphia	Tiffany, Janine	Reading Area Community College
Jones, Stephanie	South Plains College	Watt, Adrienne	Douglas College
Madsen, Donna	Kirkwood Community College	Weaver, Paul	Bossier Parish Community College
Meck, Kari	Harrisburg Area Community College	Weber, Sandy	Gateway Technical College
Miller, Cindy	Ivy Tech	Wood, Dawn	
Nowakowski, Tony	Buffalo State	Weissman, Jonathan	Finger Lakes Community College
Pace, Phyllis	Queensborough Community College		

Super Reviewers

Brotherton, Cathy	Riverside Community College		
Cates, Wally	Central New Mexico Community College		
Cone, Bill	Northern Arizona University		
Coverdale, John	Riverside Community College		
Foster, Nancy	Baker College		
Helfand, Terri	Chaffey College	Rodgers, Gwen	Southern Nazarene University
Hibbert, Marilyn	Salt Lake Community College	Smolenski, Robert	Delaware Community College
Holliday, Mardi	Community College of Philadelphia	Spangler, Candice	Columbus State Community College
Jerry, Gina	Santa Monica College		
Martin, Carol	Harrisburg Area Community College	Thompson, Joyce	Lehigh Carbon Community College
Maurer, Trina	Odessa College		
Meck, Kari	Harrisburg Area Community College	Weber, Sandy	Gateway Technical College
Miller, Cindy	Ivy Tech Community College	Wells, Lorna	Salt Lake Community College
Nielson, Phil	Salt Lake Community College	Zaboski, Maureen	University of Scranton

Technical Editors

Janice Snyder
Joyce Nielsen
Colette Eisele
Janet Pickard
Mara Zebest
Lindsey Allen
William Daley
LeeAnn Bates

Student Reviewers

Allen, John	Asheville-Buncombe Tech Community College	Davis, Brandon	Northern Michigan University
		Davis, Christen	Central Washington University
Alexander, Steven	St. Johns River Community College	Den Boer, Lance	Central Washington University
Alexander, Melissa	Tulsa Community College	Dix, Jessica	Central Washington University
Bolz, Stephanie	Northern Michigan University	Moeller, Jeffrey	Northern Michigan University
Berner, Ashley	Central Washington University	Downs, Elizabeth	Central Washington University
Boomer, Michelle	Northern Michigan University	Erickson, Mike	Ball State University
Busse, Brennan	Northern Michigan University	Gadomski, Amanda	Northern Michigan University
Butkey, Maura	Central Washington University	Gyselinck, Craig	Central Washington University
Christensen, Kaylie	Northern Michigan University	Harrison, Margo	Central Washington University
Connally, Brianna	Central Washington University	Heacox, Kate	Central Washington University

Hill, Cheretta	Northwestern State University
Innis, Tim	Tulsa Community College
Jarboe, Aaron	Central Washington University
Klein, Colleen	Northern Michigan University
Moeller, Jeffrey	Northern Michigan University
Nicholson, Regina	Athens Tech College
Niehaus, Kristina	Northern Michigan University
Nisa, Zaibun	Santa Rosa Community College
Nunez, Nohelia	Santa Rosa Community College
Oak, Samantha	Central Washington University
Oertii, Monica	Central Washington University
Palenshus, Juliet	Central Washington University
Pohl, Amanda	Northern Michigan University
Presnell, Randy	Central Washington University
Ritner, April	Northern Michigan University
Rodriguez, Flavia	Northwestern State University
Roberts, Corey	Tulsa Community College
Rossi, Jessica Ann	Central Washington University
Shafapay, Natasha	Central Washington University
Shanahan, Megan	Northern Michigan University
Teska, Erika	Hawaii Pacific University
Traub, Amy	Northern Michigan University
Underwood, Katie	Central Washington University
Walters, Kim	Central Washington University
Wilson, Kelsie	Central Washington University
Wilson, Amanda	Green River Community College

Series Reviewers

Abraham, Reni	Houston Community College
Agatston, Ann	Agatston Consulting Technical College
Alexander, Melody	Ball Sate University
Alejandro, Manuel	Southwest Texas Junior College
Ali, Farha	Lander University
Amici, Penny	Harrisburg Area Community College
Anderson, Patty A.	Lake City Community College
Andrews, Wilma	Virginia Commonwealth College, Nebraska University
Anik, Mazhar	Tiffin University
Armstrong, Gary	Shippensburg University
Atkins, Bonnie	Delaware Technical Community College
Bachand, LaDonna	Santa Rosa Community College
Bagui, Sikha	University of West Florida
Beecroft, Anita	Kwantlen University College
Bell, Paula	Lock Haven College
Belton, Linda	Springfield Tech. Community College
Bennett, Judith	Sam Houston State University
Bhatia, Sai	Riverside Community College
Bishop, Frances	DeVry Institute—Alpharetta (ATL)
Blaszkiewicz, Holly	Ivy Tech Community College/Region 1
Branigan, Dave	DeVry University
Bray, Patricia	Allegany College of Maryland
Brotherton, Cathy	Riverside Community College
Buehler, Lesley	Ohlone College
Buell, C	Central Oregon Community College
Byars, Pat	Brookhaven College
Byrd, Lynn	Delta State University, Cleveland, Mississippi
Cacace, Richard N.	Pensacola Junior College
Cadenhead, Charles	Brookhaven College
Calhoun, Ric	Gordon College
Cameron, Eric	Passaic Community College
Carriker, Sandra	North Shore Community College
Cannamore, Madie	Kennedy King
Carreon, Cleda	Indiana University—Purdue University, Indianapolis
Chaffin, Catherine	Shawnee State University
Chauvin, Marg	Palm Beach Community College, Boca Raton
Challa, Chandrashekar	Virginia State University
Chamlou, Afsaneh	NOVA Alexandria
Chapman, Pam	Wabaunsee Community College
Christensen, Dan	Iowa Western Community College
Clay, Betty	Southeastern Oklahoma State University
Collins, Linda D.	Mesa Community College
Conroy-Link, Janet	Holy Family College
Cosgrove, Janet	Northwestern CT Community
Courtney, Kevin	Hillsborough Community College
Cox, Rollie	Madison Area Technical College
Crawford, Hiram	Olive Harvey College
Crawford, Thomasina	Miami-Dade College, Kendall Campus
Credico, Grace	Lethbridge Community College
Crenshaw, Richard	Miami Dade Community College, North
Crespo, Beverly	Mt. San Antonio College
Crossley, Connie	Cincinnati State Technical Community College
Curik, Mary	Central New Mexico Community College
De Arazoza, Ralph	Miami Dade Community College
Danno, John	DeVry University/Keller Graduate School
Davis, Phillip	Del Mar College
DeHerrera, Laurie	Pikes Peak Community College
Delk, Dr. K. Kay	Seminole Community College
Doroshow, Mike	Eastfield College
Douglas, Gretchen	SUNYCortland
Dove, Carol	Community College of Allegheny
Driskel, Loretta	Niagara Community College
Duckwiler, Carol	Wabaunsee Community College
Duncan, Mimi	University of Missouri-St. Louis
Duthie, Judy	Green River Community College
Duvall, Annette	Central New Mexico Community College
Ecklund, Paula	Duke University
Eng, Bernice	Brookdale Community College
Evans, Billie	Vance-Granville Community College
Feuerbach, Lisa	Ivy Tech East Chicago
Fisher, Fred	Florida State University
Foster, Penny L.	Anne Arundel Community College
Foszcz, Russ	McHenry County College
Fry, Susan	Boise State University
Fustos, Janos	Metro State
Gallup, Jeanette	Blinn College
Gelb, Janet	Grossmont College
Gentry, Barb	Parkland College
Gerace, Karin	St. Angela Merici School
Gerace, Tom	Tulane University
Ghajar, Homa	Oklahoma State University
Gifford, Steve	Northwest Iowa Community College
Glazer, Ellen	Broward Community College
Gordon, Robert	Hofstra University
Gramlich, Steven	Pasco-Hernando Community College
Graviett, Nancy M.	St. Charles Community College, St. Peters, Missouri
Greene, Rich	Community College of Allegheny County
Gregoryk, Kerry	Virginia Commonwealth State
Griggs, Debra	Bellevue Community College

Grimm, Carol	Palm Beach Community College	Lindberg, Martha	Minnesota State University
Hahn, Norm	Thomas Nelson Community College	Linge, Richard	Arizona Western College
Hammerschlag, Dr. Bill	Brookhaven College	Logan, Mary G.	Delgado Community College
Hansen, Michelle	Davenport University	Loizeaux, Barbara	Westchester Community College
Hayden, Nancy	Indiana University—Purdue University, Indianapolis	Lopez, Don	Clovis-State Center Community College District
Hayes, Theresa	Broward Community College	Lord, Alexandria	Asheville Buncombe Tech
Helfand, Terri	Chaffey College	Lowe, Rita	Harold Washington College
Helms, Liz	Columbus State Community College	Low, Willy Hui	Joliet Junior College
Hernandez, Leticia	TCI College of Technology	Lucas, Vickie	Broward Community College
Hibbert, Marilyn	Salt Lake Community College	Lynam, Linda	Central Missouri State University
Hoffman, Joan	Milwaukee Area Technical College	Lyon, Lynne	Durham College
Hogan, Pat	Cape Fear Community College	Lyon, Pat Rajski	Tomball College
Holland, Susan	Southeast Community College	MacKinnon, Ruth	Georgia Southern University
Hopson, Bonnie	Athens Technical College	Macon, Lisa	Valencia Community College, West Campus
Horvath, Carrie	Albertus Magnus College		
Horwitz, Steve	Community College of Philadelphia	Machuca, Wayne	College of the Sequoias
Hotta, Barbara	Leeward Community College	Madison, Dana	Clarion University
Howard, Bunny	St. Johns River Community	Maguire, Trish	Eastern New Mexico University
Howard, Chris	DeVry University	Malkan, Rajiv	Montgomery College
Huckabay, Jamie	Austin Community College	Manning, David	Northern Kentucky University
Hudgins, Susan	East Central University	Marcus, Jacquie	Niagara Community College
Hulett, Michelle J.	Missouri State University	Marghitu, Daniela	Auburn University
Hunt, Darla A.	Morehead State University, Morehead, Kentucky	Marks, Suzanne	Bellevue Community College
		Marquez, Juanita	El Centro College
Hunt, Laura	Tulsa Community College	Marquez, Juan	Mesa Community College
Jacob, Sherry	Jefferson Community College	Martyn, Margie	Baldwin-Wallace College
Jacobs, Duane	Salt Lake Community College	Marucco, Toni	Lincoln Land Community College
Jauken, Barb	Southeastern Community	Mason, Lynn	Lubbock Christian University
Johnson, Kathy	Wright College	Matutis, Audrone	Houston Community College
Johnson, Mary	Kingwood College	Matkin, Marie	University of Lethbridge
Johnson, Mary	Mt. San Antonio College	McCain, Evelynn	Boise State University
Jones, Stacey	Benedict College	McCannon, Melinda	Gordon College
Jones, Warren	University of Alabama, Birmingham	McCarthy, Marguerite	Northwestern Business College
Jordan, Cheryl	San Juan College	McCaskill, Matt L.	Brevard Community College
Kapoor, Bhushan	California State University, Fullerton	McClellan, Carolyn	Tidewater Community College
Kasai, Susumu	Salt Lake Community College	McClure, Darlean	College of Sequoias
Kates, Hazel	Miami Dade Community College, Kendall	McCrory, Sue A.	Missouri State University
		McCue, Stacy	Harrisburg Area Community College
Keen, Debby	University of Kentucky	McEntire-Orbach, Teresa	Middlesex County College
Keeter, Sandy	Seminole Community College	McLeod, Todd	Fresno City College
Kern-Blystone,		McManus, Illyana	Grossmont College
Dorothy Jean	Bowling Green State	McPherson, Dori	Schoolcraft College
Keskin, Ilknur	The University of South Dakota	Meiklejohn, Nancy	Pikes Peak Community College
Kirk, Colleen	Mercy College	Menking, Rick	Hardin-Simmons University
Kleckner, Michelle	Elon University	Meredith, Mary	University of Louisiana at Lafayette
Kliston, Linda	Broward Community College, North Campus	Mermelstein, Lisa	Baruch College
		Metos, Linda	Salt Lake Community College
Kochis, Dennis	Suffolk County Community College	Meurer, Daniel	University of Cincinnati
Kramer, Ed	Northern Virginia Community College	Meyer, Marian	Central New Mexico Community College
Laird, Jeff	Northeast State Community College	Miller, Cindy	Ivy Tech Community College, Lafayette, Indiana
Lamoureaux, Jackie	Central New Mexico Community College	Mitchell, Susan	Davenport University
		Mohle, Dennis	Fresno Community College
Lange, David	Grand Valley State	Monk, Ellen	University of Delaware
LaPointe, Deb	Central New Mexico Community College	Moore, Rodney	Holland College
		Morris, Mike	Southeastern Oklahoma State University
Larson, Donna	Louisville Technical Institute		
Laspina, Kathy	Vance-Granville Community College	Morris, Nancy	Hudson Valley Community College
Le Grand, Dr. Kate	Broward Community College	Moseler, Dan	Harrisburg Area Community College
Lenhart, Sheryl	Terra Community College	Nabors, Brent	Reedley College, Clovis Center
Letavec, Chris	University of Cincinnati	Nadas, Erika	Wright College
Liefert, Jane	Everett Community College	Nadelman, Cindi	New England College
Lindaman, Linda	Black Hawk Community College	Nademlynsky, Lisa	Johnson & Wales University
Lindberg, Martha	Minnesota State University	Ncube, Cathy	University of West Florida
Lightner, Renee	Broward Community College		

Nagengast, Joseph — Florida Career College
Newsome, Eloise — Northern Virginia Community College Woodbridge
Nicholls, Doreen — Mohawk Valley Community College
Nunan, Karen — Northeast State Technical Community College
Odegard, Teri — Edmonds Community College
Ogle, Gregory — North Community College
Orr, Dr. Claudia — Northern Michigan University South
Otieno, Derek — DeVry University
Otton, Diana Hill — Chesapeake College
Oxendale, Lucia — West Virginia Institute of Technology
Paiano, Frank — Southwestern College
Patrick, Tanya — Clackamas Community College
Peairs, Deb — Clark State Community College
Prince, Lisa — Missouri State University-Springfield Campus
Proietti, Kathleen — Northern Essex Community College
Pusins, Delores — HCCC
Raghuraman, Ram — Joliet Junior College
Reasoner, Ted Allen — Indiana University—Purdue
Reeves, Karen — High Point University
Remillard, Debbie — New Hampshire Technical Institute
Rhue, Shelly — DeVry University
Richards, Karen — Maplewoods Community College
Richardson, Mary — Albany Technical College
Rodgers, Gwen — Southern Nazarene University
Roselli, Diane — Harrisburg Area Community College
Ross, Dianne — University of Louisiana in Lafayette
Rousseau, Mary — Broward Community College, South
Samson, Dolly — Hawaii Pacific University
Sams, Todd — University of Cincinnati
Sandoval, Everett — Reedley College
Sardone, Nancy — Seton Hall University
Scafide, Jean — Mississippi Gulf Coast Community College
Scheeren, Judy — Westmoreland County Community College
Schneider, Sol — Sam Houston State University
Scroggins, Michael — Southwest Missouri State University
Sever, Suzanne — Northwest Arkansas Community College
Sheridan, Rick — California State University-Chico
Silvers, Pamela — Asheville Buncombe Tech
Singer, Steven A. — University of Hawai'i, Kapi'olani Community College
Sinha, Atin — Albany State University
Skolnick, Martin — Florida Atlantic University
Smith, T. Michael — Austin Community College
Smith, Tammy — Tompkins Cortland Community College
Smolenski, Bob — Delaware County Community College
Spangler, Candice — Columbus State
Stedham, Vicki — St. Petersburg College, Clearwater
Stefanelli, Greg — Carroll Community College
Steiner, Ester — New Mexico State University

Stenlund, Neal — Northern Virginia Community College, Alexandria
St. John, Steve — Tulsa Community College
Sterling, Janet — Houston Community College
Stoughton, Catherine — Laramie County Community College
Sullivan, Angela — Joliet Junior College
Szurek, Joseph — University of Pittsburgh at Greensburg
Tarver, Mary Beth — Northwestern State University
Taylor, Michael — Seattle Central Community College
Thangiah, Sam — Slippery Rock University
Thompson-Sellers, Ingrid — Georgia Perimeter College
Tomasi, Erik — Baruch College
Toreson, Karen — Shoreline Community College
Trifiletti, John J. — Florida Community College at Jacksonville
Trivedi, Charulata — Quinsigamond Community College, Woodbridge
Tucker, William — Austin Community College
Turgeon, Cheryl — Asnuntuck Community College
Turpen, Linda — Central New Mexico Community College
Upshaw, Susan — Del Mar College
Unruh, Angela — Central Washington University
Vanderhoof, Dr. Glenna — Missouri State University-Springfield Campus
Vargas, Tony — El Paso Community College
Vicars, Mitzi — Hampton University
Villarreal, Kathleen — Fresno
Vitrano, Mary Ellen — Palm Beach Community College
Volker, Bonita — Tidewater Community College
Wahila, Lori (Mindy) — Tompkins Cortland Community College
Waswick, Kim — Southeast Community College, Nebraska
Wavle, Sharon — Tompkins Cortland Community College
Webb, Nancy — City College of San Francisco
Wells, Barbara E. — Central Carolina Technical College
Wells, Lorna — Salt Lake Community College
Welsh, Jean — Lansing Community College Nebraska
White, Bruce — Quinnipiac University
Willer, Ann — Solano Community College
Williams, Mark — Lane Community College
Wilson, Kit — Red River College
Wilson, Roger — Fairmont State University
Wimberly, Leanne — International Academy of Design and Technology
Worthington, Paula — Northern Virginia Community College
Yauney, Annette — Herkimer County Community College
Yip, Thomas — Passaic Community College
Zavala, Ben — Webster Tech
Zlotow, Mary Ann — College of DuPage
Zudeck, Steve — Broward Community College, North

About the Authors

Shelley Gaskin, author and Series Editor, is a Professor of Business Information Technology at Pasadena City College in Pasadena, California. She holds a bachelor's degree in Business Administration from Robert Morris College (Pennsylvania), a master's degree in Business from Northern Illinois University, and a doctorate in Education from Ball State University. Before joining Pasadena City College, she spent twelve years in the computer industry where she was a systems analyst, sales representative, and Director of Customer Education with Unisys Corporation. She also worked for Ernst & Young on the development large systems applications for their clients. She has written and developed training materials for custom systems applications in both the public and private sector, and has written and edited numerous computer application textbooks.

This book is dedicated to my students at Pasadena City College, who inspire me every day.

—Shelley Gaskin

Carol L. Martin is an adjunct faculty member at Harrisburg Area Community College. She holds a bachelor's degree in secondary education—mathematics from Millersville University and a master's degree in training and development from Pennsylvania State University. For over 30 years she has instructed individuals in the use of various computer applications and has co-authored several training manuals for use in Pennsylvania Department of Education in-service courses.

This book is dedicated with all my love to my husband Ron—a constant source of encouragement and technical support; and to my delightful grandsons, Tony and Josh, who keep me young at heart.

—Carol L. Martin

chapterone

Introduction to Outlook 2007 and E-mail

OBJECTIVES

At the end of this chapter you will be able to:

1. Start and Navigate Outlook
2. Compose and Send E-mail
3. Read and Respond to E-mail Messages
4. Use Mail Options and Signatures
5. Manage E-mail
6. Use Outlook Help and Close Outlook

OUTCOMES

Mastering these objectives will enable you to:

PROJECT 1A
Read and Respond to E-mail Using Outlook 2007

Lake Michigan City College

Lake Michigan City College is located along the lakefront of Chicago—one of the country's most exciting cities. The college serves its large and diverse student body and makes positive contributions to the community through relevant curricula, partnerships with businesses and nonprofit organizations, and learning experiences that allow students to be full participants in the global community. The college offers three associate degrees in 20 academic areas, adult education programs, and continuing education offerings on campus, at satellite locations, and online.

Getting Started with Microsoft Office Outlook 2007

One of the most common uses of the personal computer is to send and receive e-mail. E-mail is a convenient way to communicate with coworkers, business contacts, friends, and family members. Outlook combines all the features of a personal information manager with e-mail capabilities in one program that you can use with other programs within Microsoft Office.

Outlook's e-mail features enable you to send, receive, and forward e-mail messages. With optional features, you can personalize and prioritize sent messages and received messages. After you have started using e-mail on a regular basis, you will need to manage your e-mail by deleting messages you no longer need, sorting your messages, and performing other tasks that will keep your Inbox organized.

In this chapter, you will become familiar with Outlook and practice using Outlook's e-mail capabilities. You will practice sending and replying to e-mail messages, creating signatures, using the mail options, and managing e-mail messages.

Project 1A College Staff

In Activities 1.1 through 1.25, you will start Microsoft Office Outlook 2007 and become familiar with the parts of Outlook. Then you will compose, send, read, and respond to e-mail messages for Darron Jacobsen, Vice President of Administrative Affairs at Lake Michigan City College. You will use various Outlook options and manage his Inbox. The messages you send, reply to, and forward will be stored in your Outbox rather than being sent to actual recipients. You will also print a forwarded message. Upon completion, your Inbox, Outbox, and one of the printed messages will look similar to the ones shown in Figure 1.1

For Project 1A, you will need the following files:

New blank message form

o01A_College_Staff_Inbox

o01A_College_Staff_Schedule

You will print three files with the following footers:
1A_College_Staff_Inbox_Firstname_Lastname
1A_College_Staff_Outbox_Firstname_Lastname
1A_College_Staff_Message_Firstname_Lastname

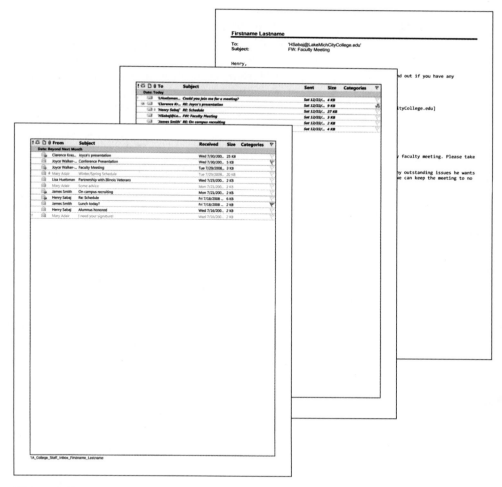

Figure 1.1
Project 1A—College Staff

Objective 1
Start and Navigate Outlook

Microsoft Office Outlook 2007 has two functions: It is an e-mail program, and it is a *personal information manager*. Among other things, a personal information manager enables you to store information about your contacts in electronic form. *Contacts* are the names of your friends, family members, coworkers, customers, suppliers, or other individuals with whom you communicate. By using a personal information manager, you can also keep track of your daily schedule, tasks you need to complete, and other personal and business-related information. Thus, Outlook's major parts include Mail for e-mail and Calendar, Contacts, and Tasks for personal information management.

Your e-mail and personal information in Outlook is stored in folders, and there are separate folders for each of Outlook's components. For example, the Mail component is stored in a folder called *Inbox*. Outlook presents information in *views*, which are ways to look at similar information in different formats and arrangements. Mail, Contacts, Calendar, and Tasks all have different views.

Alert!

Starting Project 1A

Because Outlook stores information on the hard drive of the computer at which you are working, it is recommended that you schedule enough time to complete this project in one working session, unless you are working on a computer that is used only by you. Allow approximately one to two hours for Project 1A.

Activity 1.1 Starting Outlook

Start Outlook in the same manner as you start other Microsoft Office 2007 programs.

1 On the Windows taskbar, click the **Start** button .

2 From the displayed **Start** menu, locate the **Outlook** program, and then click **E-mail: Microsoft Office Outlook 2007**. If necessary,

Maximize the Outlook window.

Organizations and individuals store computer programs in a variety of ways. The Outlook program might be located under *All Programs* or *Microsoft Office* or at the top of the Start menu. See Figure 1.2 for an example.

Figure 1.2

Click to start Outlook

Start button

3 Look at the opening Outlook screen, and take a moment to study the main parts of the screen as shown in Figure 1.3 and as described in the table in Figure 1.4.

Alert!

Does your Outlook screen differ from the one shown in Figure 1.3?

If your Outlook data is stored in a personal folders file, it will likely be named *Personal Folders*. If your data is stored on a Microsoft Exchange Server, it will be named *Mailbox*. To see Outlook Today, click either Personal Folders or Mailbox in the Navigation Pane.

The default view when you open Outlook is **Outlook Today**, which is a summary view of your schedule, tasks, and e-mail for the current day. Your Outlook screen might differ from the one shown in Figure 1.3. Your program window might display the Inbox instead of Outlook Today. The starting appearance of the screen depends on various settings that were established when Outlook was installed on the computer you are using.

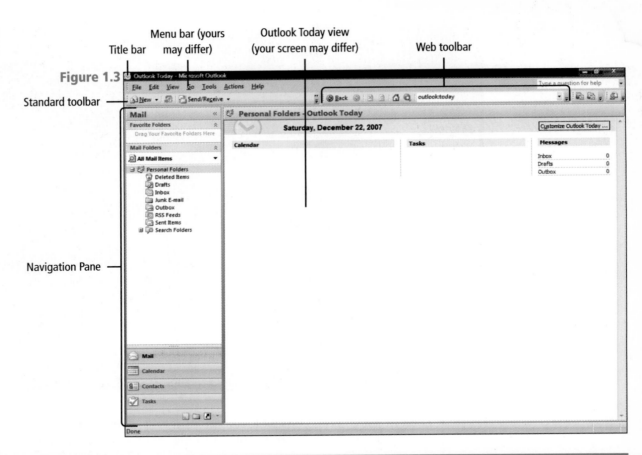

Figure 1.3

Microsoft Outlook Screen Elements

Screen Element	Description
Navigation Pane	Displays a list of shortcuts to Outlook's components and folders. The top position of the Navigation Pane consists of two smaller panes. The lower portion contains buttons for frequently used folders.
Title bar	Displays the program name and the name of the currently displayed folder. The Minimize, Maximize/Restore Down, and Close buttons display on the right side of the title bar.
Menu bar	Contains the lists of commands by category. To display a menu, click the menu name.
Standard toolbar	Contains buttons for the most commonly used commands in Outlook. There are different buttons on the Standard toolbar, depending on which Outlook folder is currently displayed.
Web toolbar	Contains buttons for navigating the Internet, similar to the navigation buttons in Microsoft Internet Explorer. The Web toolbar is displayed by default only in the Outlook Today view.

Figure 1.4

Note — Outlook Express

You may be familiar with **Microsoft Outlook Express**, which is a different program from Microsoft Office Outlook. Outlook Express is a basic, no-cost e-mail program that is included with Microsoft Internet Explorer. It enables you to send and receive e-mail and store contact information, but it does not contain many of the features found in Microsoft Office Outlook.

Activity 1.2 Exploring Outlook Using the Navigation Pane

A convenient way to move among—navigate—Outlook's different components is to use the **Navigation Pane**, which is located on the left side of the Outlook window. The Navigation Pane provides quick access to Outlook's components and folders. As you manage the e-mail activities of Darron Jacobsen, the Navigation Pane will be your primary tool for moving around Outlook.

1 Be sure that your **Navigation Pane** is displayed as shown previously in Figure 1.3. If necessary, click **View** on the menu bar, and then point to **Navigation Pane** and then click **Normal** to display it.

The Navigation Pane displays as a column on the left side of the Outlook window. The upper portion of the Navigation Pane contains two smaller panes. The lower portion contains buttons to quickly display frequently used folders.

2 In the upper portion of the **Navigation Pane**, in the **Personal Folders**, click **Inbox**.

The Inbox folder displays as shown in Figure 1.5. The middle pane of the Outlook window shows any e-mail messages you have received. On the right side of the screen is the **Reading Pane**, a window in which you can preview an e-mail message without actually opening it. If your Inbox contains no messages, the Reading Pane is blank. If you have messages, the contents of the first message display in the Reading Pane. On the far right of the screen is the **To-Do Bar**, which provides a consolidated view of appointments, tasks, and e-mail that has been flagged for follow-up. It allows you to set your priorities for the day.

Figure 1.5

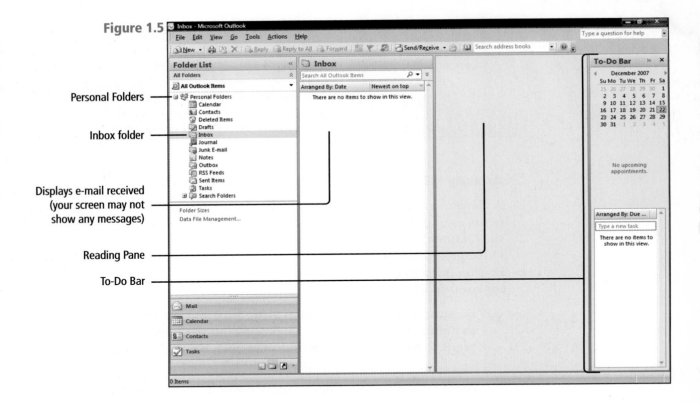

Personal Folders

Inbox folder

Displays e-mail received
(your screen may not
show any messages)

Reading Pane

To-Do Bar

Alert!

Does your screen differ?

Depending on the configuration of Outlook on your system, your Reading Pane and To-Do Bar may not display. To show the Reading Pane, from the View menu, point to Reading Pane and click Right. To show the To-Do Bar, from the View menu, point to To-Do Bar and click Normal.

3 In the **Navigation Pane**, click the **Calendar** button to display the Calendar folder.

The right portion of the Outlook window displays the calendar for the current day, and the upper two panes of the Navigation Pane display calendar-related information. The Web toolbar is no longer displayed, and available commands on the Standard toolbar change based on the current view. In this manner, each of Outlook's folder views displays different information.

4 In the **Navigation Pane**, click the **Contacts** button to display the Contacts folder.

Depending on whether contacts have been created, contact names may or may not display in the middle pane of the Outlook window.

5 In the **Navigation Pane**, click the **Tasks** button to display the Tasks folder.

The To-Do List shows any pending tasks. If no tasks have been created, the list is blank. The Reading Pane may or may not be visible.

6 In the lower portion of the **Navigation Pane**, locate the three small buttons that have *icons*—graphic representations of objects you can select and open. Point to each one to display its **ScreenTip**—a small box that displays the name of a screen element. Then click the **Notes** button ⬜ to display the Notes folder.

Use the Notes component to keep track of information you might use later, such as directions or a question you have for someone.

Activity 1.3 Exploring Outlook Using the Folder List

Outlook uses folders to organize information. Individual folders store **items**. An item is an element of information in Outlook, such as a message, a contact name, a task, or an appointment. Data in your Outlook folders is stored in a data file called the **Personal Folders** file. Outlook uses the *.pst* file name extension for the Personal Folders file. If you are working in an **Exchange Server environment**, a special shared environment set up by your system administrator, your Outlook information is probably stored in an Exchange Server mailbox rather than a local pst file. In either case, you can use the folder list to navigate in Outlook.

1 In the **Navigation Pane**, click the **Contacts** button [🔳 Contacts] to display the Contacts folder. Locate the three buttons in the lower portion of the **Navigation Pane**, and then click the **Folder List** button ⬜ to display the Folder List in the upper portion of the **Navigation Pane**, as shown in Figure 1.6.

The right portion of the Outlook window continues to display the Contacts folder; the upper portion of the Navigation Pane displays the folder list.

Figure 1.6

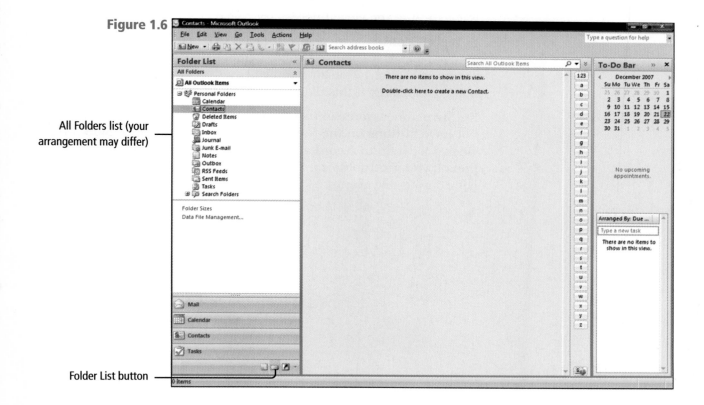

All Folders list (your arrangement may differ)

Folder List button

2 In the upper portion of the **Navigation Pane**, under **All Folders**, locate the top folder. Click either **Personal Folders** or **Mailbox**.

The Outlook Today view displays. Folders shown in the Navigation Pane may contain more folders than can fit in the All Folders pane. If necessary, you can scroll down the pane to view the additional folders. *Scrolling* is the action of moving a pane or window vertically (up or down) or horizontally (side to side) to bring unseen areas into view.

Alert!

Does your screen differ?

Depending on the configuration of Outlook on your system, the Folder List shown in the Navigation Pane might differ from the one shown in Figure 1.6. No scroll bar displays if the folder list fits within the boundaries of the pane.

3 In the **All Folders** pane, click **Inbox** to display the Inbox folder.

4 At the far right, notice that the **To-Do Bar** is displayed in **Normal** view. At the top of the **To-Do Bar**, click on the **Minimize the To-Do Bar** button `»` to display the To-Do Bar in a minimized view.

This minimized view will be used for all related figures in the remainder of this book.

5 If a scroll bar displays on the right side of the **Navigation Pane**, point to the scroll box, press and hold down the left mouse button, and then drag it downward to display the lower portion of the **All Folders** pane.

You can also use the scroll arrows at the top and bottom of the scroll bar to adjust the view if necessary.

6 In the **All Folders** pane, click **Journal** to display the contents of the Journal folder. A Microsoft Office Outlook dialog box might display, as shown in Figure 1.7, asking you whether you want to turn on automatic journaling; if this dialog box displays, click **No**.

In this manner, you can use the Folder List to display folders that do not have buttons on the Navigation Pane. The *Journal* folder provides a location to record and track all your activities and interactions if you want to do so. Like a personal journal, it is a record of your day-to-day events.

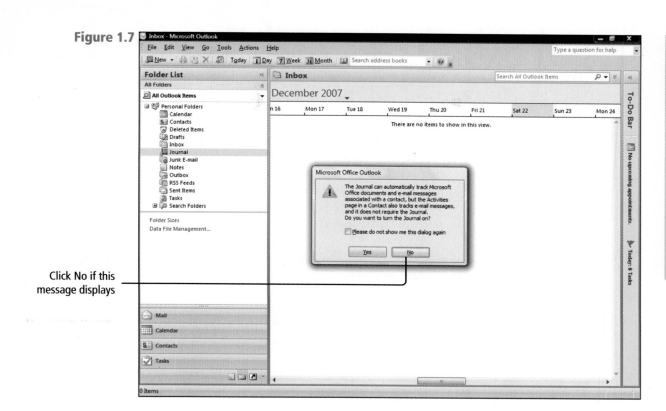
Figure 1.7

Click No if this
message displays

7 In the **Navigation Pane**, click the **Mail** button [Mail] to display the Inbox folder, and then notice that Outlook hides the Folder List when you click a button on the Navigation Pane.

More Knowledge

Servers and Exchange Server Accounts

Your e-mail account may be a Microsoft Exchange Server account. Exchange Server is an e-mail–based communications *server* for businesses and organizations. A server is a computer or device on a network that handles shared network resources. Microsoft Exchange Server functions as a mail server for a business or organization. In an Exchange Server environment, Outlook functions as a *client* of the server. A client is a program that runs on a personal computer and relies on the server to perform some of its operations. A few Outlook features require an Exchange Server e-mail account. Home users typically do not have Exchange Server accounts. Most home users of Outlook have a *POP3* e-mail account with an Internet service provider. POP3 is a protocol that provides a simple, standardized way for users to access mailboxes and download messages to their computers.

Activity 1.4 Identifying and Displaying Menus, Toolbars, and ScreenTips

Outlook commands are organized in *menus*—lists of commands within a category. You perform menu commands by using the menu bar. *Toolbars* are rows of buttons from which you can perform commands using a single click of the mouse; this is faster than performing the command from the menu. Toolbars are usually located below the menu bar. Recall that a ScreenTip is a small box that contains the name or a descriptive label of a screen element, such as a toolbar button. As you move around Darron Jacobsen's Inbox, the menus, toolbars, and ScreenTips will be available to you.

1 On the menu bar, click **File**.

The File menu displays either in a short format (as shown in Figure 1.8) or in a full format, displaying all the File menu commands. The short menus are **adaptive**, meaning that they adapt to the way you work by displaying the commands you most frequently use. If you want to see the full format, you can wait a moment, and the full menu will display. You can also click the Expand arrows, which are located in the lower portion of the menu.

Figure 1.8

Short menu format

Expand arrows

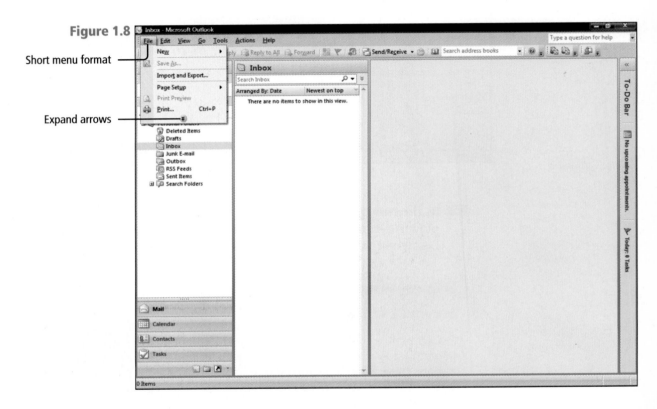

Note — Displaying the Full Menu

Many Outlook users prefer the automatic display of full menus. To set the system to always display the full menu, display the Tools menu, click Customize, and then click the Options tab. Under Personalized Menus and Toolbars, click the Always show full menus check box. Click the Close button.

2 On the displayed **File** menu, point to, but do not click, the **New** command to display the **submenu** as shown in Figure 1.9.

When you point to a command on the menu, the command is shaded and surrounded by a border. Commands that have triangles next to their names will display a submenu—a second-level menu activated by selecting a main menu option.

3 Without clicking, move the pointer down the list of commands on the **File** menu.

Commands that are shaded or gray indicate that the command is currently unavailable. Commands that display an ellipsis (...) after the name will display a dialog box or a task pane.

4 Look to the right of the **Print** command and notice the **keyboard shortcut**, *Ctrl+P*. To the left of this command, notice the image of the toolbar button that represents the Print command on the toolbar, as shown in Figure 1.9.

A keyboard shortcut is a combination of keys on the keyboard that performs a command. Many Outlook commands can be accomplished in more than one way. To use the keyboard shortcut for the Print command, press and hold down Ctrl and then press P. The result is the same as starting on the menu bar, clicking on the **File** menu, and then clicking on **Print**.

Triangle indicates that a submenu will appear

Figure 1.9

Gray lettering indicates that the command is currently unavailable

Toolbar button for Print command

Keyboard shortcut for Print command

Ellipsis (...) indicates the command will display a dialog box or task pane

Submenu

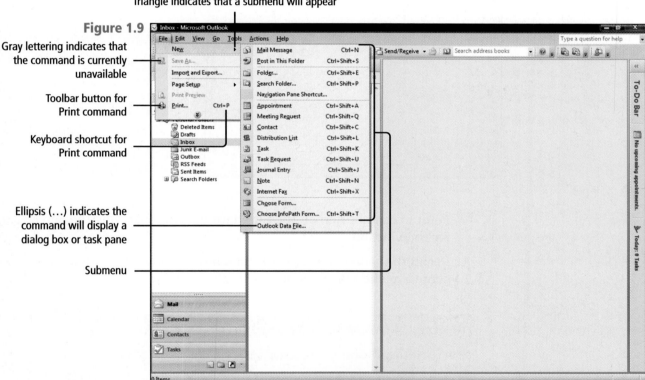

5 Move the pointer away from the menu, and click anywhere in the Outlook window to close the menu without executing any commands.

6 On the menu bar, click **View**.

The View menu displays. Notice the check mark to the left of the Status Bar command. A check mark indicates that a command is turned on or active. Because the Status Bar is displayed, this command is active.

7 Move the pointer away from the menu, and click anywhere in the Outlook window to close the menu.

8 On the Standard toolbar, point to the **New Mail Message** button New .

When you position the pointer over a button, Outlook highlights the button and displays a ScreenTip, which describes the button as *New Mail Message* as shown in Figure 1.10.

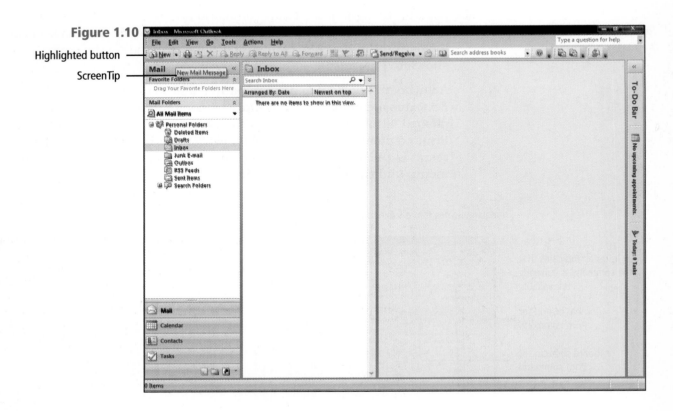

Figure 1.10

Highlighted button —

ScreenTip —

9 Point to each button on the Standard toolbar, observing the ScreenTip for each button.

Recall that shaded or gray buttons indicate that the command represented by the button is not currently available.

More Knowledge

Performing Menu Commands Using the Keyboard

In addition to keyboard shortcuts, there are other ways to perform menu commands using the keyboard. Every menu name, every menu command, and most dialog box elements have an underlined character. To perform commands on the menu bar, first press [Alt] and then press the underlined letter of the menu name, and then press the underlined letter of the command on the menu. When a submenu displays, perform a command by typing the underlined letter of the submenu command. For example, if you press [Alt] and then press [F], the File menu is displayed; then, if you press [P], the Print dialog box displays. This action is the same as starting on the menu bar, clicking on the File menu, and then clicking on Print.

Objective 2
Compose and Send E-mail

Outlook uses an e-mail **profile** to identify which e-mail account you use and where the related data is stored. When Outlook is initially configured, a single profile is created. You might choose to create separate profiles to keep your work data and personal information separate.

To send an e-mail message to someone, you must know the recipient's e-mail address. There are two parts to an e-mail address, with each part separated by the **at sign (@)**. The first part is the user name of the recipient. The second part of the e-mail address is the **domain name**. A domain name is the host name of the recipient's mail server. For example, if the mail server is MSN Hotmail, the domain is hotmail.com.

You create an e-mail message using an Outlook **form**, which is a window for displaying and collecting information. There are forms for messages, contacts, tasks, and appointments.

Activity 1.5 Creating a Profile

In the projects in this book, you will be importing a variety of data into Outlook. If you are working in a lab situation, this will not be an issue; skip to Activity 1.6. However, if you are working on your own, personal computer, you will want to create a new profile in order to segregate your personal Outlook files from the data you will use in the projects. In this activity you will create a student profile, including a new e-mail account.

1 From the **File** menu, click **Exit** to close Outlook.

2 Click the **Start** button 🔵, and then click **Control Panel**.

3 Click **User Accounts**, and then click **Mail**. If you have Vista set to **Classic view**, you will not see User Accounts, simply double-click **Mail**.

4 In the **Mail Setup** dialog box, click the **Show Profiles** button; and then click **Add**.

5 For the name of the profile, type **Student** and then click **OK**.

6 In the **Auto Account Setup** screen, at the lower left, click the box to **Manually configure server settings or additional server types**, and then click **Next** two times.

7 In the **Your Name** box, using your own name, type **Firstname Lastname**. In the **E-mail Address** box, type **Firstname_Lastname@ GOMAIL.com**

8 If necessary set the **Account Type** to **POP3**. In the **Incoming mail server** box, type **GOMAIL.com** and for the **Outgoing mail server (SMTP)** box, type **PHMAIL.com** Accept the user name and set the **Password** to **123456** Your password will display as asterisks. Compare your screen with Figure 1.11.

Figure 1.11

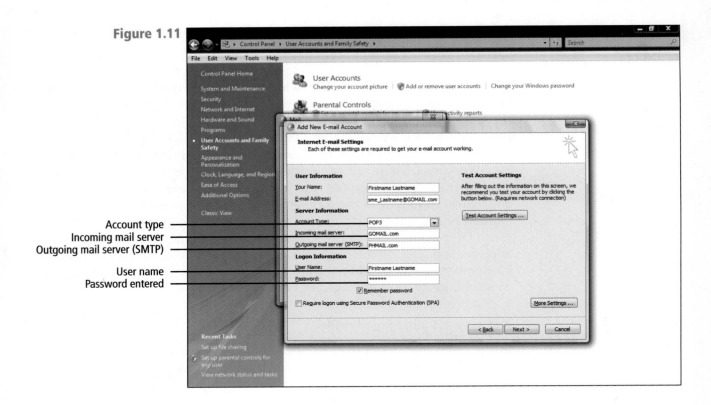

Account type
Incoming mail server
Outgoing mail server (SMTP)

User name
Password entered

Note — **Testing Your Account Settings**

Although it is not necessary to do this in this instruction, when setting up a new e-mail account, it is good practice to click the Test Account Settings command button before clicking Next in order to test the specified settings. If the account information is correct you will receive a sample e-mail message to your Inbox.

9 Click **Next**. In the screen indicating *Congratulations!*, click **Finish** to redisplay the **Mail** dialog box.

10 Under **Always use this profile**, click **Student** and then click **OK**.

If you use multiple profiles, you can be prompted to select a profile each time that you start Outlook, or you can always use the same profile. Switching to a different profile will change the e-mail accounts and settings that are available to you in an Outlook session. You cannot switch from one e-mail profile to another while Outlook is running.

11 Click the **Close** button to close the **Control Panel**.

12 On the Windows taskbar, click the **Start** button, and then from the displayed **Start** menu, locate the **Outlook** program, and then click **Microsoft Office Outlook 2007**. If necessary, **Maximize** the Outlook window.

13 In the **Navigation Pane**, if necessary, click on the **Mail** button .

Note that there are no e-mail messages or contacts because you are in the **Student** profile.

Activity 1.6 Configuring Outlook for Sending and Receiving Messages

If your computer is connected and **online**—connected to your organization's network or to the public Internet—Outlook's default setting is to send messages immediately when the Send button in the Message form is clicked. Copies of sent messages are then stored in the Sent Items folder. If you are **offline**—*not* connected to a network or to the public Internet—messages are stored in the Outbox. In this activity, you will configure Outlook to store all your sent messages in the Outbox instead of actually sending the messages. You will be handling the e-mail activities of Darron Jacobsen. You can create and send his messages even if your computer is not actually connected and online.

1 From the **Tools** menu, click **Options**. In the **Options** dialog box, click the **Mail Setup** tab.

2 Under **Send/Receive**, click to remove the check mark from the **Send immediately when connected** check box, and then compare your screen with Figure 1.12.

Figure 1.12

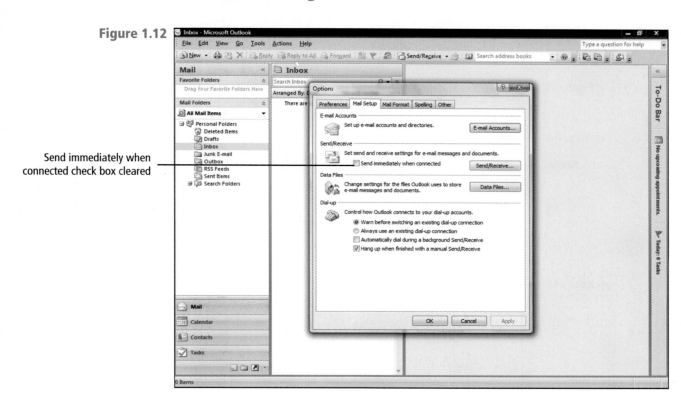

Send immediately when connected check box cleared

3 Click **Send/Receive**.

4 In the displayed **Send/Receive Groups** dialog box, under **Setting for group "All Accounts"**, clear *both* **Include this group in send/receive (F9)** check boxes. If necessary, clear *both* **Schedule an automatic send/receive** check boxes. Click **Close**.

5 In the **Options** dialog box, click **OK** to close the dialog box.

Activity 1.7 Creating a New E-mail Message

You can use two *editors*—programs with which you can create or make changes to existing files—to create and view messages in Outlook. These are the Outlook editor and the Microsoft Word editor. The default e-mail editor is the Microsoft Word editor, with which you can use many Word features when creating your messages, for example, the spelling checker, tables, and bullets and numbering. In this activity, you will create a message for Darron Jacobsen using the Word editor and send it to one of his colleagues at Lake Michigan City College.

1 In the **Navigation Pane**, under **Mail Folders**, click **Inbox** to select it. Then, on the Standard toolbar, click the **New Mail Message** button ⌐ New, and compare your screen with Figure 1.13.

The top of the form contains an area called the *Ribbon*. The Ribbon is an area above an Outlook form that displays commands, organized by groups and *tabs*. Tabs are part of the user interface in Office 2007 that provide access to different commands based on particular activities, such as setting message options or formatting text.

Options tab

Figure 1.13

Message tab —

Ribbon —

Message area —

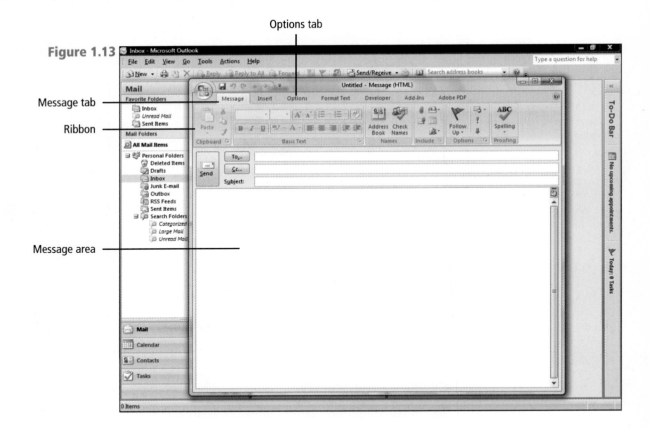

Alert!

Does your Ribbon look different?

The size of the Outlook window determines how much information appears with each command on the Ribbon. Users with larger screen resolutions will notice both icons and words for all commands while those with small screens may see only the icons for certain commands.

2 Click the **Options tab** and locate the **Format group**. Notice the **HTML** button Aa HTML is selected. Compare your screen with Figure 1.14.

The default message format in Outlook is **HTML**, which allows your message to include numbering, bullets, lines, backgrounds, HTML styles, and multimedia features that can be viewed in a Web browser. **Rich Text** format can include character and paragraph formatting and embedded graphics. **Plain Text** allows no special formatting.

Options tab   HTML button

Figure 1.14

Plain Text button

Rich Text button

Format group

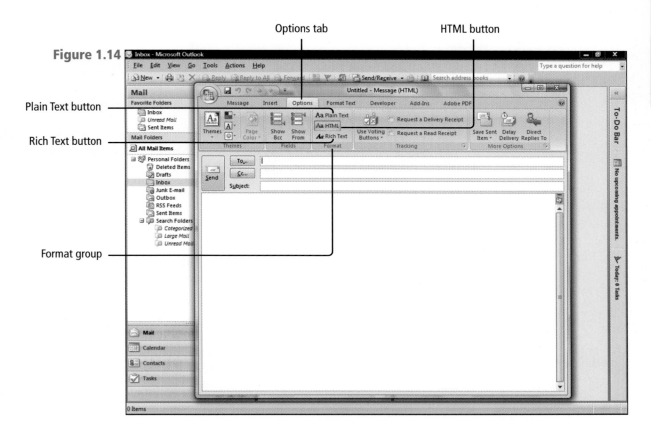

3 In the **Format group**, click the **Plain Text** button Aa Plain Text.

It is a good practice to use Plain Text for messages you create because the recipient of your message might have an e-mail program that can only read messages written in Plain Text.

4 In the **To** box, type **LHuelsman@LakeMichCityCollege.edu**

This is the e-mail address of the recipient. Notice the **syntax**—the way in which the parts of the e-mail address are put together. The user name is to the left of the @ symbol, and the domain name is on the right. If another student has used this computer, you may see Ms. Huelsman's e-mail address display in blue.

5 In the **Cc** box, click to place the insertion point, and then type **HSabaj@LakeMichCityCollege.edu**

This sends a **courtesy copy**, or **carbon copy**, of the message to the address specified in the Cc box. In both the To and the Cc boxes, you can enter multiple addresses, separating each address with a semicolon. Send a courtesy copy to others who need to see the message.

More Knowledge

Carbon Copies

Old fashioned carbon paper is rarely used anymore, but the term *carbon copy* has remained. Sometimes Cc is referred to as a *courtesy copy*.

6 Press `Tab` move the insertion point to the **Subject** box.

You can move the insertion point from one box to another either by clicking in the box or by pressing `Tab`.

Note — Underlined E-mail Addresses

Outlook may display an underlined e-mail address after you type it in the box. Outlook remembers previously typed addresses, and this change in its appearance shows that this address has been used before, either by you or a previous user. Your system may also be set to automatically underline all e-mail addresses that use correct syntax.

7 In the **Subject** box, type **Your speech at the Chamber of Commerce** and then press `Tab`.

Always include a brief, meaningful subject for your messages. This makes it easier for people who receive your e-mail messages to quickly know the contents of your message.

8 On the Message form title bar, click the **Maximize** button to enlarge the viewing area of the form. You can type the text of your message without enlarging the viewing area of the Message form, but it is easier to see your text as you type it when the form is maximized.

9 With the insertion point in the message area of the Message form, type **Hi Lisa,** and then press `Enter` **two** times.

This is the beginning of your message. It is considered good etiquette to address the recipient(s) by name and add an appropriate salutation. Keep your messages short and to the point. It is usually helpful to the recipient if you restrict your message to one subject. If you have another topic to discuss, send another e-mail message.

10 Type **I received confirmation today from the Chamber of Commerce for you to speak at their monthly member meeting next month. Let's arrange a time for you, Henry, and me to talk about what you'd like to say.**

As you type, the insertion point moves left to right. When it reaches the right margin, Outlook determines whether the next word will fit within the established margin. If the word does not fit, the insertion point moves the whole word down to the next line. This feature is called ***wordwrap***.

11 Press `Enter` **two** times and type **You might want to take a look at the presentation Joyce prepared for her talk last month to the Illinois**

Special Needs Teachers conference. Mary has a copy of it if you don't have one.

To leave a single blank line between paragraphs, press Enter **two** times. Keep paragraphs short and single-spaced. Do not indent the first line of paragraphs, and press Spacebar only one time following the punctuation at the end of a sentence.

12 Press Enter **two** times, type **Darron** and then click somewhere in the text of the message.

Darron is flagged with a wavy red line, indicating the word is not in Word's dictionary. Proper names are often not in Word's dictionary; however, this is the correct spelling of Mr. Jacobsen's name.

13 Right-click on **Darron** and then click **Ignore**. Read through your message, checking for errors, and then compare your screen with Figure 1.15.

Always double-check the addresses of your recipients. Address errors result in either the return of the message or delivery to the wrong person. Edit and proofread your messages carefully. Messages containing errors in style, grammar, and punctuation reflect poorly on you, the sender. E-mail messages can use a more casual tone than you would use in a formal business letter; but, as in any business communication, keep the tone of your message courteous and professional.

Figure 1.15

Your lines of text may wrap differently

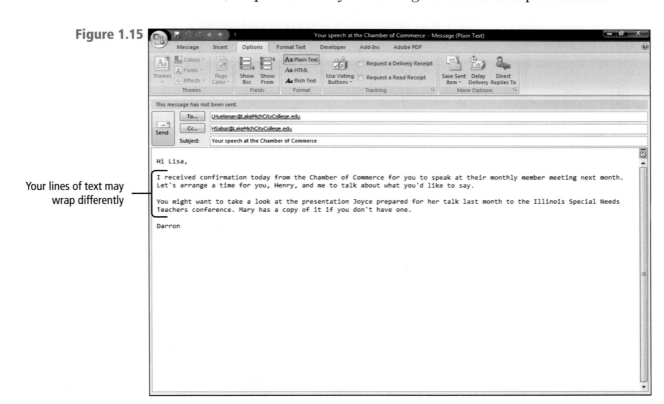

14 On the Message form title bar, click the **Restore Down** button to restore the Message form to its original size.

Activity 1.8 Sending a Message and Checking the Outbox

Recall that you configured Outlook to store all your sent messages in the Outbox. This allows you to send Darron Jacobsen's messages even if your computer is not actually online. When opening a message, you can either double-click it or you can *right-click*—the action of clicking the right mouse button, and then click Open. Right-clicking displays a *shortcut menu*—a list of context-related commands.

1 In the message header, to the left of **To...**, click the **Send** button .

The message is sent to the Outbox folder, and the Message form closes.

Alert!

Is your Send button missing?

If the Outlook program you are using has never been set up for an e-mail account, the Send button will not display. For the purpose of displaying the button, you can set up an e-mail account even if you are not online. Minimize the e-mail message that is on your screen. In the Outlook window, click the Tools menu, and then click Account Settings. Click the New... button. The option Microsoft Exchange, POP3, IMAP, or HTTP is selected by default. Click Next. Click the Manually configure server settings box, and click Next two times. To add a fictitious account, type your name in the Your Name box. In the E-mail Address box type **Firstname_Lastname@ GOMAIL.com**. In the Account Type, select POP3. In the Incoming mail server box, type **GOMAIL.com** and in the Outgoing mail server (SMTP) box type **PHMAIL.com** As the password, type **123456**. Alternatively, select one of the options to set an account for your personal or college e-mail address, or consult your instructor or lab coordinator. Click No if prompted to set the account as a permanent setting. Click Next, and then click Finish.

2 In the **Navigation Pane** under **Mail Folders**, locate and then click the **Outbox** folder. Compare your screen with Figure 1.16.

The contents of the Outbox folder display. When the Outbox folder contains unsent messages, the folder name is displayed in bold followed by the number of items in brackets.

Figure 1.16

Contents of the displayed folder (yours may differ)

Number of items in the folder (yours may differ)

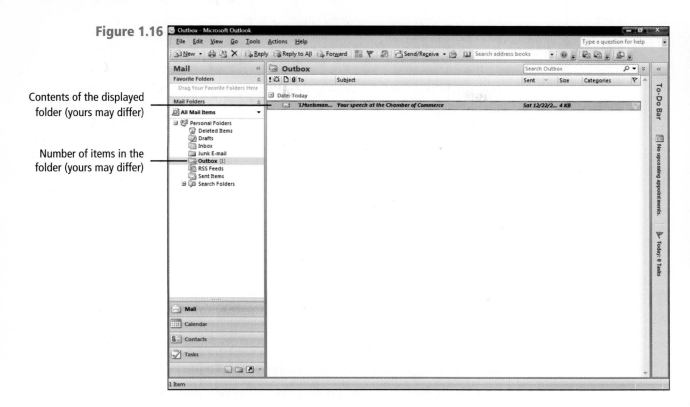

3 In the **Outbox**, double-click the *LHuelsman* message to open it. Alternatively, right-click the message, and from the displayed shortcut menu, click **Open**. In the open message, notice the banner under the Ribbon indicating that *This message has not been sent.*

4 On the Message toolbar, click the **Send** button.

The Message form closes. If you open an unsent message in the Outbox, you must send it again to include it with your outgoing messages. If you close an Outbox message without clicking the Send button, Outlook stores the message in the Outbox, but the message is not sent when the Send/Receive button is clicked.

More Knowledge
Using the Send/Receive Button

Outlook receives messages sent to you many times a day. This may occur at automatic intervals, or manually, when you click the Send/Receive button on the Standard toolbar. By default, automatic send/receive is disabled. To set Outlook to receive your messages automatically, go to the Tools menu, click Send/Receive, click Send/Receive Settings, and then click Define Send/Receive Groups. Select appropriate options and adjust the time to indicate how you would like Send/Receive to occur. Close the dialog box. When you click the Send/Receive button, Outlook checks for any received messages and places them in your Inbox. It also sends any messages in your Outbox and places a copy of the sent message in the Sent Items folder. Recall that Outlook normally sends messages as soon as you click the Send button in the Message form, but you have configured Outlook to place your sent messages in the Outbox instead. If you click the Send/Receive button while not actually online, Outlook attempts to send the message and will display an error message.

Objective 3
Read and Respond to E-mail Messages

Messages you receive are stored in Outlook's Inbox folder. Each message displays the name of the message sender, the subject, and the date and time sent. You can respond to a received message by either replying to the message or forwarding the message to another individual.

In Activities 1.9 through 1.14, you will work with messages that you will import into your Inbox. This will enable you to work with different types of received messages.

Activity 1.9 Importing Messages to the Inbox

Importing data into your Inbox involves the same steps, regardless of whether you are importing the data into the Personal Folders or into an Exchange Server mailbox. In this activity, you will import Darron Jacobsen's received messages into your Inbox.

1 In the **Navigation Pane**, under **Mail Folders**, click **Inbox**.

2 From the **File** menu, click **Import and Export**.

The Import and Export Wizard dialog box displays. A *wizard* is a tool that walks you through a process in a step-by-step manner.

3 In the **Import and Export Wizard** dialog box, under **Choose an action to perform**, click **Import from another program or file**, and then click **Next**.

4 In the **Import a File** dialog box, under **Select file type to import from**, click the **down scroll arrow** until the lower portion of the list displays.

5 Click **Personal Folder File (.pst)**, and then click **Next**. In the displayed **Import Personal Folders** dialog box, click **Browse**.

6 In the displayed **Open Personal Folders** dialog box, in the **Folders** list at the left side of the window, click **Computer** to view a list of the drives and folders available on your system. See Figure 1.17 as an example—the drives and folders displayed on your screen will differ.

Figure 1.17

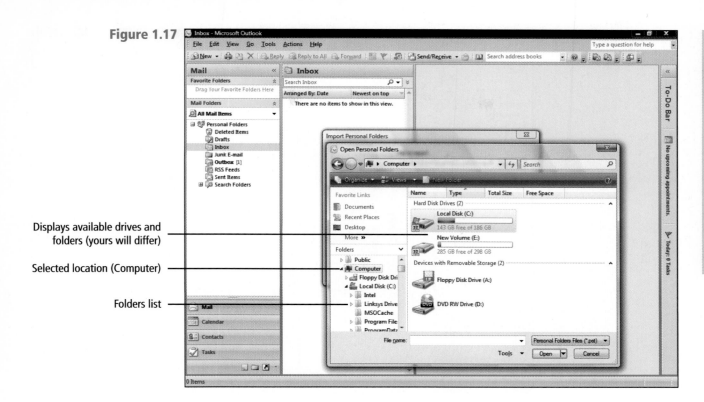

Displays available drives and folders (yours will differ)

Selected location (Computer)

Folders list

7 Navigate to the location where the student files that accompany this textbook are stored. Locate **o01A_College_Staff_Inbox**, and click one time to select it. Then, in the lower right corner of the **Open Personal Folders** dialog box, click **Open**.

The Open Personal Folders dialog box closes, and the path and file name display in the File to import box.

8 Click **Next** and compare your screen with Figure 1.18.

The Import Personal Folders dialog box displays the folder structure for the file you are going to import.

Figure 1.18

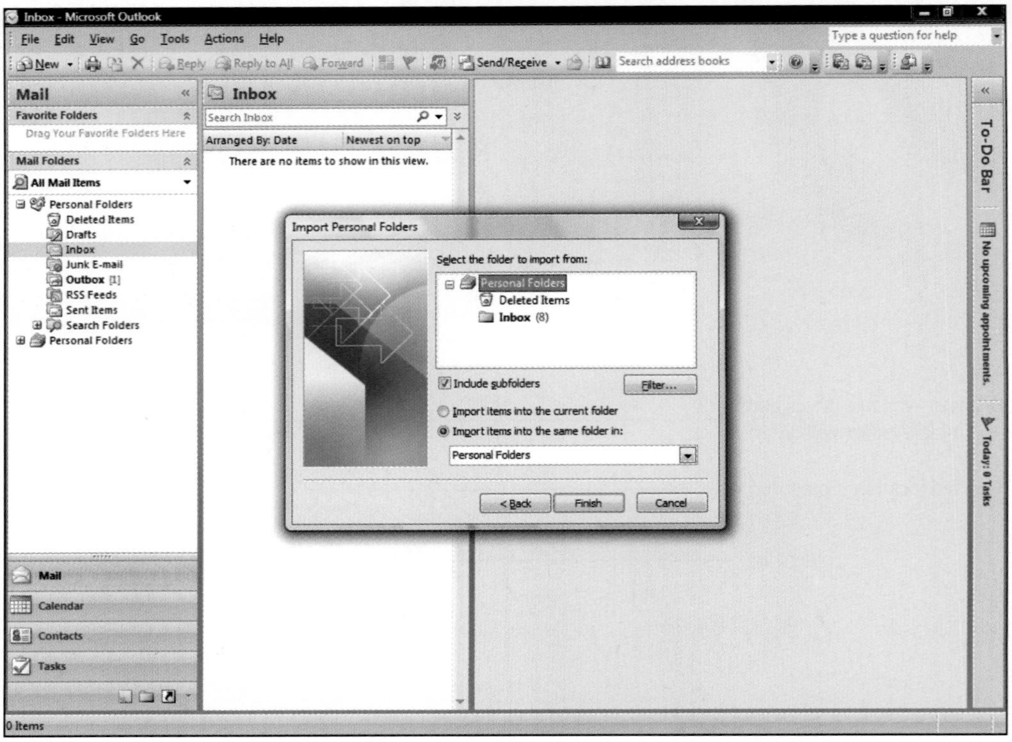

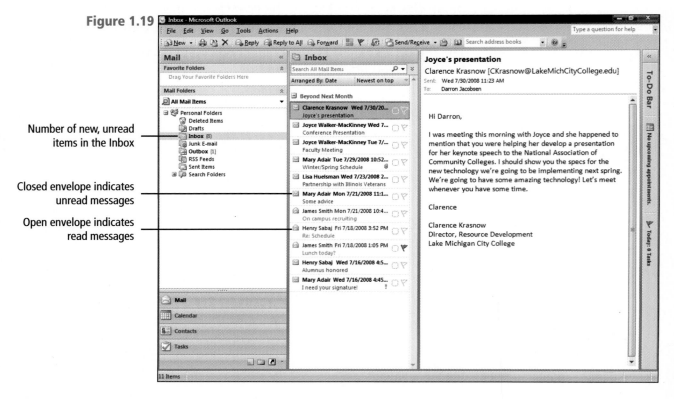

> **9** Under **Select the folder to import from**, click **Inbox**, and then click the **Import items into the current folder** option button.

> **10** Click **Finish**. If a Translation Warning dialog box displays, click OK. Compare your screen with Figure 1.19.

Figure 1.19

Number of new, unread items in the Inbox

Closed envelope indicates unread messages

Open envelope indicates read messages

Activity 1.10 Opening, Navigating, and Closing an E-mail Message

You can read messages in two ways. You can read the text of shorter messages in the Reading Pane without opening the message. When the Reading Pane is not displayed or the text of the message is too long to fit in the Reading Pane, you can open the message. In this activity, you will view Darron Jacobsen's messages in several ways.

1 Look at the **Inbox**, and take a moment to study the messages shown in Figure 1.19.

In the Navigation Pane, the number in parentheses found to the right of Inbox displays the number of unread messages. The Inbox pane lists the *message header* for each message. Message headers include basic information about an e-mail message such as the sender's name, the date sent, and the subject. The message header for an e-mail that has not yet been read or opened is displayed in bold, and the icon at the left shows a closed envelope. After a message has been read, the bold is removed and the icon changes to an open envelope.

2 Locate the second message in the **Inbox**, which is from *Joyce Walker-MacKinney* and has as its subject **Conference Presentation**. Click it one time to display it in the Reading Pane.

After you view a message in the Reading Pane, Outlook considers its status as *read* after you move to another message. The first message indicates that you have read it—the bold has been removed and the icon displays an open envelope. The *Conference presentation* message is too long to display entirely in the Reading Pane; however, you can scroll down to view the remainder of the message. Or, you may prefer to open the message to read it.

3 Double-click the **Conference Presentation** message to open it. Alternatively, **right-click** the message, and click **Open**. Compare your screen with Figure 1.20.

The Message form displays the message. The area above the text of the message contains the message header information, which includes the sender's name and the date of the message.

In the Message form title bar, the Quick Access Toolbar is displayed. This allows you to perform frequently used commands such as saving an item, viewing a previous item, or viewing the next item.

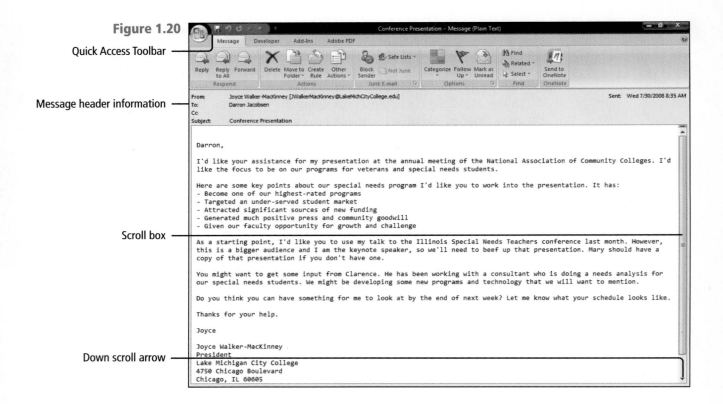

Figure 1.20

Quick Access Toolbar

Message header information

Scroll box

Down scroll arrow

Figure 1.20

Conference Presentation - Message (Plain Text)

From: Joyce Walker-MacKinney [JWalkerMacKinney@LakeMichCityCollege.edu]   Sent: Wed 7/30/2008 8:35 AM
To: Darron Jacobsen
Cc:
Subject: Conference Presentation

Darron,

I'd like your assistance for my presentation at the annual meeting of the National Association of Community Colleges. I'd like the focus to be on our programs for veterans and special needs students.

Here are some key points about our special needs program I'd like you to work into the presentation. It has:
- Become one of our highest-rated programs
- Targeted an under-served student market
- Attracted significant sources of new funding
- Generated much positive press and community goodwill
- Given our faculty opportunity for growth and challenge

As a starting point, I'd like you to use my talk to the Illinois Special Needs Teachers conference last month. However, this is a bigger audience and I am the keynote speaker, so we'll need to beef up that presentation. Mary should have a copy of that presentation if you don't have one.

You might want to get some input from Clarence. He has been working with a consultant who is doing a needs analysis for our special needs students. We might be developing some new programs and technology that we will want to mention.

Do you think you can have something for me to look at by the end of next week? Let me know what your schedule looks like.

Thanks for your help.

Joyce

Joyce Walker-MacKinney
President
Lake Michigan City College
4750 Chicago Boulevard
Chicago, IL 60605

4 In the vertical scroll bar of the Message form, click the **down scroll arrow** or drag the scroll box down until the lower portion of the message displays.

5 Press End to move to the end of the message.

You can use Home or End to move to the beginning or end of a message you are reading. In a message you are writing, you can move the insertion point within the message, as described in the table in Figure 1.21.

Keystrokes for Moving the Insertion Point in a Message

Keystrokes	Result
Ctrl + End	Moves to the end of the message
Ctrl + Home	Moves to the beginning of the message
End	Moves to the end of the line
Home	Moves to the beginning of the line
Page Up	Moves up one window
PgDn	Moves down one window
↑	Moves up one line
↓	Moves down one line

Figure 1.21

6 Press [Home], and then, on the Message form title bar, click the **Close** button [X].

7 Locate the third message in the **Inbox**, which is the message from *Joyce Walker-MacKinney* with the subject heading **Faculty Meeting**, and then open it by double-clicking. Alternatively, click one time to select the message, and then from the File menu, click Open; or right-click and click Open.

8 On the Message form title bar, click the **Restore Down** button [image] so the message does not fill the screen.

9 On the Quick Access Toolbar, click the **Previous Item** button [image].

The message is closed, and the Message form displays the previous message in your Inbox, which is the message from *Joyce Walker-MacKinney* with the subject **Conference Presentation**.

10 On the Quick Access Toolbar, click the **Next Item** button [image].

11 Click the **Next Item** button [image] again.

The displayed message is closed, and the next message in your Inbox displays. You can view all the messages in your Inbox in the Message form by using this toolbar button. When you do so, the current message is closed, and the next message in the list displays.

12 Use the **Next Item** button [image] to view the remaining messages in your Inbox. The last message is from *Mary Adair* and has the subject heading **I need your signature!**.

13 **Close** [X] the Message form, and notice that no unread items remain in the Inbox.

Activity 1.11 Opening a Message with an Attachment

A message might include an ***attachment***, which is a separate file that is included with the message. The attachment could be information in a Word file, an Excel spreadsheet file, or an image file. Outlook blocks the receipt of files that might contain viruses. For example, any file that has the file name extension of *.bat*, *.vbs*, or *.exe* is blocked. One of the messages Darron has received includes an attachment.

1 In the **Inbox**, locate the message from *Mary Adair* with the subject heading **Winter/Spring Schedule** and click it one time to display it in the Reading Pane. Compare your screen with Figure 1.22.

In the Inbox, a small paper clip icon displays under the date of the message. This indicates that the message has an attachment. In the Reading Pane, the name of the attachment file displays. The icon representing the Word program indicates that the attachment is a Word document.

Figure 1.22

Attached file ——

Word icon ——

Paper clip icon ——

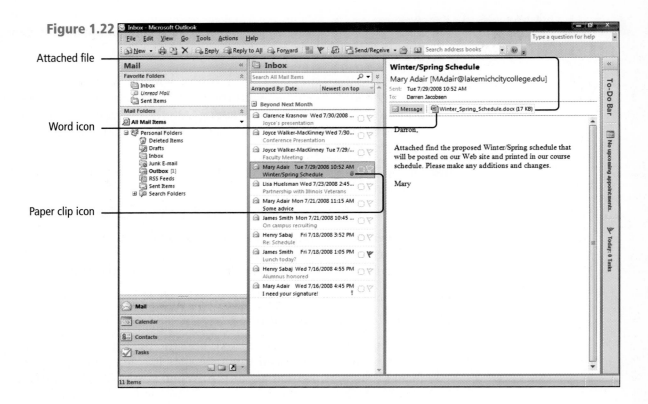

2 Open the **Winter/Spring Schedule** message.

The message displays in the Message form. The attachment file name displays in the message header.

3 Double-click the **Word icon** in the attachment file name to open the attachment. Alternatively, right-click the attachment, and then click **Open**. Compare your screen with Figure 1.23.

The Opening Mail Attachment dialog box displays. Outlook displays this dialog box to remind you that attachments might contain viruses. You have the choice of opening an attachment or saving it as a file. You should not open an attachment unless it is from a known source. Your system may include an antivirus program that scans attachments, but unless you are certain that this is the case, it is safer to save the attachment as a file and scan it with an antivirus program before opening it.

Figure 1.23

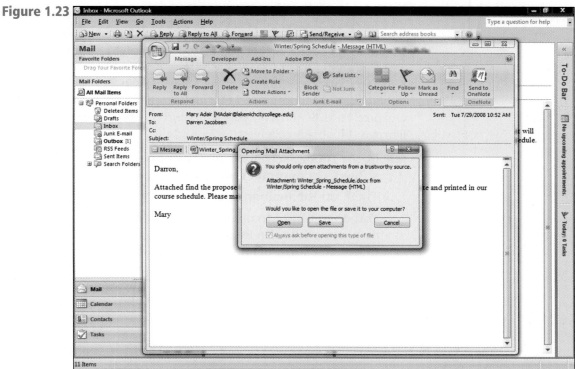

4 In the **Opening Mail Attachment** dialog box, click **Open**. If Microsoft Word displays a dialog box containing information about the Full Screen Reading view, click OK.

Microsoft Word starts the Word program and displays the attached file, which is a Word document.

Alert! — **Is the Word attachment in Reading view?**

The Word attachment may open in Full Screen Reading view. You can click on the Close button at the top right of your screen to close this view.

---

5 In the **Microsoft Word** title bar, click the **Close** button to close the attachment.

The Winter/Spring Schedule message displays. Note that an attachment is part of an e-mail message unless you save it separately. You can save an attachment separately by right-clicking the Word icon in the attachment file name and then clicking Save As. You will not save this attachment separately.

6 **Close** the **Winter/Spring Schedule** message.

Another Way — **To Open Messages**

You can also open a selected message using the keyboard shortcut Ctrl + O. Finally, recall that you can right-click a message to display a shortcut menu and then click Open.

Activity 1.12 Replying to an E-mail Message

You can reply to an e-mail message from the Inbox or while viewing it in the Message form. A toolbar button for replying to messages is available when replying from the Inbox. When viewing the message, a Reply button is located on the Ribbon on the Message tab in the Respond group. Recall that you configured Outlook to place your sent messages in the Outbox. In this activity, you will send a reply to one of the messages that Darron Jacobsen received.

1 In the **Inbox**, select the message from *James Smith* that has the subject **On campus recruiting** to display it in the Reading Pane. Then, on the toolbar, click the **Reply** button Reply.

You do not have to open a message to reply to it—selecting and displaying it in the Reading Pane is sufficient to create a reply. A Message form displays. Outlook adds the prefix *RE:* to the subject and title of the message. **RE:** is commonly used to mean *in regard to* or *regarding*. The text of the original message is included in the message area of the form, and Outlook places the sender's e-mail address in the To box. Compare your screen with Figure 1.24.

Figure 1.24

RE: Reply message prefix

Original message text

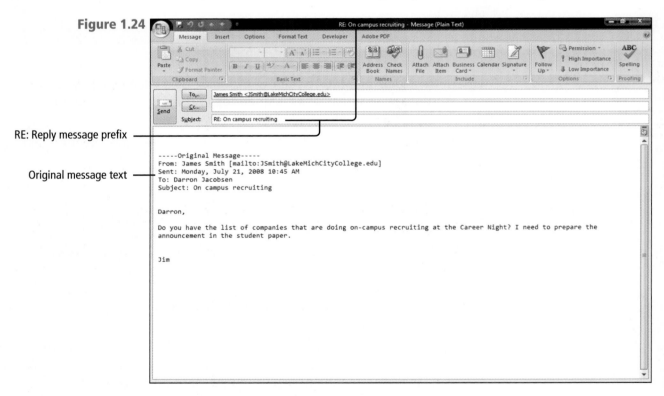

2 With the insertion point at the top of the message area, type **Jim**, and press Enter **two** times. Type **I will have the list ready for you by the end of the day.** Press Enter **two** times, and type **Darron**

A message reply is typed above the original message so that the recipient does not have to scroll down to see your reply.

3 On the Message form, click the **Send** button.

The message is sent to the Outbox, and the Message form closes.

4 In the **Inbox**, locate the *James Smith*, **On campus recruiting** message, and then compare your screen with Figure 1.25.

The red arrow on the message in the Inbox shows that you have replied to the message. In the Reading Pane, a banner tells you the date and time that you replied to the message.

Figure 1.25

Banner indicates when the reply was sent (your date will differ)

Icon indicates that a reply has been sent

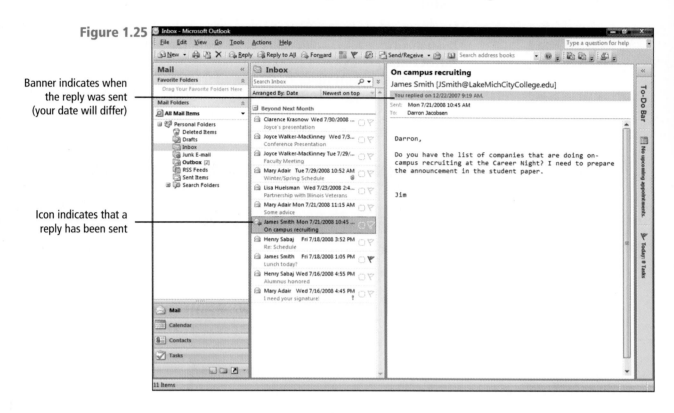

More Knowledge

Replying to Multiple Recipients

When you receive a message that has been sent to a group of individuals including you, you can use the Reply to All button to send your reply to everyone who received the original message. To reply only to the sender of the original message, use the Reply button as you did in this activity.

Activity 1.13 Forwarding an E-mail Message

You can forward an e-mail message you receive to someone else—commonly referred to as a ***third party***. This is called ***forwarding***. However, do not forward messages to others unless you are sure the sender of the original message would approve of forwarding the message. You can forward a message from the Inbox or while viewing the opened message. Darron Jacobsen has received a message that he wants to forward to a third party, Henry Sabaj at Lake Michigan City College.

1 In the **Inbox**, click the *Joyce Walker-MacKinney* **Faculty Meeting** message to display it in the Reading Pane.

2 On the toolbar, click the **Forward** button .

You do not have to open a message to forward it. A Message form displays. Outlook adds the prefix *FW:* to the subject and title of the message. The text of the original message is included in the message area of the form.

3 In the **To** box, type the first letter of the recipient's address, which is **h** and then compare your screen with Figure 1.26.

Under the To box, Outlook displays the address *HSabaj@ LakeMichCityCollege.edu.* This is an example of Outlook's *AutoComplete* feature; Outlook remembers addresses you have typed previously. If more than one address begins with the first character you type, Outlook displays all suggested addresses. You may continue typing the address if you do not want to use any of the displayed addresses.

Figure 1.26

AutoComplete suggests address (one or more suggestions may display)

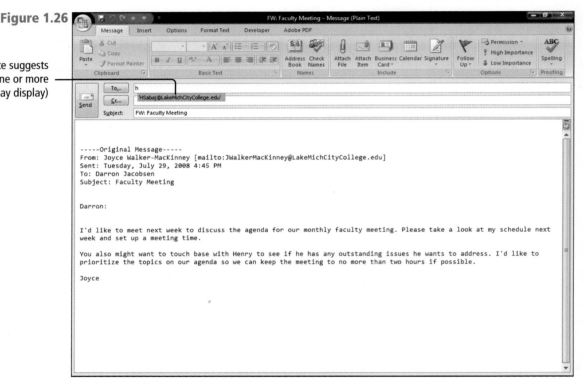

4 Point to *Henry Sabaj's* address and click once, or, if his address is highlighted, press Enter to accept the suggested address. Then, click to place the insertion point at the top of the message area, type **Henry,** and press Enter **two** times.

5 Type **As you can see from Joyce's message below, she's asked me to find out if you have any outstanding issues for the next faculty meeting. Let me know.**

6 Press Enter **two** times and type **Darron** Then, on the Message form, click the **Send** button.

The message is sent to the Outbox, and the Message form closes. The blue arrow on the message in the Inbox and the Reading Pane indicates that you have forwarded the message. Notice that the icons for the forwarded and replied messages are different and that they are the same as their respective buttons on the toolbar.

Activity 1.14 Sending an Attachment and Deleting Text in a Message

You can attach one or more files to any message you send. When you reply to a message, you may prefer *not* to include some of, or the entire, previous message. You can delete portions of text by **selecting text** and pressing [Delete]. Selecting text refers to highlighting areas of the text by dragging with the mouse.

1 In the **Inbox**, click the *Henry Sabaj* **RE: Schedule** message to display it in the Reading Pane, and then, on the Standard toolbar, click the **Reply** [⤺ Reply].

The Message form displays. The message area displays text from two previous messages. You can delete the earlier message, which is the lower half of the Message form text.

2 **Maximize** [▫] the viewing area, if necessary, and then click to place the insertion point at the beginning of the line *Original Message*. Drag downward to the lower portion of the message area to select the lower portion of the text, as shown in Figure 1.27.

Figure 1.27

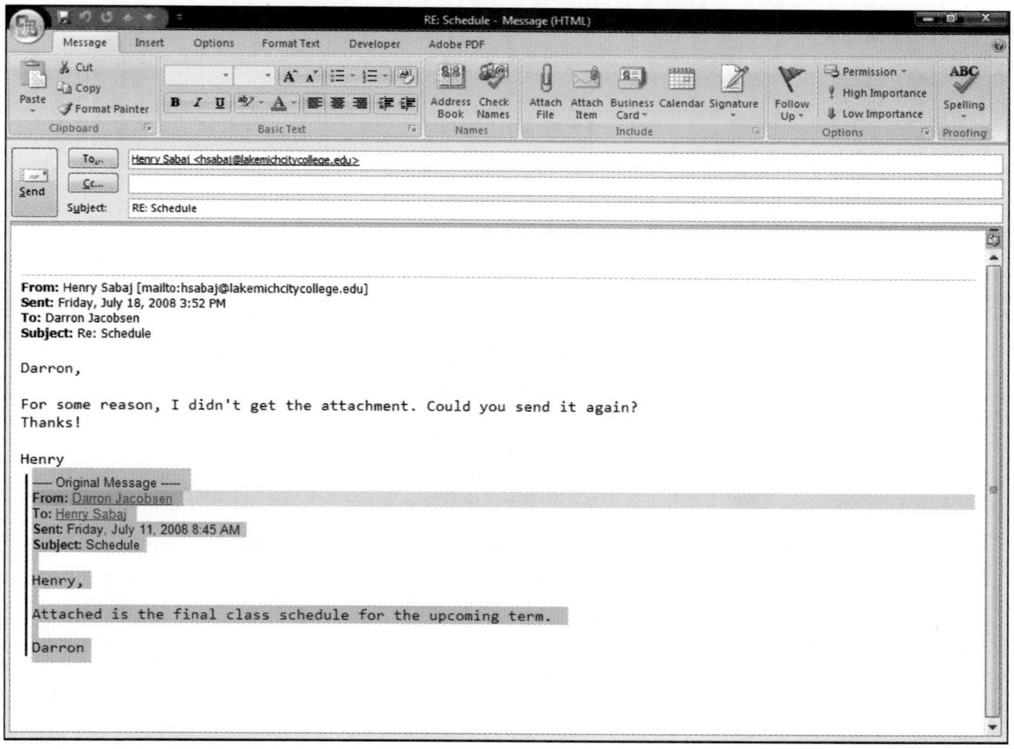

3 Press Delete to delete the selected text. Press Ctrl + Home to place the insertion point at the top of the message area. Type **Henry,** and then press Enter **two** times.

4 Type **Here it is again.** Press Enter **two** times and then type **Darron** On the **Message tab**, in the **Include group**, click the **Attach File**

button [paperclip icon], and then compare your screen with Figure 1.28.

The Insert File dialog box displays a list of the drives available on your system. The drives and folders displayed on your screen will differ.

Figure 1.28

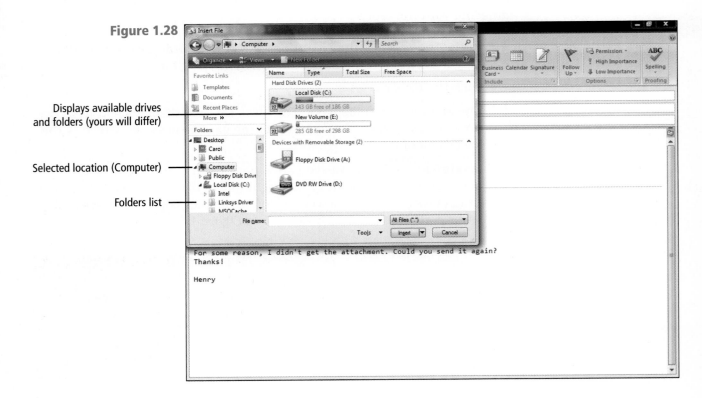

Displays available drives and folders (yours will differ)

Selected location (Computer)

Folders list

5 At the left side of the **Insert File** dialog box, in the **Folders** list, click on **Computer**, and then navigate to the location where the student files that accompany this textbook are stored. Locate the Word file **o01A_Office_Staff_Schedule** and click **one** time to select it. Then, in the lower right corner of the **Insert File** dialog box, click **Insert**.

The Insert File dialog box closes, and the Message form redisplays. Outlook attaches the document to the message. The Word icon and the name of the attached file display in the Attached box.

If you decide later you do not want to attach the file to the message, you can click the attachment icon and press Delete. Also, the attachment icon will displace the position of the salutation if this message is printed, but you can add a blank line before the salutation to prevent this.

6 On the Message title bar, click the **Restore Down** button 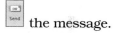 to restore the Message form to its original size, and then **Send** the message.

The message is sent to the Outbox, and the Message form closes. The Inbox and the Reading Pane indicate that you have replied to the message.

> **Note** — Deleting Original Text in Messages
>
> Many Outlook users prefer not to include the original text of a message when they reply to or forward a message, especially when the original text is lengthy or contains multiple responses. You can manually delete the original text of a message. You can also have Outlook delete the original text of messages automatically. To automatically delete original text, display the Tools menu, click Options, and then, on the Preferences page, click E-mail Options. In the E-Mail Options dialog box, you can choose how you want Outlook to handle original text for replies and forwarded messages.

Objective 4
Use Mail Options and Signatures

Outlook has options that you can apply to messages. For example, you can mark a message to remind yourself or the message recipient to take some follow-up action. You can check the spelling of every message you compose. A message can be marked for *sensitivity* or *importance*. Sensitivity refers to a security label applied to messages that should not be read by others because of the message content—for example, information about employee salaries. Importance refers to marks that are applied to messages based on the urgency of the message—for example, information that should be read immediately or information that can be read later.

You can create *signatures* for your messages. A signature is a block of text that is added at the end of your message and can be inserted manually or automatically. A signature commonly includes your name, title, address, and phone number. It might also include a paragraph informing a recipient how to reach you or respond to your message.

Activity 1.15 Flagging Messages and Formatting Text

Marking a message with a flag—referred to as *flagging*—gives you a way to draw attention to a message and to include additional information with it. You can also use a flag to remind the recipient to follow up the message in some way. You can flag both sent and received messages. ***Formatting text*** refers to the process of setting the appearance of the text in a message by changing the color, shading, or size of the text. In this activity, you will reply to one of Darron Jacobsen's received messages, adding a flag and formatting the reply.

1 In the **Inbox**, click to display the **Joyce's presentation** message from *Clarence Krasnow* in the Reading Pane, and then click **Reply** 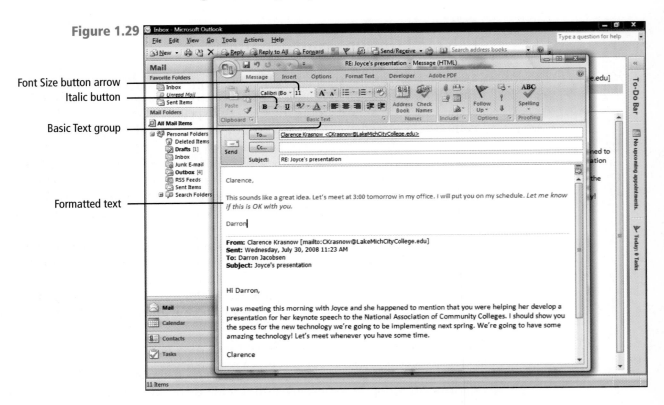.

The Message form displays. This message is in HTML format because this was the format of the original message. Because the text is in HTML format, you can apply formatting to the text.

2 With the insertion point at the top of the message area, and using the technique you have practiced for spacing the parts of an e-mail message, type **Clarence, This sounds like a great idea. Let's meet at 3:00 tomorrow in my office. I will put you on my schedule. Let me know if this is OK with you. Darron**

3 Select the sentence *Let me know if this is OK with you.* On the **Message tab** in the **Basic Text group**, click the **Italic** button *I* to apply the italic style to the selected text. In the **Basic Text group**, click the **Font Size button arrow** and then click **12** to increase the font size. Click anywhere in the message to cancel the text selection. If **Darron** has a red wavy underline, right-click on **Darron**, and then click **Ignore**. Compare your screen with Figure 1.29.

Figure 1.29

Font Size button arrow
Italic button
Basic Text group
Formatted text

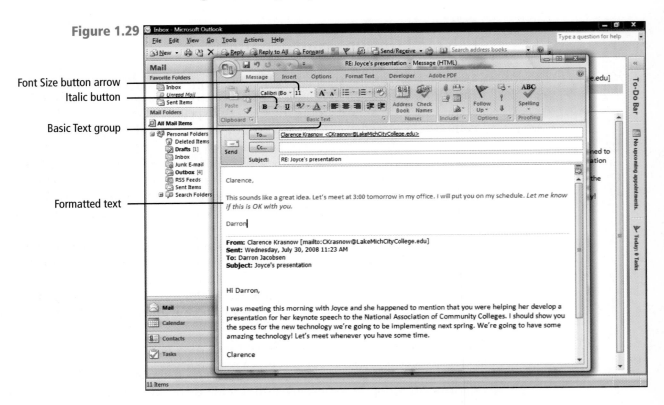

4 On the **Message tab**, in the **Options group**, click the **Follow Up** button, and then click **Flag for Recipients**. Compare your screen with Figure 1.30.

Figure 1.30

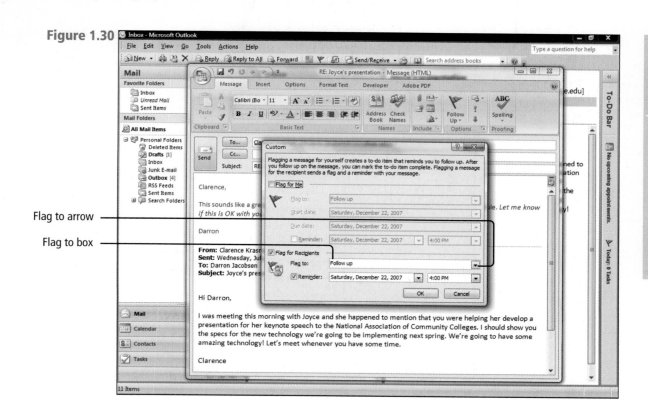

Flag to arrow

Flag to box

5 In the **Custom** dialog box, click the **Flag to arrow** to view a predefined list of requested actions you can add to the message. From the **Flag to** list, click **Reply**.

You can use any of the predefined messages. Notice that you can also specify a date and time. If the message recipient uses Outlook, a reminder will display on the recipient's system at the appropriate time.

6 At the lower portion of the **Custom** dialog box, click **OK**, and then,

on the Message form, click the **Send** button. Compare your screen with Figure 1.31.

The message is sent to the Outbox, and the Message form closes. Both the Inbox and the Reading Pane indicate that you have replied to the message.

Figure 1.31

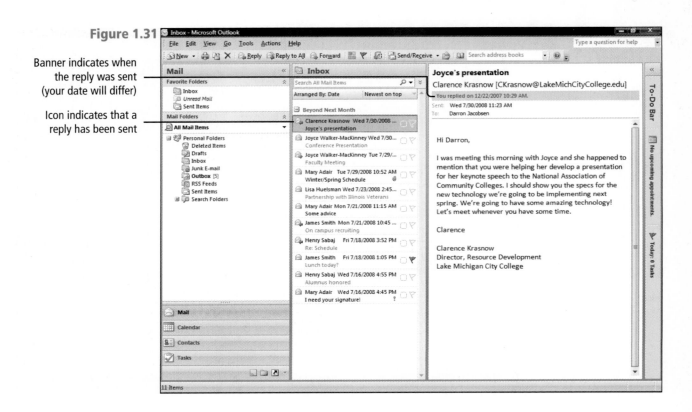

Banner indicates when the reply was sent (your date will differ)

Icon indicates that a reply has been sent

7 In the **Inbox**, select the message from *James Smith* with the subject **Lunch today?** Notice that a red flag displays to the right of the date.

This is how a flagged message appears to you, the recipient. At the top of the Reading Pane, a banner indicates *Follow up*.

8 Select the message from *Joyce Walker-MacKinney* with the subject **Conference presentation**. On the Standard toolbar, click the **Follow Up** button [icon], and then click the **Tomorrow** flag.

The message displays a flag. You can choose from a variety of flags to call attention to messages you have received, as described in the table in Figure 1.32.

Outlook Message Flags

Flag	Start Date	Due Date
Today	Current date	Current date
Tomorrow	Current date plus one day	Current date plus one day
This Week	Current date plus two days, but no later than the last work day of this week	Last work day of this week
Next Week	First work day of next week	Last work day of next week
No Date	No date	No date
Custom	Choose a custom date if desired	Choose a custom date if desired

Figure 1.32

9 At the extreme right of the Outlook window, on the **To-Do Bar**, click

the **Expand the To-Do Bar** button ⌈ « ⌉. Compare your screen with Figure 1.33. Your screen will differ.

Notice the subject names for flagged e-mail messages are listed at the bottom of the To-Do Bar. Recall that the To-Do Bar is designed to give you a consolidated view for appointments, tasks, and flagged e-mail. Double-clicking the subject name will open the related e-mail, regardless of your current folder view.

Figure 1.33

Calendar

Expanded view of To-Do Bar

Flagged e-mail displays (yours may differ)

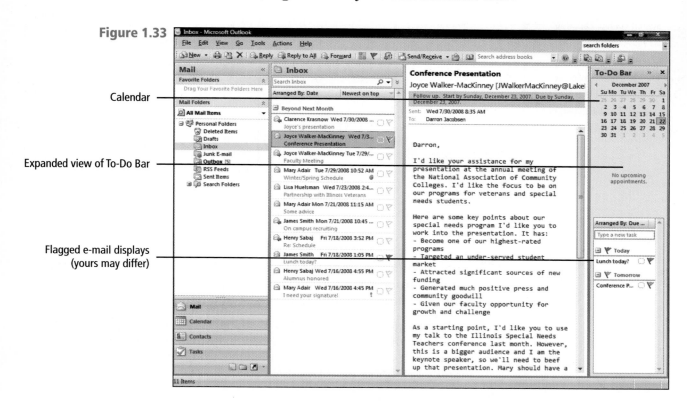

10 On the **To-Do Bar**, click the **Minimize the To-Do Bar** button ⌈ » ⌉.

11 In the **Navigation Pane**, in the **Mail Folders** section, locate **Search Folders**, scrolling if necessary. If this folder is not expanded, click the **plus symbol** next to it to display the folders within **Search Folders**. Compare your screen with Figure 1.34. Your screen may differ.

A Search Folder is a virtual folder that allows you to view all e-mail items that match specific conditions. For example, the *Unread Mail* folder allows you to view all unread messages, regardless of where the messages may be located.

Figure 1.34

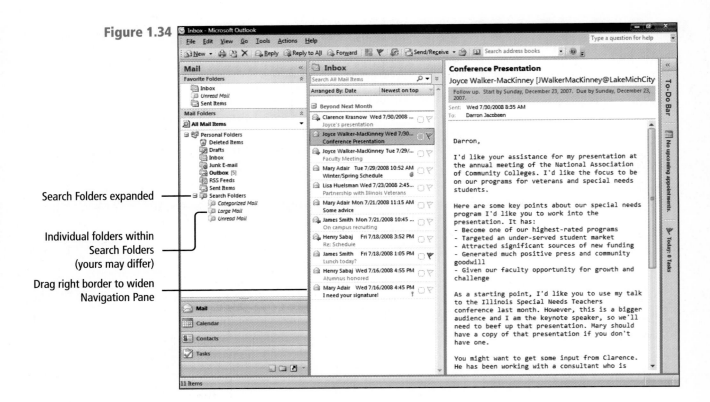

Search Folders expanded

Individual folders within Search Folders (yours may differ)

Drag right border to widen Navigation Pane

12 If the **Navigation Pane** is too narrow to show the folders in **Search Folders**, place the insertion point on the right border of the Navigation Pane, and drag it slightly to the right to widen it.

13 In the **Navigation Pane**, in the **Mail Folders** section, click on **Inbox**. Locate the message from *Mary Adair* with the subject **I need your signature!**. Right-click on the message, and then from the shortcut menu, click **Mark as Unread**.

14 Click on the **Unread Mail** folder.

Notice the Search Folder named *Unread Mail* is now active and the message from Mary Adair is displayed.

15 Click the **Inbox** folder, click the message from *Mary Adair* with the subject **I need your signature!**.

The message is now displayed in the Reading Pane, and is considered read. It is no longer indicated in the *Unread Mail* folder.

Activity 1.16 Using the Spelling Checker

Outlook's automatic spelling and grammar checker is active when Outlook is installed. Outlook indicates a misspelled word by underlining it with a wavy red line. To manually check the spelling of a word that has a wavy red line in a message, point to the word and right-click. In this activity, you will send a new message for Darron Jacobsen to one of his colleagues and use the spelling checker to correct spelling errors.

1 Click the **New Mail Message** button [New] to display a new, blank Message form. In the **To** box, type **LHuelsman@ LakeMichCityCollege.edu** As you type, if the e-mail address displays in blue, indicating that Outlook remembers it, you can press Enter to have the AutoComplete feature fill in the address for you.

2 Press Tab **two** times to move the insertion point to the **Subject** box, and then type **Could you join me for a meeting?** Press Tab **one** time to place the insertion point in the message area.

Recall that it is a good e-mail practice to create a subject that is brief and informative for recipients when they view your message in a list of other received messages.

3 In the message area, type **Lisa,** and then press Enter **two** times.

4 Type, but do not correct any spelling errors, as follows: **I'm arranging a meeting with the Illanois Veterans Association to discuss our partnerchip program. Could you join me?** Press Enter **two** times and type **Darron**

If you typed *Illanois*, Outlook indicates this word as misspelled by underlining it with a wavy red line. You can also have Outlook find the correct spelling.

5 Point to the word **Illanois** and right-click. Compare your screen with Figure 1.35.

A shortcut menu displays near the pointer. At the top of the shortcut menu, Outlook suggests a correct spelling of the word. If there is more than one possible correct spelling, the shortcut menu displays multiple choices.

Figure 1.35

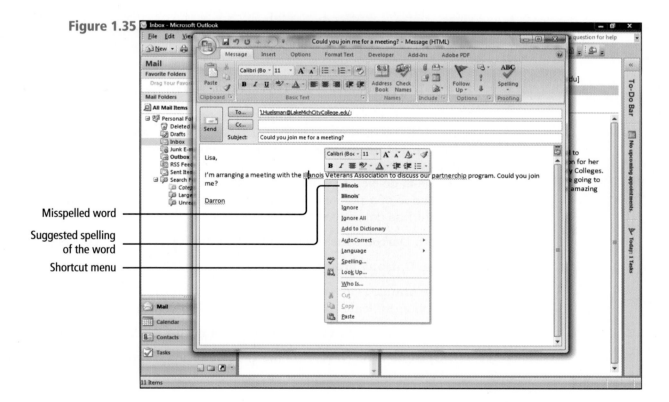

Misspelled word

Suggested spelling of the word

Shortcut menu

6 From the shortcut menu, click **Illinois** to correct the spelling.

7 Point to the word **partnerchip** and right-click to display the shortcut menu. At the top of the shortcut menu, click **partnership**.

8 Point to the name **Darron** at the end of the message and right-click.

A shortcut menu displays. There are multiple spellings of this name. However, the name as it is typed is correct. Using the shortcut menu command, you can add the word to the dictionary. You can have Outlook add a word to its dictionary so that it will not appear as misspelled in this or future documents. The spelling checker feature functions in the same manner across all the Microsoft Office programs, so if you are familiar with how this feature works in Word, for example, you will find that it works in the same way in Outlook.

9 Click **Ignore** to close the shortcut menu without adding Darron to the dictionary.

More Knowledge

Checking the Spelling of an Entire Message

You can have Outlook check all the misspelled words in a message at one time. From the Ribbon, on the Message tab, in the Proofing group, click the Spelling & Grammar button. The Spelling and Grammar dialog box displays the first misspelled word and displays suggested corrections. You can proceed through the entire message, correcting each misspelled word. When you click Options in the Spelling and Grammar dialog box, you can adjust how Outlook corrects spelling and grammar in a more precise manner.

Activity 1.17 Modifying Message Settings and Delivery Options

Recall that setting message importance and message sensitivity are options that you can use with messages. You can also set various *message delivery options*, such as the time a message is sent or an address that should be used for replies. These are applied at the time a message is delivered. One of the messages you will send for Darron Jacobsen is of a personal nature, and he also wants to know when the recipient has actually read it.

1 With Darron's message to Lisa still displayed, on the **Message tab**, in the **Options group**, click the **High Importance** button.

The orange color and black line border around the button on the Ribbon indicate that the *Importance: High* status is active.

2 On the **Message tab**, in the **Options group**, click the **Message Options** dialog box launcher, and then compare your screen with Figure 1.36.

Figure 1.36

Importance level set to *High*

Delivery and read
receipt options

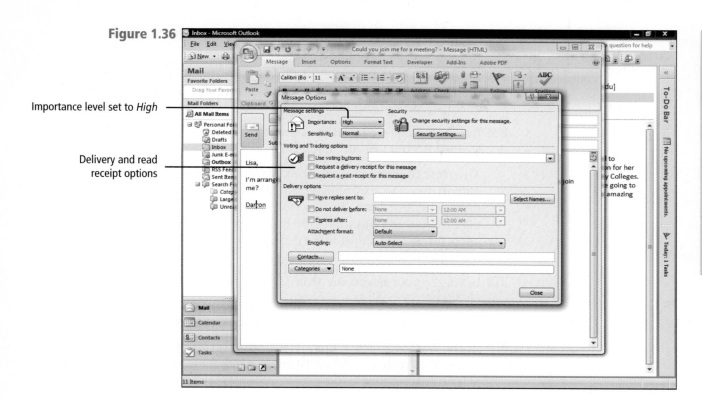

3 In the displayed **Message Options** dialog box, notice that under **Message settings**, **Importance** is set to **High**. Click the **Sensitivity arrow**, and then click **Personal**.

It is good practice to use discretion when discussing confidential or personal information in your e-mail messages. Recall that the privacy of your e-mail messages cannot be guaranteed.

4 Under **Voting and Tracking** options, click to select the **Request a read receipt for this message** check box.

By selecting this option, you will be notified when the recipient reads this message.

5 In the lower right corner of the **Message Options** dialog box, click

Close. **Send** the message.

6 Be sure the **Inbox** folder is displayed, and then locate and select the message from *Mary Adair* with the subject **I need your signature!** to display it in the Reading Pane.

When Mary sent this message, she applied the *Importance: High* setting. In the Inbox folder list, an Importance icon displays under the date, and a banner displays at the top of the message in the Reading Pane.

Activity 1.18 Creating and Adding Signatures for Messages

Recall that an e-mail signature is a block of text that can be automatically added to the end of your messages. It can also include a picture. It is common to include your name, title, address, or phone number in a signature. In this activity, you will create a signature for Darron Jacobsen and add it to a new message.

1 From the **Tools** menu, click **Options**. In the displayed **Options** dialog box, click the **Mail Format** tab. In the **Signatures** section, click **Signatures…**.

2 In the displayed **Signatures and Stationery** dialog box, on the **E-mail Signature** tab, click **New**.

The **New Signature** dialog box displays. You can create multiple signatures. For example, you might have a signature that contains only your first name to use with friends and family, and another signature that contains your full name and title to use with business associates. You should use a name or descriptive text to identify each signature.

3 In the **Type a name for this signature** box, type **Darron** and then click **OK**.

The name Darron appears in the **Select signature to edit** box.

4 In the **Edit signature** box, type **Darron Jacobsen** and then press Enter. Type **Vice President, Administrative Affairs** and then compare your screen with Figure 1.37.

Figure 1.37

New Messages arrow

Select signature to edit box

Edit signature box

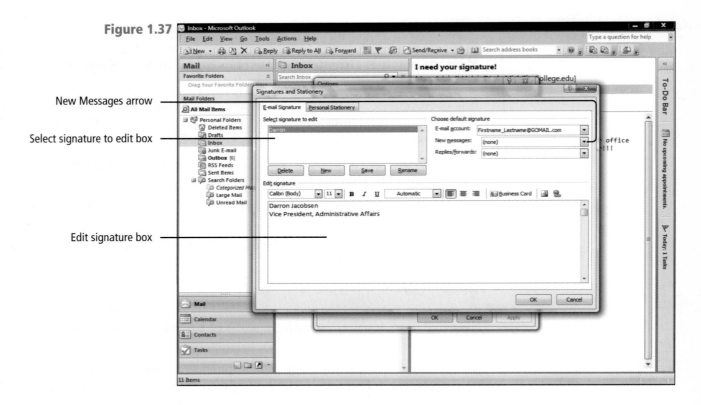

5 To indicate when you want to use the new signature, at the top right of the dialog box, click the **New messages** arrow. From the displayed list, click *Darron*, and then click **OK** to close the Signatures and Stationery dialog box. Click **OK** to close the **Options** dialog box.

The new signature will be applied only to new messages. Replied messages and forwarded messages normally will not display your signature. An option in the Signatures and Stationery dialog box enables you to apply a signature to replies and forwards if you want to do so.

6 Open a **New Mail Message** , and notice that Outlook adds the signature text to the message area of the Message form.

You add text to the message above the signature as you would with any message. New messages are created in HTML format. You can change the format to Plain Text for the message.

7 On the **Options tab**, in the **Format group**, click the **Plain Text** button **Aa Plain Text**, and then compare your screen with Figure 1.38.

The Microsoft Office Outlook Compatibility Checker dialog box appears. There is a warning that the text of the signature will be reformatted as Plain Text. Recall that it is good practice to use Plain Text because not all e-mail programs display formatted text, such as text with bold or italic applied.

Figure 1.38

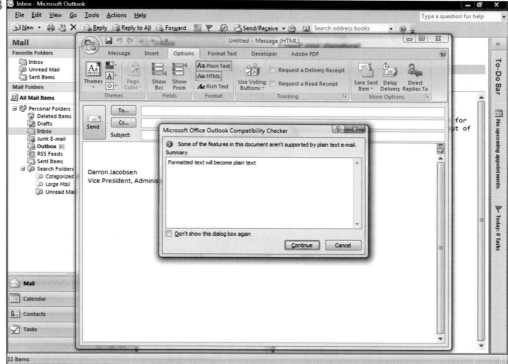

8 In the **Microsoft Office Outlook Compatibility Checker** dialog box, click **Continue**.

The signature is reformatted as Plain Text.

9 **Close** the Message form, and then click **No** when asked whether you want to save the message.

Activity 1.19 Editing a Signature

You can make changes to signatures you have created. In this activity, you will add the organization name and telephone number to Darron's signature.

1 From the **Tools** menu, click **Options**. In the **Options** dialog box, click the **Mail Format** tab. In the **Signatures** section click **Signatures**.

The Signatures and Stationery dialog box displays. Under Signature, the signature named *Darron* that you created in the previous activity is selected.

2 In the **Edit signature** box, click to place the insertion point at the end of the word *Affairs* and press (Enter). Type **Lake Michigan City College** and then press (Enter). Type **(312)-555-0134** Compare your screen with Figure 1.39.

Figure 1.39

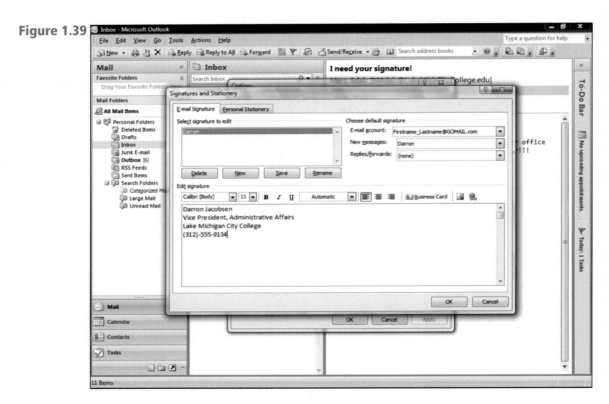

3 Click **OK two** times to close the dialog boxes.

Activity 1.20 Discontinuing or Deleting a Signature

You may want to create a signature, use it selectively, and discontinue it when it is not needed. You can also delete it completely.

1 From the **Tools** menu, display the **Options** dialog box, and then click the **Mail Format** tab. In the **Signatures** section, click **Signatures**.

The Signatures and Stationery dialog box opens. The current setting applies the *Darron* signature to all new messages.

2 Click the **New messages** arrow, and then click **(None)**.

The *Darron* signature is discontinued. It is still available on the list if you want to renew its automatic use in this manner. You can delete it completely if you no longer need it.

3 If necessary, in the **Select signature to edit** box, click to select **Darron**.

The *Darron* signature that you created is selected. If more than one signature displays, you must select the signature you want to remove or edit.

4 Below the **Select signature to edit** box, click **Delete**, and then compare your screen with Figure 1.40.

A warning message asks you whether you are sure you want to delete the signature.

Figure 1.40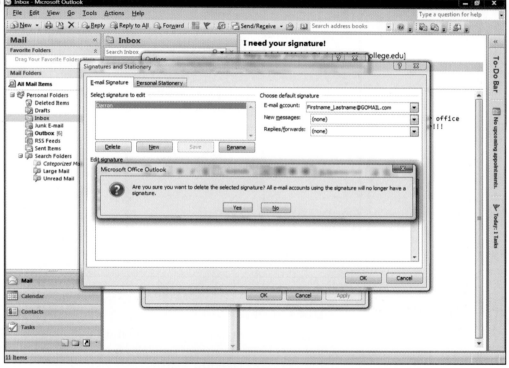

5 In the **Microsoft Office Outlook** dialog box, click **Yes** to delete the signature. Click **OK** two times to close the dialog boxes.

Objective 5
Manage E-mail

After you have started receiving a large number of e-mail messages, you will need to manage the contents of your Inbox and other mail folders. Outlook has tools that you can use to quickly find a specific e-mail message. You can sort and organize your mail folders, and you can print your e-mail messages.

Activity 1.21 Finding E-mail Messages

Outlook provides an Instant Search feature that is a fast way to find your information, no matter where it is located. Instant Search will display results immediately, as you are typing your search criteria. You can search for all messages from one person. You can also search for the occurrence of a specific word or phrase in all your messages. In this activity, you will search Darron's Inbox folder for messages containing a specific phrase.

1 Be sure the **Inbox** folder is displayed. At the top of the **Inbox** pane, locate the **Instant Search** pane, and then place your insertion point in the **Instant Search** box, as shown in Figure 1.41.

Figure 1.41

Instant Search box ⎯

Instant Search pane ⎯

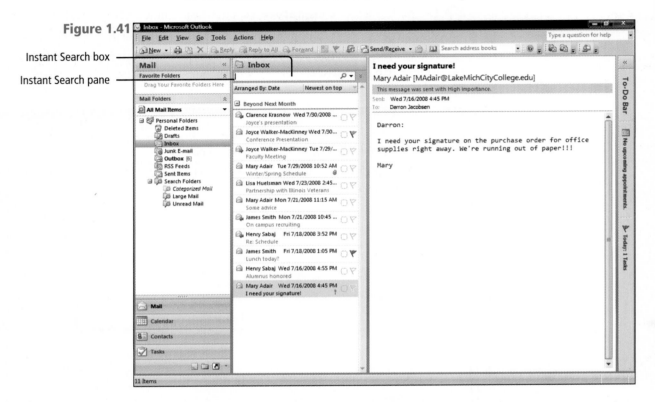

Alert!

Does your screen differ?

If you are using Windows XP, you must download and install the search components to enable Instant Search. Go to *www.microsoft.com* and download the Windows Desktop Search component.

---

2 In the **Instant Search** box, type **veterans** Do not be concerned if displayed messages change as you type.

The Inbox displays two e-mail messages that contain the word *veterans*.

3 In the **Instant Search** box, click the **Clear Search** button ⊠ to clear the search and redisplay the entire Inbox. In the **Instant Search** box, type **schedule**

The Inbox displays five e-mail messages, all of which have text that contains the word *schedule*.

4 Click the **Clear Search** button ⊠ to clear the search and redisplay the entire Inbox.

More Knowledge

Performing More Detailed Searches

You can perform more detailed searches by clicking the Expand the Query Builder button to the right of the search box. In this expanded view, you can also click the Add Criteria button in the lower left corner. For example, you might want to search for messages sent to or received from a specific person or for messages sent during a specific time period.

Activity 1.22 Sorting and Organizing Inbox Messages

Sometimes you will want to sort your messages. For example, you may want to see all the messages you received on a specific date or all the messages you received from a specific person. Additionally, you can organize your messages using folders, colors, and different views. As you will see while working with Darron's Inbox, different arrangements offer a more visually oriented way to work with messages.

1 From the **View** menu, point to **Reading Pane**, click **Bottom**, and then compare your screen with Figure 1.42.

The Reading Pane displays in the lower portion of the Outlook window. When the Reading Pane is turned off or is displayed in the lower portion of the Outlook window, you can see the message **column headings**. The column headings identify the message **fields**, which are categories of information within an item, such as the subject of a message or the date and time received.

Column headings

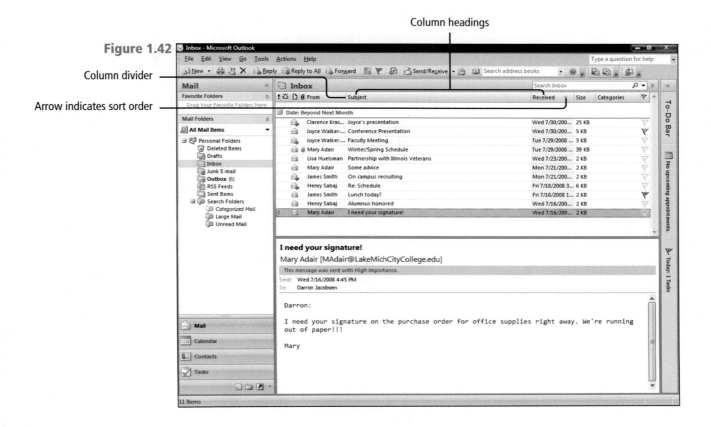

Figure 1.42

Column divider

Arrow indicates sort order

2 Point to the column heading **Subject**, and notice the ScreenTip *Sort by: Subject.*

Use the column headings to sort your messages. The column heading used by default to sort Inbox messages is the *Received* field, with the most recent messages displayed first. The leftmost column headings are icons for sorting by Importance, by Reminder, by Icon, or by Attachment.

3 In the **Inbox**, click the **From** column heading, and notice that a pale upward-pointing arrow displays to the right of *From.*

The Inbox messages are sorted alphabetically by the sender's first name. The up arrow in the *From* header indicates that this is ascending order—from A to Z.

4 In the **Inbox**, click the **From** column heading again to change the sort order to descending—from Z to A.

The downward-pointing arrow in the *From* header indicates that the sort order is descending.

5 In the **Inbox**, click the **up scroll arrow** and notice that the messages are grouped by the person they are from.

6 In the **Inbox**, click the **Received** column heading to restore sorting by the date and time received.

Recall that received messages flow into your Inbox by the date and time received, which is the default sort order.

More Knowledge
Grouping Messages by Date

By default, Outlook displays messages in your Inbox by the date received in groups. Your Inbox will likely display a single group, Older. As you receive messages over a period of days, you will likely see additional groups such as Today, Yesterday, and Last Month. You can turn the grouping feature on and off. From the View menu, point to Arrange By, and then click Show in Groups.

7 In the **Inbox**, click any message from *Mary Adair.* Then, from the **Tools** menu, click **Organize**, and then compare your screen with Figure 1.43.

The ***Ways to Organize Inbox pane*** displays. Use this pane to manage your Inbox using Folders, Colors, or Views. For example, you can apply color to messages from specific senders.

Figure 1.43

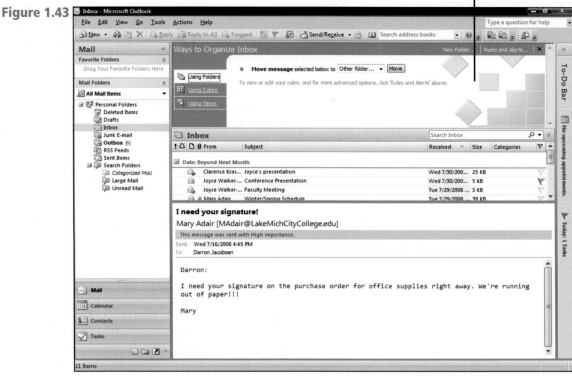

8 In the **Ways to Organize Inbox** pane, click **Using Colors**.

Options display for applying color to messages from Mary Adair—the selected sender. The default color is red.

9 Click the arrow to the right of **Red** and notice that there are a number of colors from which you can select. Click **Red** to retain it as the color for messages from *Mary Adair*, and then click **Apply Color**.

10 In the **Ways to Organize Inbox** pane, click the **Close Organize** button ![x] and notice that all the messages from Mary Adair display in red.

11 On the menu bar, click **View**, point to **Reading Pane**, and then click **Right** to display the Reading Pane in its default position.

More Knowledge

Resizing Inbox Column Widths

When the Reading Pane is displayed in the lower portion of the Outlook screen or is turned off, you can resize the column widths for the Inbox. Point to the divider that separates the message column headers and drag it left or right to increase or decrease the width of the column.

Activity 1.23 Printing Messages

Recall that Outlook organizes its information in folders. To print information in Outlook, each folder type has one or more predefined print styles associated with it. A **print style** is a combination of paper and page settings that determines the way items print. For the Inbox folder, there are two predefined print styles—Table Style and Memo Style. You can also customize a combination of paper and page settings for a unique print style. In this activity, you will print Darron's Inbox, Outbox, and one of his sent messages.

1 Be sure your **Inbox** folder is displayed so that the contents of the Inbox display in the center pane. From the **File** menu, point to **Page Setup**, and then click **Table Style**. In the displayed **Page Setup: Table Style** dialog box, and then notice the **Preview** image of what your printed document will look like.

To print a folder list, use the **Table Style**. Table Style prints selected items or all the items in a list with the visible columns displayed. Use Table Style to print multiple items, such as the contents of the Inbox.

2 Click the **Header/Footer** tab. In the **Page Setup: Table Style** dialog box, under **Footer**, click to position the insertion point in the first white box. Delete any existing text. Using your own first and last name, type **1A_College_Staff_Inbox_Firstname_Lastname** Do not be concerned if your text wraps to another line. Delete any existing information in the center and right footer boxes. Under **Header**, delete any existing text in the three boxes. Compare your screen with Figure 1.44.

Print styles may include the user name, the page number, and the print date in the footer, or they may include other information. Although the text you type in the Footer box may wrap to two lines, when the page is printed, the footer appears on a single line.

Figure 1.44

Footer information

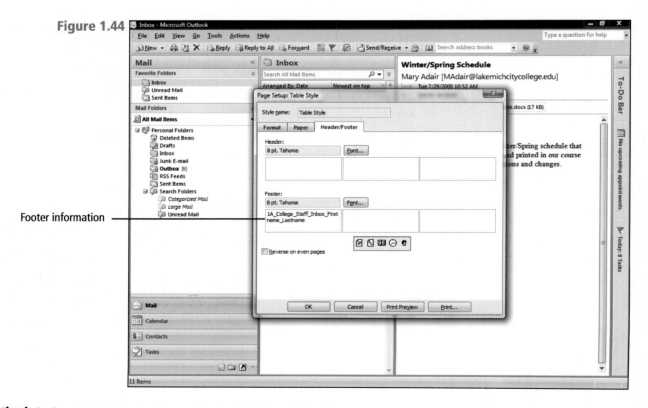

Alert! — **Does your screen show a different header or footer?**

Outlook remembers previously entered headers and footers. The boxes for this information in the Page Setup dialog box may indicate a previous user's name or some other information. You can enter new information in these boxes and Outlook will retain this information for the next header or footer you print in this print style.

3 In the **Page Setup: Table Style** dialog box, click the **Paper** tab. Under **Orientation**, click **Portrait** if this option is not already selected.

Here you can also control the margins and paper size of your documents.

4 At the bottom of the **Page Setup: Table Style** dialog box, click **Print Preview**.

The Inbox list displays as it will appear when printed. The pointer displays as a magnifying glass with a plus sign in it, indicating that you can magnify the view.

5 Point to the lower portion of the document, and click **one** time to enlarge the lower portion of the preview.

The lower portion of the document is enlarged and easier to read. The pointer changes to a magnifying glass with a minus sign in it.

6 Click **one** time anywhere in the document to return the view to its previous magnification. On the **Print Preview** toolbar, click the

Print button [🖨 Print...] and then compare your screen with Figure 1.45.

The print preview closes, and the Print dialog box displays. In the Print dialog box, you can specify the rows of the Inbox to print, the number of copies to print, and the printer to use. The printer that displays will be the printer that is configured for your computer.

Figure 1.45

Selected printer

Number of copies

Rows of the Inbox to print

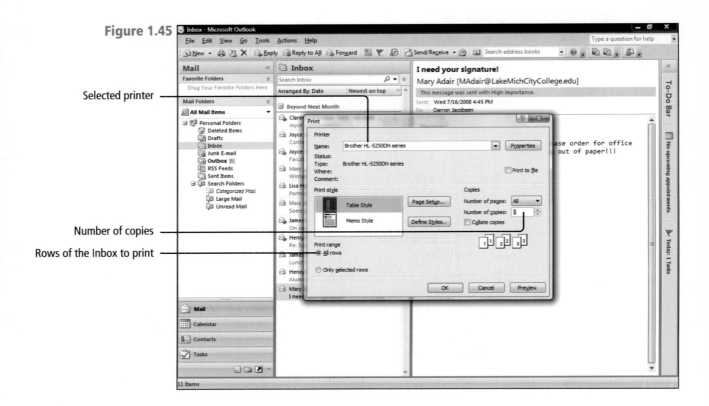

7 In the **Print** dialog box, under **Copies**, change the number of copies to **2** by clicking the **up arrow** in the spin box or by typing **2** in the box. In the lower portion of the **Print** dialog box, click **OK**.

From the printer connected to your system, collect your two copies of the Inbox list. Submit the end results to your instructor as directed.

8 In the **Navigation Pane**, under **Mail Folders**, click **Outbox** to display the Outbox folder. Click the first message in the Outbox **one** time to select it. Press and hold down ⇧Shift, and then click the last message in the Outbox.

All the Outbox messages are selected. Use this technique to select a group of items in any Windows-based program, such as Outlook.

More Knowledge

Selecting Nonadjacent Items

In any Windows-based program, to select nonadjacent items, press and hold down Ctrl, and then click the individual items.

9 From the **File** menu, click **Print**. In the **Print** dialog box, under **Print style**, click **Table Style**, and then click the **Page Setup** button.

10 In the **Page Setup: Table Style** dialog box, click the **Header/Footer** tab. Under **Footer**, delete the existing information in the left box. Using your own name, type **1A_College_Staff_Outbox_Firstname_Lastname** Click **OK**.

11 In the **Print** dialog box, click **OK**.

The list of messages in the Outbox prints in Table Style. Your dates will differ from those shown in Figure 1.1. Submit the end result to your instructor as directed.

12 In the **Outbox**, click to select the message from *Henry Sabaj* with the subject **FW: Faculty Meeting**. Recall that the *FW:* prefix indicates that this is a forwarded message.

13 From the **File** menu, click **Print**.

The Print dialog box displays. When you select an individual message to print, Outlook uses the Memo Style by default; thus, ***Memo Style*** is already selected. Memo Style prints the text of the selected items one at a time. Use Memo Style to print individual items, such as an entire e-mail message.

> **Note** — **Account Names in Printouts**
>
> Depending on the print style you use, your printout may include the name associated with the e-mail account that you are using on your computer. In the Memo Style print style, it displays in bold just under the header. It may be different from your own name.

14 In the **Print dialog box**, click **Page Setup**. In the **Page Setup: Memo Style dialog box**, click the **Header/Footer tab**. Under **Footer**, delete any existing information in the three boxes. In the left box, using your own first and last name, type **1A_College_Staff_Message_Firstname_Lastname** Compare your screen with Figure 1.46.

Figure 1.46

Footer information (use your own first and last name)

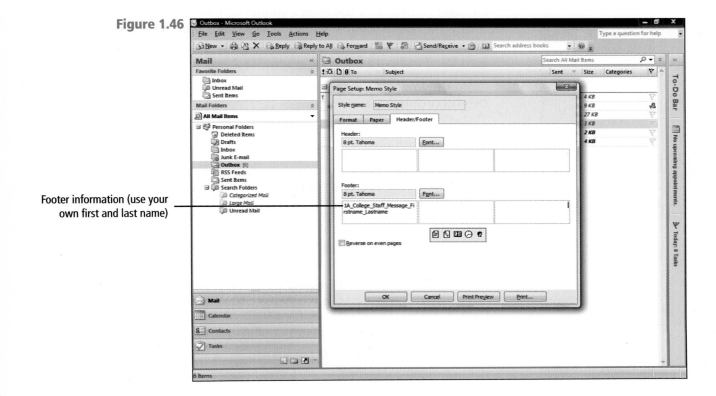

15 In the lower left corner of the dialog box, click **OK**, and then, in the Print dialog box, click **OK**. Submit the end result to your instructor as directed.

Another Way ── **To Print**

You can print a message while viewing it in the Message form by clicking the Office button, and then clicking Print. This method displays the Print dialog box, from which you can choose the appropriate setup options for the message. You can also use the Print button on the Standard toolbar. The toolbar button bypasses the Print dialog box and sends the selected item directly to the printer using the most recently used Print dialog box settings.

Activity 1.24 Deleting Messages

After you read and reply to a message, it is good practice to either delete it or store it in another folder for future reference. Doing so keeps your Inbox clear of messages that you have already handled. When you delete a message in your Inbox folder, Outbox folder, or any other mail folder, it is placed in the Deleted Items folder. Items remain in this folder until you delete them from this folder, at which time they are permanently deleted. You can see that this is helpful in case you delete a message by mistake; you can still retrieve it from the Deleted Items folder until that folder is emptied. Periodically empty the Deleted Items folder to conserve your disk space. You can delete messages in a variety of ways—from the toolbar, from the keyboard, and from a menu.

1 Display your **Inbox** folder, and then select the message from *Mary Adair* with the subject **Some advice**.

Outlook remembers the colors you assign to specific messages. All future messages from Mary Adair will display in red. Before you delete Mary's message, you will restore its default color so that the next user will not see them in red.

2 From the **Tools** menu, click **Organize** to display the **Ways to Organize Inbox** pane.

Recall that the Ways to Organize Inbox pane is used to manage messages with colors, folders, and views.

3 In the **Ways to Organize Inbox** pane, click **Using Colors**. In the rightmost **Color messages** box, click the **down arrow**, and then click **Auto**. Click **Apply Color**.

Done! displays to the right of the Apply Color button. This sets all messages from Mary Adair to display in the default color; future messages from Mary will not display in red.

4 In the **Ways to Organize Inbox** pane, click the **Close Organize** button ☒ .

5 With Mary's message still selected, click **Delete** ☒ to move the message to the **Deleted Items** folder.

6 Be sure the message from *James Smith* with the subject **On campus recruiting** is selected. Hold down Ctrl and click the message from

James Smith with the subject **Lunch today? Delete** 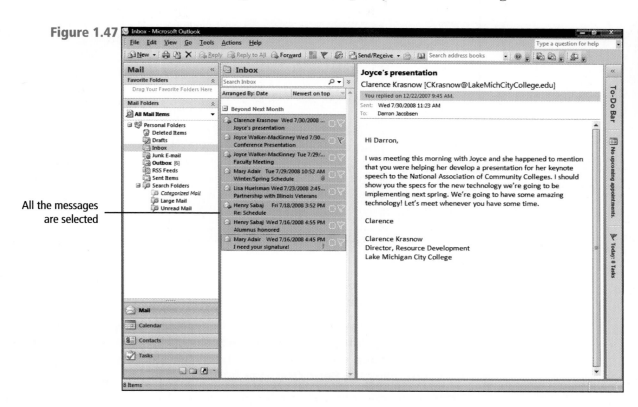 the selected messages.

Use this technique to select nonadjacent (not next to each other) items in any Windows-based program.

7 In the **Inbox**, click the first message, hold down ⟨⇧ Shift⟩ and click the last message, and then compare you screen with Figure 1.47.

Figure 1.47

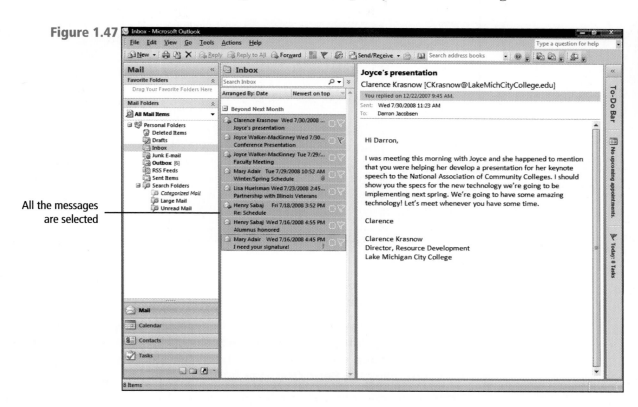

All the messages are selected

8 From the menu bar, display the **Edit** menu, and notice the **Delete** command. To the left of the command is a reminder that this command can be performed using one click from the toolbar. To the right of the command is a reminder that a keyboard shortcut is available for the command. From the displayed menu, click **Delete**.

The selected messages are deleted, and the Inbox is empty.

9 Display the **Outbox** folder. Using the technique you just practiced, select all the messages and then delete them.

10 Display the **Deleted Items** folder, and then scroll as necessary to view all the items. To the left of each item, notice the icons, which indicate the type of Outlook item, such as a received message or a message you forwarded.

11 Select all the items in the folder, and then use any method to delete them. Alternatively, in the Navigation Pane, right-click the **Deleted Items** folder, from the shortcut menu click **Empty "Deleted Items"** Folder. Compare your screen with Figure 1.48.

Outlook displays a warning box indicating that you are permanently deleting the selected items.

Figure 1.48

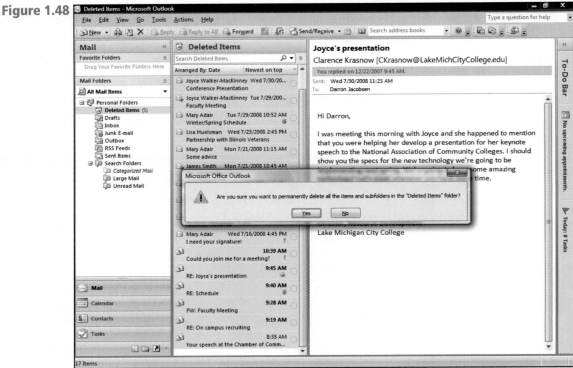

12 In the **Microsoft Office Outlook** dialog box, click **Yes** to permanently delete the items and empty the folder.

13 From the **Tools** menu, display the **Options** dialog box, and then click the **Mail Setup** tab. Under **Send/Receive**, select the **Send immediately when connected** check box. Then, to the right of the check box, click the **Send/Receive** button.

14 In the **Send/Receive Groups** dialog box, under **Setting for group "All Accounts"**, select both **Include this group in send/receive (F9)** check boxes. Select both **Schedule an automatic send/receive** check boxes if this is a default setting on your computer. Click **Close** and then click **OK**.

Outlook's default setting is restored. With no items in the folder list, the Reading Pane displays in light blue.

15 From the **File** menu, point to **Page Setup**, and then click **Define Print Styles**.

The Define Print Styles dialog box displays. Recall that Outlook remembers any header or footer information that you type. You can use this dialog box to restore the print styles you used to their default settings. You used both the Table Style and Memo Style print styles.

16 In the **Define Print Styles** dialog box, with **Table Style** selected, click **Reset**. In the displayed **Microsoft Office Outlook** dialog box, click **OK**. Click **Memo Style**, click **Reset**, and then click **OK**. In the **Define Print Styles** dialog box, click **Close**.

The headers and footers in the Table Style and Memo Style print styles are restored to their default settings.

More Knowledge

Using Outlook Web Access

If you have an Exchange Server e-mail account, you may be able to use Outlook Web Access. This feature enables you to access your Microsoft Exchange Server mailbox from any computer that has an Internet connection, using Microsoft Internet Explorer or any other Web browser. There are different versions of Outlook Web Access, and each version has its own set of features. Outlook Web Access is a useful program for individuals who work in different computer environments, such as Apple Macintosh or UNIX. It is also useful for individuals who require remote access. Outlook Web Access is usually set up by a network administrator or Internet service provider. You must have an Exchange Server e-mail account to use Outlook Web Access.

Objective 6
Use Outlook Help and Close Outlook

As you work with Outlook, you can get assistance by using the Help feature. You can ask questions, and Outlook Help will provide you with information and step-by-step instructions for performing tasks.

Activity 1.25 Using Outlook Help

The quickest way to use Help is to type a question in the Type a question for help box, which is located on the right side of the menu bar.

1 Move your pointer to the right side of the menu bar, and click in the **Type a question for help** box. Type **How do I open an attachment?** and then press Enter. Compare your screen with Figure 1.49.

The Outlook Help window displays a list of related Help topics with hyperlinks in blue text. Clicking these hyperlinks displays additional information about the topic. Your display may look different.

Note — Outlook Help

You must be connected online to access the online help. Somewhat more limited help is available if you are not online.

Figure 1.49

The Type a question
for help box

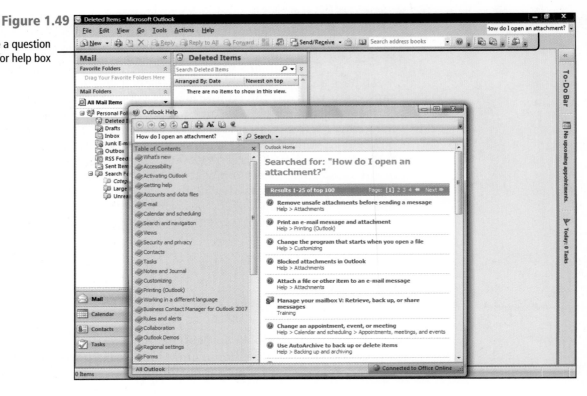

2 In the **Results** list, search for and click **View, open, and save attachments**.

General information related to viewing, opening, and saving attachments is displayed in the Outlook Help window. Included in the article are hyperlinks for additional information.

3 Click on the hyperlink **Open an attachment**.

Specific instructions are given for opening an attachment in several ways.

4 In the **Outlook Help** window, click the **Close** button [X].

5 From the **File** menu, click **Exit** to close Outlook. Alternatively, click the **Close** button [X] on the Outlook title bar.

Alert!

Did you create a Student profile?

If you created a Student profile in Activity 1.5, change it back to the default (Outlook) profile. To do this click Start, and then click Control Panel. Click User Accounts and then click Mail; or in classic view, double-click Mail. Under Always use this profile, select Outlook (or the default name) and then click OK. Close the Control Panel.

End You have completed Project 1A —————————

Content-Based Assessments

Summary

Microsoft Outlook 2007 is a personal information manager and an e-mail program. Use Outlook to manage your schedule, store information about your contacts, keep track of tasks you need to complete, and send and receive e-mail messages.

In this chapter, you practiced using Outlook's e-mail capabilities, started Outlook and navigated through its various components using the Navigation Pane and the folder list, and identified and displayed menus, toolbars, and ScreenTips. You composed and sent e-mail messages and viewed your sent messages. Additionally you replied to messages, forwarded a message, worked with attachments, and set levels of importance and sensitivity for specific messages.

Key Terms

Content-Based Assessments

Matching

Match each term in the second column with its correct definition in the first column by writing the letter of the term on the blank line in front of the correct definition.

_____ **1.** Of the two functions of Microsoft Office Outlook 2007, the function that enables you to store information about your contact names and addresses, your calendar, and tasks you need to complete electronically.

_____ **2.** A summary view of your schedule, tasks, and e-mail for the current day—the default view when you open the Outlook program.

_____ **3.** Located on the left side of the Outlook screen, a pane containing buttons and smaller panes that provides quick access to Outlook's components and folders.

_____ **4.** Located on the right side of the Outlook screen when the Inbox and some other mail folders are open, a pane that lets you read an e-mail item without actually opening it.

_____ **5.** The name of the file in which Outlook information, organized into various folders, is stored and has the file extension _pst_.

_____ **6.** A copy of an e-mail message sent to one or more individuals who need to see the message.

_____ **7.** A separate file included with a message, such as a Word document or an Excel spreadsheet.

_____ **8.** The action of sending an e-mail message that you receive to someone else; _FW:_ displays to indicate this action.

_____ **9.** A security label that can be applied to messages that should not be read by others because of the message content, for example, information about employee salaries.

_____ **10.** Marks that can be applied to a message to indicate its urgency, for example, information that should be read immediately or that can be read later.

_____ **11.** A block of text that is added, manually or automatically, at the end of your message that commonly includes your name, title, address, and phone number.

_____ **12.** The print option used to print multiple items in a list, for example, the contents of your Inbox.

_____ **13.** Options that you can apply to messages, such as the time a message is sent or the address to use for replies.

_____ **14.** A pane used to manage messages by the use of colors, folders, and views.

_____ **15.** The print option used to print an individual message.

A Attachment

B Courtesy copy

C Forwarding

D Importance

E Memo Style

F Message delivery options

G Navigation Pane

H Outlook Today

I Personal Folders

J Personal information manager

K Reading Pane

L Sensitivity

M Signature

N Table Style

O Ways to Organize Inbox pane

Content-Based Assessments

Fill in the Blank

Write the correct answer in the space provided.

1. The names of your friends, family members, coworkers, customers, suppliers, or other individuals with whom you communicate are referred to as _____.

2. Ways to look at similar Outlook information in different formats and arrangements are _____.

3. An element of information in Outlook, such as a message, a contact name, a task, or an appointment is a(n) _____.

4. A computer or device on a network that handles shared network resources is a(n) _____.

5. The second part of an e-mail address, which indicates the recipient's mail system, is called the _____ _____

6. An Outlook window for displaying and collecting information is a(n) _____

7. Programs with which you can create or make changes to existing files are _____.

8. The way in which the parts of an e-mail address are put together is referred to as the _____.

9. The Outlook feature in which text typed in the Message form is moved automatically from the end of one line to the beginning of the next line in order to fit within the established margins is known as the _____ feature.

10. A tool that walks you through a process in a step-by-step manner is a(n) _____.

11. The prefix that Outlook adds to the subject and title of a mail message, commonly used to mean *in regard to*, is _____.

12. The term commonly used to describe a person to whom you forward an e-mail message is _____ _____.

13. The Outlook feature that assists you in typing addresses by suggesting previously typed addresses based on the first character you type, is the _____ feature.

14. Categories of information within an item, such as the subject of a message or the date and time received, and displayed in a column heading are called _____.

15. A second-level menu activated by selecting a main menu option is called a(n) _____.

Content-Based Assessments

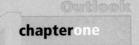
Project 1B — Career Fair

Objectives: 1. *Start and Navigate Outlook;* **2.** *Compose and Send E-mail;*
4. *Use Mail Options and Signatures;* **5.** *Manage E-mail;* **6.** *Use Outlook Help
and Close Outlook.*

In the following Skills Review, you will send an e-mail message for James
Smith, Vice President of Student Affairs at Lake Michigan City College.
Your completed message will look similar to the one shown in Figure 1.50.

For Project 1B, you will need the following file:

New message form

You will print one file with the following footer:
1B_Career_Fair_Firstname_Lastname

Figure 1.50

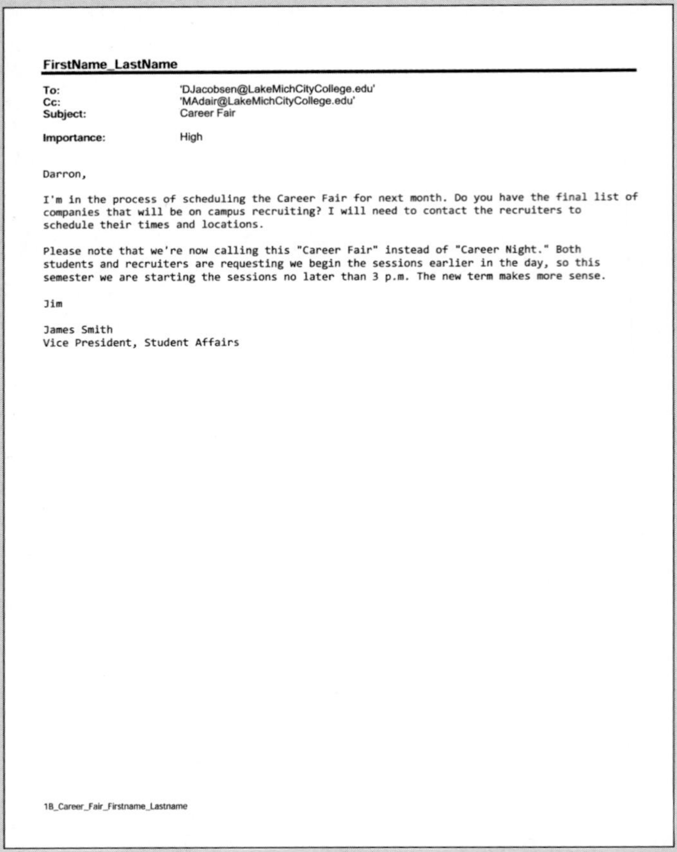

> **FirstName_LastName**
>
> To: 'DJacobsen@LakeMichCityCollege.edu'
> Cc: 'MAdair@LakeMichCityCollege.edu'
> Subject: Career Fair
>
> Importance: High
>
> Darron,
>
> I'm in the process of scheduling the Career Fair for next month. Do you have the final list of
> companies that will be on campus recruiting? I will need to contact the recruiters to
> schedule their times and locations.
>
> Please note that we're now calling this "Career Fair" instead of "Career Night." Both
> students and recruiters are requesting we begin the sessions earlier in the day, so this
> semester we are starting the sessions no later than 3 p.m. The new term makes more sense.
>
> Jim
>
> James Smith
> Vice President, Student Affairs
>
> 1B_Career_Fair_Firstname_Lastname

(Project 1B–Career Fair continues on the next page)

Content-Based Assessments

(Project 1B–Career Fair continued)

1. **Start** Outlook and be sure the **Navigation Pane** is displayed on the left. If necessary, to display the Navigation Pane, from the View menu, click Navigation Pane.

2. In the lower portion of the **Navigation Pane**, click the **Mail** button to display the Mail component of Outlook, and then, at the top of the pane, click **Inbox** to display the Inbox folder list.

3. From the **Tools** menu, click **Options**. In the **Options** dialog box, click the **Mail Setup tab**.

4. Under **Send/Receive**, clear the **Send immediately when connected** check box if necessary. To the immediate right, click the **Send/Receive** button. In the **Send/ Receive Groups** dialog box, under **Setting for group "All Accounts"**, clear both **Include this group in send/receive (F9)** check boxes if necessary. Clear both **Schedule an automatic send/receive** check boxes if necessary. Click **Close**, and then click **OK**.

5. From the **Tools** menu, display the **Options** dialog box again, click the **Mail Format** tab, and then, in the lower right corner of the **Options** dialog box, click **Signatures**.

6. In the **Signatures and Stationery** dialog box, click **New**. In the **New Signature** dialog box, in the **Enter a name for your new signature** box, type **Jim** and then click **OK**.

7. In the **Edit signature – [Jim]** box, type **James Smith** and then press Enter. Type **Vice President, Student Affairs**

8. At the top right of the dialog box, click the **New messages arrow**. From the displayed list, click **Jim**, and then click **OK** to close the **Signatures and Stationery** dialog box.

9. Click **OK** to close the **Options** dialog box.

10. On the Standard toolbar, click the **New Mail Message** button. On the **Options tab**, in the **Format group**, click the **Plain Text** button. In the **Microsoft Office Outlook Compatibility Checker** dialog box, click **Continue**.

11. In the **To** box, type **DJacobsen@ LakeMichCityCollege.edu** and recall that if the name displays in blue, you can press Enter to have AutoComplete fill in the address for you.

12. Click in the **Cc** box, and then type **MAdair@LakeMichCityCollege.edu**

13. Press Tab to move the insertion point to the **Subject** box. In the **Subject** box, type **Career Fair** and then press Tab.

14. In the message area, notice that the signature you created has been automatically inserted. On the Message form title bar, click the **Maximize** button to enlarge the viewing area of the form for better viewing while typing. With the insertion point in the message area of the Message form, type **Darron,** and then press Enter **two** times.

15. Recall that the wordwrap feature will wrap long lines of text automatically as you type. Type **I'm in the process of scheduling the Career Fair for next month. Do you have the final list of companies that will be on campus recruiting? I will need to contact the recruiters to schedule their times and locations.** Press Enter **two** times.

16. Type **Please note that we're now calling this "Career Fair" instead of "Career Night." Both students and recruiters are requesting we begin the sessions earlier in the day, so this semester we are starting the sessions no later than 3 p.m. The new term makes more sense.** Press Enter **two** times. Type **Jim**

(Project 1B–Career Fair continues on the next page)

Content-Based Assessments

(Project 1B–Career Fair continued)

17. On the Message form title bar, click the **Restore Down** button to restore the Message form to its original size.

18. On the **Message tab**, in the **Options group**, click the **High Importance** button, and then click the **Send** button. In the **Navigation Pane**, under **Mail Folders**, click the **Outbox** folder.

19. In the **Outbox**, click the message you just created to **DJacobsen** one time to select it. Note that the full name and e-mail address might not display, depending on the width of the column setting.

20. From the **File** menu, click **Print**. In the **Print** dialog box, click **Page Setup**. In the **Page Setup: Memo Style** dialog box, click the **Header/Footer tab**. Recall that if you select a single message to print, the print style defaults to the Memo Style.

21. In the **Page Setup: Memo Style** dialog box, under **Footer**, delete any existing text in the three boxes. Delete any existing text in the **Header** boxes. In the left **Footer** box, using your own name, type **1B_Career_Fair_Firstname_Lastname** Although your text may wrap in the box, it will print on one line.

22. At the bottom of the dialog box, click **OK**, and then, in the **Print** dialog box, click **OK** to print the e-mail. Submit the end result to your instructor as directed.

23. On the Standard toolbar, click the **Delete** button to delete the message to **DJacobsen**.

24. In the **Navigation Pane**, point to the **Deleted Items** folder and right-click. From the displayed shortcut menu, click **Empty "Deleted Items" Folder**. In the **Microsoft Office Outlook** box, click **Yes**.

25. From the **Tools** menu, click **Options**. Click the **Mail Setup tab**, and under **Send/Receive**, select the **Send immediately when connected** check box.

26. In the **Options** dialog box, click **Send/Receive**. In the **Send/Receive Groups** dialog box, under **Setting for group "All Accounts"**, select both **Include this group in send/receive (F9)** check boxes. Select both **Schedule an automatic send/receive** check boxes if this is a default setting on your computer. Click **Close**, and then click **Apply**.

27. Click the **Mail Format tab**. At the lower portion of the **Options** dialog box, click **Signatures**. In the **Signatures and Stationery** dialog box, be sure the signature for **Jim** is selected, click **Delete**, and then click **Yes**.

28. In the **Signatures and Stationery** dialog box, click **OK**. In the **Options** dialog box, click **OK**.

29. From the **File** menu, point to **Page Setup**, and then click **Define Print Styles**. Recall that you can use this dialog box to restore any print style you used to its default settings. Click **Memo Style**, click **Reset**, and then click **OK**. Click **Close**. On the Outlook title bar, click the **Close** button.

End **You have completed Project 1B**

Content-Based Assessments

Skills Review

Project 1C—Enrollments

Objectives: 1. *Start and Navigate Outlook;* **3.** *Read and Respond to E-mail Messages;* **4.** *Use Mail Options and Signatures;* **5.** *Manage E-mail;* **6.** *Use Outlook Help and Close Outlook.*

In the following Skills Review, you will handle the e-mail correspondence for Lisa Huelsman, Associate Dean, Adult Basic Education at Lake Michigan City College. You will import her messages into your Inbox. Then you will reply and forward messages. Your completed messages will look similar to the ones shown in Figure 1.51.

For Project 1C, you will need the following files:

New blank message form

o01C_Enrollments_Inbox

o01C_Enrollments_Schedule

You will print two files with the following footers:
1C_Enrollments_ESL_Program_Firstname_Lastname
1C_Enrollments_Increased_Firstname_Lastname

Figure 1.51

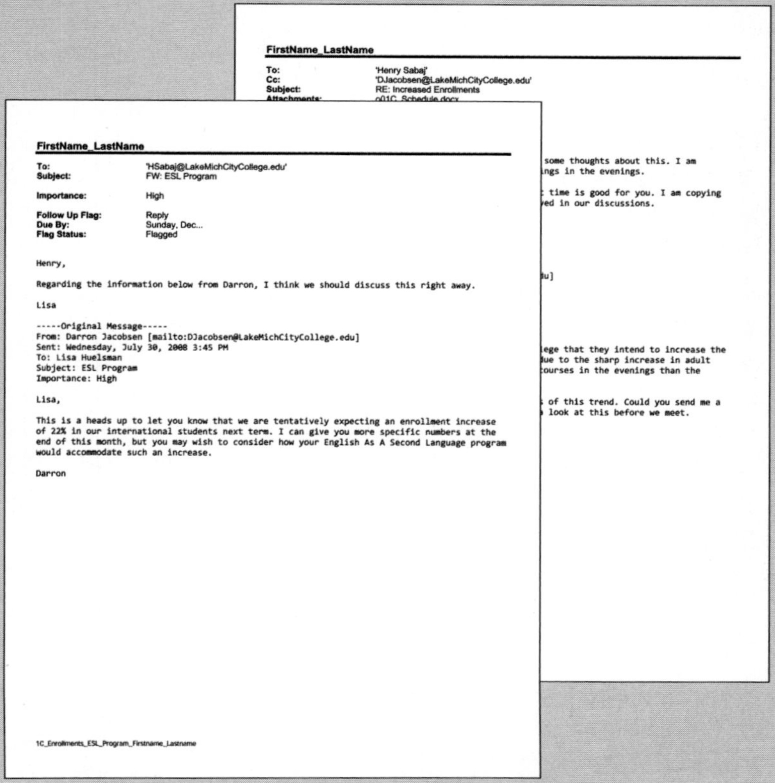

(Project 1C–Enrollments continues on the next page)

Content-Based Assessments

(Project 1C–Enrollments continued)

1. **Start** Outlook. If the Navigation Pane is not displayed, click **View** on the menu bar, and then click **Navigation Pane**. In the lower portion of the **Navigation Pane**, click the **Mail** button to display the Mail component of Outlook, and then, at the top of the pane, click **Inbox**.

2. From the **Tools** menu, display the **Options** dialog box, and then click the **Mail Setup tab**. Under **Send/Receive**, clear the **Send immediately when connected** check box. To the immediate right, click **Send/ Receive**. In the **Send/Receive Groups** dialog box, under **Setting for group "All Accounts"**, clear both **Include this group in send/receive (F9)** check boxes. Clear both **Schedule an automatic send/ receive** check boxes if this is a default setting on your computer. **Close** the dialog box, and in the **Options** dialog box, click **OK.**

3. From the **File** menu, display the **Import and Export Wizard** dialog box. Under **Choose an action to perform**, click **Import from another program or file**, and then click **Next**.

4. In the **Import a File** dialog box, under **Select file type to import from**, scroll as necessary and click **Personal Folder File (.pst)**, and then click **Next**. In the **Import Personal Folders** dialog box, click **Browse**. In the **Open Personal Folders** dialog box, click the **Look in arrow**, and then navigate to the student files that accompany this textbook.

5. Click **o01C_Enrollments_Inbox one** time to select it, and then, in the lower right corner of the **Open** dialog box, click **Open**. Click **Next**. Under **Select the folder to import from**, click **Inbox**, and then click the **Import items into the current folder** option button. Click **Finish**. If a Translation

Warning dialog box displays, click OK. Mail items are placed in Lisa's Inbox.

6. Be sure that the **Inbox** folder list is displayed. Select the **Increased Enrollments** message from *Henry Sabaj*, and then on the Standard toolbar, click the **Reply** button. In the **Cc** box, type **DJacobsen@ LakeMichCityCollege.edu** and press Tab as necessary to position the insertion point at the top of the message area. Recall that if the address displays in blue as you begin to type, you can press Enter to have AutoComplete fill in the address for you.

7. Type **Henry,** and then press Enter **two** times. Type **Yes, I have been hearing about this trend also. I have some thoughts about this. I am wondering if we will have to open more classroom buildings in the evenings.** Press Enter **two** times.

8. Type **I can meet with you any day next week. Let me know what time is good for you. I am copying Darron in my reply in case he feels he should be involved in our discussions.** Press Enter **two** times. Type **I have attached the winter/spring schedule.** Press Enter **two** times and type **Lisa**

9. On the Message **tab**, in the **Include group**, click the **Attach File** button. In the **Insert File** dialog box, in the Folders pane, click on **Computer**, and then navigate to the location where the student files that accompany this textbook are stored.

10. Locate the Word file **o01C_Enrollments_ Schedule** and click **one** time to select it. Then, in the lower right corner of the **Insert File** dialog box, click **Insert**. On the Message toolbar, click the **Send** button. In the **Inbox** folder list, notice the small arrow to the left of *Henry Sabaj* indicating that you have replied to the message.

11. Click the **ESL Program** message from *Darron Jacobsen* **one** time to select it

(Project 1C–Enrollments continues on the next page)

Content-Based Assessments

(Project 1C–Enrollments continued)

without opening it. After reading the message in the Reading Pane, on the Standard toolbar, click the **Forward** button. Recall that you can forward a message to someone else—known as a third party—if you think the information is important for them to know.

12. In the **To** box, type **HSabaj@ LakeMichCityCollege.edu** and then press Tab as necessary to position the insertion point at the top of the message area. Type **Henry,** and then press Enter **two** times. Type **Regarding the information below from Darron, I think we should discuss this right away.** Press Enter **two** times and type **Lisa**

13. On the **Message tab**, in the **Options group**, click the **Follow Up** button, and then click **Flag for Recipients**. In the **Custom** dialog box, click the **Flag to** arrow, and then click **Reply**. Click **OK**. This action will apply a flag to remind Henry to follow up on this issue.

14. On the Message form, click the **Send** button. In the **Navigation Pane**, under **Mail Folders**, click **Outbox** to display the Outbox folder list. Recall that *RE:* indicates a message that you have replied to and *FW:* indicates a message that you have forwarded to a third party.

15. In the **Outbox** folder list, select the **ESL Program** message from *Henry Sabaj*. From the **File** menu, display the **Print** dialog box, and then click **Page Setup**. In the **Page Setup: Memo Style** dialog box, click the **Header/Footer tab**.

16. In the **Page Setup: Memo Style** dialog box, under **Footer**, delete any existing information in the three boxes. Delete any existing information in the **Header** boxes. In the left **Footer** box, type **1C_Enrollments_ ESL_Program_Firstname_Lastname** using your own name.

17. In the **Page Setup: Memo Style** dialog box, click **OK**. In the **Print** dialog box, click **OK** to print the message. Submit the end result to your instructor as directed.

18. In the **Outbox** folder list, select the message from *Henry Sabaj* with the subject **Increased Enrollments**.

19. From the **File** menu, display the **Print** dialog box, and then click **Page Setup**. In the **Page Setup: Memo Style** dialog box, click the **Header/Footer tab**.

20. In the **Page Setup: Memo Style** dialog box, under **Footer**, in the left box, delete the existing information. Using your own name, type **1C_Enrollments_Increased_ Firstname_Lastname** In the **Page Setup: Memo Style** dialog box, click **OK**. In the **Print** dialog box, click **OK** to print the message. Submit the end result to your instructor as directed.

21. In the **Outbox** folder list, click the first message, hold down ⇧Shift, and then click the last message. On the toolbar, click the **Delete** button to delete the messages. In the **Navigation Pane**, click **Inbox**. In the **Inbox** folder list, select all the messages, and then delete them. In the **Navigation Pane**, point to **Deleted Items**, right-click, click **Empty "Deleted Items" Folder**, and then click **Yes**.

22. From the **Tools** menu, click **Options**. Click the **Mail Setup tab**, and then, under **Send/Receive**, select the **Send immediately when connected** check box.

23. In the **Options** dialog box, click **Send/Receive**. In the **Send/Receive Groups** dialog box, under **Setting for group "All Accounts"**, select both **Include this group in send/receive (F9)** check boxes. Select both **Schedule an automatic send/receive** check boxes if this is

(Project 1C–Enrollments continues on the next page)

Content-Based Assessments

(Project 1C–Enrollments continued)

a default setting on your computer. Click **Close**. Click **OK**.

24. From the **File** menu, point to **Page Setup**, and then click **Define Print Styles**. Click

Memo Style, click **Reset**, and then click **OK**. Click **Close**. On the Outlook title bar, click the **Close** button.

End You have completed Project 1C ─────────────────────

Content-Based Assessments

Project 1D—Merit Increases

Objectives: 1. *Start and Navigate Outlook;* **2.** *Compose and Send E-mail;*
4. *Use Mail Options and Signatures;* **5.** *Manage E-mail;* **6.** *Use Outlook Help
and Close Outlook.*

In the following Mastering Outlook project, you will create and send an
e-mail message for Darron Jacobsen, Vice President, Administrative Affairs
at Lake Michigan City College that contains confidential information. Your
completed message will look similar to the one shown in Figure 1.52.

For Project 1D, you will need the following file:

New blank message form

You will print one file with the following footer:
1D_Merit_Increases_Firstname_Lastname

Figure 1.52

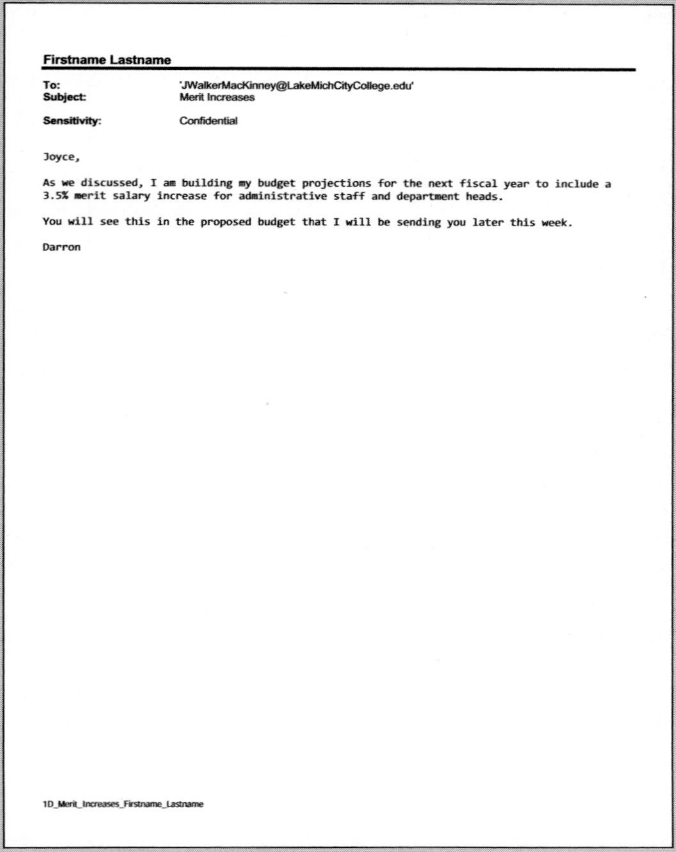

Firstname Lastname

To:	'JWalkerMacKinney@LakeMichCityCollege.edu'
Subject:	Merit Increases
Sensitivity:	Confidential

Joyce,

As we discussed, I am building my budget projections for the next fiscal year to include a
3.5% merit salary increase for administrative staff and department heads.

You will see this in the proposed budget that I will be sending you later this week.

Darron

1D_Merit_Increases_Firstname_Lastname

(Project 1D–Merit Increases continues on the next page)

Content-Based Assessments

(Project 1D–Merit Increases continued)

1. **Start** Outlook, and be sure the **Navigation Pane** is displayed. From the **Tools** menu, display the **Options** dialog box, click the **Mail Setup tab**, and then, under **Send/Receive**, clear the **Send immediately when connected** check box. Click **Send/Receive**. In the **Send/Receive Groups** dialog box, under **Setting for group "All Accounts"**, clear both **Include this group in send/receive (F9)** check boxes. Clear both **Schedule an automatic send/receive** check boxes if necessary. Click **Close**. Click **OK**.

2. Display the **Inbox** folder list and click the **New Mail Message** button. In the **To** box, type **JWalkerMacKinney@ LakeMichCityCollege.edu** As the **Subject**, type **Merit Increases** Change the **Message format** to **Plain Text**.

3. In the message area, using the appropriate spacing for a message that you have practiced in this chapter and not correcting any spelling errors, type **Joyce, As we discussed, I am building my budget projections for the next fiscle year to include a 3.5% merit salary increase for administrative staff and department heads.**

4. Start a new paragraph, and type **You will see this in the proposed budget that I will be sending you later this week.** Type **Darron**

5. On the **Message tab**, in the **Options group**, click the **Message Options dialog box launcher**. In the **Message Options** dialog box, set **Sensitivity** to **Confidential**. Locate the word **fiscle**, right-click it, and on the shortcut menu, click **fiscal**.

6. **Send** the message. From the **Navigation Pane**, display the **Outbox** folder list, and then select the message you just created. Display the **Print** dialog box, and then click **Page Setup**. Click the **Header/ Footer tab**, and delete any existing header or footer information. Use your own name, in the left footer box, type **1D_Merit_ Increases_Firstname_Lastname**

7. **Print** the message and then delete the contents of the **Outbox**. In the **Navigation Pane**, right-click the **Deleted Items** folder and empty its contents. Submit the end result to your instructor as directed.

8. From the **Tools** menu, display the **Options** dialog box. Click the **Mail Setup tab**, and under **Send/Receive**, select the **Send immediately when connected** check box. Click **Send/Receive**. In the **Send/Receive Groups** dialog box, under **Setting for group "All Accounts"**, select both **Include this group in send/receive (F9)** check boxes. Select both **Schedule an automatic send/receive** check boxes if this is a default setting on your computer. Click **Close**. Click **OK**.

9. From the **File** menu, point to **Page Setup**, and then click **Define Print Styles**. Reset the **Table Style** print style, and then **Close** the dialog box. **Close** Outlook.

End **You have completed Project 1D** _____

Content-Based Assessments

chapterone

Mastering Outlook

Project 1E—Needs Analysis

Objectives: 1. *Start and Navigate Outlook;* **3.** *Read and Respond to E-mail Messages;* **4.** *Use Mail Options and Signatures;* **5.** *Manage E-mail;* **6.** *Use Outlook Help and Close Outlook.*

In the following Mastering Outlook project, you will import the messages of Darron Jacobsen, Vice President, Administrative Affairs at Lake Michigan City College into the Inbox, locate a specific message, and then forward it to a third party. Your completed message will look similar to the one shown in Figure 1.53.

For Project 1E, you will need the following files:

New blank message form
o01E_Needs_Analysis_Inbox

You will print one file with the following footer:
1E_Needs_Analysis_Firstname_Lastname

Figure 1.53

```
FirstName_LastName

To:              'CKrasnow@LakeMichCityCollege.edu'
Subject:         FW: NACC Conference Presentation

Importance:      High


Clarence,

When it is completed, could I see the needs analysis Joyce refers to below? Thanks!

Darron

-----Original Message-----
From: Joyce Walker-MacKinney [mailto:JWalkerMacKinney@LakeMichCityCollege.edu]
Sent: Wednesday, July 30, 2008 1:35 PM
To: Darron Jacobsen
Subject: NACC Conference Presentation

Darron,

As we discussed, I'll be making a presentation at the annual meeting of the National
Association of Community Colleges. I'd appreciate your assistance in preparing it. I'd like
the focus to be on our programs for veterans and special needs students.

Here are some key points about our special needs program. It has:
- Become one of our highest-rated programs
- Targeted an under-served student market
- Attracted significant sources of new funding
- Generated much positive press and community goodwill
- Given our faculty opportunity for growth and challenge

I'd like you to work these features into the presentation.

Use my talk to the Illinois Special Needs Teachers conference last month as a starting point.
However, this is a bigger audience and I am the keynote speaker, so we'll need to beef up
that presentation. Mary should have a copy of that presentation if you don't have one.

You might want to get some input from Clarence. He has been working with a consultant who is
doing a needs analysis for our special needs students. We might be developing some new
programs and technology that we will want to mention.

Do you think you can have something for me to look at by the end of next week? Let me know
what your schedule looks like.

Thanks for your help.

Joyce

Joyce Walker-MacKinney
President
Lake Michigan City College
4750 Chicago Boulevard
Chicago, IL 60605

1E_Needs_Analysis_Firstname_Lastname
```

(Project 1E–Needs Analysis continues on the next page)

(Project 1E–Needs Analysis continued)

1. **Start** Outlook and display the **Navigation Pane**. Then, from the **Mail** component, display the **Inbox** folder list.

2. From the **Tools** menu, display the **Options** dialog box, click the **Mail Setup tab**, and then, under **Send/Receive**, clear the **Send immediately when connected** check box. Click **Send/Receive**. In the **Send/Receive Groups** dialog box, under **Setting for group "All Accounts"**, clear both **Include this group in send/receive (F9)** check boxes. Clear both **Schedule an automatic send/receive** check boxes if necessary. Click **Close**. Click **OK**.

3. From the **File** menu, display the **Import and Export Wizard** dialog box. Under **Choose an action to perform**, click **Import from another program or file**, and then click **Next**.

4. In the **Import a File** dialog box, click **Personal Folder File (.pst)** as the file type to import from. Click **Next**. In the **Import Personal Folders** dialog box, click **Browse**, and in the **Open Personal Folders** dialog box, navigate to the location where the student files that accompany this textbook are stored.

5. Locate and select **o01E_Needs_Analysis_Inbox**, and then click **Open**. Click **Next**. In the **Import Personal Folders** dialog box, under **Select the folder to import from**, click **Inbox**, and then click the **Import items into the current folder** option button. Click **Finish**. If a Translation Warning dialog box displays, click **OK**.

6. Place your insertion point in the **Instant Search** box. Type **needs analysis**. In the **Inbox** folder list, click the displayed message **one** time to select it.

7. **Forward** the message to **CKrasnow@ LakeMichCityCollege.edu** and then, using the appropriate message spacing, type **Clarence**, Type **When it is completed, could I see the needs analysis Joyce refers to below? Thanks!** Type **Darron**

8. Set the importance by clicking the **High Importance** button, and then **Send** the message. Click the **Clear Search** button to redisplay the entire Inbox.

9. From the **Navigation Pane**, display the **Outbox** folder list, and then click the message you just created **one** time to select it without opening it.

10. From the **File** menu, display the **Print** dialog box, and then click **Page Setup**. On the **Header/Footer tab**, delete any existing header and footer information, and then create a left footer by typing **1E_ Needs_Analysis_Firstname_Lastname**

11. Print the message and then delete the contents of the **Outbox**. From the **Navigation Pane**, display the **Inbox** folder list, and delete the contents of that folder. Then, right-click the **Deleted Items** folder and empty it. Submit the end result to your instructor as directed.

12. From the **Tools** menu, display the **Options** dialog box. Click the **Mail Setup tab**, and under **Send/Receive**, select the **Send immediately when connected** check box. Click **Send/Receive**. In the **Send/Receive Groups** dialog box, under **Setting for group "All Accounts"**, select both **Include this group in send/receive (F9)** check boxes. Select both **Schedule an automatic send/receive** check boxes if this is a default setting on your computer. Click **Close**. Click **OK**.

13. From the **File** menu, point to **Page Setup**, and then click **Define Print Styles**. **Reset** the **Memo Style** print style, and then **Close** the dialog box. **Close** Outlook.

End You have completed Project 1E

Content-Based Assessments

Mastering Outlook

Project 1F—Schedule Change

Objectives: 1. *Start and Navigate Outlook;* **2.** *Compose and Send E-mail;*
4. *Use Mail Options and Signatures;* **5.** *Manage E-mail;* **6.** *Use Outlook Help
and Close Outlook.*

In the following Mastering Outlook project, you will compose and send an
e-mail message from Darron Jacobsen, Vice President, Administrative
Affairs at Lake Michigan City College. The message will include a signature, an attachment, and other message options. Your completed message
will look similar to the one shown in Figure 1.54.

For Project 1F, you will need the following files:

New blank message form
o01F_Schedule_Change

You will print one file with the following footer:
1F_Schedule_Change_Firstname_Lastname

Figure 1.54

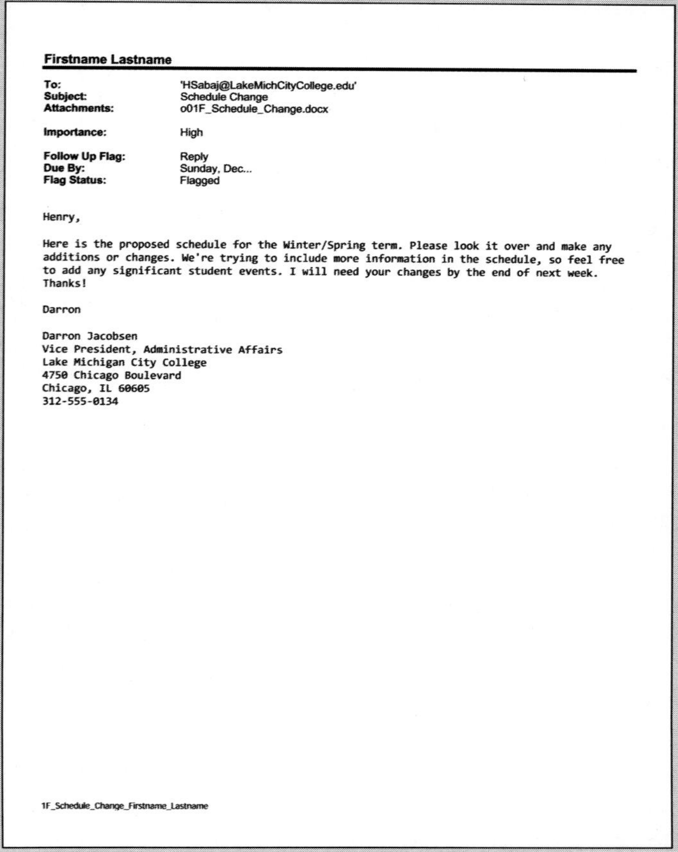

Firstname Lastname

To:	'HSabaj@LakeMichCityCollege.edu'
Subject:	Schedule Change
Attachments:	o01F_Schedule_Change.docx
Importance:	High
Follow Up Flag:	Reply
Due By:	Sunday, Dec...
Flag Status:	Flagged

Henry,

Here is the proposed schedule for the Winter/Spring term. Please look it over and make any
additions or changes. We're trying to include more information in the schedule, so feel free
to add any significant student events. I will need your changes by the end of next week.
Thanks!

Darron

Darron Jacobsen
Vice President, Administrative Affairs
Lake Michigan City College
4750 Chicago Boulevard
Chicago, IL 60605
312-555-0134

1F_Schedule_Change_Firstname_Lastname

(Project 1F–Schedule Change continues on the next page)

Content-Based Assessments

(Project 1F–Schedule Change continued)

1. **Start** Outlook and display the **Navigation Pane**. Open **Mail**, and then display the **Inbox** folder list.

2. From the **Tools** menu, display the **Options** dialog box, click the **Mail Setup tab**, and then, under **Send/Receive**, clear the **Send immediately when connected** check box. Click **Send/Receive**. In the **Send/Receive Groups** dialog box, under **Setting for "All Accounts"**, clear both **Include this group in send/receive (F9)** check boxes. Clear both **Schedule an automatic send/receive** check boxes if necessary. Click **Close**. Click **Apply**.

3. Click the **Mail Format tab**. Click **Signatures**. Create a new signature, typing **Darron Jacobsen** as the name for the signature. The text of the Darron Jacobsen signature is as follows:

   Darron Jacobsen
   Vice President, Administrative Affairs
   Lake Michigan City College
   4750 Chicago Boulevard
   Chicago, IL 60605
   312-555-0134

4. In the **Signatures and Stationery** dialog box, apply the new signature to new messages, and then close the **Signatures and Stationery** dialog box, and then close the **Options** dialog box.

5. Create a new message to **HSabaj@ LakeMichCityCollege.edu** As the **Subject**, type **Schedule Change** Change the message format to **Plain Text**.

6. Create the following message using appropriate spacing: **Henry, Here is the proposed schedule for the Winter/Spring term. Please look it over and make any additions or changes. We're trying to include more information in the schedule, so feel free to add any significant student events. I will need**

your changes by the end of next week. **Thanks! Darron**

7. Be sure that the information entered in the message area is spaced as shown in Figure 1.54. Click to place the insertion point to the left of *Henry* and press Enter **one** time so that the attachment icon will not displace the salutation when the message is printed.

8. Set the message to **High Importance**. Flag the message for the recipient for **Reply**. Insert a file as an attachment by displaying the **Insert File** dialog box, and then navigating to the student files that accompany this textbook. Insert the file **o01F_Schedule_Change**.

9. **Send** the message. Display the **Outbox**, select the message without opening it, and then display the **Print** dialog box. Click **Page Setup**, and then, in the **Header/Footer tab**, delete any existing header and footer text. Create a left footer that contains the text **1F_Schedule_Change_Firstname_Lastname** and then print the message. Submit the end result to your instructor as directed.

10. Delete the contents of the **Outbox**, and then empty the **Deleted Items** folder.

11. From the **Tools** menu, display the **Options** dialog box, click the **Mail Setup tab**, and under **Send/Receive**, select the **Send immediately when connected** check box. Click **Send/Receive**. In the **Send/Receive Groups** dialog box, under **Setting for group "All Accounts"**, select both **Include this group in send/receive (F9)** check boxes. Select both **Schedule an automatic send/receive** check boxes if this is a default setting on your computer. Click **Close**, and then click **Apply**.

(Project 1F–Schedule Change continues on the next page)

Content-Based Assessments

(Project 1F–Schedule Change continued)

12. Click the **Mail Format tab**, click **Signatures**, and then remove the **Darron Jacobsen** signature. Close all dialog boxes.

13. Display the **Define Print Styles** dialog box. **Reset** the **Memo Style**, and then **Close** the dialog box. **Close** Outlook.

End You have completed Project 1F

Content-Based Assessments

Project 1G—Jacobsen Inbox

Objectives: 1. *Start and Navigate Outlook;* **3.** *Read and Respond to E-mail Messages;* **4.** *Use Mail Options and Signatures;* **5.** *Manage E-mail;* **6.** *Use Outlook Help and Close Outlook.*

In the following Mastering Outlook project, you will manage received e-mail for Darron Jacobsen, Vice President, Administrative Affairs at Lake Michigan City College. You will import his messages into the Inbox, sort them, reply to one message, and forward another message to a third party. Your Inbox and completed messages will look similar to the ones shown in Figure 1.55.

For Project 1G, you will need the following files:

New blank message form
o01G_Jacobsen_Inbox

You will print three files with the following footers:
1G_Jacobsen_Inbox_Firstname_Lastname
1G_Jacobsen_Inbox_Alumnus_Honored_Firstname_Lastname
1G_Jacobsent_Inbox_Faculty_Meeting_Firstname_Lastname

Figure 1.55

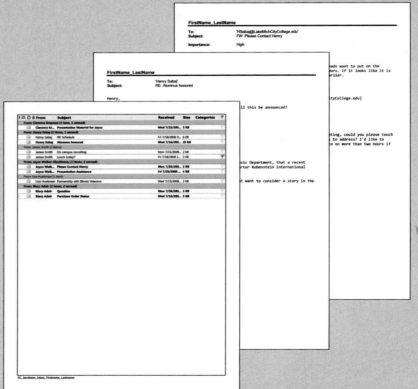

(Project 1G–Jacobsen Inbox continues on the next page)

(Project 1G–Jacobsen Inbox continued)

1. **Start** Outlook and display the **Navigation Pane**. Select Outlook's **Mail** component, and then display the **Inbox** folder list.

2. From the **Tools** menu, display the **Options** dialog box, and then click the **Mail Setup tab**. Under **Send/Receive**, clear the **Send immediately when connected** check box. Click **Send/Receive**. In the **Send/Receive Groups** dialog box, under **Setting for group "All Accounts"**, clear both **Include this group in send/receive (F9)** check boxes. Clear both **Schedule an automatic send/receive** check boxes if necessary. Click **Close**. Click **OK**.

3. From the **File** menu, display the **Import and Export Wizard** dialog box, click **Import from another program or file**, and then click **Next**.

4. In the **Import a File** dialog box, under **Select file type to import from**, click **Personal Folder File (.pst)**, and then click **Next**. In the **Import Personal Folders** dialog box, navigate to the student files that accompany this textbook, locate and then open **o01G_Jacobson_Inbox**, and then click **Next**.

5. In the **Import Personal Folders** dialog box, under **Select the folder to import from**, click **Inbox**, and then click the **Import items into current folder** option button. Click **Finish**. If a Translation Warning dialog box displays, click **OK**.

6. From the **View** menu, point to **Reading Pane**, and then click **Bottom** to display the pane at the bottom of the Outlook screen. In the **Inbox**, click the **From** column header to sort the messages alphabetically by sender.

7. Display the **Print** dialog box, and set the **Print style** to **Table Style**. In the **Page Setup** dialog box, click the **Paper tab** and

set the orientation to **Portrait**. Delete any existing header or footer information, create a left footer that contains the text **1G_Jacobsen_Inbox_Firstname_Lastname** and then print the **Inbox** list. Submit the end result to your instructor as directed.

8. In the **Inbox**, click the **Received** column header to sort the Inbox by date. Redisplay the Reading Pane on the right side of the screen.

9. In the **Inbox**, locate and click the **Alumnus honored** message from *Henry Sabaj*. On the Standard toolbar, click **Reply**. Change the message format to **Plain Text**. In the message area, type the text of the message as follows, using appropriate spacing as shown in Figure 1.54:

   Henry, Quite an honor indeed! I will issue a press release. When will this be announced? Darron

10. **Send** the message. In the **Inbox**, select the **Please Contact Henry** message from *Joyce Walker-MacKinney*. On the Standard toolbar, click **Forward**. Send the message to **HSabaj@LakeMichCityCollege.edu** In the message area, type the text of the message as follows, using appropriate spacing:

    Henry, Can you give me an idea of what topics you and the department heads want to put on the agenda? Joyce is keen to keep the meeting to no more than two hours. If it looks like it is going to run longer than that, I am going to propose we start earlier. Darron

11. Set the message to **High Importance**, and then **Send** the message.

12. Display the **Outbox**, select the message to **Henry Sabaj** with the subject **Alumnus honored**, and then display the **Print** dialog box. In the **Page Setup** dialog box, delete any existing header or footer text,

(Project 1G–Jacobsen Inbox continues on the next page)

Content-Based Assessments

(Project 1G–Jacobsen Inbox continued)

and then create a left footer that contains the text **1G_Jacobsen_Inbox_Alumnus_Honored_Firstname_Lastname** Print the message. Submit the end result to your instructor as directed.

13. In the **Outbox**, select the **Please Contact Henry** message to *Henry Sabaj*, and then display the **Print** dialog box. In the **Page Setup** dialog box, delete any existing header or footer text, and then create a left footer that contains the text **1G_Jacobsen_Inbox_Faculty_Meeting_Firstname_Lastname** Print the message. Submit the end result to your instructor as directed.

14. Delete the contents of the **Outbox** folder, the **Inbox** folder, and then empty the **Deleted Items** folder.

15. From the **Tools** menu, display the **Options** dialog box. Click the **Mail Setup tab**, and under **Send/Receive**, select the **Send immediately when connected** check box. Click **Send/Receive**. In the **Send/Receive Groups** dialog box, under **Setting for group "All Accounts"**, select both **Include this group in send/receive (F9)** check boxes. Select both **Schedule an automatic send/receive** check boxes if this is a default setting on your computer. Click **Close**. Click **OK**.

16. Display the **Define Print Styles** dialog box, and **Reset** the **Memo Style** print style. **Close** the dialog box and then **Close** Outlook.

End **You have completed Project 1G** ——————

Outcomes-Based Assessments

Rubric

The following outcomes-based assessments are *open-ended assessments*. That is, there is no specific correct result; your result will depend on your approach to the information provided. Make *Professional Quality* your goal. Use the following scoring rubric to guide you in *how* to approach the problem and then to evaluate *how well* your approach solves the problem.

The *criteria*—Software Mastery, Content, Format and Layout, and Process—represent the knowledge and skills you have gained that you can apply to solving the problem. The *levels of performance*—Professional Quality, Approaching Professional Quality, or Needs Quality Improvement—help you and your instructor evaluate your result.

	Your completed project is of Professional Quality if you:	Your completed project is Approaching Professional Quality if you:	Your completed project Needs Quality Improvements if you:
1-Software Mastery	Choose and apply the most appropriate skills, tools, and features and identify efficient methods to solve the problem.	Choose and apply some appropriate skills, tools, and features, but not in the most efficient manner.	Choose inappropriate skills, tools, or features, or are inefficient in solving the problem.
2-Content	Construct a solution that is clear and well organized, contains content that is accurate, appropriate to the audience and purpose, and is complete. Provide a solution that contains no errors of spelling, grammar, or style.	Construct a solution in which some components are unclear, poorly organized, inconsistent, or incomplete. Misjudge the needs of the audience. Have some errors in spelling, grammar, or style, but the errors do not detract from comprehension.	Construct a solution that is unclear, incomplete, or poorly organized; contains some inaccurate or inappropriate content; and contains many errors of spelling, grammar, or style. Do not solve the problem.
3-Format and Layout	Format and arrange all elements to communicate information and ideas, clarify function, illustrate relationships, and indicate relative importance.	Apply appropriate format and layout features to some elements, but not others. Overuse features, causing minor distraction.	Apply format and layout that does not communicate information or ideas clearly. Do not use format and layout features to clarify function, illustrate relationships, or indicate relative importance. Use available features excessively, causing distraction.
4-Process	Use an organized approach that integrates planning, development, self-assessment, revision, and reflection.	Demonstrate an organized approach in some areas, but not others; or, use an insufficient process of organization throughout.	Do not use an organized approach to solve the problem.

Outcomes-Based Assessments

Outlook

Problem Solving

Project 1H — Child Center

Objectives: 1. *Start and Navigate Outlook;* **2.** *Compose and Send E-mail;* **4.** *Use Mail Options and Signatures;* **5.** *Manage E-mail;* **6.** *Use Outlook Help and Close Outlook.*

> **For Project 1H, you will need the following file:**
>
> New blank message form

You will print one file with the following footer:
1H_Child_Center_Firstname_Lastname

Lake Michigan City College operates a fully staffed child development center for use by its students, faculty, and staff. Because of the college's large adult education program, the center is an important resource for students. The child development center falls under the control of Clarence Krasnow, Director of Resource Development. Compose an e-mail message from Krasnow to James Smith, Vice President of Student Affairs. Dr. Smith is creating an information sheet about the child development center that will be included in the student packet for incoming adult students. Mr. Krasnow's message describes the facility, staff, and hours of operation of the center.

Start Outlook and display the Options menu. Using the techniques you have practiced in this chapter, configure the Send/Receive settings so that your sent messages will be placed in the Outbox instead of the Sent Items folder. Compose a new message to James Smith, whose e-mail address is **JSmith@LakeMichCityCollege.edu** Change the message format to Plain Text and type a subject for the message that defines the purpose of the message, which is a description of the child development center.

For the text of the message, write three paragraphs of general information—an introductory paragraph describing the facility, a second paragraph describing the staff, and a third paragraph that covers the hours of operation. Close the message using the name **Clarence** Suggestion: To help you compose your paragraphs, visit the Web site of your college to see whether it has a child development center or go to *www.pasadena.edu* and click **Student Services**. Then click **Child Development Center**.

Change the message importance to high and then send the message. Display the Outbox and print the message, using the Memo Style print style with **1H_Child_Center_Firstname_Lastname** as the footer. Submit the end result to your instructor as directed.

Delete the Outbox message and then empty the Deleted Items folder. Restore the Send/Receive options to their default settings. Reset the Memo Style to its default settings. Close Outlook.

End **You have completed Project 1H**

Problem Solving

Project 1I — Athletic Center

Objectives: 1. *Start and Navigate Outlook;* **2.** *Compose and Send E-mail;* **4.** *Use Mail Options and Signatures;* **5.** *Manage E-mail;* **6.** *Use Outlook Help and Close Outlook.*

> ### For Project 1I, you will need the following file:
>
> New blank message form

You will print one file with the following footer:
1I_Athletic_Center_Firstname_Lastname

James Smith, Vice President of Student Affairs at Lake Michigan City College, is preparing a brochure for incoming students that describes the college's athletic facilities. The college has recently received a very large donation from a wealthy alumnus for a new athletic center. Darron Jacobsen is responsible for facilities management. Dr. Smith has asked Mr. Jacobsen for a brief summary of the new facility. Construction has not yet begun. The facility has yet to be named. It is expected that it will bear the name of the donor, but this is a matter of some debate and is not yet public. Compose an e-mail message from Darron Jacobsen to James Smith describing the features of the new facility.

Start Outlook and display the Options menu. Using the techniques you have practiced in this chapter, configure the Send/Receive settings so that your sent messages will be placed in the Outbox instead of the Sent Items folder. Compose a new message to James Smith, whose e-mail address is **JSmith@LakeMichCityCollege.edu** Change the message format to Plain Text and type a subject for the message that defines the purpose of the message, which is a description of the new athletic center.

For the text of the message, type three paragraphs—an introductory paragraph describing the facility, a second paragraph describing the expected start and completion dates of construction, and a third paragraph that discusses how the college has not made a decision yet on the name of the facility. Close the message using the name **Darron** Suggestion: Conduct an Internet search using *www.google.com* and the search term **construction+ athletic center** to find some information for your paragraphs.

Change the message sensitivity to confidential and importance to high. Send the message, and then display the Outbox. Print the message using the Memo Style print style, using **1I_Athletic_Center_Firstname_Lastname** as the footer. Submit the end result to your instructor as directed.

Delete the contents of the Outbox and the Deleted Items folder. Restore the Send/Receive options to their default settings, and reset the print style you used when you printed your message. Close Outlook.

End **You have completed Project 1I**

Outcomes-Based Assessments

Problem Solving

Project 1J — Marathon

Objectives: 1. *Start and Navigate Outlook;* **3.** *Read and Respond to E-mail Messages;* **4.** *Use Mail Options and Signatures;* **5.** *Manage E-mail;* **6.** *Use Outlook Help and Close Outlook.*

> **For this project, you will need the following files:**
>
> New blank message form
> o01J_Marathon_Inbox

You will print one file with the following footer:
1J_Marathon_Firstname_Lastname

Mary Adair, who works in the president's office at Lake Michigan City College, enjoys recreational running. She is considering entering her first marathon, and has solicited advice from Darron Jacobsen, who is a long-time runner and has participated in many marathons. In this project, you will respond to an e-mail message Mary has sent to Darron asking for advice.

Start Outlook. In the Options dialog box, configure the Send/Receive options to place your sent messages in the Outbox instead of the Sent Items folder. Then, import the file **o01J_Marathon_Inbox** into your Inbox folder, using the techniques you have practiced in this chapter. In your Inbox, locate the message from Mary Adair in which she mentions running the Chicago Marathon. Reply to the message, congratulating her on her decision and offering her encouragement. Offer to do some training runs with her, and also share five running tips. Conduct an Internet search using the term **running tips** to find some information for your message. Assign the Personal sensitivity message setting. Send the message.

Display the Outbox and print the message, adding **1J_Marathon_ Firstname_Lastname** as the footer. Submit the end result to your instructor as directed.

Delete the message in the Outbox. Delete the contents of the Inbox folder and the Deleted Items folder. Restore the Send/Receive options to their default settings, and reset the print style you used when you printed your message. Close Outlook.

End You have completed Project 1J _____

Outcomes-Based Assessments

GO! with Help

Project 1K — *GO!* with Help

The Outlook Help system can help you as you work. In the following steps, you will view information about getting help as you work in Outlook.

1 **Start** Outlook. In the **Type a question for help** box, type **How can I get Outlook help?** and press ⏎.

2 In the **Outlook Help** window, click the **Outlook 2007 Help and How-to Home Page** link. On the **Microsoft Office Online** Web page, in the **Browse Outlook 2007 Help and How-to** section, click **Getting Help**. Notice there is a two-page list of topics on various ways to access Help.

3 Using the **Print** button at the top of the Help window, print the contents of the two pages to save for future reference. Your name will not display on this printout.

4 **Close** the Help window, **Close** the **Search Results** task pane, and then **Close** Outlook.

End **You have completed Project 1K** ————————

chaptertwo

Working with Contacts and Tasks

OBJECTIVES

At the end of this chapter you will be able to:

OUTCOMES

Mastering these objectives will enable you to:

1. Create Contacts
2. Use Contacts with E-mail
3. Edit Contacts
4. Manage Distribution Lists
5. Organize Contacts
6. Manage Contacts

PROJECT 2A
Create a Contacts List

7. Create and Update Tasks
8. Manage Tasks

PROJECT 2B
Create a To-Do List

The City of Desert Park

Desert Park, Arizona, is a thriving city with a population of just under one million in an ideal location serving major markets in the western United States and Mexico. Desert Park's temperate year-round climate attracts both visitors and businesses, making it one of the most popular vacation destinations in the world. The city expects long-term growth and has plenty of space for expansion. Most of the undeveloped land already has a modern infrastructure and assured water supply in place.

Working with Contacts and Tasks

The Contacts component of Outlook is a tool for storing information—for example, addresses, phone numbers, e-mail addresses, and so on—about individuals, organizations, and businesses with whom you communicate. The Contacts folder displays a list of these individuals and organizations. Used in conjunction with Outlook's Mail, Calendar, and Tasks components, you can click a button to have Outlook use contact information to address an e-mail message, send a task request, or send a meeting invitation.

In addition to helping you manage your contacts, Outlook also helps you monitor personal or work-related activities that you want to track until they are completed.

Project 2A Mayor's Office

In Activities 2.1 through 2.19, you will create a Contacts list for Linda Hobson, who is the assistant to City Manager Madison Romero. The list will contain the names of members of the city government of Desert Park, Arizona. You will use the Contacts list to send e-mail, create lists of contacts, and track the activities of specific contacts. You will link, sort, change the views, and organize your Contacts list in various ways. On completion, you will have a number of contacts in your Contacts list, similar to the individual contact and Contacts list shown in Figure 2.1

For Project 2A, you will need the following files:

New blank contact form

o02A_Mayor's_Office_Contacts

You will print two files with the following footers:
2A_Mayor's_Office_Assistant_Firstname_Lastname
2A_Mayor's_Office_Firstname_Lastname

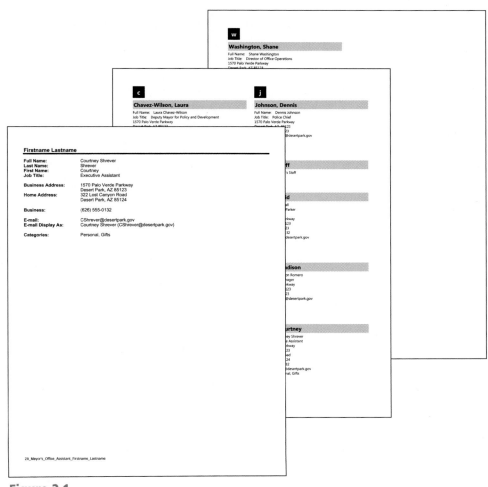

Figure 2.1
Project 2A—Mayor's Office

Objective 1
Create Contacts

A *contact* is a person or organization, inside or outside your own organization, about whom you can save information such as street and e-mail addresses, telephone and fax numbers, Web page addresses, birthdays, and even pictures. The *Contacts* component of Outlook is your e-mail address book for storing information about people, organizations, and businesses with whom you communicate.

The default location for Outlook's Contacts information is the *Contacts folder*. To create, edit, or display the contents of your Contacts list, you must display this folder. Build your Contacts list by entering your contact information one person, one company, or one organization at a time, adding as much or as little information about the contact as you want.

Alert!

Starting Project 2A

Because Outlook stores information on the hard drive of the computer at which you are working, unless you are working on your own computer, it is recommended that you complete Project 2A in one working session. Allow approximately one to one and a half hours.

Activity 2.1 Exploring Contacts

As you manage the contacts for the members of the Desert Park city government, you will use the Navigation Pane to *navigate*—move around within—Outlook.

1 **Start** Outlook. If the Navigation Pane is not displayed, display the **View** menu, point to **Navigation Pane**, and then click **Normal**. At the bottom of the **Navigation Pane**, click the **Folder List** button 🗀, display the **Inbox** folder. Delete any existing messages in the folder by selecting the messages, and then clicking the **Delete** button ✕.

2 In the **Navigation Pane**, click the **Contacts** button [🔲 Contacts] and **Delete** ✕ any existing items in the folder. Compare your screen with Figure 2.2.

In the Navigation Pane, you can control how your Contacts list is displayed. The default view is Business Cards. Recall that *views* provide different ways to look at the same information by putting it in different formats or arrangements.

Figure 2.2

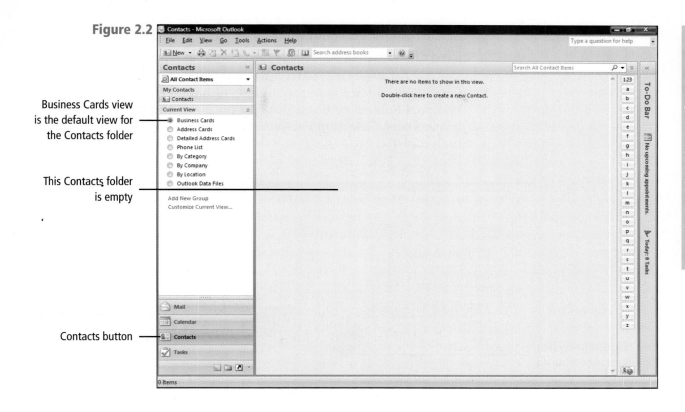

Business Cards view is the default view for the Contacts folder

This Contacts folder is empty

Contacts button

3 At the bottom of the **Navigation Pane**, click the **Folder List** button ▢ to display the **Folder List** in the upper portion of the **Navigation Pane**. Notice that the **Contacts** folder is selected.

4 In the **Navigation Pane**, click the **Contacts** button [⬛ Contacts] to redisplay the **Current View** pane within the Navigation Pane.

Activity 2.2 Importing Contacts into Your Contacts Folder

In this activity, you will **import** contacts into your Contacts folder. To import means to bring the information into Outlook from another program in which the information already exists. The imported contacts contain information about various members of the Desert Park city government.

1 From the **File** menu, click **Import and Export**. In the displayed **Import and Export Wizard** dialog box, under **Choose an action to perform**, click **Import from another program or file**, and then click **Next**.

2 In the **Import a File** dialog box, under **Select file type to import from**, scroll as necessary, and then click **Personal Folder File (.pst)**. Click **Next**.

3 In the **Import Personal Folders** dialog box, click the **Browse** button. In the **Open Personal Folders** dialog box, in the **Folders** list, click **Computer**, and then navigate to the location where the student files for this textbook are stored.

4 Locate **o02A_Mayor's_Office_Contacts** and click one time to select it. Then, in the lower right corner of the **Open Personal Folders** dialog box, click **Open**, and notice that the path and file name display in the **File to import** box.

5 In the **Import Personal Folders** dialog box, click **Next**, and then compare your screen with Figure 2.3.

The Import Personal Folders dialog box displays the folder structure for the file you are about to import. Although not visible here, Personal Folders contains data for both a Contacts folder and an Inbox folder. Selecting Personal Folders imports information into both folders.

Figure 2.3

List of folders from which information can be imported

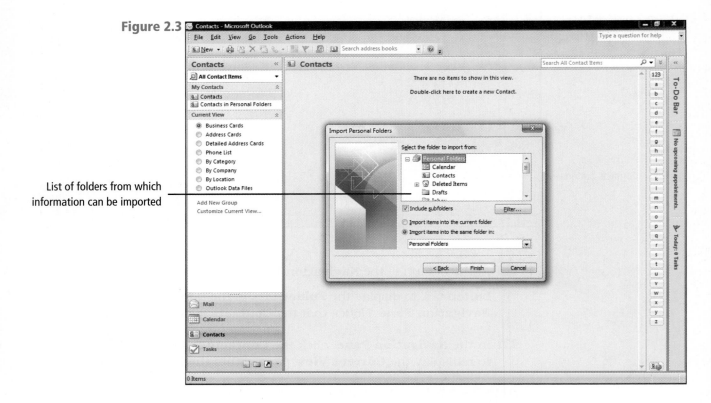

6 In the **Import Personal Folders** dialog box, click **Finish**. If a Translation Warning dialog box displays, click **OK**. Compare your screen with Figure 2.4.

Five contacts are imported into your Contacts folder and displayed in the Business Cards view. Depending upon your screen resolution, your layout may differ.

Figure 2.4

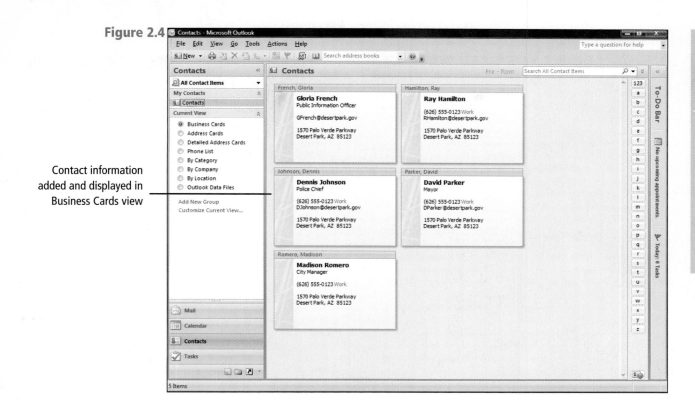

Contact information added and displayed in Business Cards view

Activity 2.3 Creating Contacts

When you create a new contact, you add it to your Contacts list. In this activity, you will add Shane Washington, Director of Office Operations for the mayor of Desert Park, to the Contacts list.

1 In the **Navigation Pane**, be sure your **Contacts** folder is displayed. If necessary, click **Contacts** 🔲 Contacts to display the Contacts folder.

2 On the Standard toolbar, click the **New Contact** button 🔲 New , and then compare your screen with Figure 2.5.

The *Untitled – Contact* form displays. By default the form is displayed in *General* view. By using different commands, displayed on the Ribbon, you can store a variety of information about a person or an organization. A blank area of the form, called the ***Notes area***, can be used for any information about the contact that is not otherwise specified in the form.

General view   Notes area

Figure 2.5

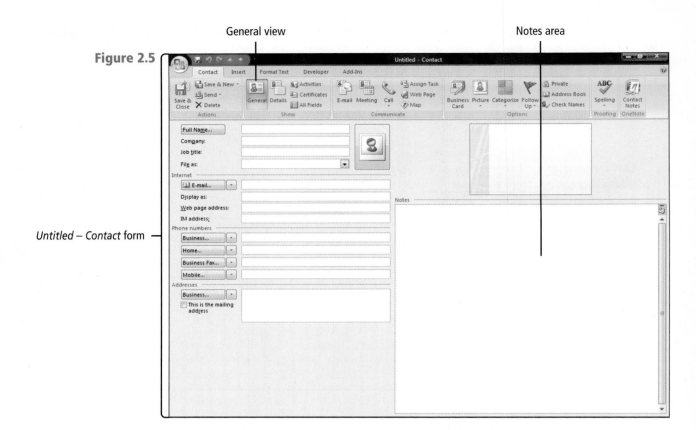

Untitled – Contact form ⟶

3 In the **Untitled – Contact** form, in the **Full Name** box, type **Shane Washington** and then press ⏎Tab⏎ **two** times.

The insertion point moves to the *Job title* box, and the form title bar displays *Shane Washington – Contact*. Notice that the *File as* box displays the contact name as *Washington, Shane*. This is how it will appear in the Contacts list. Outlook displays items in the Contacts list in alphabetical order based on last names, a common method for arranging groups of names.

4 In the **Job title** box, type **Director of Office Operations** In the **E-mail** box, type **SWashington@desertpark.gov** and then press ⏎Tab⏎.

The *Display as* box shows the contact's name with the e-mail address in parentheses. When you use the contact's address in an e-mail message, this is how Outlook will display the address. Sometimes a contact's e-mail address may be completely unrelated to the person's actual name. When viewing e-mail messages, this feature helps you recall the person associated with the e-mail address.

5 Under **Phone numbers**, in the **Business** box, type **626-555-0129** and then press ⏎Tab⏎. If a Location Information dialog box displays, select your country or region. Compare your screen with Figure 2.6.

The phone number displays with parentheses around the area code portion of the number. You can also type a phone number without hyphens, and Outlook will format it correctly.

Figure 2.6

Title bar indicates contact
name *Shane Washington*

Contact's name

Contact's e-mail address
in parentheses

Parentheses added
to phone number

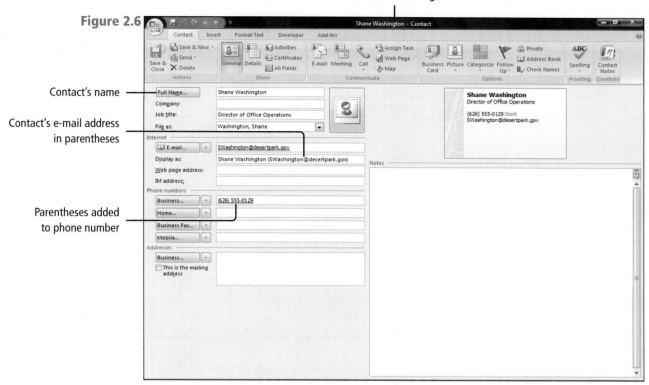

More Knowledge

Verifying and Adding Information to Names, Internet, Phone Numbers, and Addresses

The Contact form contains the Full Name command button and command buttons under Internet, Phone numbers, and Addresses. These command buttons display dialog boxes that enable you to add more information to a name, Internet information, phone number, or address. For example, the Full Name command button displays the Check Full Name dialog box, in which you can add a prefix such as Dr. or Ms. to the contact's name. These dialog boxes also verify the accuracy of the information. Outlook displays these boxes automatically if a name, phone number, address, or Internet address is incomplete or unclear.

6 Under **Addresses**, in the **Business** box, type the following information, and then compare your screen with Figure 2.7:

1570 Palo Verde Parkway
Desert Park, AZ 85123

Figure 2.7

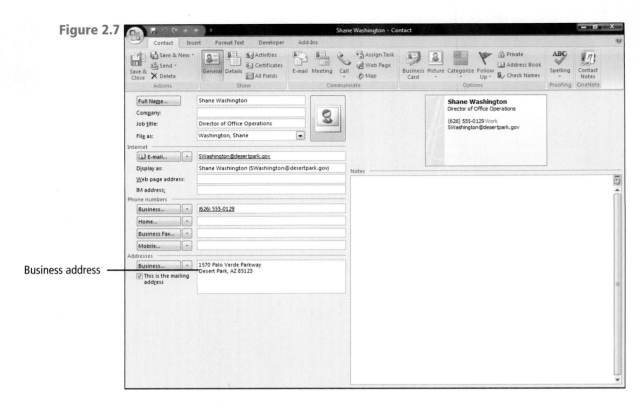

Business address

---

7 On the Ribbon, in the **Actions group**, click the **Save & Close** button [Save & Close].

Outlook saves the new contact and the Contacts folder displays in Business Cards view. The new contact displays in either the first or the second column, depending on your screen resolution.

8 On the Standard toolbar, click the **New Contact** button [New].

Another Way ── **To Open a Blank Contact Form**

You can display a blank Contact form in several ways. In addition to the toolbar button, you can use the keyboard shortcut Ctrl + N. Or, from the File menu, point to New, and then click Contact. Finally, you can right-click in a blank area of the Contacts folder and click New Contact on the shortcut menu.

9 In the **Untitled – Contact** form, use the technique you just practiced to add the following new contact, using **Business** for the phone number and address information.

Laura Chavez-Wilson
Deputy Mayor for Policy and Development
LChavezWilson@desertpark.gov
626-555-0131
1570 Palo Verde Parkway
Desert Park, AZ 85123

After typing the address in the **Business** box, press Tab and compare your screen with Figure 2.8.

Figure 2.8

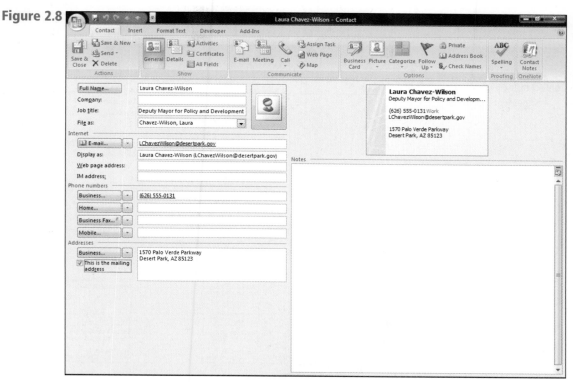

10 On the Ribbon in the **Actions group**, click the **Save & New** button [Save & New ▾].

Outlook saves the new contact and displays a new, blank Contact form. When you enter multiple new contacts, you can use this button to save a new contact and then display another blank form.

11 Add the following new contact, using Business for the e-mail, phone number, and address information:

**Courtney Shrever
Executive Assistant
CShrever@desertpark.gov
626-555-0132
1570 Palo Verde Parkway
Desert Park, AZ 85123**

12 On the **Courtney Shrever – Contact** form, under **Addresses**, click the **Business arrow**, and then click **Home**.

The adjacent box clears and changes to Home. You can store multiple addresses for a contact.

13 Type the following home address information for the contact:

**322 Lost Canyon Road
Desert Park, AZ 85124**

14 On the Ribbon, click the **Save & Close** button [Save & Close]. Compare your Contacts list with the one displayed in Figure 2.9.

The new contacts are added to the Contacts list.

Figure 2.9

Contact Index—your letter arrangement may differ

Contact information for Chavez-Wilson and Shrever added

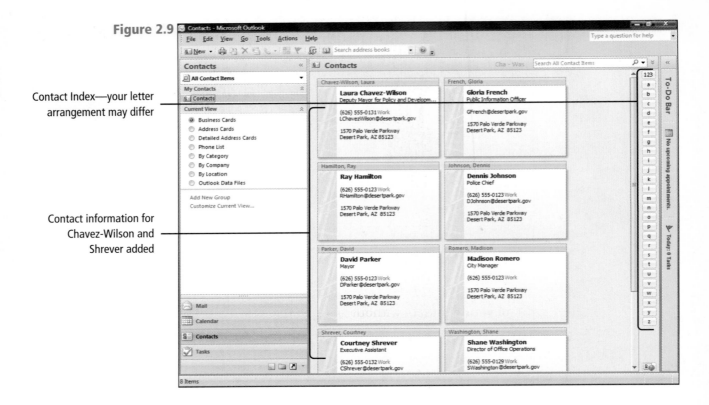

15 On the right side of the Outlook window, locate the buttons with the letters of the alphabet.

The lettered buttons form a **Contact Index**, which is a set of buttons used to move through contact items displayed in Business Cards view. The Contact Index moves the focus to the first contact whose name begins with selected character. In a large Contacts list, you can use the buttons on the Contact Index to quickly display a specific section of the list. Depending on the size of your monitor and screen resolution, instead of a single letters, the letters may be grouped in pairs.

16 In the **Contacts** list, click Ray Hamilton to select this contact. In the **Contact Index**, click **r**, and then notice that the business card for *Madison Romero* is selected. Then in the **Contact Index**, click **f**—or **ef** if your display shows pairs of letters—and notice that the business card for *Gloria French* is highlighted—currently no contact last names begin with the letter *e*.

Although this is a fairly short list of contacts, you can see that with a very long list, it is convenient to use the Contact Index to jump to a specific section of the list.

More Knowledge

Creating Contacts with the Same Address

If you have several contacts from the same company or contacts who use the same address and phone number, you can use the information from an existing contact for the new entry. Select an existing contact with the same information. From the Actions menu, click New Contact from Same Company. Outlook displays the Contact form with the phone number, address, and company name (if any) already completed. You need only add the new name and e-mail address, and adjust other information as necessary.

Objective 2
Use Contacts with E-mail

When viewing your Contacts list, you can send an e-mail message to one of your contacts without switching to the Inbox folder. Conversely, you can use the information in a received e-mail message to create a new entry in your Contacts list using the sender's e-mail address. In this manner, Outlook is designed to make it easy to enter new contacts without switching to different screens and without extra typing on your part.

Activity 2.4 Sending an E-mail Message to a Contact

You can send an e-mail message to a contact either from the Contacts list or while viewing the contact information in the Contact form. You can also use the Contacts list to address messages in the Message form. In this activity, you will practice sending e-mail messages to the Desert Park contacts using both techniques.

1 In the **Contacts** list, click the **Ray Hamilton** contact one time to select it.

2 From the **Actions** menu, point to **Create**, and then click **New Message to Contact**.

A blank Untitled Message form displays. The *To* box displays the e-mail address taken from the e-mail information for the contact. You can see that this requires fewer steps than switching to the Mail component and starting a new message.

Alert!

Is the New Message to Contact command missing?

If you do not see the New Message to Contact command on your menu, it is because no e-mail accounts have been set up on the computer on which you are working. From the Tools menu, click Options, click the Mail Setup tab, and then click E-mail Accounts. Click Add a new e-mail account, click Next, click POP3, and then click Next. On the E-mail tab, click the New... button. Click Next, and select Manually configure server settings or additional server types, and then click Next two times. Type your name, any real or fictitious e-mail address, any fictitious incoming and outgoing server name (for example, GOmail.com), and any user name and password. Click Next, and then click Finish. Then return to this activity.

3 On the **Message** form title bar, click the **Close** button ![X]. In the **Microsoft Office Outlook** dialog box, click **No** to close the Message form without sending a message or saving a draft of the message.

The Contacts folder redisplays.

4 In the **Contacts list**, right-click the **Shane Washington** contact, and then point to **Create**. Compare your screen with Figure 2.10.

A shortcut menu displays. The Create option displays a submenu with the New Message to Contact command.

Figure 2.10

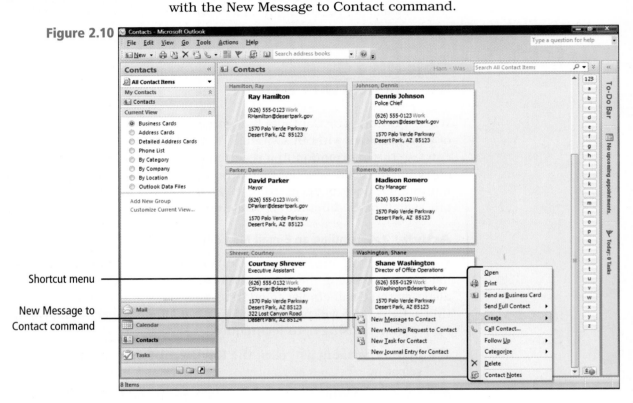

Shortcut menu

New Message to Contact command

5 Click anywhere outside the shortcut menu to close it.

6 In the **Navigation Pane**, click the **Mail** button ![Mail]. Click the **New Mail Message** button ![New] to display a blank Untitled Message form.

7 In the **Message** form, point to, and then click the word **To**, and then compare your screen with Figure 2.11.

The Select Names: Contacts box displays, and all entries in your Contacts list that contain e-mail addresses also display.

Figure 2.11

Select Names:
Contacts dialog box

Names of contacts that
have an e-mail address
associated with them

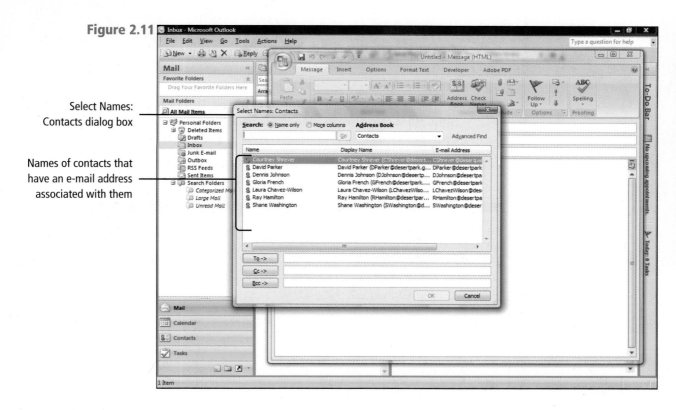

8 In the **Select Names: Contacts** dialog box, click **David Parker** one time to select it. Click the **To** button.

The David Parker address displays in the To box.

9 In the **Select Names: Contacts** dialog box, locate the **Bcc** box.

Bcc is an abbreviation for *blind courtesy copy*, or *blind carbon copy*. When you add a message recipient in the Bcc box, the Bcc recipient receives a copy of the message, but the Bcc recipient's name is not visible to other recipients of the message. Recall that *Cc* is an abbreviation for *courtesy copy*. If you place a name in this box, that person will receive a copy of the message, and everyone will see that this person was copied on the message.

10 In the **Select Names: Contacts** dialog box, click **OK**.

The Select Names: Contacts dialog box closes. The David Parker address displays in the To box of the Message form.

11 **Close** [X] the Message form. In the **Microsoft Office Outlook** dialog box, click **No** to close the Message form without sending a message or saving a draft of the message.

Activity 2.5 Creating a Contact from an E-mail Message

If you receive an e-mail message from someone whose name is not on your Contacts list, you can add the name to your Contacts list directly from the message. In this activity, you will add another individual from Desert Park's city government to the Contacts list.

1 From the **Navigation Pane**, click **Mail** [Mail], and be sure the Inbox displays.

The Inbox contains a message from Simone Daley. This message was imported into your Inbox when you imported the contacts into your Contacts folder. There is no listing in your Contacts list for the individual.

2 In the **Reading Pane**, point to **Simone Daley's** e-mail address, and right click. On the displayed shortcut menu, click **Add to Outlook Contacts**, and then compare your screen with Figure 2.12.

A Contact form displays with Simone's name in the title bar, and the form displays the name and e-mail address of the new contact.

Figure 2.12

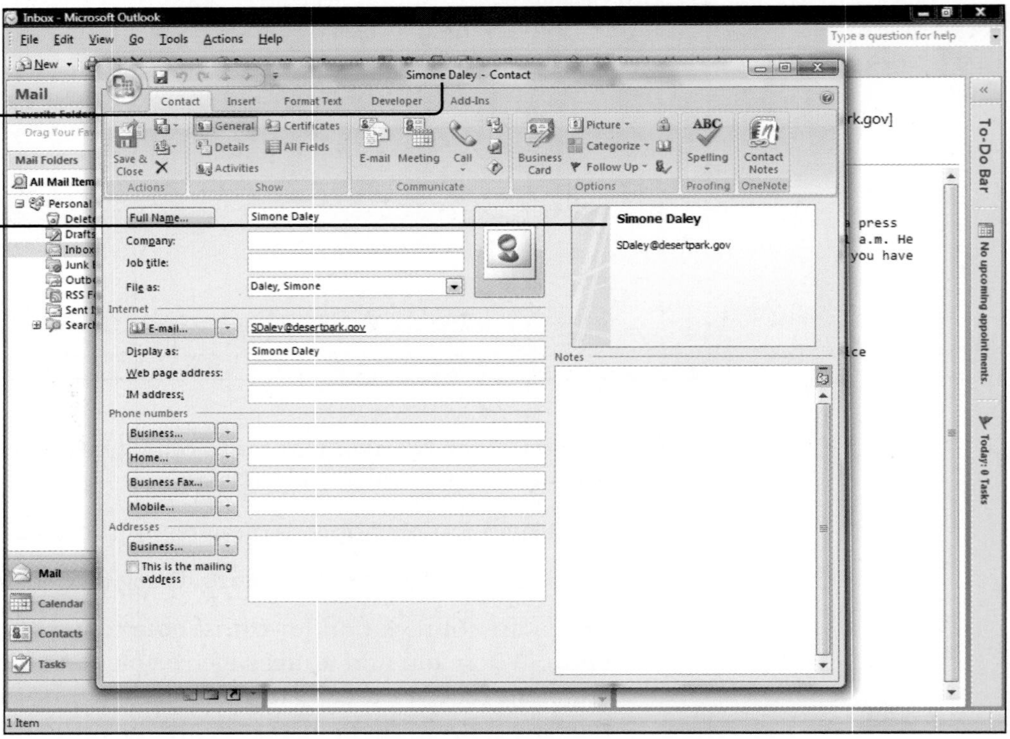

New contact's name in title bar

Name and e-mail address display

3 Complete the form by typing the following contact information:

626-555-0128
1570 Palo Verde Parkway
Desert Park, AZ 85123

4 **Save & Close**  to add the new contact and redisplay the Inbox.

5 In the **Reading Pane**, right-click the e-mail address of **Simone Daley** to display the shortcut menu again.

Notice the *Look up Outlook Contact* command. If you receive a message from someone already on your Contacts list, you can use this command to display his or her contact information. This could be useful if you wish to contact an individual immediately by phone; the contact's phone number is readily available.

6 Click anywhere outside the shortcut menu to close it.

Objective 3
Edit Contacts

When information about a specific contact changes, you can easily add details, change addresses and phone numbers, or add a flag for follow-up to remind you of something related to the contact.

Activity 2.6 Editing a Contact

It is common to create a contact and then add more information later as it becomes available. Two members of Desert Park's government are new in their positions. In this activity, you will edit the existing entries by adding more information.

1 From the **Navigation Pane**, display the **Contacts** folder [Contacts]. Point to the contact **Madison Romero**, and then double-click to open the Contact form. Alternatively, point to the contact, right-click, and from the shortcut menu, click **Open**.

2 In the **E-mail** box, type **MRomero@desertpark.gov** and then

Save & Close [Save & Close] the form.

The new information is added to the contact, and the Contacts list redisplays.

3 In the **Contacts list**, use the technique you just practiced to open the Contact form for **Gloria French**. Under **Phone numbers**, in the

Business box, type **626-555-0123** and then **Save & Close** [Save & Close] the form.

4 In the **Navigation Pane**, under **Current View**, click **Address Cards**.

5 In the displayed **Contacts list**, click the phone number portion of the **Gloria French** contact, and then compare your screen with Figure 2.13.

Depending on where you clicked, a blinking insertion point displays in the phone number, which indicates that you can edit the phone number directly in the Contacts list without actually opening the Contact form.

Figure 2.13

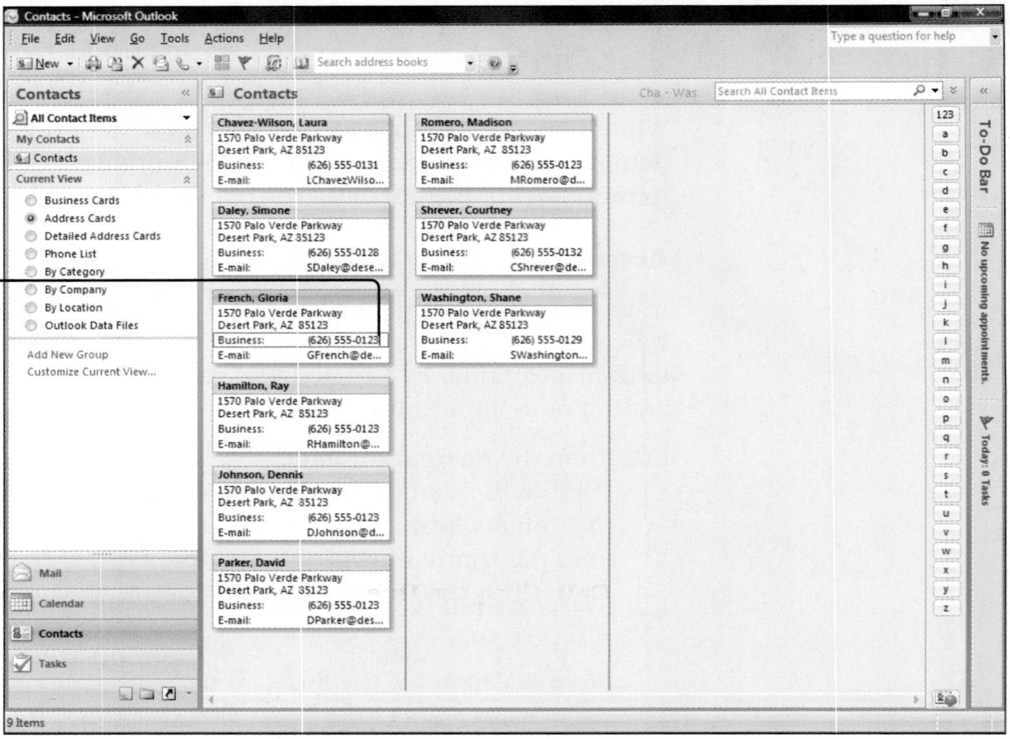

Blinking insertion point indicates that you can edit the list

6 Move the insertion point to the end of the phone number. Press `←Bksp` and then type **8** so that the phone number displays as 626-555-0128. Click any blank area in the Contacts list to complete the editing for the Gloria French contact.

7 In the **Navigation Pane**, under **Current View**, click **Business Cards**.

Recall that *Business Cards* view is the default view for the Contact list.

Another Way ── **To Open an Existing Contact**

You can open a selected contact in several ways. In addition to double-clicking the contact in the Contacts list, you can select the contact and then use the keyboard shortcut `Ctrl` + `O`. Or select the contact, and then, from the File menu, point to Open and click Selected Items. You can also point to the contact, right-click, and from the displayed shortcut menu, click Open.

Activity 2.7 Adding Detail to a Contact

In addition to addresses and phone numbers, you can store additional details about a contact, for example, the name of the contact's assistant or the contact's birthday. You can flag a contact to remind yourself of a follow-up action related to the contact, for example, to remind yourself to call a contact for a dinner meeting. In this activity, you will add details to the contact information for Desert Park's mayor, David Parker.

1 From the **Contacts list**, open the contact form for **David Parker**. If necessary, **maximize** 🔲 the Contact form. Under **Phone numbers**, click the **Business arrow**, and then click **Assistant**.

The contact form provides space for four phone numbers, which are set to the defaults *Business*, *Home*, *Business Fax*, and *Mobile*. By clicking the arrow, you can select other names, for example, Assistant, and then insert appropriate phone numbers.

2 In the Assistant box, type **626-555-0132**

3 On the **Contact tab**, in the **Show group**, click the **Details** button. In the **Assistant's name** box, type **Courtney Shrever**

4 On the Ribbon, in the **Options group**, click the **Follow Up** button, and then click **Custom**.

The *Custom* dialog box displays. If you want, for example, to be reminded to call David Parker on a specific day, you can set a date, and Outlook will display a reminder when the date arrives.

5 In the **Custom** dialog box, click the **Flag to arrow**, and then click **Call**. Click the **Due date arrow**, and then compare your screen with Figure 2.14.

Due date arrow

Figure 2.14

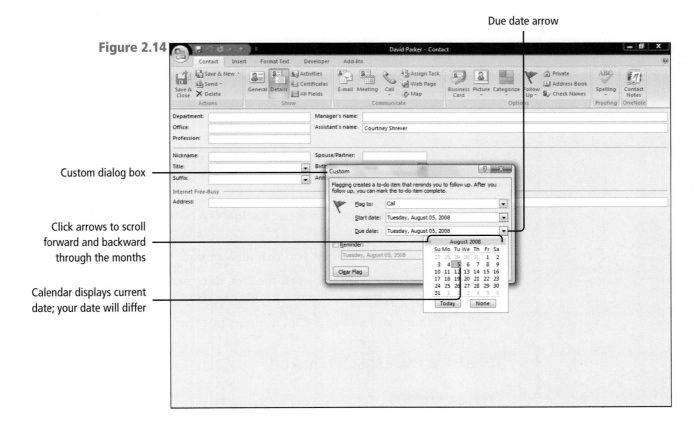

Custom dialog box

Click arrows to scroll forward and backward through the months

Calendar displays current date; your date will differ

6 On the calendar, next to the month name, click the **right arrow** once, advancing the calendar to the next month. Click **25**. In the **Reminder** section, click the **Reminder** check box, then click the **time arrow** and click **8:00 AM** for the time. Click **OK**.

The Custom dialog box closes. Outlook will display a reminder when the date arrives.

7 On the Ribbon, in the **Show group**, click the **General** button 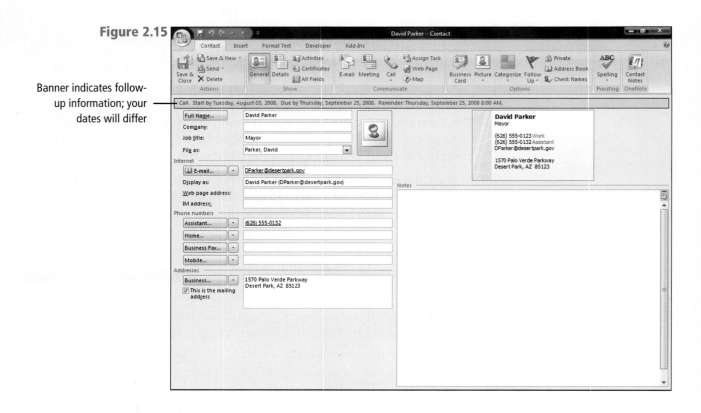, and then compare your screen with Figure 2.15.

The Contact form displays a follow-up banner under the Ribbon.

Figure 2.15

Banner indicates follow-up information; your dates will differ

8 In the **Options group**, click the **Follow Up** button , and then click **Custom**.

In the *Custom* dialog box you can also remove reminders.

9 In the **Custom** dialog box, click the **Due date arrow**. On the displayed calendar, click **None**. Clear the **Reminder** check box, and then click **OK**.

The contact still shows a Call banner, but the reminder has been removed.

10 **Save & Close** the contact.

Objective 4
Manage Distribution Lists

You can develop ***distribution lists*** from your contacts. A distribution list is a collection of contacts to whom you send e-mail messages. A distribution list is an easy way to send an e-mail message to a group of people all at one time. For example, if you frequently send messages to a group of people on a marketing team, you can create a distribution list called *Marketing* and include in the list the e-mail addresses of all the people on the team. A message sent to the *Marketing* distribution list goes to every address on the list.

Activity 2.8 Creating a Distribution List

Distribution lists are created and displayed in the Contacts folder. In this activity, you will create a distribution list containing all the names of the Desert Park mayor's staff.

1 Be sure the **Contacts list** is displayed, and then, from the **File** menu point to **New**, and click **Distribution List**.

2 In the **Distribution List** form, in the **Name** box, type **Mayor's Staff** as the name for the list.

This is the name of the distribution list as it will display in your Contacts list. This is also the name you will use to address e-mail messages to all the members in the list.

3 On the **Distribution List tab**, in the **Members group**, click **Select Members**.

The Select Members: Contacts dialog box displays with the first member of the list selected. The dialog box displays only names from your Contacts list that have e-mail addresses.

4 At the bottom of the dialog box, click **Members**.

Outlook adds the first name in the list, *Courtney Shrever*, to the distribution list.

5 Under **Name**, click **Laura Chavez-Wilson**, and then click **Members** to add her to the distribution list.

6 Using the technique you just practiced, add **Shane Washington** and **Simone Daley** to the distribution list, and then compare your screen with Figure 2.16. If necessary to see the entire name, you can widen the right edge of the dialog box using the Horizontal resize pointer ↔.

Figure 2.16

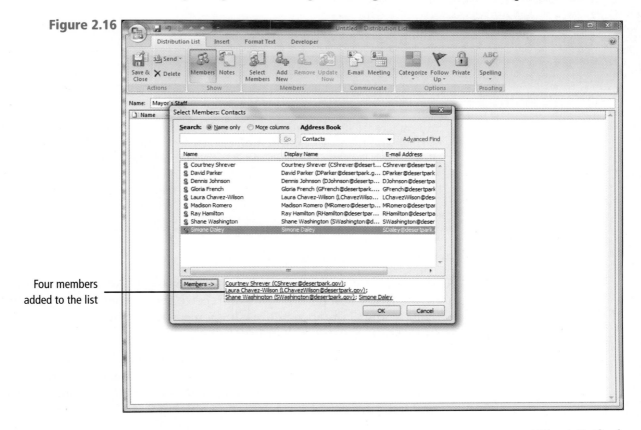

Four members added to the list

7 At the bottom of the **Select Members: Contacts** dialog box, click **OK**.

On the **Distribution List** form, click the **Save & Close** button . Compare your screen with Figure 2.17.

The Contacts list redisplays. The distribution list displays as an entry in the Contacts list. The word *Group* below the name indicates that this is a distribution list.

Figure 2.17

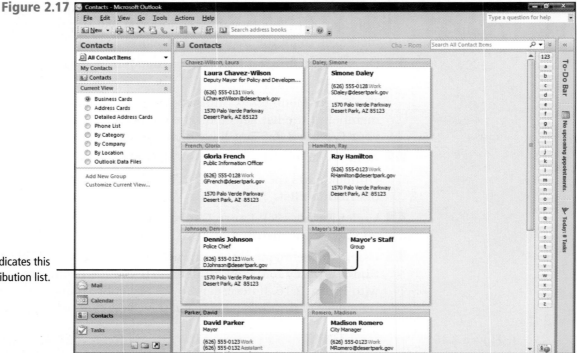

The word *Group* indicates this contact is a distribution list.

Another Way — **To Create a Distribution List**

You can create a distribution list in various ways. From the File menu, point to New, and then click Distribution List. Or from the Actions menu, click New Distribution list. Another method is the keyboard shortcut Ctrl + Shift + L. Still another method is clicking the New button arrow and then clicking Distribution List. Finally, you can right-click a blank area of the Contacts list and then click New Distribution List on the shortcut menu.

Activity 2.9 Using a Distribution List

After you create a distribution list, you can use it like any other e-mail address. Every name in the list will receive the message you send. In this activity, you will practice addressing a message to the members of the mayor's staff by using a distribution list.

1 On the Standard toolbar, click the **New Contact button arrow** 📇 New, and then click **Mail Message**. In the **Untitled Message** form, click **To**, and notice that *Mayor's Staff* displays as one of the available e-mail addresses.

2 In the **Select Names: Contacts** dialog box, under **Name**, click **Mayor's Staff** one time to select it. In the lower portion of the dialog box, click **To**. Compare your screen with Figure 2.18.

Figure 2.18

Select Names: Contacts dialog box

Mayor's Staff distribution list selected

Mayor's Staff indicated in the To box

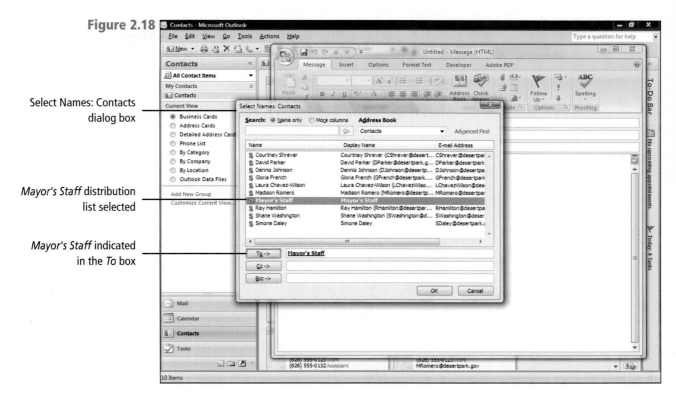

3 Click **OK**, and in the box to the left of *Mayor's Staff*, notice the small plus (+) sign. Position the pointer over the plus (+) sign and click.

The *Expand List* dialog box displays. You can use this dialog box to replace the *Mayor's Staff* distribution list name in the *To* box with the actual e-mail addresses contained in the list. This can be useful if you would like to add or remove a specific name in the list as a recipient of the message.

4 In the **Expand List** dialog box, read the information, and then click **Cancel** to close the dialog box without expanding the list.

5 In the **To** box, position the pointer over the text *Mayor's Staff*, and double-click.

The Distribution List form displays, listing the members of the distribution list. This is useful if you want to see and confirm the names on a distribution list before you send the message. This is also another way to add or remove names as recipients of the message. If you choose to add or remove names from the distribution list, you will need to Save & Close for those changes to be applied to the message.

6 **Close** ☒ the **Distribution List** form, and then **Close** ☒ the **Message** form without sending the message. In the **Microsoft Office Outlook** dialog box, click **No**.

Activity 2.10 Modifying a Distribution List

To keep a distribution list up-to-date, you can add or delete names. In this activity, you will update the distribution list you created for the mayor's staff.

1 With the **Contacts list** still displayed, open the **Mayor's Staff** contact. In the **Distribution List** form, on the Ribbon, in the **Members group**, click **Select Members**.

The *Select Members: Contacts* dialog box displays. Recall that the names that display represent all the contacts with e-mail addresses in your Contacts list, including the names that are already members of the *Mayor's Staff* distribution list.

2 In the **Select Members: Contacts** dialog box, click **Madison Romero**, and then click **Members**. Click **OK** and notice that *Madison Romero* is added to the list.

3 In the **Distribution List** form, under **Name**, click **Courtney Shrever**. On the Ribbon, in the **Members group**, click **Remove** to remove her from the distribution list.

4 In the **Distribution List** form, in the **Members group**, click **Add New**.

The *Add New Member* dialog box displays. Use this option if you want to add a name to the distribution list that is not on your Contacts list.

5 In the displayed **Add New Member** dialog box, in the **Display Name** box, type **Andrew Gore** In the E-mail address box, type **AGore@desertpark.gov** Select the **Add to Contacts** check box, and then compare your screen with Figure 2.19.

Figure 2.19

New name added

Add New Member dialog box

New member's e-mail address inserted

Add to Contacts check box selected

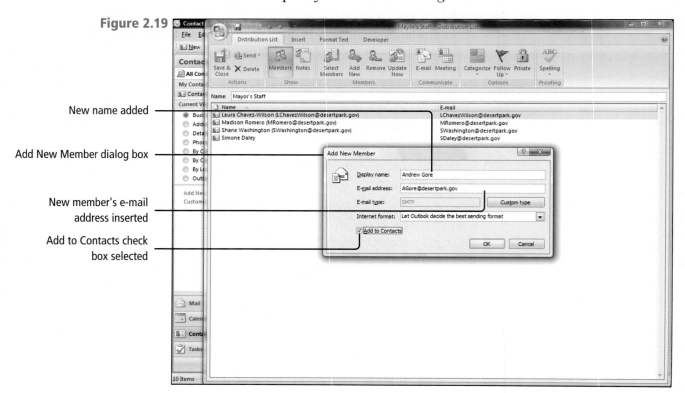

6 Click **OK**, and then **Save & Close** [icon] the distribution list.

More Knowledge
Using the Update Now Option

If you change e-mail addresses in your Contacts list, you can have those e-mail addresses automatically changed in a distribution list. To do so, open the Distribution List form, and on the Ribbon, in the Members group, click Update Now. Outlook will scan your Contacts list and make any changes for e-mail addresses that have been modified.

Objective 5
Organize Contacts

In a short Contacts list, it is easy to find the information you need. As the number of contacts increases, Outlook has tools to assist you in finding a contact if you are unsure of a name, company, or some other detail relating to the contact. You can assign contacts to *categories*, which are colors, with optional words or phrases, applied to Outlook items for the purpose of finding, sorting, filtering, or grouping them. You can also apply various views to the Contacts folder.

Activity 2.11 Creating Categories in Outlook

Outlook has a variety of color categories that you can rename with descriptions such as *Customers* or *Family*. In this activity, you will assign descriptive names to particular colors.

1 With the **Contacts list** displayed, on the Standard toolbar, click the **Categorize** button [icon], and then click **All Categories**.

The *Color Categories* dialog box displays. Use this option when you want to rename an existing color category or create a new one.

2 In the **Color Categories** dialog box, select the text **Red Category** and then click the **Rename** button. Compare your screen with Figure 2.20.

Notice the box containing the Red Category is now active, so you can type a more descriptive name.

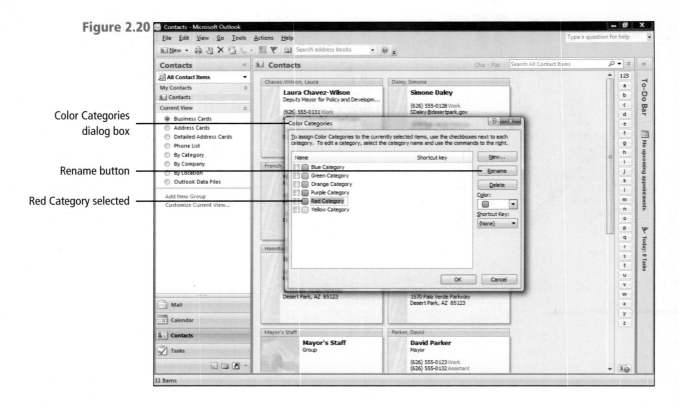

Figure 2.20

Color Categories dialog box — Color Categories

Rename button — Rename

Red Category selected — Red Category

3 In the box with **Red Category** selected, type **Personal**

4 In the **Color Categories** dialog box, select the text **Purple Category**, click **Rename**, and then type **VIP**

5 Using the technique you just practiced, rename the **Green Category** as **Holiday Cards** and the **Orange Category** as **Gifts**

You now have four color categories renamed with descriptive words. You should not have any selection boxes checked.

6 Click **OK** to close the **Color Categories** dialog box.

Activity 2.12 Assigning Contacts to Categories

Outlook provides the option to assign categories to a contact or any other Outlook item. Assign categories to a contact in the Contact form or by using a shortcut menu in the Contacts list. In this activity, you will assign the Desert Park city employees to different categories.

1 With the **Contacts list** displayed, open **Courtney Shrever's** contact form, and if necessary, **Maximize** [button] the form. On the Ribbon, in the **Options group**, click **Categorize**, and then click **All Categories**.

2 In the displayed **Color Categories** dialog box, select the **Gifts** and **Personal** check boxes, and then compare your screen with Figure 2.21.

The Gifts category is a useful way to group individuals for whom you regularly buy birthday or holiday gifts. The Personal category is a good way to separate family and friends from work-related contacts in your Contacts list.

Figure 2.21

Categorize button

Color Categories dialog box

Gifts and *Personal* check boxes selected

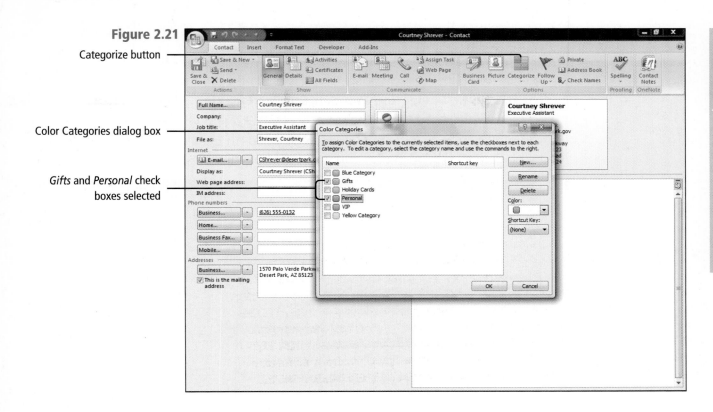

3 Click **OK**, and then **Save & Close** the contact form.

4 In the **Contacts list**, point to **Andrew Gore**, right-click, and then on the displayed shortcut menu, point to **Categorize**, and then on the submenu click **Personal**.

This is another method to assign a category to a contact.

5 In the **Contacts list**, click one time to select **Dennis Johnson**. Hold down Ctrl, and then click **David Parker** and **Madison Romero**. Release Ctrl.

Three contacts are selected. Use this technique to select two or more contacts and perform an action on all of them at one time; for example, assigning all the selected contacts to a category.

6 Right-click any of the three selected contacts, and then, from the short-cut menu, point to **Categorize**, and then on the submenu click **VIP**.

All three contacts are assigned to the *VIP*—Very Important Person—category.

7 Click on Laura Chavez-Wilson and notice that the other three contacts are deselected. Then, using the technique you just practiced to select multiple contacts, select **Laura Chavez-Wilson**, **Gloria French**, and **Shane Washington**. Display the **Categorize** submenu, and select **Holiday Cards**.

The three contacts are assigned to the Holiday Cards category. When the time comes to send holiday cards, you can sort your contacts by category and be reminded of those people to whom you want to send a card.

Activity 2.13 Changing the View of the Contacts List

In this activity, you will change the view and display the Desert Park Contacts list in a different arrangement.

1 In the **Navigation Pane**, under **Current View**, click **Detailed Address Cards**. Compare your screen with Figure 2.22.

The Contacts list displays in Detailed Address Cards view. In this view, the categories you assigned to contacts are displayed.

Figure 2.22

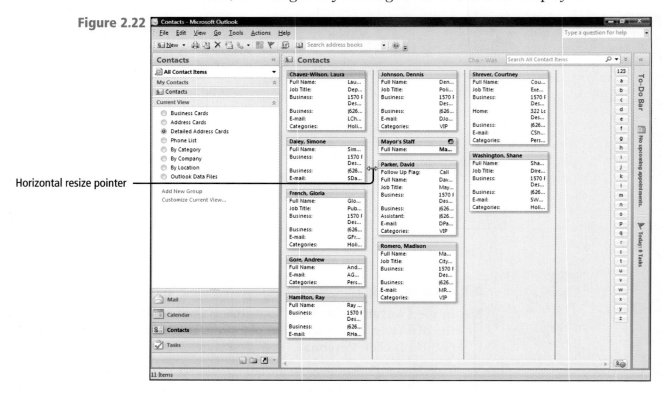

Horizontal resize pointer

2 On the vertical dividing line between the first and second columns, position the pointer until it changes to a Horizontal resize pointer ⟷ as shown in Figure 2.22.

3 Drag the column divider to the right so that all the information for the contacts in the first column displays.

Widening the columns enables you to see more of the address card information. Outlook retains the width you apply to the columns until you change to a different width.

4 At the bottom of the screen, drag the horizontal scroll box to view the rightmost column if necessary, and then press Ⓒ.

The first item in the Contacts list, the entry for *Linda Chavez-Wilson*, is selected, and the first column of the Contacts list displays. Using this technique, you can jump to different areas of the Contacts list by typing letters on the keyboard. You can also jump to different areas by clicking the Contact Index tabs on the right side of the screen.

5 On the right side of the screen, on the **Contact Index**, click the **w** button.

The last item in the Contacts list, the entry for *Shane Washington*, is selected, and the last column of the Contacts list displays.

6 On the **Contacts Index**, click the **a** button—or the **ab** button if your computer displays only this button.

The first item in the Contacts list is selected, and the first column in the Contacts list displays. When there is no contact that begins with the clicked letter button, Outlook selects the item closest to that letter in the alphabet.

7 On the column divider, drag to the left so that three columns display and the first column is returned to its approximate original width. Compare your screen with Figure 2.23.

Figure 2.23

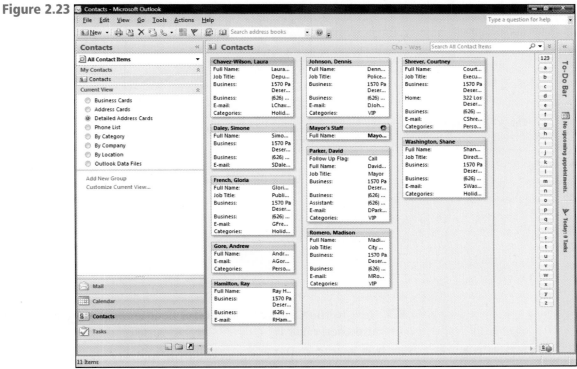

Activity 2.14 Sorting the Contacts List by Category and Field

Some views display items in a **table**—an arrangement of information with a separate row for each item and a separate column for each **field**. A field is an element of information within an Outlook item, such as company name or state. You can use the column headings to sort by fields. You can also sort the Contacts list by Category, provided that you have assigned categories to your contacts in the manner you did for your Desert Park Contacts list.

1 Change the **Current View** to **By Category**.

The Contacts list switches to a table view in which the contact items are grouped by category. There are groups for every category that has been assigned to a contact.

2 To the left of the **Categories** headings, locate the plus (+) or minus (–) symbols. If the plus (+) displays, click each to display the items in the groups, as shown in Figure 2.24.

Outlook uses a ***plus symbol*** and a ***minus symbol*** to display or hide groups of items, such as categories. Within Microsoft Vista programs such as Outlook, the + symbol is used to ***expand*** (show) and the – symbol is used to ***collapse*** (hide) displayed items.

Figure 2.24

Collapse (minus) symbols

Category groups

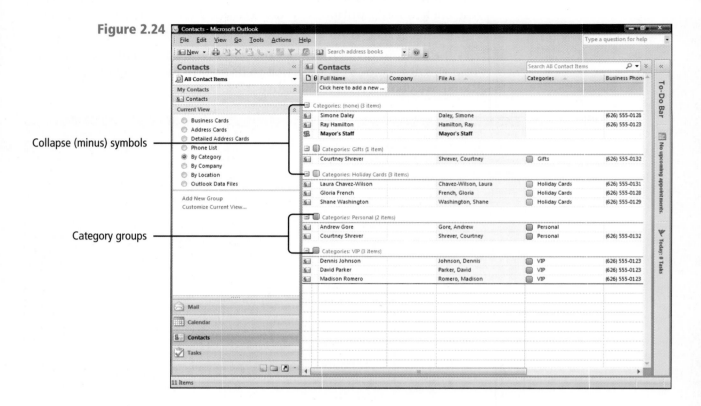

3 Next to the **Categories: (none)** heading, point to the **collapse** button, and then click it.

The items in the Contacts list having no category assignments are collapsed (hidden). The symbol changes to a plus sign. Notice that some contacts display more than once, because they have multiple category assignments.

4 Next to the **Categories: (none)** heading, click the **expand** button again to expand (show) the items. Then, change the **Current View** to **Phone List**.

The Contacts list displays in a table, arranged alphabetically by name and displaying the phone numbers. In a large Contact list, this view is a convenient way to quickly locate a contact's phone number.

More Knowledge

Customizing the Columns in Table Views

You can change the columns displayed in tables. For example, in the Outlook Data Files view, you can remove the Flag Status column and add a Department column. Or, you can create a new column. This enables you to create views that display exactly the contact information you want to see. To customize the columns in table views, display the view you want to customize, and from the View menu, point to Current View, and then click Customize Current View. In the Customize Current View dialog box, click Fields. In the displayed Show Fields dialog box, you can add, remove, and create new fields.

5 At the top of the table, point to the **File As** column heading to display the ScreenTip *Sort by: File As*. Click once, and then compare your screen with Figure 2.25.

The sort order of the Contacts list is changed to descending, Z to A, as indicated by the downward-pointing arrow next to the *File As* heading. Depending on the size of your monitor and screen resolution, the Categories field may also display.

Figure 2.25

Downward pointing arrow indicates reverse sort order

Column headings

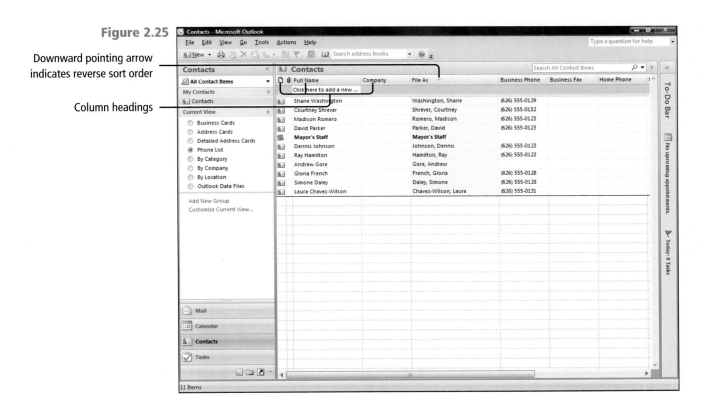

6 At the top of the table, click the **File As** heading again to restore the sort order to ascending, A to Z.

7 Change the **Current View** to **Business Cards** to restore the Contacts list to its default view.

Activity 2.15 Searching for Contacts

In this activity, you will use the Search address books box to locate specific contacts in the Desert Park Contacts list.

1 Change the **Current View** to **Detailed Address Cards**. On the Standard toolbar, click in the **Search address books** box, and then type **Washington** Compare your screen with Figure 2.26.

Figure 2.26

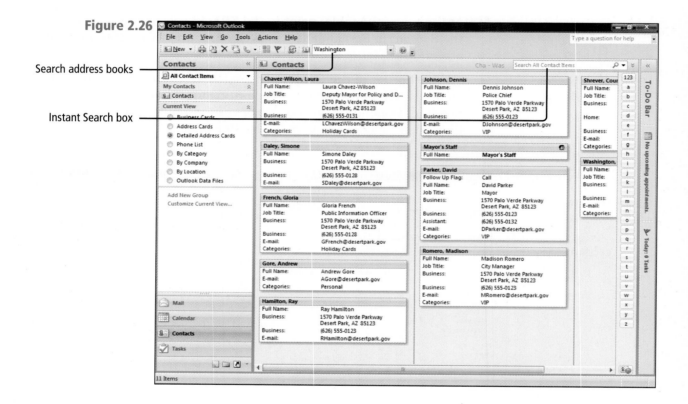

Search address books

Instant Search box

2 Press Enter.

Outlook searches the Contacts folder and then locates and displays Shane Washington's contact form. Outlook can perform searches like this using a contact's first name, last name, or company name.

3 **Close** the **Contact** form. In the **Search address books** box, type **Courtney** and then press Enter.

4 **Close** Courtney Shrever's **Contact** form. At the top of the **Contacts** list, on the right, click in the **Instant Search** box.

The difference between the Instant Search box and the Find a Contact box is that the Instant Search feature will perform a search on the current folder, using *any* information you type—not just a name. If you have done an instant search before, Search All Contact

Items displays in the Instant Search box. If you have not done a search, Search Contacts appears. If you select the arrow next to Search Contacts, you can select Search All Contact Items.

5 In the **Instant Search** box, type **Lost Canyon Road**

Outlook displays the contact containing this address.

6 In the **Instant Search** box, click on the **Clear Search** button ☒ to display the entire Contacts list. Change the **Current View** to **Business Cards** to restore the Contacts list to its default view.

The Contacts list displays in Business Cards view. Depending on the size of your screen, one or more entries in the Contacts list might move out of view. Use the scroll bar at the bottom of the screen to scroll to the right or left to adjust the viewing area.

Objective 6
Manage Contacts

As your Contacts list grows, you can manage it in other ways. You can create subfolders within the Contacts folder, for example, a folder for personal contacts and a folder for work-related contacts. You can also use a contact's information to create a vCard, a separate, special file, and then send the entire file in an e-mail message. Finally, you can delete contacts from your Contacts list and print information stored in your Contacts list.

Activity 2.16 Creating a Personal Folder for Contacts

When you create a separate folder within your Contacts folder, it displays as a subfolder. You can create contacts that are stored only in this folder. You can also copy and move contacts into the new folder. In this activity, you will create a folder for Personal contacts and include in it the Desert Park contacts assigned to the Personal category.

1 With the **Contacts list** displayed in **Business Cards** view, at the bottom of the **Navigation Pane**, click the **Folder List** button 🗀.

The Navigation Pane displays Outlook's folder structure, and the Contacts folder is selected.

2 From the **File** menu, point to **New**, and then click **Folder**.

The Create New Folder dialog box displays. Because you are creating this as subfolder within the Contacts folder, Outlook assumes that this folder will contain contact information.

3 In the **Create New Folder** dialog box, in the **Name** box, type **Personal Contacts** and then click **OK**. In the Folder List, if necessary, click the expand button (+ symbol) to the left of the Contacts folder to display the Personal Contacts subfolder. Compare your screen with Figure 2.27.

Outlook creates a folder called Personal Contacts and displays it as a subfolder of the Contacts folder.

Figure 2.27

Click expand (+) and collapse (−) buttons to display and hide subfolders

Personal Contacts subfolder

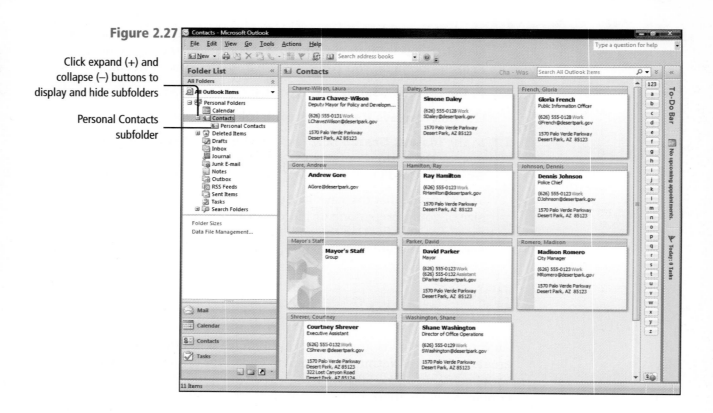

4 In the **Navigation Pane**, click the **collapse** button (−) next to the **Contacts** folder, and then compare your results with Figure 2.28.

The Personal Contacts folder is hidden. The minus symbol changes to a plus sign.

Figure 2.28

Expand button indicates the Personal Contacts subfolder is hidden.

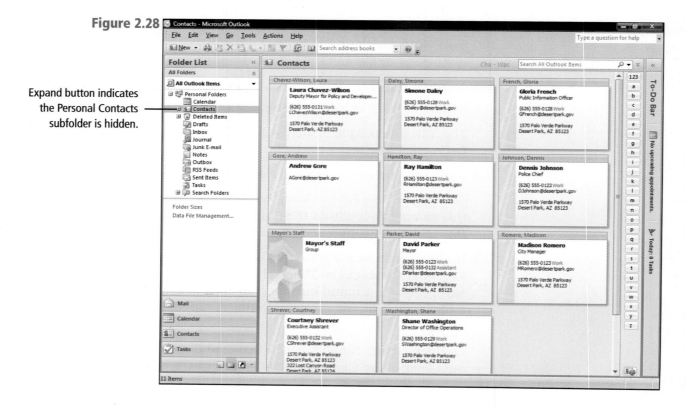

5 In the **Navigation Pane**, click the **Contacts** button ⬚ Contacts .

The Navigation Pane switches back to the two-pane view above the buttons. The My Contacts pane displays two entries—*Contacts* and *Personal Contacts*. All the items in your Contacts list are contained in the Contacts folder.

6 In the **Navigation Pane**, under **My Contacts**, click **Personal Contacts**.

The Contacts list in this folder is empty. If you create any new contacts while this is the current folder, they will be stored here. You can also copy and move existing contacts from your Contacts folder into this folder.

7 In the **Navigation Pane**, under **My Contacts**, click **Contacts** to display your existing **Contacts list**.

8 In the **Contacts list**, click one time to select **Andrew Gore**, and then, from the **Edit** menu, click **Copy to Folder**.

The Copy Items dialog box displays. The *Personal Contacts* folder is selected as the target folder—the folder to copy to—because currently it is the only other folder for contact information.

9 Click **OK**.

Outlook copies Andrew Gore's contact information to the Personal Contacts folder.

10 In the **Navigation Pane**, under **My Contacts**, click **Personal Contacts**.

The Personal Contacts folder displays a copy of Andrew Gore's contact information.

Activity 2.17 Saving a Contact in a Different File Format

You can send information about one of your contacts to someone else in an e-mail message. The most efficient way to do this is to save the contact information in a special file format. Outlook supports a file format called *vCard*—an Internet standard for creating and sharing virtual business cards. Any program that supports vCard format can share contact information. In this activity, you will save one of the Desert Park contacts as a vCard.

1 In the **Navigation Pane**, under **My Contacts**, click **Contacts** to display your primary **Contacts list**.

2 Click one time to select **David Parker's** contact information. Then, from the **Actions** menu, click **Send as Business Card**.

3 In the displayed **Message** form, notice that the Message form displays an attachment, the file **David Parker.vcf**. Compare your screen with Figure 2.29.

The attachment contains the contact information for David Parker. The recipient of the message will receive this attachment with the message. When the recipient opens the attachment, Outlook will display David Parker's contact form, which can be saved in the recipient's own Contacts list.

Figure 2.29

Contact information
as a vCard attachment
(your file size may differ)

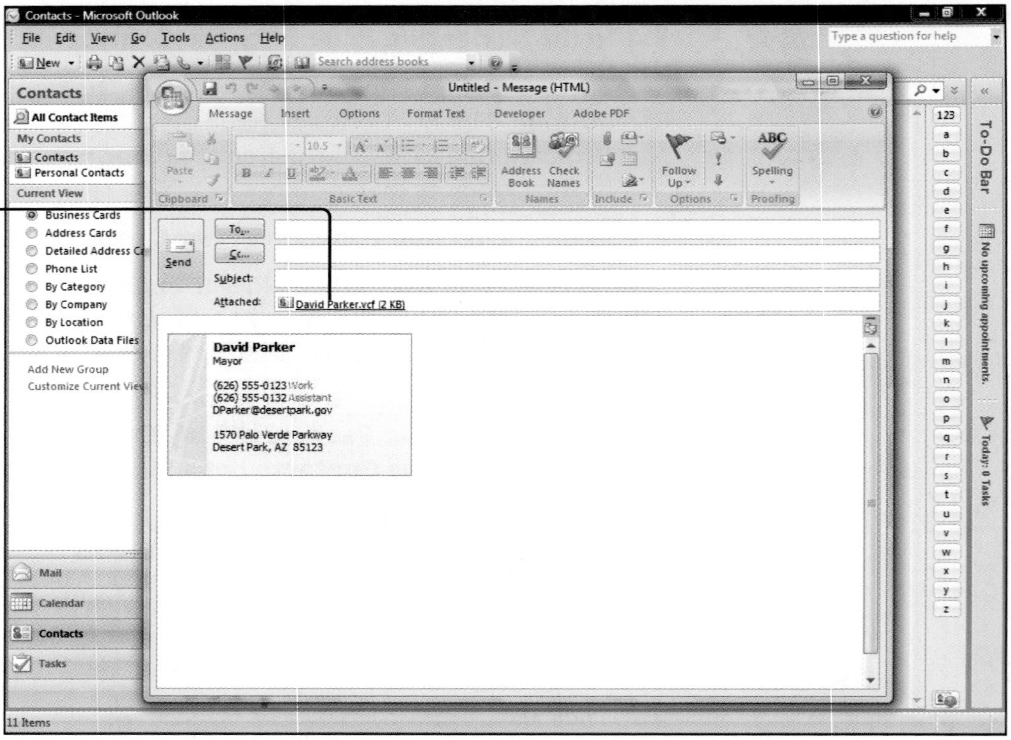

4 **Close** [X] the **Message** form without sending or saving the message.

More Knowledge

Attaching Your vCard in a Signature

You can automatically include a vCard with your own contact information in any e-mail messages you send by adding it to your signature. Recall that a signature is a block of text that is added at the end of your message. To include your vCard, create a new contact for yourself in your Contacts list. Create or edit your signature, and in the Signatures and Stationery dialog box, in the Edit Signature section, click Business Card (vCard). In the Insert Business Card dialog box, select your name in your Contacts list. Click OK three times to close all dialog boxes. When you create a new message, your vCard file is automatically entered in the Attach box. It is good practice to delete the vCard attachment if the message recipient already has your information so you do not add unnecessary attachments to the messages you send.

Activity 2.18 Printing Contacts

You can print the information for a single contact, a list of selected contacts, or a list of all the contacts. There are different print styles for contacts, depending on what you want to print. In this activity, you will print information for one of the Desert Park contacts, and then you will print the entire Desert Park Contacts list.

1 With your primary **Contacts list** displayed, select **Courtney Shrever's** contact information. From the **File** menu, click **Print**. Under **Print styles**, click the down scroll arrow to view the available print styles.

Each of the different print styles arranges the contact information in a different format. You can preview how the contact information will display when you print it. You cannot preview Small Booklet Style or Medium Booklet Style unless your selected printer supports two-sided printing.

2 Under **Print style**, click **Card Style**, if necessary, and then, in the lower right corner, click **Preview**.

The preview displays the entire Contacts list in the Card Style print style.

3 Point to the document, click one time to increase the magnification, use the bottom and right scroll bars to scroll as necessary, and then compare your screen with Figure 2.30.

This print style displays the information as it currently displays in the Contacts list, which is in the Business Cards view. Footer information may display at the bottom of the page. In its default setting, the Card Style print style includes a *blank form* page, which is a lined page added to the printout of this print style that you can use to manually list new contacts if you want to do so.

Figure 2.30

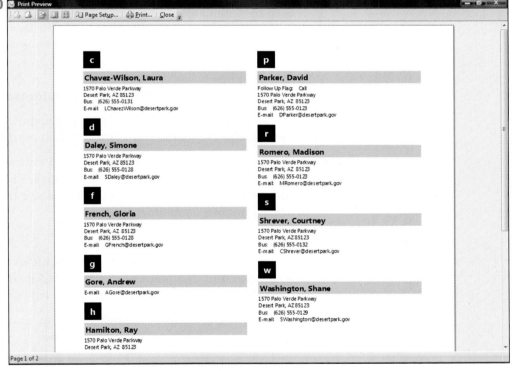

4 On the **Print Preview** toolbar, click the **Print** button [Print...] to redisplay the **Print** dialog box.

5 In the **Print** dialog box, under **Print style**, select the **Phone Directory Style**, and then click **Preview**.

This print style displays only the contact names and the phone numbers.

6 On the Print Preview toolbar, click the **Print** button ⟨🖨 Print...⟩ to redisplay the **Print** dialog box.

7 In the **Print** dialog box, under **Print style**, click **Memo Style**, and then click **Preview**.

To print a single contact, you must use Memo Style. You can also use Memo Style to print multiple items on the Contacts list.

8 Redisplay the **Print** dialog box, and in the center of the dialog box, click **Page Setup**. Click the **Header/Footer tab**, and delete any existing header or footer information, including dates and page numbers. In the left footer box, using your own first and last names, type **2A_Mayor's_Office_Assistant_Firstname_Lastname** Click **OK** to redisplay the **Print** dialog box.

9 In the **Print** dialog box, click **Preview** to preview the printed document. In the **Print Preview** window, click **Print** to return to the **Print** dialog box, and then click **OK**. Submit the end result to your instructor as directed.

Note — Names on Printed Documents

The name that appears at the top of a printed document and in Print Preview may differ from your own name. It is the name associated with your specific computer. Your name is printed in the document footer.

---

10 Change the **Current View** to **Detailed Address Cards**.

When printing your contacts, display the contacts as you want them to be printed. This view will print detailed contact information.

11 From the **File** menu, click **Print**. Under **Print style**, click **Card Style**. Click **Page Setup**. Click the **Header/Footer tab**. Delete any existing header or footer information. In the left footer box, type **2A_Mayor's_Office_Firstname_Lastname**

12 In the **Page Setup: Card Style** dialog box, click the **Format tab**.

Recall that the Card Style print style includes a blank form page. You can exclude this page from the printout. If this page has been previously excluded, Outlook will retain this setting.

13 Under **Options**, locate the **Blank forms at end** box, click the **Blank forms at end arrow**, and then click **None**.

The blank form at the end of the printout will be excluded.

14 In the **Page Setup: Card Style** dialog box, click **Print** to redisplay the **Print** dialog box. In the **Print** dialog box, click **Preview** to preview the printed document. In the **Print Preview** window, click **Print** to return to the **Print** dialog box, and then click **OK**. Submit the end result to your instructor as directed.

More Knowledge

Print a Group of Contacts

If you want to print more than one contact on your Contacts list but not all of them, select the first contact you want to print. Then hold down Ctrl on the keyboard and click each of the additional contacts you want to include in the printout. In the Print dialog box, under Print range, click the Only selected items option button. Use the Phone Directory Style, the Memo Style, or the Card Style as the print style.

Activity 2.19 Deleting Contacts and Restoring Default Settings

In a manner similar to messages and other Outlook items, you can delete contacts. When you delete a contact in your Contacts folder or any other contact folder, it moves to the Deleted Items folder. Items remain in this folder until you empty the Deleted Items folder, at which time they are permanently deleted. You can also restore the default settings for print style headers and footers, and change the categories to their original names.

1 Select any contact. On the Standard toolbar, click the **Categorize** button 🔳, and then click **All Categories**.

2 In the **Color Categories** dialog box, select **Gifts**, click **Rename**, and then type **Orange Category**

Outlook retains the most recent name change, so renaming is required to restore the category to its original, default name. You must rename the categories prior to deleting all contacts, messages or tasks.

3 Using the same technique, rename **Holiday Cards** as **Green Category**, **Personal** as **Red Category**, and **VIP** as **Purple Category** Click **OK**.

4 Display your primary **Contacts folder** and change the **Current View** to **Business Cards**. In the **Navigation Pane**, under **My Contacts**, click **Personal Contacts two** times to select the folder.

You can delete any folder you create. When you delete a folder, you also delete its contents.

5 On the Standard toolbar, click the **Delete** button ☒.

Outlook displays an information box asking whether you are sure you want to delete the folder and move its contents to the Deleted Items folder.

6 In the **Microsoft Office Outlook** dialog box, click **Yes**.

Outlook moves the folder to the Deleted Items folder. The Navigation Pane displays only one folder in the My Contacts pane.

7 In the **Contacts list**, click **Laura Chavez-Wilson's** contact one time to select it. Hold down ⇧ Shift, scroll horizontally if necessary, and then click **Shane Washington's** contact information.

8 With all the items in your **Contacts list** selected, from the **Edit** menu, click **Delete**.

The Contacts list is deleted. You can undo any deletion if you make a mistake or change your mind.

9 From the **Edit** menu, click **Undo Delete**.

The deleted items are restored. You can use this technique only on the most recent deletion. You can recover deleted items from the Deleted Items folder if they have not been permanently deleted.

10 From the **Edit** menu, click **Select All**.

This is an alternative method to select all the items in your Contacts list.

11 Right-click any of the selected items, and then, from the displayed shortcut menu, click **Delete**.

12 In the **Navigation Pane**, click the **Folder List** button 🗀. To the left of the **Deleted Items** folder, click the **expand** (+) button to display the subfolders in the **Deleted Items** folder. Compare your screen with Figure 2.31.

The Deleted Items folder displays the deleted subfolder *Personal Contacts.*

Figure 2.31

Click expand and collapse buttons to display or hide Deleted Items subfolders

Personal Contacts subfolder

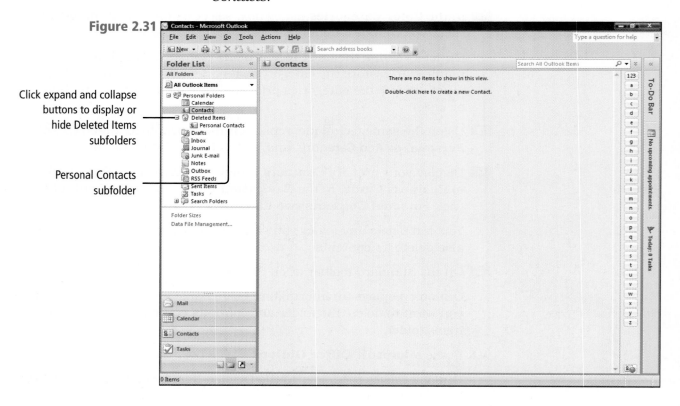

13 In the **Folder List**, click the **Personal Contacts** subfolder **two** times to select it, and then click the **Delete** button ✕.

Outlook displays a Microsoft Office Outlook box, warning you that you are permanently deleting the Personal Contacts folder.

14 In the **Microsoft Office Outlook** box, click **Yes**. Compare your screen with Figure 2.32.

The Personal Contacts subfolder is deleted, and the Deleted Items folder displays. The first item in the folder is displayed in the Reading Pane.

Figure 2.32

Deleted Items folder selected in the Folder List

First item in the folder displays in the Reading Pane

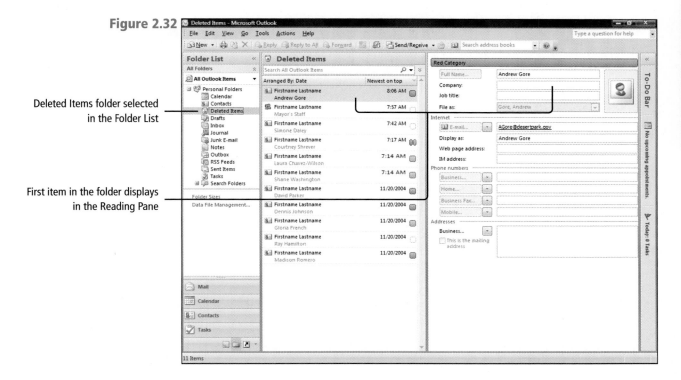

15 In the **Folder List**, right-click the **Deleted Items** folder, and then click **Empty "Deleted Items" Folder**. Alternatively, use any method that you have practiced to select all the items in the Deleted Items folder, and then click the **Delete** button ⊠. In the **Microsoft Office Outlook** box, click **Yes**.

The Deleted Items folder is emptied. There is still an item in the Inbox.

16 In the **Folder List**, click **Inbox** to display the Inbox folder. Click the message from **Simone Daley**, and then **Delete** ⊠ it.

17 In the **Folder List**, click the **Deleted Items** folder to select it. Delete the item in this folder using any technique you have practiced.

18 In the **Folder List**, click **Contacts** to display the Contacts folder. From the **File** menu, point to **Page Setup**, and then click **Define Print Styles** to display the **Define Print Styles** dialog box.

Recall that Outlook remembers header and footer information. You can restore the print style you used to its default setting.

19 In the **Define Print Styles** dialog box, click **Memo Style**, click **Reset**, and then click **OK**.

20 In the **Folder List**, click **Contacts** to display the Contacts folder. From the **File** menu, point to **Page Setup**, and then click **Define Print Styles** to display the **Define Print Styles** dialog box.

21 In the **Define Print Styles** dialog box, click **Card Style**, click **Reset**, and then click **OK**. **Close** the dialog box, and then **Close** Outlook.

End **You have completed Project 2A** ——————————

Project 2B Mayor's Tasks

In Activities 2.20 through 2.26, you will create and manage a To-Do list for Simone Daley, who is Chief of Staff for the mayor of Desert Park. You will create a To-Do list and make changes and updates to tasks on the list. You will print a task and the To-Do list, which will look similar to the ones shown in Figure 2.33.

For Project 2B, you will need the following file:

New blank task form

You will print two files with the following footers:
2B_Mayor's_Tasks_Firstname_Lastname
2B_Mayor's_Tasks_Japan_Trip_Firstname_Lastname

Firstname Lastname

Subject:	Prepare mayor's Japan travel itinerary
Due Date:	Tuesday, August 19, 2008
Status:	Waiting on someone else

☐ ! 0 Task Subject	Status	Due Date	% Complete	Categories	In Folder	▽
Categories: (none) (5 items)						
Write press release for mayor...	Not Started	Mon 8/4/2008	0%		Tasks	▽
Complete mayor's staff budg...	In Progress	Tue 8/5/2008	25%		Tasks	▽
Call Japanese embassy to dis...	Completed	Wed 8/6/2008	100%		Tasks	✓
Schedule press conference	Not Started	Wed 8/6/2008	0%		Tasks	▽
Draft mayor's position paper ...	Not Started	Tue 8/26/2008	0%		Tasks	▽
Categories: Waiting (2 items)						
Review and forward EPA air q...	Waiting o...	Thu 8/7/2008	0%	Waiting	Tasks	▽
Prepare mayor's Japan travel ...	Waiting o...	Tue 8/19/2008	50%	Waiting	Tasks	▽

2B_Mayor's_Tasks_Firstname_Lastname

Figure 2.33
Project 2B—Mayor's Tasks

Objective 7
Create and Update Tasks

In Outlook, a **task** is a personal or work-related activity that you want to keep track of until it is complete. For example, writing a report, creating a memo, making a sales call, and organizing a staff meeting are all tasks. Use Outlook's Tasks folder to create and manage a list of tasks, create one-time tasks or **recurring tasks**, and set reminders for tasks. A recurring task occurs repeatedly, for example, a weekly staff meeting or a monthly haircut.

Task items are added to the To-Do List as you create them, and, of course, some tasks take longer to complete than others. You can organize your To-Do List by due dates, by category, and by status. Updates to tasks, such as completing the task, modifying its due date, or changing the task to a recurring task, can be made directly on the To-Do List.

Alert!

Starting Project 2B

Because Outlook stores information on the hard drive of the computer at which you are working, unless you are working on your own computer, it is recommended that you complete Project 2B in one working session. Allow approximately 45 minutes to one hour.

Activity 2.20 Creating Tasks

You can create a new task using a Task form or enter a new task directly in the To-Do List. In this activity, you will create tasks for Simone Daley, who is the mayor's Chief of Staff.

1 **Start** Outlook. In the **Navigation Pane**, click the **Tasks** button
[Tasks] to display the Tasks folder. If necessary, change the **Current View** to **Simple List**. If the Tasks folder is not empty, click a blank area of the **To-Do List**, press Ctrl + A, and then click the **Delete** button [X]. Compare your screen with Figure 2.34.

The To-Do List displays in Simple List view. The To-Do List is used to display tasks, as well as other items; for example, a message that has been flagged for follow-up. The Navigation Pane for the Tasks folder has the same two-pane structure as the Contacts folder. Notice in the Navigation Pane, under My Tasks, that To-Do List is selected. This is the default format to view tasks. In Simple List view, individual task items are displayed in a table with column headings for five fields: Icon, Complete, Task Subject, Due Date, and Flag Status, which are summarized in the table in Figure 2.35.

Figure 2.34

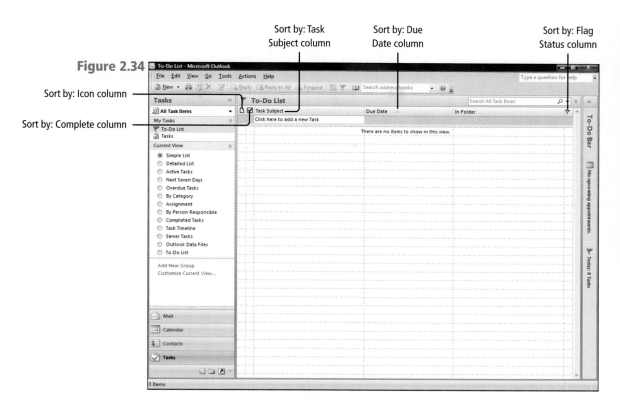

Sort by: Task Subject column

Sort by: Due Date column

Sort by: Flag Status column

Sort by: Icon column

Sort by: Complete column

2 Take a moment to study the main parts of the screen as shown in Figure 2.34 and as described in the table in Figure 2.35. Move the pointer over the five column headings in the **To-Do List** and observe the ScreenTip for each heading.

The ScreenTips for each column heading are prefixed with Sort by. Use the column headings to sort the To-Do List either by icon type, the completed status, the task subject, the due date, or the flag status.

To-Do List Column Headings

To-Do List Column Heading ScreenTip	Sort Purpose
Sort by: Icon	Enables you to sort the To-Do List by task type. The column displays an icon—a small graphic representation of an item type. There are four different types of tasks, each with a distinctive icon. The four task types include a task that you own, a recurring task, a task you assigned to someone else, and a task assigned to you by someone else.
Sort by: Complete	Enables you to sort the To-Do List by whether or not a task is complete. An empty box indicates that a task is not complete. A check mark indicates that a task is complete.
Sort by: Task Subject	Enables you to sort the To-Do List alphabetically by the Subject name of the task.
Sort by: Due Date	Enables you to sort the To-Do List in chronological order by the task's due date.
Sort by: Flag Status	Enables you to sort the To-Do List by the flag status of the task.

Figure 2.35

3 On the Standard toolbar, click the **New Task** button. In the **Untitled - Task** form, in the **Subject** box, type **Prepare mayor's Japan travel itinerary** Click the **Due date arrow**. On the displayed calendar, click a date **ten *business days***—days that are not Saturday, Sunday, or a holiday—from today's date.

4 On the Task form toolbar, click the **Save & Close** button, and notice that the **To-Do List** displays the new task.

Recall that there are four types of tasks, each represented by an icon. The icon assigned to this task represents a task that you own. Notice the flag for this task has a custom status because you specified a particular date.

5 Using the technique you just practiced, open a new, untitled Task form, and as the **Subject** type **Review and forward EPA air quality report for city to mayor** Click the **Due date arrow**, and then click a date **two** business days from today's date.

6 In the **Task** form, locate the **Reminder** check box.

You can set a date and time to be reminded of a task. The reminder is a small dialog box that appears in the middle of the Outlook screen. You can be working in any Outlook folder when a reminder displays. By default Outlook does not display a reminder—the check box is clear. If you want to use the Reminder feature, you can click in the Reminder check box, and then select the date and time of day when you would like to be reminded of the task.

7 In the **Task** form, click the **Priority arrow**, and then click **High**. In the *comments area*—the blank area in the lower half of the form in which you can add information not otherwise specified in the form—type **David needs this before the weekly press conference** and then compare your screen with Figure 2.36.

Figure 2.36

Outlook | chapter 2

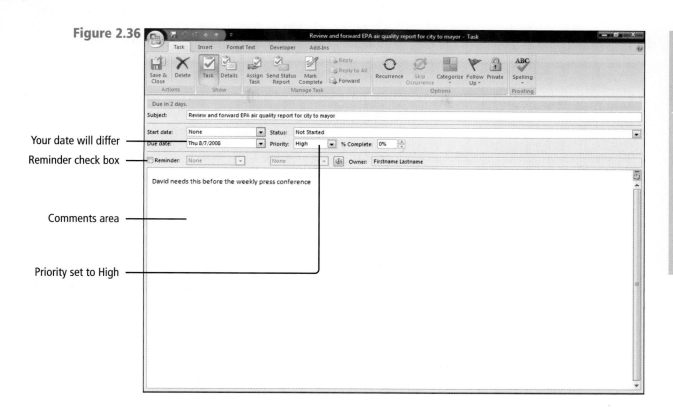

Your date will differ

Reminder check box

Comments area

Priority set to High

---

8 **Save & Close** the task. In the **To-Do List** under the column headings, click in the **Click here to add a new Task** box, and then type **Call Japanese embassy to discuss mayor's trip** Press Tab, and in the **Due Date** box, type **Tomorrow** and then press Enter.

The task is added to the list. Notice that the insertion point is still located in the *Click here to add new Task* box, and the text no longer displays. Use this box to quickly create a new task with only a subject and due date. You can see that you can use **natural language** phrases such as *Tomorrow* to specify dates, and then Outlook converts the phrases to actual dates. ***Natural language*** is a language spoken or written by humans, as opposed to a computer programming language. Other examples of natural language phrases that Outlook can convert to actual dates include *next Tuesday* or *two weeks from today*.

9 In the **Click here to add a new Task** box, type **Complete staff budget** Press Tab, in the **Due Date** box, type **One week from today** and then press Enter.

Note — Natural Language and Nonbusiness Days

When Outlook converts natural language into actual dates, it makes no distinction between business days and nonbusiness days. For example, if the current day of the week is Sunday, and you type *one week from today*, Outlook will use the calendar date of the next Sunday.

10 In the **Click here to add a new Task** box, type **Write press release for mayor's new staff appointments** Press Tab to make the **Due Date** box active, type **Tomorrow** and then press Enter.

11 In the **Click here to add a new Task** box, type **Draft mayor's position paper for new airport development** Press Tab to make the **Due Date** box active, type **Three weeks from today** and then press Enter.

12 Click anywhere in the **To-Do List**, and then compare your screen with Figure 2.37.

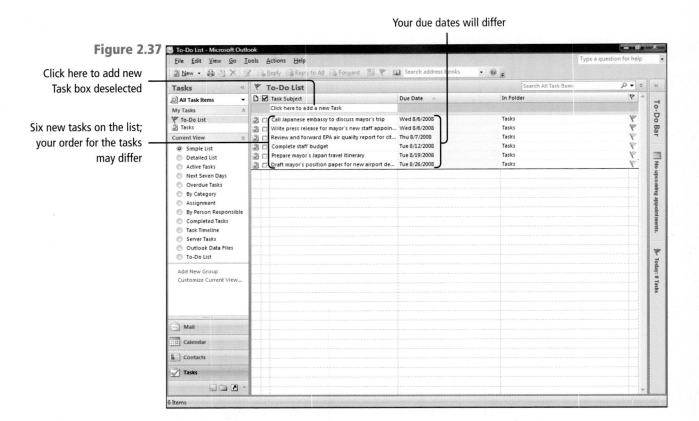

Your due dates will differ

Figure 2.37

Click here to add new Task box deselected

Six new tasks on the list; your order for the tasks may differ

More Knowledge
Creating a Personal Folder for Tasks

In the same manner as you create a personal folder for your contacts, you can create a subfolder within the Tasks folder for tasks. This is useful if you want to separate your work-related tasks from your personal tasks. To create a subfolder for your tasks, first display the Tasks folder. From the File menu, point to New, and then click Folder. Type a name for your folder, and then click OK.

Activity 2.21 Changing and Updating Tasks

You can make changes to a task in the To-Do List or on the Task form. In this activity, you will add more details to Simone Daley's tasks.

1 In the **To-Do List**, click anywhere in the words *Complete staff budget* to select the task and to activate the insertion point.

2 Position the insertion point so that it displays just before the word *staff*. Type **mayor's** and then press ⎵Spacebar⎵.

Use this technique to edit both the Subject text and the Due Date directly in the To-Do List.

3 In the **Write press release for mayor's new staff appointments** task, click the **Due date** box. Change the date to two days *prior* to the current date. Press ⏎Enter⏎ or click in a blank area of the **To-Do List**, and then compare your screen with Figure 2.38.

You cannot change a due date to occur before the date when the task was created—today's date. Outlook displays the message box and sounds a tone if your computer's sound is enabled.

Figure 2.38

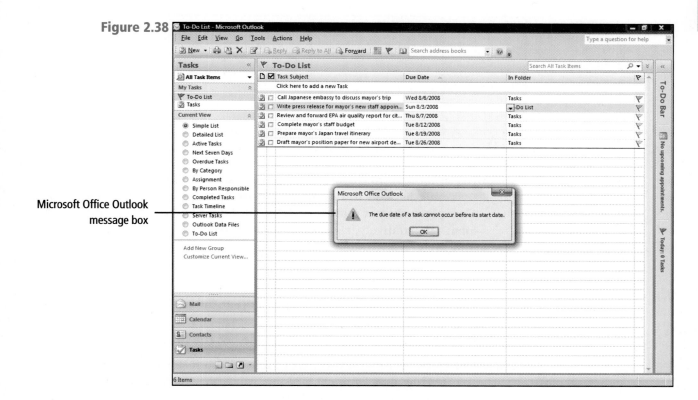

Microsoft Office Outlook message box

4 **Close** ⨯ the message box.

Notice that the task is still selected. Outlook will not allow you to create contradictory dates for tasks.

5 With the **Write press release for mayor's new staff appointments** task still selected, double-click the task to open the **Task** form. Click the **Start date arrow**, and select a date two days *prior* to today's date, and then click the **Due date arrow** and select a date one day prior to today's date. **Save & Close** the task, and then compare your screen with Figure 2.39.

This task is displayed in red because it is now overdue. Notice that the To-Do Bar indicates that there is one task due today.

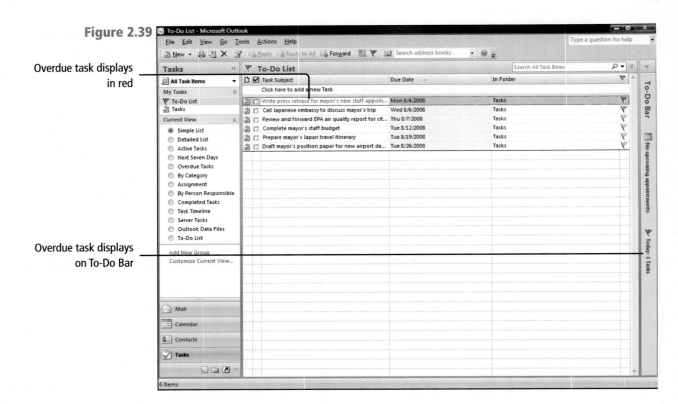

Figure 2.39

Overdue task displays in red

Overdue task displays on To-Do Bar

6 Select a different task in the **To-Do List**, and notice that the overdue task still displays in red. In the **To-Do List**, point to the subject text **Complete mayor's staff budget**, and double-click to open the task's form. Alternatively, right-click the *Complete mayor's staff budget* text, and then click **Open**.

7 In the right center portion of the **Task** form, click the **% Complete up arrow** to display **25%**. Click the **Priority arrow**, and set the level to **High**. Click the **Due date arrow**, and at the bottom of the displayed calendar, click **Today**. **Save & Close** [icon] the task.

8 Using the technique you just practiced, from the **To-Do List**, display the **Review and forward EPA air quality report for city to mayor** Task form. In the displayed form, click the **Status arrow**, and then click **Waiting on someone else**. On the Ribbon, click the **Categorize** button [icon], and then click **All Categories**. Select the text **Orange Category** and then click **Rename**. Type **Waiting** Click the **Waiting** check box, and then click **OK**.

Use Status to show the progress of your tasks. Assigning tasks to categories provides a way to organize your To-Do List. For this task, the Waiting category is a good category because it relates to its current status. Thus, you could sort your tasks by those that are awaiting action or information from someone else.

9 On the Quick Access Toolbar, click the **Next Item** button [icon].

A Microsoft Office Outlook dialog box displays. You can use this button to display the next item in your To-Do List without redisplaying the list. Before closing this task and displaying the next one, Outlook will prompt you to save the changes you have made in the current task.

10 In the **Microsoft Office Outlook** dialog box, click **Yes** to save the changes and display the next task in the list, which is the **Prepare mayor's Japan travel itinerary** task.

11 In the displayed **Task** form, use the techniques you have practiced to change the **Status** to **Waiting on someone else** and the **% Complete** to **50%**. In the comments area of the Task form, type **Waiting to hear from Governor's chief of staff** Click on **Categorize**, and then click on

Waiting. Save & Close the task.

12 In the **To-Do List**, locate the **Call Japanese embassy to discuss mayor's trip** task, and in the second column of the table, click in the check box to indicate that the task has been completed. Compare your screen with Figure 2.40.

The task is marked as complete, and a line is drawn through the task.

Figure 2.40

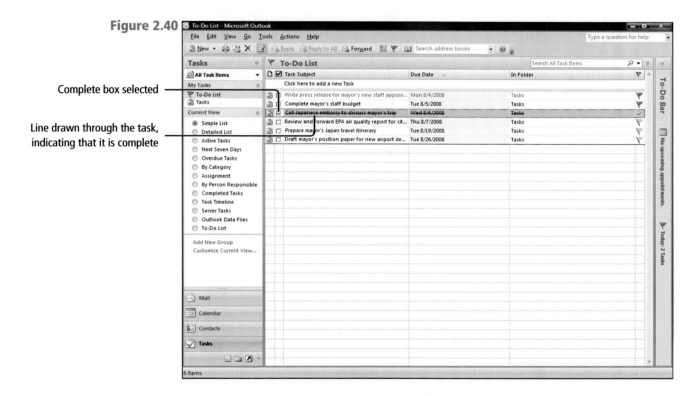

Complete box selected

Line drawn through the task, indicating that it is complete

Activity 2.22 Creating a Recurring Task

Recall that a recurring task is one that occurs repeatedly on a regular schedule, such as preparing a weekly status report or attending a monthly staff meeting. In this activity, you will make one of Simone Daley's tasks recurring.

1 Display a new, untitled Task form, and in the **Subject** box type **Schedule press conference**

2 On the Ribbon, in the **Options group**, click the **Recurrence** button .

Here you define when and how frequently the task will recur. For example, a task can recur every day, every week, every month, or every year. Additionally, you can define a range of time for the task to recur, for example, a weekly meeting for the period January through June.

3 In the **Task Recurrence** dialog box, click **Weekly** if it is not already selected, and then select the **Wednesday** check box if it is not already selected. Clear any other check boxes, and then compare your screen with Figure 2.41.

Figure 2.41

Task Recurrence dialog box

Recurrence pattern set to Weekly on Wednesdays

Your dates will differ

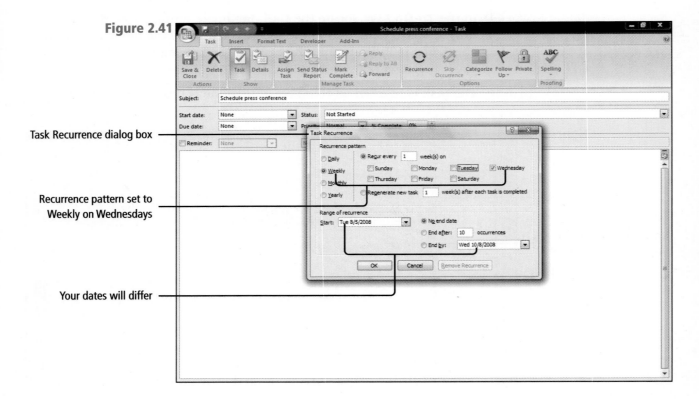

4 Click **OK**, and notice the banner at the top of the form, which indicates that the task is set to recur every week. **Save & Close** the task. Compare your screen with Figure 2.42.

The recurring task is added to the To-Do List. The icon for the task indicates that it is a recurring task.

Figure 2.42

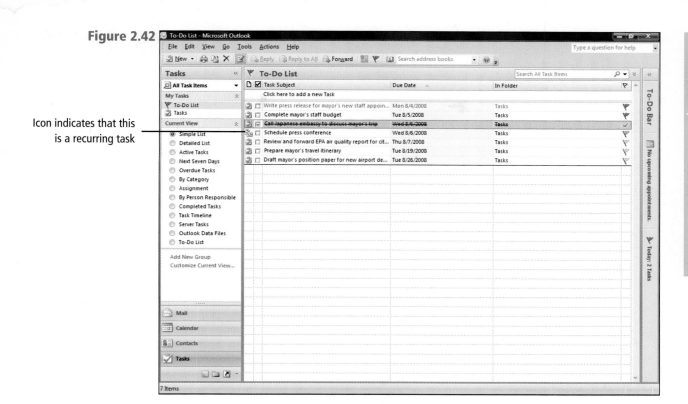

Icon indicates that this is a recurring task

Objective 8
Manage Tasks

Various tools and views are available to help you manage a large and complex To-Do List. For example, the Navigation Pane provides various views so that you can look at your list of tasks in different ways. You can also sort the To-Do List by priority, by due date, or by status. Finally, you can print specific tasks or the entire To-Do List so that you can refer to them without looking at your computer screen. You will organize your To-Do List in different ways and then print both a single task and the entire To-Do List.

Activity 2.23 Viewing Tasks

Outlook allows you to view tasks in three different places—in the To-Do List, on the To-Do Bar, and in a calendar. In this activity, you will view Simone Daley's tasks from these three locations.

1 In the **Navigation Pane**, under **Current View**, make certain that **Simple List** is selected.

2 On the **To-Do Bar**, at the far right of your screen, click the **Expand To-Do Bar** button ⟨⟨ . Compare your screen with Figure 2.43.

Notice that all tasks not completed are displayed in the lower portion of the bar. The tasks are arranged based on the due dates.

Figure 2.43

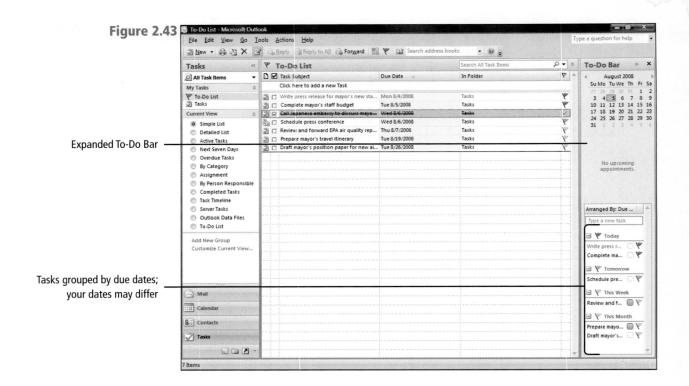

Expanded To-Do Bar

Tasks grouped by due dates; your dates may differ

3 On the **To-Do Bar**, click **the Minimize To-Do Bar** button ⟫ .

4 In the **Navigation Pane**, click the **Calendar** button 🗓 Calendar . Compare your screen with Figure 2.44.

The Calendar folder opens. By default, the Calendar displays the current date. At the bottom of the screen, notice the Tasks section, showing the overdue task, the task due today, and the task that was completed today.

Figure 2.44

Calendar displays current date, your date will differ

Task section

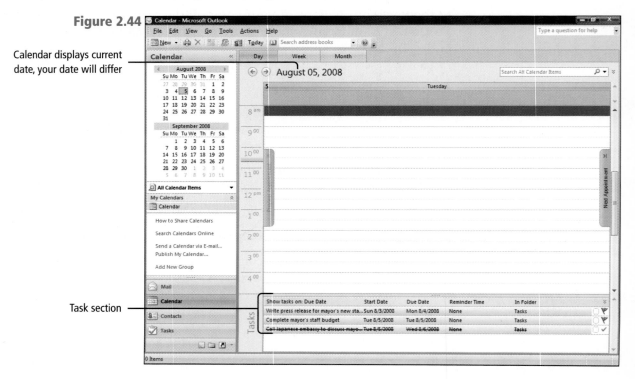

5 In the **Navigation Pane**, click the **Tasks** button 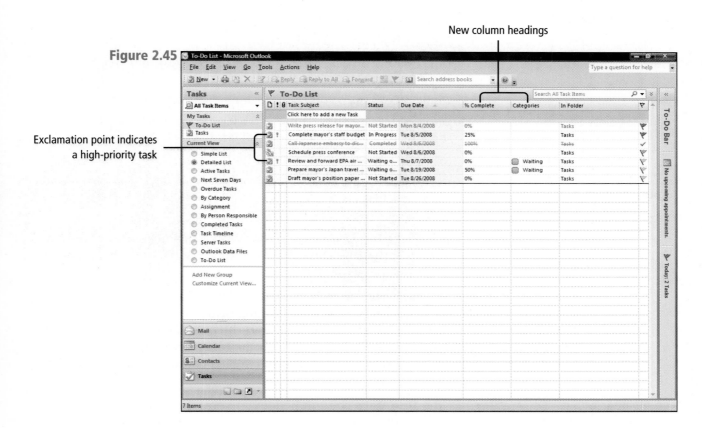 to display the **To-Do List**.

Activity 2.24 Sorting the To-Do List

You can sort the To-Do List from either the Navigation Pane or the column headings in the To-Do List. In this activity, you will display different views of Simone Daley's To-Do List.

1 In the **Navigation Pane**, under **Current View**, click **Detailed List**, and then compare your screen with Figure 2.45.

The Tasks list includes several new fields in its display. High-priority tasks display an exclamation point under the Priority heading, and you can see the % Complete information. Tasks with category assignments can be grouped by category.

New column headings

Figure 2.45

Exclamation point indicates a high-priority task

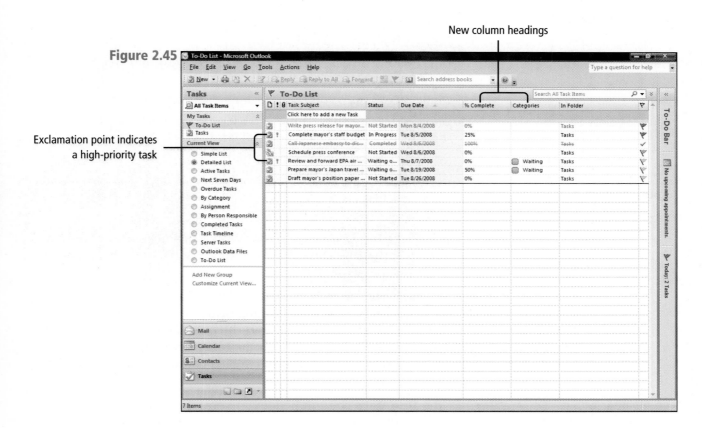

2 In the **Navigation Pane**, under **Current View**, click each of the remaining views, and view the arrangement of the information. As you do so, take a moment to study the view descriptions in the table in Figure 2.46.

To-Do List Views

To-Do List View	Description
Simple List	Displays the Icon (type), Complete status, Subject, Due Date, In Folder, and Flag Status for all tasks in the To-Do List.
Detailed List	Displays the Icon, Priority, Attachment, Task Subject, Status, Due Date, % Complete, Categories, In Folder (location), and Flag Status for all tasks in the To-Do List.
Active Tasks	Displays all tasks not marked *Completed* or *100% Complete*.
Next Seven Days	Displays all tasks due within the next seven days.
Overdue Tasks	Displays all currently overdue tasks.
By Category	Displays all tasks grouped by categories.
Assignment	Displays tasks you have assigned to others.
By Person Responsible	Displays tasks grouped by task owner.
Completed Tasks	Displays tasks marked *Completed*.
Task Timeline	Displays tasks on a daily time scale, arranged from left to right, according to the task Due Date.
Server Tasks	Displays tasks stored on a server running Microsoft Sharepoint.
Outlook Data Files	Displays tasks based on Outlook file location, which only applies if there is more than one Personal Folders file.
To-Do List	Displays all active tasks according to the task Due Date, with the most recent date at the top of the list. To-Do List is the default view.

Figure 2.46

3 Click the **Detailed List** view. In the column headings area of the **To-Do List**, click the **Due Date** heading, and observe the small, shaded arrow next to the heading name.

The To-Do List is sorted by Due Date. When the arrow is pointing up, the tasks are sorted in ascending order—tasks closest in time to the current date are listed first, and the overdue task is listed first. When the arrow is pointing down, the tasks are sorted in descending order. This arrow displays in other sorted column headings and works the same way in all cases.

4 Click the **Due Date** column heading several times to observe the change in sort order and the direction of the shaded arrow.

5 In the **To-Do List**, click the **Priority** column heading—the column with the exclamation point—to sort the list by priority.

6 In the **To-Do List**, click the **Icon** column heading—the first column—until the **Prepare mayor's Japan travel itinerary** task is at the top of the list.

This is the default, or original, sort order, which arranges tasks by the order in which they were entered.

More Knowledge

Changing the Default Sort Order

You can change Outlook's default view for displaying your tasks. With the To-Do List displayed, arrange your tasks in the sort order you prefer. On the Standard toolbar, click Actions, and then click Save Task Order. Your default view is changed to the current sort order.

Activity 2.25 Printing Tasks

Printing the entire To-Do List or individual tasks is similar to printing other Outlook items, such as messages and contacts. In the following activity, you will print some of the tasks you created for Simone Daley.

1 In the **Navigation Pane**, display the **To-Do List** in the **By Category** view. If necessary, click the **expand** button next to **Categories: (none)** and **Categories: Waiting** to display all the items in each group. Compare your screen with Figure 2.47.

The tasks are arranged in two groups. Outlook uses the current view when you print an entire To-Do List.

Figure 2.47

Tasks are arranged in two groups in Category view

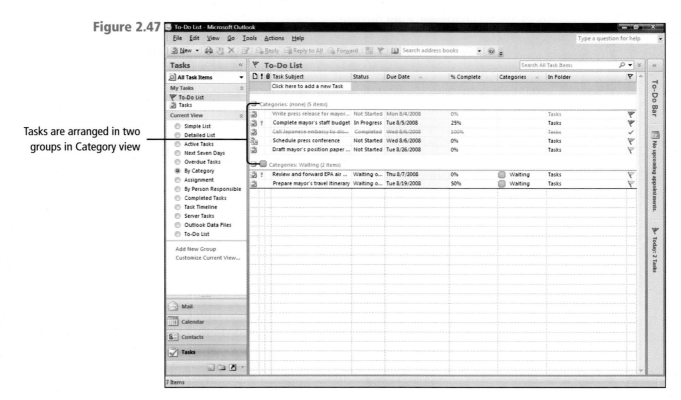

2 To print the entire **To-Do List**, from the **File** menu, display the **Print** dialog box. Under **Print style**, be sure that **Table Style** is selected.

Use the Table style to print the entire To-Do List.

3 Click **Page Setup**, click the **Header/Footer tab**, and delete any existing header or footer information. In the left **Footer** box, type **2B_Mayor's_ Tasks_Firstname_Lastname** In the **Page Setup: Table Style** dialog box, click **Print** to return to the **Print** dialog box. In the **Print** dialog box, click **Preview** to preview the document. Click **Print** to return to the **Print** dialog box, and then click **OK**. Submit the end result to your instructor as directed.

4 In the **To-Do List**, click one time to select the **Prepare mayor's Japan travel itinerary** task without opening the Task form. From the **File** menu, click **Print**.

5 In the displayed **Print** dialog box, under **Print style**, locate the two styles available for tasks.

Memo Style is appropriate for printing individual tasks. Recall that the Table Style is used to print the entire To-Do-List.

6 Under **Print style**, click **Memo Style**, and then, to the right, click **Page Setup**. In the **Page Setup: Memo Style** dialog box, click the **Header/Footer tab**, and then delete any existing header or footer information, including dates and page numbers. In the left **Footer** box and using your own name, type **2B_Mayor's_Tasks_Japan_Trip_Firstname_Lastname** In the lower right corner of the dialog box, click **Print**. In the **Print** dialog box, click **Preview** to preview the printed document. In the **Print Preview** window, click **Print** to return to the **Print** dialog box, and then click **OK**. Submit the end result to your instructor as directed.

Activity 2.26 Deleting Tasks and Restoring Default Settings

After you complete a task, you will likely want to delete it from your To-Do List. When you delete a task in your To-Do List, it moves to the Deleted Items folder and remains there, along with other deleted items, until the Deleted Items folder is emptied. After an item is deleted from the Deleted Items folder, it is permanently deleted. In this activity, you will use various methods to delete Simone Daley's tasks. You will also restore print style headers and footers, and category names to their default settings.

1 In the **To-Do List**, select any task. On the Standard toolbar, click the **Categorize** button, and then click **All Categories**.

2 In the **Color Categories** dialog box, select **Waiting**, click **Rename**, and then type **Orange Category**.

Recall that Outlook retains the most recent name change, so renaming is required to restore the category to its default name.

3 Click **OK** to close the dialog box, and then change the **Current View** to **Simple List**, which is the default view. In the **To-Do List**, click the first task one time to select it, hold down ⧉ Shift, and then click the last task to select all the tasks in the list. Alternatively, press Ctrl + A.

4 From the **Edit** menu, click **Delete**.

A Microsoft Office Outlook dialog box appears warning you that deleting these items will also delete associated e-mail messages and/or contacts.

5 Click **OK**, and then compare your screen with Figure 2.48.

Outlook displays a dialog box asking whether you want to delete all occurrences of the *Schedule press conference* task. Recall that this is a recurring task with no end date.

All the tasks in the list selected

Figure 2.48

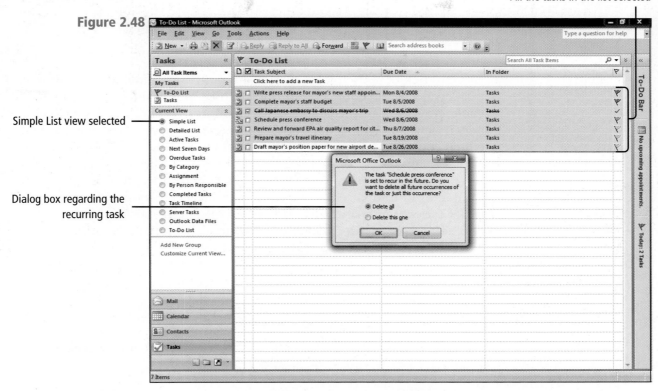

Simple List view selected

Dialog box regarding the recurring task

6 In the **Microsoft Office Outlook** dialog box, click **OK** to delete all future occurrences of the task. Display the **Folder List** , right-click the **Deleted Items** folder, and then click **Empty "Deleted Items" Folder**.

Outlook displays a warning box indicating that you are permanently deleting the selected items.

7 In the **Microsoft Office Outlook** dialog box, click **Yes**.

The items are permanently deleted and the Deleted Items folder is empty.

8 In the **Folder List**, click **Tasks** to display the Tasks folder. From the **File** menu, point to **Page Setup**, and then click **Define Print Styles**. Click **Memo Style**, click **Reset**, and then click **OK**. Click **Table Style**, click **Reset**, and then click **OK**. **Close** the dialog box.

The two print styles you used are restored to their default settings.

9 **Close** ☒ Outlook.

End You have completed Project 2B

Content-Based Assessments

Summary

Use Outlook to store information about your contacts and keep track of tasks you need to complete. In this chapter, you practiced creating a Contacts list, used the Contacts list to address e-mail messages, and added new contacts to the Contacts list from received messages. You also edited contacts, added details to contacts, and linked contacts with one another. You created, used, and modified a distribution list. To organize the Contacts list, you assigned contacts to categories, sorted the Contacts list in different ways with different views, created a separate folder for contacts, and then printed and deleted items in the Contacts list. You created a To-Do List, updated tasks, created a recurring task, sorted tasks, and printed and deleted tasks.

Key Terms

Content-Based Assessments

Matching

Match each term in the second column with its correct definition in the first column by writing the letter of the term on the blank line in front of the correct definition.

_____ **1.** Individuals, organizations, or companies with whom you communicate.

_____ **2.** To bring information into Outlook from another program in which the information already exists.

_____ **3.** A set of lettered buttons on the right side of the screen with which you can move through contact items displayed in Business Cards view.

_____ **4.** An e-mail feature in which you can have a copy of the message sent to another recipient, but the recipient's name is not visible to other recipients of the message.

_____ **5.** A graphic representation that indicates an item type in a To-Do List.

_____ **6.** A collection of contacts to whom you send e-mail messages.

_____ **7.** Colors, words, or phrases applied to Outlook items for the purpose of finding, sorting, filtering, or grouping them.

_____ **8.** Different screen arrangements of similar information; for example, information organized by company name or by individual's names.

_____ **9.** An arrangement of information with a separate row for each item and a separate column for each field.

_____ **10.** An element of information within an item, such as company name or state.

_____ **11.** The action of clicking a displayed minus sign to hide the items within a category or similar list.

_____ **12.** The Internet standard for creating and sharing virtual business cards.

_____ **13.** A personal or work-related activity that you want to keep track of until it is complete.

_____ **14.** A task that occurs repeatedly, for example, a weekly meeting.

_____ **15.** A language written or spoken by humans, as opposed to a computer programming language.

A Blind courtesy copy

B Categories

C Collapse

D Contact Index

E Contacts

F Distribution list

G Field

H Icon

I Import

J Natural language

K Recurring task

L Table

M Task

N vCard

O Views

Content-Based Assessments

Fill in the Blank

Write the correct word in the space provided.

1. A person or organization, inside or outside your own organization, about whom you can save information, such as street and e-mail addresses, telephone and fax numbers, Web page addresses, birthdays, and even pictures is called a(n) _____.

2. A blank area of the Contact form, which can be used for any information about the contact that is not otherwise specified, is called the _____ _____.

3. Use the _____ _____ print style to print a single contact.

4. The _____ _____ print style for contacts includes a blank form page, a lined page for manually listing new contacts.

5. In a Message form, you can display the Contacts list and find the e-mail address of a contact by clicking the word _____.

6. When displaying an Inbox message in the Reading Pane, you can add the sender's name and e-mail address to your Contacts list by pointing to the message in the Reading Pane and right-clicking the _____ _____.

7. To display your Contacts list in a format that displays the names and phone numbers, change the Current View to _____ _____.

8. To locate a specific contact in a large Contacts list, use the _____ _____ feature.

9. The print style that prints an entire list of tasks in the To-Do List is the _____ Style.

10. Days that are not Saturday, Sunday, or a holiday are known as _____ _____.

11. A blank area of the Task form, which can be used for any information about the task that is not otherwise specified, is called the _____ _____.

12. In the To-Do List, Outlook indicates that a task is overdue by displaying the task in _____.

13. In Detailed List view, the symbol in the Status column of a To-Do List that indicates a high priority item is a(n) _____ _____.

14. Tasks that are sorted by due date with tasks closest in time to the current date listed first are sorted in _____ order.

15. To select a contiguous group of tasks in a To-Do List for deletion, hold down the _____ key and then click the first and last message.

Content-Based Assessments

Skills Review

Project 2C—Music Festival

Objectives: 1. *Create Contacts;* **6.** *Manage Contacts;* **7.** *Create and Update Tasks;* **8.** *Manage Tasks.*

In the following Skills Review, you will create additions to the Contacts list and the To-Do List for Ray Hamilton, Desert Park's Director of Fine Arts and Parks. The additions relate to a new summer music festival that the department is developing. Your completed To-Do List and Contacts list will look similar to the ones shown in Figure 2.49.

For Project 2C, you will need the following files:

New blank contact form
New blank task form

You will print three files with the following footers:
2C_Music_Festival_Contact_Firstname_Lastname
2C_Music_Festival_Police_Firstname_Lastname
2C_Music_Festival_Tasks_Firstname_Lastname

Figure 2.49

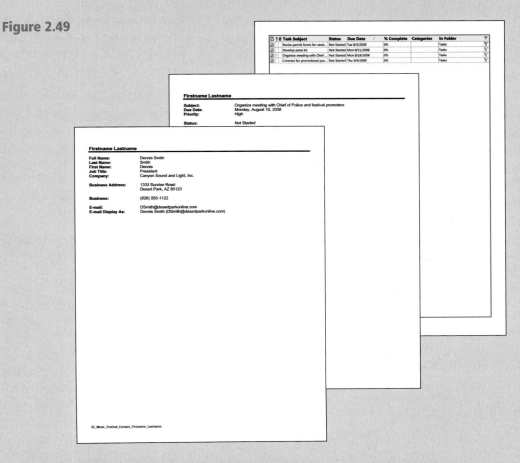

(Project 2C–Music Festival continues on the next page)

Content-Based Assessments

(Project 2C–Music Festival continued)

1. **Start** Outlook. Be sure the **Navigation Pane** is displayed; if necessary, on the menu bar, click View, and then click Navigation Pane. In the **Navigation Pane**, click the **Contacts** button to display the **Contacts** folder. On the Standard toolbar, click the **New Contact** button.

2. In the **Contact** form, in the **Full Name** box, type **Dennis Smith** In the **Company** box, type **Canyon Sound and Light, Inc.** In the **Job title** box, type **President**

3. In the **E-mail** box, type **DSmith@desertparkonline.com** Under **Phone numbers**, in the **Business** box, type **626-555-1122**

4. Under **Addresses**, in the **Business** box, type the following information:

   1333 Sunrise Road
   Desert Park, AZ 85123

5. **Save & Close** the form.

6. From the **File** menu, click **Print**. Under **Print style**, select **Memo Style**. Click **Page Setup**. On the **Header/Footer tab**, delete any existing header or footer information, including page numbers or dates. In the left **Footer** box, using your own name, type **2C_Music_Festival_Contact_Firstname_Lastname** Click **OK** to redisplay the **Print** dialog box. Click **Preview** to preview the printed document. In the **Print Preview** window, click **Print** to return to the **Print** dialog box, and then click **OK**. Submit the end result to your instructor as directed.

7. In the **Navigation Pane**, click the **Tasks** button, and then be sure the **Current View** is **Simple List**. On the Standard toolbar, click the **New Task** button. In the **Task** form, as the **Subject**, type **Organize meeting with Chief of Police and festival promoters** Click the **Due date arrow**. On

the displayed calendar, click a date **ten business days** from the current date.

8. Click the **Priority arrow**, and then click **High**. In the comments area of the Task form, type **Dennis needs to develop police overtime schedule Save & Close** the task.

9. In the **To-Do List**, under the column headings, click in the **Click here to add a new Task** box, and then type **Revise permit forms for vendors** In the **Due Date** box, type **Tomorrow** and then press Enter.

10. With the insertion point still located in the **Click here to add a new Task** box, type **Develop press kit** In the **Due Date** box, type **One week from today** and press Enter.

11. With the insertion point still located in the **Click here to add a new Task** box, type **Contract for promotional posters** and as the **Due Date**, type **One month from today** and press Enter.

12. Change the **Current View** to **Detailed List**, if necessary. In the **To-Do List** point to the **Due Date** heading, and click until the tasks are sorted in ascending order—the shaded arrow is pointing up. In the **To-Do List**, click the **Organize meeting with Chief of Police** task one time to select it without opening it.

13. From the **File** menu, point to **Page Setup**, and then click **Memo Style**. On the **Header/Footer tab**, delete any existing header or footer information. In the left **Footer** box, type **2C_Music_Festival_Police_Firstname_Lastname** and then click **Print**. In the **Print** dialog box, click **Preview** to preview the printed document. In the **Print Preview** window, click **Print** to return to the **Print** dialog box, and then click **OK**. Submit the end result to your instructor as directed.

(Project 2C–Music Festival continues on the next page)

Content-Based Assessments

(Project 2C–Music Festival continued)

14. Display the **Page Setup: Table Style** dialog box, click the **Header/Footer tab**, and then delete any existing header or footer information. In the left **Footer** box, type 2C_Music__Festival_Tasks_Firstname_Lastname Click **Print**. In the **Print** dialog box, **Preview** the document, and then **Print** it. Submit the end result to your instructor as directed.

15. Change the **Current View** to **Simple List**, if necessary. Click the first item in the **To-Do List** one time to select it without opening it. Hold down ⇧Shift and click the last item in the **To-Do List**. From the **Edit** menu, click **Delete**. In the **Microsoft Office Outlook** dialog box, click **OK**.

16. In the **Navigation Pane**, click the **Contacts** button. Click the **Dennis Smith** contact one time to select it. Click the **Delete** button.

17. In the **Navigation Pane**, click the **Folder List** button. In the **Folder List**, point to the **Deleted Items** folder and right-click. Click **Empty "Deleted Items" Folder**, and then in the **Microsoft Office Outlook** box, click **Yes**.

18. In the **Folder List**, click **Tasks** to display the Tasks folder. From the **File** menu, point to **Page Setup**, and then click **Define Print Styles**. Click **Memo Style**, click **Reset**, and then click **OK**. Click **Table Style**, click **Reset**, and then click **OK**. **Close** the dialog box. **Close** Outlook.

End You have completed Project 2C

Content-Based Assessments

Skills Review

Project 2D — New Assistant

Objectives: 1. *Create Contacts;* **2.** *Use Contacts with E-mail;* **6.** *Manage Contacts.*

In the following Skills Review, you will create contacts for Madison Romero, the City Manager of Desert Park. Ms. Romero has hired a new assistant, and she is sending contact information to him by using an e-mail message. Your completed contact and e-mail message will look similar to the ones shown in Figure 2.50.

For Project 2D, you will need the following file:

New blank contact form

You will print two files with the following footers:
2D_New_Assistant_vCard_Firstname_Lastname
2D_New_Assistant_Epstein_Contact_Firstname_Lastname

Figure 2.50

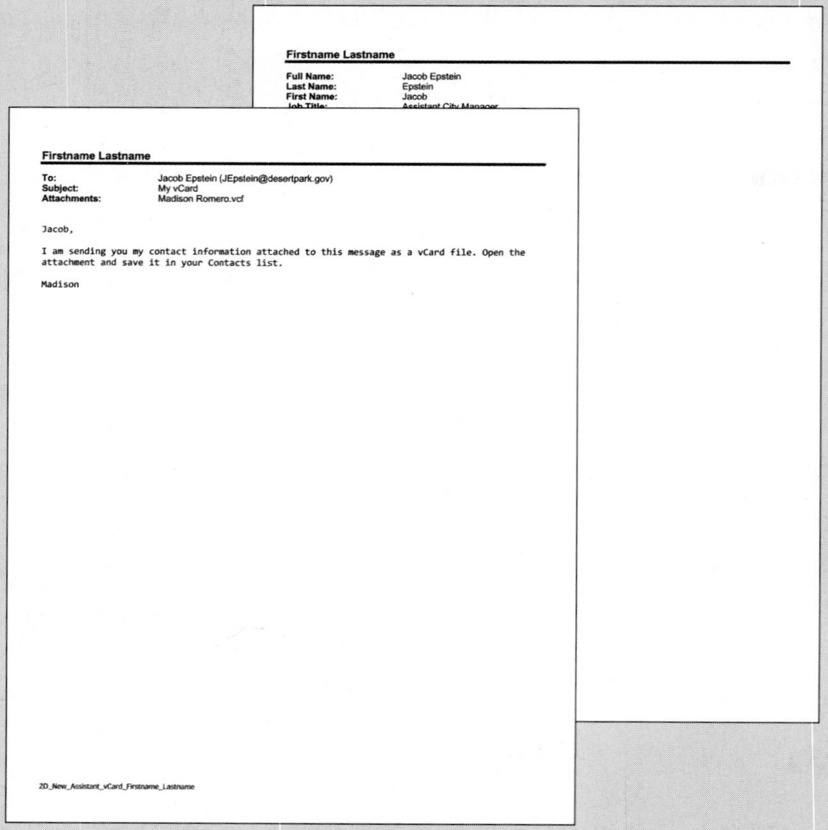

(Project 2D–New Assistant continues on the next page)

Content-Based Assessments

Skills Review

(Project 2D–New Assistant continued)

1. **Start** Outlook. Be sure the **Navigation Pane** is displayed; if necessary, from the View menu, click Navigation Pane. From the **Tools** menu, click **Options**. In the **Options** dialog box, click the **Mail Setup tab**.

2. Under **Send/Receive**, if necessary, clear the Send immediately when connected check box. To the immediate right, click the **Send/Receive** button. In the **Send/Receive Groups** dialog box, under **Setting for group "All Accounts"**, clear both Include this group in send/receive (F9) check boxes if necessary. Clear both Schedule an automatic send/receive check boxes if necessary. Click **Close**, and then click **OK**.

3. In the **Navigation Pane**, click the **Contacts** button to display the **Contacts** folder. On the Standard toolbar, click the **New Contact** button.

4. As the **Full Name**, type Jacob Epstein As the **Job title**, type Assistant City Manager

5. In the **E-mail** box, type JEpstein@desertpark .gov

6. Under **Phone numbers**, in the **Business** box, type 626-555-0143

7. Under **Addresses**, in the **Business** box, type the following:

   1570 Palo Verde Parkway
   Desert Park, AZ 85123

8. Click **Save&New**. In the **Contact** form, type the following information for the new contact, using **Business** for the phone and address information:

   Madison Romero
   City Manager
   MRomero@desertpark.gov
   626-555-0133
   1570 Palo Verde Parkway
   Desert Park, AZ 85123

9. On the Ribbon, click the **Details** button. In the **Assistant's name** box, type Jacob Epstein and then **Save & Close** the form.

10. In the **Contacts list**, click the **Madison Romero** contact one time to select it. From the **Actions** menu, click **Send as Business Card**. In the **Message** form, click **To**. In the **Select Names** dialog box, select **Jacob Epstein** if it is not already selected, and click the **To** button, and then click **OK**.

11. In the **Message** form, on the Ribbon, click the **Options tab**. In the **Format group**, click **Plain Text**. In the **Microsoft Office Outlook Compatibility Checker** dialog box, click **Continue**. Click in the **Subject** box, type **My vCard** Click in the message area, press Enter to start your message on the second line, and then type Jacob, Press Enter **two** times. Type **I am sending you my contact information attached to this message as a vCard. Open the attachment and save it in your Contacts list.** Press Enter **two** times and then type Madison On the Message form toolbar, click the **Send** button.

12. In the **Navigation Pane**, click the **Folder List** button. In the **Folder List**, click **Outbox**, and then click the **Jacob Epstein** message one time to select it without opening it. From the **File** menu, point to **Page Setup**, and then click **Memo Style**. On the **Header/Footer tab**, delete any existing header or footer information. In the left **Footer** box, type 2D_New_Assistant_vCard_Firstname_Lastname Click **Print**. In the **Print** dialog box, click **Preview** to preview the printed document. In the **Print Preview** window, click **Print** to return to the **Print** dialog box, and then click **OK**. Submit the end result to your instructor as directed.

13. With the **Outbox** still displayed and the **Jacob Epstein** message still selected, click the **Delete** button.

(Project 2D–New Assistant continues on the next page)

Content-Based Assessments

Skills Review

(Project 2D–New Assistant continued)

14. In the **Navigation Pane**, click the **Contacts** button. Click the **Jacob Epstein** contact one time to select it without opening it.

15. From the **File** menu, point to **Page Setup**, and then click **Memo Style**. In the **Header/Footer tab**, delete any header or footer information. In the left **Footer** box, type **2D_New_Assistant_Epstein_Contact_Firstname_Lastname** Click **Print**. In the **Print** dialog box, preview the printed document, and then print the document. Submit the end result to your instructor as directed.

16. In the **Contacts list**, click the first item one time to select it without opening it. Hold down ⇧Shift and click the second item in the **Contacts list**. From the **Edit** menu, click **Delete**.

17. Redisplay the **Folder List**, right-click the **Deleted Items** folder, and then click

Empty **"Deleted Items" Folder**. In the **Microsoft Office Outlook** box, click **Yes**.

18. From the **Tools** menu, click **Options**. Click the **Mail Setup tab**, and then, under **Send/Receive**, select the **Send immediately when connected** check box.

19. In the **Options** dialog box, click **Send/Receive**. In the **Send/Receive Groups** dialog box, under **Setting for group "All Accounts"**, select both **Include this group in send/receive (F9)** check boxes. Select both **Schedule an automatic send/receive** check boxes if this is a default setting on your computer. Click **Close**. Click **OK**.

20. Display the **Contacts** folder. From the **File** menu, point to **Page Setup**, and then click **Define Print Styles**. **Reset** the **Memo Style** print style, and then **Close** the dialog box. **Close** Outlook.

End **You have completed Project 2D** —————————————

Content-Based Assessments

Mastering Outlook

Project 2E — New Responsibilities

Objectives: 1. *Create Contacts;* **3.** *Edit Contacts;* **4.** *Manage Distribution Lists;* **5.** *Organize Contacts;* **6.** *Manage Contacts.*

In the following Mastering Outlook project, you will work with the Contacts list for Courtney Shrever, the Executive Assistant for Desert Park's mayor, David Parker. Ms. Shrever handles the affairs of other members of the mayor's staff. She will be editing some contacts, organizing her Contacts list, and creating a distribution list for the mayor's staff. Your completed Contacts list will look similar to the one shown in Figure 2.51.

For Project 2E, you will need the following files:

New blank contact form
o02E_New_Responsibilities_Contacts

You will print one file with the following footer:
2E_New_Responsibilities_Shrever_Contacts_Firstname_Lastname

Figure 2.51

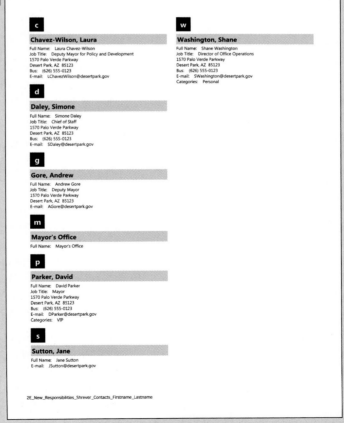

(Project 2E–New Responsibilities continues on the next page)

Content-Based Assessments

(Project 2E–New Responsibilities continued)

1. **Start** Outlook. Be sure the **Navigation Pane** is displayed; if necessary, from the View menu, click Navigation Pane. In the **Navigation Pane**, click the **Contacts** button. From the **File** menu, click **Import and Export**. In the **Import and Export Wizard** dialog box, under **Choose an action to perform**, click **Import from another program or file**, and then click **Next**. In the **Import a File** dialog box, under **Select file type to import from**, scroll down as necessary, and then click **Personal Folder File (.pst)**. Click **Next**.

2. In the **Import Personal Folders** dialog box, click **Browse**. In the **Open Personal Folders** dialog box, click the **Look in arrow**, and then navigate to the location where the student files for this textbook are stored. Locate **o02E_New_Responsibilities_Contacts**, and click one time to select it. Click **Open**.

3. In the **Import Personal Folders** dialog box, click **Next**. Under **Select the folder to import from**, be sure **Personal Folders** is selected. Click **Finish**. If a Translation Warning dialog box displays, click **OK**.

4. In the **Navigation Pane**, click the **Inbox** folder. Make certain the e-mail from **Jane Sutton** is displayed.

5. In the **Reading Pane**, point to Jane Sutton's e-mail address. Right-click on the address, and click **Add to Outlook Contacts**. **Save & Close** the Contact form.

6. Click the **Contacts** button. In the **Contacts list**, double-click the **Shane Washington** contact to open it. In the **Contact** form, in the **E-mail** box, type SWashington@desertpark.gov In the **Options group**, click **Categorize**. In the **Color Categories** dialog box, rename **Blue Category** as **Personal**. Select the **Personal**

check box and click **OK**. **Save & Close** the form.

7. From the **File** menu, point to **New**, and then click **Distribution List**. In the **Distribution List** form, in the **Name** box, type **Mayor's Office** Click **Select Members**.

8. In the **Select Members** dialog box, click **Laura Chavez-Wilson**, and then click **Members**. In the same manner, add **Shane Washington** and **Simone Daley** as **Members**. Click **OK**. **Save & Close** the distribution list.

9. From the **Contacts list**, open the **David Parker** contact. Display the **Color Categories** dialog box, rename the **Purple Category** as **VIP**. Select the **VIP** check box, and then click **OK**. **Save & Close**.

10. Change the **Current View** to **Detailed Address Cards**. From the **File** menu, point to **Page Setup**, and then click **Card Style**. With the **Format tab** displayed, under **Options**, locate the **Blank forms at end** box. Click the **Blank forms at end arrow**, and then click **None**.

11. Click the **Header/Footer tab**, and delete any header or footer information. In the left **Footer** box, type **2E_New_Responsibilities_Shrever_Contacts_Firstname_Lastname** using your own name. Click **Print**. In the **Print** dialog box, click **Preview** to preview the printed document. In the **Print Preview** window, click **Print** to return to the **Print** dialog box, and then click **OK**. Submit the end result to your instructor as directed.

12. In the **Contacts list**, select any contact. Display the **Color Categories** dialog box, select **Personal**, click **Rename**, and then type **Blue Category**. Rename **VIP** as **Purple Category**, and then **close** the dialog box.

(Project 2E–New Responsibilities continues on the next page)

Mastering Outlook

(Project 2E–New Responsibilities continued)

13. Change the **Current View** to **Business Cards**. In the **Contacts list**, click the first item one time to select it without opening it. Hold down ⇧ Shift and click the last item in the **Contacts list**. From the **Edit** menu, click **Delete**.

14. In the **Navigation Pane**, click the **Folder List** button, and then click the **Inbox** folder. Right-click on the message from **Jane Sutton**, and then click **Delete**.

15. In the **Folder List**, right-click the **Deleted Items** folder, and then click **Empty "Deleted Items" Folder**. In the **Microsoft Office Outlook** box, click **Yes**.

16. Display the **Contacts** folder. From the **File** menu, point to **Page Setup**, and then click **Define Print Styles**. **Reset** the **Card Style** print style, and then **Close** the dialog box. **Close** Outlook.

End **You have completed Project 2E** ─────────────────────

Content-Based Assessments

Mastering Outlook

Project 2F—Holiday Party

Objectives: 1. *Create Contacts;* **5.** *Organize Contacts;* **6.** *Manage Contacts;* **7.** *Create and Update Tasks;* **8.** *Manage Tasks.*

In the following Mastering Outlook project, you will develop a To-Do List and Contacts list for Courtney Shrever, who has been asked by the Desert Park mayor, David Parker, to organize a holiday party for his office and other members of city government. Your completed To-Do List and Contacts list will look similar to the ones shown in Figure 2.52.

For Project 2F, you will need the following file:

New blank contact form

You will print two files with the following footers:
2F_Holiday_Party_Suppliers_Firstname_Lastname
2F_Holiday_Party_List_Firstname_Lastname

Figure 2.52

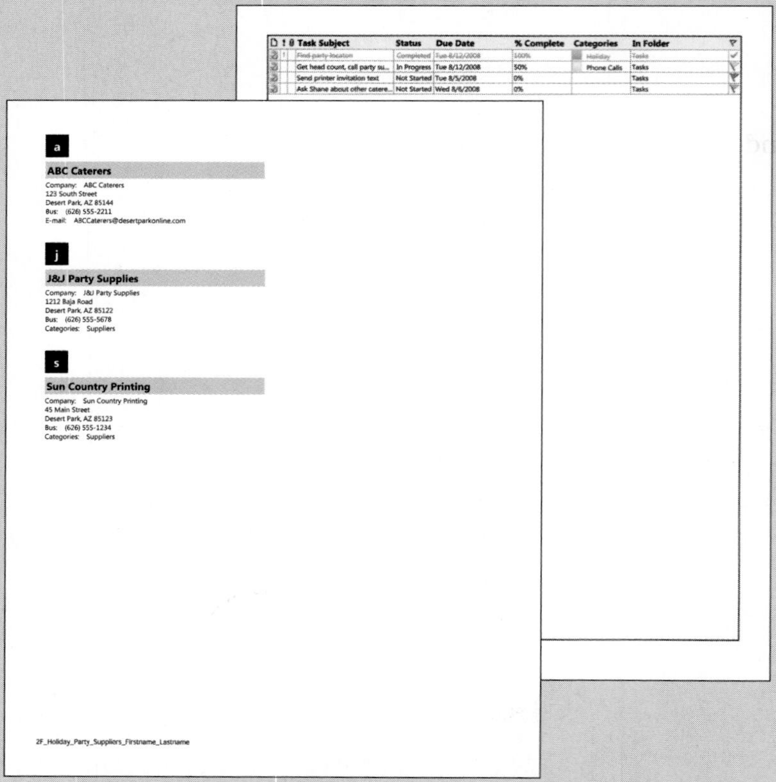

(Project 2F—Holiday Party continues on the next page)

Content-Based Assessments

chapter two   **Mastering Outlook**

(Project 2F–Holiday Party continued)

1. **Start** Outlook, display the **Navigation Pane**, click the **Contacts** button, and then open a new Contact form. As the **Company** name, type **ABC Caterers** Type the following information for the new contact, using **Business** for the address and phone information:

   ABCCaterers@desertparkonline.com
   626-555-2211
   123 South Street
   Desert Park, AZ 85144

2. Click **Save & New**, and then, in the **Contact** form, type the following information in the appropriate boxes for this company:

   Sun Country Printing
   626-555-1234
   45 Main Street
   Desert Park, AZ 85123

3. Display the **Color Categories** dialog box, rename the **Green Category** as **Suppliers**, and then assign this category to this contact. **Save & Close** the contact. Open a new contact, and add the following company:

   J&J Party Supplies
   626-555-5678
   1212 Baja Road
   Desert Park, AZ 85122

4. Assign this contact to the **Suppliers** category, and then **Save & Close** the form. Change the **Current View** to **Detailed Address Cards**. From the **File** menu, display the **Page Setup: Card Style** dialog box. On the **Format tab**, click the **Blank forms at end arrow**, and then click **None**. On the **Header/Footer tab**, delete any existing header or footer information, and in the left **Footer** box, type **2F_Holiday_Party_Suppliers_Firstname_Lastname Preview** and **Print** the document. Submit the end result to your instructor as directed.

5. Change to **Business Cards** view. Display the **Tasks** folder, and then click the **New**

Task button. As the **Subject**, type **Find party location** Set the **Due date** as one week from the current date. Clear the **Reminder** check box, if necessary, and then set the **Priority** to **High**. In the comments area of the Task form, type **Look at restaurants in neighborhood** Display the **Color Categories** dialog box, rename the **Red Category** as **Holiday**, and then assign this category to the task. **Save & Close** the task.

6. In the **To-Do List** under the column headings, click in the **Click here to add a new Task** box, and then type **Ask Shane about other caterers** In the **Due Date** box, type **Tomorrow** and then press [Enter].

7. Directly in the **To-Do List**, create a new task with the **Subject Send printer invitation text** In the **Due Date** box, type **Today** and then press [Enter]. Create another new task with the **Subject Get head count, call party suppliers** In the **Due Date** box, type **One week from today** and then press [Enter].

8. In the **To-Do List**, double-click the **Get head count** task to open its form. Display the **Color Categories** dialog box, rename the **Yellow Category** as **Phone Calls**, and assign this category to the task. Change the **% Complete** to **50%**, and then **Save & Close** the form.

9. In the **To-Do List**, mark the **Find party location** task as **Completed**.

10. Change the **Current View** to **Detailed List**. From the **Priority** column heading, sort the **Tasks list** with the highest priority tasks first.

11. From the **File** menu, display the **Page Setup: Table Style** dialog box. Delete any header or footer information. In the left **Footer** box, type **2F_Holiday_Party_List_Firstname_Lastname Preview** and then

(Project 2F–Holiday Party continues on the next page)

Project 2F: Holiday Party | **Outlook**   161

Content-Based Assessments

(Project 2F–Holiday Party continued)

> **Print** the document. Submit the end result to your instructor as directed.

12. In the **To-Do List**, select any task. Display the **Color Categories** dialog box, select **Suppliers**, click **Rename**, and then type **Green Category**. Rename **Holiday** as **Red Category**, and **Phone Calls** as **Yellow Category Close** the dialog box.

13. Change the **Current View** to **Simple List**. Delete the contents of the **Tasks folder**. Then display the **Contacts** folder, and delete its contents.

14. In the **Navigation Pane**, click the **Folder List** button. Empty the **Deleted Items** folder. Display the **Contacts** folder, and then display the **Define Print Styles** dialog box. **Reset** the **Card Style** print style and then **Close** the dialog box. Display the **Tasks** folder, and then display the **Define Print Styles** dialog box. **Reset** the **Table Style** print style, and then **Close** the dialog box. **Close** Outlook.

End **You have completed Project 2F**

Mastering Outlook

Project 2G — Computer Network

Objectives: 1. *Create Contacts;* **2.** *Use Contacts with E-mail;* **3.** *Edit Contacts;* **6.** *Manage Contacts.*

In the following Mastering Outlook project, you will create contacts and send an e-mail message for Shane Washington, the Director of Office Operations in the mayor's office. Shane is directing an upgrade of the office computer network and will be creating contacts for the consultants implementing the project. Your completed Contacts list and message will look similar to the ones shown in Figure 2.53.

For Project 2G, you will need the following files:

New blank contact form
New blank message form

You will print two files with the following footers:
2G_Computer_Network_Proposal_Firstname_Lastname
2G_Computer_Network_Contacts_Firstname_Lastname

Figure 2.53

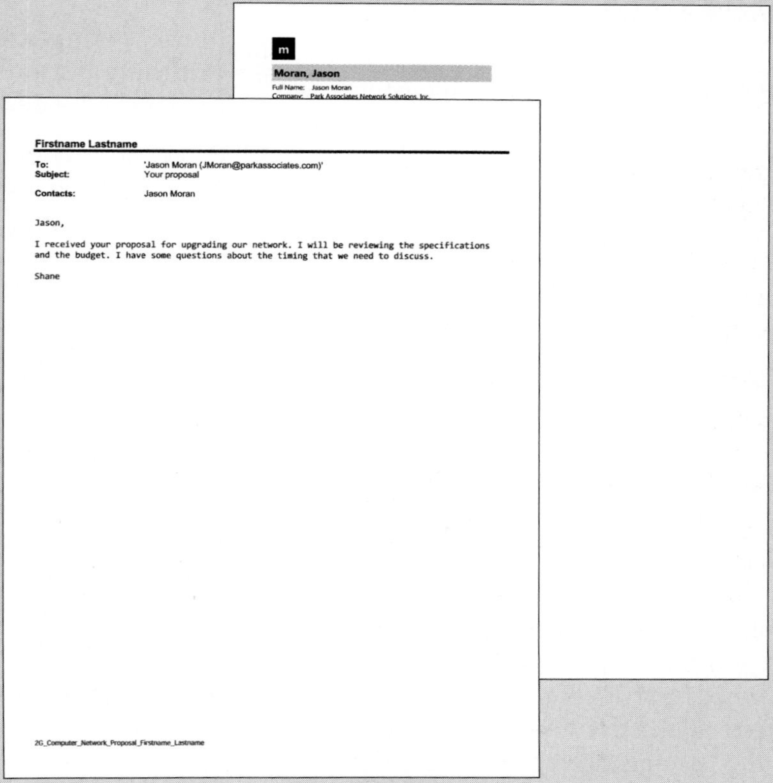

(Project 2G–Computer Network continues on the next page)

(Project 2G–Computer Network continued)

1. **Start** Outlook. From the **Tools** menu, display the **Options** dialog box, and then click the **Mail Setup tab**. Under **Send/Receive**, clear the Send immediately when connected check box if necessary. To the immediate right, click the **Send/Receive** button. In the **Send/Receive Groups** dialog box, under **Setting for group "All Accounts"**, clear both Include this group in send/receive (F9) check boxes if necessary. Clear both Schedule an automatic send/receive check boxes if necessary. Click **Close**, and then click **OK**.

2. Display the **Contacts** folder, and open a new Contact form. Complete the form with the following information:

   Shane Washington
   Director of Office Operations
   SWashington@desertpark.gov
   626-555-0129
   1570 Palo Verde Parkway
   Desert Park, AZ 85123

3. Click **Save & New**, and enter the following contact:

   Jason Moran
   Park Associates Network Solutions, Inc.
   JMoran@parkassociates.com
   626-555-3434
   333 Rio Grande Avenue
   Desert Park, AZ 95123

4. **Save & Close** the contact. In the **Contacts list**, right-click the **Jason Moran** contact. On the displayed shortcut menu, point to **Create**, and then click **New Message to Contact**.

5. In the **Message** form, change the **Message format** to **Plain Text**. As the **Subject**, type Your proposal In the message area, using the format you have practiced for e-mail messages, type Jason, I received your proposal for upgrading our network. I will be reviewing the specifications and the budget.

I have some questions about the timing that we need to discuss. Shane On the Message form toolbar, click the **Send** button.

6. Display the **Folder List** and click **Outbox**. Select the **Jason Moran** message, and then, from the **File** menu, display the **Page Setup: Memo Style** dialog box. Delete any header or footer information, and then, in the left **Footer** box, type 2G_Computer_Network_Proposal_Firstname_Lastname Click **Print**. In the **Print** dialog box, **Preview** the document, and then **Print** it. Submit the end result to your instructor as directed.

7. Delete the contents of the **Outbox**. Display the **Contacts** folder, and open the **Contact** form for **Jason Moran**. Move the insertion point to the postal code. Change the postal code from **95123** to **85123 Save & Close** the form.

8. In the **Navigation Pane**, click the **Contacts** button. Change the current view to **Detailed Address Cards**.

9. Select both contacts. From the **File** menu, display the **Print** dialog box. Under **Print style**, click **Card Style**. Click **Page Setup**. On the **Format tab**, change the **Blank forms at end** box to **None**. Click the **Header/Footer tab**. Delete any header or footer information. In the left **Footer** box, type 2G_Computer_Network_Contacts_Firstname_Lastname **Preview** and **Print** the document. Submit the end result to your instructor as directed.

10. Display the **Contacts** folder, and then display the **Define Print Styles** dialog box. **Reset** the **Card Style** print style, and then **Close** the dialog box.

11. In the **Contacts list**, delete both items. Then, empty the **Deleted Items** folder.

(Project 2G–Computer Network continues on the next page)

Mastering Outlook

(Project 2G–Computer Network continued)

12. From the **Tools** menu, click **Options**. Click the **Mail Setup tab**, and then, under **Send/Receive**, select the **Send immediately when connected** check box.

13. In the **Options** dialog box, click **Send/Receive**. In the **Send/Receive Groups** dialog box, under **Setting for** group "**All Accounts**", select both **Include this group in send/receive (F9)** check boxes. Select both **Schedule an automatic send/receive** check boxes if this is a default setting on your computer. Click **Close**. Click **OK**. **Close** Outlook.

End You have completed Project 2G ——————————————————————

Content-Based Assessments

Mastering Outlook

Project 2H—Job Fair

Objectives: 1. *Create Contacts;* **3.** *Edit Contacts;* **4.** *Manage Distribution Lists;* **5.** *Organize Contacts;* **6.** *Manage Contacts.*

In the following Mastering Outlook project, you will create contacts and a distribution list for Gloria French, who is the Public Information Officer for the city of Desert Park. Ms. French is organizing a job fair for city agencies and departments using both internal and external personnel. Your completed Contacts list will look similar to the one shown in Figure 2.54.

For Project 2H, you will need the following files:

New blank distribution list form

o02H_Job_Fair_Contacts

You will print two files with the following footers:
2H_Job_Fair_Managers_Firstname_Lastname
2H_Job_Fair_Firstname_Lastname

Figure 2.54

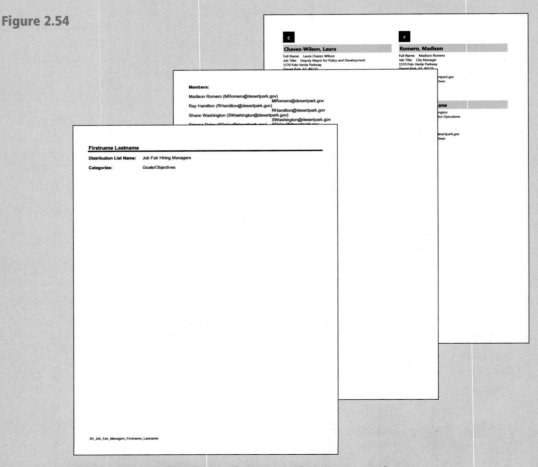

(Project 2H–Job Fair continues on the next page)

Content-Based Assessments

(Project 2H–Job Fair continued)

1. **Start** Outlook and display the **Contacts** folder. Display the **Import and Export Wizard** dialog box. In the **Import and Export Wizard** dialog box, click **Import from another program or file**, and then click **Next**. In the **Import a File** dialog box, scroll as necessary, and then click **Personal Folder File (.pst)**. Click **Next**.

2. In the **Import Personal Folders** dialog box, click **Browse**. In the **Open Personal Folders** dialog box, navigate to the location where the student files for this textbook are stored. Locate **o02H_Job_Fair_Contacts**, and click **Open**. In the **Import Personal Folders** dialog box, click **Next**.

3. In the **Import Personal Folders** dialog box, under **Select the folder to import from**, click **Contacts**. Click **Import items into the current folder**. Click **Finish**. If a Translation Warning dialog box displays, click **OK**.

4. Begin a new distribution list, and name it **Job Fair Hiring Managers** Add the following names to the distribution list: **Ray Hamilton**, **Madison Romero**, **Simone Daley**, and **Shane Washington**.

5. In the **Distribution List** form, display the **Color Categories** dialog box, rename **Orange Category** as **Goals/Objectives** Select the **Goals/Objectives** check box, and then click **OK**. **Save & Close** the distribution list.

6. If necessary, display the **Contacts** folder, Select **Ray Hamilton**, hold down Ctrl, and then select **Madison Romero**, **Simone**

Daley, and **Shane Washington**. Right-click one of the selected items, click **Categorize**, display the **Color Categories** dialog box, and assign the **Goals/Objectives** category. The individual contacts and the distribution list are assigned to the category Ms. French is using for her job fair activities.

7. Change the **Current View** to **Detailed Address Cards**. In the **Contacts list**, click the **Job Fair Hiring Managers** contact one time to select it. Display the **Page Setup: Memo Style** dialog box. Delete any header or footer information, and then, in the left **Footer** box, type **2H_Job_Fair_Managers_Firstname_Lastname Preview** and **Print** the document. Submit the end result to your instructor as directed.

8. Display the **Page Setup: Card Style** dialog box. Set **Blank forms at end** to **None**. Delete any header or footer information. In the left **Footer** box, type **2H_Job_Fair_Firstname_Lastname Preview** and **Print** the document. Submit the end result to your instructor as directed.

9. In the **Contacts list**, select any contact. Display the **Color Categories** dialog box, select **Goals/Objectives**, click **Rename**, and then type **Orange Category**. Click **OK**.

10. Change to **Business Cards** view. Delete all the items in the **Contacts list**. Display the **Define Print Styles** dialog box and **Reset** the **Card Style** and **Memo Style** print styles. Empty the **Deleted Items** folder, and then **Close** Outlook.

End **You have completed Project 2H**

Content-Based Assessments

Project 2I—Property Managers Forum

Objectives: 1. *Create Contacts;* **2.** *Use Contacts with E-mail;* **5.** *Organize Contacts;* **6.** *Manage Contacts;* **7.** *Create and Update Tasks;* **8.** *Manage Tasks.*

In the following Mastering Outlook project, you will create tasks and contacts for Gloria French, the Public Information Officer for the city of Desert Park. Her department is sponsoring a forum for the city's property managers to hear a panel discussion with heads of various city agencies. Your completed message, contact, and To-Do List will look similar to the ones shown in Figure 2.55.

For Project 2I, you will need the following files:

New blank contact form

New blank message form

You will print three files with the following footers:
2I_Property_Managers_Forum_Firstname_Lastname
2I_Property_Managers_Forum_Tasks_Firstname_Lastname
2I_Property_Managers_Forum_Contact_Firstname_Lastname

Figure 2.55

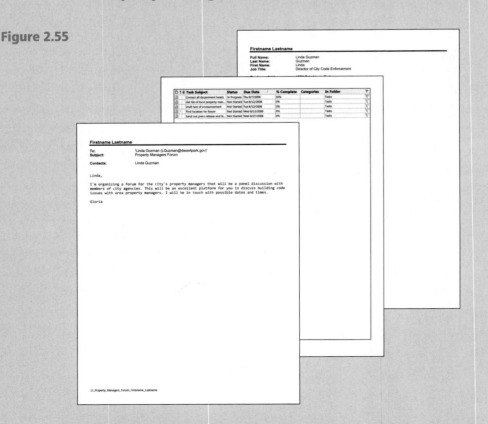

(Project 2I–Property Managers Forum continues on the next page)

Content-Based Assessments

(Project 2I–Property Managers Forum continued)

1. **Start** Outlook. From the **Tools** menu, display the **Options** dialog box, and click the **Mail Setup tab**. Under **Send/Receive**, clear the Send immediately when connected check box if necessary. To the immediate right, click the **Send/Receive** button. In the **Send/Receive Groups** dialog box, under **Setting for group "All Accounts"**, clear both Include this group in send/receive (F9) check boxes if necessary. Clear both Schedule an automatic send/receive check boxes if necessary. Click **Close**, and then click **OK**.

2. Display the **Contacts** folder, and then create the following new contact:

   Linda Guzman
   Director of City Code Enforcement
   LGuzman@desertpark.gov
   626-555-0151
   1570 Palo Verde Parkway
   Desert Park, AZ 85123

3. Display the **Color Categories** dialog box, rename the **Orange Category** as Goals/Objectives Assign the contact to the **Goals/Objectives** category. Ms. French is using this category to organize all her Outlook contacts and activities for the forum. Under **Phone numbers**, change the **Home** box to **Assistant**, and then type **626-555-0111** On the Ribbon, click **Details**, and add **John Stevens** as the **Assistant's name**. **Save & Close** the contact.

4. Right-click the **Linda Guzman** contact, click **Create**, and then click **New Message to Contact**. Change the **Message format** to **Plain Text**. As the **Subject**, type Property Managers Forum Using the spacing technique you have practiced for typing messages, create the following message in the message area:

   Linda, I'm organizing a forum for the city's property managers that will be a panel discussion with members of city agencies. This will be an excellent platform for you to discuss building code issues with area property managers. I will be in touch with possible dates and times. Gloria

5. **Send** the message, display the **Folder List**, and then display the **Outbox folder**. Select the **Linda Guzman** message without opening it, display the **Print** dialog box, and then display the **Page Setup: Memo Style** dialog box. Delete any existing header or footer information, and then create a left footer by typing 2I_Property_Managers_Forum_Firstname_Lastname **Preview** and **Print** the message. Submit the end result to your instructor as directed.

6. Display the **Tasks** folder. Using the **Click here to add a new Task** box, create five tasks, using the following information:

Subject	**Due Date**
Find location for forum	One week from today
Contact all department heads	Tomorrow
Get list of local property managers from Tax Dept.	Next Tuesday
Draft text of announcement	Next Tuesday
Send out press release and letters to property managers	Three weeks from today

(Project 2I–Property Managers Forum continues on the next page)

Content-Based Assessments

Mastering Outlook

(Project 2I–Property Managers Forum continued)

7. Open the task **Contact all department heads**, and change the **% Complete** to **50%**. Open the task **Find location for forum**, and change the **Priority** to **High**.

8. Change the **Current View** to **Detailed List**, and then sort the **To-Do List** by **Due Date** so that the tasks with the nearest due dates are first. Prepare to print the list of tasks in **Table Style** with the footer 2I_Property_Managers_Forum_Tasks_Firstname_Lastname and then **Preview** and **Print** the list. Submit the end result to your instructor as directed.

9. Display the **Contacts** folder. Prepare to print the contact in **Memo Style** with the footer 2I_Property_Managers_Forum_Contact_Firstname_Lastname **Preview** and **Print** the contact. Submit the end result to your instructor as directed.

10. In the **Contacts list**, select the contact. Display the **Color Categories** dialog box, select **Goals/Objectives**, click **Rename**, and then type **Orange Category**. Click **OK.**

11. Delete the contents of the **Contacts** folder, the **Tasks** folder, and the **Outbox** folder, and then empty the **Deleted Items** folder.

12. From the **Tools** menu, click **Options**. Click the **Mail Setup tab**, and then, under **Send/Receive**, select the **Send immediately when connected** check box.

13. In the **Options** dialog box, click **Send/Receive**. In the **Send/Receive Groups** dialog box, under **Setting for group "All Accounts"**, select both **Include this group in send/receive (F9)** check boxes. Select both **Schedule an automatic send/receive** check boxes if this is a default setting on your computer. Click **Close**. Click **OK.**

14. Display the **Tasks** folder, and then reset the **Table Style** and **Memo Style** print styles, and then **Close** Outlook.

End **You have completed Project 2I**

Mastering Outlook

Project 2J — City Council

Objectives: 3. *Edit Contacts;* **4.** *Manage Distribution Lists;* **5.** *Organize Contacts;* **6.** *Manage Contacts.*

In the following Mastering Outlook project, you will manage the Contacts list for Simone Daley, the Chief of Staff for Desert Park's mayor, David Parker. Simone is creating a distribution list to notify staff members and other key officials of city council meetings. You will import contacts, organize the Contacts list, and create a distribution list. Your completed distribution list and Contacts list will look similar to the ones shown in Figure 2.56.

For Project 2J, you will need the following files:

New blank distribution list form

o02J_City_Council_Contacts

You will print two files with the following footers:
2J_City_Council_Firstname_Lastname
2J_City_Council_List_Firstname_Lastname

Figure 2.56

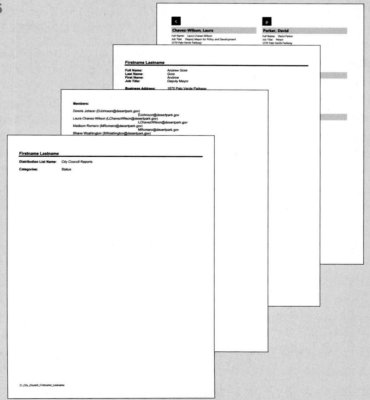

(Project 2J–City Council continues on the next page)

Content-Based Assessments

Mastering Outlook

(Project 2J–City Council continued)

1. **Start** Outlook, and display the **Contacts** folder. Display the **Import and Export Wizard** dialog box, and then, using the techniques you have practiced, import **o02J_City_Council_Contacts** into the **Contacts folder**.

2. In the **Color Categories** dialog box, rename **Red Category** as Status, **Purple Category** as VIP, and **Blue Category** as Personal

3. Create a new distribution list named **City Council Reports** Add the following names to the list: **Madison Romero**, **Dennis Johnson**, **Shane Washington**, and **Laura Chavez-Wilson**. Apply the **Status** category to the distribution list. Ms. Daley organizes and displays her Contacts list using categories. She uses this category for regular meetings and report-related activities and contacts.

4. In the **Contacts list**, apply the category **VIP** to **David Parker**, **Andrew Gore**, and **Dennis Johnson**. Ms. Daley uses this category for important contacts. Open the **David Parker** contact and add **Sean Fogerty** as the **Assistant's name**.

5. In the **Andrew Gore** contact, assign the contact to the **Personal** category.

Ms. Daley uses this category for friends and family members in her Contacts list.

6. Display the **Contacts list** in **Detailed Address Cards** view. Select the **City Council Reports** and **Andrew Gore** contacts. Prepare to print these in **Memo Style** with the footer 2J_City_Council_Firstname_Lastname **Preview** and **Print** the contacts. Submit the end result to your instructor as directed.

7. Prepare to print all the contacts in **Card Style** with the footer 2J_City_Council_List_Firstname_Lastname Set the **Blank forms at end** to **None**. **Preview** and **Print** the Contacts list. Submit the end result to your instructor as directed.

8. In the **Contacts list**, select any contact. Display the **Color Categories** dialog box, rename all categories to their default color names. Click **OK**.

9. Display the **Contacts list** in **Business Cards** view. Delete the contents of the **Contacts** folder and empty the **Deleted Items** folder. Display the **Contacts** folder and reset the **Card Style** and **Memo Style** print styles, and then **Close** Outlook.

End You have completed Project 2J

Rubric

The following outcomes-based assessments are *open-ended assessments*. That is, there is no specific correct result; your result will depend on your approach to the information provided. Make *Professional Quality* your goal. Use the following scoring rubric to guide you in *how* to approach the problem and then to evaluate *how well* your approach solves the problem.

The *criteria*—Software Mastery, Content, Format and Layout, and Process—represent the knowledge and skills you have gained that you can apply to solving the problem. The *levels of performance*—Professional Quality, Approaching Professional Quality, or Needs Quality Improvement—help you and your instructor evaluate your result.

	Your completed project is of Professional Quality if you:	Your completed project is Approaching Professional Quality if you:	Your completed project Needs Quality Improvements if you:
1-Software Mastery	Choose and apply the most appropriate skills, tools, and features and identify efficient methods to solve the problem.	Choose and apply some appropriate skills, tools, and features, but not in the most efficient manner.	Choose inappropriate skills, tools, or features, or are inefficient in solving the problem.
2-Content	Construct a solution that is clear and well organized, contains content that is accurate, appropriate to the audience and purpose, and is complete. Provide a solution that contains no errors of spelling, grammar, or style.	Construct a solution in which some components are unclear, poorly organized, inconsistent, or incomplete. Misjudge the needs of the audience. Have some errors in spelling, grammar, or style, but the errors do not detract from comprehension.	Construct a solution that is unclear, incomplete, or poorly organized; contains some inaccurate or inappropriate content; and contains many errors of spelling, grammar, or style. Do not solve the problem.
3-Format and Layout	Format and arrange all elements to communicate information and ideas, clarify function, illustrate relationships, and indicate relative importance.	Apply appropriate format and layout features to some elements, but not others. Overuse features, causing minor distraction.	Apply format and layout that does not communicate information or ideas clearly. Do not use format and layout features to clarify function, illustrate relationships, or indicate relative importance. Use available features excessively, causing distraction.
4-Process	Use an organized approach that integrates planning, development, self-assessment, revision, and reflection.	Demonstrate an organized approach in some areas, but not others; or, use an insufficient process of organization throughout.	Do not use an organized approach to solve the problem.

Outcomes-Based Assessments

Problem Solving

Project 2K—Recreation Center

Objectives: 1. *Create Contacts;* **2.** *Use Contacts with E-mail;* **4.** *Manage Distribution Lists;* **6.** *Manage Contacts;* **7.** *Create and Update Tasks;* **8.** *Manage Tasks.*

For Project 2K, you will need the following files:

New blank distribution list form   o02K_Recreation_Center_Contacts

New blank message form

You will print three files with the following footers:
2K_Recreation_Center_Message_Firstname_Lastname
2K_Recreation_Center_Contacts_Firstname_Lastname
2K_Recreation_Center_Tasks_Firstname_Lastname

Desert Park, Arizona is opening a new downtown recreation center. Ray Hamilton, Desert Park's Director of Fine Arts and Parks, is coordinating the opening with other departments in the city government. You will manage his Contacts list and tasks for this project. You will import contacts, send an e-mail message to a contact, create a distribution list, and create a To-Do List. Start Outlook. Configure the Send/Receive settings to place your e-mail messages in the Outbox instead of the Sent Items folder. Using the techniques you have practiced in this chapter, import **o02K_Recreation_ Center_Contacts** into your Contacts folder. Using the Gloria French contact, create a new mail message to her, using a Plain Text message format. Type a subject for the message that briefly defines the purpose of the message, which is a request for assistance in publicizing the opening of the new recreation center.

For the text of the message, type a salutation of **Gloria,** followed by two paragraphs—an introductory paragraph describing the facility, and a second paragraph asking her for her help in publicizing the opening. End the text of the message with the name **Ray** Send the message. Display the Outbox and print the message in Memo Style with **2K_Recreation_Center_ Message_Firstname_Lastname** as a footer. Submit the end result to your instructor as directed.

Create a distribution list with three names from the Contacts list. Display the Contacts list in a view that shows the contacts' details. Print the Contacts list in Card Style with **2K_Recreation_Center_Contacts_ Firstname_Lastname** as a footer. Submit the end result to your instructor as directed. Display the Contacts list in its default view.

Create a To-Do List with four tasks relating to the opening of the recreation center. Give all the tasks a due date within the next two weeks. Print the To-Do List in Table Style with **2K_Recreation_Center_Tasks_ Firstname_Lastname** as a footer. Submit the end result to your instructor as directed. Delete the contents of the Task folder, the Contacts folder, the Outbox folder, and the Deleted Items folder. Restore the Send/Receive options to their default settings. Reset the print styles you used.

End **You have completed Project 2K**

Outcomes-Based Assessments

chapter two

Problem Solving

Project 2L—Visitor Center

Objectives: 1. *Create Contacts;* **3.** *Edit Contacts;* **4.** *Manage Distribution Lists;* **5.** *Organize Contacts;* **6.** *Manage Contacts.*

> **For Project 2L, you will need the following file:**
>
> New blank contact form

You will print one file with the following footer:
2L_Visitor_Center_Contacts_Firstname_Lastname

Gloria French, the Director of Public Information for the city of Desert Park, has hired consultants to assist in the remodeling of the city's Visitor Center. You will manage her Contacts list for the project. You will create new contacts and a distribution list and organize the Contacts list.

Create three new contacts. Each of the three contacts works for the Desert Park design consulting firm of Oasis Design Associates, Inc. Create a Desert Park address for the company. All three contacts may have the same address and phone numbers. Assign all three Oasis Design contacts to a category, and rename that category with a more descriptive name. Create a distribution list with the three contacts from Oasis Design Associates, Inc.

Create a new contact for Madison Romero, using the address and phone number information in Project 2D. Assign the Madison Romero contact to a category, renaming the category with an appropriate name.

Display the Contacts list in a view that shows the contacts' details. Add **2L_Visitor_Center_Contacts_Firstname_Lastname** as a footer. Print the Contacts list in an appropriate print style. Submit the end result to your instructor as directed. Restore categories to their default color names. Display the Contacts list in its default view. Delete the contents of the Contacts folder and the Deleted Items folder. Reset the print style you used.

End **You have completed Project 2L** ————————————

Outcomes-Based Assessments

Problem Solving

Project 2M — Skate Park

Objectives: 1. *Create Contacts;* **3.** *Edit Contacts;* **4.** *Manage Distribution Lists;* **5.** *Organize Contacts;* **6.** *Manage Contacts;* **7.** *Create and Update Tasks;* **8.** *Manage Tasks.*

> **For Project 2M, you will need the following file:**
>
> New blank contact form

You will print two files with the following footers:
2M_Skate_Park_Contacts_Firstname_Lastname
2M_Skate_Park_Tasks_Firstname_Lastname

Ray Hamilton, Desert Park's Director of Fine Arts and Parks, has decided to build a skate park in the city's main park. Its design includes ramps, rails, boxes, and jumps for skateboarding, rollerblading, and BMX biking. He has asked his assistant, Steve Bouchard, to manage the project. Mr. Bouchard has hired consultants to assist in developing this attraction. You will manage his Contacts list and tasks for the project. You will create new contacts and a distribution list, organize the Contacts list, and create a To-Do List.

Create three new contacts. Each of the three contacts works for the Desert Park design consulting firm of Stunts&Jumps Design, Inc. Create a Desert Park address for the company. All three contacts may have the same address and phone numbers, but also include a home address and phone number for at least two of the contacts. Assign all three contacts to an appropriately named category. Create a distribution list with the three contacts from Stunts&Jumps Design, Inc.

Create a new contact for Ray Hamilton, Director of Parks and Fine Arts. Use the following address information:

**1570 Palo Verde Parkway
Desert Park, AZ 05123**

Add a home address and phone number for this contact, using a Desert Park address. Ray's e-mail address is **RHamilton@desertpark.gov** Assign the contact to an appropriately named category.

Display the Contacts list in a view that shows the contacts' details. Add a footer of **2M_Skate_Park_Contacts_Firstname_Lastname** Print the Contacts list in an appropriate print style and submit the end result to your instructor as directed.

Create a To-Do List with four tasks relating to the opening of the skate park. Give all the tasks a due date within the next three weeks. Assign all tasks to an appropriately named category. Display the To-Do List in a view that shows task details. Add the footer **2M_Skate_Park_Tasks_ Firstname_Lastname** to the file. Print the To-Do List and submit the end result to your instructor as directed.

(Project 2M–Skate Park continues on the next page)

Problem Solving

(Project 2M–Skate Park continued)

Restore the categories to their default color names. Display the To-Do List in its default view. Delete the contents of the Tasks folder. Display the Contacts list in its default view, and then delete the contents of the Contacts folder. Delete the contents of the Deleted Items folder. Reset the print styles you used.

End **You have completed Project 2M** ─────────────

Outcomes-Based Assessments

chaptertwo   *GO!* with Help

Project 2N — *GO!* with Help

If you have a mobile phone, you can access urgent e-mail messages and other Outlook items. Use Outlook Help to help you redirect items to your mobile phone.

1. **Start** Outlook. In the **Type a question for help** box, type **Can I use my mobile phone with Outlook?**

2. In the **Outlook Help** window, click **Redirect Outlook items to your mobile phone**.

   The Outlook Help window displays a detailed list of various ways to redirect Outlook items.

3. Read the information and click the displayed links. **Close** the Help window, and **Close** the task pane.

End **You have completed Project 2N** ————————

chapterthree

Using the Calendar

OBJECTIVES

At the end of this chapter you will be able to:

1. Navigate the Calendar
2. Schedule Appointments
3. Edit Appointments
4. Work with Events
5. Organize and Customize the Calendar
6. Manage a Calendar

OUTCOMES

Mastering these objectives will enable you to:

PROJECT 3A
Managing Your Work Day

Jefferson Inn

About two-and-a-half hours outside Washington, D.C., the Jefferson Inn is located in Charlottesville, Virginia. The Inn's proximity to Washington, D.C. and Richmond, Virginia, makes it a popular weekend getaway for locals and a convenient base for out-of-town vacationers. The Inn offers 12 rooms, all individually decorated. A fresh country breakfast and afternoon tea are provided each day. Meeting rooms offering the latest high-tech amenities, such as high-speed Internet connections, have made the Inn an increasingly popular location for day-long corporate meetings and events.

Working with the Calendar

The Calendar is Outlook's tool for storing information about your schedule. Many people's workdays consist of a constant flow of meetings, appointments, and events. Each workday can be divided into blocks of time, with different time slots reserved for these activities. For each activity, you can record when, where, why, and with whom the activity occurs.

If your schedule contains many activities, keeping track of everything is a critical task. You may find that your job and your coworkers depend on your being organized and efficient in managing your schedule. Using Outlook's Calendar, you can schedule appointments, events, and meetings. You can use it to quickly and easily see the activities you have scheduled for the day, the week, the month, or longer. Used in conjunction with Outlook's other components, the Calendar can help you stay organized and productive.

In this chapter, you will become familiar with Outlook's Calendar. You will practice scheduling appointments, working with events, and managing your calendar activities.

Project 3A **Travel Plans**

In Activities 3.1 through 3.17, you will create calendar entries related to activities and out-of-town trips for Carmen Jeffries, one of the co-owners of the Jefferson Inn. You will add appointments to the calendar. Some appointments will be recurring, and some will include reminders. You will make changes to scheduled appointments, moving them to different times or different days. You will work with events, scheduling annual events and multiple-day events. You will organize the calendar in different ways, using colors, fonts, and categories to differentiate calendar items. Upon completion, your calendar, for several time periods, will look similar to the ones shown in Figure 3.1.

For Project 3A, you will need the following files:

New blank Appointment form
New blank Event form

You will print two files with the following footers:
3A_Travel_Plans_Week_Firstname_Lastname
3A_Travel_Plans_Breakfast_Firstname_Lastname

Figure 3.1
Project 3A—Travel Plans

Objective 1
Navigate the Calendar

The **Calendar** component of Outlook stores your schedule and calendar-related information. The default location for Outlook's calendar information is the Calendar folder. To add an item to your calendar, display this folder by clicking the Calendar button in the Navigation Pane or by clicking the Calendar folder in the folder list. You can also create other calendar folders as subfolders of the Calendar folder in the folder list.

In Activities 3.1 and 3.2, you will explore the Calendar. You will create your own calendar folder and will use this folder to create a schedule in subsequent activities.

Alert!

Starting Project 3A
Because Outlook stores information on the hard drive of the computer at which you are working, unless you are working on your own computer, it is recommended that you complete Project 3A in one working session. Allow approximately two hours.

Activity 3.1 Exploring the Calendar

In this activity, you will use the Navigation Pane and the Date Navigator to explore the calendar. These are the main tools you will use to manage the calendar activities of Carmen Jeffries, one of the co-owners of the Jefferson Inn.

1 **Start** Outlook. Be sure the **Navigation Pane** displays; if necessary, from the View menu, click Navigation Pane. In the **Navigation Pane**, click the **Calendar** button [Calendar]. On today's date, delete any existing calendar items by clicking the appointment and then clicking the **Delete** button [X]. Compare your screen with Figure 3.2.

The Calendar folder displays. On the right side of the screen is the **appointment area**, which is a one-day view of the current day's calendar entries. An **appointment** is a calendar activity occurring at a specific time and day that does not require inviting other people or reserving a room or equipment. The **banner area** displays important calendar information including Day, Week, and Month view buttons. The **Time Bar** displays one-hour time increments.

The upper pane of the Navigation Pane is the **Date Navigator**, which is a one-month, or multiple-month, view of the calendar that you can use to display specific days in a month. The highlighted date in the Date Navigator and at the top of the appointment area is the selected date that you are viewing, which is, by default, the current date. On each side of the appointment area are two buttons, Previous Appointment and Next Appointment, which allow quick movement to one's previous appointment or next appointment, respectively. On the Standard toolbar, the **Today button** changes the calendar to display the date based on your computer's system clock.

Below the appointment area is a Task pane, a pane that can be used to schedule tasks, or display tasks currently due. Depending on your screen resolution, the Task pane may be maximized or minimized.

Click to move to current
date, your date will differ   View buttons   Banner area

Figure 3. 2

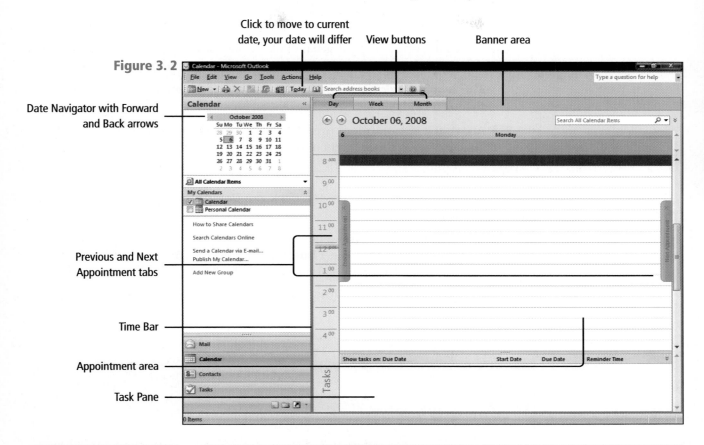

Date Navigator with Forward
and Back arrows

Previous and Next
Appointment tabs

Time Bar

Appointment area

Task Pane

Alert!

Does your screen differ?

The time range for your appointment area may differ from Figure 3.2. Larger computer screens and screens with a higher resolution may display a much larger time span. For example, a high-resolution setting for your computer screen may show 8:00 a.m. to 11:00 p.m. in the appointment area. Your Date Navigator also may display two or three months instead of one. Clicking the arrows to move forward and backward in the Date Navigator displays different months based on what you click.

If you do not see the current date displayed in the format shown in Figure 3.2, from the View menu, point to Current View, and then click Day/Week/Month. Alternatively, click the Day view button above the appointment area.

2 In the **Navigation Pane**, in the **Date Navigator**, click a different day of the month.

The date displayed in the appointment area changes to the day of the month you selected in the Date Navigator. In the Date Navigator, the current date remains outlined in red, and the selected date is highlighted in orange.

3 In the **Date Navigator**, click the **left arrow** next to the month name.

The Date Navigator displays the past month. The appointment area adjusts to the same day in the past month.

4 In the **Date Navigator**, click the **right arrow** several times, moving forward in the calendar two or three months.

The Date Navigator displays future months, and the appointment area adjusts to the same day in the future month.

5 Above the appointment area, click the **Week** button Week . Notice this view has two options: *Show work week* and *Show full week*.

The **work week view** option shows only the weekdays, Monday through Friday.

6 Above the appointment area, click the **Month** button Month . This view provides three levels of detail: *Low*, *Medium*, and *High*.

7 On the Standard toolbar, click the **Today** button Today to return to the current day. If necessary, click the **Day** button Day to return to Day view.

8 In the appointment area, click a different time in the calendar grid, and then notice that the **Time Bar** displays an orange bar across the current time. Compare your screen with Figure 3.3.

Use the scroll bar to adjust the times displayed in the appointment area.

Figure 3.3

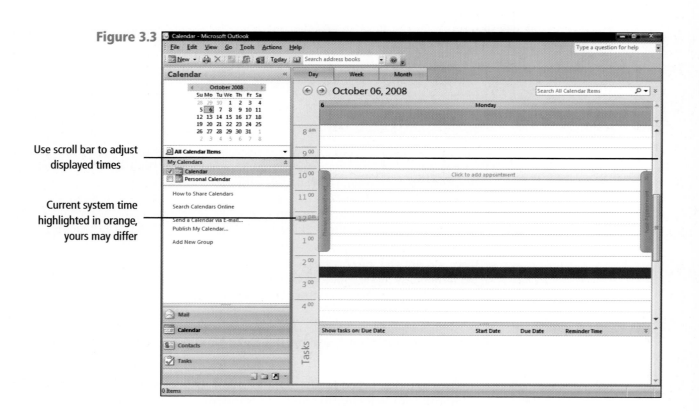

Use scroll bar to adjust displayed times

Current system time highlighted in orange, yours may differ

9 In the appointment area, drag the **scroll box** up and down to display different times of day.

Outlook displays the normal workday hours by default, but you can schedule and view appointments in any time period.

Activity 3.2 Creating a Personal Calendar Folder

You can create subfolders within the Calendar folder for separate calendar activities, for example, a folder for personal calendar items and a folder for work-related calendar items. Creating a personal calendar can be especially useful in organizations where business calendars are shared, and you want to keep your personal activities private. In this activity, you will create a separate subfolder for personal calendar items and name the subfolder *Personal Calendar*. You will use this for personal calendar items you create for Carmen Jefferies.

1 In the lower right area of the **Navigation Pane**, click the **Folder List** button ☐ to display the folder list in the middle portion of the **Navigation Pane**. From the **File** menu, point to **New**, and then click **Folder**. Alternatively, from the File menu, click Folder, and then click New Folder.

2 In the displayed **Create New Folder** dialog box, in the **Name** box, type **Personal Calendar** and then compare your screen with Figure 3.4.

The *Folder contains* box shows that this folder will contain Calendar Items. Outlook applies this setting because you are creating this as a subfolder in the Calendar folder.

New folder contains   Create New Folder
Calendar items   dialog box

Figure 3. 4

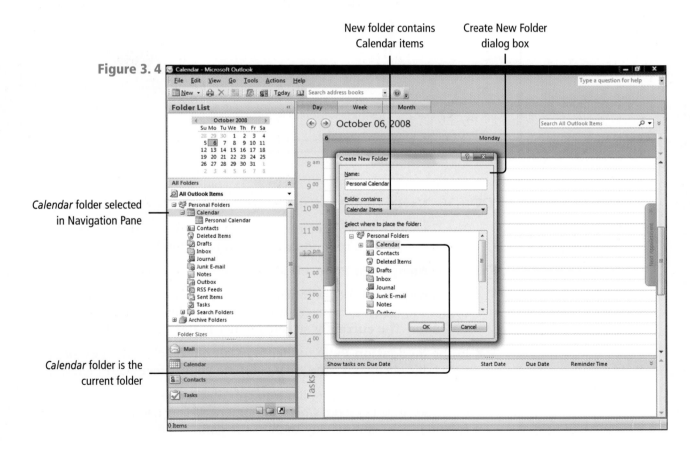

Calendar folder selected in Navigation Pane

Calendar folder is the current folder

3 In the **Create New Folder** dialog box, click **OK**.

Outlook creates a folder named *Personal Calendar*. The collapse (–) button next to the Calendar folder indicates that the new folder is a subfolder of the Calendar folder.

4 In the **Navigation Pane**, under **All Folders**, click **Personal Calendar**, and then, if necessary, click the **Day** button [Day] to return to Day view. Compare your screen with Figure 3.5.

The Personal Calendar becomes the current folder. Outlook changes the default color scheme for the appointment area to green to distinguish it from the Calendar folder.

Figure 3.5

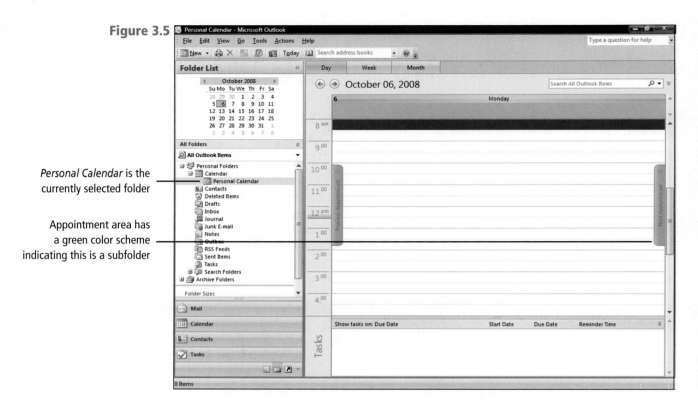

Personal Calendar is the currently selected folder

Appointment area has a green color scheme indicating this is a subfolder

5 In the **Navigation Pane**, under **All Folders**, click **Calendar**.

The Calendar folder becomes the current folder, and the color of the appointment area reminds you that this is the default calendar.

6 In the **Navigation Pane**, click the **Calendar** button [Calendar].

The Navigation Pane switches to a two-pane view above the buttons. Under *My Calendars* two entries display: *Calendar* and *Personal Calendar*. The currently selected folder is the *Calendar* folder.

7 In the **Navigation Pane**, under **My Calendars**, click the **Personal Calendar** check box, and then compare your screen with Figure 3.6.

The appointment area splits into two sections, showing both the *Calendar* and *Personal Calendar* folders. If you use more than one calendar, you can display both at the same time.

Figure 3.6

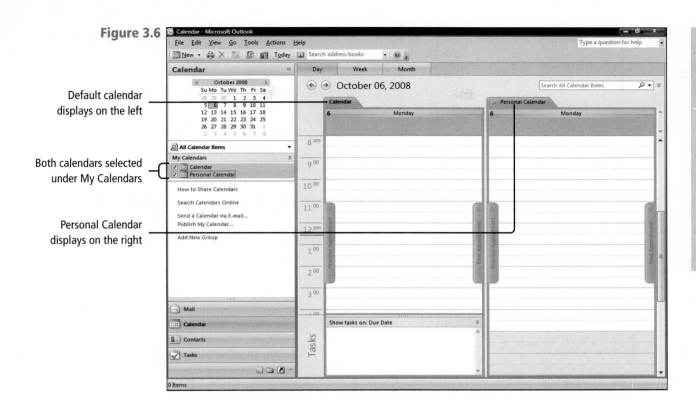

Default calendar displays on the left

Both calendars selected under My Calendars

Personal Calendar displays on the right

8 In the **Navigation Pane**, clear the **Calendar** check box to display only the Personal Calendar.

Objective 2
Schedule Appointments

Recall that an appointment occurs at a specific time and day and does not require inviting other people or reserving a room or equipment. For example, meeting with a coworker or supervisor could be considered an appointment. Some appointments are ***recurring appointments***, meaning that they occur regularly on specific dates and times and at specific intervals and have associated reminders, such as a weekly staff meeting. Outlook uses the term ***meeting*** to refer to a calendar activity that requires inviting other people, reserving a room, or ordering equipment. As you progress in your study of Outlook, you will practice scheduling meetings.

In Activities 3.3 through 3.6, you will practice scheduling appointments in the Personal Calendar folder. You will enter appointments directly into the appointment area and into the Appointment form. You will also create a recurring appointment and an appointment with a reminder.

Activity 3.3 Adding Appointments in the Appointment Area

You can create a new appointment directly in the calendar by typing it in a blank time slot in the appointment area. In this activity, you will schedule some appointments in the Personal Calendar for Jefferson Inn co-owner, Carmen Jeffries.

1 In the **Date Navigator**, click the **right arrow** one time, advancing the calendar to the next month. Click the **Monday** of the first full week of the displayed month.

The selected date displays at the top of the appointment area.

2 In the appointment area, click the **11:00 am** time slot, type **Weekly meeting with Bradley** and notice that as you type, the time slot displays green shading surrounded by a black border. Compare your screen with Figure 3.7.

Figure 3.7

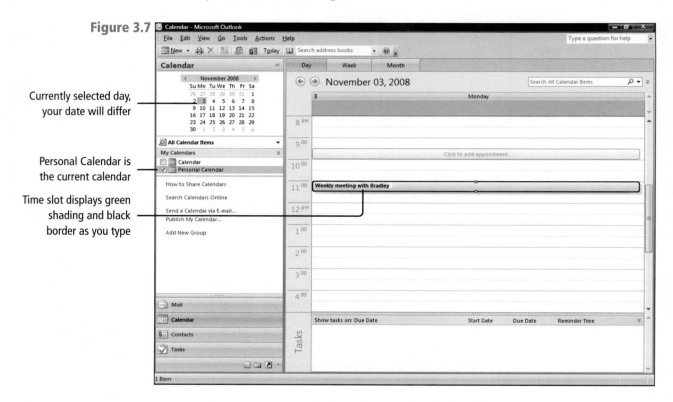

Currently selected day, your date will differ

Personal Calendar is the current calendar

Time slot displays green shading and black border as you type

3 Click any other time slot in the appointment area.

The appointment is scheduled from 11:00 to 11:30. When you use this method to enter an appointment, Outlook automatically makes it a 30-minute appointment.

4 In the appointment area, click the **12:30 pm** time slot—that is, the lower half of the 12:00 pm time slot—to enter an appointment on the half hour.

5 Type **Lunch with Marty** Click any other time slot in the appointment area, and then compare your screen with Figure 3.8.

The appointment is scheduled from 12:30 to 1:00. Notice that the day number of a date in the Date Navigator changes to bold when an appointment is scheduled on that day.

Figure 3.8

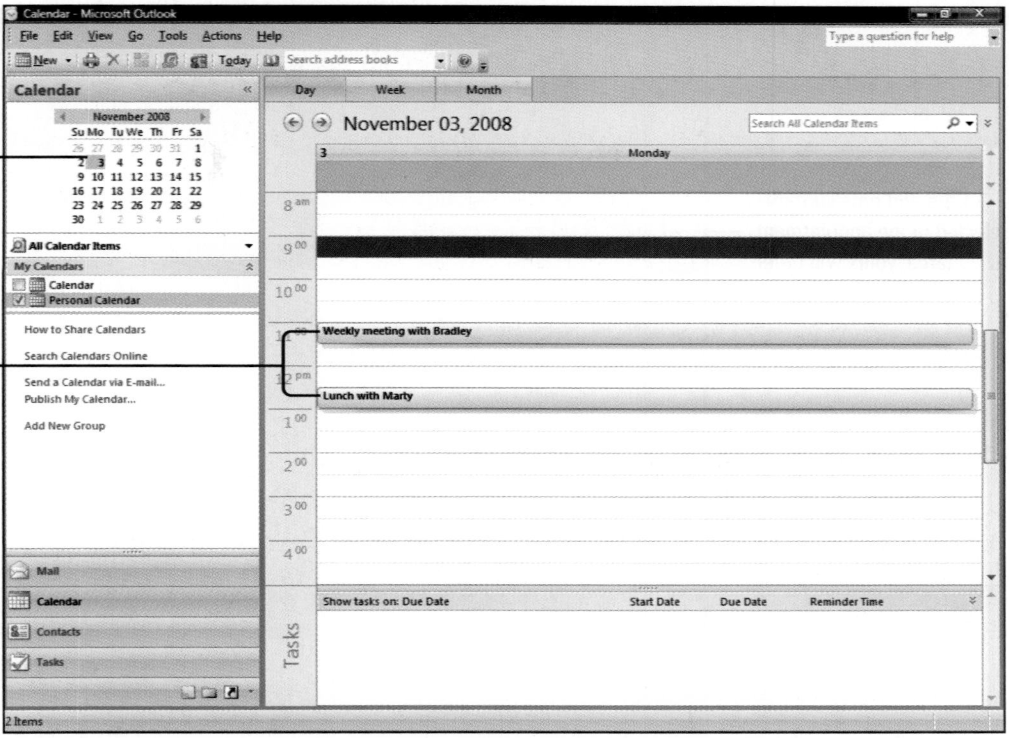

Bold number in Date Navigator indicates an appointment scheduled that day

Two appointments scheduled

Activity 3.4 Adding Appointments by Using the Appointment Form

In addition to typing directly into the appointment area, you can also use an Appointment form to create new appointments. By using an Appointment form, you can enter more detailed information about an appointment. In this activity, you will schedule appointments for Carmen Jeffries using the Appointment form.

1 On the Standard toolbar, click the **New Appointment** button ▦ **New** ▾, and then compare your screen with Figure 3.9.

The Untitled - Appointment form displays. You can store a variety of information about an appointment, including its subject, location, starting time, and ending time. Notice that the starting and ending times for the new appointment default to the time you clicked in the appointment area. A *comments area* in the lower half of the form enables you to enter information about the appointment not otherwise specified in the form.

Figure 3.9

Date and time currently
selected in the appointment
area; yours will differ

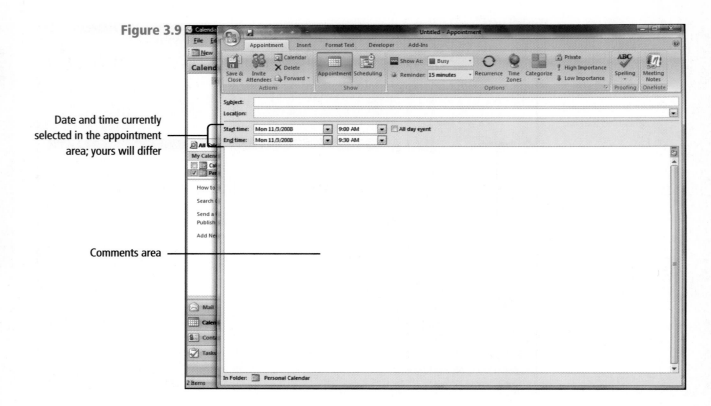

Comments area

2 As the **Subject** of the appointment, type **Meet with Dominique** In the **Location** box, type **My office**

3 In the right **Start time** box, click the **time arrow**, and then locate and click **9:00 AM**. In the right **End time** box, click the **time arrow**, and then locate and click **10:00 AM (1 hour)**.

4 On the Ribbon, in the **Action group**, click the **Save & Close** button , and then compare your screen with Figure 3.10.

The new appointment is added to the calendar. The appointment occupies the 9:00 to 10:00 am time slot, and the location of the appointment displays below the subject.

Figure 3.10

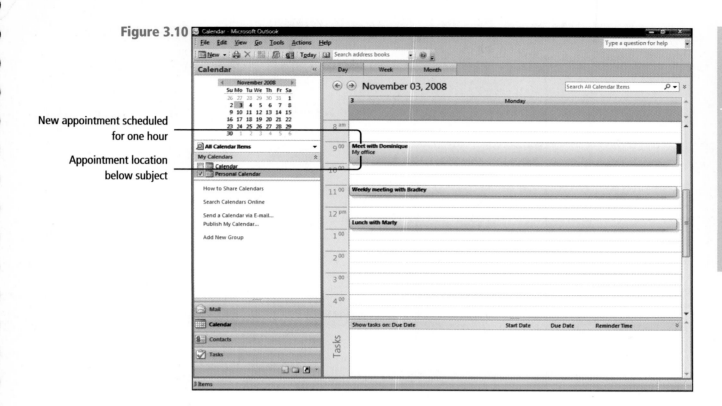

New appointment scheduled for one hour

Appointment location below subject

5 From the **File** menu, point to **New**, and then click **Appointment**. Alternatively, press Ctrl + N or click the **New Appointment** button 🗓 **New** ▾.

A blank Appointment form displays. As you have done in other Outlook components, in the Calendar component it is often possible to start a command from a menu, from a toolbar button, or by using a keyboard shortcut.

6 In the **Appointment** form, in the **Subject** box, type **Chamber of Commerce Orientation** In the **Location** box, type **Wellesley Hotel** Set the **Start time** to **3:00 PM** and **End time** to **5:00 PM (2 hours)**.

7 Save & Close 💾 the appointment, and then compare your screen with Figure 3.11.

Figure 3.11

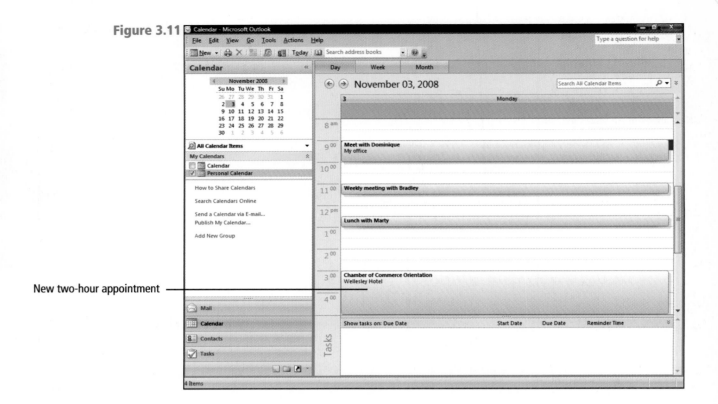

New two-hour appointment

Activity 3.5 Scheduling Recurring Appointments

Appointments, events, and meetings may be recurring, which means that these items occur repeatedly over time. Examples of recurring appointments might be weekly staff meetings or monthly haircuts. When you create a recurring appointment, Outlook automatically places the appointment in the calendar every day it is set to recur. In this activity, you will create a recurring appointment for Carmen Jeffries.

1 In the **Date Navigator**, click the **Tuesday** of the same week in which you are working, and then click the **New Appointment** button ▦ **New** ▾ to display a blank Appointment form. Alternatively, double-click a blank time slot in the appointment area.

2 As the **Subject**, type **Travel & Lodging Technology Seminar** and as the **Location**, type **Richmond** Set the **Start time** for **9:00 AM** and the **End time** for **12:00 PM (3 hours)**.

3 On the Ribbon, in the **Options group**, click the **Recurrence** button ↻ Recurrence, and then compare your screen with Figure 3.12.

The Appointment Recurrence dialog box displays. You can set the *recurrence pattern*—the frequency—of an appointment, which may be daily, weekly, monthly, or yearly. You can also set the *range of recurrence*, which is the date of the final occurrence of the appointment based on its end date or the number of times an appointment occurs.

Another Way

To Create a New, Recurring Appointment

There are several ways to create a new, recurring appointment in the calendar. On the Standard toolbar, you can display the Actions menu, and then click New Recurring Appointment. Outlook opens a blank Appointment form and then displays the Appointment Recurrence dialog box. You can also right-click any blank time slot in the appointment area and, from the displayed shortcut menu, click New Recurring Appointment.

Figure 3.12

Appointment Recurrence dialog box

Recurrence pattern sets the frequency of the appointment

Range of recurrence sets the end of the recurring appointments

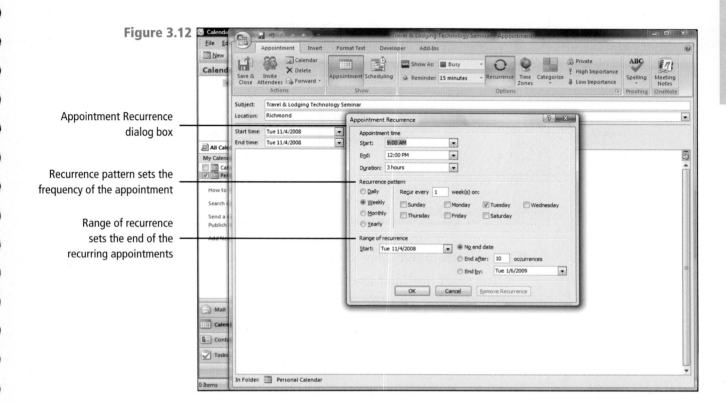

4 In the **Appointment Recurrence** dialog box, under **Recurrence pattern**, select **Weekly**, and then next to **Recur every**, type **2** and select the **Tuesday** check box if it is not already selected. Under **Range of recurrence**, select **End after** and type **3** in the **occurrences** box. Compare your screen with Figure 3.13.

The recurrence is set for every two weeks, for three occurrences.

Figure 3.13

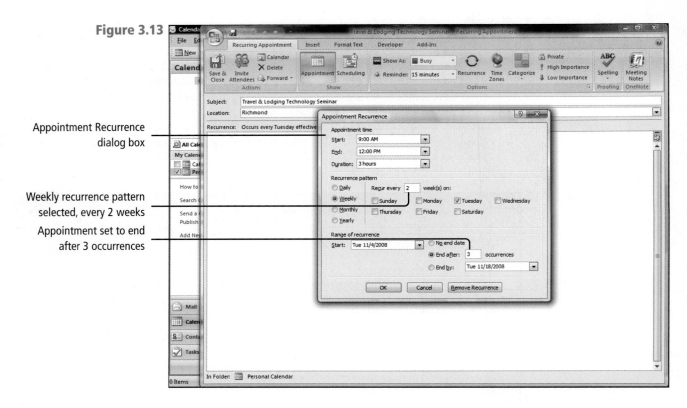

Appointment Recurrence
dialog box

Weekly recurrence pattern
selected, every 2 weeks

Appointment set to end
after 3 occurrences

5 Click **OK** to redisplay the Appointment form.

The Start time and End time boxes have been replaced by Recurrence information. The appointment is set to repeat every *two* weeks.

6 **Save & Close** the appointment, and then compare your screen with Figure 3.14.

The new appointment is added to the calendar. The recurrence icon in the lower right corner of the appointment in the calendar indicates that this is a recurring appointment. The Date Navigator for the day displays in bold, indicating that this date has an appointment scheduled. The days on which the appointment repeats also display in bold.

Figure 3.14

Dates display in bold,
indicating appointments
are scheduled on these dates

Second occurrence of recurring
appointment indicated

Icon indicates that this is a
recurring appointment

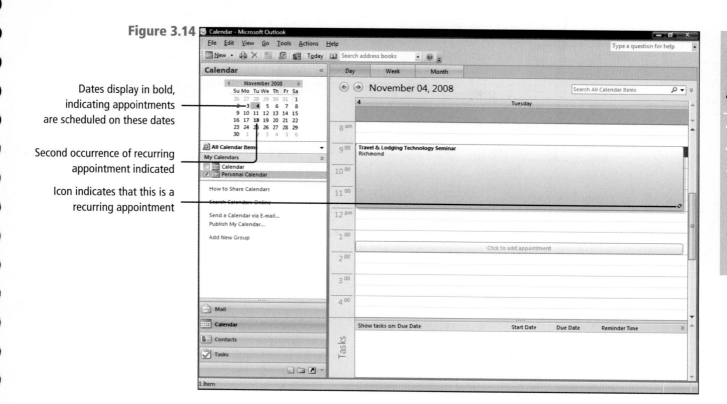

More Knowledge

Removing or Changing Appointment Recurrence

If you need to change or remove an appointment's recurrence information, open the appointment by double-clicking one of its occurrences in the appointment area, and then select *Open the series*. In the Appointment form, click the Recurrence button to display the Appointment Recurrence dialog box. Change the recurrence pattern or the range of recurrence. Use Remove Recurrence to remove all the recurrence information.

Activity 3.6 Using Reminders

Just as you can have Outlook remind you of a task, you can have Outlook remind you of appointments and events that you do not want to forget. Recall that a **reminder** is an Outlook window, accompanied by a tone, that displays automatically at a designated date and time before appointments or tasks. Calendar reminders are identical to task reminders. All appointments you have created in this project have been set to Outlook's default reminder time of 15 minutes. In this activity, you will modify a reminder for one of Carmen Jeffries' appointments.

1 In the **Date Navigator**, click the **Wednesday** of the same week in which you are working and then click the **10:00 am** time slot.

2 Using the techniques you have practiced, open a blank **Appointment** form, and create a new appointment with the **Subject Dentist**

3 The Start time is already correct, because Outlook uses the time slot selected in the appointment area as the **Start time**. Set the **End time** as **11:00 AM (1 hour)**.

4 On the Ribbon, in the **Options group**, click the **Reminder arrow**, and then click **30 minutes**. Compare your screen with Figure 3.15.

Figure 3.15

Reminder time ────
Subject ────

End time ────

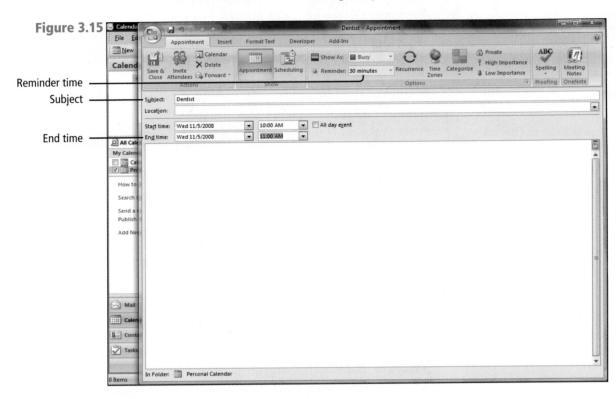

5 Click **Save & Close** . Compare your screen with Figure 3.16.

The new appointment is added to the calendar.

Figure 3.16

New appointment in
Personal Calendar ────

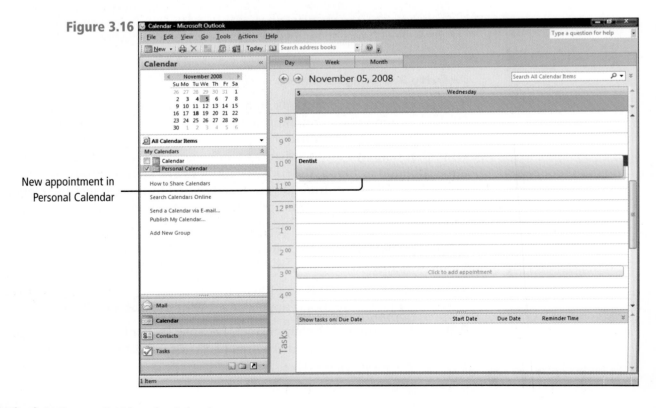

More Knowledge

Default Reminder Setting

When you are working in the Calendar folder, the Reminder box is automatically set to 15 minutes for all new appointments, including appointments you type directly in the appointment area. You can change this default setting. From the Tools menu, click Options. On the Preferences tab, in the Calendar group, clear the Default reminder check box so that reminders are not automatically created. You can also modify the default time with the Reminder check box selected.

Objective 3
Edit Appointments

After you schedule an appointment, you may need to change the time, location, or other details. You can edit appointments similarly to any other Outlook item. One way to change an appointment's date or time is by dragging it to a new location. You can also open calendar items and edit them directly in the Appointment form.

In Activities 3.7 through 3.9, you will modify existing appointments using various methods.

Activity 3.7 Editing an Appointment in the Appointment Area

In this activity, you will change some of the appointments in Carmen Jeffries' calendar.

1 In the **Date Navigator**, click the **Monday** of the same week in which you are working. Click the **2:00 pm** time slot. On the right side of the appointment area, click the **down scroll arrow** until the **Meet with Dominique** appointment moves out of the viewing area, as shown in Figure 3.17.

Depending on the size of your screen and the screen resolution, some appointments may not appear in your viewing area. If that is the case, at the top right of the appointment area, a small gray arrow displays above 10:00 am in the appointment area, indicating that an appointment is scheduled that does not appear in the viewing area. When you point to the arrow it changes to yellow and a ScreenTip appears: *Click for more appointments*. A similar arrow will display at the bottom of the appointment area when later appointments are not visible in the viewing area.

Figure 3.17

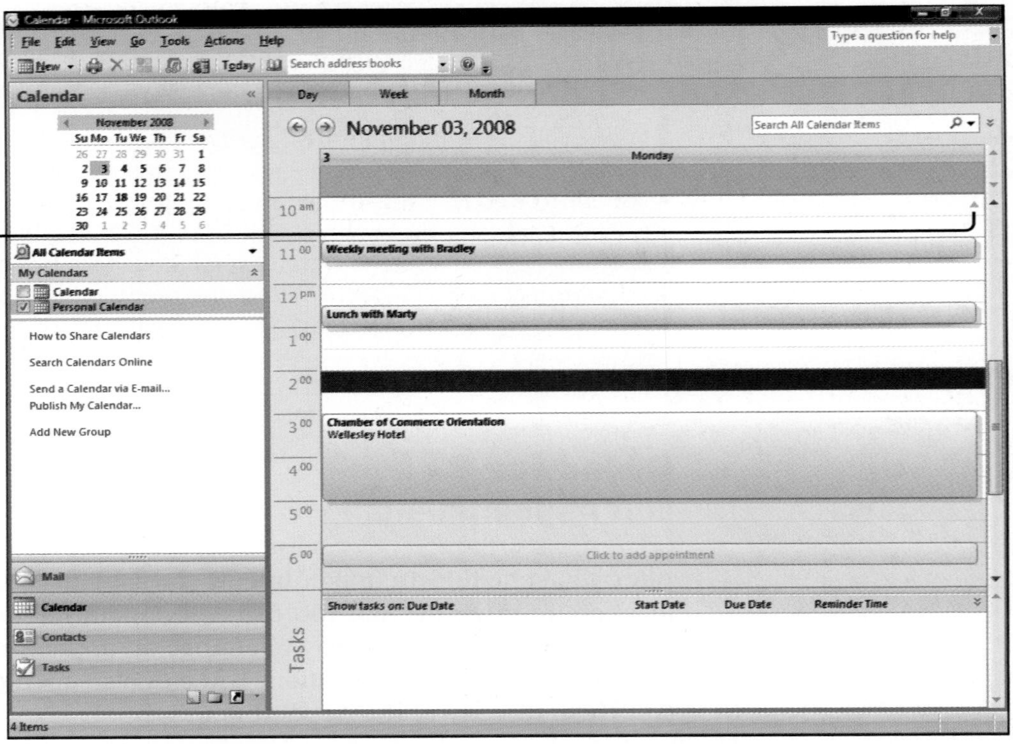

Arrow indicates earlier
appointments are out of view

2 Click the **up scroll arrow** until the **Chamber of Commerce Orientation** appointment moves out of the viewing area, if possible.

Depending on the size and resolution of your screen, at the bottom right of the appointment area, the gray arrow displays in a similar manner to indicate that some appointments are out of view.

3 Click the **down scroll arrow** until your viewing area contains the appointment times from 8:00 am until 5:00 pm. In the appointment area, click the **Lunch with Marty** appointment to select it.

The appointment is outlined by a **_black border_**, which is the indication that an appointment is selected.

4 Point to the top border until the vertical resize pointer [⇕] displays, and then compare your screen with Figure 3.18.

You can increase or decrease the specified time of an appointment by dragging the upper and lower borders.

Figure 3.18

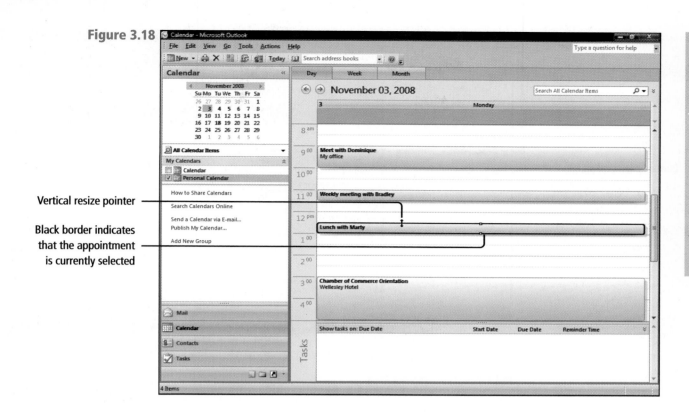

Vertical resize pointer

Black border indicates
that the appointment
is currently selected

5 With the vertical resize pointer displayed, drag the upper border of the selected appointment up to **12:00 pm**, and then release the mouse button.

The appointment is now scheduled to last from 12:00 to 1:00 pm.

6 Click at the beginning of the text in the **Meet with Dominique** appointment one time to select it. To edit this appointment, click at the same place again.

The blinking insertion point indicates that the subject can be edited. Although the location displays it cannot be modified. You can change the location of an appointment only when editing it in the Appointment form.

7 Press Delete until all the existing text of the subject is deleted, and then type **Dominique's performance review** Press Enter, or click a blank time slot in the appointment area to end the editing of the appointment.

Activity 3.8 Moving Appointments

In this activity, you will move some of Carmen Jeffries' appointments to different dates and times.

1 In the **Monday** of the same week in which you are working, click the **Weekly meeting with Bradley** appointment to select it.

2 Point to the selected appointment. Drag the appointment until the Move pointer ⊕ displays with the appointment attached, as shown in Figure 3.19.

You can drag an appointment to a new day or time.

Figure 3.19

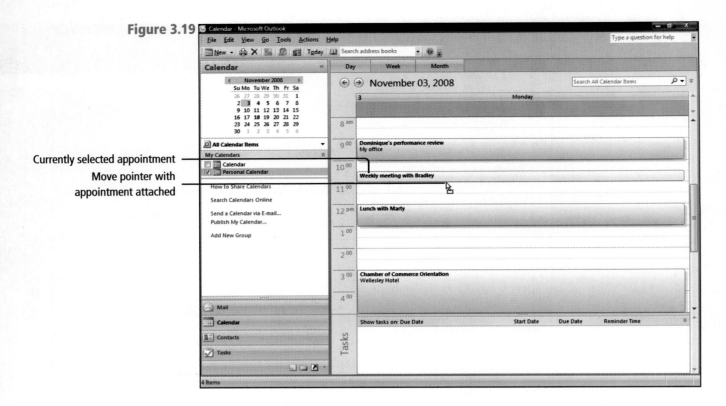

Currently selected appointment
Move pointer with
appointment attached

3 Drag the appointment to the **2:00 pm** time slot, and then release the mouse button.

The *Weekly meeting with Bradley* appointment is scheduled for 2:00 to 2:30 pm.

4 Click the **Weekly meeting with Bradley** appointment again. Drag the selected appointment to the **Date Navigator**, and position the insertion point over the **Wednesday** of the same week in which you are working. Release the mouse button.

The calendar displays Wednesday of that week, with the *Weekly meeting with Bradley* appointment scheduled for 2:00 to 2:30 pm of that day. When you move an appointment to a different day, Outlook uses the same time slot of the new day. If the time slot is already occupied by another appointment, Outlook displays the two appointments side by side in the calendar.

5 In the **Date Navigator**, click the **Monday** of the same week in which you are working, and then click the **Chamber of Commerce Orientation** appointment.

Notice that the insertion point is not blinking. Recall that clicking an appointment one time selects it without making it available for editing.

6 From the **Edit** menu, click **Cut**.

Outlook copies the information to the *Office Clipboard*, a memory area in which you can collect text and graphics from any Office program and then place them in another area of the same program or in a different program. Outlook leaves the cut item in the original location until you paste it in the new location.

7 In the **Date Navigator**, if only one month displays, click the **right arrow** beside the month name, advancing the calendar one month ahead of the month in which you are working. Click the first **Monday** in that month, and then compare your screen with Figure 3.20.

The time slot for the new date is already selected, matching the appointment's original time slot.

Click right arrow to advance
Date Navigator to the next month

Figure 3.20

First Monday in the
next month is selected,
your date will differ

Time slot of new date
matches appoinment's
original time slot

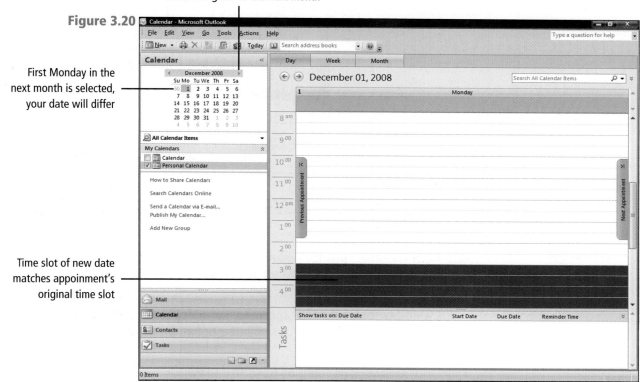

8 From the **Edit** menu, click **Paste**.

The *Chamber of Commerce Orientation* appointment is moved to the new date. In this manner, you can move appointments to different calendars.

9 Click the **Chamber of Commerce Orientation** appointment you just moved, display the **Edit** menu, and then click **Cut** again.

10 In the **Navigation Pane**, under **My Calendars**, click the **Calendar** check box to display both the **Personal Calendar** and **Calendar** folders.

The appointment area splits into two sections, showing both the Calendar and Personal Calendar folders.

11 In the **Date Navigator**, if only one month displays (some large screens will display two or three complete months in the Date Navigator), click the **left arrow** to display the previous month. Using the bold day numbers to locate the week in which you have been working, click the **Monday** of that week. In the **Calendar** folder (the default calendar), click the **2:00 pm** time slot. Compare your screen with Figure 3.21.

Figure 3.21

Click left arrow to display a previous month

Bold dates indicate the week in which you have been working

Selected check boxes display both calendar folders

Time slot selected is 2:00 pm in the Calendar folder

Next and Previous Assignment tabs may not display

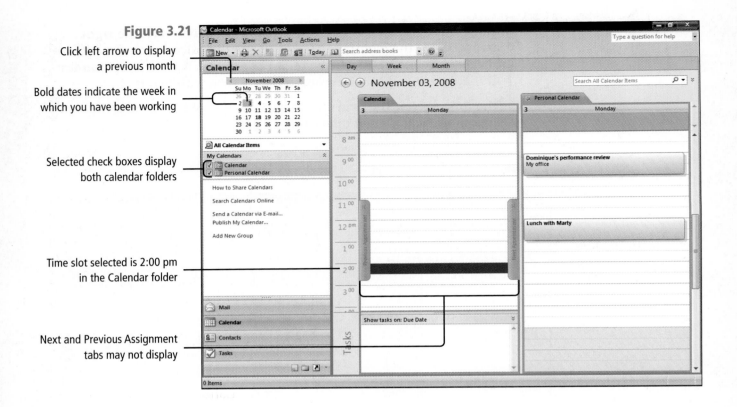

12 With the **2:00 pm** time slot selected in the **Calendar** folder, display the **Edit** menu, and then click **Paste**.

The *Chamber of Commerce Orientation* appointment is pasted to the Calendar folder. In this manner, you can cut and paste items within a specific calendar folder and also between two different calendar folders.

13 On the Standard toolbar, from the **View** menu, click **View in Overlay Mode**.

The *Calendar* displays on top of the *Personal Calendar*, with all appointments visible. You can use **overlay mode** to display multiple calendars in an overlapping view. Using this mode quickly allows you to see any conflicts and free time.

14 To return to the default view, from the **View** menu, click **View in Side-By-Side Mode**.

15 Click the **Chamber of Commerce Orientation** appointment to select it. Press and hold your right mouse button down and drag the appointment from the **Calendar** folder to the same day and time in the **Personal Calendar** folder. Release the mouse button, and from the shortcut menu click **Move**.

Notice that after the drag operation is complete, the appointment is removed from its *Calendar* location and appears in the *Personal Calendar* folder in the 2:00 pm time slot.

16 In the **Navigation Pane**, under **My Calendars**, clear the **Calendar** check box to display only the **Personal Calendar** folder.

More Knowledge

Moving Recurring Appointments

When you move recurring appointments, only the selected appointment is moved. The item will still show a recurrence icon next to it, but the icon will have a line drawn through it, which indicates that it is a recurring appointment that has been moved. If you want to change all instances of a recurring appointment's date or time, you must open the Appointment Recurrence dialog box for the appointment. You can change all the appointments in the series from that dialog box.

Activity 3.9 Opening an Appointment

You can edit an existing appointment by opening it and changing the information in the Appointment form. In this activity, you will open several of Carmen Jeffries' appointments and make changes.

1 In the **Date Navigator**, click the **Wednesday** of the same week in which you have been working (next week). Point to the **Dentist** appointment and right-click. Then, from the displayed shortcut menu, click **Open**.

2 Change the **Start time** to **9:00 AM**, and notice that the **End time** automatically changes to **10:00 AM**.

3 On the Ribbon, in the **Options group**, click the **Reminder arrow** and select **None**.

4 In the comments area of the **Appointment** form, type **Remember to get directions to the new office location** and then compare your screen with Figure 3.22.

Use the comments area of the form for any details about an appointment you want to include.

Figure 3.22

Reminder time set to None ——

Location arrow ——

Comments area ——

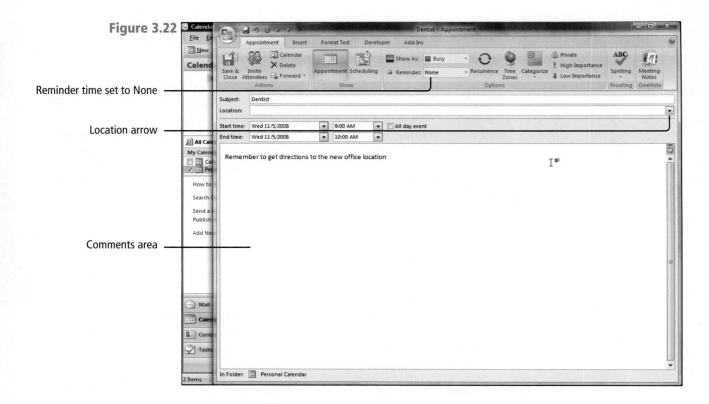

5 **Save & Close** the appointment. Double-click the **Weekly meeting with Bradley** appointment to open the Appointment form. Alternatively, right-click, and from the shortcut menu, click **Open**. In the **Appointment** form, change the **End time** to **3:00 PM (1 hour)**, and notice that the **Start time** did not change.

6 Click the **Location arrow**, and click **My office**.

Outlook remembers locations you type in the Locations box after you have entered them once. Instead of typing a previously used location, you can click the Location box arrow to display the list of past locations, and then select the one you need.

7 In the comments area of the **Appointment** form, type **Print out next month's conference schedule for his review Save & Close** the appointment.

More Knowledge
Opening Multiple Appointments at Once

You can open more than one appointment at a time. Select the first appointment, press Ctrl, and then select the additional appointments you want to open. After selecting all the appointments, right-click any selected appointment. From the displayed shortcut menu, click Open Items. An Appointment form for each selected appointment displays. You can then make changes to each appointment. For example, you might do this if you wanted to remove the Reminder for all the selected appointments.

Objective 4
Work with Events

Outlook defines any calendar activity that lasts 24 hours or longer as an *event*. Rather than displaying as blocks of time in your calendar, events are indicated by a banner across the top appointment area on days in which they occur. For example, attending a conference for one or more days is indicated as an event in Outlook.

In Activities 3.10 and 3.11, you will create a multiday event and an annual event.

Activity 3.10 Scheduling Events

In this activity, you will schedule some events for Carmen Jeffries.

1 From the **Actions** menu, click **New All Day Event**.

The Untitled - Event form displays. The only difference in the Event form and the Appointment form is the time-of-day boxes for the start and end times of an event are grayed out. Although you can change the times, events normally are scheduled for an entire 24-hour day, or over several days where start and end times may vary.

2 As the **Subject**, type **Southeast Lodging Association Conference** and in the **Location** box, type **Atlanta** Click the **Start time arrow**, and then click the **Thursday** of the same week in which you have been working. Click the **End time arrow**, and then click the **Friday** of the

same week. **Save & Close** the event.

The event is scheduled for two days.

3 In the **Date Navigator**, click the **Friday** of the week in which you have been working, and then compare your screen with Figure 3.23.

The banner across the top of the calendar displays the event information. Notice in the Date Navigator that the two days of the event are not shown in bold. Outlook still considers these days as free because no specific time slots are occupied.

Figure 3.23

Event dates do not display in bold ——

Event banner ——

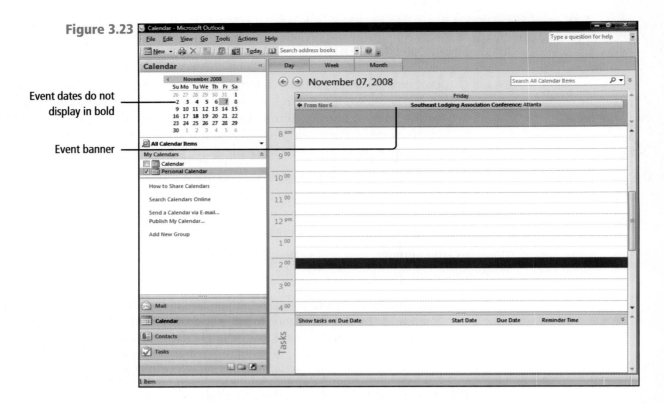

4 With **Friday** still displayed in the calendar, create a new appointment using the techniques you have practiced. For the **Subject**, type **Breakfast at the conference with John McCarthy & Sonia Friedman** In the Location box, type **TBA** The **Start time** is **8:30 AM**, and the **End time** is **9:30 AM**.

TBA is a common abbreviation for To Be Arranged or To Be Announced.

5 In the comments area of the **Appointment** form, type **Call Sonia and John at hotel to arrange location Save & Close** the appointment.

The calendar redisplays. You can see that you can schedule appointments at the same time as events.

6 Double-click the event banner to display the event form. In the comments area of the **Event** form, type **Breakfast with John McCarthy and Sonia Friedman on Friday morning Save & Close** the event.

More Knowledge

Converting Appointments and Events

You can change appointments into events and events into appointments. On both the Appointment form and the Event form, you can select or clear the All day event check box to convert the activity. The start times are added to an event to make it an appointment, the banner is then removed, and the activity displays in the specified time slot. When you convert an appointment to an event, the times are removed and only the dates remain; a banner displays in the calendar.

Activity 3.11 Scheduling an Annual Event

An *annual event* is a recurring event that happens once each year. Birthdays, anniversaries, or holidays are typical annual events.

1 In the **Date Navigator**, click the **Tuesday** in the same week in which you have been working. From the **Actions** menu, click **New All Day Event**. In the **Subject** box, type **Elaine's birthday** On the Ribbon, in

the **Options group**, click the **Recurrence** button .

2 In the displayed **Appointment Recurrence** dialog box, under **Recurrence pattern**, click **Yearly**. Compare your screen with Figure 3.24.

The default setting for the Range of recurrence is for the event to start on the currently selected day in the Date Navigator, and to never end—*No end date* is selected.

Figure 3.24

Range of recurrence set to *No end date*

Yearly selected

Your dates will differ

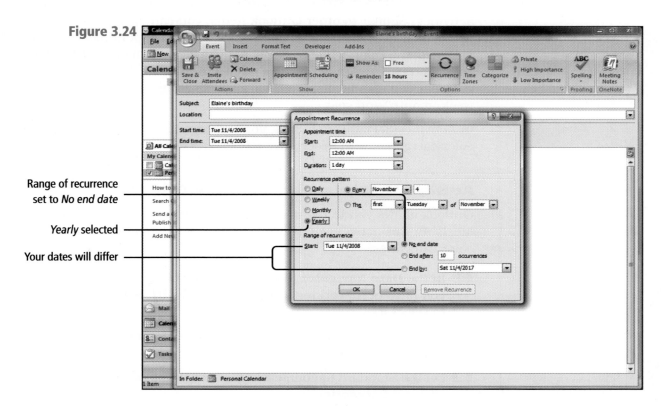

3 Click **OK**, and then **Save & Close** the event.

A banner for the birthday displays in the calendar. A recurrence icon indicates that it is a recurring event. The event is set to display on this date with no end date.

More Knowledge

Displaying Holidays

Outlook 2007 provides holiday information during calendar years 2006 through 2012. To display holidays in the calendar, from the Tools menu, click Options, and then click Calendar Options. Under Calendar options, click Add Holidays. Select the check box next to each country/region whose holidays you want to add to your calendar, and then click OK. By default, your own country/region is automatically selected.

Objective 5
Organize and Customize the Calendar

Outlook provides a variety of useful ways to organize your calendar activities. Similar to other Outlook items, you can assign color categories to calendar activities. For example, must-attend appointments can be assigned one color, while personal activities can be assigned another color. You can assign descriptive names to color categories. Your calendar can also be displayed for a specific time period, such as day, week, month, and year.

In Activities 3.12 through 3.14, you will organize your calendar using color categories with descriptive names and different views.

Activity 3.12 Assigning Descriptive Names to Categories

Outlook allows you to rename color categories with more descriptive labels. In this activity you will assign descriptive names to particular color categories.

1 In the **Date Navigator**, click on **Monday** of the same week in which you have been working. Click the **Lunch with Marty** appointment to select it.

When working in Calendar view, an appointment or event must be selected in order to rename categories.

2 On the Standard toolbar, click the **Categorize** button 🔲, and then click **All Categories**.

The *Color Categories* dialog box displays. Recall, you can use this option when you want to rename an existing category or create a new one.

3 In the **Color Categories** dialog box, select **Blue Category**, and then click the **Rename** button.

4 In the box with **Blue Category** selected, type **Travel Required**. Press [Enter].

5 Using the technique you just practiced, rename **Green Category** as **Personal**, **Red Category** as **Important**, **Orange Category** as **Status**, and **Yellow Category** as **Time & Expenses**. Compare your screen with Figure 3.25.

Figure 3.25

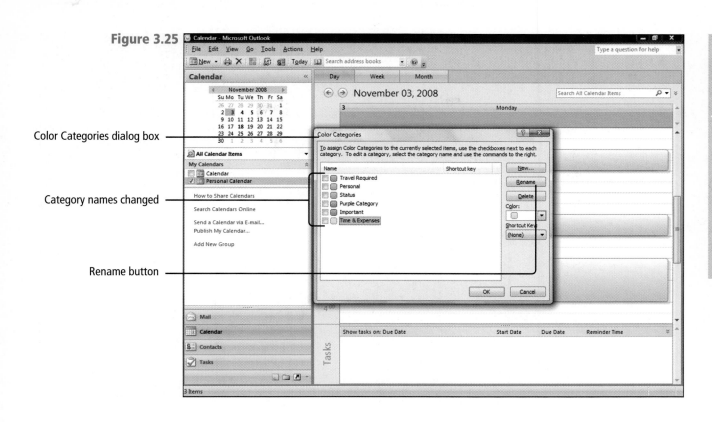

Color Categories dialog box

Category names changed

Rename button

6 Click **OK** to close the **Color Categories** dialog box.

More Knowledge

Adding Descriptive Names without Color

You can create new categories that do not use color. In the Color Categories dialog box, click the New button. In the Add New Category dialog box, in the Name box, type a descriptive name. Click the Color box arrow and click None. Click OK two times to close the dialog boxes.

Activity 3.13 Assigning Appointments to Categories

Calendar entries can be assigned to categories in the Appointment or Event forms or by using the shortcut menu. Carmen Jeffries organizes her calendar items using categories. In the following activity, you will assign categories to activities in her calendar.

1 Open the **Lunch with Marty** appointment. On the Ribbon, in the **Options group**, click **Categorize** and then click **Personal**. Compare your screen with Figure 3.26.

The appointment is assigned to the Personal category.

Figure 3.26

Personal category assigned ———

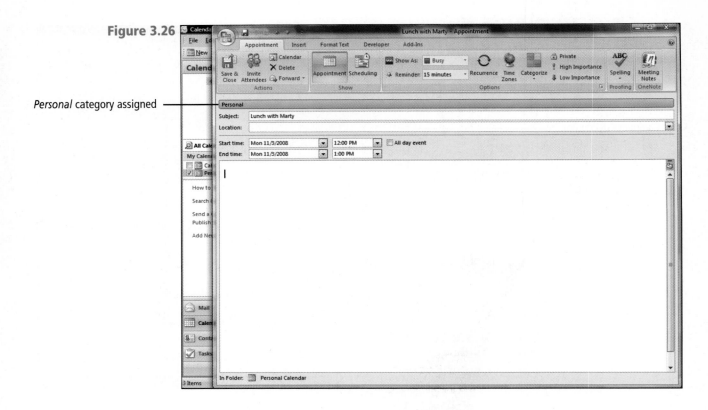

---

2 **Save & Close** the appointment.

3 Right-click the **Chamber of Commerce Orientation** appointment, point to **Categorize**, and then click **Time & Expenses** to assign this category. Compare your screen with Figure 3.27.

Figure 3.27

Personal category assigned ———

Time & Expenses category assigned ———

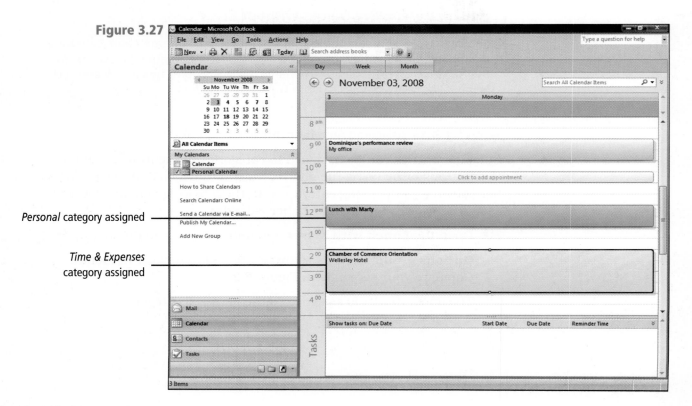

Carmen Jeffries assigns the Time & Expenses category to all her appointments in which she will be incurring business expenses such as travel and meals. She finds that this helps her keep track of expenses for her monthly expense reports. In Day view, the calendar displays the appointment with the color of the assigned category.

4 In the **Date Navigator**, click the **Tuesday** of the same week in which you have been working. Assign the **Travel & Lodging Technology Seminar** appointment to the **Time & Expenses** category.

5 In the **Date Navigator**, click the **Wednesday** of the same week in which you have been working. Assign the **Dentist** appointment to the **Personal** category. Assign the **Weekly meeting with Bradley** to the **Status** category.

6 In the **Date Navigator**, click the **Friday** of the same week in which you have been working. Click the **Southeast Lodging Association Conference** banner one time to select it. Hold down Ctrl and click the **Breakfast at the conference with John McCarthy and Sonia Friedman** appointment.

This technique selects both calendar items. As in other areas of Outlook, you can assign multiple items to categories at one time. You can also assign events to categories.

7 Right-click either selected item, point to **Categorize**, and then assign both to the **Time & Expenses** category.

The calendar items for the week are assigned to various categories. Category assignments are useful when displaying the calendar in different views.

8 Select only the **Southeast Lodging Association Conference** banner and assign the **Travel Required** category.

When an appointment or event is assigned to a second category, the first category displays as a colored square on the right side of the appointment or event.

9 In the **Date Navigator**, click the **Monday** of the same week in which you have been working. Select the **Dominique's performance review** appointment and assign the **Important** category.

10 In the **Date Navigator**, click the **Tuesday** of the same week in which you have been working. Select the **Travel & Lodging Seminar** appointment and assign the **Travel Required** category.

More Knowledge

Viewing Calendar Items by Category

If you assign calendar items to categories, you can display your calendar entries in a table, grouped by category. From the View menu, point to Current View, and then click By Category. Next to each category name are expand and collapse buttons, which can be used to display or hide the items in a category. To restore the calendar to its default view, click View, point to Current View, and then click Day/Week/Month.

Activity 3.14 Changing the Calendar View

Outlook has a number of views you can use to organize your calendar and display its various periods of time. In this activity, you will change the views of Carmen Jeffries' calendar.

1 In the **Date Navigator**, click any day of the same week in which you have been creating appointments, if one is not already displayed.

2 Above the appointment area, click the **Week** view button ⬛ Week, and select the **Show work week** option. Compare your screen with Figure 3.28.

The Personal Calendar folder displays the five days of the selected week in work week view, Monday through Friday. This is a good way to see your work week at a glance. The color coding of appointments is especially effective in this view. Notice that some appointment descriptions may be too long to display all their text, depending on the size of your screen and its resolution.

Figure 3.28
Week view button
Show work week option
Show full week option

3 In the **Friday** column, point to the **Breakfast at the conference with John McCarthy & Sonia Friedman** appointment, if its description is truncated.

Calendar items, whose full descriptions are not visible in the appointment area, display the time, subject, and location information as a ScreenTip. You also can view all the details of an appointment by opening it.

4 Above the appointment area, select the **Show full week** option.

The calendar displays in **full week view**, which arranges the calendar in a weekly, seven-day view in frames. In the Date Navigator, the entire week is highlighted in orange, indicating that the entire week is displayed in the appointment area. Some of the appointment descriptions may also be truncated in this view, depending on your screen size and resolution. You can view the truncated appointment information as a ScreenTip.

5 In the **Friday** frame, point to the **Breakfast at the conference with John McCarthy & Sonia Friedman** appointment, if its description is truncated, to display the ScreenTip for this appointment. Compare your screen with Figure 3.29.

Forward and Back buttons

Calendar in full week view, your dates will differ

Figure 3.29

Date Navigator indicates the week displayed in the appointment area

Color-coded calendar items

ScreenTip showing date, time, and location for truncated descriptions

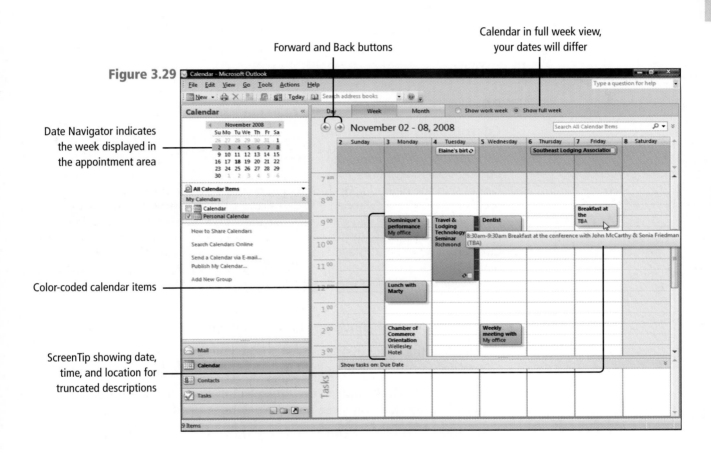

6 Locate the **Forward** and **Back** buttons to the left of the Date in the appointment area. Click the **Forward** button ▶ one time to display the next week of the month.

You can use the Forward and Back buttons to move forward and backward by week in this view. Notice that the Date Navigator changes the highlighted week. Alternatively, you can use the scroll bar to move forward or backward.

7 Click the **Back** button ◀ one time to redisplay the week in which you have been working. Above the appointment area, click the **Month** button Month to display the calendar in Month view.

By default, the Month displays in High detail view. High detail view displays calendar events and appointments including the subject. Medium detail view displays events with the subject and shows appointments only as colored bars. Low detail view displays events only.

8 In the **scroll bar**, drag the **scroll box** down to move forward in the calendar.

Notice as you drag the scroll box, Outlook displays a ScreenTip that identifies the week of the month. This ScreenTip is useful when you want to jump ahead or back in the calendar by many weeks or months.

9 Drag the **scroll box** up so that the ScreenTip shows the same week in which you have been working.

10 In the **Date Navigator**, click the **Wednesday** in the week in which you have been working. The Calendar is restored to Day view, the default view.

More Knowledge
Customizing the Calendar

You can change the appearance of the Calendar folder in a number of different ways. From the Tools menu, click Options, and then click Calendar Options. In the Calendar Options dialog box, you can change the background color of the calendar. You can also set the days and time of your calendar work week. You can customize individual views within the Calendar folder by right-clicking in the appointment area, and then clicking Customize Current View in the displayed shortcut menu. In the Customized View dialog box, click Other Settings to display options for changing the fonts, time scale, and other settings in the view.

11 From the **View** menu, point to **Reading Pane**, and then click **Right**.

The Reading Pane displays next to the calendar. The Reading Pane enables you to view details of an appointment without opening it.

12 Click the **Dentist** appointment to select it. Point to the border between the Reading Pane and the calendar until the pane resize pointer ⊹ displays, and then compare your screen with Figure 3.30.

The Dentist Appointment form displays in the Reading Pane. You can increase the size of the Reading Pane by dragging the left border if necessary.

Figure 3.30

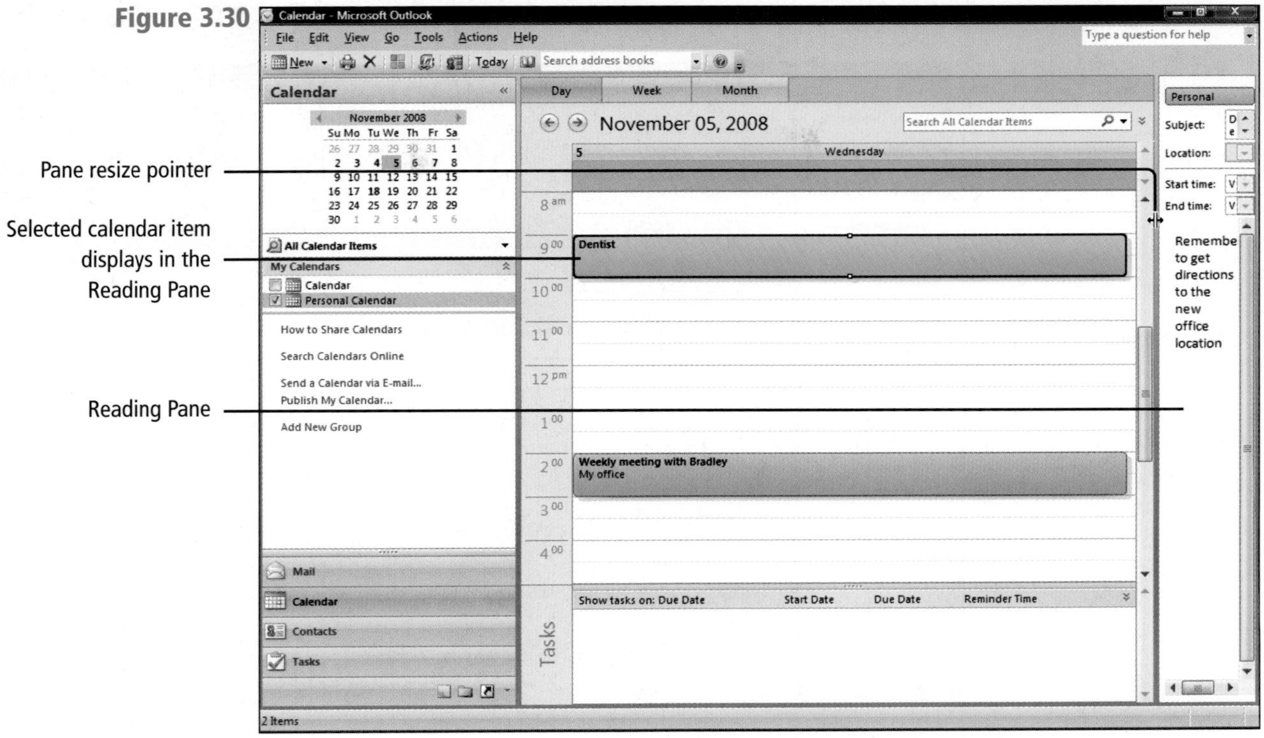

Pane resize pointer

Selected calendar item
displays in the
Reading Pane

Reading Pane

13 To widen the **Reading Pane**, point to the left border of the **Reading Pane** until the pane resize pointer ⊞ displays, drag the border to the left, releasing the mouse button when most of the Reading Pane is visible.

14 Restore the **Reading Pane** to its default width by dragging the left border to the right to its original location.

15 From the **View** menu, point to **Reading Pane**, and then click **Off**. Display the **View** menu again, point to **To-Do Bar**, and then click **Normal**. Compare your screen with Figure 3.31.

Outlook rearranges the calendar screen. The right side of the screen displays the To-Do Bar. Note that the Date Navigator is contained in the To-Do Bar, and is no longer displayed on the left side of your screen. Recall that the To-Do bar is used to display current tasks and appointments located in the *Calendar* folder. Because all of your appointments are stored in the Personal Calendar folder, they are not visible on the To-Do Bar.

Figure 3.31

Date Navigator   To-Do Bar

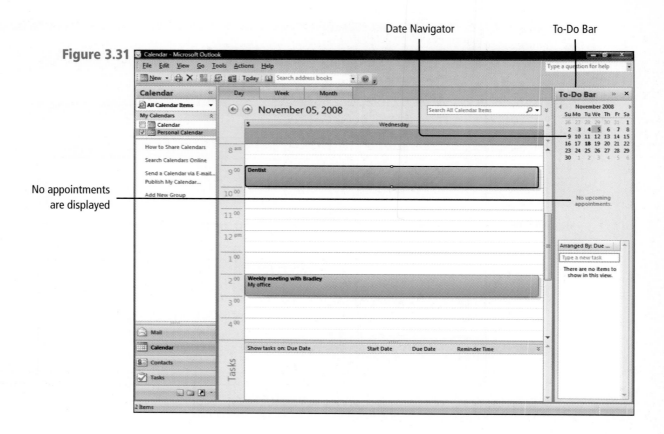

No appointments are displayed

16 From the **View** menu, point to **To-Do Bar**, and then click **Off** to turn off the display of the To-Do Bar and restore the calendar to its default view.

> ## Note — Default Setting for the To-Do Bar
>
> When viewing the Calendar folder, the To-Do Bar is not displayed, by default. Calendar view includes the Date Navigator on the left and the Task Pane below the appointment area, which displays all currently due tasks. Therefore, there is really no need to have the To-Do Bar displayed.

Objective 6
Manage a Calendar

From time to time, you will find it useful to print portions of your calendar. The procedures for printing a calendar and setting print options are similar to printing from other areas of Outlook. And, as with other Outlook folders, you may need to delete calendar items from time to time to keep it current.

In Activities 3.15 through 3.17, you will configure Outlook for printing calendar information, print several calendars, and then delete the contents of your Personal Calendar folder.

Activity 3.15 Configuring and Viewing Calendar Print Options

Depending on what you want to print in your calendar, Outlook has a variety of print styles. You can print a range of hours, a day, a week, or a month. You can also print an individual appointment or event. In this activity, you will set up the print options for Carmen Jeffries' calendar.

1 In the **Date Navigator**, click the **Wednesday** in the week in which you have been entering appointments.

2 From the **File** menu, display the **Print** dialog box, and then, under **Print style**, click the **down scroll arrow** to view the available print styles.

Each print style arranges calendar information in a different format. You can preview how the information will display when you print it.

3 Under **Print style**, click **Weekly Style**. In the **Print** dialog box, click **Preview**. Point to the top of the document, click one time to increase the magnification, and then compare your screen with Figure 3.32.

The *Weekly Style* print style arranges the appointments in frames, one frame per day, similar to the Week view in the calendar.

Your dates will differ

Figure 3.32

Top half of Weekly Style print style

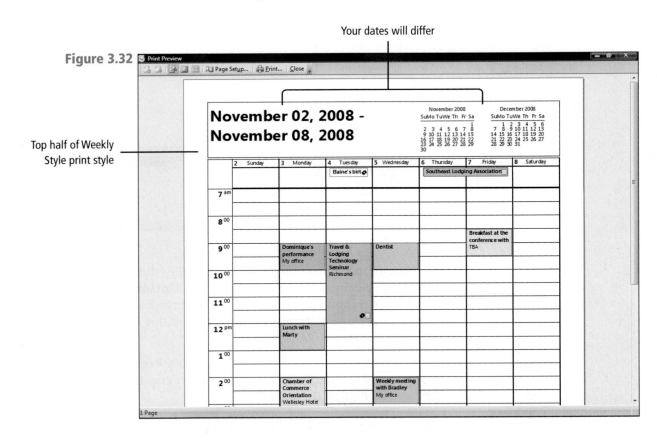

4 On the Print Preview toolbar, click the **Print** button to redisplay the **Print** dialog box. Under **Print style**, click **Monthly Style**, click **Preview**, and then notice that the Print Preview shows how the calendar will look when this print style is used.

5 On the Print Preview toolbar, click the **Print** button to redisplay the **Print** dialog box. Under **Print style**, click **Tri-fold Style**, and then click **Preview**. Point to the top of the document, click one time to increase the magnification, and then compare your screen with Figure 3.33.

In the **_Tri-fold Style_**, the printout includes three sections. The default layout includes the daily calendar, the Daily Task List, and the weekly calendar. The content of each section is controlled in the Format tab of the Page Setup dialog box.

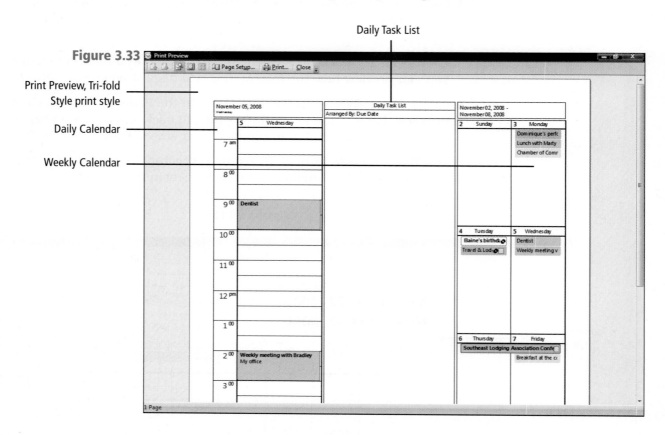

Figure 3.33

Daily Task List

Print Preview, Tri-fold Style print style

Daily Calendar

Weekly Calendar

6 Click the **Print** button [🖨 Print...] to redisplay the **Print** dialog box. Click **Page Setup**, and notice that under **Options**, you can control which information prints in each of the three sections of the Tri-fold Style. In the **Page Setup: Tri-fold Style** dialog box, click **Print** to return to the **Print** dialog box.

7 Under **Print style**, click **Daily Style**. Click **Preview**. When you finish previewing the document, click **Close** to close the Print Preview window and redisplay the calendar.

Activity 3.16 Printing Calendar Information

In this activity, you will print different portions of Carmen Jeffries' calendar.

1 Be sure that the same week in which you have been working is displayed in the calendar. From the **File** menu, display the **Print** dialog box. Under **Print style**, click **Weekly Style**. Click **Page Setup**, and then click the **Header/Footer tab**. Delete any existing header or footer information, including dates and page numbers. In the left **Footer** box, using your own first and last name, type **3A_Travel_Plans_ Week_Firstname_Lastname** and then compare your screen with Figure 3.34

Figure 3.34

Page Setup: Weekly Style dialog box

Footer information

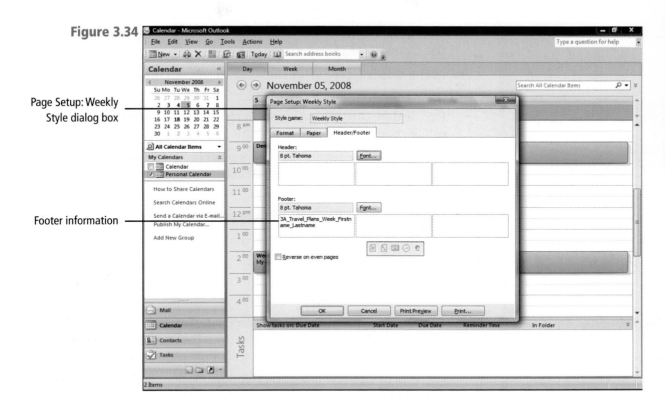

2 Click **Print** to return to the **Print** dialog box. In the **Print** dialog box, click **OK** to print the currently displayed week. Submit the end result to your instructor as directed.

3 In the **Date Navigator**, click the **Friday** of the week in which you have been entering appointments. Click the **Breakfast at the conference with John McCarthy & Sonia Friedman** appointment one time to select it.

To print an individual appointment, you must first select it.

4 From the **File** menu, display the **Print** dialog box, and then, under **Print style**, click **Memo Style**, which is used to print individual calendar items.

5 Click **Page Setup**, and then click the **Header/Footer tab**. Delete any existing header or footer information. In the left **Footer** box, type **3A_Travel_Plans_Breakfast_Firstname_Lastname** Click **Print** to redisplay the **Print** dialog box. Preview and print the document. Submit the end result to your instructor as directed.

Activity 3.17 Deleting Calendar Information

You can delete calendar information in a manner similar to any other Outlook item. In this activity, you will delete some of the calendar items you have created for Carmen Jeffries, and then you will delete the entire calendar folder you created for her.

1 In the **Date Navigator**, click the **Monday** of the week in which you have been entering appointments. Click the **Lunch with Marty** appointment, and then, on the Standard toolbar, click the **Categorize** button 🔲, and then click **All Categories** to display the **Color Categories** dialog box.

2 In the **Color Categories** dialog box, select **Travel Required**, click the **Rename** button, and type **Blue Category**.

Recall that Outlook retains the most recent name change, so renaming is required to restore the category to its default name.

3 Using the same technique, rename **Personal** as **Green Category**, **Important** as **Red Category**, **Status** as **Orange Category**, and **Time & Expenses** as **Yellow Category**. Click **OK**.

4 Make certain the **Lunch with Marty** appointment is still selected.

On the Standard toolbar, click the **Delete** button ❎ to delete the appointment.

5 In the **Date Navigator**, click the **Tuesday** of the same week in which you have been working. Click the **Travel & Lodging Technology Seminar** appointment, and then click **Delete** ❎. Alternatively, right-click the appointment, and from the displayed shortcut menu, click **Delete**. Compare your screen with Figure 3.35.

A Confirm Delete dialog box displays. Because this is a recurring appointment, Outlook asks whether you want to delete all the occurrences of the appointment.

Figure 3.35

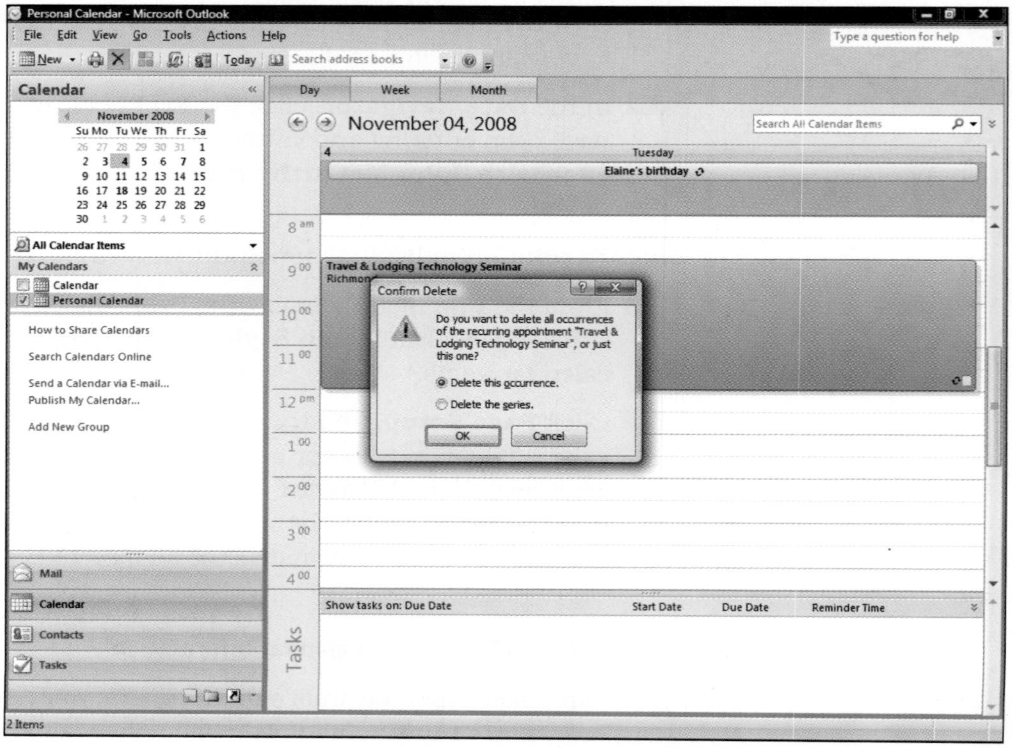

6 In the **Confirm Delete** dialog box, click **Delete the series**, and then click **OK**.

All occurrences of the appointment are deleted. Recurring events are deleted in the same way.

7 At the top of the calendar, click the **Elaine's birthday** event banner, and then click **Delete** ☒. In the displayed **Confirm Delete** dialog box, click **Delete the series**, and then click **OK** to delete all occurrences of the event.

More Knowledge
Displaying and Deleting All Calendar Items

An easy way to display and clear your calendar of all entries is to use the Active Appointments view. With the calendar displayed, from the View menu, point to Current View, and then click Active Appointments. All your appointments, events, and meetings display in a table. Press Ctrl + A to select all the items in the table and then click Delete. To restore the calendar to its default view, click View, point to Current View, and then click Day/Week/Month.

8 In the **Navigation Pane**, click the **Folder List** button ▢. Under **All Folders**, click **Personal Calendar** if it is not already selected. Click **Delete** ☒.

Outlook displays an information box asking whether you are sure you want to delete the folder and move its contents to the Deleted Items folder.

9 In the **Microsoft Office Outlook** dialog box, click **Yes**.

Outlook moves the folder to the Deleted Items folder, and the Calendar folder displays.

10 In the **Navigation Pane**, click **Deleted Items** to display the **Deleted Items** folder.

The Reading Pane displays next to the Deleted Items folder, displaying the first deleted item in the folder.

11 Under **All Folders**, to the left of the **Deleted Items** folder, if necessary, click the expand button (+) to display the subfolders in the Deleted Items folder. Compare your screen with Figure 3.36.

Figure 3.36

Deleted Items, your order may differ

Click expand (+) or collapse (−) to display or hide Deleted Items subfolders

Personal Calendar subfolder

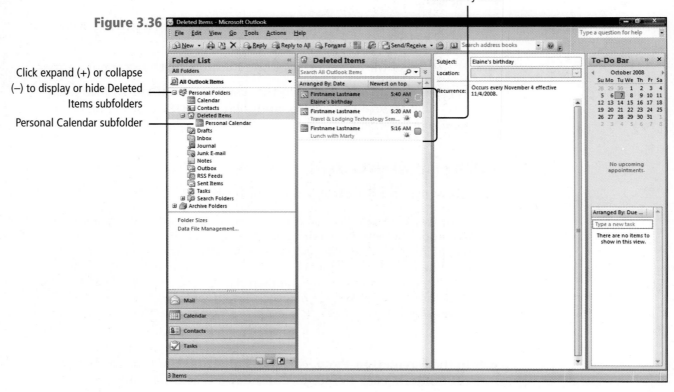

12 In the **Folder List**, right-click the **Deleted Items** folder, and then click **Empty "Deleted Items" Folder**.

Outlook displays a warning box indicating that you are permanently deleting all the items and subfolders in the Deleted Items folder.

13 In the **Microsoft Office Outlook** box, click **Yes**.

The items are permanently deleted, including the Personal Calendar subfolder. The Deleted Items folder is now empty.

14 In the **Navigation Pane**, click the **Calendar** button ⬛ Calendar . From the **File** menu, point to **Page Setup**, and then click **Define Print Styles**.

15 In the **Define Print Styles** dialog box, click **Weekly Style**, click **Reset**, and then click **OK**. Click **Memo Style**, click **Reset**, and then click **OK**. Close the **Define Print Styles** dialog box. **Close** ⬛ Outlook.

The two print styles you used are restored to their default settings.

End You have completed Project 3A ——————

Content-Based Assessments

Summary

The calendar is Outlook's tool for managing your schedule. Use the calendar to store information about appointments and events, including the time, place, location, purpose, and other details of the activity.

In this chapter, you created, edited, and moved appointments. You created a recurring appointment and an appointment with a reminder. You moved appointments to different times and different days of the month. You also worked with events, creating one-day events and multiple-day events. You used various ways to customize and organize your calendar activities. You assigned calendar items to categories and also assigned colors. You worked with various calendar views, and you displayed the calendar with the Reading Pane and the To-Do Bar. You printed a week of the calendar and an individual appointment. Finally, you deleted calendar items and the personal calendar folder you created at the beginning of the chapter.

Key Terms

Content-Based Assessments

Matching

Match each term in the second column with its correct definition in the first column. Write the letter of the term on the blank line in front of the correct definition.

_____ **1.** The Outlook folder that contains all calendar-related items.

_____ **2.** The right portion of the Calendar folder, which displays a one-day view of a day's calendar entries.

_____ **3.** In the Calendar folder, the upper pane in the Navigation Pane that displays a one-month view of the calendar and is used to display specific days in a month.

_____ **4.** A calendar activity occurring at a specific time and day that does not require inviting other people or reserving a room or equipment.

_____ **5.** An appointment type that occurs regularly on specific dates and times and at specific intervals.

_____ **6.** A calendar activity that requires inviting other people or reserving a room.

_____ **7.** An Outlook window, accompanied by a tone, that displays automatically at a designated date and time before appointments or tasks.

A Appointment

B Appointment area

C Black border

D Calendar

E Comments area

F Date Navigator

G Event

H Meeting

I Office Clipboard

J Overlay mode

K Recurring

L Reminder

M Task Pane

N Tri-fold

O Work week

_____ **8.** The lower portion of an Appointment form enabling you to enter information not otherwise specified in the form.

_____ **9.** Multiple calendars are displayed overlapping one another.

_____ **10.** The outline around an appointment that indicates that the appointment is selected.

_____ **11.** An Office term for a memory area in which you can collect text and graphics from any Office program and then place them in another area of the same program or in a different program.

_____ **12.** Any calendar activity that lasts 24 hours or longer.

_____ **13.** A calendar view showing Monday through Friday.

_____ **14.** An abbreviated list of current tasks stored in the Tasks folder that is displayed below the appointment area.

_____ **15.** A calendar print style with three sections: a default layout that includes the daily calendar, the Daily Task List, and the weekly calendar.

Content-Based Assessments

Fill in the Blank

Write the correct word in the space provided.

1. In the Appointment form, add details or other information about an appointment in the _____ area.

2. In the appointment area of the calendar, you can drag the _____ _____ of an appointment to extend the end time.

3. In the appointment area of the calendar, the location of a scheduled appointment appears _____ the subject of the appointment.

4. The frequency of a recurring appointment, which may be daily, weekly, monthly, or yearly, is referred to as the _____ _____.

5. An appointment or event that is a recurring appointment or recurring event displays a(n) _____ in the lower right corner of the appointment.

6. To indicate that an appointment is scheduled beyond the time currently shown in the viewing area, a small gray _____ displays at the top right or bottom right of the appointment area.

7. You can move an appointment to a different day by dragging it to the _____ _____.

8. To indicate that an event is scheduled for the day, an event _____ displays across the top of the calendar.

9. Unlike appointments, days with events scheduled do not display in _____ in the Date Navigator.

10. A color category can be assigned to an appointment by using a shortcut menu command or the _____ button.

11. The calendar view that displays all seven days of the week is the _____ _____ view.

12. You can view the details of an appointment in the calendar without opening it by using the View menu to display the _____ _____.

13. Recurring events that happen each year, for example, a birthday or anniversary, are called _____ events.

14. The print style you use to print individual calendar items is the _____ Style.

15. When you delete a subfolder of the Calendar folder, in the folder list it appears as a subfolder of the _____ _____ folder.

Content-Based Assessments

Skills Review

Project 3B — Travel Conference

Objectives: 1. *Navigate the Calendar;* **2.** *Schedule Appointments;* **3.** *Edit Appointments;* **4.** *Work with Events;* **6.** *Manage a Calendar.*

In the following Skills Review, you will manage the weekly schedule of Jefferson Inn co-owner, Carmen Jeffries. Every spring, the Jefferson Inn hosts a conference for area travel agents, which the inn uses to promote its unique blend of country charm and first-rate guest services. Your completed calendar information will look similar to the ones shown in Figure 3.37.

For Project 3B, you will need the following files:

New blank Appointment form
New blank Event form

You will print two files with the following footers:
3B_Travel_Conference_Firstname_Lastname
3B_Travel_Conference_Appointment_Firstname_Lastname

Figure 3.37

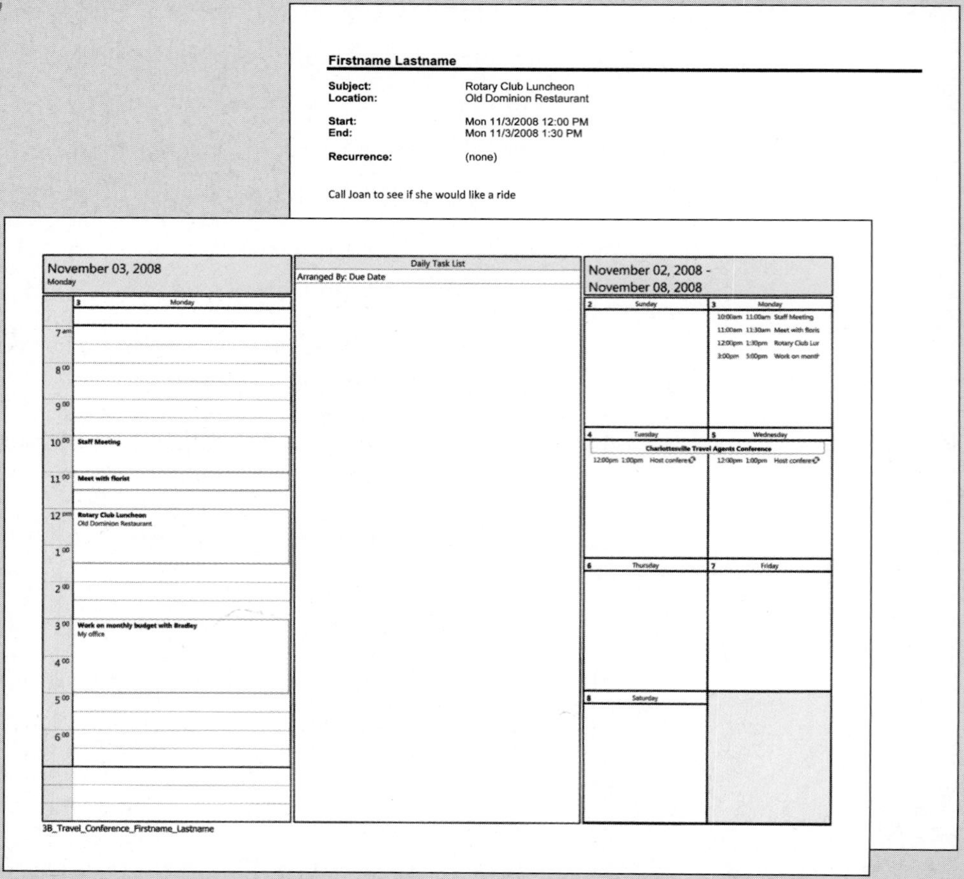

(Project 3B–Travel Conference continues on the next page)

Content-Based Assessments

(Project 3B–Travel Conference continued)

1. **Start** Outlook and display the **Navigation Pane**. In the **Navigation Pane**, click the **Calendar** button to display the **Calendar** folder. If you are working in a college lab or other classroom environment, clear all previous calendar entries made by others as follows: From the **View** menu, point to **Current View**, and then click **Active Appointments**. If any appointments display, press Ctrl + A, and then click **Delete**. Return to the **Current View**, using the same steps, and then clicking **Day/Week/Month**.

2. In the **Date Navigator**, click the **right arrow** as necessary to advance the calendar to next month. Click the **Monday** of the first full week of next month.

3. In the appointment area, click the **10:00 am** time slot, and type **Staff Meeting** Click the **11:00 am** time slot and type **Meet with florist**

4. On the Standard toolbar, click the **New Appointment** button. In the **Appointment** form, in the **Subject** box, type **Rotary Club Luncheon** In the **Location** box, type **Old Dominion Restaurant**

5. Set the **Start time** to **12:00 PM** and the **End time** to **1:30 PM (1.5 hours)**. In the comments area of the **Appointment** form, type **Call Joan to see if she would like a ride** Click the **Reminder arrow**, and then click **None** to remove the reminder. **Save & Close** the Appointment form.

6. Open another new **Appointment** form. As the **Subject**, type **Work on monthly budget with Bradley** In the **Location** box, type **My office** Set the **Start time to 3:00 PM** and the **End time** to **5:00 PM (2 hours)**. Click the **Reminder arrow**, and then click **None** to remove the reminder. **Save & Close** the appointment.

7. In the appointment area, click the **Staff Meeting** appointment one time to select it. Point to the bottom border until the vertical resize pointer displays. With the vertical resize pointer displayed, drag the bottom border of the selected appointment down to **11:00 am**.

8. In the appointment area, double-click the **Meet with florist appointment** to open the appointment. Recall that Outlook automatically includes a reminder with new appointments. In the **Appointment** form, set the **Reminder** to **None**, and then **Save & Close** the appointment.

9. In the **Date Navigator**, click the **Tuesday** of the same week in which you have been entering appointments. From the **Actions** menu, click **New All Day Event**. In the **Event** form, in the **Subject** box, type **Charlottesville Travel Agents Conference**

10. Click the **End time arrow**, and then click the **Wednesday** of the same week in which you are working to make the event a two-day event. Set the **Reminder** to **None**. **Save & Close** the event.

11. Open a new **Appointment** form. As the **Subject**, type **Host conference lunch** In the **Location** box, type **Magnolia Room** Set the **Start time** for **12:00 PM** and the **End time** for **1:00 PM (1 hour)**.

12. On the Ribbon, click the **Recurrence** button. In the **Appointment Recurrence** dialog box, under **Recurrence pattern**, click **Daily**. Under **Range of recurrence**, click **End after**, and in the adjacent box type **2** Click **OK**. In the **Appointment** form, set the **Reminder** to **None**, and then **Save & Close** the Appointment form.

13. In the **Date Navigator**, click the **Monday** of the week in which you have been entering appointments. From the **File** menu,

(Project 3B–Travel Conference continues on the next page)

Content-Based Assessments

(Project 3B–Travel Conference continued)

point to **Page Setup**, and then click **Tri-fold Style**. In the **Page Setup: Tri-fold Style** dialog box, click the **Header/Footer tab**, and delete any existing header or footer information, including page numbers and dates. In the left **Footer** box, using your own first and last name, type **3B_Travel_Conference_Firstname_Lastname** Click **Print** to display the **Print** dialog box.

14. In the **Print** dialog box, click **Preview**. On the Print Preview toolbar, click the **Print** button to return to the **Print** dialog box. Click **OK** to print the calendar. Submit the end result to your instructor as directed.

15. In the appointment area, click the **Rotary Club Luncheon** appointment one time to select it. From the **File** menu, display the **Page Setup: Memo Style** dialog box. Display the **Header/Footer tab**, delete any existing header or footer information, and then, in the left **Footer** box, type **3B_Travel_Conference_Appointment_Firstname_Lastname** Click **Print** to display the **Print** dialog box. **Preview** and then **Print** the document. Submit the end result to your instructor as directed.

16. In the appointment area, select the **Staff Meeting** appointment, and then, on the

Standard toolbar, click the **Delete** button. Delete the remaining appointments for the day. Recall that you can select a group of appointments by holding down Ctrl and that you can right-click a selected appointment and then click **Delete** from the displayed shortcut menu.

17. In the **Date Navigator**, click the **Tuesday** for the week in which you are entering appointments. Select and then delete the event banner. Click the **Host conference lunch** appointment, and then click the **Delete** button. In the **Confirm Delete** dialog box, click **Delete the series**, and then click **OK**.

18. In the **Navigation Pane**, click the **Folder List** button. Under **All Folders**, right-click the **Deleted Items** folder, and then click **Empty "Deleted Items" Folder**. In the **Microsoft Office Outlook** box, click **Yes**.

19. In the **Navigation Pane**, click the **Calendar** button. From the **File** menu, point to **Page Setup**, and then click **Define Print Styles**. In the **Define Print Styles** dialog box, click **Tri-fold Style**, click **Reset**, and then click **OK**. Click **Memo Style**, click **Reset**, and then click **OK**. **Close** the dialog box. **Close** Outlook.

End **You have completed Project 3B**

Skills Review

Project 3C — Landscaping

Objectives: 1. *Navigate the Calendar;* **2.** *Schedule Appointments;* **3.** *Edit Appointments;* **5.** *Organize and Customize the Calendar;* **6.** *Manage a Calendar.*

In the following Skills Review, you will manage the weekly calendar of Dominique Amerline, the manager of the Jefferson Inn. One very attractive feature of the Jefferson Inn is its beautiful grounds. The Inn is currently relandscaping its patio gardens, and the project is being supervised by Ms. Amerline. Your completed calendar will look similar to the one shown in Figure 3.38.

For Project 3C, you will need the following file:

New blank Appointment form

You will print one file with the following footer:
3C_Landscaping_Week_Firstname_Lastname

Figure 3.38

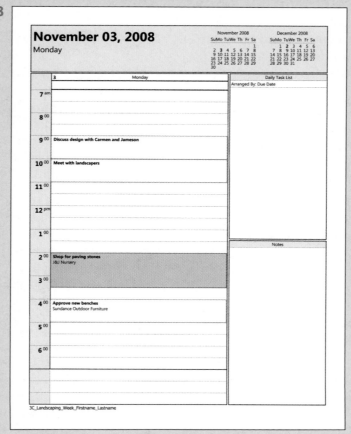

(Project 3C–Landscaping continues on the next page)

Content-Based Assessments

(Project 3C–Landscaping continued)

1. **Start** Outlook and display the **Navigation Pane**. In the **Navigation Pane**, click the **Calendar** button to display the **Calendar** folder. If you are working in a college lab or other classroom environment, clear all previous calendar entries made by others as follows: From the **View** menu, point to **Current View**, and then click **Active Appointments**. If any appointments display, press Ctrl + A, and then click **Delete**. Return to the **Current View**, using the same steps, and then clicking **Day/Week/Month**.

2. In the **Date Navigator**, click the **right arrow** once, advancing the calendar to next month. Click the **Monday** of the first full week of the month. In the appointment area, click the **9:00 am** time slot, and type **Discuss design with Carmen and Jameson** Click the **10:00 am** time slot, and type **Meet with landscapers**

3. On the Standard toolbar, click the **New Appointment** button. As the **Subject**, type **Shop for paving stones** and as the **Location**, type **J&J Nursery** Set the **Start time** to **2:00 PM** and the **End time** to **3:30 PM (1.5 hours)**. Set the **Reminder** to **None**. **Save & Close** the appointment.

4. Open another new **Appointment** form. As the **Subject**, type **Approve new benches** and as the **Location**, type **Sundance Outdoor Furniture** Set the **Start time** to **4:00 PM** and the **End time** to **5:00 PM (1 hour)**. Set the **Reminder** to **None**, and then **Save & Close** the appointment.

5. In the appointment area, click the **Meet with landscapers** appointment one time to select it. Point to the bottom border of the appointment until the pointer changes to a vertical resize pointer, and then drag the bottom border of the appointment to **11:00 am**.

6. Right-click the **Discuss design with Carmen and Jameson** appointment, and then click **Open** from the displayed shortcut menu. Alternatively, double-click the appointment to open it. In the **Appointment** form, change the **End time** to **10:00 AM (1 hour)**. Set the **Reminder** to **None**, and then **Save & Close** the appointment.

7. In the appointment area, right-click the **Shop for paving stones** appointment. Point to **Categorize**, and then click **All Categories**. Select the **Red Category**, click **Rename**, and then type **Important** Select the **Important** check box, and then click **OK**.

8. From the **File** menu, display the **Page Setup: Daily Style** dialog box. Click the **Header/Footer tab**. Delete any existing header or footer information. In the left **Footer** box, type **3C_Landscaping_Week_Firstname_Lastname** Click **Print** to display the **Print** dialog box.

9. In the **Print** dialog box, click **Preview**. When you have finished previewing the calendar, on the Print Preview toolbar, click the **Print** button to return to the **Print** dialog box. Click **OK** to print the calendar. Submit the end result to your instructor as directed.

10. In the appointment area, select the **Meet with landscapers** appointment. On the Standard toolbar, click the **Categorize** button, and then click **All Categories**. Rename the **Important** category as **Red Category**, and then click **OK**. With the

(Project 3C–Landscaping continues on the next page)

Content-Based Assessments

chapterthree **Skills Review**

(Project 3C–Landscaping continued)

appointment still selected, on the Standard toolbar, click the **Delete** button. Click the first remaining appointment, hold down Ctrl, and then click all the remaining appointments. Use the method of your choice to delete the remaining appointments for the day.

11. In the **Navigation Pane**, click the **Folder List** button. Under **All Folders**, right-click the **Deleted Items** folder, and then

click **Empty "Deleted Items" Folder**. In the **Microsoft Office Outlook** box, click **Yes**.

12. In the **Navigation Pane**, click the **Calendar** button. From the **File** menu, point to **Page Setup**, and then click **Define Print Styles**. In the **Define Print Styles** dialog box, click **Daily Style**, click **Reset**, and then click **OK**. **Close** the dialog box, and then **Close** Outlook.

End **You have completed Project 3C** _____

chapterthree

Skills Review

Project 3D — Gala

Objectives 1. *Navigate the Calendar;* **2.** *Schedule Appointments;* **3.** *Edit Appointments;* **5.** *Organize and Customize the Calendar;* **6.** *Manage a Calendar.*

In the following Skills Review, you will manage the calendar schedule of Jefferson Inn's chef, Bradley Matteson, during the New Year's Eve holiday. Every year the Jefferson Inn hosts a festive New Year's Eve holiday gala, which is one of the Inn's most popular and successful events. The gala includes a gourmet dinner on New Year's Eve, live entertainment, car service, and a lavish brunch the following morning. Chef Bradley Matteson supervises all aspects of this gala. His schedule will include hiring additional staff for the event. Your completed calendar will look similar to the one shown in Figure 3.39.

For Project 3D, you will need the following file:

New blank Appointment form

You will print two files with the following footers:
3D_Gala_Week_Firstname_Lastname
3D_Gala_Month_Firstname_Lastname

Figure 3.39

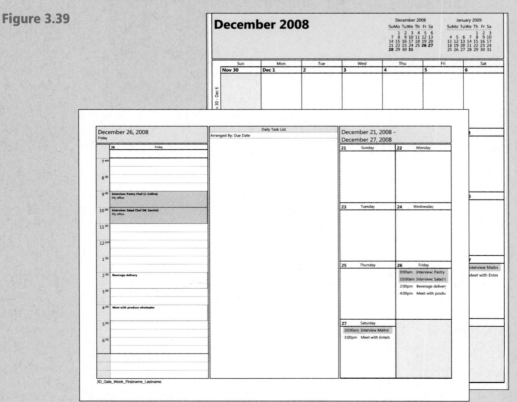

(Project 3D–Gala continues on the next page)

Content-Based Assessments

(Project 3D–Gala continued)

1. **Start** Outlook, and display the **Navigation Pane**. In the **Navigation Pane**, click the **Calendar** button to display the **Calendar** folder. If you are working in a college lab or other classroom environment, clear all previous calendar entries made by others as follows: From the **View** menu, point to **Current View**, and then click **Active Appointments**. If any appointments display, press Ctrl + A, and then click **Delete**. Return to the **Current View**, using the same steps, and then clicking **Day/Week/Month**.

2. In the **Date Navigator**, click the right arrow to advance the calendar to **December** of the current year. Click **26** to display the day's calendar for December 26. On the Standard toolbar, click the **New Appointment** button. As the **Subject**, type Interview: Pastry Chef (J. Collins) As the **Location**, type My office Set the **Start time** to **9:00 AM** and the **End time** to **10:00 AM (1 hour)**. On the Ribbon, click the **Categorize** button, and then click **All Categories**. Rename **Orange Category** as Important. Select the **Important** check box, and then click **OK**. Set the **Reminder** to **None**. **Save & Close** the appointment.

3. Open another new **Appointment** form. As the **Subject**, type Interview: Salad Chef (M. Santini) and as the **Location**, type My office Set the **Start time** to **10:00 AM**. Set the **End time** to **11:00 AM (1 hour)**. Assign the **Important** category. Set the **Reminder** to **None**, and then **Save & Close** the appointment.

4. In the appointment area, click the **2:00 pm** time slot, and type Beverage delivery Point to the bottom border until the pointer changes to a vertical resize pointer, and then drag the bottom border of the selected appointment down to **3:00 pm**.

In the appointment area, click the **4:00 pm** time slot, type Meet with produce wholesaler and then drag the bottom border down to **5:00 pm**.

5. In the **Date Navigator**, click **27** to display December 27, and then open a new **Appointment** form. As the **Subject**, type Interview: Maitre d' (F. Smith) As the **Location**, type My office Set the **Start time** to **10:00 AM**. Set the **End time** to **11:00 AM (1 hour)**. Assign the **Important** category. Set the **Reminder** to **None**, and then **Save & Close** the appointment.

6. In the appointment area, click the **3:00 pm** time slot, and type Meet with Entertainment Manager Drag the bottom border down to **4:00 pm**, and then press Enter. Alternatively, double-click the appointment to open it. In the **Appointment** form, set the **Reminder** to **None**, and then **Save & Close** the appointment.

7. In the **Date Navigator**, click **28** to display December 28. In the appointment area, click the **10:30 am** time slot, and type Meet with Carmen and Jameson Open a new **Appointment** form, and as the **Subject**, type Waitstaff Meeting As a **Location**, type Music Room Set the **Start time** to **2:00 PM** and the **End time** to **3:00 PM (1 hour)**. Set the **Reminder** to **None**, and then **Save & Close** the appointment.

8. In the **Date Navigator**, click **31** to display December 31. Open a new **Appointment** form. As the **Subject**, type Ballroom Setup Set the **Start time** to **1:00 PM** and the **End time** to **4:00 PM (3 hours)**. Click the **Categorize** button, and then click **All Categories**. Rename the **Yellow Category** as Needs Preparation. Assign the **Needs Preparation** category to this appointment.

(Project 3D–Gala continues on the next page)

(Project 3D–Gala continued)

Set the **Reminder** to **None**, and then **Save & Close** the appointment.

9. In the **Date Navigator**, click **26** to display December 26. From the **File** menu, display the **Page Setup: Tri-fold Style** dialog box. On the **Header/Footer tab**, delete any existing header or footer information. In the left **Footer** box type **3D_Gala_Week_ Firstname_Lastname** Click **Print** to return to the **Print** dialog box. In the **Print** dialog box, click **Preview**. On the Print Preview toolbar, click **Print** to return to the **Print** dialog box. Click **OK**. Submit the end result to your instructor as directed.

10. From the **File** menu, display the **Page Setup: Monthly Style** dialog box. On the **Header/Footer tab**, delete any existing header or footer information. In the left **Footer** box type **3D_Gala_Month_ Firstname_Lastname** Click **Print** to return to the **Print** dialog box. In the **Print** dialog box, click **Preview**. On the Print Preview toolbar, click **Print** to return to the **Print** dialog box. Click **OK**. Submit the end result to your instructor as directed.

11. Click the **Interview: Pastry Chef** appointment one time to select it. On the Standard toolbar, click the **Categorize** button, and then click **All Categories**. Rename the **Important** category as **Orange Category**, rename the **Needs Preparation**

category as **Yellow Category**, and then click **OK**.

12. With the same appointment selected, on the Standard toolbar, click the **Delete** button. Delete the remaining appointments for December 26. Recall that you can select an appointment, hold down Ctrl, and then select the remaining appointments, and then delete the entire group at once. In the **Date Navigator**, click **27** to display December 27. **Delete** the appointments for that day. **Delete** the appointments for December 28 and December 31. Notice that as you delete all the appointments for a given day, the day no longer displays in bold on the Date Navigator.

13. In the **Navigation Pane**, click the **Folder List** button. Under **All Folders**, right-click the **Deleted Items** folder, and then click **Empty "Deleted Items" Folder**. In the **Microsoft Office Outlook** box, click **Yes**.

14. In the **Navigation Pane**, click the **Calendar** button. From the **File** menu, point to **Page Setup**, and then click **Define Print Styles**. In the **Define Print Styles** dialog box, click **Tri-fold Style**, click **Reset**, click **OK**, click **Monthly Style**, click **Reset**, and then click **OK**. **Close** the dialog box, and then **Close** Outlook.

End You have completed Project 3D

Mastering Outlook

Project 3E — Wedding

Objectives 1. *Navigate the Calendar;* **2.** *Schedule Appointments;* **3.** *Edit Appointments;* **4.** *Work with Events;* **5.** *Organize and Customize the Calendar;* **6.** *Manage a Calendar.*

In the following Mastering Outlook project, you will manage the weekly calendar activities of Dominique Amerline, the manager of Jefferson Inn. The Jefferson Inn's small size allows it to promote itself as an ideal location for wedding parties. Several times a year, especially in the late spring and early summer, the inn reserves its entire facility for weddings. Out-of-town visitors stay in the guest rooms, and the beautiful gardens serve as a backdrop for outdoor weddings. Ms. Amerline supervises these events. Your completed calendar and one appointment will look similar to the ones shown in Figure 3.40.

For Project 3E, you will need the following files:

New blank Appointment form
New blank Event form

You will print two files with the following footers:
3E_Wedding_Appointment_Firstname_Lastname
3E_Wedding_Week_Firstname_Lastname

Figure 3.40

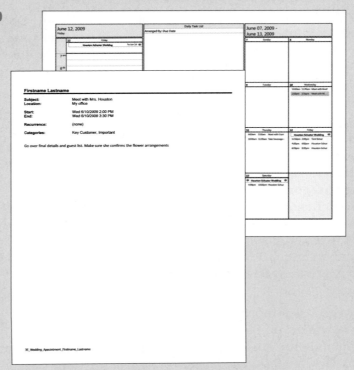

(Project 3E–Wedding continues on the next page)

Content-Based Assessments

(Project 3E–Wedding continued)

1. **Start** Outlook and display the **Calendar** folder. If you are working in a college lab or other classroom environment, clear all previous calendar entries made by others as follows: From the **View** menu, point to **Current View**, and then click **Active Appointments**. If any appointments display, press [Ctrl] + [A], and then click **Delete**. Return to the **Current View**, using the same steps, and then clicking **Day/Week/Month**.

2. In the **Date Navigator**, click the **right arrow** next to the month name as necessary to advance the calendar to **June**. Click the **Wednesday** of the first full week. Open a new **Appointment** form, and as the **Subject**, type **Meet with Bradley to discuss weekend menu** As the **Location**, type **Bradley's office** Set the **Start time** to **10:00 AM** and the **End time** to **11:00 AM**. Set the **Reminder** to **None**, and then **Save & Clos**e the appointment.

3. Open another new **Appointment** form. As the **Subject**, type **Meet with Mrs. Houston** and as the **Location**, type **My office** Set the **Start time** to **2:00 PM** and the **End time** to **3:30 PM**.

4. In the comments area, type **Go over final details and guest list. Make sure she confirms the flower arrangements** Ms. Amerline organizes her calendar items by category. Click **Categorize**, and then click **All Categories**. Rename the **Green Category** as **Important** and the **Purple Category** as **Key Customer** Assign both categories to this appointment. Set the **Reminder** to **None** and then **Save & Close** the appointment.

5. In the **Date Navigator**, click the **Thursday** of the same week in which you have been entering appointments. In the appointment area, click the **9:00 am** time slot and type **Meet with Carmen to discuss Houston wedding** Click the **10:30 am** time slot and type **Take beverage delivery** Open both appointments and set the **Reminder** to **None** in each Appointment form.

6. In the **Date Navigator**, click the **Friday** of the same week in which you have been entering appointments. From the **Actions** menu, click **New All Day Event**. In the **Event** form, as the **Subject**, type **Houston-Schuster Wedding** Set the **End time** for the **Sunday** of the week in which you have been working so that it is a three-day event. Set the **Reminder** to **None**, and then **Save & Close** the appointment.

7. In the appointment area, click the **12:00 pm** time slot, and type **Tent Setup** Drag the bottom border of the appointment to **2:00 pm**. Open a new **Appointment** form. As the **Subject**, type **Houston-Schuster Rehearsal** Set the **Start time** for **4:00 PM** and the **End time** for **6:00 PM**. Set the **Reminder** to **None**, and then **Save & Close** the appointment.

8. Enter another new appointment with the **Subject Houston-Schuster Rehearsal Dinner** Set the **Start time** at **6:00 PM** and the **End time** at **8:00 PM**. Set the **Reminder** to **None**. **Save & Close** the appointment.

9. In the **Date Navigator**, click the **Saturday** of the same week in which you have been entering appointments. Open a new appointment, and as the **Subject**, type **Houston-Schuster Wedding** Set the **Start time** for **4:00 PM** and the **End time** for **10:00 PM**. Set the **Reminder** to **None**. **Save & Close** the appointment.

10. In the **Date Navigator**, click the **Wednesday** of the same week in which you have been

(Project 3E–Wedding continues on the next page)

Content-Based Assessments

(Project 3E–Wedding continued)

working. Click the **Meet with Mrs. Houston** appointment. From the **File** menu, display the **Page Setup: Memo Style** dialog box. On the **Header/Footer tab**, delete any existing header or footer information, and then, in the left **Footer** box, type **3E_Wedding_ Appointment_Firstname_Lastname** Click **Print** to display the **Print** dialog box. Preview and then print the document. Submit the end result to your instructor as directed.

11. In the **Date Navigator**, click the **Friday** of the same week in which you have been working. From the **File** menu, display the **Page Setup: Tri-fold Style** dialog box. On the **Header/Footer tab**, delete any existing header or footer information. In the left **Footer** box, type **3E_Wedding_Week_ Firstname_Lastname** Click **Print** to return the **Print** dialog box. **Preview** and **Print** the document. Submit the end result to your instructor as directed.

12. Select the **Houston-Schuster Wedding** event. Click the **Categorize** button, and then click **All Categories**. Rename **Important** as **Green Category** and **Key Customer** as **Purple Category** Close the dialog box.

13. From the **View** menu, point to **Current View**, and then click **Active Appointments**. Press Ctrl + A, and then click **Delete**. Return to the **Current View**, using the same steps, and then click **Day/Week/Month**. In the **Navigation Pane**, click the **Folder List** button. Under **All Folders**, right-click the **Deleted Items** folder, and then empty it.

14. Display the **Calendar** folder. Display the **Define Print Styles** dialog box and **Reset** the **Tri-fold Style** and **Memo Style**. **Close** the dialog box, and then **Close** Outlook.

End **You have completed Project 3E**

Project 3F — Remodeling

Objective: 1. *Navigate the Calendar;* **2.** *Schedule Appointments;* **3.** *Edit Appointments;* **5.** *Organize and Customize the Calendar;* **6.** *Manage a Calendar.*

In the following Mastering Outlook project, you will schedule calendar activities for Dominique Amerline, the manager of the Jefferson Inn. The inn is remodeling and redecorating its dining room, meeting rooms, and several guest rooms. Ms. Amerline, is directing the project. The renovations include wiring the facility for high-speed Internet connections and other business services. The consultant performing the technical work will also be training the staff. Your completed calendar will look similar to the one shown in Figure 3.41.

For Project 3F, you will need the following file:

New blank Appointment form

You will print one file with the following footer:
3F_Remodeling_Week_Firstname_Lastname

Figure 3.41

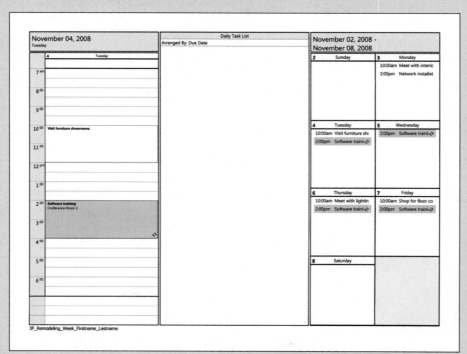

(Project 3F—Remodeling continues on the next page)

Content-Based Assessments

(Project 3F–Remodeling continued)

1. **Start** Outlook and display the **Calendar** folder. If you are working in a college lab or other classroom environment, clear all previous calendar entries made by others as follows: From the **View** menu, point to **Current View**, and then click **Active Appointments**. If any appointments display, press Ctrl + A, and then click **Delete**. Return to the **Current View**, using the same steps, and then clicking **Day/Week/Month**.

2. In the **Date Navigator**, click the **right arrow** to advance to next month. Click the **Monday** of the first full week. Open a new appointment. As the **Subject**, type **Meet with interior designers** As the **Location**, type **Conference Room 1** Set the **Start time** to **10:00 AM** and the **End time** to **12:00 PM**. Set the **Reminder** to **None**, and then **Save & Close** the appointment. Open another new **Appointment** form. As the **Subject**, type **Network installation** Set the **Start time** to **2:00 PM** and the **End time** to **5:00 PM**. Set the **Reminder** to **None**, and then **Save & Close** the appointment.

3. In the **Date Navigator**, click the **Tuesday** of the week in which you are entering appointments. Open a new **Appointment** form, and as the **Subject**, type **Software training** As the **Location**, type **Conference Room 2** Click **Categorize**, and then click **All Categories**. Rename the **Blue Category** as **Important**, and assign to this appointment. Set the **Start time** to **2:00 PM** and the **End time** to **4:00 PM**. Set the **Reminder** to **None**.

4. Display the **Appointment Recurrence** dialog box. Set the **Recurrence pattern** to **Daily** and the **Range of recurrence** to **End after 4 occurrences**. **Save & Close** the appointment. Still working in **Tuesday** of the same week, click the **10:00 am** time slot. Type **Visit furniture showrooms** Drag the bottom border to **12:00 pm**. Open the appointment, and set the **Reminder** to **None**. **Save & Close** the appointment.

5. In the **Date Navigator**, click **Thursday** of the week in which you are working, and then open a new **Appointment** form. As the **Subject**, type **Meet with lighting designer** In the **Location** box, type **Conference Room 1** Set the **Start time** to **10:00 AM** and the **End time** to **11:00 AM**. Set the **Reminder** to **None**, and then **Save & Close** the appointment.

6. In the **Date Navigator**, click **Friday** of the week in which you have been working. Click the **10:00 am** time slot and type **Shop for floor coverings** Drag the bottom border to **12:00 pm**. Open the appointment and set the **Reminder** to **None**. **Save & Close** the appointment.

7. In the **Date Navigator**, click the **Tuesday** of the same week in which you have been working. From the **File** menu, display the **Page Setup: Tri-fold Style** dialog box. On the **Header/Footer tab**, delete any existing header or footer information. In the left **Footer** box, type **3F_Remodeling_Week_ Firstname_Lastname** Click **Print** to return to the **Print** dialog box. **Preview** and **Print** the document. Submit the end result to your instructor as directed.

8. Select the **Software training** appointment. On the Standard toolbar, click **Categorize**, and then **All Categories**. Rename **Important** as **Blue Category** and then **Close** the dialog box.

9. From the **View** menu, point to **Current View**, and then click **Active Appointments**. Press Ctrl + A to select all the appointments,

(Project 3F–Remodeling continues on the next page)

(Project 3F–Remodeling continued)

and then click **Delete**. Return to the **Current View**, using the same steps, and then click **Day/Week/Month**.

10. In the **Navigation Pane**, click the **Folder List** button. Under **All Folders**, right-click the **Deleted Items** folder, and

then empty it. Display the **Calendar** folder, and then display the **Define Print Styles** dialog box. Reset the **Tri-fold Style**. **Close** the dialog box, and then **Close** Outlook.

End You have completed Project 3F ——————————————

Content-Based Assessments

chapter three Mastering Outlook

Project 3G — Magazine Story

Objectives: 1. *Navigate the Calendar;* **2.** *Schedule Appointments;* **3.** *Edit Appointments;* **4.** *Work with Events;* **5.** *Organize and Customize the Calendar;* **6.** *Manage a Calendar.*

In the following Mastering Outlook project, you will manage the calendar activities of Jameson Taylor, the co-owner of the Jefferson Inn. A national travel and leisure magazine is preparing a cover story on the Charlottesville area, and the Jefferson Inn will be prominently featured. The inn's owners, Carmen Jeffries and Jameson Taylor, are thrilled to be receiving this exposure. The magazine is sending a writer and photographer for a two-day photo shoot. They will also use the inn as a base during their week-long stay in the Charlottesville area. The week of their visit will be a busy one for Mr. Taylor. You will create appointments and an event. One of your appointments and your completed calendar will look similar to the ones shown in Figure 3.42.

For Project 3G, you will need the following files:

New blank Appointment form
New blank Event form

You will print two files with the following footers:
3G_Magazine_Story_Week_Firstname_Lastname
3G_Magazine_Story_Event_Firstname_Lastname

Figure 3.42

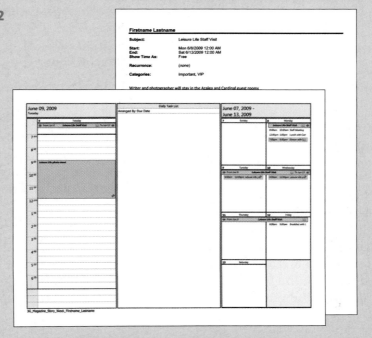

(Project 3G–Magazine Story continues on the next page)

Content-Based Assessments

(Project 3G–Magazine Story continued)

1. **Start** Outlook and display the **Calendar** folder. If you are working in a college lab or other classroom environment, clear all previous calendar entries made by others as follows: From the **View** menu, point to **Current View**, and then click **Active Appointments**. If any appointments display, press Ctrl + A, and then click **Delete**. Return to the **Current View**, using the same steps, and then clicking **Day/Week/Month**.

2. In the **Date Navigator**, click the **right arrow** to advance the calendar to **June** of the next year. Click the **Monday** of the first full week of June. From the **Actions** menu, click **New All Day Event**. In the **Event** form, as the **Subject**, type Leisure Life Staff Visit Set the **End time** to **Friday** of the same week. Mr. Taylor likes to organize his calendar using categories. Click **Categorize**, and then click **All Categories**. Rename **Red Category** as Important and rename **Purple Category** as VIP which Mr. Taylor uses for very important people. Assign both the **Important** and **VIP** categories to this event. Set the **Reminder** to **None**. In the comments area, type Writer and photographer will stay in the Azalea and Cardinal guest rooms Save & Close the appointment.

3. In the appointment area, click the **9:00 am** time slot, and then type Staff Meeting Drag the bottom border down to **10:00 am**. Open the appointment, set the **Reminder** to **None**, and then **Save & Close** the appointment. In the appointment area, click in the **12:00 pm** time slot, and type Lunch with Carmen Drag the bottom border down to **1:00 pm**. Open the appointment and set the **Reminder** to **None**. **Save & Close** the appointment.

4. Open a new **Appointment** form. As the **Subject**, type Dinner with Leisure Life staff Set the **Start time** to **7:00 PM** and the **End time** to **9:00 PM**. Assign the **Important** and **VIP** categories. Set the **Reminder** to **None**. **Save & Close** the appointment.

5. In the **Date Navigator**, click the **Tuesday** of the same week in which you are entering appointments, and then open a new **Appointment** form. As the **Subject**, type Leisure Life photo shoot Assign the **Important** category. Set the **Start time** to **9:00 AM** and the **End time** to **12:00 PM**. Set the **Reminder** to **None**. Display the **Appointment Recurrence** dialog box. Set the **Recurrence pattern** to **Daily** and the **Range of recurrence** to **End after 2 occurrences**. Click **OK**. **Save & Close** the appointment.

6. In the **Date Navigator**, click the **Friday** of the same week in which you are working. Open a new appointment. As the **Subject**, type Breakfast with Leisure Life staff Set the **Start time** to **8:00 AM** and the **End time** to **9:00 AM**. Set the **Reminder** to **None**. **Save & Close** the appointment.

7. In the **Date Navigator**, click the **Tuesday** of the same week in which you have been working. From the **File** menu, display the **Page Setup: Tri-fold Style** dialog box. On the **Header/Footer tab**, delete any existing header or footer information. In the left **Footer** box, type 3G_Magazine_Story_Week_Firstname_Lastname Click **Print** to return to the **Print** dialog box. **Preview** and **Print** the calendar. Submit the end result to your instructor as directed.

8. Click the **event banner** one time to select it. From the **File** menu, display the **Page**

(Project 3G–Magazine Story continues on the next page)

Mastering Outlook

(Project 3G–Magazine Story continued)

Setup: Memo Style dialog box. Delete any existing header or footer information. In the left **Footer** box, type **3G_Magazine_Story_Event_Firstname_Lastname** Click **Print** to return to the **Print** dialog box. **Preview**, and then **Print** the event. Submit the end result to your instructor as directed.

9. Select the **event banner**, click **Categorize**, and then click **All Categories**. Rename **Important** as **Red Category** and **VIP** as **Purple Category**. **Close** the dialog box.

10. From the **View** menu, point to **Current View**, and then click **Active**

Appointments. Press Ctrl + A to select all the appointments, and then click **Delete**. Return to the **Current View**, using the same steps, and then click **Day/Week/Month**.

11. In the **Navigation Pane**, click the **Folder List** button. Under **All Folders**, right-click the **Deleted Items** folder and empty it. Display the **Calendar** folder, and then display the **Define Print Styles** dialog box. Reset both the **Tri-fold Style** and the **Memo Style**. **Close** the dialog box, and then **Close** Outlook.

End **You have completed Project 3G** ——————————————————

Outlook

Mastering Outlook

Project 3H — Football Weekend

Objectives: 1. *Navigate the Calendar;* **2.** *Schedule Appointments;* **3.** *Edit Appointments;* **4.** *Work with Events;* **5.** *Organize and Customize the Calendar;* **6.** *Manage a Calendar.*

In the following Mastering Outlook project, you will manage the calendar activities of Dominique Amerline, the manager of the Jefferson Inn. Every year for the national football championship game, the Jefferson Inn runs a Football Sunday weekend special for private parties. Guests are treated to a gourmet dinner, game-time snacks and beverages, a post game buffet, and overnight accommodations. The inn's conference rooms, music room, and dining room are each converted into large-screen theaters for fun and relaxing viewing of the game. Each room accommodates private Football Sunday parties of 15 to 25 guests. Ms. Amerline is responsible for coordinating this event. Your completed calendar will be similar to the one shown in Figure 3.43.

For Project 3H, you will need the following files:

New blank Appointment form
New blank Event form

You will print two files with the following footers:
3H_Football_Weekend_Saturday_Firstname_Lastname
3H_Football_Weekend_Sunday_Firstname_Lastname

Figure 3.43

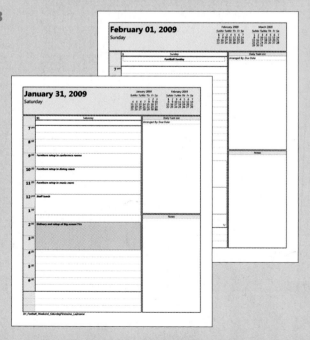

(Project 3H–Football Weekend continues on the next page)

Content-Based Assessments

Outlook

Mastering Outlook

(Project 3H–Football Weekend continued)

1. **Start** Outlook and display the **Calendar** folder. If you are working in a college lab or other classroom environment, clear all previous calendar entries made by others as follows: From the **View** menu, point to **Current View**, and then click **Active Appointments**. If any appointments display, press `Ctrl` + `A`, and then click **Delete**. Return to the **Current View**, using the same steps, and then clicking **Day/Week/Month**.

2. Advance the calendar to **February**, and then click the first **Sunday** in February. Schedule an event for that day. As the **Subject**, type **Football Sunday** Set the **Reminder** to **None**, and then **Save & Close** the event. Display the **Saturday** *before* Football Sunday. By typing directly in the appointment area and extending as necessary, create four appointments as follows: In the **9:00 am–10:00 am** time slot, create an appointment for **Furniture setup in conference rooms** From **10:00 am–11:00 am** Furniture setup in dining room From **11:00 am–12:00 pm** Furniture setup in music room From **12:00 pm–1:30 pm** Staff lunch

3. To open all four appointments at one time, select the first appointment, hold down `Ctrl`, and then click the remaining appointments. Right-click any selected appointment, and then from the displayed shortcut menu, click **Open Items**. Remove the reminders in all four appointments.

4. Create a new appointment, using a form, with the **Subject Delivery and setup of big screen TVs** Set the **Start time** to **2:00 PM** and the **End time** to **4:00 PM**. Rename

the **Orange Category** as **Important** and assign it to this appointment. Remove the reminder.

5. In the **Date Navigator**, click the **Sunday** for Football Sunday game day. In a new **Appointment** form, make the **Subject Beverages and snacks** Set the **Start time** to **2:00 PM** and the **End time** to **4:00 PM**. Remove the reminder.

6. Create the following three new appointments on Sunday, and remove the reminder from each one as you create it: **Football Sunday Dinner** starting at **4:00 PM** and ending at **6:00 PM**; **Pre-game & Game** starting at **6:00 PM** and ending at **10:00 PM**; and **Post-game buffet** starting at **10:00 PM** and ending at **11:30 PM**.

7. Display the **Saturday** before Football Sunday. Prepare to print in **Daily Style** with the footer **3H_Football_Weekend_ Saturday_Firstname_Lastname Preview** and **Print** the schedule for this day. Display **Sunday**, the day of the game. Prepare to print using the **Daily Style** and the footer **3H_Football_Weekend_Sunday_Firstname_ Lastname Preview**, and then **Print** the schedule for this day. Submit the end results to your instructor as directed.

8. Rename the **Important** category to its default name. Using a method of your choice, delete all the appointments and the event for the Saturday and Sunday of the Football Sunday weekend. Be sure the final view is **Day/Week/Month**. Empty the **Deleted Items** folder. Display the **Calendar** folder, and **Reset** the **Daily Style** print style. **Close** Outlook.

End **You have completed Project 3H**

Content-Based Assessments

Mastering Outlook

Project 3I — Virginia History Festival

Objectives: 1. *Navigate the Calendar;* **2.** *Schedule Appointments;* **3.** *Edit Appointments;* **4.** *Work with Events;* **5.** *Organize and Customize the Calendar;* **6.** *Manage a Calendar.*

In the following Mastering Outlook project, you will manage the calendar activities of Jameson Taylor, the co-owner of the Jefferson Inn, during the Virginia History Festival. Mr. Taylor is a long-time supporter of historic preservation and local history. Every spring, the Jefferson Inn participates in the Virginia History Festival. Middle-school and high-school students from around the state gather in Charlottesville to exhibit their history projects in a juried competition. The inn is the host for some of these events. You will create an event and appointments. Your completed calendar for the week will look similar to the one shown in Figure 3.44.

For Project 3I, you will need the following files:

New blank Appointment form
New blank Event form

You will print one file with the following footer:
3I_History_Festival_Week_Firstname_Lastname

Figure 3.44

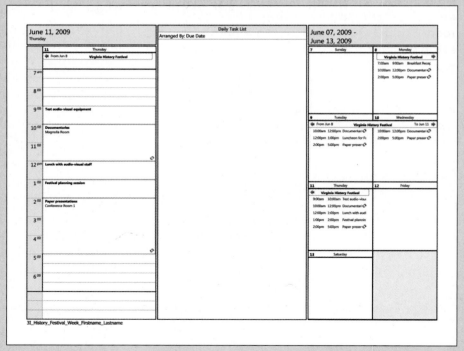

(Project 3I–Virginia History Festival continues on the next page)

Content-Based Assessments

Mastering Outlook

(Project 3I–Virginia History Festival continued)

1. **Start** Outlook and display the **Calendar** folder. If you are working in a college lab or other classroom environment, clear all previous calendar entries made by others as follows: From the **View** menu, point to **Current View**, and then click **Active Appointments**. If any appointments display, press Ctrl + A, and then click **Delete**. Return to the **Current View**, using the same steps, and then click **Day/Week/Month**.

2. Advance the calendar to the next **June**. Display **Monday** in the first full week in June, and schedule an event for that day. Make the **Subject Virginia History Festival** Set the event to start on **Monday** and end on the **Thursday** of the same week. Remove the reminder.

3. On **Monday** of the week in which you are working, create three new appointments as follows, removing the reminders for each: **Breakfast Reception** in **Conference Room 1** starting at **7:00 AM** and ending at **9:00 AM** and **Paper presentations** in **Conference Room 1** starting at **2:00 PM** and ending at **5:00 PM**. Make this appointment a recurring appointment, with a **Daily** recurrence pattern ending after **4** occurrences. Create the third appointment with a subject of **Documentaries** in the **Magnolia Room** starting at **10:00 AM** and ending at **12:00 PM**. Make this appointment a **Daily** recurring appointment ending after **4** occurrences.

4. Display the **Tuesday** of the week in which you are entering appointments. In the appointment area, create an appointment at **12:00 pm** for **Luncheon for Festival Directors** and extend the time to **1:00 pm**. Remove the reminder.

5. Display **Thursday** of the week in which you are working. Create three new appointments as follows, removing the reminders for each: **Test audio-visual equipment** starting at **9:00 am** and ending at **10:00 am**, **Lunch with audio-visual staff** starting at **12:00 pm** and ending at **1:00 pm**, and **Festival planning session** starting at **1:00 pm** and ending at **2:00 pm**.

6. With **Thursday** of the same week displayed in the calendar, display the **Page Setup: Tri-fold Style** dialog box. On the **Header/Footer tab**, delete any existing header or footer information. For the footer, type **3I_History_Festival_Week_Firstname_Lastname Preview** and **Print** the document. Submit the end result to your instructor as directed.

7. Delete all the appointments, including the event, Monday through Thursday of the same week in which you have been working. To make sure the calendar is empty, click **View**, point to **Current View**, and then click **Active Appointments**. Delete any appointments. To restore the calendar to its default view, click **View**, point to **Current View**, and then click **Day/Week/Month**.

8. Empty the **Deleted Items** folder. Display the **Calendar** folder, and reset the **Tri-fold Style** print style. **Close** Outlook.

End You have completed Project 3I

Outcomes-Based Assessments

Rubric

The following outcomes-based assessments are *open-ended assessments*. That is, there is no specific correct result; your result will depend on your approach to the information provided. Make *Professional Quality* your goal. Use the following scoring rubric to guide you in *how* to approach the problem and then to evaluate *how well* your approach solves the problem.

The *criteria*—Software Mastery, Content, Format and Layout, and Process—represent the knowledge and skills you have gained that you can apply to solving the problem. The *levels of performance*—Professional Quality, Approaching Professional Quality, or Needs Quality Improvement—help you and your instructor evaluate your result.

	Your completed project is of Professional Quality if you:	Your completed project is Approaching Professional Quality if you:	Your completed project Needs Quality Improvements if you:
1-Software Mastery	Choose and apply the most appropriate skills, tools, and features and identify efficient methods to solve the problem.	Choose and apply some appropriate skills, tools, and features, but not in the most efficient manner.	Choose inappropriate skills, tools, or features, or are inefficient in solving the problem.
2-Content	Construct a solution that is clear and well organized, contains content that is accurate, appropriate to the audience and purpose, and is complete. Provide a solution that contains no errors of spelling, grammar, or style.	Construct a solution in which some components are unclear, poorly organized, inconsistent, or incomplete. Misjudge the needs of the audience. Have some errors in spelling, grammar, or style, but the errors do not detract from comprehension.	Construct a solution that is unclear, incomplete, or poorly organized; contains some inaccurate or inappropriate content; or contains many errors of spelling, grammar, or style. Do not solve the problem.
3-Format and Layout	Format and arrange all elements to communicate information and ideas, clarify function, illustrate relationships, and indicate relative importance.	Apply appropriate format and layout features to some elements, but not others. Overuse features, causing minor distraction.	Apply format and layout that does not communicate information or ideas clearly. Do not use format and layout features to clarify function, illustrate relationships, or indicate relative importance. Use available features excessively, causing distraction.
4-Process	Use an organized approach that integrates planning, development, self-assessment, revision, and reflection.	Demonstrate an organized approach in some areas, but not others; or, use an insufficient process of organization throughout.	Do not use an organized approach to solve the problem.

Problem Solving

Project 3J — Youth Softball

Objectives: 1. *Navigate the Calendar;* **2.** *Schedule Appointments;* **3.** *Edit Appointments;* **5.** *Organize and Customize the Calendar;* **6.** *Manage a Calendar.*

For Project 3J, you will need the following file:

New blank Appointment form

You will print one file with the following footer:
3J_Youth_Softball_Calendar_Firstname_Lastname

Jameson Taylor, the co-owner of the Jefferson Inn, is an avid softball player, and he plays regularly in an adult league. He also coaches a youth softball team, and the Jefferson Inn sponsors the team. At the end of every season, the inn hosts a barbeque for the team members. This year, his team has made the playoffs. You will manage Mr. Taylor's calendar for the week of the playoffs and the barbeque, creating appointments for the practices, games, and barbeque.

Start Outlook. In the Calendar, display the first full week of May to create Mr. Taylor's schedule for the week. Clear the reminders for all appointments. Create a new appointment for Tuesday for **Softball Practice** from 5:30 to 7:30 p.m. Create an hour-long appointment on Wednesday morning with the team's assistant coach, with a playoff-related subject. Create an appointment on Wednesday with the subject **Youth Softball practice** from 3:30 to 5:30 p.m.

On Thursday of that same week, create a recurring appointment for **Playoffs** from 3:30 to 6:00 p.m. Assign a category named Important, and make the appointment a daily recurrence, ending after two occurrences— on Friday. On Friday morning of that same week, create an hour-long appointment with the inn's chef, Bradley Matteson, with a subject related to the barbeque. On Friday, create a new appointment for the barbeque from 6:00 to 8:00 p.m.

Print the calendar for the week in a print style that shows both Thursday and the entire week, adding the footer **3J_Youth_Softball_Calendar_ Firstname_Lastname** to the file. Submit the end result to your instructor as directed. Change the Important category to its default name. Delete the calendar entries for the week in which you have been working. Empty the contents of the Deleted Items folder, and reset the print style you used.

End You have completed Project 3J

chapter three   ## Problem Solving

Project 3K — Charity Art Show

Objectives: 1. *Navigate the Calendar;* **2.** *Schedule Appointments;* **3.** *Edit Appointments;* **4.** *Work with Events;* **5.** *Organize and Customize the Calendar;* **6.** *Manage a Calendar.*

For Project 3K, you will need the following files:

New blank Appointment form
New blank Event form

You will print one file with the following footer:
3K_Art_Show_Calendar_Firstname_Lastname

A unique feature of the Jefferson Inn is its fine collection of American antiques and art. Many of America's best nineteenth-century artists are represented in the inn's collection of oil paintings and watercolors. A local charity is staging an art show, auction, and gala, and has asked the inn to donate its space for the event. The inn's collection would complement the art show and draw art lovers from around the area. In this project, you will manage the schedule of the inn's co-owner, Carmen Jeffries, during the week of the gala.

Start Outlook. In the Calendar, display the first full week of March to create Ms. Jeffries' schedule for the week. Clear the reminders for all appointments, and assign a location for all appointments, except for the art show and the pre-auction showing.

Create a new appointment for Tuesday with the subject **Meet with gala chairwoman** from 10:00 to 11:00 a.m. Create a new appointment for Wednesday with the subject **Lunch with art director** from 12:00 to 1:00 p.m. Create a new appointment for Thursday with the subject **Meet with auction master** from 11:00 to 12:00 p.m. On Thursday afternoon, create a new, hour-long appointment with the inn's co-owner, Jameson Taylor, with an auction-related subject.

On Friday of that same week, create an event with the subject **Charlottesville Hospice Art Show and Gala** Make it a two-day event, ending on Saturday. On Friday morning, create a new, hour-long appointment with the inn's chef, Bradley Matteson, with a gala-related subject. On Friday, create a new appointment with the subject **Pre-auction Showing** from 5:00 to 8:00 p.m. Assign a category named Important. On Saturday of that same week, create a new appointment with the subject **Auction and Dinner** from 6:00 p.m. to 11:00 p.m. Assign a category named Important.

Print the calendar using a print style that shows both Friday and the entire week, adding the footer **3K_Art_Show_Calendar_Firstname_ Lastname** to the file. Submit the end result to your instructor as directed. Change the Important category to its default name. Delete the calendar

(Project 3K–Charity Art Show continues on the next page)

Problem Solving

(Project 3K–Charity Art Show continued)

items for Tuesday through Saturday of the week in which you have been working. Delete the contents of the Deleted Items folder, and reset the print style you used.

End **You have completed Project 3K** ———————————

Problem Solving

Project 3L—Plant Swap

Objectives: 1. *Navigate the Calendar;* **2.** *Schedule Appointments;* **3.** *Edit Appointments;* **4.** *Work with Events;* **5.** *Organize and Customize the Calendar;* **6.** *Manage a Calendar.*

> **For Project 3L, you will need the following files:**
>
> New blank Appointment form
> New blank Event form

You will print one file with the following footer:
3L_Plant_Swap_Calendar_Firstname_Lastname

The Jefferson Inn's extensive gardens draw gardening enthusiasts from around the area. One of the secrets of the inn's large variety of flowers and shrubs is the annual plant swap the inn sponsors each spring. The inn's gardeners trade bulbs, specimens, and advice with other gardeners. Over the years, Carmen Jeffries has turned this informal weekend activity into a fun and popular event. The swap occurs on Saturday and Sunday morning and includes brunch. In this project, you will manage Ms. Jeffries' schedule during the plant swap weekend.

Start Outlook. In the Calendar, display the first full week of March to create Ms. Jeffries' schedule for the week. Clear the reminders for all appointments.

Create a new appointment for Wednesday with the subject **Meet with gardeners to discuss setup** from 10:00 to 11:00 a.m., and choose an appropriate location. Create a new appointment for Thursday with the subject **Go over brunch menu with Bradley** from 2:00 to 3:00 p.m. with a location of **Bradley's office** On Friday morning, create a new, hour-long appointment with the inn's co-owner, Jameson Taylor, with a brunch-related subject, and choose an appropriate location. Create a new appointment for Friday with the subject **Tent setup** from 2:00 to 4:00 p.m. and assign an appropriate category name to it.

On Saturday of that same week, create an event with the subject **Plant Swap and Brunch** Make it a two-day event, ending on Sunday. For Saturday, create a new appointment with the subject **Plant Swap** from 10:00 a.m. to 1:00 p.m. Assign an appropriate category name, and make it a daily recurrence, ending after two occurrences—on Sunday.

Print the calendar using a print style that shows both Saturday and the entire week, adding the footer **3L_Plant_Swap_Calendar_Firstname_Lastname** to the file. Submit the end result to your instructor as directed. Change the categories to their default names. Delete the calendar items for Wednesday through Sunday of the week in which you have been working. Empty the contents of the Deleted Items folder, and reset the print style you used.

End You have completed Project 3L

GO! with Help

Project 3M — *GO!* with Help

You can create a calendar and share it with others as a Web page. You might want to do this when, for example, you are involved in a project that has many activities and events that you want other project team members to know about. You could also create a Web page for personal activities such as a soccer team schedule.

1. **Start** Outlook. In the **Type a question for help** box, type **Publish calendar online** and press Enter.

   An Outlook Help window displays information about calendars.

2. In the **Outlook Help** window, locate the link **Publish a calendar on Office Online**. Click this link.

3. Read the information, and click related links, if necessary.

4. When you are through, **Close** the Help window, and then **Close** Outlook.

End **You have completed Project 3M**

chapter**four**

Planning Meetings

OBJECTIVES

At the end of this chapter you will be able to:

1. Publish Free/Busy Information
2. Schedule a Meeting
3. Respond to Meeting Requests
4. Schedule an Office Resource
5. Manage Meeting Information

OUTCOMES

Mastering these objectives will enable you to:

PROJECT 4A
Managing Meetings

Owens Family Builders

Owens Family Builders was founded in 1968 as Owens and Sons Builders; in 1980, the name was changed to reflect the extended family that had joined the business. Today the company has more than 300 employees, including about 50 members of the Owens family. Focusing on home building, the company is known for quality construction, innovative design, and customer service. Owens Family Builders has built more than 3,000 homes in the Orlando area and has also built many schools, shopping centers, and government buildings.

Planning Meetings

Meetings are similar to appointments. They are stored in your Calendar folder, and they appear in your schedule resembling appointments. You create, edit, and view them like appointments. Appointments involve only your own schedule and time, but meetings involve the schedules of all meeting participants. Outlook helps you plan meetings by enabling you to share your calendar information with others. You can organize a meeting based on the participants' availability as shown in their Outlook calendars. Similarly, your calendar can be made available to others who need your participation in a meeting. You can also use Outlook to reserve resources for meetings, such as a conference room or audiovisual equipment.

Project 4A New Construction

In Activities 4.1 through 4.16, you will plan meetings for members of the management team of Owens Family Builders. You will make the calendar of Warren Owens available on the Internet, and you will schedule meetings for him. You will send meeting invitations, add and remove meeting attendees, send updates, check the response status for scheduled meetings, and cancel meetings. Warren Owens will receive invitations to attend various meetings. You will accept and decline invitations, tentatively accept invitations, and propose new meeting times. You will also book office resources and schedule a resource for a meeting. Upon completion, your calendar and one of your invitations will look similar to the ones shown in Figure 4.1.

For Project 4A, you will need the following files:

o04A_New_Construction_Contacts
o04A_New_Construction_Inbox
BrianFong.vfb
JohnZeidler.vfb
JenniferOwens.vfb
BrianFong2011.vfb
JohnZeidler2011.vfb
JenniferOwens2011.vfb

You will print two files with the following footers:
4A_New_Construction_Calendar_Firstname_Lastname
4A_New_Construction_Meeting_Firstname_Lastname

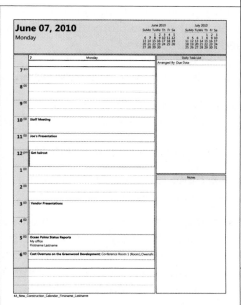

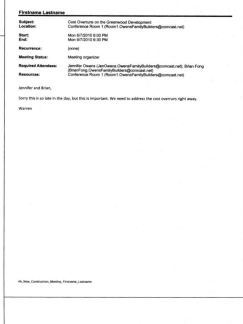

Figure 4.1
Project 4A—New Construction

Objective 1
Publish Free/Busy Information

When you create an appointment in your calendar, Outlook displays one of four indicators associated with your availability for that date and time: Busy, Free, Tentative, or Out of Office. This is referred to as your *free/busy information*. Outlook's default setting for all appointments is Busy. These indicators display in your *local calendar*—the calendar stored on the hard drive of your computer. The free/busy indicators also display when others view your calendar on a shared server.

Microsoft's system for sharing Outlook information among members on a network is the *Exchange Server*—special server software for networks. In an Exchange Server environment, your free/busy schedule is shared automatically with all other users on the Exchange Server. If you want others who are *not* on the Exchange Server to see your free/busy schedule or you do not use an Exchange Server, you can still share your free/busy information by publishing it on any server to which you have *read/write access*—a server on which you can view and store information. For example, your company may have a server that you can use to make this information available to all your coworkers. You can configure Outlook to use such a server to show this information.

Alert!

Starting Project 4A

Because Outlook stores information on the hard drive of the computer at which you are working, unless you are working on your own computer, it is recommended that you complete Project 4A in one working session. Allow approximately one and a half to two hours.

Activity 4.1 Exploring the Free/Busy Schedule

In this activity, you will create appointments for Warren Owens of Owens Family Builders and then explore his free/busy schedule for the day of the scheduled appointments.

1 **Start** Outlook and display the **Navigation Pane**. In the **Navigation Pane**, click the **Mail** button [Mail], display the **Inbox** folder, and then delete any existing messages in the Inbox by clicking the message, and then clicking the **Delete** button [X]. From the **Navigation Pane**, display the **Contacts** [Contacts] folder, and then delete any existing contacts.

2 From the **Navigation Pane**, display the **Calendar** [Calendar] folder. In the **Date Navigator**, click the **right arrow**, and then advance the calendar to next **June** or **December**, *whichever month is closest to the current month*. Click the **first Monday** in the month. Delete any existing calendar items for that day, and then compare your screen with Figure 4.2.

Outlook displays free/busy information for only 10 months into the future, so the first Monday in either June or December will be less than 10 months in the future.

Figure 4.2

Right arrow advances the calendar

December or June displayed; your year may differ

First Monday in either December or June selected

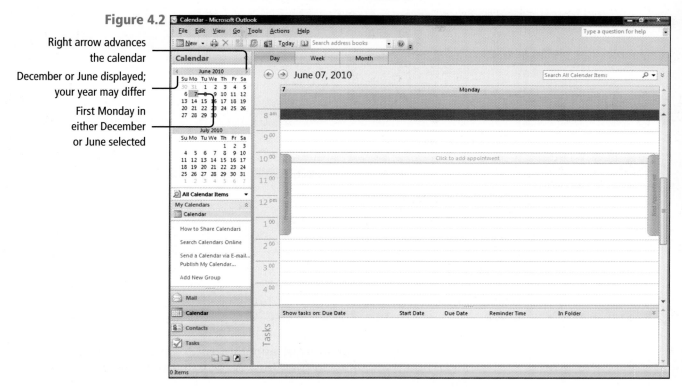

3 In the appointment area, click the **10:00 am** time slot, and type **Staff Meeting** Extend the bottom border of the appointment to **11:00 am**. In the **11:00 am** time slot, type **Joe's Presentation** In the **12:00 pm** time slot, type **Get haircut** and then extend the bottom border of this appointment to **1:00 pm**.

4 In the **3:00 pm** time slot, type **Vendor Presentations** and extend the time to **5:00 pm**. Click any blank area of the calendar, and compare your screen with Figure 4.3.

Figure 4.3

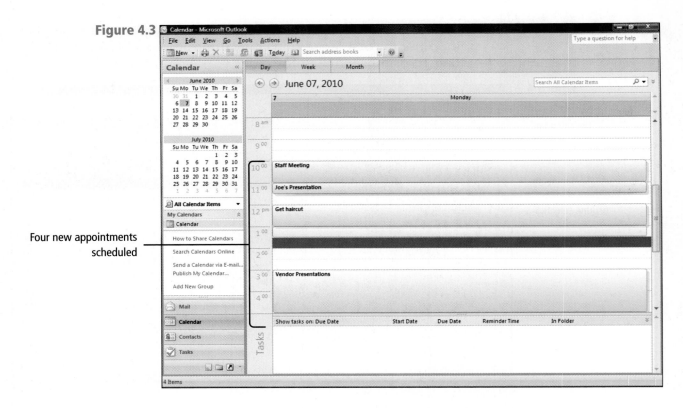

Four new appointments scheduled

5 Double-click the **Get haircut** appointment to open its appointment form, and then notice in the **Show As** box that the setting is set as *Busy*.

By default, Outlook assigns the ***Busy*** setting to all new appointments, which indicates that you have an appointment or meeting scheduled for that time. Others on the network who can view your calendar cannot see the specific details of your appointment, but they see that your time is scheduled—you are *busy*.

6 Click the **Show As arrow** and notice that for each of the four choices, a colored or patterned box displays; for example, *Out of Office* has a purple box. Click **Out of Office**. On the Appointment form toolbar,

click the **Save & Close** button [icon], click in a blank time slot, and then compare your screen with Figure 4.4.

The left border for the *Get haircut* appointment changes to purple, which indicates an ***Out of Office*** status. Use this setting to indicate when you are away from your office and not available for other meetings or appointments. Outlook assigns a different border color or pattern to each of the four different free/busy availability options. The default blue border indicates a *Busy* status.

Figure 4.4

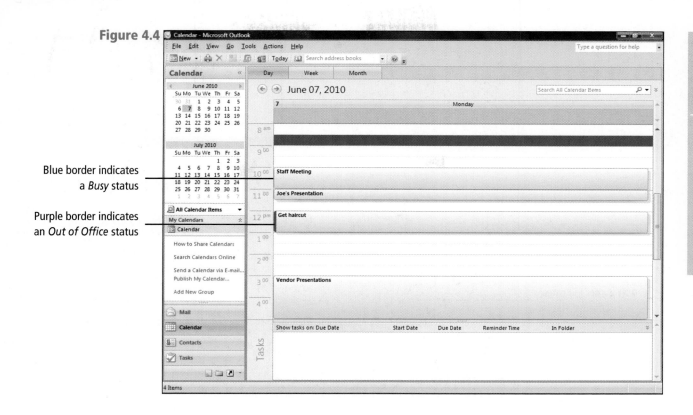

Blue border indicates a *Busy* status

Purple border indicates an *Out of Office* status

Note — Using the Out of Office and Busy Settings

The *Busy* and *Out of Office* settings for appointments and meetings are most meaningful when you apply them so that your coworkers can predict your availability. Use *Busy* for appointments and meetings in which you are in the building but are busy in appointments or meetings. Use *Out of Office* when you are out of the building and possibly some distance away—in other words, you are not necessarily available right after that time for another appointment or meeting.

7 Open the **Vendor Presentations** appointment form, click the **Show As arrow**, and then click **Tentative**. Click the **Reminder arrow** and then click **None**. **Save & Close** the appointment, and then click in a blank time slot. Compare your screen with Figure 4.5.

The left border for the *Vendor Presentations* appointment indicates that the appointment is ***Tentative***—the appointment is scheduled but not confirmed. Use *Tentative* when you want to indicate that the specified time might be available or that your attendance at an appointment or meeting is uncertain.

Figure 4.5

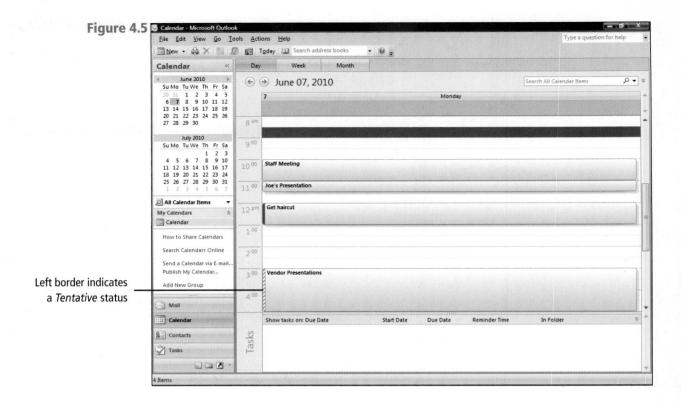

Left border indicates a *Tentative* status

8 In the appointment area, click the **2:00 pm** time slot. On the Standard toolbar, click the **New Appointment** button.

The *Start time* for the appointment is indicated as *2:00 PM*. Recall that the default Start time for an appointment is the currently selected time in the appointment area.

9 In the Appointment form, click the **Scheduling** button. Take a moment to study the parts of the screen as shown in Figure 4.6.

The free/busy schedule for this day is displayed as a table. Your schedule for the day displays as the second row in the table, with your name listed under *All Attendees*—or the user name Outlook is currently configured to display on your computer. Notice that Outlook uses the different color codes associated with the appointments to show your availability for this day. The shaded column at 2:00 pm is the currently selected time for the new appointment. As you add *attendees*—meeting participants—to a meeting, their names will display under *All Attendees*, and their free/busy schedules will display in the adjacent rows.

Appointment form with the
Scheduling button selected

Column for current
start time selected

Figure 4.6

Current date—your
date may differ

Your name—or the user
name for your computer

Your scheduled
appointments
for this day

Use scroll bar to adjust
date and time displayed

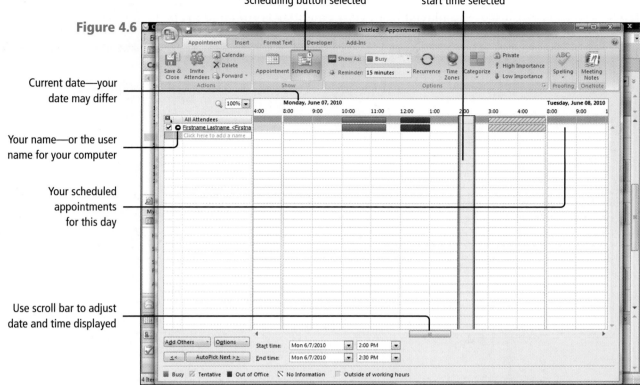

10 Locate the scroll bar at the bottom of the schedule, and then click the **left scroll arrow** several times to adjust the displayed time for the day.

You can use the horizontal scroll bar at the bottom of the schedule to adjust both the time and day displayed.

11 Close the appointment form *without* saving the new appointment.

Activity 4.2 Publishing Your Free/Busy Information

If you work in an Exchange Server environment, your free/busy information is automatically available to anyone who uses the server and displays your calendar. If you want to make your free/busy information available to others *not* on this server or you do not use an Exchange Server, you can make this information available on any server to which you have read/write access. Thus, people who need to include you in meetings can see your availability. In this activity, you will configure Outlook to make Warren Owens's free/busy schedule available to his coworkers at Owens Family Builders.

1 From the **Tools** menu, display the **Options** dialog box. Under **Calendar**, click **Calendar Options**. In the displayed **Calendar Options** dialog box, at the bottom, under **Advanced options**, click the **Free/Busy Options** command button. Compare your dialog box with Figure 4.7.

The Free/Busy Options dialog box displays. If you do not have an Exchange Server e-mail account, use this dialog box to specify the server that contains your calendar information. Under Options, you can specify how many months of calendar information you want to make available. The default is two months, and the information displayed from your calendar is updated every 15 minutes.

Figure 4.7

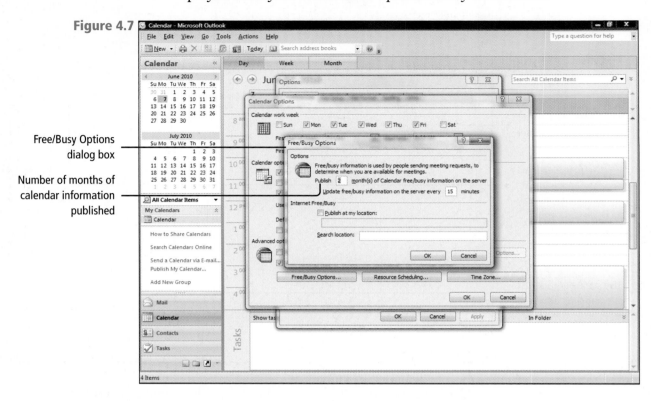

Free/Busy Options dialog box

Number of months of calendar information published

2 In the **Free/Busy Options** dialog box, select the **Publish at my location** check box if it is not already selected.

The text box under this option becomes available. A *virtual free/busy* file stores the calendar information for an individual. In this box, you specify the file that contains your calendar information. The file name is your user name, and it must include the file name extension *.vfb*—which is an abbreviation for virtual free/busy. You must also include the location of the file, which can be a local file server on your network or an address on the World Wide Web. Warren Owens's calendar information is stored on the company's local area network.

3 In **Publish at my location,** delete any existing text and type **file:\\g:\Schedules\WarrenOwens.vfb** Compare your dialog box with Figure 4.8.

This tells Outlook where to store Warren Owens's free/busy information for others to use. The specified location is a server on Owens Family Builders' local area network, on drive *g* in a folder called *Schedules*. In an actual work environment, the drive letter, folder name (if any), and user name that you would specify depend on your specific work environment—in other words, your drive letter and folder would likely differ, and you would use your own name. The address *must* begin with the prefix *file:* and your file name *must* include the *.vfb* file name extension.

Figure 4.8

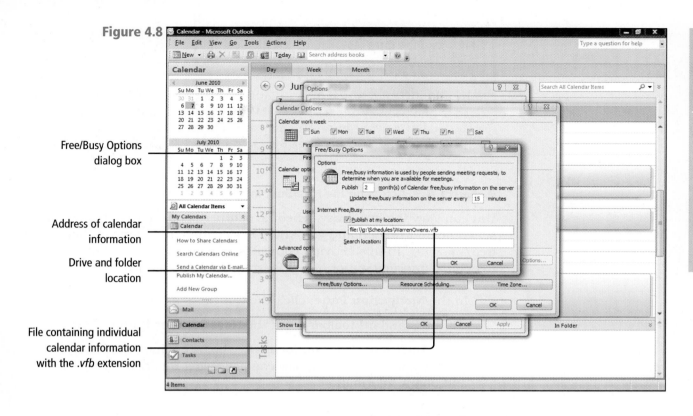

Free/Busy Options
dialog box

Address of calendar
information

Drive and folder
location

File containing individual
calendar information
with the *.vfb* extension

Note — Specifying a Location for Calendar Information

When you specify a location for your calendar information, it may be a server on your local network or an address on the World Wide Web. An example of a Web address would be *http://OwensFamilyBuilders.com/ Schedules/Warren_Owens.vfb*. The address, drive, and folder location you specify depends on your particular work environment, and you would use your own user name. Your network administrator can identify the location you would use to store your calendar information if you are not working in an Exchange Server environment.

4 In the **Free/Busy Options** dialog box, click **OK**. Click **OK** to close the **Calendar Options** dialog box, and then click **OK** to close the **Options** dialog box.

Outlook will post two months of Warren Owens's schedule information every 15 minutes to the specified server. Outlook does *not* actually use the address you specified in the previous step because this is a fictional server; *it is not necessary that your calendar information be available for others in this activity.*

More Knowledge

Updating Free/Busy Information

You can have Outlook update your free/busy information immediately if you need to make this information available to others right away. To immediately update your free/busy information, display the Tools menu, point to Send/Receive, and then click Free/Busy Information.

Activity 4.3 Accessing the Free/Busy Information of Others

You can view the free/busy schedule of other people if they publish their schedule information and you know the location and name of their free/busy file. In this activity, you will specify the location of the free/busy information for one of Warren Owens's contacts.

1 In the **Navigation Pane**, click the **Contacts** button [Contacts].

On the Standard toolbar, click the **New Contact** button [New].

2 In the **Untitled - Contact** form, use the techniques you have practiced to add the following new contact, using **Business** for the address and phone information:

Juan Sanchez
Owens Family Builders
JuanSanchez.OwensFamilyBuilders@comcast.net
407-555-0159
5000 South Orange Avenue
Orlando, FL 32835

3 Click the **Details** button [Details]. Under **Internet Free-Busy**, in the **Address** box, type **file:\\g:\Schedules\JuanSanchez.vfb** and then compare your Contact form with Figure 4.9.

The location is a file server on the Owens Family Builders local area network, on drive *g* in a folder called *Schedules*. This contact has configured his Free/Busy Options dialog box to store his schedule information in this location using this file name. If this were an actual work environment, Warren Owens and Juan Sanchez could view each other's free/busy information.

Juan Sanchez – Contact form

Figure 4.9

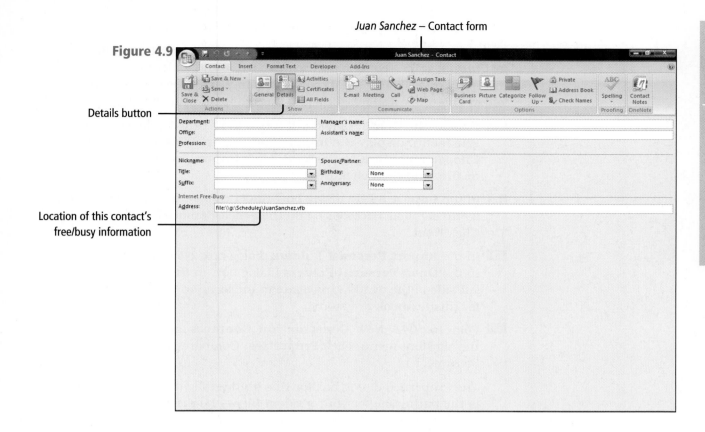

Details button

Location of this contact's
free/busy information

More Knowledge
Performing a Search for All Contacts' Free/Busy Information

If all your contacts use the same server to post their free/busy information, you can have Outlook perform a global search for free/busy information instead of specifying the location for each contact individually. Display the Tools menu, click Options, and then click Calendar Options. In the displayed Calendar Options dialog box, click Free/Busy Options and then, in the Search location box, type the location for your contacts' free/busy information using the file name *%name%.vfb*. Using a Web address, an example would be *http://OwensFamilyBuilders.com/Schedules/%name%.vfb*.

Objective 2
Schedule a Meeting

Outlook uses the term **meeting** to refer to a calendar activity that requires inviting other people or reserving a room. You can schedule meetings with other Outlook users or anyone who uses an e-mail program. Meeting invitations occur as e-mail messages. Planning a meeting involves finding an available time in your schedule and inviting the meeting attendees. After you have scheduled the meeting, you can add additional attendees. You may also need to remove attendees, send updates, check the response status, or even cancel the meeting altogether.

Activity 4.4 Importing Contacts and Copying Pathname Information

In this activity, you will copy the path location of your student files. A *pathname* is the sequence of the drive letter and folder names that lead to the files. You will also import contacts into Warren Owens's Contacts folder. This will establish some existing contacts with which you can work.

1 Display the **Contacts** folder if it is not already displayed. From the **File** menu, display the **Import and Export Wizard** dialog box. Under **Choose an action to perform**, click **Import from another program or file**, and then click **Next**.

2 In the **Import a File** dialog box, under **Select file type to import from**, scroll as necessary, and then click **Personal Folder File (.pst)**. Click **Next**.

3 In the **Import Personal Folders** dialog box, click the **Browse** button. In the **Open Personal Folders** dialog box, in the **Folders** list at the left side of the window, navigate to the location where the student files for this textbook are stored.

4 Point to **o04A_New_Construction_Contacts** and right-click. From the shortcut menu, click **Properties**. Compare your screen with Figure 4.10.

The Properties dialog box for this student file displays. The *Location* is the pathname for your student files—the drive and folder location for all your student files.

Figure 4.10

o04_New_Construction_Contacts.pst Properties dialog box

Pathname for this file; your drive and folder information will differ

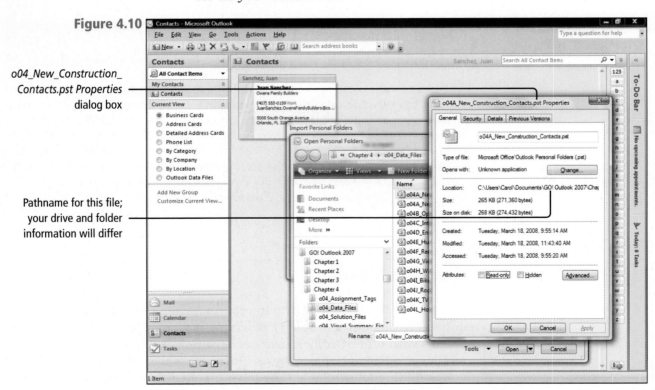

5 In the **o04A_New_Construction_Contacts.pst Properties** dialog box, place the insertion point at the beginning of the pathname. Dragging to the right, select the entire pathname (the pathname may seem to extend beyond the border of the dialog box). Compare your screen with Figure 4.11.

Figure 4.11

o04_New_Construction_Contacts.pst Properties dialog box

Pathname selected

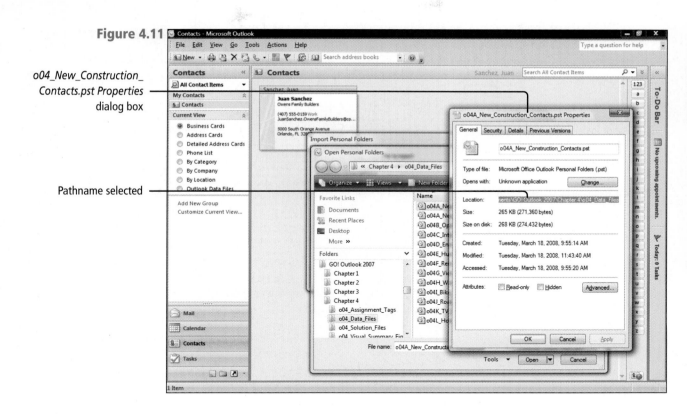

6 Right-click the selected pathname. From the displayed shortcut menu, click **Copy**.

The pathname information is copied to the Office Clipboard. Recall that the Office Clipboard is a memory area in which you can collect text and graphics from any Office program and then place them in another area of the same program or a different program. It is necessary to copy the pathname information so that it can be pasted into the Contact form at a later time in this activity.

7 In the **o04A_New_Construction_Contacts.pst Properties** dialog box, click **Cancel** to close the dialog box.

The Open Personal Folders dialog box redisplays. The file o04A_New_Construction_Contacts is still selected.

8 In the displayed **Open Personal Folders** dialog box and with the file **o04A_New_Construction_Contacts** selected, in the lower right corner of the dialog box, click **Open**. Notice that the file name displays in the **File to import** box.

9 In the **Import Personal Folders** dialog box, click **Next**. Under **Select the folder to import from**, click **Contacts**, and then click **Import items into the current folder**. Compare your screen with Figure 4.12.

The Import Personal Folders dialog box displays the folder structure for the file you are about to import.

Figure 4.12

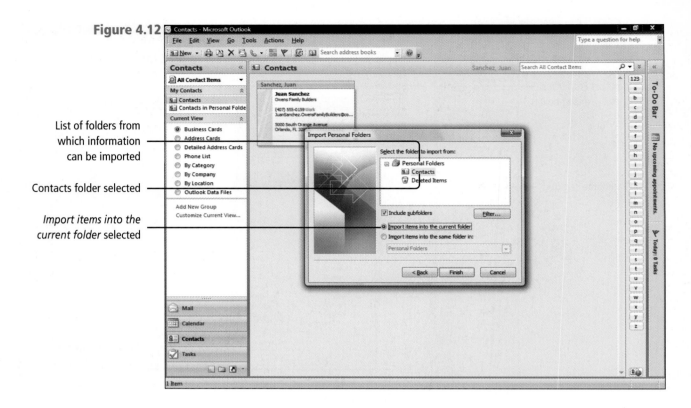

List of folders from
which information
can be imported

Contacts folder selected

Import items into the
current folder selected

10 In the **Import Personal Folders** dialog box, click **Finish**. If a
Translation Warning dialog box displays, click OK. Compare your
screen with Figure 4.13.

The contacts are imported into your Contacts folder and displayed in
Business Cards view. Your layout may differ.

Figure 4.13

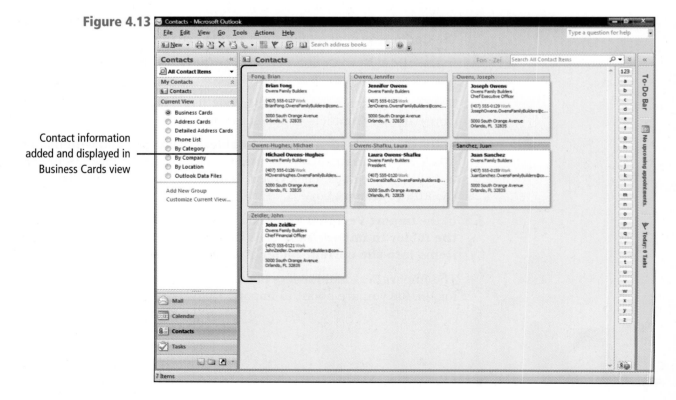

Contact information
added and displayed in
Business Cards view

11 In the **Contacts list**, double-click the **John Zeidler** contact to open it, and then click the **Details** button [image]. Under **Internet Free-Busy**, in the **Address** box, type **file:**

12 With the insertion point still located in the **Address** box, right-click, and from the displayed shortcut menu, click **Paste**.

The pathname information is copied from the Office Clipboard to the Address box.

13 With the insertion point still located in the **Address** box, after the pathname information, type **\JohnZeidler.vfb** to complete the address information for this contact's free/busy file. Compare your screen with Figure 4.14.

The address begins with the prefix *file:* and the file name includes the *.vfb* extension.

Details button   *John Zeidler – Contact* form

Figure 4.14

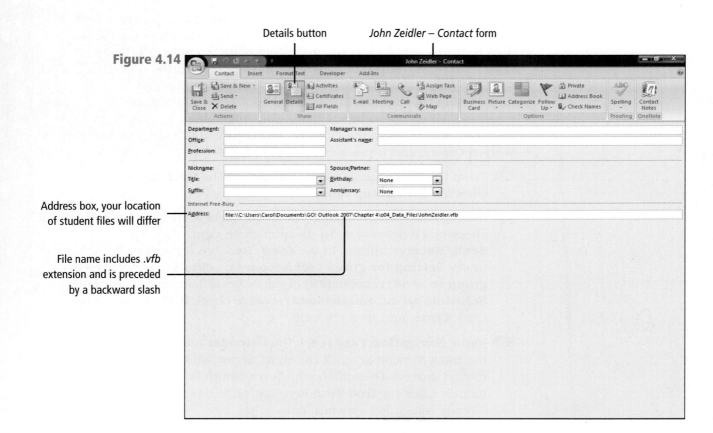

Address box, your location of student files will differ

File name includes *.vfb* extension and is preceded by a backward slash

---

Alert!   **Is the current year 2011 or later?**

If the current year is 2011 or later, you will need to use an alternate *.vfb* file for the John Zeidler contact. Outlook stores only three years of calendar information in the *.vfb* files, and the *JohnZeidler.vfb* file contains calendar information from 2008 through 2010. For the years 2011 through 2013, specify his file as *JohnZeidler2011.vfb* using the format described in the preceding step. Similarly, for the next two contacts you will edit, if the year is 2011 or later, use the files *BrianFong2011.vfb* for Brian Fong, and *JenniferOwens2011.vfb* for Jennifer Owens.

14 **Save & Close** [icon] the contact.

15 Open the **Brian Fong** contact and click the **Details** button [icon]. Under **Internet Free-Busy**, in the **Address** box, type **file:** With the insertion point still in the **Address** box, right-click, click **Paste**, and then type **\BrianFong.vfb Save & Close** [icon] the contact.

16 Open the **Jennifer Owens** contact and click the **Details** button [icon]. In the **Address** box, type **file:** With the insertion point still in the **Address** box, right-click, click **Paste**, and then type **\JenniferOwens.vfb Save & Close** [icon] the contact.

Activity 4.5 Planning a Meeting

Planning a meeting involves finding an available time in your schedule and the schedules of the meeting attendees and then inviting the attendees to the meeting. Outlook notifies meeting attendees of the meeting via e-mail, so anyone you invite to a meeting must have an e-mail address. Recall that you can configure Outlook to store all your sent messages in the Outbox. Thus, you do not have to be online to send your meeting invitations. In this activity, you will configure Outlook to place your sent messages in the Outbox, and then you will set up a meeting for Warren Owens and three of his colleagues.

1 From the **Tools** menu, click **Options**. In the **Options** dialog box, click the **Mail Setup tab**.

2 Under **Send/Receive**, clear the **Send immediately when connected** check box if necessary. To the immediate right, click the **Send/Receive** button. In the **Send/Receive Groups** dialog box, under **Setting for group "All Accounts"**, clear both **Include this group in send/receive (F9)** check boxes if necessary. Clear both **Schedule an automatic send/receive** check boxes if necessary. Click **Close**, and then click **OK**.

3 In the **Navigation Pane**, click the **Calendar** button [Calendar icon]. In the **Date Navigator**, click the **right arrow**, and advance the calendar to next June or December, whichever month is closest to the current month. Click the **first Monday**—the same day for which you have already scheduled appointments.

4 Click the **2:00 pm** time slot. From the **Actions** menu, click **Plan a Meeting**, and then compare your screen with Figure 4.15.

The Plan a Meeting dialog box displays. It is similar to the Scheduling view of the Appointment form. Your schedule for the day displays as the first name under *All Attendees*. The shaded column with a green left border and a red right border represents the currently selected time for the meeting.

Shaded column represents
currently selected time

Red border
indicates end time

Figure 4.15

Plan a Meeting dialog box

Your schedule for the day
appears as first name
under *All Attendees*

Green border indicates
start time

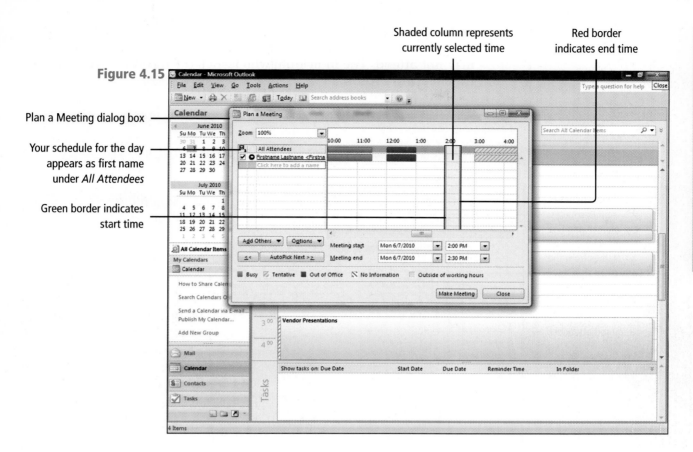

5 In the **Plan a Meeting** dialog box, click different time blocks on the time grid.

As you click various time blocks, the shaded column moves in the selected time grid. The *Meeting start time* and the *Meeting end time* boxes change as you click various time blocks.

6 Click the time block under **1:00** so that the meeting is set to run from 1:00 PM to 1:30 PM.

You can click different time blocks to adjust the time of the meeting. You may need to change the time as you add meeting attendees and you see their availability.

7 Click the time block between **11:30** and **12:00** so that the meeting is set to run from 11:30 AM to 12:00 PM.

This is your desired time for the meeting.

8 In the lower left, click **Add Others**, click **Add from Address Book**, and then compare your screen with Figure 4.16.

The Select Attendees and Resources: Contacts dialog box displays. All the names from your Contacts list that have e-mail addresses display in this dialog box, and you can select meeting attendees from the names on this list. You can also specify attendees who are required or who are optional. ***Required attendees*** must be able to attend the meeting for the meeting to take place—their knowledge and association with the meeting's topic is required.

Optional attendees are not considered critical for the meeting; if they cannot attend, the meeting can still be held and they may or may not attend. The individual who issues the meeting invitations is the *meeting organizer*.

Figure 4.16

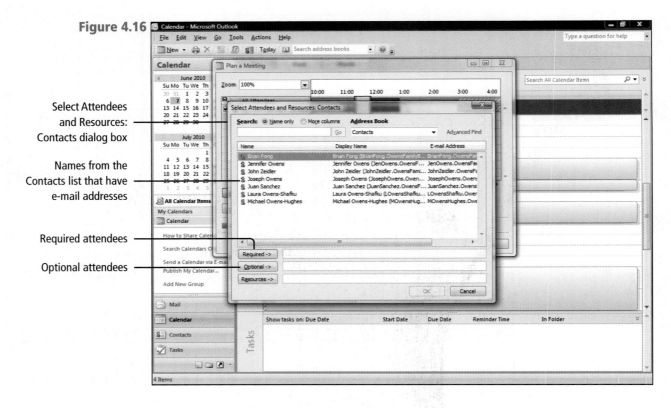

Select Attendees and Resources: Contacts dialog box

Names from the Contacts list that have e-mail addresses

Required attendees

Optional attendees

9 In the **Select Attendees and Resources: Contacts** dialog box, under **Name**, click **John Zeidler** one time to select that name, and then click **Required** to add the name to the Required box.

10 Select **Jennifer Owens**, and then click **Required**. Click **Brian Fong**, and then click **Required**.

The Required box contains three names. These are all the individuals who *must* be able to attend if the meeting is to take place. Outlook assumes that you, as the meeting organizer, will attend the meeting.

11 In the **Select Attendees and Resources: Contacts** dialog box, click **OK**. If the Microsoft Office Internet Free/Busy dialog box displays, click **Cancel**. Compare your screen with Figure 4.17.

The Plan a Meeting dialog box redisplays and shows each attendee's free/busy information. Notice that Jennifer Owens is busy at the time of your meeting. You will need to find a different time. You can have Outlook find a time at which everyone is available.

Free/busy information
of meeting attendees

Figure 4.17

Plan a Meeting
dialog box

Three names added
to meeting

AutoPick Next button

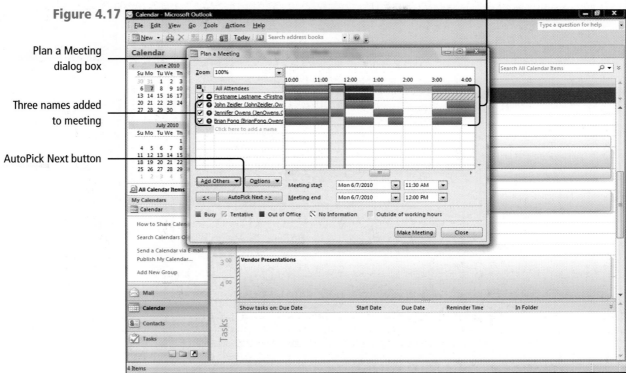

Are you using an Exchange Server?

If you are working in an Exchange Server environment, the meeting attendees may show no free/busy information. Although free/busy information is displayed automatically for Exchange Server users, this information may not display for the fictional users in this instruction.

12 At the lower left of the **Plan a Meeting** dialog box, click **AutoPick Next**.

Outlook scans the free/busy information of the meeting attendees and selects the first time that everyone is available, which is 2:00 to 2:30 PM. When the attendees have busy schedules, this can be a quick way to find a time for everyone to meet. Notice that the available times in the schedule are only *working hours*—8:00 AM until 5:00 PM. You can schedule meetings for later in the day.

13 In the **Plan a Meeting** dialog box, click **Options**, and then click **Show Only My Working Hours** to clear the check mark.

14 Click the **right scroll arrow**, and click the column under **5:00**. Position the pointer on the red border of the shaded column until it changes to the **Horizontal resize pointer** ⟷ as shown in Figure 4.18.

You can drag the green (for start) and red (for end) borders of the shaded column to change the start and end times of a meeting.

Figure 4.18

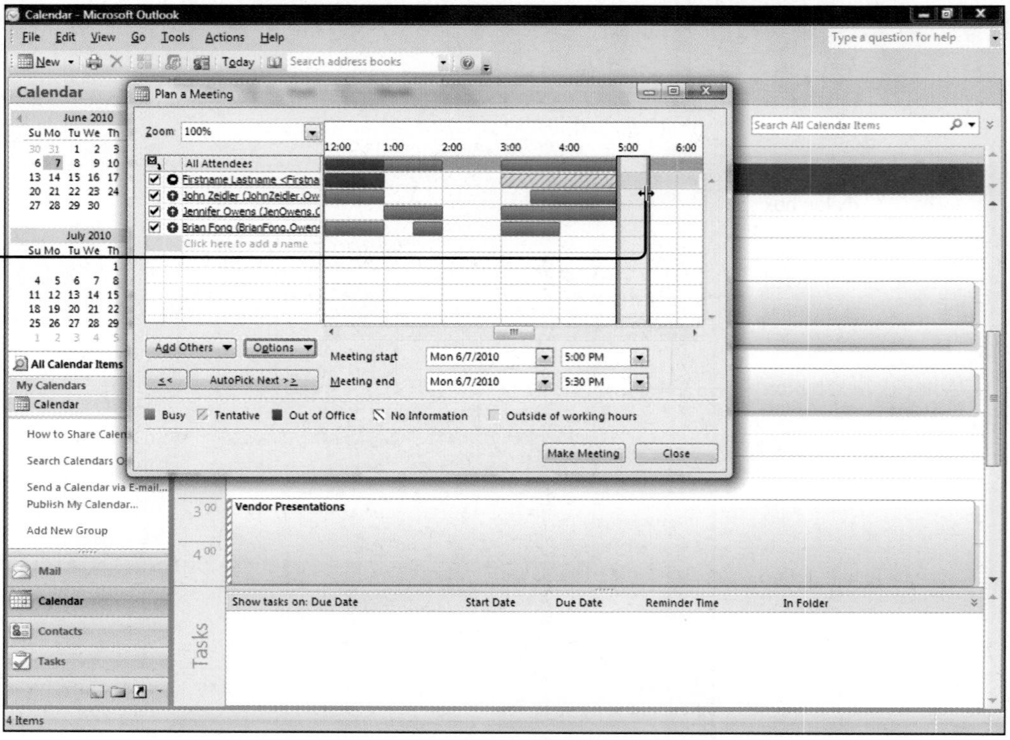

Horizontal resize pointer

15 Drag the red border to **6:00** to make the time of the meeting 5:00 PM to 6:00 PM. Then, in the lower right corner of the dialog box, click **Make Meeting**.

An Untitled - Meeting form displays. A *Meeting form*, similar to an Appointment form, includes a To: box, a Send button, and a Cancel Invitation button. The *To* box contains the e-mail addresses of the meeting attendees. In the meeting form you can add a Subject and other information in the same manner as you would any other e-mail message.

16 In the **Subject** box, type **Ocean Palms Status Reports** In the **Location** box, type **My office** Click the **Reminder arrow**, and then click **None**. In the comments area, type **Status reports on Ocean Palms condominium development** Compare your screen with Figure 4.19.

The *To* box contains the e-mail addresses of all the meeting attendees. Depending on the size and resolution of your screen, up and down arrows may display on the right side of the *To* box, indicating there are more names in the box than are visible.

Figure 4.19

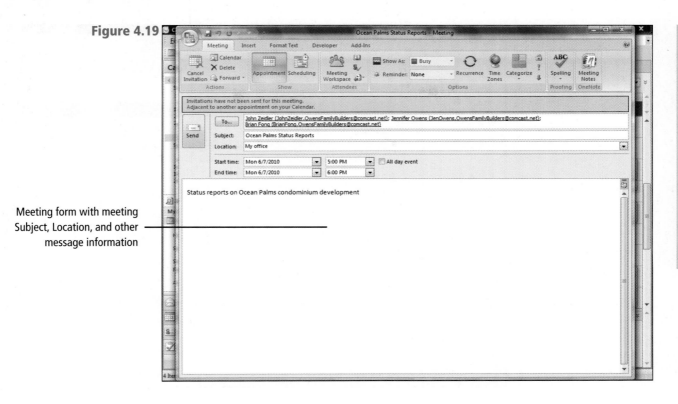

Meeting form with meeting Subject, Location, and other message information

17 On the Meeting form, click the **Send** button [Send].

The invitations are sent to the Outbox, and the Meeting form closes. The Plan a Meeting dialog box remains open. The time slot for your name—the meeting organizer—displays the 5:00 PM to 6:00 PM time slot as Busy.

18 **Close** the **Plan a Meeting** dialog box, and compare your screen with Figure 4.20, scrolling if necessary.

The meeting is added to your calendar. Notice your name is displayed as the meeting organizer. Compare this with *Staff Meeting*, which is an appointment, not a meeting, despite its name. Because you did not invite people or reserve a room for *Staff Meeting*, it is simply an appointment for something you plan to do.

Figure 4.20

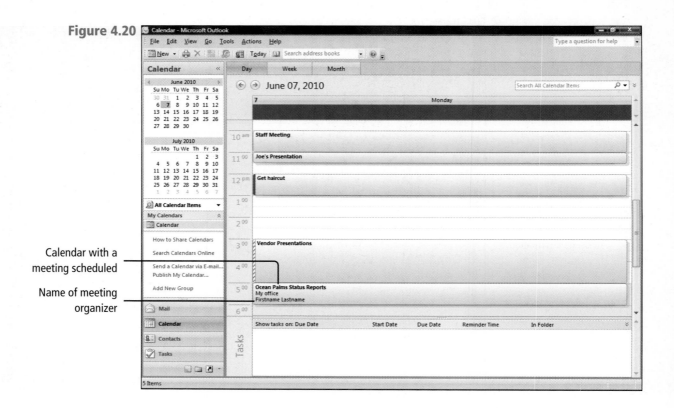

Calendar with a meeting scheduled

Name of meeting organizer

Activity 4.6 Adding Meeting Attendees

You can add more people to a scheduled meeting after you have scheduled a time and issued invitations. In this activity, you will add two more individuals at Owens Family Builders to the meeting.

1 With your calendar still showing the first Monday in June or December, open the **Ocean Palms Status Reports** meeting. Compare your screen with Figure 4.21.

The Meeting form displays. A banner at the top of the form describes the responses of the meeting attendees. The banner indicates that you have not yet received any responses. The banner also reminds you that this appointment is adjacent to another time slot in the calendar.

Figure 4.21

Banner indicates meeting
attendees' responses
not yet received

Ocean Palms Status
Reports – Meeting form

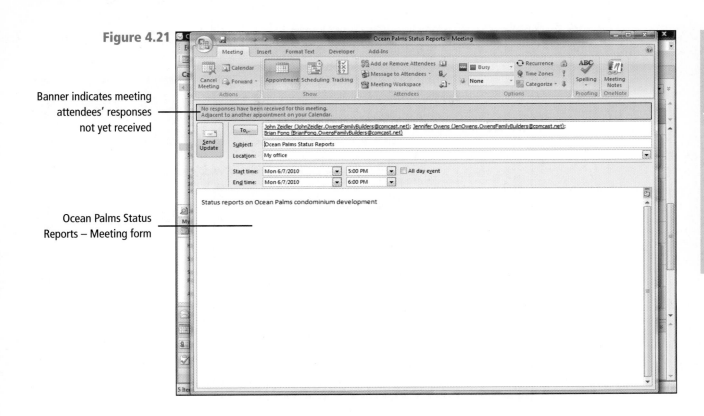

2 On the Ribbon, click the **Add or Remove Attendees** button
 Add or Remove Attendees . In the displayed **Select Attendees and
Resources: Contacts** dialog box, click **Joseph Owens**, and then in
the lower left portion of the dialog box, click **Optional**.

Joseph Owen's name displays in the Optional box. The attendance of
an optional attendee is not critical to the meeting—the meeting can
take place with or without the optional attendee.

3 Click **Michael Owens-Hughes**, and then click **Optional**. Click **OK** to
close the **Select Attendees and Resources: Contacts** dialog box and
redisplay the **Meeting** form.

4 In the Meeting form, if not all names appear in the **To** box, click the
To down arrow to see the two additional names you added to your
meeting.

5 Click the **Scheduling** button Scheduling , and compare your screen with
Figure 4.22.

In the *Meeting* form, the ***Scheduling button*** changes the view to
display available free/busy information for all meeting attendees.
The schedule shows the two new names you added to the meeting.
No free/busy information displays for the two new names. Joseph
Owens and Michael Owens-Hughes have not made their free/busy
information available. The column adjacent to All Attendees shows
icons indicating the type of attendee.

Figure 4.22

Scheduling button

Ocean Palms Status
Reports – Meeting form

Free/busy information not
available for these attendees

Icons indicating the type
of attendee—organizer,
required, or optional

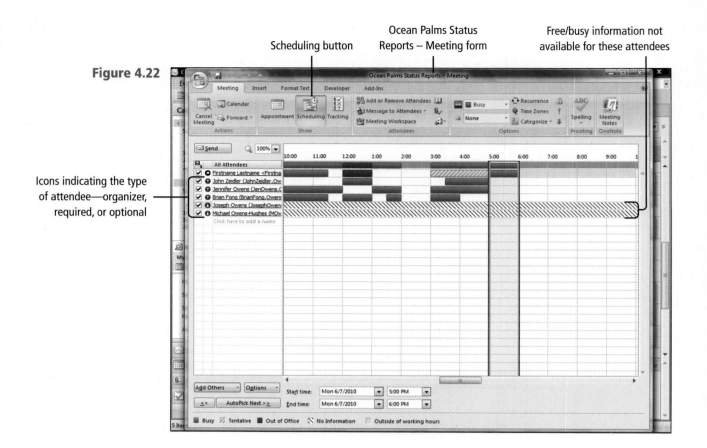

6 Point to each of the icons to see the ScreenTip that describes an attendee either as Meeting Organizer, Required Attendee, or Optional Attendee.

7 On the **Meeting** form, click **Send** [Send].

The Send Updates to Attendees dialog box displays. You have the option of sending updates to all meeting attendees or only to those individuals you have added or deleted. If you expect to make additional changes to the individuals attending a meeting, you can wait until you have finalized the meeting to send the update to all attendees.

8 Click **Send updates only to added or deleted attendees**, and then click **OK**.

The Meeting form closes. Meeting invitations are sent to the two additional meeting attendees.

Activity 4.7 Removing Meeting Attendees

After you have organized a meeting, you may decide that one or more of the individuals you have invited do not need to attend the meeting. You can remove an attendee from a meeting. In this activity, Warren Owens, the meeting organizer, has learned that Joseph Owens will not be available for the meeting, so you will remove him from the list of meeting attendees.

1 In the calendar, open the **Ocean Palms Status Reports** meeting. On the Ribbon, click the **Add or Remove Attendees** button [Add or Remove Attendees].

2 In the displayed **Select Attendees and Resources: Contacts** dialog box, in the **Optional** box, click **Joseph Owens**, and then be sure Joseph's name is selected, as shown in Figure 4.23.

Figure 4.23

Select Attendees and Resources: Contacts dialog box

Joseph Owens selected in the Optional box

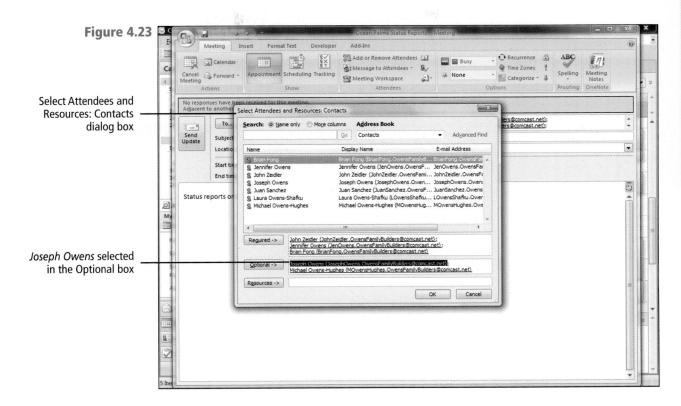

3 Press Delete, and then click **OK**. In the redisplayed Meeting form, if not all names appear in the **To** box, at the right edge of the **To** box, click the **To down arrow** and notice that Joseph Owen's name is no longer included.

4 Click the **Send Update** button. If the **Send Update to Attendees** dialog box displays, click **Send updates only to added or deleted attendees,** and then click **OK**.

The Meeting form closes. A meeting update is sent only to Joseph Owens. As the meeting organizer, you would, of course, update the meeting attendees after the list of attendees is finalized.

Activity 4.8 Checking the Response Status

When an invited meeting attendee responds to a meeting request, a message is returned to you indicating his or her response. You can keep track of which attendees have responded to your request in the Meeting form. In this activity, you will check and modify the response status for the meeting Warren Owens has planned.

1 Open the **Ocean Palms Status Reports** meeting.

2 On the Ribbon, click the **Tracking** button, and then compare your screen with Figure 4.24.

The ***Tracking button*** changes the view to display a list of each meeting attendee, his or her status as a required or optional attendee, and the attendee's response status. As you receive responses to the meeting invitation, Outlook updates the Response column for each meeting attendee. You can also update the responses manually. You might want to do this if a meeting attendee verbally accepts a meeting invitation.

Ocean Palms Status
Reports – Meeting form

Figure 4.24

Tracking button

Response status of
meeting attendees

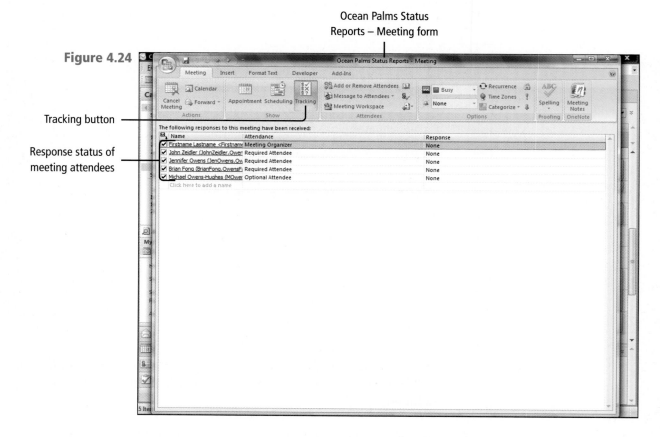

□3 Under **Response**, in the row for **Michael Owens-Hughes**, click **None**, and then click **Tentative**.

□4 Using the technique you just practiced, change the response statuses for **Brian Fong**, **Jennifer Owens**, and **John Zeidler** to **Accepted**.

The default status of the Meeting Organizer indicates *None* because you—the meeting organizer—would not be responding to your own meeting invitation.

□5 **Close** ❎ the meeting. In the **Microsoft Office Outlook** dialog box, click **Save changes but don't send**, and then click **OK**.

Objective 3
Respond to Meeting Requests

When you are invited to a meeting by someone, the invitation displays in your Inbox as an e-mail message. An icon differentiates it from ordinary e-mail messages. You can reply to a meeting invitation in one of four ways: Accept, Tentative, Propose New Time, and Decline. Outlook notifies the meeting organizer of your response. If your response is Accept or Tentative, Outlook places an item in your calendar for the meeting.

Activity 4.9 Importing Meeting Invitations into Your Inbox Folder

In this activity, you will import e-mail messages into Warren Owens's Inbox folder so that you will have some meeting invitations to which you will respond.

1 In the **Navigation Pane**, click the **Mail** button [Mail]. From the **File** menu, display the **Import and Export Wizard** dialog box. Under **Choose an action to perform**, click **Import from another program or file**, and then click **Next**.

2 In the **Import a File** dialog box, under **Select file type to import from**, scroll as necessary, and then click **Personal Folder File (.pst)**. Click **Next**.

3 In the **Import Personal Folders** dialog box, click the **Browse** button. In the **Open Personal Folders** dialog box, click the **Look in arrow**, and then navigate to the location where the student files for this textbook are stored.

4 Locate **o04A_New_Construction_Inbox**, and click one time to select it. Then, in the lower right corner of the **Open Personal Folders** dialog box, click **Open**, and notice that the file name displays in the **File to import** box.

5 In the **Import Personal Folders** dialog box, click **Next**. In the **Import Personal Folders** dialog box, click **Finish**. If a Translation Warning dialog box displays, click OK. If necessary, in the Navigation Pane under Favorite Folders, click to display the Inbox folder contents. Compare your screen with Figure 4.25.

One message and four meeting invitations are imported into your Inbox folder. Notice the different icons for the messages. The first four items in the Inbox are meeting invitations. The remaining item is a normal e-mail message.

Figure 4.25

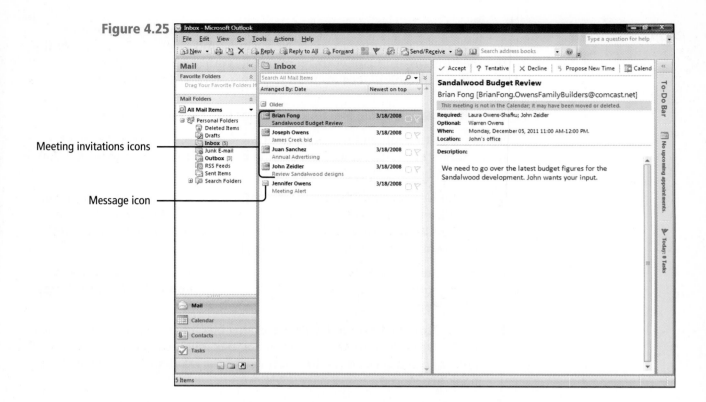

Meeting invitations icons

Message icon

---

6 Select the message from **Brian Fong**, if necessary, without opening it, and look at the message in the **Reading Pane**. If the **Reading Pane** is not visible, from the **View** menu, point to **Reading Pane**, and then click **Right**. Notice the commands that appear at the top of the message.

When you view meeting invitations in the Reading Pane, the four possible responses to the meeting invitation appear as commands at the top of the message: Accept, Tentative, Decline, and Propose New Time. Not all the commands may display in the Reading Pane in this screen position.

7 From the **View** menu, point to **Reading Pane**, and then click **Bottom**. Compare your screen with Figure 4.26.

With the Reading Pane displayed at the bottom of the screen, all the meeting invitation commands display at the top of the message.

Figure 4.26

Reading Pane in
Bottom position

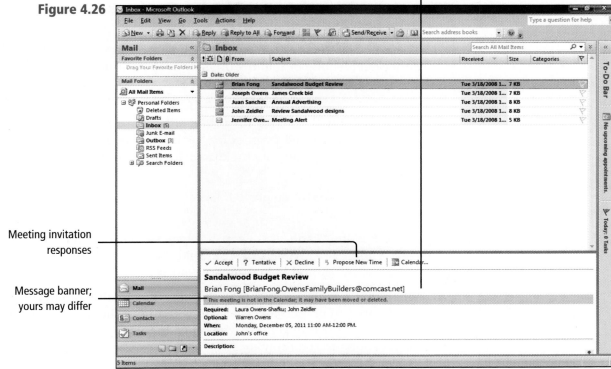

Meeting invitation
responses

Message banner;
yours may differ

8 Select each of the remaining meeting invitations and take a moment to examine each one in the Reading Pane. Then, select the e-mail message from **Jennifer Owens** and notice how, in the Reading Pane, it differs from a meeting invitation.

The format for all the meeting invitations is the same. Each contains the commands at the top of the Reading Pane, and each states the time, location, required attendees, and optional attendees, if any. When you receive a meeting invitation as an e-mail message, the banner reads *Please respond*. However, your banner will be different because you imported your messages into your Inbox instead of actually receiving them as e-mail messages. It may indicate that there is no calendar entry for the meeting.

Note — Calendar Entries with Meeting Invitations

A meeting invitation normally arrives in your Inbox as a sent e-mail message. The incoming message adds a tentative appointment to your calendar for the date and time of the meeting. This calendar item is linked to the Inbox message, and it changes depending on how you respond to the invitation. Your messages do not have the calendar entries because you imported your meeting invitations.

9 Select each of the meeting invitations, and look at the dates of the meetings.

All the meetings occur on December 5, 2011. If the current date is later than this date, the message banner for the meeting may indicate that the meeting occurs in the past. For the purpose of this instruction, you can still respond to meeting invitations if they occur in the past.

10 Compare the meeting times for the **John Zeidler** meeting and the **Juan Sanchez** meeting.

There is a conflict for the two afternoon meetings. You will have to either decline one of the meetings or propose a new time.

Activity 4.10 Accepting and Declining Meeting Invitations

You can respond to a meeting invitation either in the Reading Pane or by opening the message and responding in the Message form. In this activity, you will accept one of the invitations for Warren Owens and decline another.

1 With the **Inbox** still displayed, select the message from **John Zeidler**.

2 In the **Reading Pane**, at the top of the message, click **Accept**. In the displayed **Microsoft Office Outlook** dialog box, click **Edit the response before sending**, and then compare your screen with Figure 4.27.

When you *accept* a meeting invitation, the meeting organizer is notified in an e-mail message that you will attend the meeting. Editing the response before sending the reply enables you to add comments or questions to the reply message.

Figure 4.27

Meeting accepted

Microsoft Office Outlook dialog box

Edit response before sending selected

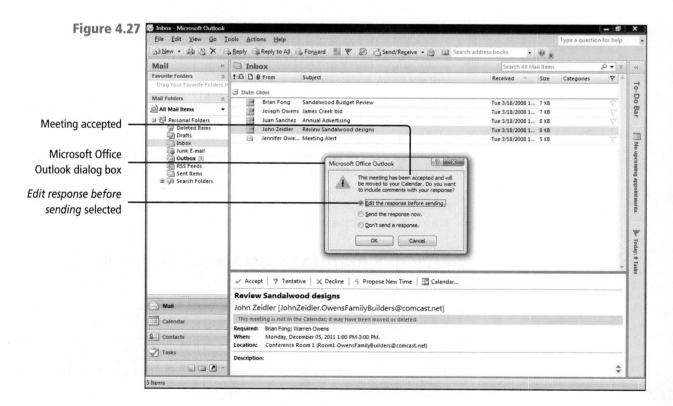

3 In the **Microsoft Office Outlook** dialog box, click **OK**.

A Meeting Response form displays. The banner under the toolbar indicates *Yes, I will attend*, and at the beginning of the Subject box, the prefix *Accepted* is indicated. You can type your comments in the comments area of the form.

4 Using the spacing technique you have practiced for typing messages, create the following message in the comments area: **John, Could you have Brian bring along the Deerfield Farms designs? I would like to compare them to the Sandalwood designs. Warren** Compare your screen with Figure 4.28.

Figure 4.28

Banner text and prefix indicate you have accepted the meeting invitation

Added comments

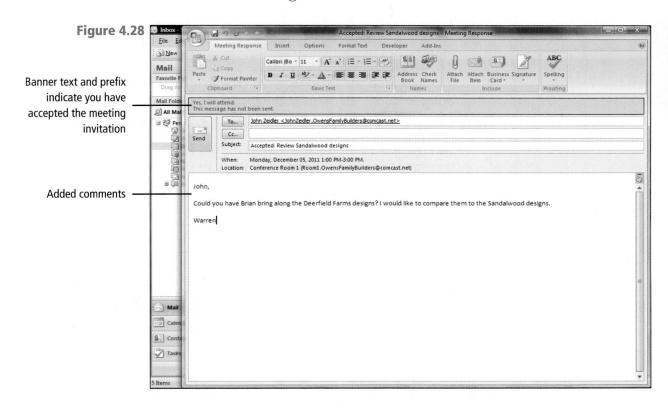

5 On the **Meeting Response** form, click the **Send** button.

The Meeting Response form closes. The message is sent to the Outbox, and the Inbox redisplays. The John Zeidler message has been removed from your Inbox, and the accepted meeting is now a calendar entry on the date of the meeting.

6 In the **Navigation Pane**, click the **Calendar** button. From the **Go** menu, click **Go to Date**. In the **Go To Date** dialog box, type **12/05/11** and then click **OK**.

Recall that the Go to Date command is an alternative way to jump to dates in the calendar. The calendar for December 5, 2011 displays. Outlook has created an appointment for the time of the meeting invitation.

Note — Dates for Received Meeting Invitations

The dates for your accepted meetings may vary significantly from the date you have been using to schedule your own meetings. A fixed date was necessary in the received meeting invitation. Depending on the current date, these meetings may take place far in the future, or they may occur in the past. Outlook will enter the accepted meeting into your calendar regardless of its date.

7 **Open** the **Review Sandalwood designs - Meeting** form.

The Meeting form displays. The banner indicates the date on which you accepted the invitation. The name of the meeting organizer— John Zeidler—displays at the top of the form.

8 **Close** ❎ the **Review Sandalwood designs - Meeting** form. In the **Navigation Pane**, click the **Mail** button 📨 Mail , select the message from **Brian Fong**, and then, in the **Reading Pane**, notice that *Warren Owens* is an optional attendee. If he declines to attend, the meeting can still take place.

9 Open the **Brian Fong** message. On the Meeting form, click the **Decline** button ❌ Decline , and then compare your screen with Figure 4.29.

A Microsoft Office Outlook dialog box displays. When you *decline* a meeting invitation, the meeting organizer is notified in an e-mail message that you will not attend the meeting. When declining a meeting invitation, it is polite to include comments with your response. The option to edit the response before sending is already selected.

Figure 4.29

Decline button —

Microsoft Office Outlook dialog box —

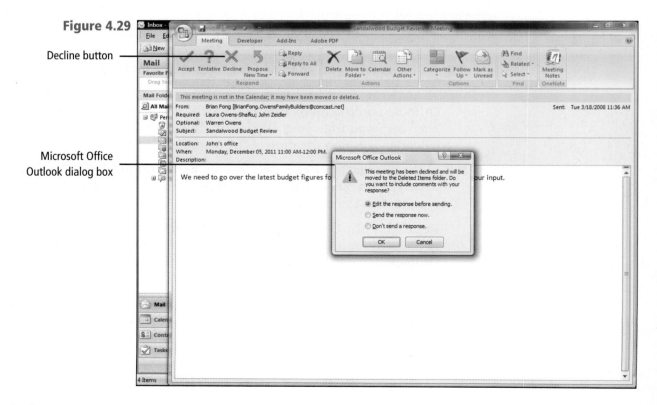

10 In the **Microsoft Office Outlook** dialog box, click **OK**.

A Meeting Response form displays. The banner indicates that you will not attend, and the prefix *Declined* is placed at the beginning of the Subject text.

11 Using the spacing technique you have practiced for typing messages, create the following message in the comments area: **Brian, I really need this time to prepare for a presentation the next day. Laura can handle any of the budget questions that might arise. Warren** Compare your screen with Figure 4.30.

Figure 4.30

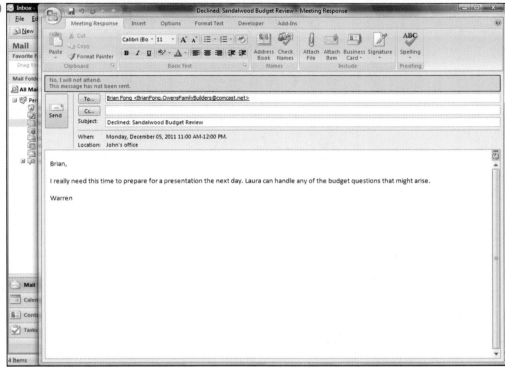

12 **Send** the message.

The Meeting Response form closes. The message is sent to the Outbox, and the Inbox redisplays. The Brian Fong message has been removed from your Inbox.

Activity 4.11 Replying with a Tentative Status

If your schedule is especially busy, you might need to tentatively accept a meeting invitation. In this activity, you will tentatively accept one of Warren Owens's meeting invitations.

1 In the **Inbox**, open the **Joseph Owens** message. On the Ribbon, in the **Respond group**, click the **Tentative** button.

When your response to a meeting invitation is tentative, the meeting organizer is notified by an e-mail message that you might attend the meeting.

2 In the **Microsoft Office Outlook** dialog box, click **Edit the response before sending**, and then click **OK**.

A Meeting Response form displays. The banner indicates *Yes, I might attend*, and the prefix *Tentative* is placed at the beginning of the Subject text.

3 Using the proper format for typing messages, create the following message in the comments area: **Joe, As luck would have it, I have a 7:30 a.m. dentist appointment that morning. I should be able to reschedule it; I will let you know. Warren** Compare your screen with Figure 4.31.

Figure 4.31

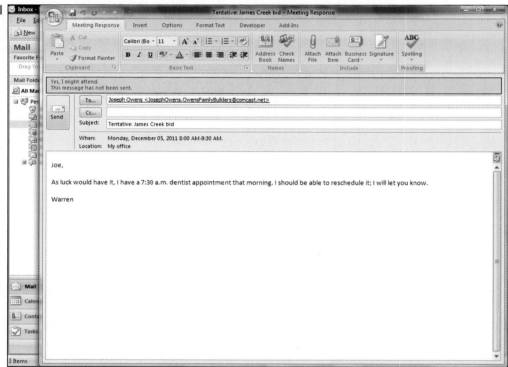

4 **Send** the message.

The Meeting Response form closes. The message is sent to the Outbox, and the Inbox redisplays. The Joseph Owens message has been removed from your Inbox. The tentatively accepted meeting is now a calendar entry on the meeting date.

5 In the **Navigation Pane**, click the **Calendar** button [Calendar]. From the **Go** menu, click **Go to Date**. In the **Go To Date** dialog box, type **12/05/11** and then click **OK**. Compare your screen with Figure 4.32.

This date now contains two meetings. Outlook has created an appointment for the time of the Joseph Owens meeting invitation. The icon indicates that this is a meeting, and the patterned border indicates that the meeting's status is Tentative.

Figure 4.32

Calendar with two
scheduled meetings

Patterned border indicates
that the status of this
meeting is *Tentative*

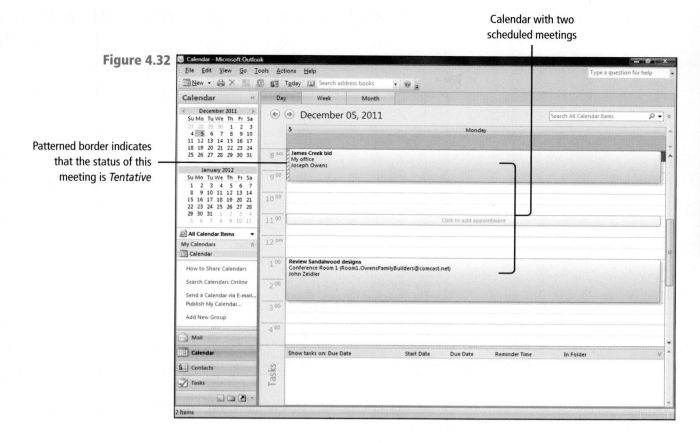

Activity 4.12 Proposing a New Meeting Time

It is likely that you will, from time to time, receive meeting invitations
that conflict with other activities. Outlook enables you to respond to a
meeting invitation by proposing a different time. In this activity, you will
propose a different meeting time for a meeting invitation that Warren
Owens received.

1 In the **Navigation Pane**, click the **Mail** button [Mail], and
then select the **Juan Sanchez** message. Compare your screen with
Figure 4.33.

When displayed on the bottom, the Reading Pane shows the
Calendar command at the top of the meeting invitation. This command is especially useful if you want to see the calendar date for a
meeting. Depending on the size and resolution of your screen, the
Calendar command is not always visible when the Reading Pane is
displayed on the right.

Figure 4.33

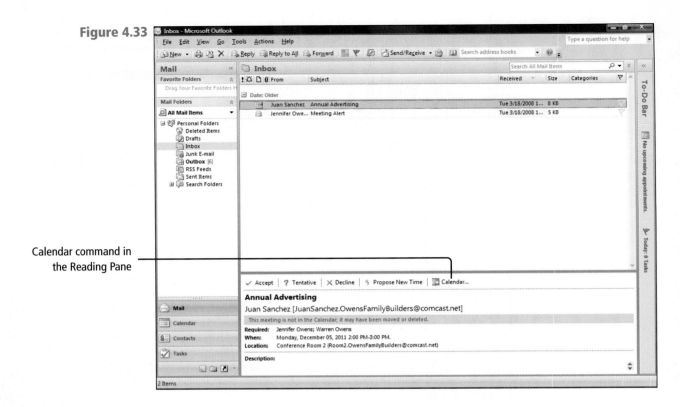

Calendar command in
the Reading Pane

2 In the **Reading Pane**, look at the date and time of the proposed meeting message.

The meeting organizer has scheduled the meeting for December 5, 2011, from 2:00 PM to 3:00 PM.

3 In the **Reading Pane**, at the top of the message, click **Calendar**.

Outlook opens *a new window* in which the calendar displays December 5, 2011. You already have a meeting occurring at 2:00 pm, but the time slot from 3:00 to 4:00 pm is available. You can propose this alternative time to the meeting organizer by choosing the ***Propose New Time*** response—a meeting invitation response in which you request that the meeting organizer change the meeting to a time at which you can attend.

4 In the title bar, **Close** the calendar window.

The Inbox redisplays, and the Juan Sanchez message is still selected.

Another Way ── To Display a Meeting Date in the Calendar

In addition to the Calendar command in the Reading Pane, you can see a calendar date for a meeting by using a shortcut menu command. Select the meeting invitation in the Inbox, right-click it, and then click Check Calendar. Outlook opens a separate window displaying the calendar day of the meeting. When you close the calendar window, the Inbox is redisplayed.

5 In the **Reading Pane**, click **Propose New Time**. If the Microsoft Internet Free/Busy Service dialog box displays, click **Cancel**. Compare your screen with Figure 4.34.

The Propose New Time: Annual Advertising dialog box displays. The yellow column shows the current meeting time. You can adjust the borders of the column to set a different time. Note that no schedule information is available for the meeting attendees because the meeting invitation was imported.

No schedule information available for the meeting attendees

Figure 4.34

Propose New Time dialog box

Drag borders to set different start and end times

Yellow column indicates current meeting time

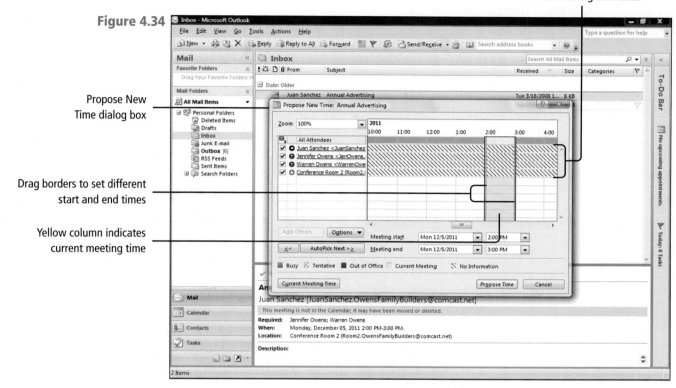

6 Position the pointer on the red border of the column, and drag it to **4:00**. Position the pointer on the green border, and drag it to **3:00**.

7 In the lower right corner of the **Propose New Time: Annual Advertising** dialog box, click **Propose Time**.

A Meeting Response form displays. The banner indicates the current and proposed times for this meeting, and the prefix *New Time Proposed* is placed at the beginning of the Subject text.

8 Create the following message in the comments area: **Juan, I'm already in a meeting at your proposed time. Can we move it to 3 PM? I really want to see the Web site! Warren** Compare your screen with Figure 4.35.

New Time Proposed: Annual
Advertising Meeting Response form

Figure 4.35

Prefix indicates that
a new time is being
proposed for the meeting

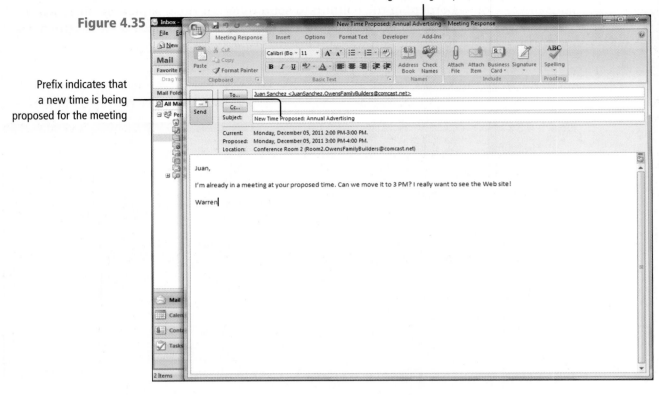

9 **Send** the message.

The Meeting Response form closes, the message is sent to the Outbox, and the Inbox redisplays. The Juan Sanchez message is removed from your Inbox. The meeting is now a calendar entry on the meeting date.

10 In the **Navigation Pane**, click the **Calendar** button [Calendar]. Use the **Date Navigator** or the **Go** menu to display **December 5, 2011** in the calendar.

Notice that the meeting time for the *Annual Advertising* meeting is still at the original time proposed by the meeting organizer and that it occurs at the same time as the *Review Sandalwood designs* meeting. It has a *Tentative* status. Only the actual meeting organizer—not you—can change the meeting time.

11 Open the **Annual Advertising** meeting.

The banner indicates that you have proposed a new time. The date shown in the banner is the current date—the date on which you proposed a new time for this meeting.

12 **Close** the **Annual Advertising** meeting.

Objective 4
Schedule an Office Resource

If you work in an Exchange Server environment, you may be able to schedule—reserve—a resource when you are planning your meetings.

A **resource** might be a conference room or audiovisual equipment. To schedule a resource, it must have its own mailbox on the server—an e-mail address. Your network administrator sets up the resource mailbox and then gives others permission to schedule the resource. In some organizations, only managers have permission to schedule a resource.

Activity 4.13 Setting Up an Office Resource

To reserve a resource such as a conference room, it must appear as a contact in your contact list. A resource must have an e-mail address, and you must have permission to reserve it. In this activity, you will add a resource to Warren Owens's Contacts list.

1 In the **Navigation Pane**, click the **Contacts** button [Contacts], and then open a new contact form.

2 In the **Contact** form, in the **File as** box, type **Conference Room 1**

When creating a contact that is a resource, type in the *File as* box rather than the *Full Name* box. Otherwise, Outlook will reformat the name in a *Lastname, Firstname* format and then will alphabetize the conference room name as *1, Conference Room*.

3 In the **E-mail** box, type **Room1.OwensFamilyBuilders@comcast.net** Click in the **Display as** box, and then compare your screen with Figure 4.36.

A resource must have an e-mail address. Your network administrator sets up the mailbox for the resource and assigns permission for specific individuals to schedule it.

4 **Save & Close** [Save & Close] the contact.

Figure 4.36

Conference Room 1 – Contact form

Use *File as* box for a resource name

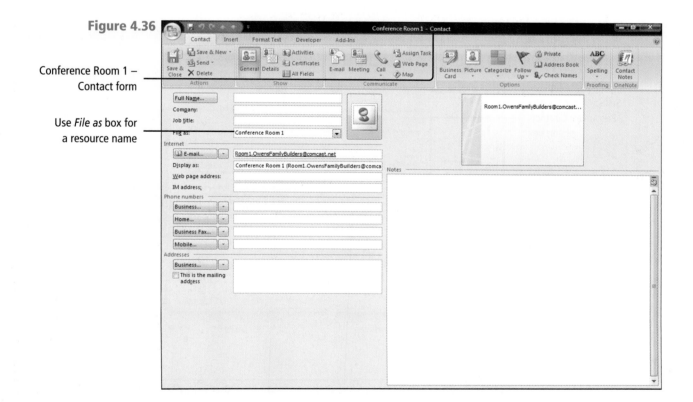

Activity 4.14 Reserving a Resource for a Meeting

After your resource has been set up with an e-mail address by your network administrator and you have added it to your contact list, you can schedule it for meetings as necessary. In this activity, you will plan a meeting for Warren Owens and two of his colleagues, using the Conference Room 1 resource.

1 In the **Navigation Pane**, click the **Calendar** button 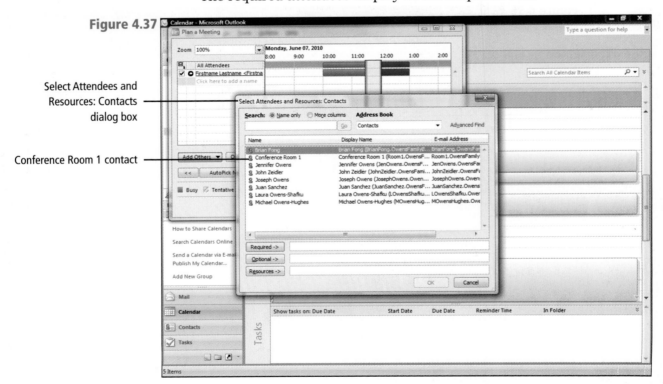. On the Standard toolbar, click the **Today** button Today.

Clicking the *Today* button will ensure that the current date is selected.

2 In the **Navigation Pane**, in the **Date Navigator**, click the **right arrow**, and advance the calendar to next June or December, whichever month is closest to the current month. Click the **first Monday**, a day for which you have already scheduled appointments.

3 Click the **11:30 am** time slot. From the **Actions** menu, click **Plan a Meeting**.

The Plan a Meeting dialog box displays. The free/busy information reflects the appointments in your calendar for that day.

4 In the **Plan a Meeting** dialog box, click **Add Others**, and then click **Add from Address Book**. Compare your screen with Figure 4.37.

The Select Attendees and Resources: Contacts dialog box displays. The list includes the *Conference Room 1* contact you just added.

5 In the **Select Attendees and Resources: Contacts** dialog box, click **Jennifer Owens**, and then click **Required**. Click **Brian Fong**, and then click **Required**.

The required attendees display in the Required box.

Figure 4.37

Select Attendees and
Resources: Contacts
dialog box

Conference Room 1 contact

6 Click **Conference Room 1**, and then click **Resources**. Click **OK**. If the **Microsoft Free/Busy Service** dialog box displays, click **Cancel**. Compare your screen with Figure 4.38.

The Plan a Meeting dialog box redisplays and shows the free/busy information for the meeting attendees. No schedule information is available for the conference room resource. Under All Attendees, the icon for the conference room indicates that it is a resource. Notice that Jennifer Owens is not free at the desired meeting time.

Conference Room 1 schedule information is unavailable

Schedule information of meeting attendees

Figure 4.38

Icon indicates that this is a resource

Use scroll arrows to display the remainder of the work day

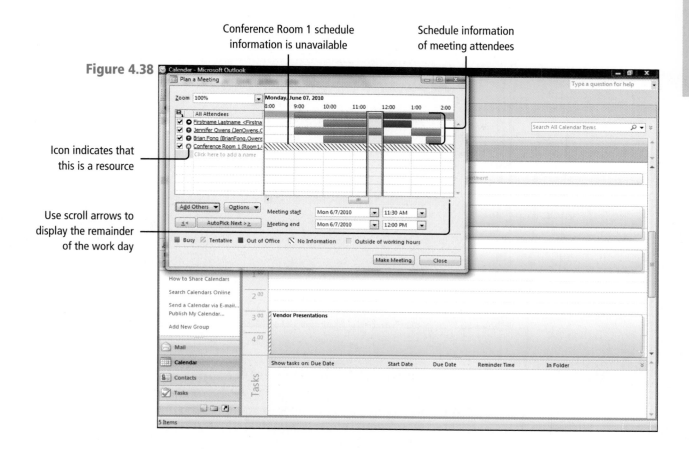

7 Use the **right scroll arrow** and **left scroll arrow** to see the rest of the work day.

Although 2 PM to 3 PM is available for all attendees, Warren Owens does not want Jennifer and Brian to have a full afternoon of meetings without a break. You decide to schedule the meeting after regular working hours—8 AM to 5 PM. Recall that you can display the entire day.

8 In the **Plan a Meeting** dialog box, click **Options**, and then click **Show Only My Working Hours** to clear the check mark.

9 Click the **right scroll arrow**, and then click the column under **6:00** so that the meeting time is 6:00 to 6:30 PM. Click **Make Meeting**.

A Meeting form displays. The *To* box contains the e-mail addresses of all the invited meeting attendees. The *Location* box displays *Conference Room 1*.

10 In the **Subject** box, type **Cost Overruns on the Greenwood Development** Click the **Reminder arrow**, and then click **None**. Create the following message in the comments area: **Jennifer and Brian, Sorry this is so late in the day, but this is important. We need to address the cost overruns right away. Warren** Compare your screen with Figure 4.39.

Figure 4.39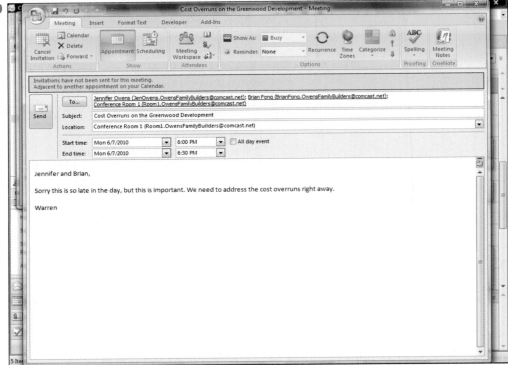

Are you using an Exchange Server?

If you are working in an Exchange Server environment, you should remove Conference Room 1 as a recipient of your meeting invitation. You must be granted permission from your network administrator to use resources in Outlook when using Exchange Server accounts. Outlook may not send the meeting invitation if you include a resource as a meeting attendee.

11 **Send** the meeting invitation, and then **Close** the Plan a Meeting dialog box.

Outlook adds the meeting to your calendar. The resource will accept the invitation if it is free and decline it if it is already busy. If it accepts the invitation, the time is automatically scheduled in the resource's calendar. Depending on the size and resolution of your screen, a small, gray arrow may display at the bottom right of the Appointment area. Recall that this indicates an appointment that does not appear in the viewing area.

12 If necessary, scroll down to 6:00 pm to view the Cost Overruns on the Greenwood Development meeting.

Objective 5
Manage Meeting Information

If your schedule includes many meetings, you may find it helpful to print meeting invitations and calendar information. Printing meeting information is similar to printing other items in Outlook. Deleting meetings in your calendar must be handled somewhat differently because they may be linked to sent invitations.

Activity 4.15 Printing Meeting Information

In this activity, you will print Warren Owens's calendar for the day of the meetings he has planned, as well as one of his invitations.

1 Display the same Monday in June or December in which you have been working, which now shows six meetings and appointments. Compare your screen with Figure 4.40.

Figure 4.40

Calendar contains two meetings and four appointments

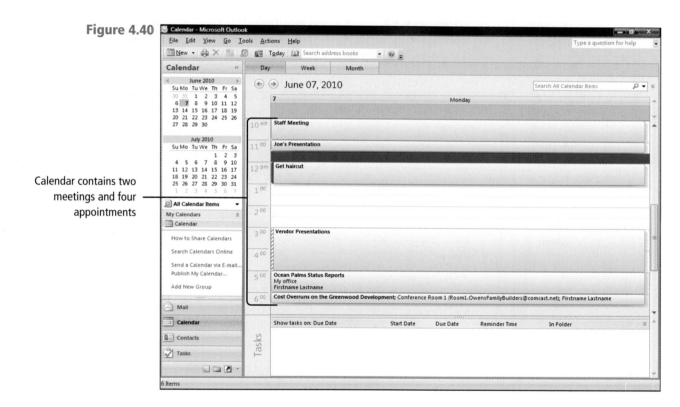

2 From the **File** menu, display the **Page Setup: Daily Style** dialog box. Click the **Header/Footer tab**, and then delete any existing header or footer information, including dates and page numbers. In the left **Footer** box, using your own name, type **4A_New_Construction_Calendar_Firstname_Lastname** Preview the calendar, and then print it. Submit the end result to your instructor as directed.

3 In the calendar, click the **Cost Overruns on the Greenwood Development** meeting.

4 From the **File** menu, display the **Page Setup: Memo Style** dialog box. On the **Header/Footer tab**, delete any existing header or footer information, including dates and page numbers. In the left **Footer** box, using your own name, type **4A_New_Construction_Meeting_ Firstname_Lastname** Preview the meeting, and then print it. Submit the end result to your instructor as directed.

Activity 4.16 Deleting Meetings

When you delete meetings from your calendar, you may need to update meeting attendees to let them know the meeting has been cancelled. In this activity, you will delete Warren Owens's meetings and other Outlook information.

1 With the same **Monday** in June or December still displayed, click the **Cost Overruns on the Greenwood Development** meeting.

2 On the Standard toolbar, click the **Delete** button ☒. Compare your screen with Figure 4.41.

The Meeting form opens and a banner indicates that the meeting attendees have not been notified that the meeting is cancelled. As the meeting organizer, you should notify meeting attendees when a meeting is cancelled.

Figure 4.41

Banner indicates cancellation has not been sent for this meeting

Send Cancellation button

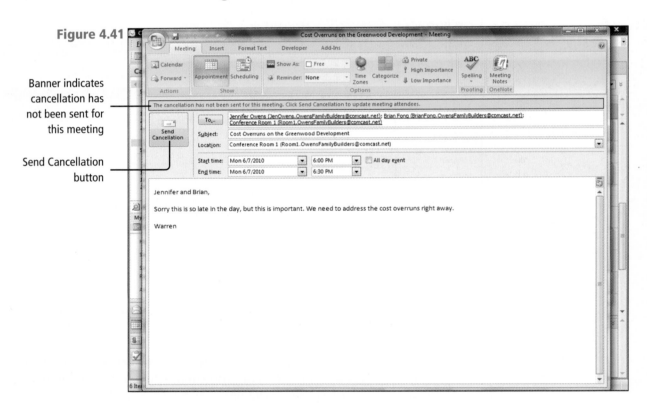

3 Click the **Send Cancellation** button to send an update to all attendees and remove the meeting from your calendar.

4 Click the **Ocean Palms Status Reports** meeting. On the Standard toolbar click the **Delete** button ☒.

5 In the **Meeting** form, click the **Send Cancellation** button .

6 Hold down Ctrl while selecting the remaining appointments in the calendar for this day, display the shortcut menu, and then click **Delete**.

7 From the **Go** menu, click **Go to Date**. In the **Go To Date** dialog box, type **12/05/11** and then click **OK**.

The calendar displays December 5, 2011. This date contains the meeting invitations that you accepted and tentatively accepted or for which you proposed a new time.

8 Click the **Review Sandalwood designs** meeting, and then click

Delete ☒. Click **Delete without sending a response**, and then compare your screen with Figure 4.42.

The Confirm Delete dialog box indicates that you have already accepted this meeting invitation. It is good manners to inform the meeting organizer when you are unable to attend a meeting for which you have already accepted an invitation; however, for purposes of this instruction, it is not necessary to do so.

Figure 4.42

Confirm Delete dialog box

Delete without sending a response selected

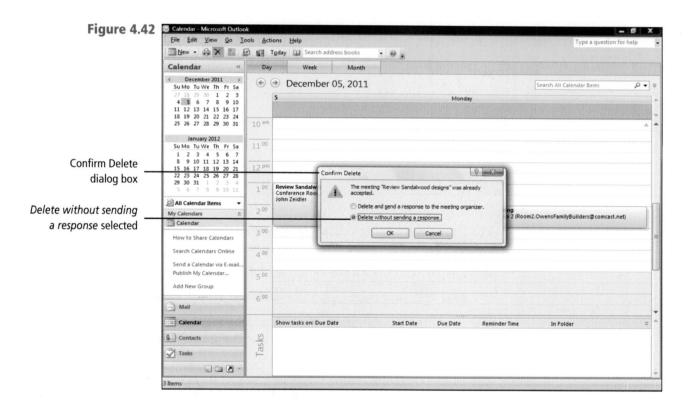

9 Click **OK**. **Delete** ☒ the remaining meeting for this date without sending a response.

10 Click the **Mail** button ▨ Mail. From the **View** menu, point to **Reading Pane**, and then click **Right**. **Delete** ☒ the contents of the **Inbox**.

11 Display the **Outbox**, select all the items in the folder, and then click the **Delete** button ⊠. Compare your screen with Figure 4.43.

A Microsoft Office Outlook dialog box indicates that the meeting organizer will not be sent a response. Because some of these outgoing messages are responses to meeting invitations you received, you are prompted to confirm that you are deleting the messages without sending a reply.

Figure 4.43

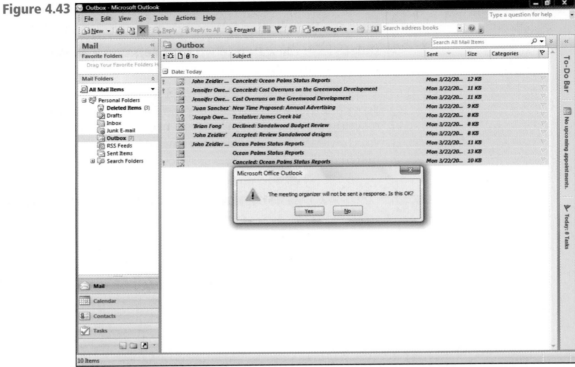

12 In the **Microsoft Office Outlook** dialog box, click **Yes**, and then click **Yes** for each remaining meeting response that is deleted.

13 Display the **Contacts** folder, and delete its contents. Display the **Folder List** ▣, and then empty the **Deleted Items** folder.

14 From the **Tools** menu, click **Options**. Click the **Mail Setup tab**, and then, under **Send/Receive**, select the **Send immediately when connected** check box.

15 In the **Options** dialog box, click **Send/Receive**. In the **Send/Receive Groups** dialog box, under **Setting for group "All Accounts"**, select both **Include this group in send/receive (F9)** check boxes. Select both **Schedule an automatic send/receive** check boxes if this is a default setting on your computer. Click **Close**.

16 Click the **Preferences tab**, click **Calendar Options**, and then click **Free/Busy Options**. In the **Free/Busy Options** dialog box, clear the **Publish at my location** box. Click **OK**. If you changed your time zone, in the **Calendar Options** dialog box, click the **Time Zone** command button, click the **Time zone arrow**, locate and click your time zone. Click **OK** as needed to close the dialog boxes. If you manually changed the time on your computer, right-click the time in the taskbar, click **Adjust Date/Time**, change the time to your local time, and then click **OK**.

17 On the **Navigation Pane**, click **Mail**. From the **File** menu, point to **Page Setup**, and then click **Define Print Styles**. Click **Table Style**, click **Reset**, and then click **OK**. Click **Memo Style**, click **Reset**, and then click **OK**. **Close** the dialog box, and then **Close** Outlook.

End **You have completed Project 4A** —————————————

Content-Based Assessments

Summary

Use Outlook to schedule meetings and coordinate your schedule with others. In this chapter, you created appointments and examined how Outlook stores your free/busy information. You practiced publishing your free/busy schedule on a file server and accessed the free/busy schedule of others. You organized a meeting, planned a meeting, and invited meeting participants, as well as adding and deleting meeting attendees.

Outlook also assists in responding to meetings. You practiced accepting and declining meetings and responded to a meeting invitation with a *Tentative* reply. You practiced responding to a meeting invitation by proposing a different meeting time when the original invitation conflicted with another appointment in your calendar. You also set up and scheduled a meeting using a resource. Finally, you practiced printing meeting information and deleting meetings from your calendar.

Key Terms

Content-Based Assessments

Matching

Match each term in the second column with its correct definition in the first column by writing the letter of the term on the blank line in front of the correct definition.

_____ **1.** A group of four indicators displayed by Outlook, which can be viewed by others who have the ability to view your calendar, to indicate your availability for a date and time in your calendar.

_____ **2.** The Outlook calendar stored on the hard drive of your computer.

_____ **3.** Special server software that provides a system for sharing Outlook information among members on a network.

_____ **4.** The default free/busy setting that Outlook assigns to all new appointments, which is indicated by an appointment with a blue border.

_____ **5.** A free/busy setting that indicates you are away from your office and not available for other meetings or appointments and that is indicated by an appointment with a purple border.

_____ **6.** A meeting response in which the meeting organizer is notified that you might attend the meeting and that places the text *Yes, I might attend* in a banner at the top of the sent reply.

_____ **7.** A calendar activity that requires inviting other people and/or scheduling a room or equipment.

_____ **8.** A term used to refer to meeting attendees without whom, because of their special knowledge or input, a meeting cannot take place.

_____ **9.** The individual who plans a meeting and issues the meeting invitations.

_____ **10.** A person whose attendance at a meeting is not critical and without whom the meeting can still take place.

_____ **11.** A meeting invitation response in which you agree to attend a meeting and that notifies the meeting organizer, by sending an e-mail message, that you will attend.

_____ **12.** A meeting invitation response in which you do not agree to attend a meeting and that notifies the meeting organizer, by sending an e-mail message, that you will not attend.

_____ **13.** A meeting invitation response in which you request that the meeting organizer change the meeting to a time at which you can attend.

_____ **14.** A facility, such as conference room, or a piece of equipment, such as a projector, whose availability and use you can schedule within Outlook.

_____ **15.** The weekday hours between 8:00 a.m. and 5:00 p.m.

A Accept

B Busy

C Decline

D Exchange Server

E Free/busy information

F Local calendar

G Meeting

H Meeting organizer

I Optional attendee

J Out of Office

K Propose New Time

L Required attendee

M Resource

N Tentative

O Working hours

Content-Based Assessments

Fill in the Blank

Write the correct answer in the space provided.

1. Meetings are displayed in your calendar at the date and time they are scheduled and appear similar to a(n) _____.

2. For an appointment in your calendar for which you want to indicate that you are away from your office and are not available for other appointments or meetings, use the _____ _____ _____ status.

3. The people who participate in meetings are referred to as the meeting _____.

4. To display a list of each meeting attendee, his or her status as required or optional, and the attendee's response status, click the _____ button on the Meeting form.

5. The meeting organizer is always considered a(n) _____ meeting attendee.

6. The ability to both view and store information on a server is known as _____ access.

7. When you receive a meeting invitation, it arrives in your Inbox as a(n) _____ message.

8. Outlook assigns a different color or pattern to the _____ of an appointment in the appointment area depending on which of the four free/busy options is selected.

9. In the Plan a Meeting dialog box, the shaded column indicating the meeting time has a green border to indicate the meeting's start time and a(n) _____ border to indicate the meeting's end time.

10. There are _____ different ways in which you can respond to a meeting invitation, all of which display in the Reading Pane.

11. When the Reading Pane is displayed on the bottom of the screen, meeting invitations show an additional command at the top of the pane that enables you to view dates for a proposed meeting; this command is the _____ command.

12. When you decline a meeting invitation, it is polite to include the reason why you cannot attend in the _____ area of the Meeting Response form.

Content-Based Assessments

13. To schedule a resource for a meeting, it is necessary that the resource appear in your contact list and have a(n) _____ address.

14. The sequence of a drive letter and folders that identifies the location of a *.vfb* file is the _____.

15. When you add or delete meeting attendees or delete the meeting, Outlook gives you the option of sending a(n) _____ to all the meeting attendees.

Skills Review

Project 4B—Open House

Objectives: 1. *Publish Free/Busy Information;* **2.** *Schedule a Meeting;*
5. *Manage Meeting Information.*

In the following Skills Review, you will schedule a meeting for Warren
Owens at Owens Family Builders. The company has scheduled an open
house for several model homes in a new development in Orlando. Mr.
Owens wants to discuss this event with other senior managers. Your
completed document will look similar to the one shown in Figure 4.44.

For Project 4B, you will need the following files:

o04B_Open_House_Contacts
JohnZeidler.vfb
JosephOwens.vfb
JohnZeidler2011.vfb
JosephOwens2011.vfb

You will print one file with the following footer:
4B_Open_House_Firstname_Lastname

Figure 4.44

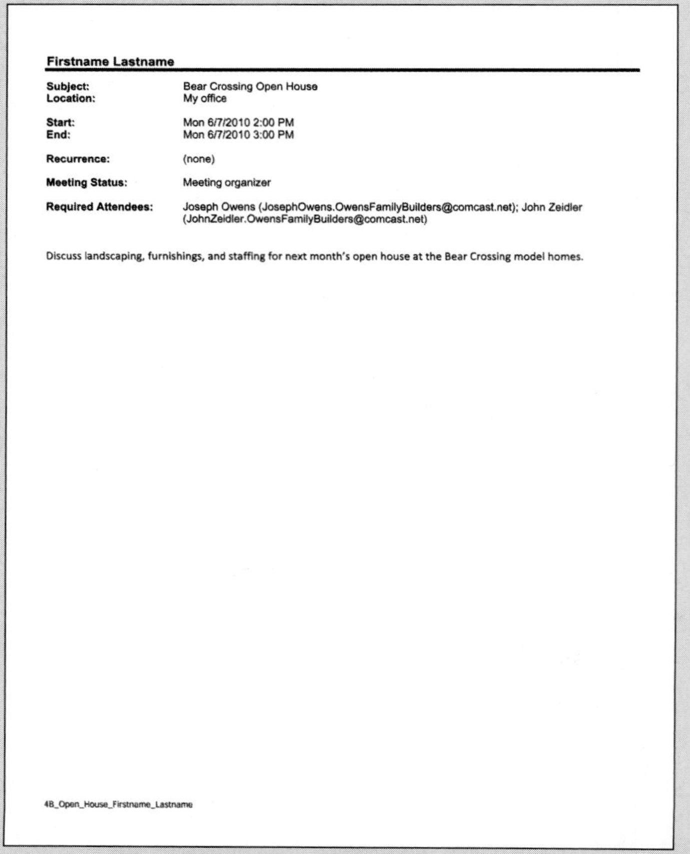

Firstname Lastname

Subject:	Bear Crossing Open House
Location:	My office
Start:	Mon 6/7/2010 2:00 PM
End:	Mon 6/7/2010 3:00 PM
Recurrence:	(none)
Meeting Status:	Meeting organizer
Required Attendees:	Joseph Owens (JosephOwens.OwensFamilyBuilders@comcast.net); John Zeidler (JohnZeidler.OwensFamilyBuilders@comcast.net)

Discuss landscaping, furnishings, and staffing for next month's open house at the Bear Crossing model homes.

4B_Open_House_Firstname_Lastname

(Project 4B–Open House continues on the next page)

Content-Based Assessments

(Project 4B–Open House continued)

1. **Start** Outlook. From the **Tools** menu, display the **Options** dialog box, and then click the **Mail Setup tab**.

2. Under **Send/Receive**, clear the **Send immediately when connected** check box if necessary. To the immediate right, click the **Send/Receive** button. In the **Send/Receive Groups** dialog box, under **Setting for group "All Accounts"**, clear both **Include this group in send/receive (F9)** check boxes if necessary. Clear both **Schedule an automatic send/receive** check boxes if necessary. Click **Close**, and then click **OK**.

3. In the **Navigation Pane**, click the **Contacts** button. From the **File** menu, display the **Import and Export Wizard** dialog box. Under **Choose an action to perform**, click **Import from another program or file**, and then click **Next**. In the **Import a File** dialog box, scroll as necessary, and then click **Personal Folder File (.pst)**. Click **Next**.

4. In the **Import Personal Folders** dialog box, click **Browse**. In the **Open Personal Folders** dialog box, navigate to the location where the student files for this textbook are stored. Point to **o04B_Open_ House_Contacts** and right-click. From the displayed shortcut menu, click **Properties**.

5. In the **o04B_Open_House_Contacts.pst Properties** dialog box, next to **Location**, place the insertion point at the beginning of the pathname. Dragging to the right, select the entire pathname (the pathname may extend beyond the border of the dialog box). Right-click the selected pathname. From the displayed shortcut menu, click **Copy**. Recall that this copies the pathname to the Office Clipboard. In the **o04B_Open_House_Contacts.pst Properties** dialog box, click **Cancel** to close the dialog box. In the **Open Personal Folders** dialog box, with the file **o04B_Open_House_Contacts** selected, click **Open**. In the **Import Personal Folders** dialog box, click **Next**.

6. In the **Import Personal Folders** dialog box, under **Select the folder to import from**, click **Contacts**. Click **Import items into the current folder**. Click **Finish**. If a Translation Warning dialog box displays, click OK.

7. Open the **John Zeidler** contact and click the **Details** button. Under **Internet Free/Busy**, in the **Address** box, type **file:** With the insertion point still in the **Address** box, right-click, and then click **Paste** to insert the pathname from the Office Clipboard. With the insertion point still in the **Address** box after the pasted pathname, if the current year is 2010 or earlier, type **\JohnZeidler.vfb** If the current year is 2011 or later, type **\JohnZeidler2011 .vfb Save & Close** the contact.

8. Open the **Joseph Owens** contact. Click the **Details** button. Under **Internet Free/ Busy**, in the **Address** box, type **file:** Right-click, and click **Paste**. If the year is 2010 or earlier, type **\JosephOwens.vfb** If the year is 2011 or later, type **\JosephOwens2011 .vfb Save & Close** the contact.

9. In the **Navigation Pane**, click **Calendar**. In the **Date Navigator**, click the **right arrow**, and then advance the calendar to next **June** or **December**, whichever month is closest to the current month. Click the **first Monday** in the month. Click the **11:00 am** time slot.

10. From the **Actions** menu, display the **Plan a Meeting** dialog box, click **Add Others**, and then click **Add from Address Book**. In the **Select Attendees and Resources:**

(Project 4B–Open House continues on the next page)

Content-Based Assessments

(Project 4B–Open House continued)

Contacts dialog box, under **Name**, select **Joseph Owens**, and then click **Required**. Click **John Zeidler**, and then click **Required**. Click **OK**.

11. In the **Plan a Meeting** dialog box, notice that Joseph Owens is not available at 11:00 am. Change the start time for the meeting to 2:00 pm. Position the pointer on the red border of the shaded column, and then drag to **3:00**. Click **Make Meeting**.

12. In the **Subject** box, type Bear Crossing Open House In the **Location** box, type **My office** Click the **Reminder arrow**, and then click **None**. In the comments area of the form, type **Discuss landscaping, furnishings, and staffing for next month's open house at the Bear Crossing model homes.** On the **Meeting** form, click the **Send** button. **Close** the **Plan a Meeting** dialog box.

13. With the calendar still displayed on the same date, select the **Bear Crossing Open House** meeting. From the **File** menu, display the **Page Setup: Memo Style** dialog box. On the **Header/Footer tab**, delete any existing header or footer information, including dates and page numbers. In the left **Footer** box, type **4B_Open_House_ Firstname_Lastname Preview** and **Print** the meeting information. Submit the end result to your instructor as directed.

14. Delete the meeting in the calendar. In the **Meeting** form, click **Send Cancellation**. In the **Navigation Pane**, click the **Mail** button. Display the **Outbox** folder, and then delete the contents of the **Outbox** folder. Open the **Contacts** folder, and delete its contents. In the **Folder List**, right-click the **Deleted Items** folder. From the displayed shortcut menu, click **Empty "Deleted Items" Folder**, and then click **Yes**.

15. From the **Tools** menu, click **Options**. Click the **Mail Setup tab**, and then, under **Send/Receive**, select the **Send immediately when connected** check box.

16. In the **Options** dialog box, click **Send/Receive**. In the **Send/Receive Groups** dialog box, under **Setting for group "All Accounts"**, select both **Include this group in send/receive (F9)** check boxes. Select both **Schedule an automatic send/receive** check boxes if this is a default setting on your computer. Click **Close**. Click **OK**.

17. From the **File** menu, point to **Page Setup**, and then click **Define Print Styles**. Click **Memo Style**, click **Reset**, and then click **OK**. **Close** the dialog box, and **Close** Outlook.

End **You have completed Project 4B**

Content-Based Assessments

Skills Review

Project 4C—Interviews

Objectives: 3. *Respond to Meeting Requests;* **5.** *Manage Meeting Information.*

In the following Skills Review, you will handle the meeting invitations received by Jennifer Owens. Owens Family Builders is hiring several new staff architects. Ms. Owens is a member of the hiring committee. The hiring committee typically interviews each candidate as a group, and then individual committee members interview each candidate individually. Ms. Owens has received several meeting invitations for the group interviews. You will handle her responses to these invitations. Your completed documents will look similar to the ones shown in Figure 4.45.

> ## For Project 4C, you will need the following file:
>
> o04C_Interviews_Inbox

You will print three files with the following footers:
4C_Interviews_Firstname_Lastname
4C_Interviews_Meeting_Firstname_Lastname
4C_Interviews_Acceptance_Firstname_Lastname

Figure 4.45

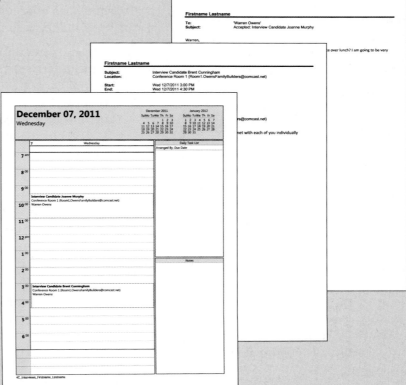

(Project 4C–Interviews continues on the next page)

Content-Based Assessments

(Project 4C–Interviews continued)

1. **Start** Outlook. From the **Tools** menu, display the **Options** dialog box, and then click the **Mail Setup tab**.

2. Under **Send/Receive**, clear the **Send immediately when connected** check box if necessary. To the immediate right, click the **Send/Receive** button. In the **Send/Receive Groups** dialog box, under **Setting for group "All Accounts"**, clear both **Include this group in send/receive (F9)** check boxes if necessary. Clear both **Schedule an automatic send/receive** check boxes if necessary. Click **Close**, and then click **OK**.

3. If your time zone is not Eastern time (US & Canada), from the **Tools** menu, display the **Options** dialog box, and click **Calendar Options**. In the **Calendar Options** dialog box, at the bottom of the box, click **Time Zone**. Click the **Time zone arrow**, locate and click **(GMT-05:00) Eastern Time (US & Canada)**, and then click **OK**. **Close** the remaining dialog boxes. If you are not permitted to change time zones, your times may vary slightly.

4. From the **Navigation Pane**, click **Mail**, and then click the **Inbox** folder. From the **File** menu, display the **Import and Export Wizard** dialog box. Under **Choose an action to perform**, click **Import from another program or file**, and then click **Next**. In the **Import a File** dialog box, scroll as necessary, and then click **Personal Folder File (.pst)**. Click **Next**.

5. In the **Import Personal Folders** dialog box, click **Browse**. In the **Open Personal Folders** dialog box, navigate to the location where the student files for this textbook are stored. Locate **o04C_Interviews_ Inbox**, and click **Open**. In the **Import Personal Folders** dialog box, click **Next**.

6. In the **Import Personal Folders** dialog box, under **Select the folder to import from**, click **Inbox**. Click **Import items into the current folder**. Click **Finish**. If a Translation Warning dialog box displays, click OK.

7. In the **Inbox**, click to select the message **Interview Candidate Joanne Murphy** from *Warren Owen*s. Notice that this meeting is scheduled for December 7, 2011. In the **Reading Pane**, at the top of the message, click **Accept**.

8. In the **Microsoft Office Outlook** dialog box, click **Edit the response before sending**, and then click **OK**.

9. Using the spacing technique you have practiced for typing messages, create the following message in the comments area: **Warren, If you haven't decided already, could you arrange for me to interview the candidate over lunch? I am going to be very busy that day. Jennifer Send** the message.

10. With the remaining message—**Interview Candidate Brent Cunningham**—from *Warren Owens* selected in the **Inbox**, in the **Reading Pane**, click **Tentative**. Notice that this meeting is also scheduled for December 7, 2011. In the **Microsoft Office Outlook** dialog box, click **Edit the response before sending**, and then click **OK**.

11. In the comments area, type **Warren, I am catching a plane later that afternoon. I can be present for only the first part of the interview. Jennifer Send** the message.

12. From the **Navigation Pane**, display the **Calendar** folder. From the **Go** menu, display the **Go To Date** dialog box, and then, as the **Date**, type **12/07/11** Click **OK**.

13. From the **File** menu, display the **Page Setup: Daily Style** dialog box. Display the **Header/Footer tab**, delete any existing

(Project 4C–Interviews continues on the next page)

Content-Based Assessments

(Project 4C–Interviews continued)

header or footer information, and then, in the left **Footer** box, type **4C_Interviews_ Firstname_Lastname** **Preview** and **Print** the calendar. Submit the end result to your instructor as directed.

14. In the appointment area, select the **Interview Candidate Brent Cunningham** meeting. From the **File** menu, display the **Page Setup: Memo Style** dialog box. Delete any existing header or footer information, create a left **Footer** by typing **4C_Interviews_Meeting_Firstname_Lastname** and then **Preview** and **Print** the meeting. Submit the end result to your instructor as directed.

15. With the **Interview Candidate Brent Cunningham** meeting selected, on the Standard toolbar, click the **Delete** button. In the **Confirm Delete** dialog box, click **Delete without sending a response**, and then click **OK**. Delete the **Interview Candidate Joanne Murphy** meeting without sending a response.

16. In the **Navigation Pane**, click the **Mail** button, and then display the **Outbox** folder. Select the message that begins **Accepted** from *Warren Owens*. Display the **Page Setup: Memo Style** dialog box, delete any existing header or footer information, and then create a left **Footer** as **4C_Interviews_Acceptance_Firstname_ Lastname** **Preview** and **Print** the message. Submit the end result to your instructor as directed.

17. In the **Outbox**, select both items in the folder and **Delete** them. In the **Microsoft Office Outlook** dialog box, click **Yes** for each item deleted. Point to the **Deleted Items** folder, right-click, from the shortcut menu, click **Empty "Deleted Items" Folder**, and then click **Yes**.

18. From the **Tools** menu, click **Options**. Click the **Mail Setup tab**, and then, under **Send/Receive**, select the **Send immediately when connected** check box.

19. In the **Options** dialog box, click **Send/Receive**. In the **Send/Receive Groups** dialog box, under **Setting for group "All Accounts"**, select both **Include this group in send/receive (F9)** check boxes. Select both **Schedule an automatic send/receive** check boxes if this is a default setting on your computer. Click **Close**. Click **OK**.

20. If you changed your time zone, from the **Tools** menu, click **Options**, click **Calendar Options**, and then click **Time Zone**. In the **Time Zone** dialog box, click the **Time zone arrow**, locate and click your time zone, and then click **OK** three times.

21. Display the **Calendar** folder. From the **File** menu, point to **Page Setup**, and then click **Define Print Styles**. Click **Daily Style**, click **Reset**, and then click **OK**. **Reset** the **Memo Style**. **Close** the dialog box, and then **Close** Outlook.

End **You have completed Project 4C** ———————————

Skills Review

Project 4D — Energy Efficiency

Objectives: 1. *Publish Free/Busy Information;* **2.** *Schedule a Meeting;*
4. *Schedule an Office Resource;* **5.** *Manage Meeting Information.*

In the following Skills Review, you will plan a meeting for Warren Owens.
Mr. Owens is organizing a meeting with his senior managers to discuss
the new energy-efficient home designs the company is developing. He is
bringing in a consultant to discuss the project with two members of his
staff. Your completed documents will look similar to the ones shown in
Figure 4.46.

For Project 4D, you will need the following files:

o04D_Energy_Efficiency_Contacts
BrianFong.vfb
MOwensHughes.vfb
BrianFong2011.vfb
MOwensHughes2011.vfb

You will print two files with the following footers:
4D_Energy_Efficiency_Meeting_Firstname_Lastname
4D_Energy_Efficiency_Contacts_Firstname_Lastname

Figure 4.46

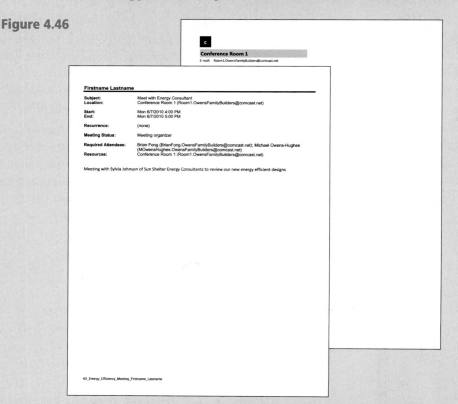

(Project 4D–Energy Efficiency continues on the next page)

Content-Based Assessments

(Project 4D–Energy Efficiency continued)

1. **Start** Outlook. From the **Tools** menu, display the **Options** dialog box, and then click the **Mail Setup tab**. Under **Send/Receive**, clear the **Send immediately when connected** check box if necessary. To the immediate right, click the **Send/Receive** button. In the **Send/Receive Groups** dialog box, under **Setting for group "All Accounts"**, clear both **Include this group in send/receive (F9)** check boxes if necessary. Clear both **Schedule an automatic send/receive** check boxes if necessary. Click **Close**, and then click **OK**.

2. In the **Navigation Pane**, click the **Contacts** button. From the **File** menu, display the **Import and Export Wizard** dialog box. Under **Choose an action to perform**, click **Import from another program or file**, and then click **Next**. In the **Import a File** dialog box, scroll as necessary, and then click **Personal Folder File (.pst)**. Click **Next**.

3. In the **Import Personal Folders** dialog box, click **Browse**. In the **Open Personal Folders** dialog box, navigate to the location where the student files for this textbook are stored. Point to **o04D_Energy_Efficiency_Contacts** and right-click. From the displayed shortcut menu, click **Properties**.

4. In the **o04D_Energy_Efficiency_Contacts .pst Properties** dialog box, place the insertion point at the beginning of the pathname. Dragging to the right, select the entire pathname (the pathname may extend beyond the border of the dialog box). Right-click the selected pathname. From the displayed shortcut menu, click **Copy**. In the **o04D_Energy_Efficiency_ Contacts.pst Properties** dialog box, click **Cancel** to close the dialog box. In the **Open Personal Folders** dialog box, with the file

   o04D_Energy_Efficiency_Contacts selected, click **Open**. In the **Import Personal Folders** dialog box, click **Next**.

5. In the **Import Personal Folders** dialog box, under **Select the folder to import from**, click **Contacts**. Click **Import items into the current folder**. Click **Finish**. If a Translation Warning dialog box displays, click OK.

6. In the **Contacts** folder, open a new contact form. In the **File as** box, type **Conference Room 1** In the **E-mail** box, type **Room1. OwensFamilyBuilders@comcast.net** and then **Save & Close** the contact. Recall that to schedule resources such as rooms and equipment, each resource must have a contact and e-mail address.

7. Open the **Brian Fong** contact. Click the **Details** button. Under **Internet Free/Busy**, in the **Address** box, type **file:** With the insertion point still in the **Address** box, right-click, and then click **Paste**. If the current year is 2010 or earlier, type **\BrianFong.vfb** If the year is 2011 or later, type **\BrianFong2011.vfb Save & Close** the contact.

8. Open the **Michael Owens-Hughes** contact. Click the **Details** button, and under **Internet Free/Busy**, in the **Address** box, type **file:** Right-click, and then click **Paste**. If the current year is 2010 or earlier, type **\MOwensHughes.vfb** If the current year is 2011 or later, type **\MOwensHughes2011 .vfb Save & Close** the contact.

9. From the **Navigation Pane**, display the **Calendar** folder. In the **Date Navigator**, click the **right arrow**, and then advance the calendar to next **June** or **December**, whichever month is closest to the current month. Click the **first Monday** in the month. From the **Actions** menu, display

(Project 4D–Energy Efficiency continues on the next page)

(Project 4D–Energy Efficiency continued)

the **Plan a Meeting** dialog box, click **Add Others**, and then click **Add from Address Book**.

10. In the **Select Attendees and Resources: Contacts** dialog box, under **Name**, click **Brian Fong**, and then click **Required**. Click **Michael Owens-Hughes**, and then click **Required**. If you are not using an Exchange Server, click **Conference Room 1**, and then click **Resources** to add a resource; recall that in an Exchange Server environment, your network administrator must give you permission to use resources. Click **OK**. If you have added the resource, it will display no schedule information.

11. In the **Plan a Meeting** dialog box, notice the available times for all attendees are either 1:00, 2:00, or 4:00 pm. Click the time block under **4:00 pm**. Position the pointer on the red border of the shaded column, and drag to **5:00**. Click **Make Meeting**. (Because only working hours are displayed, you will see 8:00 am—drag one hour.) In the **Subject** box, type **Meet with Energy Consultant** Click the **Reminder arrow**, and then click **None**. In the comments area of the form, type **Meeting with Sylvia Johnson of Sun Shelter Energy Consultants to review our new energy efficient designs**

12. **Send** the message and close the **Plan a Meeting** dialog box. With the calendar still displayed on the same date, select the **Meet with Energy Consultant** meeting. From the **File** menu, display the **Page Setup: Memo Style** dialog box, click the **Header/Footer tab**, and then delete any existing header or footer information. In the left **Footer** box, type **4D_Energy_Efficiency_Meeting_ Firstname_Lastname Preview** and **Print** the meeting. Submit the end result to your instructor as directed.

13. Delete the meeting in the calendar. In the **Meeting** form, click **Send Cancellation**.

14. From the **Navigation Pane**, display the **Contacts** folder. Change the **Current View** to **Business Cards**, if necessary. Display the **Page Setup: Card Style** dialog box. Delete any existing header or footer information, and then create a left **Footer** as **4D_Energy_Efficiency_Contacts_Firstname_ Lastname** On the **Format tab**, set **Blank forms at end** to **None**. **Preview** and **Print** the contacts list. Submit the end result to your instructor as directed.

15. Delete the contents of the **Contacts** folder. Display the **Folder List**. Delete the contents of the **Outbox** folder. Point to the **Deleted Items** folder, right-click, from the shortcut menu, click **Empty "Deleted Items" Folder**, and then click **Yes**.

16. From the **Tools** menu, click **Options**. Click the **Mail Setup tab**, and then, under **Send/Receive**, select the **Send immediately when connected** check box.

17. In the **Options** dialog box, click **Send/Receive**. In the **Send/Receive Groups** dialog box, under **Setting for group "All Accounts"**, select both **Include this group in send/receive (F9)** check boxes. Select both **Schedule an automatic send/receive** check boxes if this is a default setting on your computer. Click **Close**. Click **OK**.

18. Display the **Contacts** folder. From the **File** menu, point to **Page Setup**, and then click **Define Print Styles**. Click **Memo Style**, click **Reset**, and then click **OK**. **Reset** the **Card Style** print style. **Close** the dialog box, and **Close** Outlook.

End **You have completed Project 4D**

Content-Based Assessments

Mastering Outlook

Project 4E — Hurricanes

Objectives: 1. *Publish Free/Busy Information;* **2.** *Schedule a Meeting;* **5.** *Manage Meeting Information.*

In the following Mastering Outlook project, you will schedule a meeting for Joseph Owens, who is the president of Owens Family Builders. Mr. Owens wants to hold a meeting with his architects to discuss the effects of major hurricanes on the company's home designs. Although the company's homes have had a good track record in recent history, Mr. Owens feels that newer technology offers the possibility of improving the designs even more. Your completed documents will look similar to the ones shown in Figure 4.47.

For Project 4E, you will need the following files:

o04E_Hurricanes_Contacts
JasonMiller.vfb
LouiseFriedman.vfb
JasonMiller2011.vfb
LouiseFriedman2011.vfb

You will print two files with the following footers:
4E_Hurricanes_Meeting_Firstname_Lastname
4E_Hurricanes_Contacts_Firstname_Lastname

Figure 4.47

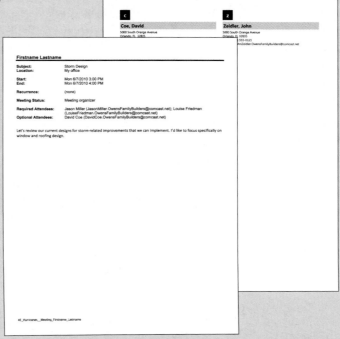

(Project 4E–Hurricanes continues on the next page)

(Project 4E–Hurricanes continued)

1. **Start** Outlook. From the **Tools** menu, display the **Options** dialog box, and then click the **Mail Setup tab**. Under **Send/Receive**, clear the **Send immediately when connected** check box if necessary. Click the **Send/Receive** button. In the **Send/Receive Groups** dialog box, under **Setting for group "All Accounts"**, clear both **Include this group in send/receive (F9)** check boxes if necessary. Clear both **Schedule an automatic send/receive** check boxes if necessary. Click **Close**, and then click **OK**.

2. Using the technique learned in previous projects, use the **Import and Export Wizard** to locate the *.pst* data file **o04E_Hurricanes_Contacts.**

3. **Copy** the pathname for the **o04E_Hurricanes_Contacts** data file from the **Properties** dialog box, and then click **Cancel**.

4. In the **Open Personal Folders** dialog box, with the file **o04E_Contacts** selected, click **Open**. In the **Import Personal Folders** dialog box, click **Next**.

5. In the **Import Personal Folders** dialog box, under **Select the folder to import from**, click **Contacts**. Click **Import items into the current folder**. Click **Finish**. If a Translation Warning dialog box displays, click OK.

6. With the **Contacts** folder displayed, open a new contact form. Complete the form with the following information:

   Louise Friedman
   Owens Family Builders
   LouiseFriedman.OwensFamilyBuilders@comcast.net
   407-555-0169
   5000 South Orange Avenue
   Orlando, FL 32835

7. Click the **Details** button. Under **Internet Free/Busy**, in the **Address** box, type **file:** Right-click, and then click **Paste**. If the current year is 2010 or earlier, type **\LouiseFriedman.vfb** If the current year is 2011 or later, type **\LouiseFriedman2011.vfb**

8. On the Ribbon, click the **Save & New arrow**, and then click **New Contact from Same Company**. Recall that this command can be used when creating a new contact from the same company. In the **Owens Family Builders - Contact** form, in the **Full Name** box, type **Jason Miller** In the **E-mail** box, type **JasonMiller.OwensFamilyBuilders@comcast.net** Change the phone number to **407-555-0179**

9. Click the **Details** button, and then under **Internet Free/Busy**, in the **Address** box, type **file:** Right-click, and then click **Paste**. If the year is 2010 or earlier, type **\JasonMiller.vfb** If the year is 2011 or later, type **\JasonMiller2011.vfb Save & Close** both contacts.

10. From the **Navigation Pane**, display the **Calendar**. In the **Date Navigator**, click the **right arrow**, and then advance the calendar to next **June** or **December**, whichever month is closest to the current month. Click the **first Monday** in the month. Click the **11:00 am** time slot for a meeting time. From the **Actions** menu, display the **Plan a Meeting** dialog box, click **Add Others**, and then click **Add from Address Book**.

11. In the **Select Attendees and Resources: Contacts** dialog box, add **Jason Miller** and **Louise Friedman** to the **Required** box. Click **OK**. In the **Plan a Meeting** dialog box, notice that both required attendees are busy at 11:00 a.m. Drag the red and green borders so that the meeting is scheduled for 3:00–4:00 pm. Click **Make Meeting**.

(Project 4E–Hurricanes continues on the next page)

Content-Based Assessments

Outlook

(Project 4E–Hurricanes continued)

12. In the **Subject** box, type **Storm Design** In the **Location** box, type **My office** Click the **Reminder arrow**, and then click **None**. In the comments area of the form, type **Let's review our current designs for storm-related improvements that we can implement. I'd like to focus specifically on window and roofing design. Send** the meeting request, and close the **Plan a Meeting** dialog box.

13. Display the **Contacts** folder, open the **Jason Miller** contact, click the **Save & New arrow**, and then click **New Contact from Same Company**. In the **Owens Family Builders - Contact** form, in the **Full Name** box, type **David Coe** Change the phone number to **407-555-0189** In the **E-mail** box, type **DavidCoe. OwensFamilyBuilders@comcast.net Save & Close** both contacts.

14. Open the **Calendar**. Display the first **Monday** in the next **December** or **June**, which is the same month in which you have been working. Open the **Storm Design** meeting. In the **Storm Design - Meeting** form, click **Add or Remove Attendees**. Add **David Coe** as an **Optional** attendee. Click **OK**, and then click **Send Update**. In the **Send Update to Attendees** dialog box, click **Send updates only to added or deleted attendees**, and then click **OK**.

15. Select the **Storm Design** meeting. Display the **Page Setup: Memo Style** dialog box. Delete any existing header or footer information, and in the left **Footer** box, type **4E_Hurricanes_Meeting_Firstname_Lastname**

Preview and **Print** the meeting. Submit the end result to your instructor as directed.

16. Delete the meeting in the calendar. In the **Meeting** form, click **Send Cancellation**.

17. Open **Contacts**; change the **Current View** to **Business Cards**, if necessary. Display the **Page Setup: Card Style** dialog box, delete any existing header or footer information, and then, in the left **Footer** box, type **4E_Hurricanes_Contacts_Firstname_ Lastname** On the **Format tab**, set the **Blank forms** at end to **None**. **Preview** and **Print** the contacts list. Submit the end result to your instructor as directed.

18. Delete the contents of the **Contacts** folder. Delete the contents of the **Outbox** folder. Delete the contents of the **Deleted Items** folder.

19. From the **Tools** menu, click **Options**. Click the **Mail Setup tab**, and then, under **Send/Receive**, select the **Send immediately when connected** check box.

20. In the **Options** dialog box, click **Send/ Receive**. In the **Send/Receive Groups** dialog box, under **Setting for group "All Accounts"**, select both **Include this group in send/receive (F9)** check boxes. Select both **Schedule an automatic send/receive** check boxes if this is a default setting on your computer. Click **Close**. Click **OK**

21. Display the **Contacts** folder. Display the **Define Print Styles** dialog box. **Reset** the **Card Style** and **Memo Style** print styles. **Close** the dialog box, and **Close** Outlook.

End **You have completed Project 4E**

Content-Based Assessments

Mastering Outlook

Project 4F — Remodeling

Objectives: 3. *Respond to Meeting Requests;* **5.** *Manage Meeting Information.*

In the following Mastering Outlook project, you will handle Jennifer Owens's meeting invitations. Although new home construction has always been the focus of Owens Family Builders, Jennifer Owens has been asked by the company's president to investigate expanding their business into remodeling services. Ms. Owens has received several meeting requests from different individuals relating to this investigation. You will reply to these meeting invitations. Your completed documents will look similar to the ones shown in Figure 4.48.

For Project 4F, you will need the following file:

o04F_Remodeling_Inbox

You will print three files with the following footers:
4F_Remodeling_Firstname_Lastname
4F_Remodeling_Acceptance_Firstname_Lastname
4F_Remodeling_New_Time_Firstname_Lastname

Figure 4.48

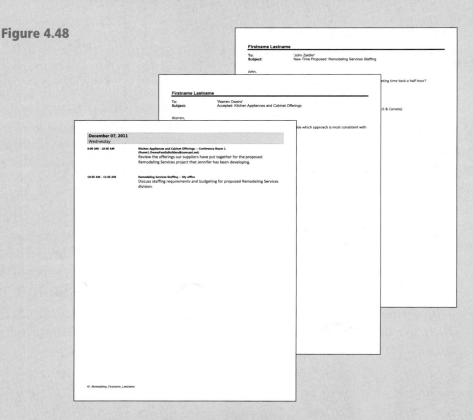

(Project 4F–Remodeling continues on the next page)

Content-Based Assessments

(Project 4F–Remodeling continued)

1. **Start** Outlook. From the **Tools** menu, display the **Options** dialog box, and then click the **Mail Setup tab**. Under **Send/Receive**, clear the **Send immediately when connected** check box if necessary. Click the **Send/Receive** button. In the **Send/Receive Groups** dialog box, under **Setting for group "All Accounts"**, clear both **Include this group in send/receive (F9)** check boxes if necessary. Clear both **Schedule an automatic send/receive** check boxes if necessary. Click **Close**, and then click **OK**.

2. If your time zone is not Eastern Time (US & Canada), from the **Tools** menu, display the **Options** dialog box. Click **Calendar Options**. Click the **Time zone arrow**, locate and click **(GMT-05:00) Eastern Time (US & Canada)**, and then click **OK** three times.

3. Use the **Import and Export Wizard** to locate the *.pst* data file **o04F_Remodeling_Inbox** and then click **Open**. In the **Import Personal Folders** dialog box, click **Next**.

4. In the **Import Personal Folders** dialog box, under **Select the folder to import from**, click **Inbox**. Click **Import items into the current folder**. Click **Finish**. If a Translation Warning dialog box displays, click OK.

5. In the **Inbox**, click the **Kitchen Appliances and Cabinet Offerings** message from *Warren Owens*. In the **Reading Pane**, at the top of the message, click **Accept**. In the **Microsoft Office Outlook** dialog box, click **Edit the response before sending**, and then click **OK**.

6. In the comments area of the **Accepted: Kitchen Appliances and Cabinet Offerings - Meeting Response** form, type **Warren, We will focus on high-end products**

(Project 4F–Remodeling continues on the next page)

versus budget offerings. We need to decide which approach is most consistent with our experience and company image. Jennifer **Send** the reply.

7. From the **View** menu, point to **Reading Pane**, and then click **Bottom**. With the **Remodeling Services Staffing** message from *John Zeidler* selected in the **Inbox**, in the **Reading Pane**, click **Propose New Time**. Because you did not import or create contacts, no free/busy times are visible. In the **Propose New Time: Remodeling Services Staffing** dialog box, drag the borders of the meeting time so that the proposed time is 11:00 to 12:00. Click **Propose Time**.

8. Create the following message in the comments area: **John, I have an appointment that is not entered on my calendar. Could we push your meeting time back a half hour? Jennifer Send** the reply. Display the **Reading Pane** on the **Right**.

9. Display the **Calendar**. From the **Go** menu, display the **Go to Date** dialog box, and then, as the date, type **12/07/11** Click **OK**. Display the **Page Setup: Calendar Details Style** dialog box. Delete any existing header or footer information, and then, in the left **Footer** box, type **4F_Remodeling_Firstname_Lastname Preview** and **Print** the calendar. Submit the end result to your instructor as directed. Delete both calendar entries for the day *without* sending a response.

10. Open **Mail** and display the **Outbox** folder. Click the **Accepted: Kitchen Appliances and Cabinet Offerings** message from *Warren Owens*. Display the **Page Setup: Memo Style** dialog box. Delete any existing header or footer information, and then create a left **Footer** as **4F_Remodeling_Acceptance_Firstname_Lastname Preview**

(Project 4F–Remodeling continued)

and **Print** the message. Submit the end result to your instructor as directed.

11. Select the **New Time Proposed: Remodeling Services Staffing** message from *John Zeidler*. Display the **Page Setup: Memo Style** dialog box. Create a left **Footer** as 4F_Remodeling_New_Time_ Firstname_Lastname **Preview** and **Print** the message. Submit the end result to your instructor as directed.

12. In the **Outbox**, delete both items. In the **Microsoft Office Outlook** dialog box, click **Yes** for each item deleted. Empty the **Deleted Items** folder.

13. From the **Tools** menu, click **Options**. Click the **Mail Setup tab**, and then, under **Send/Receive**, select the **Send immediately when connected** check box.

14. In the **Options** dialog box, click **Send/Receive**. In the **Send/Receive**

Groups dialog box, under **Setting for group "All Accounts"**, select both **Include this group in send/receive (F9)** check boxes. Select both **Schedule an automatic send/receive** check boxes if this is a default setting on your computer. Click **Close**. Click **OK**.

15. If you changed your time zone, from the **Tools** menu, click **Options**, click **Calendar Options**, and then click **Time Zone**. In the **Time Zone** dialog box, click the **Time zone arrow**, locate and click your time zone, and then click **OK** three times.

16. Display the **Calendar** folder. Display the **Define Print Styles** dialog box. **Reset** the **Calendar Details Style** and **Memo Style** print styles. **Close** the dialog box, and then **Close** Outlook.

End **You have completed Project 4F**

Content-Based Assessments

Mastering Outlook

Project 4G — Video

Objectives: 1. *Publish Free/Busy Information;* **2.** *Schedule a Meeting;* **5.** *Manage Meeting Information.*

In the following Mastering Outlook project, you will schedule a meeting for Juan Sanchez at Owens Family Builders. Mr. Sanchez has developed a video that the sales force can give to prospective customers. The video is intended to guide customers through the decision-making process after they have contracted with the company to build a new home. Mr. Sanchez is ready to show the video to the senior management team for its review. Your completed document will look similar to the one shown in Figure 4.49.

For Project 4G, you will need the following files:

o04G_Video_Contacts

FeliciaAnderson.vfb

JenniferOwens.vfb

FeliciaAnderson2011.vfb

JenniferOwens2011.vfb

You will print one file with the following footer:
4G_Video_Meeting_Firstname_Lastname

Figure 4.49

(Project 4G–Video continues on the next page)

Content-Based Assessments

(Project 4G–Video continued)

1. **Start** Outlook. From the **Tools** menu, display the **Options** dialog box, and then click the **Mail Setup tab**. Under **Send/Receive**, clear the **Send immediately when connected** check box if necessary. To the immediate right, click the **Send/Receive** button. In the **Send/Receive Groups** dialog box, under **Setting for group "All Accounts"**, clear both **Include this group in send/receive (F9)** check boxes if necessary. Clear both **Schedule an automatic send/receive** check boxes if necessary. Click **Close**, and then click **OK**.

2. From the **Navigation Pane**, display the **Contacts** folder.

3. Use the **Import and Export Wizard** to locate the *.pst* data file **o04G_Video_Contacts**.

4. **Copy** the pathname for the **o04G_Video_Contacts** data file from the **Properties** dialog box, and then click **Cancel**. Click **Open**, and then click **Next**.

5. In the **Import Personal Folders** dialog box, under **Select the folder to import from**, click **Contacts**. Click **Import items into the current folder**. Click **Finish**. If a Translation Warning dialog box displays, click OK.

6. Open the **Felicia Anderson** contact. Click the **Details** button. Under **Internet Free/Busy**, in the **Address** box, type **file:** right-click, and then click **Paste**. If the year is 2010 or earlier, type **\FeliciaAnderson.vfb** If the year is 2011 or later, type **\FeliciaAnderson2011.vfb Save & Close** the contact. Open the **Jennifer Owens** contact and click the **Details** button. Under **Internet Free/Busy**, in the **Address** box, type **file:** right-click, and then click **Paste**. If the year is 2010 or earlier, type **\JenniferOwens.vfb** If the year is 2011 or

later, type **\JenniferOwens2011.vfb Save & Close** the contact.

7. Display the **Calendar**. In the **Date Navigator**, click the **right arrow**, and then advance the calendar to next **June** or **December**, whichever month is closest to the current month. Click the **first Monday** in the month. Click the **1:00 pm** time slot for a meeting time. From the **Actions** menu, display the **Plan a Meeting** dialog box, click **Add Others**, and then click **Add from Address Book**.

8. In the **Select Attendees and Resources: Contacts** dialog box, add **Jennifer Owens** and **Felicia Anderson** to the **Required** box. Click **OK**.

9. In the **Plan a Meeting** dialog box, click **Options**, and then click **Show Only My Working Hours** to deselect this option. Notice that both required attendees are busy at 1:00 p.m. Drag the red and green borders so that the meeting is scheduled for 5:00 to 6:00 p.m. Click **Make Meeting**.

10. In the **Subject** box, type **New Video** In the **Location** box, type **My office** Click the **Reminder arrow**, and then click **None**. In the comments area of the form, type **We are showing the new Owens Custom Homes DVD. Our team has been working on this video for the last month, and we're ready for comments. Send** the meeting request, and close the **Plan a Meeting** dialog box.

11. With the calendar still displaying the same day in which you have been working, open the **New Video** meeting. In the **New Video - Meeting** form, click **Add or Remove Attendees**. Add **Michael Owens-Hughes** and **John Zeidler** as **Optional** attendees, and then click **OK**. Click **Send Update**. In the **Send Update to Attendees** dialog box,

(Project 4G–Video continues on the next page)

Content-Based Assessments

(Project 4G–Video continued)

click **Send updates only to added or deleted attendees,** and then click **OK**.

12. Select the **New Video** meeting. Display the **Page Setup: Memo Style** dialog box. Delete any existing header or footer information, and then, in the left **Footer** box, type 4G_Video_Meeting_Firstname_ **Lastname Preview** and **Print** the meeting. Submit the end result to your instructor as directed.

13. Delete the meeting in the calendar. In the **Meeting** form, click **Send Cancellation**.

14. Delete the contents of the **Contacts** folder. Delete the contents of the **Outbox** folder. Empty the **Deleted Items** folder.

15. From the **Tools** menu, click **Options**. Click the **Mail Setup tab**, and then, under

Send/Receive, select the **Send immediately when connected** check box.

16. In the **Options** dialog box, click **Send/Receive**. In the **Send/Receive Groups** dialog box, under **Setting for group "All Accounts"**, select both **Include this group in send/receive (F9)** check boxes. Select both **Schedule an automatic send/receive** check boxes if this is a default setting on your computer. Click **Close**. Click **OK**.

17. Display the **Define Print Styles** dialog box. **Reset** the **Memo Style** print style. **Close** the dialog box, and **Close** Outlook.

End **You have completed Project 4G** ——————————————

Project 4H — Water Park

Objectives: 1. *Publish Free/Busy Information;* **2.** *Schedule a Meeting;*
5. *Manage Meeting Information.*

In the following Mastering Outlook project, you will manage the meeting schedule for Warren Owens. Owens Family Builders is developing a new, family-oriented subdivision in Orlando that will boast superior recreation facilities. One of the proposals is to include a water park. This is something new for the company. Before going forward with this plan, Warren Owens would like to meet with some of his managers to discuss different aspects of this amenity. Your completed documents will look similar to the ones shown in Figure 4.50.

For Project 4H, you will need the following files:

o04H_Water_Park_Contacts
JasmineBrown.vfb
LOwensShafku.vfb
BrianFong.vfb
JasmineBrown2011.vfb
LOwensShafku2011.vfb
BrianFong2011.vfb

You will print two files with the following footers:
4H_Water_Park_Liability_Firstname_Lastname
4H_Water_Park_Design_Firstname_Lastname

Figure 4.50

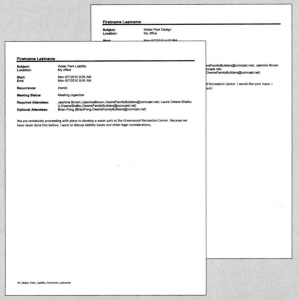

(Project 4H–Water Park continues on the next page)

Content-Based Assessments

(Project 4H–Water Park continued)

1. **Start** Outlook. From the **Tools** menu, display the **Options** dialog box, and click the **Mail Setup tab**. Under **Send/Receive**, clear the **Send immediately when connected** check box if necessary. To the immediate right, click the **Send/Receive** button. In the **Send/Receive Groups** dialog box, under **Setting for group "All Accounts"**, clear both **Include this group in send/receive (F9)** check boxes if necessary. Clear both **Schedule an automatic send/receive** check boxes if necessary. Click **Close**, and then click **OK**.

2. Open **Contacts**, display the **Import and Export Wizard** dialog box, and then, using the techniques you have practiced, display the **Properties** dialog box for **o04H_Water_Park_Contacts**, copy its pathname to the Office Clipboard, and then import the **o04H_Water_Park_Contacts** file into the **Contacts** folder.

3. Open the **Jasmine Brown** contact, click the **Details** button, and then, using the techniques you have practiced, under **Internet Free/Busy** in the **Address** box, type file:\\ and paste the pathname, and then type \JasmineBrown.vfb or \JasmineBrown2011 .vfb **Save & Close** the contact. Open the **Laura Owens-Shafku** contact, and repeat this procedure, using the file LOwensShafku.vfb or LOwensShafku2011 .vfb Be sure to separate the pathname and the file name with a backward slash (\). **Save & Close** the contact. Repeat this procedure for the **Brian Fong** contact, using the file BrianFong.vfb or BrianFong2011.vfb

4. Display the **Calendar**. In the **Date Navigator**, click the **right arrow**, and then advance the calendar to next **June** or **December**, whichever month is closest to the current month. Display the **first Monday** of the month. In the **3:00 pm**

time slot, plan a meeting. Add **Laura Owens-Shafku** and **Jasmine Brown** as **Required** attendees. Adjust the time in the **Plan a Meeting** dialog box so that the meeting time is from 4:00 to 5:00 p.m., and then make the meeting.

5. As the **Subject** of the meeting, type **Water Park Design** Make the **Location** as **My office** Set the **Reminder** to **None**. Add the following comment: **I have received some designs for the new water park at the Greenwood Recreation Center. I would like your input. I know both of you have young children, so I am counting on your feedback! Send** the meeting request, and close the **Plan a Meeting** dialog box.

6. With the calendar still displaying the same day in which you have been working, plan another meeting. Add **Jasmine Brown** and **Laura Owens-Shafku** as **Required** meeting attendees. Add **Brian Fong** as an **Optional** meeting attendee. Set the time of the meeting from 8:00 to 9:00 a.m.

7. As the meeting **Subject**, type **Water Park Liability,** and make the **Location My office** Set the **Reminder** to **None**. Add the following comment: **We are tentatively proceeding with plans to develop a water park at the Greenwood Recreation Center. Because we have never done this before, I want to discuss liability issues and other legal considerations. Send** the meeting request, and close the **Plan a Meeting** dialog box.

8. With the calendar still displaying the same day in which you have been working, open the **Water Park Design** meeting. Add **Michael Owens-Hughes** as an **Optional** attendee. Send the updated meeting to all meeting attendees.

9. Preview and then print the **Water Park Liability** meeting in **Memo Style** using

(Project 4H–Water Park continues on the next page)

(Project 4H–Water Park continued)

the footer **4H_Water_Park_Liability_ Firstname_Lastname** **Print** the **Water Park Design** meeting in **Memo Style** using the footer **4H_Water_Park_Design_Firstname_ Lastname** Submit the end results to your instructor as directed.

10. Delete the meetings in the calendar, sending cancellations. Delete the contents of the **Contacts** folder and the **Outbox** folder, and then empty the **Deleted Items** folder.

11. From the **Tools** menu, click **Options**. Click the **Mail Setup tab**, and then, under

Send/Receive, select the **Send immediately when connected** check box.

12. In the **Options** dialog box, click **Send/Receive**. In the **Send/Receive Groups** dialog box, under **Setting for group "All Accounts"**, select both **Include this group in send/receive (F9)** check boxes. Select both **Schedule an automatic send/receive** check boxes if this is a default setting on your computer. Click **Close**. Click **OK**. **Reset** the **Memo Style** print style. **Close** Outlook.

End **You have completed Project 4H**

Content-Based Assessments

Outlook

Mastering Outlook

Project 4I — Bike Path

Objectives: 3. *Respond to Meeting Requests;* **5.** *Manage Meeting Information.*

In the following Mastering Outlook project, you will manage the meeting schedule of Brian Fong at Owens Family Builders. Mr. Fong is an avid cyclist. Because of his expertise, he has been asked by the company's management to participate in the development of a series of bike paths for a large subdivision that the company is constructing. Two different groups at the company are working on the project. One is responsible for the design, and the other is involved with securing state grants for the project. Your completed documents will look similar to the ones shown in Figure 4.51.

> ### For Project 4I, you will need the following file:
>
> o04I_Bike_Path_Inbox

You will print three files with the following footers:
4I_Bike_Path_Calendar_Firstname_Lastname
4I_Bike_Path_Acceptance_Firstname_Lastname
4I_Bike_Path_Tentative_Firstname_Lastname

Figure 4.51

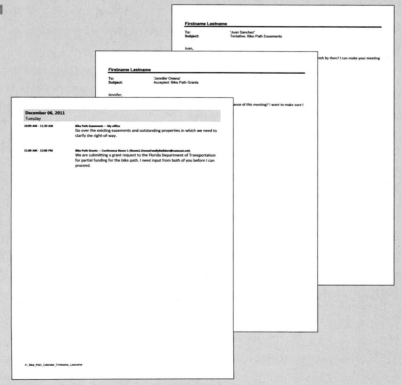

(Project 4I–Bike Path continues on the next page)

(Project 4I–Bike Path continued)

1. **Start** Outlook. From the **Tools** menu, display the **Options** dialog box, and click the **Mail Setup tab**. Under **Send/Receive**, clear the **Send immediately when connected** check box if necessary. To the immediate right, click the **Send/Receive** button. In the **Send/Receive Groups** dialog box, under **Setting for group "All Accounts"**, clear both **Include this group in send/receive (F9)** check boxes if necessary. Clear both **Schedule an automatic send/receive** check boxes if necessary. Click **Close**, and then click **OK**.

2. If your time zone is not Eastern Time (US & Canada), from the **Tools** menu, display the **Options** dialog box and click **Calendar Options**. In the **Calendar Options** dialog box, click **Time Zone**. Click the **Time zone arrow**, locate and click **(GMT-05:00) Eastern Time (US & Canada)**, and then click **OK** three times.

3. Display the **Inbox** folder. Display the **Import and Export Wizard** dialog box, and then, using the techniques you have practiced, import **o04I_Bike_Path_Inbox** into the **Inbox** folder.

4. In the **Inbox**, **Accept** the **Bike Path Grants** invitation from *Jennifer Owens*. Edit the response before sending, and add the following comment: **Jennifer, Could you be more specific about what information you need from me in advance of this meeting? I want to make sure I have everything on hand for you when we meet. Brian Send** the reply.

5. Apply a **Tentative** response to the **Bike Path Easements** invitation from *Juan Sanchez*. Edit the response before sending by adding the following comment: **Juan, I've already accepted another meeting that**

starts at 11:00. Do you think we can finish by then? I can make your meeting if we can keep it to an hour. Brian

6. After sending the reply to Juan's message, display the calendar for **December 6, 2011**. **Preview** and then **Print** the day's calendar in **Calendar Details Style** using the footer 4I_Bike_Path_Calendar_Firstname_Lastname Then delete both calendar entries for the day without sending a response. Submit the end result to your instructor as directed.

7. Display the **Outbox** folder. **Preview** and then **Print** the **Accepted: Bike Path Grants** invitation from *Jennifer Owens* in **Memo Style** using the footer 4I_Bike_Path_Acceptance_Firstname_Lastname **Preview** and then **Print** the **Tentative: Bike Path Easements** invitation from *Juan Sanchez* in **Memo Style** using the footer 4I_Bike_Path_Tentative_Firstname_Lastname Submit the end results to your instructor as directed.

8. In the **Outbox**, delete both items, and do not send a response to the organizer. Empty the **Deleted Items** folder.

9. From the **Tools** menu, click **Options**. Click the **Mail Setup tab**, and then, under **Send/Receive**, select the **Send immediately when connected** check box.

10. In the **Options** dialog box, click **Send/Receive**. In the **Send/Receive Groups** dialog box, under **Setting for group "All Accounts"**, select both **Include this group in send/receive (F9)** check boxes. Select both **Schedule an automatic send/receive** check boxes if this is a default setting on your computer. Click **Close**. Click **OK**.

(Project 4I–Bike Path continues on the next page)

Content-Based Assessments

(Project 4I–Bike Path continued)

11. If you changed your time zone, from the **Tools** menu, click **Options**, click **Calendar Options**, and then click **Time Zone**. In the **Time Zone** dialog box, click the **Time zone arrow**, locate and click your time zone, and then click **OK** three times.

12. Display the **Calendar** folder. **Reset** the **Calendar Details Style** and the **Memo Style** print style. **Close** Outlook.

End **You have completed Project 4I**

Outcomes-Based Assessments

Rubric

The following outcomes-based assessments are *open-ended assessments*. That is, there is no specific correct result; your result will depend on your approach to the information provided. Make *Professional Quality* your goal. Use the following scoring rubric to guide you in *how* to approach the problem and then to evaluate *how well* your approach solves the problem.

The *criteria*—Software Mastery, Content, Format and Layout, and Process—represent the knowledge and skills you have gained that you can apply to solving the problem. The *levels of performance*—Professional Quality, Approaching Professional Quality, or Needs Quality Improvement—help you and your instructor evaluate your result.

	Your completed project is of Professional Quality if you:	Your completed project is Approaching Professional Quality if you:	Your completed project Needs Quality Improvements if you:
1-Software Mastery	Choose and apply the most appropriate skills, tools, and features and identify efficient methods to solve the problem.	Choose and apply some appropriate skills, tools, and features, but not in the most efficient manner.	Choose inappropriate skills, tools, or features, or are inefficient in solving the problem.
2-Content	Construct a solution that is clear and well organized, contains content that is accurate, appropriate to the audience and purpose, and is complete. Provide a solution that contains no errors of spelling, grammar, or style.	Construct a solution in which some components are unclear, poorly organized, inconsistent, or incomplete. Misjudge the needs of the audience. Have some errors in spelling, grammar, or style, but the errors do not detract from comprehension.	Construct a solution that is unclear, incomplete, or poorly organized;, containing contains some inaccurate or inappropriate content; and or contains many errors of spelling, grammar, or style. Do not solve the problem.
3-Format and Layout	Format and arrange all elements to communicate information and ideas, clarify function, illustrate relationships, and indicate relative importance.	Apply appropriate format and layout features to some elements, but not others. Overuse features, causing minor distraction.	Apply format and layout that does not communicate information or ideas clearly. Do not use format and layout features to clarify function, illustrate relationships, or indicate relative importance. Use available features excessively, causing distraction.
4-Process	Use an organized approach that integrates planning, development, self-assessment, revision, and reflection.	Demonstrate an organized approach in some areas, but not others; or use an insufficient process of organization throughout.	Do not use an organized approach to solve the problem.

Problem Solving

Project 4J — Road Race

Objectives: 1. *Publish Free/Busy Information;* **2.** *Schedule a Meeting;* **4.** *Schedule an Office Resource;* **5.** *Manage Meeting Information.*

For Project 4J, you will need the following files:

o04J_Road_Race_Contacts
FeliciaAnderson.vfb
JenniferOwens.vfb
JohnZeidler.vfb
FeliciaAnderson2011.vfb
JenniferOwens2011.vfb
JohnZeidler2011.vfb

You will print two files with the following footers:
4J_Road_Race_Calendar_Firstname_Lastname
4J_Road_Race_Contacts_Firstname_Lastname

Owens Family Builders is a principal sponsor of a local 10K road race. Volunteers from the company will work the race course on the day of the race. Warren Owens is the team leader for the company, and he is calling for a meeting of the participants to discuss the preparations. You will schedule the meeting for Mr. Owens.

Start Outlook. Using the techniques you have practiced, set the Send/Receive options to place your sent e-mail messages to the Outbox. Import the file **o04J_Road_Race_Contacts** into your Contacts list. If you are not using an Exchange Server, create a new contact for Conference Room 3 at Owens Family Builders, using the e-mail address **Room3.OwensFamilyBuilders@comcast.net**. The free/busy files for Jennifer Owens, Felicia Anderson, and John Zeidler are named JenniferOwens.vfb, FeliciaAnderson.vfb, and JohnZeidler.vfb. Using the techniques you have practiced, open these contacts, and specify the Internet free/busy address for each of them. (Use the 2011 files if the current year is 2011 or later.)

Plan a meeting for the first Monday in June or December, whichever month is closest to the current date. Jennifer Owens, John Zeidler, and Felicia Anderson are required attendees for the meeting to take place. Optional attendees are Patricia Doyle and Michael Owens-Hughes. The meeting should take place in the conference room you added to your contacts list, if you created this contact. Find a meeting time that is available for the required attendees. If necessary, choose a time that is earlier or later than the usual working hours. Type a subject of the meeting that relates to the 10K road race. Choose a meeting location, if necessary. Type several lines of comments that describe the purpose of the meeting,

(Project 4J–Road Race continues on the next page)

Outcomes-Based Assessments

(Project 4J–Road Race continued)

which is to go over each team member's responsibilities and assignments on the day of the race. Send the meeting invitation.

After sending the invitation, display the date in the calendar of the meeting, and print the meeting in an appropriate print style using the footer **4J_Road_Race_Calendar_Firstname_Lastname**. Delete the meeting, sending a cancellation. Print the contacts list in an appropriate print style using the footer **4J_Road_Race_Contacts_Firstname_Lastname**. Submit the end results to your instructor as directed. Delete the contents of the Contacts folder, the Outbox folder, and the Deleted Items folder. Restore the Send/Receive options to the default settings on your computer. Reset any print styles you used. Close Outlook.

End **You have completed Project 4J** ——————————

Outcomes-Based Assessments

Problem Solving

Project 4K — TV Show

Objectives: 3. *Respond to Meeting Requests;* **5.** *Manage Meeting Information.*

> ### For Project 4K, you will need the following file:
>
> o04K_TV_Show_Inbox

You will print three files with the following footers:
4K_TV_Show_Calendar_Firstname_Lastname
4K_TV_Show_Owens_Firstname_Lastname
4K_TV_Show_Fong_Firstname_Lastname

Owens Family Builders has agreed to participate in a community television station's Do-It-Yourself TV show. The program will be broadcast over a local cable channel that is carried by the area's cable companies. Joseph Owens, the CEO of Owens Family Builders, will host the series, and Jennifer Owens is the producer. Mr. Owens is using the program to showcase the skills of the company's designers, builders, and architects while teaching viewers basic home-improvement techniques. In this project, you will handle the meeting invitations relating to the TV show that Joseph Owens receives.

Start Outlook. Using the techniques you have practiced, set the Send/Receive options to place your sent e-mail messages in the Outbox. If your time zone is not Eastern Time (US & Canada), change the Outlook time zone to GMT-5:00 Eastern Time (US & Canada). Import **o04K_TV_Show_Inbox** into the Inbox.

Accept the meeting invitation from Jennifer Owens, adding some comments before sending. For your comments, type a sentence or two indicating that you are looking forward to the meeting and have some ideas you want to share. Tentatively accept the meeting invitation from Brian Fong, adding comments to your reply. Inform Brian that your schedule is very busy that day and ask whether he could keep his meeting to an hour. After sending your replies, display the calendar for December 6, 2011, and print it in an appropriate print style using the footer **4K_TV_Show_Calendar_Firstname_Lastname**. Submit the end result to your instructor as directed. Delete both calendar entries for the day without sending a response.

Print the Outbox message to Jennifer Owens using the footer **4K_TV_Show_Owens_Firstname_Lastname**. Print the Outbox message to Brian Fong using the footer **4K_TV_Show_Fong_Firstname_Lastname**. Submit the end results to your instructor as directed. Delete both Outbox items, and do not send a response to the organizer. Delete the contents of the Deleted Items folder.

Restore your Send/Receive options to the default setting on your computer. If you changed the Outlook time zone, restore the Outlook time zone setting to its default setting. Reset any print styles you used. Close Outlook.

End **You have completed Project 4K** ───────

Problem Solving

Project 4L—Home Show

Objectives: 1. *Publish Free/Busy Information;* **2.** *Schedule a Meeting;*
5. *Manage Meeting Information.*

For Project 4L, you will need the following files:

o04L_Home_Show_Contacts
BrianFong.vbf
JohnZeidler.vfb
FeliciaAnderson.vfb
BrianFong2011.vfb
JohnZeidler2011.vfb
FeliciaAnderson2011.vfb

You will print two files with the following footers:
4L_Home_Show_Calendar_Firstname_Lastname
4L_Home_Show_Contacts_Firstname_Lastname

Every year, Owens Family Builders participates in a home show that
takes place at the local convention center. Builders, designers, architects,
landscapers, and home furnishing firms market their goods and services
to the area's homeowners and home buyers. Warren Owens is calling for
a meeting of the company's senior managers to discuss this year's exhibit
at the show. You will schedule the meeting for Mr. Owens.

Start Outlook. Set the Send/Receive options to place your sent e-mail
messages in the Outbox. Import **o04L_Home_Show_Contacts** into the
contacts list. The free/busy information for Brian Fong, Felicia
Anderson, and John Zeidler are located in the files BrianFong.vfb,
FeliciaAnderson.vfb, and JohnZeidler.vfb. Using the techniques you have
practiced, open these contacts, and specify the Internet free/busy
address for each. (Use the 2011 files if the current year is 2011 or later.)

Plan a meeting for the first Monday in June or December, whichever
month is closest to the current date. Brian Fong, John Zeidler, and
Felicia Anderson are required attendees for this meeting to take place.
Joseph Owens is an optional attendee. Schedule the meeting at a time
when all the required attendees are available. If necessary, choose a time
that is earlier or later than the usual working hours. Create an appropriate subject for the meeting, select a location, and add some comments
about its purpose, which is a brainstorming session for the company's
exhibit at the home show. Send the meeting invitation.

After sending the invitation, display the date in the calendar of the meeting, and print the meeting in an appropriate print style using the footer

(Project 4L–Home Show continues on the next page)

Problem Solving

(Project 4L–Home Show continued)

4L_Home_Show_Calendar_Firstname_Lastname. Submit the end result to your instructor as directed. Delete the meeting, sending a cancellation.

Display the Contacts list, and print the list in an appropriate print style using the footer **4L_Home_Show_Contacts_Firstname_Lastname**. Submit the end result to your instructor as directed. Delete the contents of the Contacts folder, the Outbox folder, and the Deleted Items folder. Restore the Send/Receive options to your computer's default settings. Reset any print styles you used. Close Outlook.

End **You have completed Project 4L** —————————————

chapter four

GO! with Help

Project 4M — *GO!* with Help

In addition to sharing your free/busy information, you can share your entire calendar. If you use an Exchange Server e-mail account, you may allow others to view your calendar. You can allow everyone to see your calendar details, or you can set permissions, specifying only those people you choose to see your calendar. You can also view the calendars of others.

1. **Start** Outlook. In the **Type a question for help** box, type **Share a calendar** and press **Enter**. In the **displayed Outlook Help window**, click **Share your calendar information**.

2. Read the information about sharing your calendar, and click the displayed links. Click the **Back** button, and in the **Search Results**, click **Open another person's Exchange Calendar**.

3. Read the information. When finished, **Close** the Outlook Help window, and then **Close** Outlook.

End **You have completed Project 4M** ⸺⸺⸺⸺⸺

chapterfive

Assigning Tasks and Sending Instant Messages

OBJECTIVES

At the end of this chapter you will be able to:

OUTCOMES

Mastering these objectives will enable you to:

1. Assign Tasks

2. Respond to Task Assignments

3. Manage Task Assignments

PROJECT 5A

Assign Tasks

4. Use Instant Messaging in Outlook

PROJECT 5B

Use Instant Messaging

El Cuero de Mexico

El Cuero de Mexico is a Mexico City–based manufacturer of high-quality small leather goods for men and women. Its products include wallets, belts, handbags, key chains, and travel bags. The company distributes its products to department and specialty stores in the United States and Canada through its San Diego–based subsidiary, El Cuero Specialty Wares. Plans are currently underway for a new marketing campaign focusing on several new lines that will be unveiled next year.

Working with Task Assignment and Instant Messaging

Outlook has several tools that enable you to work more efficiently with others. You can assign a task to someone and follow the task until it is completed. Likewise, you may receive a task assignment, and Outlook will let the individual who assigned the task know when you have finished it.

Outlook also enables you to use your computer to instantly communicate with your Outlook contacts from your desk. Using Windows Live Messenger, messages you send display instantly on your contact's computer screen provided that your contacts are also running this program.

Project 5A **Presentation**

In Activities 5.1 through 5.11, you will work with task assignments for Richard Kelly, the Vice President of Marketing of El Cuero Specialty Wares. Mr. Kelly has a number of tasks related to a presentation he is making to Miguel Hernandez, the Chief Executive Officer of El Cuero, who is visiting the San Diego offices next month. You will use Outlook to assign tasks to others and track their progress. You will also respond to task assignments that Mr. Kelly receives. You will accept, decline, and delegate tasks to others. You will print assigned tasks and your To-Do list, which will look similar to the ones shown in Figure 5.1.

For Project 5A, you will need the following files:

o05A_Presentation_Contacts
o05A_Presentation_Tasks

You will print four files with the following footers:
5A_Presentation_Accepted_Firstname_Lastname
5A_Presentation_Assigned_Firstname_Lastname
5A_Presentation_Outbox_Firstname_Lastname
5A_Presentation_Status_Firstname_Lastname

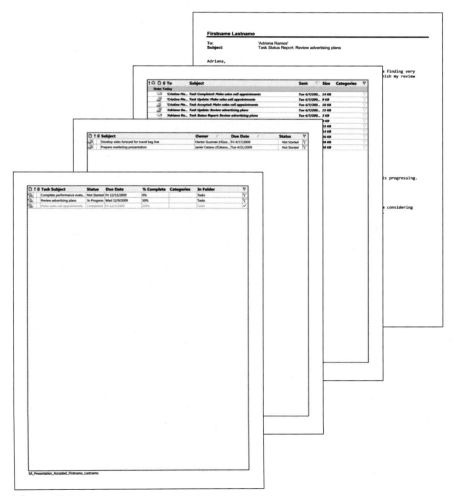

Figure 5.1

Objective 1
Assign Tasks

Recall that a **task** is a personal or work-related activity that you want to track to completion. You can assign tasks to someone else in the form of a **task request**, which is a task sent in an e-mail message asking the recipient to complete the activity. If the recipient accepts the task, the task is added to his or her To-Do List, and he or she becomes the new owner of the task.

A **task owner** is the individual currently responsible for completing an assigned task, and Outlook keeps track of task ownership. Only the task owner can make changes to the task, such as changing its due date. When a task is changed or completed, Outlook automatically sends an **update**—an e-mail message showing the changed Task form—to the person who made the task request and also to any prior owners of the task. When you make a task request, the **task assignee**—the person to whom the task has been assigned—becomes the temporary owner of the task. If the request is accepted, that individual becomes the permanent owner of the task.

Alert!

Starting Project 5A

It is recommended that you schedule enough time to complete this project in one working session. Allow approximately one and one-half hours.

Activity 5.1 Importing Contacts and Configuring Outlook

When you send a task request to a contact, the request is sent in the form of an e-mail message. Recall that you can configure Outlook to store all your sent messages in the Outbox so that you do not have to be online to send messages. In this activity, you will import some contacts for Richard Kelly at El Cuero Specialty Wares, and then you will configure Outlook to place sent messages in the Outbox.

1 **Start** Outlook. In the **Navigation Pane**, click the **Contacts** button
$\boxed{\text{Contacts}}$, and delete any existing contacts in the **Contacts list**.

2 From the **File** menu, display the **Import and Export Wizard** dialog box. Under **Choose an action to perform**, click **Import from another program or file**, and then click **Next**. In the **Import a File** dialog box, under **Select file type to import from**, click the **down scroll arrow**, and then click **Personal Folder File (.pst)**. Click **Next**.

3 In the **Import Personal Folders** dialog box, click **Browse**. In the **Open Personal Folders** dialog box, navigate to the location where the student files for this textbook are stored. Click **o05A_Presentation_Contacts**, and then click **Open**. In the **Import Personal Folders** dialog box, click **Next**, and then compare your screen with Figure 5.2.

The Import Personal Folders dialog box displays the folder structure for the file you are about to import. The folder structure includes a Contacts folder.

Figure 5.2

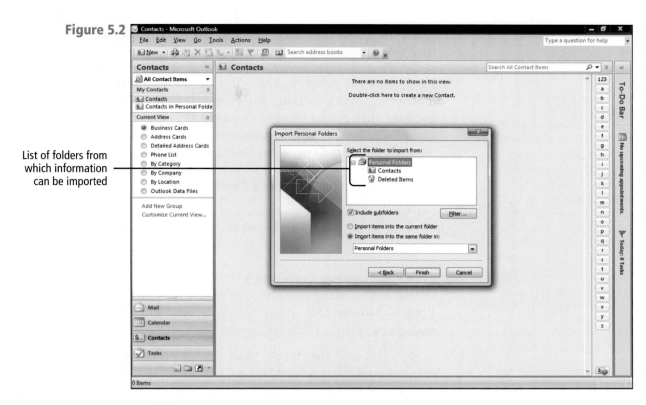

List of folders from which information can be imported

4 In the **Import Personal Folders** dialog box, under **Select the folder to import from**, click **Personal Folders**, if not already selected. Select **Include subfolders**, if necessary. Recall that selecting Personal Folders imports information into the corresponding subfolders. Click **Finish**. If a Translation Warning dialog box displays, click OK. Compare your screen with Figure 5.3. Notice that your layout may differ from this figure, but you should have the same contacts.

Figure 5.3

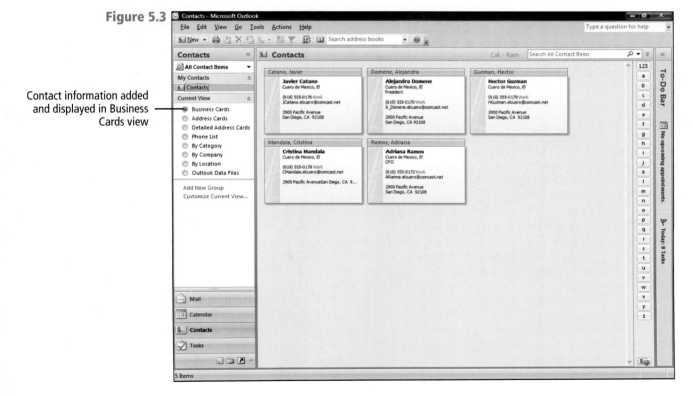

Contact information added and displayed in Business Cards view

5 From the **Tools** menu, display the **Options** dialog box, and then click the **Mail Setup tab**. Under **Send/Receive**, clear the **Send immediately when connected** check box, if necessary. To the immediate right, click the **Send/Receive** button. In the **Send/Receive Groups** dialog box, under **Setting for group "All Accounts"**, clear both **Include this group in send/receive (F9)** check boxes, if necessary. Clear both **Schedule an automatic send/receive** check boxes, if necessary. Click **Close**, and then click **OK**.

Activity 5.2 Assigning a Task to a Contact

You can assign a task to someone at the time you create the task. In this activity, you will create a task and then assign it to one of Richard Kelly's coworkers.

1 In the **Navigation Pane**, click the **Tasks** button [Tasks]. Delete any existing tasks in the **To-Do List**, and change the **Current View** to **Simple List**, if necessary. On the Standard toolbar, click the **New Task** button [New ▾].

2 In the displayed **Untitled - Task** form, in the **Subject** box, type **Prepare marketing presentation** Click the **Due date arrow**, and click a date two weeks from the current date. In the comments area of the form, type **Prepare presentation of the new travel bag line for Miguel's visit week after next.**

3 On the Ribbon, click the **Assign Task** button [Assign Task], and then compare your screen with Figure 5.4.

A *To* box displays above the *Subject* box. Options to keep a copy of the task placed in your task list and for you to receive a status report are displayed. Both options are selected by default. The banner indicates that you have not yet sent this message, and that it is due in 14 days. A **Delete** button [Delete] is added to the Ribbon in case you decide not to assign this task to anyone.

To box displays above the Subject

Figure 5.4

Delete button

Banner indicates that
this is a task request
that has not been sent

Options for you to
receive a copy of the
task and a status
report selected

Message typed in
comments area

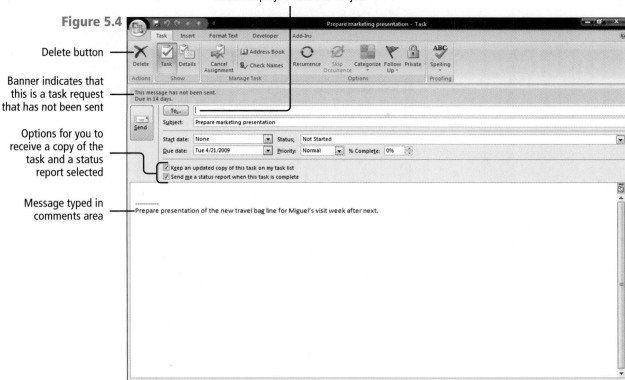

> **4** In the **Task** form, click **To**. In the displayed **Select Task Recipient:**
> **Contacts** dialog box, click **Javier Catano**. Click **To**, and then com-
> pare your screen with Figure 5.5.
>
> The Select Task Recipient: Contacts dialog box displays the names of
> those contacts in your Contacts List that have e-mail addresses.
> Because a task request is sent as an e-mail message, you must provide
> the e-mail address of the person to whom you are assigning the task.

Figure 5.5

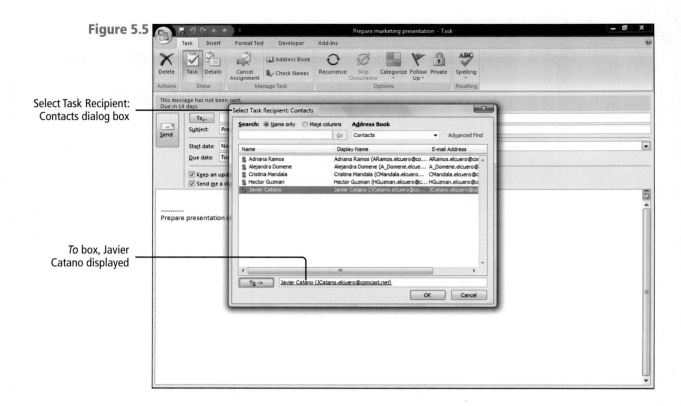

Select Task Recipient:
Contacts dialog box

To box, Javier
Catano displayed

5 In the **Select Task Recipient: Contacts** dialog box, click **OK**, and notice that the Task form redisplays with *Javier Catano* in the **To** box.

6 On the Task form, click the **Send** button.

The task request is sent to the Outbox, the Task form closes, and the task is added to your To-Do List.

7 In the **To-Do List**, open the **Prepare marketing presentation** task, and then compare your screen with Figure 5.6.

The Task form displays. The banner indicates you are waiting for a response for this task assignment. Notice that *Javier Catano* is the task owner. Also notice that the fields for *Subject*, *Due Date*, and other details cannot be changed. Only the task owner can change the details of a task.

Details that cannot be changed

Figure 5.6

Banner indicates that you are waiting for a response

Task owner

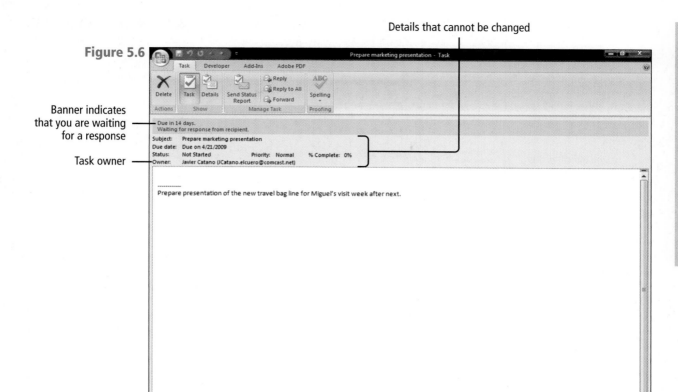

8 **Close** ☒ the Task form.

Activity 5.3 Creating a Task Request from an Existing Task

You can create a task and decide later to assign the task to someone. In this activity, you will create a task for Richard Kelly, and then you will assign the task to one of his coworkers.

1 In the **To-Do List** under the column headings, click in the **Click here to add a new Task** box, and then type **Develop sales forecast for travel bag line** Press **Tab** and in the **Due Date** box, type **one week from today** and then press Enter.

Recall that you can use natural language phrases—language spoken or written by humans, as opposed to a computer programming language—such as *Tomorrow* to specify dates. Outlook converts the phrases to actual dates.

2 In the **To-Do List**, click the **Due Date** column heading, if necessary, to sort the tasks in descending order. Locate the **Icon column**, and then notice the icons for the two tasks you have created. Compare your screen with Figure 5.7.

The first task you created has an icon containing a small hand with the clipboard, which indicates that this task has been assigned to—handed to—someone else. Someone else now owns that task. The icon for the task you just created shows the plain clipboard, which is the icon for a task that you still own.

Figure 5.7

Icon indicates you
assigned this task—
task is owned by
someone else

Icon indicates this
is a task you own

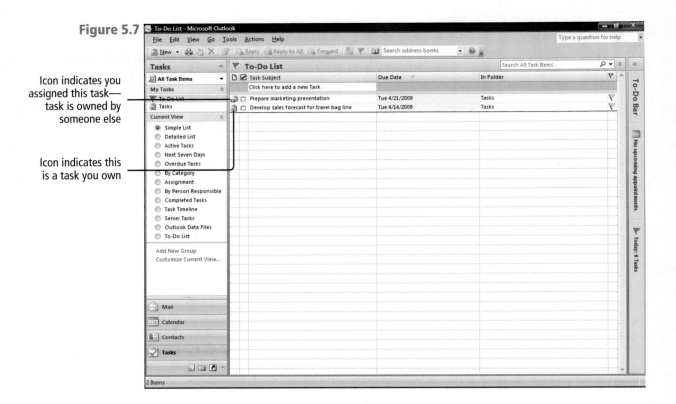

3 Open the **Develop sales forecast for travel bag line** task.

The Task form displays. Because this is a task that you created for yourself, you can change details of the task at any time.

4 Click the **Due date arrow**, and advance the due date by three more business days.

Recall that business days are days that are not Saturday, Sunday, or holidays.

5 On the Ribbon, click the **Assign Task** button .

A banner and a *To* box display over the *Subject* box.

6 In the **Task** form, click **To**. In the displayed **Select Task Recipient: Contacts** dialog box, click **Hector Guzman**, click **To**, and then click **OK**.

The Task form redisplays and shows Hector Guzman's e-mail address in the *To* box. You might want to add a message when you make a task assignment, depending on the recipient. In most situations, you typically assign tasks to subordinates. Occasionally, you might assign tasks to a coworker or equal, but rarely would you assign tasks to a supervisor.

7 Using appropriate spacing, type the following message in the comments area: **Hector, Could you handle this for me? Alejandra said you had the test market data, and you'd be able to take care of it. Thanks! Richard** Compare your screen with Figure 5.8.

Figure 5.8

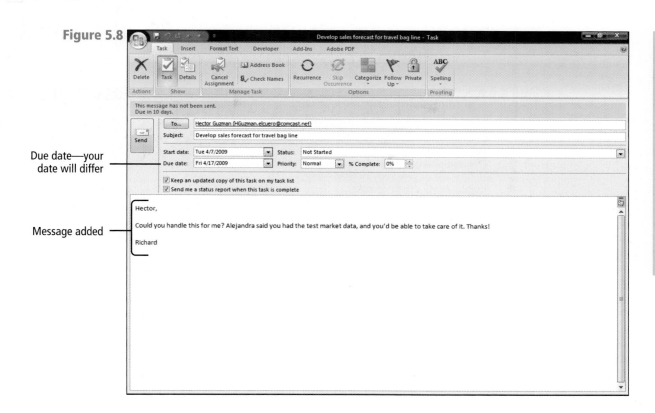

Due date—your
date will differ

Message added

8 **Send** the task request.

The task request is sent to the Outbox, and the Task form closes. The task has been added to your To-Do List. The icon for the task has changed to reflect that this is now an assigned task.

Activity 5.4 Creating an Unassigned Copy of an Assigned Task

You can create an **_unassigned copy_** of an assigned task—a duplicate of a task assigned to someone else that lists you as the task owner. Recall that you cannot change a task you have assigned to someone because the task assignee is the task owner. However, you may have times when you want to work on an assigned task yourself while someone else is also working on the task. If you create an unassigned copy of the assigned task, you can make changes to the task as you are working on it, changing the due date, completion status, and other details as needed. In this activity, you will assign a task to one of Richard Kelly's coworkers and then create an unassigned copy of the task for your task list.

1 From the **Actions** menu, click **New Task Request**. Alternatively, press Ctrl + ⇧ Shift + U.

2 In the **Untitled - Task** form, click **To**. In the displayed **Select Task Recipient: Contacts** dialog box, click **Cristina Mandala**, click **To**, and then click **OK**.

3 In the **Subject** box, type **Make travel arrangements** Click the **Due date arrow**, and click a date one month from the current date.

4 In the comments area, create the following message: **Cristina, For our sales calls next month to San Francisco and Seattle, I will make the**

plane reservations. Could you take care of the hotels and car rental? Richard Compare your screen with Figure 5.9.

Figure 5.9

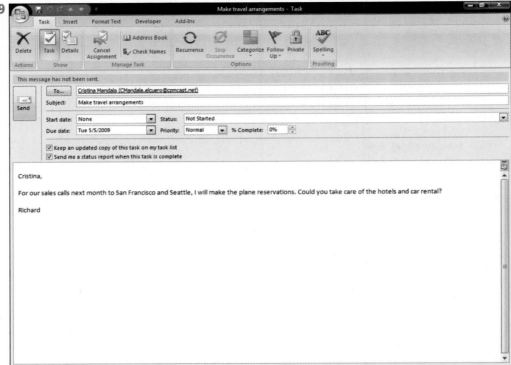

5 **Send** the task request.

The task request is sent to the Outbox, and the Task form closes. The task is added to your To-Do List.

6 To create an unassigned copy of this task, in the **To-Do List**, open the

Make travel arrangements task. Then, click the **Details** button [Details], click the **Create Unassigned Copy** button [Create Unassigned Copy], and then compare your screen with Figure 5.10.

A Microsoft Office Outlook dialog box displays indicating that you cannot receive updates for the assigned task when you create an unassigned copy. Recall that an update is an e-mail message showing the changed Task form for the task. You will not be notified when the task recipient makes any changes to the task you assigned.

Figure 5.10

Outlook | chapter 5

Make travel arrangements
—Task form, Details
button selected

Warning that no updates
will be received from the
assigned task

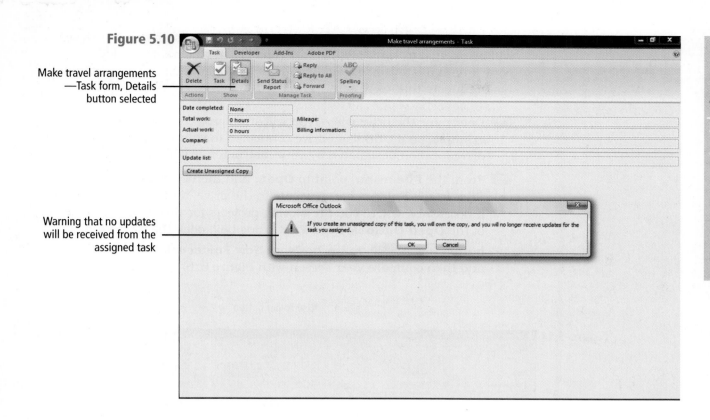

7 In the **Microsoft Office Outlook** dialog box, click **OK**, and then

Close ✕ the **Task** form.

The *Make travel arrangements* task is replaced with a new task that
has the word *(copy)* added to the Subject name. The icon indicates
that this is no longer an assigned task. The original version of this
task—the one you assigned to Cristina Mandala—is still assigned to
her, but you will not receive updates as she works on the task.

Objective 2
Respond to Task Assignments

Not only can you assign tasks to others, but you can also receive task
requests. When you receive a task request, you can take one of three
actions: You can accept the task, decline the task, or assign the task to
someone else. If you accept the task, you assume ownership of the task,
and the task is added to your To-Do List. When you make changes to the
task, such as changing the task's Due Date, an update is sent to the
person who assigned you the task—if he or she requested this option.
When you decline a task, the task is returned to the person who sent it
to you. For accepted tasks, you can also send a ***status report***, which is
an e-mail message that is sent to the originator of the task request indicating the task's progress or completion.

Activity 5.5 Creating a Folder and Opening an Outlook Data File

A task request normally arrives in your Inbox as an e-mail message. The
incoming message adds a task to your To-Do List that is linked to the

message. In this activity, the data file containing task request messages will be opened to simulate incoming mail. You will create a folder and copy a data file to that folder. Then you will open a data file containing task requests that were sent to Richard Kelly.

1 Determine the drive where you will store projects from this chapter, for example, on a USB flash drive connected to your computer or another drive location designated by your instructor or lab coordinator.

2 From the **File** menu, point to **Open**, and then click **Outlook Data File**. In the **Folders** list, navigate to the drive, and folder on the drive if necessary, where you are storing projects for this chapter. At the top of the **Open Outlook Data File** dialog box, click the **New Folder** button New Folder . In the box with **New Folder** selected, type **Chapter 5** and then compare your screen with Figure 5.11.

New Folder button

Figure 5.11

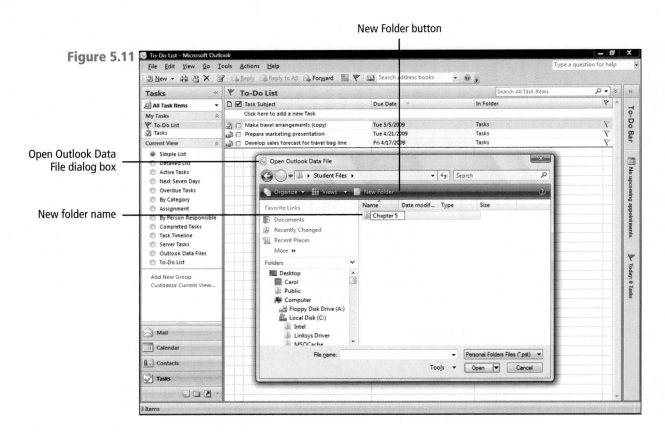

Open Outlook Data File dialog box

New folder name

3 Press Enter. If the new folder name does not display in the **Address** box, with **Chapter 5** folder selected, press Enter.

The new folder name displays in the Address box, indicating that the folder is open and ready for you to store your files.

4 In the **Open Outlook Data File** dialog box, use the **Folders** list to navigate to the location where the student files for this textbook are stored. Point to **o05A_Presentation_Tasks** and right-click. From the displayed shortcut menu, click **Copy**.

The file is copied to the *Windows Clipboard*—a temporary storage area used by Windows to hold one piece of data, such as text, a graphic, or a file. This data can then be pasted in a different location.

Alert! **Why must I make a copy of my data file?**

In this chapter it is necessary to make a copy of any *.pst* file containing task requests before opening it. After opening the file and responding to task requests, the data file is changed. Using a copy of the original data file will allow you to repeat a project, if desired. You will be instructed to make a copy of a data file for any project in which you will be modifying task requests.

5 With the **Open Outlook Data File** dialog box still displayed, use the **Folders** list to navigate back to the **Chapter 5** folder that you created.

6 Right-click in any blank area in the **Open Outlook Data File** dialog box, and then, from the displayed shortcut menu, click **Paste** to place the copy of *o05A_Presentation_Tasks* into your Chapter 5 folder. Compare your screen with Figure 5.12.

Chapter 5 location selected

Figure 5.12

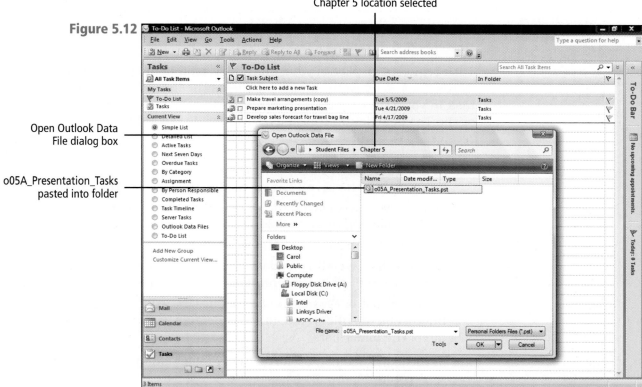

Open Outlook Data File dialog box

o05A_Presentation_Tasks pasted into folder

7 With the file **o05A_Presentation_Tasks** selected, click **OK** to open the file. Compare your screen with Figure 5.13.

In the Navigation Pane, under My Tasks, the folder *Tasks in Personal Folders* displays. Because we opened this data file, instead of importing it, a second *Personal Folders* is created and the view changes accordingly.

Figure 5.13

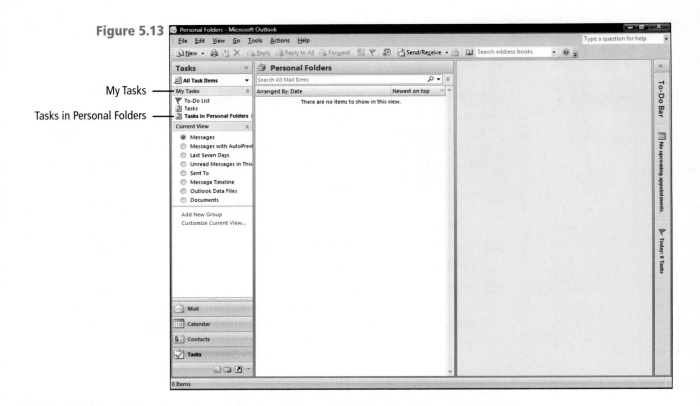

My Tasks

Tasks in Personal Folders

Activity 5.6 Accepting a Task Request

Task requests display in your Inbox as e-mail items identified by the words *Task Request* in the Subject field. The incoming message adds a task to your Tasks list. You can respond to the task request in the Inbox or the Tasks folder. In this activity, you will respond to Richard Kelly's received task requests.

1 In the **Navigation Pane**, click the **Folder List** button ⬜. Under **All Folders**, use the **scroll bar** to display the lower portion of the folder list, if necessary. Locate the **Personal Folders** file, which has the 📁 icon, displaying multiple folders, next to it. Click the **plus (+)** symbol to the left of this icon to expand the folder.

Outlook displays all open data files with the name *Personal Folders*. Therefore, the o05A_Presentation_Tasks file displays at the bottom of the folder list of *Personal Folders*. The 📁 icon next to the name distinguishes this file from Outlook's default Personal Folders file at the top of the folder list.

2 In the expanded list, click the **Inbox** folder, and then compare your screen with Figure 5.14.

The Inbox displays four received task requests. The icons for the messages and the Subject prefix *Task Request* indicate that these are task requests rather than normal e-mail messages. Commands at the top of the Reading Pane can be used to accept or decline the task.

Reading Pane commands for
responding to the task request

Figure 5.14

Task header information

Icon and prefix indicate
that this is a task request

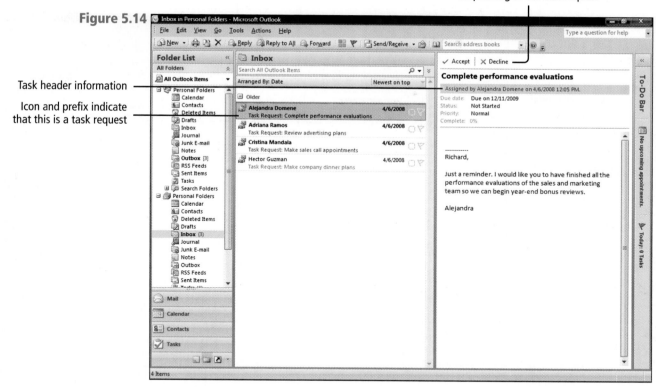

3 Click each item in the **Inbox** and make note of the Due date, Status, Priority, completion progress, and the message.

Each task request has the same header information: *Due date, Status, Priority*, and *Complete*. Every task request has a corresponding task. The corresponding tasks for these task requests are located in the Tasks in Personal Folders list. You can respond to a task request by clicking the commands in the Reading Pane, by opening the task request, or by opening the corresponding task in the Tasks list.

4 In the **Navigation Pane**, click the **Tasks** button [Tasks] , and then, under **My Tasks**, click **Tasks in Personal Folders**. Compare your screen with Figure 5.15.

The contents of the *Tasks in Personal Folders* display. The Tasks list contains the corresponding tasks for the task requests in the Inbox. The icons—a clipboard and two hands—indicate that these are tasks assigned to you by someone else.

Figure 5.15

Icons indicate that these are tasks assigned to you by someone else

Tasks in Personal Folder selected

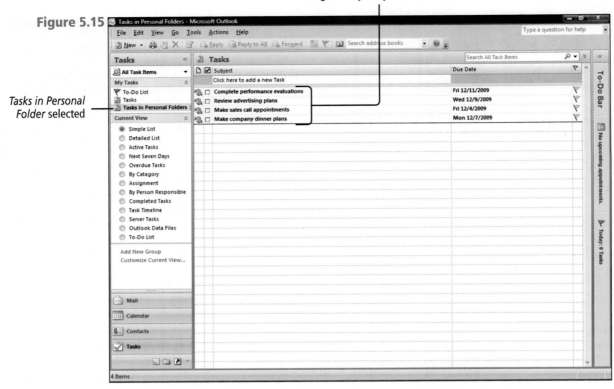

5 In the **Navigation Pane**, under **My Tasks**, click **Tasks**, and then compare the icons for the various tasks in this folder with the previous folder.

The two folders show icons for the three types of tasks: a clipboard for tasks that you own, a clipboard with one hand for tasks you have assigned to someone else, and a clipboard with two hands for tasks assigned to you by someone else.

Note — Task Folders

You have two separate folders for your tasks—one for assigned tasks and another for task requests that you have accepted. For purposes of this activity, you have a separate folder for tasks that have been assigned to you because they were opened as part of a separate data file.

---

6 Under **My Tasks**, click **Tasks in Personal Folders**, and then open the **Complete performance evaluations** task. Compare your screen with Figure 5.16.

The Task form for a received task includes Accept and Decline buttons. The task recipient, *Richard Kelly*, is the current task owner, and the banner at the top of the form indicates the name of the individual who assigned the task—*Alejandra Domene*. Details such as the Status cannot be changed. Although Richard Kelly is the task owner, he cannot change the task until he accepts it.

Figure 5.16

Accept and Decline buttons

Individual who assigned the task

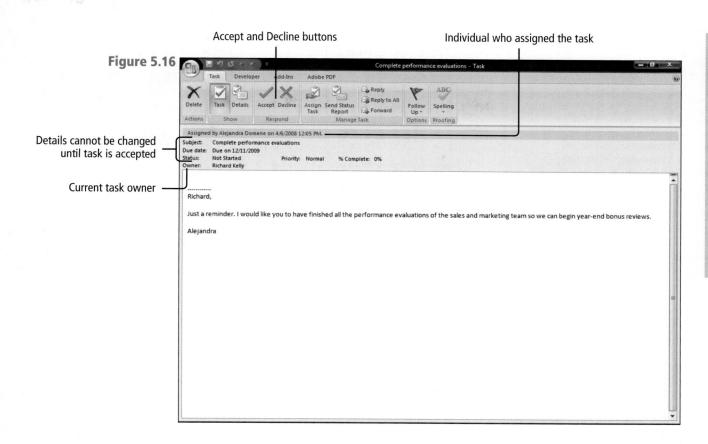

Details cannot be changed until task is accepted

Current task owner

7 In the **Task** form, click the **Details** button to view the update list.

The *update list* is a list that includes the name of the person who originally sent the task request plus the names of everyone who received the task request, reassigned the task to someone else, or chose to keep an updated copy of the task in his or her task list. The people on the update list will receive status reports and updates provided that these options were included in the original task request. This update list includes only the name of the task originator.

8 On the Ribbon, click the **Accept** button.

The Accepting Task dialog box displays. The person who assigned the task to you will be notified that you have accepted the task. You have the option of including a response with your acceptance message.

9 In the **Accepting Task** dialog box, click **Edit the response before sending**, and then click **OK**. Compare your screen with Figure 5.17.

The *To* box displays the e-mail address of the person who assigned you the task. The banner indicates that you have accepted the task, and the details can be changed because you have accepted the task. The original text of the message is separated by a dotted line for the new text you type.

Figure 5.17

Person who assigned the task

Task details can be changed because the task has been accepted

Banner indicates that you have accepted the task

Blinking insertion point above existing text

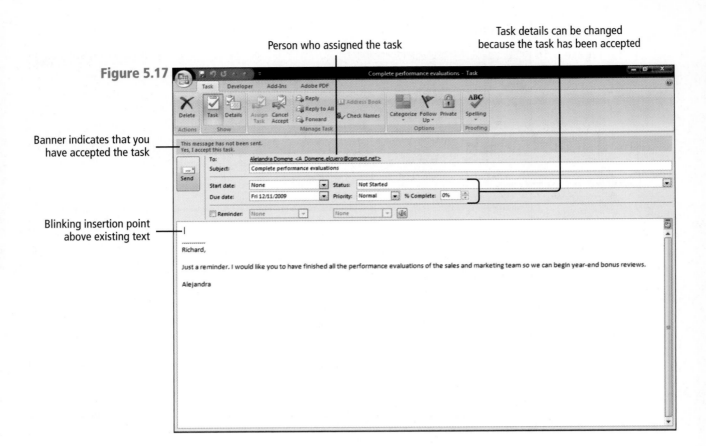

10 Using appropriate spacing, type **Alejandra, I will have these completed by the end of the week. Richard** and then compare your screen with Figure 5.18.

Figure 5.18

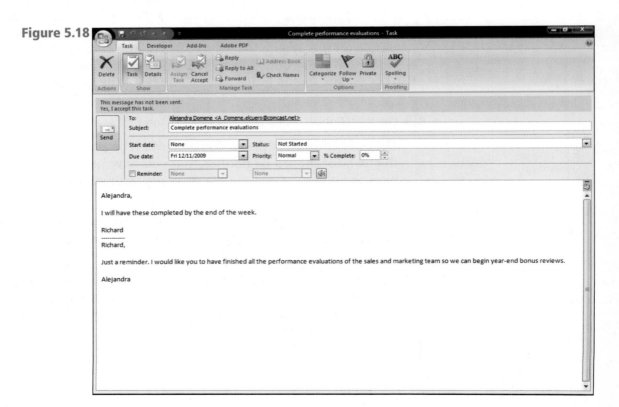

11 **Send** [Send] the message.

The task acceptance message is sent to the Outbox, and the Task form closes.

12 In the **Navigation Pane**, under **My Tasks**, click **To-Do List**.

Notice the *Complete performance evaluations* task that you accepted has been added to your To-Do List.

Activity 5.7 Declining a Task Request

Declining a task request follows a process similar to accepting a task. In this activity, you will decline a task for Richard Kelly.

1 In the **Navigation Pane**, under **My Tasks**, click **Tasks in Personal Folders**. Open the **Make company dinner plans** task.

The banner indicates that *Hector Guzman* assigned this task. *Richard Kelly* is the current task owner.

2 On the Ribbon, click the **Decline** button [X Decline].

The Declining Task dialog box displays. You have the option of adding a message to the response you send. In most circumstances, it is good business etiquette to explain why you cannot accept a task.

3 In the **Declining Task** dialog box, click **Edit the response before sending**, and then click **OK**. Notice that the banner indicates that you have declined the task.

4 In the comments area, using appropriate spacing, type **Hector, I'm really swamped preparing for this presentation. Could you possibly have Cristina take care of this? Richard** and then compare your screen with Figure 5.19.

Figure 5.19

Banner indicates that you have declined the task

Message included with the response

5 Send the message.

The message declining the task is sent to the Outbox, and the Task form closes. The task is deleted from your Tasks list and returned to Hector Guzman, who is the new owner of the task.

More Knowledge

Reassigning a Task Request

In addition to accepting or declining a task request you receive, you can also *reassign* a task—assign a received task to someone else. For example, if your supervisor assigns you a task, you might decide you would like one of your subordinates to complete the task. To reassign the task to someone else, open the task. On the Ribbon, click the Assign Task button. The Task form is reformatted with a To box. Complete the form as you would any other task assignment, and send the task request. Both you and the task originator will receive status reports and updates as the task progresses, provided that these options have been selected.

Activity 5.8 Sending a Task Status Report

As you work on a task, you might find it useful to send status reports to the person who assigned you the task. In this activity, you will accept a task for Richard Kelly and then send a status report on the task.

1 With the **Tasks list** in the **Tasks in Personal Folders** still displayed, open the **Review advertising plans** task. Notice that the banner indicates that *Adriana Ramos* assigned the task and that *Richard Kelly* is the current task owner.

2 **Accept** 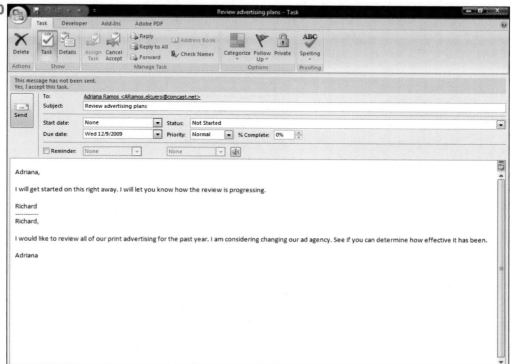 the task. In the **Accepting Task** dialog box, click **Edit the response before sending**, and then click **OK**. Then, in the comments area, using appropriate spacing, type **Adriana, I will get started on this right away. I will let you know how the review is progressing. Richard** and compare your screen with Figure 5.20.

Figure 5.20

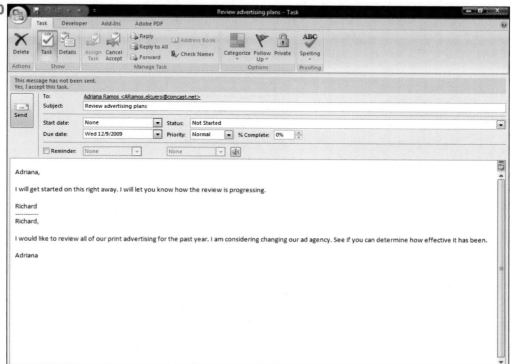

3 **Send** the message.

The task acceptance message is sent to the Outbox, and the Task form closes. The *Review advertising plans* task is permanently added to the Tasks list, and Richard Kelly is the owner of the task. As the task progresses, you can send a status report.

4 Open the **Review advertising plans** task. In the **Task** form, click the **Status arrow**, and then click **In Progress**. Click the **Start date arrow**, and select **Today** In the **% Complete** box, type **50%**

5 On the Ribbon, click the **Send Status Report** button. Compare your screen with Figure 5.21.

The Task Status Report: Review advertising plans - Message form displays, addressed to the originator of the task request. The Message form reflects all the changes you have made to the task. You can add a message that will be sent with the status report.

Figure 5.21

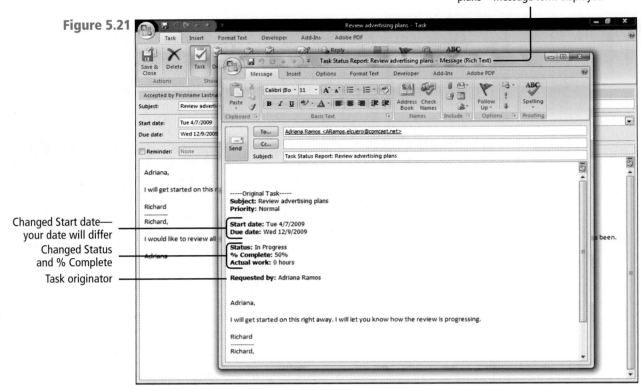

Task Status Report Review advertising plans – Message form displayed

Changed Start date— your date will differ

Changed Status and % Complete

Task originator

6 If the message format of your message is not in Plain Text, on the Ribbon, click the **Options tab**, and then click **Plain Text**. In the **Microsoft Office Outlook Compatibility Checker** dialog box, click **Continue** to convert the message to a Plain Text format.

7 On the Message form title bar, click the **Maximize** button to maximize the display so that the text is easier to view as you type. Type the following message: **Adriana, I can see why you believe we need to look at other ad agencies. So far I'm finding very little sales support for the print advertising we did last year. I will finish my review later this week. Richard** and then compare your screen with Figure 5.22. Your text may wrap differently.

Figure 5.22

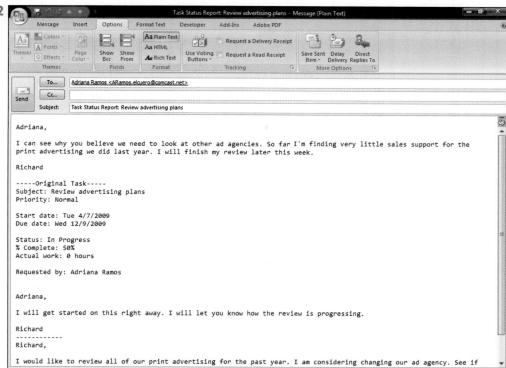

8 On the Message form title bar, click the **Restore Down** button .
Send the message, and then **Save & Close** the Task form.

Although you sent a status report, changing any detail of an assigned task generates an update that is sent to the originator of the task request, provided that this option was requested. Adriana Ramos will receive an update on the task in addition to the status report.

9 In the **Navigation Pane**, under **Current View**, click **Detailed List** to display the Status and % Complete columns. Click the **Icon** column heading to place the Tasks list in its default sort order.

Activity 5.9 Marking a Task as Complete

When you accept a task, Outlook tracks the progress of the task. The originator of the task is notified when you have completed the task. In this activity, you will accept a task for Richard Kelly and then mark the task as completed.

1 With the **Tasks in Personal Folders** list of tasks still displayed, right-click the **Make sales call appointments** task, and then compare your screen with Figure 5.23.

The displayed shortcut menu contains all the commands you can use to respond to a task request. Because the commands relate only to the item to which you are pointing, the commands are referred to as *context-sensitive*. This is an alternative way to respond to a task request.

Figure 5.23

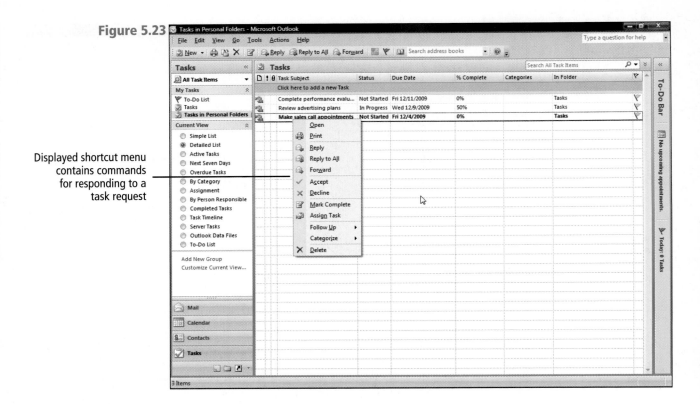

Displayed shortcut menu
contains commands
for responding to a
task request

2 From the shortcut menu, click **Accept**. In the displayed **Accepting Task** dialog box, click **OK** to send an acceptance message without any additional comments.

3 Open the **Make sales call appointments** task. On the Ribbon, click the **Mark Complete** button [Mark Complete].

The task is marked as complete, and the Task form closes. Under % Complete, the task displays 100%, and a line is drawn through the task. A Task Completed message is automatically sent to the task originator and placed in the Outbox.

Objective 3
Manage Task Assignments

Printing task requests is similar to printing other items in Outlook. Accepted tasks can be printed from the Tasks list. You may also want to print the task request messages or status reports. Task request messages can be printed from the Outbox or from the Sent Items folder. Delete task requests in the same manner as other Outlook items. Deleting assigned tasks may require that you notify task assignees that the task assignment has been cancelled.

Activity 5.10 Changing the View and Printing Task Requests

Recall that you have configured Outlook to store all your sent messages in the Outbox instead of the Sent Items folder. In this activity, you will print Richard Kelly's Outbox and some of his task requests.

1 Be sure that the **Tasks list** from the **Tasks in Personal Folders** is displayed; these are the tasks that you have accepted.

2 From the **File** menu, display the **Page Setup: Table Style** dialog box. On the **Header/Footer tab**, delete any existing header or footer information, including dates and page numbers. In the left **Footer** box, using your own name, type **5A_Presentation_Accepted_Firstname_Lastname** Preview and print the Tasks list. Submit the end result to your instructor as directed.

3 In the **Navigation Pane**, under **My Tasks**, click **Tasks**.

These are the tasks you own or that you have assigned to others. You can change the view of your task list to show only the tasks you have assigned to others.

4 With **Tasks** selected in the **Navigation Pane**, change the **Current View** to **Assignment**, and then compare your screen with Figure 5.24.

The Tasks list displays only the assigned tasks. The *Make travel arrangements (copy)* task is not included because the task is not an assigned task; unassigned copy tasks are treated as tasks you own because you will not receive updates. The *(Filter Applied)* label at the top of the list indicates that this is a filtered list. A ***filter*** is a set of instructions that causes some items in a folder to display—and others *not* to display—based on conditions you define. Outlook has filtered this folder to show only assigned tasks. This Assignment view includes a column showing the current owner of the task.

Column indicating current task owner

Label indicates that the Tasks list is filtered

Figure 5.24

Tasks selected

Tasks list in Assignment view

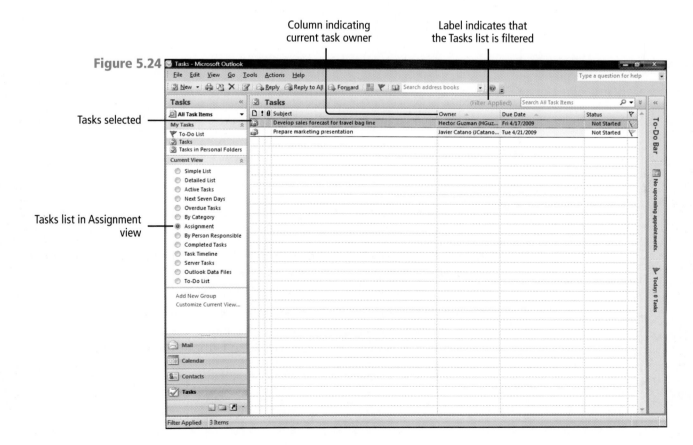

5 Display the **Page Setup: Table Style** dialog box, delete the existing footer information, and type **5A_Presentation_Assigned_Firstname_ Lastname Preview** and **Print** the Tasks list. Submit the end result to your instructor as directed.

6 In the **Navigation Pane**, click the **Mail** button ⌐ Mail ⌐, and then display the **Outbox**. If necessary, click the **Sent** column heading to sort the items in descending order. This is the default sort order for this folder. Compare your screen with Figure 5.25.

The Outbox displays all the task-related messages you have sent. Notice that the Subject prefix for each message indicates the type of task message. You can use the column divider between the Subject and Sent column headings to display more of the Subject text.

Drag column divider to
display more of the Subject text

Figure 5.25

Outbox folder—the
order of your items
may differ

Prefix identifies message
type and purpose

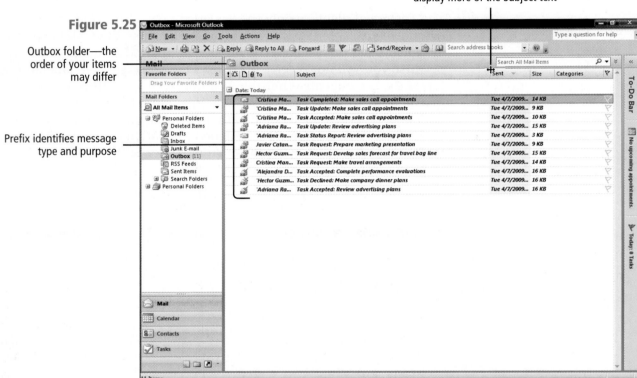

7 Position the pointer on the column divider between the **Subject** and **Sent** column, and, if necessary, drag slightly to the right so that you can read the subjects of each sent item in the **Outbox**.

8 Display the **Page Setup: Table Style** dialog box, create the left **Footer 5A_Presentation_Outbox_Firstname_Lastname** and then **Preview** and **Print** the Outbox folder. Submit the end result to your instructor as directed.

Note — Printing Outbox Items

Your printer may not print some icons displayed under the Icons column heading. Blanks may display instead of the icon. Also, once an Outbox item has been opened or printed, Outlook applies a Sent date as None, and then displays the Outbox folder in groups. By default, the Outbox folder arranges items in groups, by date sent. Your Outbox may show one or more items in a Date: None group.

9 In the **Outbox**, select the **Task Status Report: Review advertising plans** message to *Adriana Ramos*. From the **File** menu, point to **Page Setup**, and then click **Memo Style**. Delete any existing header or footer information, and create the left **Footer 5A_Presentation_ Status_Firstname_Lastname Preview** and **Print** the message. Submit the end result to your instructor as directed.

Activity 5.11 Deleting Task Requests and Closing the Outlook Data File

In most cases, you delete assigned and accepted tasks only after they are completed. For the purposes of this instruction, in this activity, you will delete Richard Kelly's task requests.

1 In the **Navigation Pane**, click the **Tasks** button [Tasks]. Under **My Tasks**, click **Tasks** if this folder is not already displayed.

2 If necessary, change the **Current View** to **Simple List**, and then Delete [X] all the tasks in the **Tasks list**.

3 In the **Navigation Pane**, under **My Tasks**, click **Tasks in Personal Folders**. Click the **Review advertising plans** task, click **Delete** [X], and then compare your screen with Figure 5.26.

A Delete Incomplete Task dialog box displays. When you delete a received task request that you have already accepted, you have the option of declining the task or marking the task as completed. In most circumstances, it is good manners to choose either of these options before deleting a task you have already accepted. Upon doing so, the person who assigned you the task will be notified of your response. For purposes of this instruction, you do need to notify the assigner of the task.

Figure 5.26

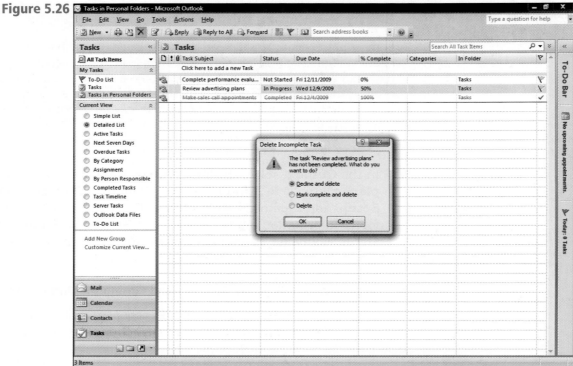

> **4** In the **Delete Incomplete Task** dialog box, click **Delete**, and then click **OK**.

> **5** Delete the **Complete performance evaluations** task. In the **Delete Incomplete Task** dialog box, click **Delete**, and then click **OK**.

> **6** Delete the **Make sales call appointments** task.

Because this task is already completed, the Delete Incomplete Task dialog box does not display. The Tasks list is empty.

> **7** In the **Navigation Pane**, click the **Folder List** button ⬜. Under **All Folders**, use the **scroll bar** to display the lower portion of the folder list, if necessary. Locate the **Personal Folders** file, which has the 📁 icon, next to it, and then compare your screen with Figure 5.27. Your list of folders may differ.

Recall that Outlook displays all open data files with the name *Personal Folders*. The icon distinguishes the *Personal Folders* for the o05A_Presentation_Tasks file you opened from the default *Personal Folders*. Outlook data files are opened every time Outlook is started until they are closed in the folder list.

Figure 5.27

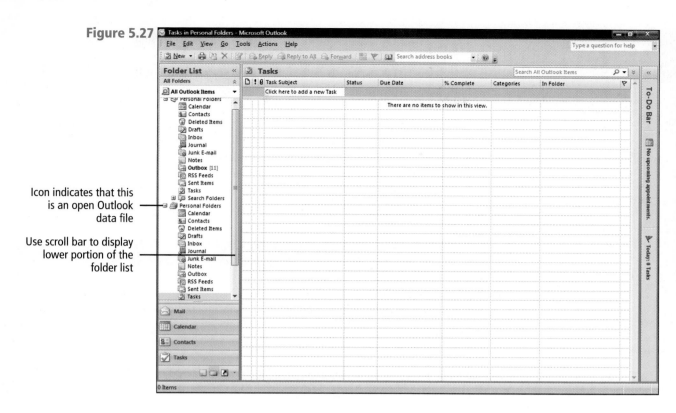

Icon indicates that this is an open Outlook data file

Use scroll bar to display lower portion of the folder list

8 In the **Folder List**, right-click the second (bottom) occurrence of **Personal Folders**. From the shortcut menu, click **Close "Personal Folders"** to close the Outlook data file.

9 In the **Navigation Pane**, click **Outbox**.

The Outbox still contains the task request e-mail messages and task responses. Because in this instruction you are not actually sending messages, they were not deleted.

10 Delete the contents of the **Outbox** folder. Delete the contents of the **Contacts** folder. Empty the **Deleted Items** folder.

11 Display the **Inbox** folder. From the **File** menu, point to **Page Setup**, and then click **Define Print Styles**. In the **Define Print Styles** dialog box, click **Table Style**, click **Reset**, and then click **OK**. Click **Memo Style**, click **Reset**, and then click **OK**. Close the dialog box.

Recall that Outlook retains header and footer information that you use in its print styles. Resetting the print styles returns them to their default settings.

12 From the **Tools** menu, click **Options**, and then click the **Mail Setup** tab. Under **Send/Receive**, select the **Send immediately when connected** check box.

13 In the **Options** dialog box, click **Send/Receive**. In the **Send/Receive Groups** dialog box, under **Setting for group "All Accounts"**, select both **Include this group in send/receive (F9)** check boxes. Select both **Schedule an automatic send/receive** check boxes if this is a default setting on your computer. Click **Close**, and then click **OK**.

End **You have completed Project 5A**

Project 5B Instant Messaging

In Activities 5.12 through 5.21, you will set up Outlook for instant messaging. You will enable Windows Live Messenger in Outlook, start the program, and add contacts to Windows Live Messenger. Then, with a student partner, you will use Windows Live Messenger to conduct an instant messaging session between Richard Kelly and Javier Catano at El Cuero Specialty Wares. You will print your dialogue with your partner. If you are playing the role of Richard Kelly, your solution will look similar to the document shown in Figure 5.28. If you are playing the role of Javier Catano, your solution will differ slightly.

For Project 5B, you will need the following files:

o05B_Instant_Messaging_Contacts
o05B_Instant_Messaging_Caterers
o05B_Instant_Messaging_Restaurants
o05B_Instant_Messaging_Inbox_JC
o05B_Instant_Messaging_Inbox_RK

You will print one file with the following footer:
5B_Instant_Messaging_Firstname_Lastname

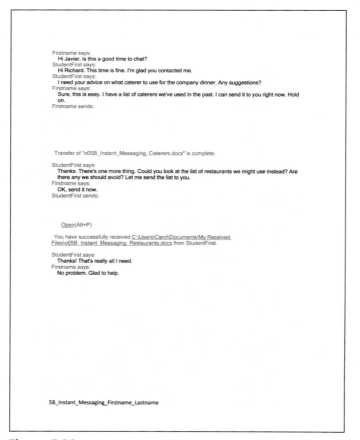

Figure 5.28

Alert!

Starting Project 5B

It is recommended that you schedule enough time to complete this project in one working session. You will need a partner to complete this project. Allow approximately one and one-half hours.

Objective 4
Use Instant Messaging in Outlook

Integrated into Outlook is a Windows communication program called **Windows Live Messenger**, which is an instant messaging program. **Instant messaging**—often abbreviated as **IM**—is a form of online, real-time communication over the Internet in which users communicate with each other in a private, text-based dialogue. This type of communication is also referred to as **chat**—a real-time conversation on a computer whereby one participant types and then presses the Enter key, and the typing displays on the other participant's computer. An instant messaging session is like a telephone conversation, except that the dialogue is typed, not spoken. Windows Live Messenger also supports voice and video conferencing in addition to text chat.

To use instant messaging in Outlook, Windows Live Messenger must be installed on your computer. You must also have a Windows Live ID account. You can also use your ID from an MSN account, Hotmail, Messenger, or Microsoft Passport account for Windows Live. **Hotmail** is Microsoft's free, Web-based e-mail service with which you can read and write e-mail messages on any computer with a Web browser that is connected to the Internet. **Windows Live** is a free Microsoft service that enables you to sign into several different Web sites for services, such as instant messaging and e-mail, using a single user name. After starting Windows Live Messenger, you can add your Outlook contacts to your Windows Live Messenger contact list. Your contacts must also have a Windows Live or related account.

Note — Using Instant Messaging with Windows Live Messenger or Windows Messenger

You must be online and connected to the Internet to complete this project. To conduct the chat session, you will need a partner. Check with your instructor or lab assistant to see if there are specific instructions for selecting a partner for the chat session.

This instruction assumes you are using Windows Live Messenger, which is an enhanced version of Windows Messenger. If you use Windows Messenger, the screens and dialog boxes will differ slightly from those shown in this instruction. If neither program is installed on the computer you are using, consult your instructor for specific instructions.

Activity 5.12 Starting Windows Live Messenger

You must first start Windows Live Messenger to use instant messaging in Outlook. You start Windows Live Messenger in the same manner as you start any Microsoft Office program.

1 **Start** Outlook if necessary. Display the **Inbox**, and delete any existing messages. Display the **Contacts** folder, and delete any existing contacts. **Close** Outlook.

2 On the Windows taskbar, click the **Start** button to display the **Start** menu. On the computer you are using, locate the **Windows Live Messenger** program on the **Start** or **All Programs** menu. See Figure 5.29.

Organizations and individuals store computer programs in a variety of ways. The Windows Live Messenger program might be located under All Programs or at the top of the Start menu. You may also find the program under such headings as Accessories or Online Services. Alternatively, you might have to open Windows Live in order to access Windows Live Messenger.

Figure 5.29

Click to Start Windows Live Messenger

Start button

3 Click Windows Live Messenger. Compare your screen with Figure 5.30.

The Windows Messenger log-in window displays. The screen may show the user name of the last person who logged into the program. Your screen may be maximized.

Note — Windows Live Messenger Log-In Window

The log-in window for Windows Live Messenger may display differently, depending on your computer or whether Windows Live Messenger has been used before. If the program has never been run on your computer, there will be no previous sign-in name—only the message "Click here to sign in." The screen may also display a previous user's sign-in name. Upon logging in, you may be asked to update to a newer version. Check with your instructor or lab coordinator before updating the program. Your log-in procedure may also vary in other ways.

Figure 5.30

User name of last person to use Windows Live Messenger

Click here to create a Windows Live ID

4 If you already have a Windows Live, Hotmail, Messenger, Microsoft Passport, or MSN account ID, log in to Windows Live Messenger, and then skip to Activity 5.14.

Activity 5.13 Setting Up a Windows Live Account

You must have a Windows Live account to use Windows Live Messenger. In this activity, you will create a Windows Live account.

1 With the Windows Live Messenger log-in window displayed, click **Sign up for a Windows Live ID**. If a user is already signed in, click File, and then click Sign Out. Compare your screen with Figure 5.31.

The Web browser opens and displays the Get Windows Live Web page.

Note — Opening a New Windows Live Account

Depending on the configuration of your computer or network, or if Windows Live Messenger has never been used on your computer, you may have several intervening screens and prompts before you arrive at the Get Windows Live Web page shown in Figure 5.31.

Figure 5.31

Get Windows Live Web page

Sign up button

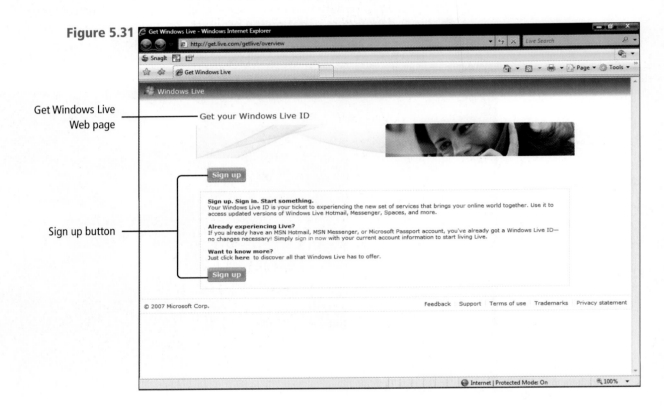

2 Click the **Sign Up** button and then compare your screen with Figure 5.32.

The Sign up for Windows Live Web page is displayed in your browser. You must fill in the information on this page and subsequent pages to open your Windows Live account. First, you must create a Windows Live ID, which is, in essence, your Windows Live e-mail address, and a Password. The domain name for your e-mail address will be *@live.com*. Recall that a ***domain name*** is the portion of an e-mail address that defines the e-mail system or Internet Service Provider—in this case, Windows Live. You will be choosing your user name—for example, *YourName@live.com*. Select a user name of your choice. If that name is not available, you will be asked to choose another. Use the scroll bar to see the lower portion of the page.

Figure 5.32

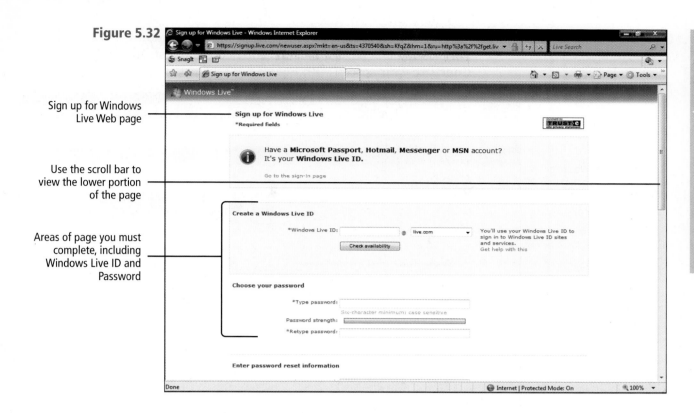

Sign up for Windows Live Web page

Use the scroll bar to view the lower portion of the page

Areas of page you must complete, including Windows Live ID and Password

---

Alert!

Do your screens differ?

Your Web pages may differ from those shown in this instruction. The Windows Live sign-up page may change in appearance and content. Microsoft may request different information, and the order of the information may vary.

---

3 Type the required information in the boxes provided, starting with the **Windows Live ID** and **Password**. Click the Check Availability button to make sure your e-mail address is not being used by another person. Use the **scroll bar** to display the lower portions of the page. When you have completed the page, at the bottom of the page, click **I accept**.

Note — Completing the Sign-Up

The Windows Live sign-up form requests personal information, including your name, birth year, and zip code. The name you provide will be sent with your outgoing e-mail messages. As with most reputable online services, Microsoft provides assurances that this information is held in the company's confidence. You may read Microsoft's privacy statement by clicking the *Privacy Statement*. When you click the *I Accept* button, Microsoft checks for the completeness of the information you have typed. If you have chosen a user name for the E-mail Address box that is already in use, the form will redisplay, and you will be asked to pick a different name. If you have not filled in a required box, the form will redisplay with a request that you fill in the box(es).

4 When the Web browser window displays the *Windows Live ID - Congratulations* page, you have finished the registration process. Compare your screen with Figure 5.33.

Figure 5.33

Congratulations Web page indicates that the sign-up is complete

Link to *home.live.com*

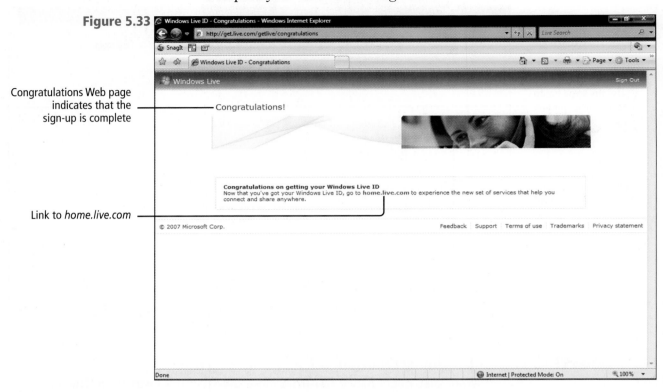

5 On the **Windows Live ID - Congratulations** page, click **home.live.com**. Compare your screen with Figure 5.34.

The Windows Live home page displays. Your first name, which you entered in the sign-up form, appears at the top right of the window, indicating that you are signed in.

Figure 5.34

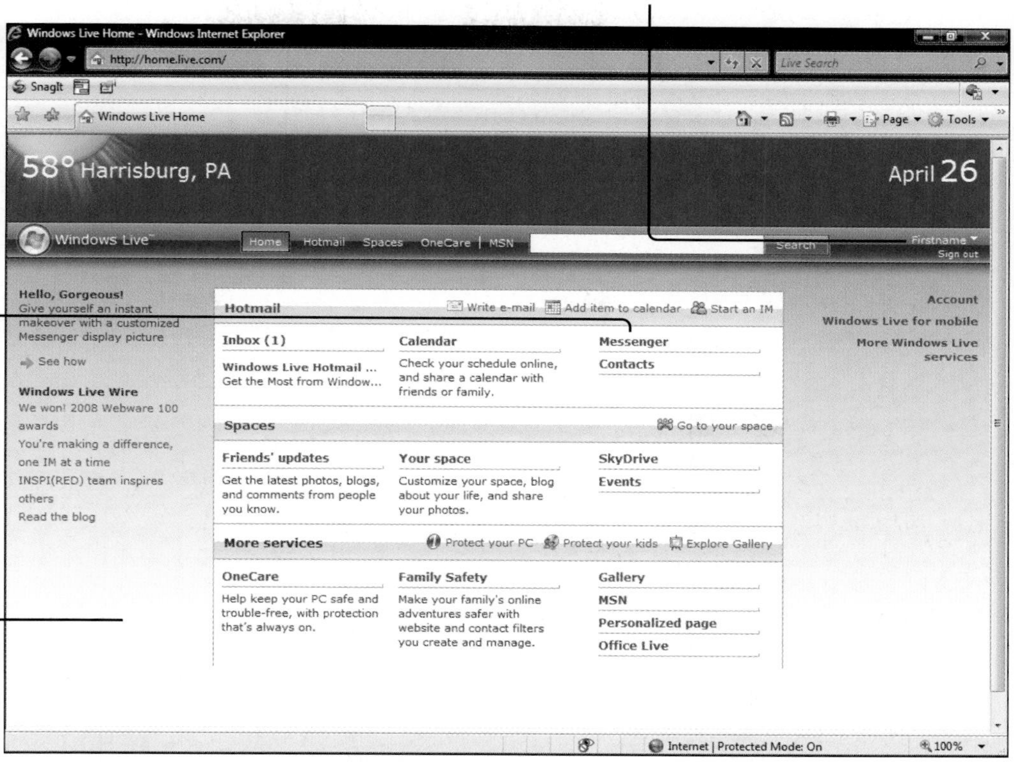

Click to display Windows
Live Messenger dialog box

Windows Live home page

6 In the middle right of the page, click **Messenger** to display the
Windows Live Messenger dialog box. **Close** [X] the **Windows Live**
home page.

The Windows Live Messenger dialog box is still displayed.

7 In the **Windows Live Messenger** dialog box, in the **E-mail address**
box, type your new Windows Live ID. In the **Password** box, type your
password. If you are using a public computer, make certain that the
three options for signing in are unchecked. Click **Sign In**. **Maximize**
[□] the window if necessary. Compare your screen with Figure 5.35,
noting that advertising at the bottom of the page has been removed
from the figure.

The Windows Live Messenger dialog box closes, and Windows Live
Messenger logs in by using your new Windows Live ID. The *(Online)*
indicator after your user name indicates that you are connected and
online in Windows Live Messenger, which means that you can communicate with other Windows Live Messenger users who are also
online.

> ## Note — Viewing Your Screen
>
> Because Windows Live is a free Microsoft service, advertisements display at
> the bottom of your screen. The advertising content has been removed from
> the images in this project. Your screens will differ slightly.

Windows Live Messenger menu bar

Figure 5.35

Your first name— yours will differ

(Online) status indicates that you are online in Windows Live Messenger

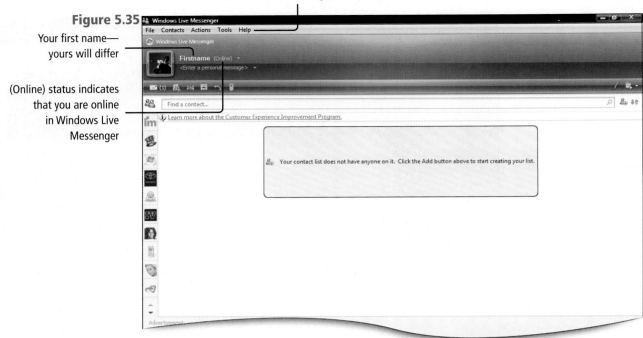

More Knowledge

Changing Your Display Name

Windows Live Messenger uses your first name as the displayed name by default. This is the name other Windows Live Messenger users will see when they have your name on their Windows Live Messenger contact list. The name is often referred to as your *screen name*. You can change your screen name. From the Windows Live Messenger Tools menu, click Options. In the Display Name box, type the screen name you want to use, and then click OK.

Activity 5.14 Configuring Outlook to Use Windows Live Messenger

Outlook has several settings related to Windows Live Messenger. These must be enabled before you can use Windows Live Messenger in Outlook. In this activity, you will configure Outlook to show when your El Cuero contacts are online in Windows Live Messenger.

1 On the Windows Live Messenger title bar, click the **Minimize** button.

The window is minimized; however, Windows Live Messenger is still running, and you are still online in Windows Live Messenger.

2 **Start** Outlook, and display the **Contacts** folder. From the **File** menu, display the **Import and Export Wizard** dialog box, and then, using the techniques you have practiced, import **o05B_Instant_Messaging_Contacts** into the **Contacts** folder.

3 From the Outlook **Tools** menu, click **Options**, and then click the **Other tab**. Under **Person Names**, check to see if the **Display online**

status next to a person name and **Display online status in the To and Cc fields only when mouse pointer rests on a person name** check boxes are selected; select them if necessary. Compare your screen with Figure 5.36.

Outlook checks the online status in Windows Live Messenger of a contact and displays the status in e-mail messages you send to and receive from the contact. The online status of the contact is displayed in his or her *Person Names online presence indicator*, which is a small button displayed next to the contact's e-mail address.

Other tab selected

Figure 5.36

Options dialog box

Person Names options selected

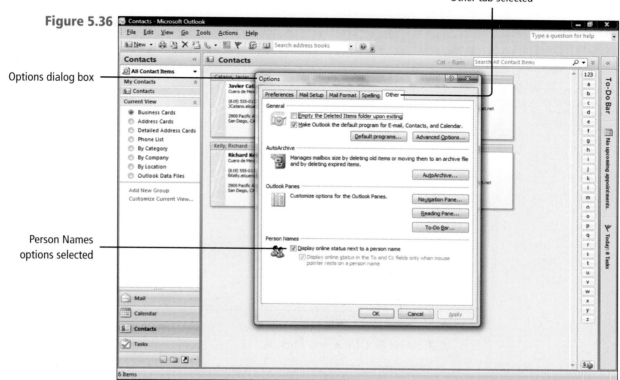

4 In the **Options** dialog box, click **OK**.

Outlook can check the Windows Live Messenger online status of the contacts in your contact list. In order for Outlook to check a contact's online status, you must specify the IM address—Windows Live Messenger address—in the IM address box.

Alert!

Are your Person Names Option boxes unavailable?

Depending on your computer settings, the Person Names Option Boxes may be unchecked and unavailable. If you are working on your own computer, you will need to call Microsoft Support to enable these options. If you are working in a lab situation, consult your instructor. Otherwise, you can continue with the project, but some of the features will not be activated.

5 With the **Contacts** folder displayed, open the **Alejandra Domene** contact. In the **IM address** box, type **Alejandra.elcuero@live.com** and then compare your screen with Figure 5.37.

This is *Alejandra Domene's* Windows Live ID. Recall that the contact must have a Windows Live ID, or other related account, to use Windows Live Messenger.

Alejandra Domene – Contact form

Figure 5.37

IM address box, Windows
Live ID for this contact

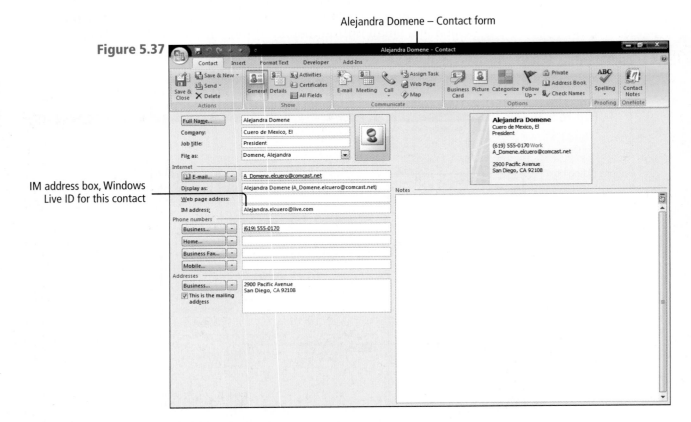

6 **Save & Close** the contact.

The IM address for the contact is saved. Outlook will indicate when this contact is online in Windows Live Messenger in her Person Names online presence indicator, which is displayed in the *To* and *From* boxes of any e-mail message containing her address.

7 Display the **Inbox** folder, and click the **New Mail Message** button [New].

8 In the **Message** form, click **To**. In the **Select Names: Contacts** dialog box, click **Alejandra Domene**, click **To** and then click **OK**.

9 Point to the **Alejandra Domene** address until the **Person Names online presence indicator**—a small gray circle—displays to the left of the address. Point to the **Person Names online presence indicator** until the ScreenTip displays. Compare your screen with Figure 5.38.

The ScreenTip indicates that Alejandra Domene's presence is unknown—either her address has not been added to your Windows Live Messenger contact list or she is not online. You can add her address to your Windows Live Messenger contact list in Outlook.

Figure 5.38

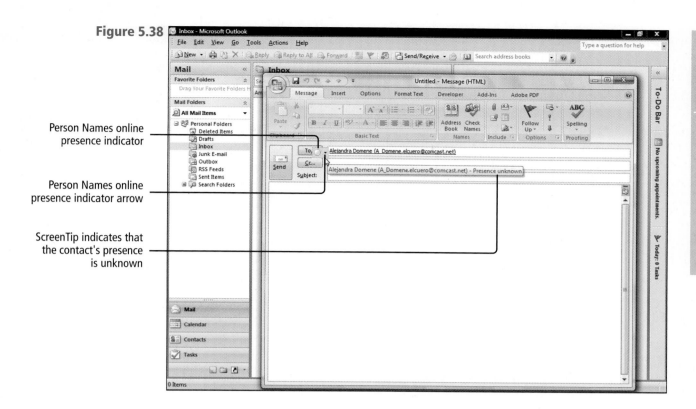

Person Names online presence indicator

Person Names online presence indicator arrow

ScreenTip indicates that the contact's presence is unknown

Alert!

Did the Person Names online presence indicator display?

In some instances, the Person Names online presence indicators and commands do not display as shown in this instruction. The online presence indicators may not display next to the e-mail addresses, or they may not accurately show when contacts are online, or some commands on the online presence indicators shortcut menu may not display. Sometimes it is necessary to start Windows Live Messenger before starting Outlook in order for the Person Names online presence indicator to display properly. Close Outlook and, with Windows Live Messenger running, start Outlook again. The Person Names online presence indicators will likely display properly. If they do not, you can still proceed with the project.

10 Click the **Person Names online presence indicator arrow**, and then click **Add to Instant Messaging Contacts**. If necessary, at the bottom of your screen, click the **Add a Contact** button in the Windows taskbar if this button displays. Compare your screen with Figure 5.39.

Windows Live Messenger displays an Add a Contact dialog box, indicating that you are able to add the IM address for Alejandra Domene to your Windows Live Messenger contact list.

Figure 5.39

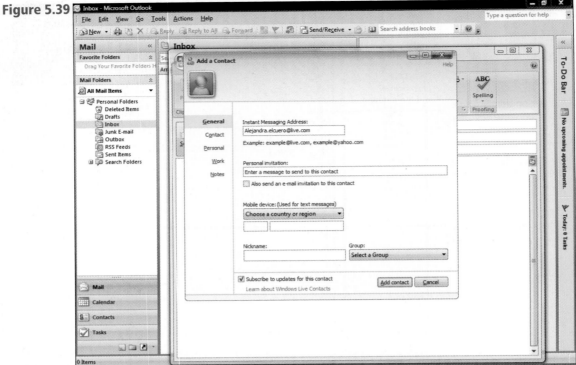

Note — Messenger's Screens and Dialog Boxes

Depending on the version of Windows Live Messenger that you are using and the options you have selected, your screens and dialog boxes may differ from the ones shown in this instruction. Your Messenger screens and dialog boxes also will differ if you are using Windows Messenger instead of Windows Live Messenger. Microsoft frequently updates Windows Live Messenger and Windows Messenger. The functionality is the same in all versions.

11 In the **Add a Contact** dialog box, click **Add contact**.

The contact is added to Windows Live Messenger contact list, and the Add a Contact dialog box closes.

12 On the Windows taskbar, click the **Windows Live Messenger** button to bring that window to the front of the desktop.

Notice that *Alejandra.elcuero@live.com*—Alejandra Domene's IM address—has been added to your Windows Live Messenger contacts.

13 **Minimize** 🗖 the **Windows Live Messenger** window, and then click on the **Message** form to make it active.

14 In the **Message** form **To** box, point to **Alejandra Domene**, and compare your screen with Figure 5.40.

The Person Names online presence indicator for Alejandra Domene displays in red, which means that she is on your Windows Live Messenger contact list but is not currently online.

Figure 5.40

Red color indicates that the contact is on your list but is not currently online

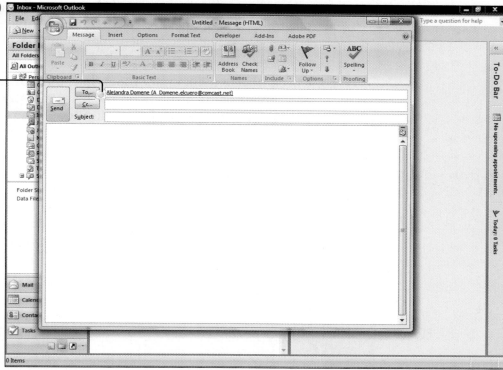

15 In the **To** box, point to the address for **Cristina Mandala**, and notice the gray Smart Tag for this contact.

This contact is not on your Windows Messenger contacts list.

16 **Close** ❌ the **Message** form without saving.

More Knowledge

Using Person Names Online Presence Indicators in Received Messages

Person Names online presence indicators are found in e-mail messages you receive as well as those you send. When you have messages in your Inbox, the online presence indicators may display next to the e-mail address in the Reading Pane of a selected message. If the message sender is on your Windows Live Messenger contact list, viewing the online presence indicator in the message is a quick way of seeing when a contact is online or not.

Activity 5.15 Configuring Windows Live Messenger

You must configure Windows Live Messenger to allow other Outlook users to see your online status. In this activity, you will configure your Windows Live Messenger settings so that El Cuero employees will be able to see your online status.

1 Maximize the **Windows Live Messenger** window. Click **Show menu** 🔳, click **Tools** to display the Tools menu, and then click **Options**. In the displayed **Options** dialog box, in the **Options** list, click **Privacy**.

Here you control who sees you online. The default setting is for no one to see you online. For your Outlook contacts to see when you are online, you must specify them individually or allow all Windows Live Messenger users to see you online.

2 Check the contents under **Block list**. If **All others** or **All .NET Messenger users** displays on the list, click **All others** or **All .NET Messenger users**, and then click **Allow**. Compare your screen with Figure 5.41.

The All others or All .NET Messenger users is placed under the Allow list. When you are online, all Windows Live Messenger users who have your name on their contact list will see you online and will be able to start a conversation with you. Use the Block command to prevent specific users from seeing you online and starting conversations with you. When you *block* a user, you prevent that person from contacting you or seeing when you are online.

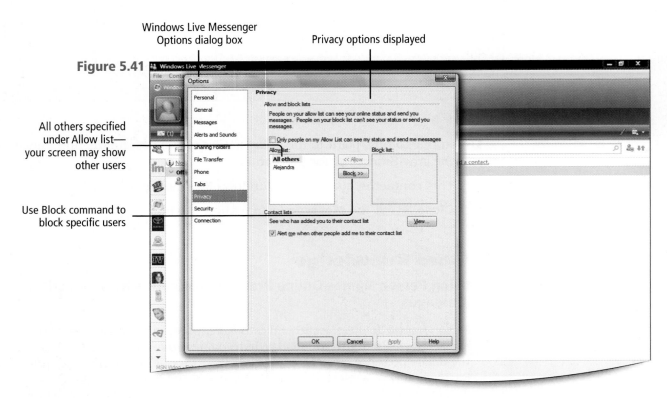

Figure 5.41

Windows Live Messenger Options dialog box

Privacy options displayed

All others specified under Allow list— your screen may show other users

Use Block command to block specific users

3 In the **Options** dialog box, click **OK**.

All Windows Live Messenger users who have your IM address on their contact lists now will see when you are online.

Activity 5.16 Adding Outlook Contacts in Windows Live Messenger

Recall that you can add Outlook contacts to your Windows Live Messenger contact list by using the Person Names online presence indicator in Outlook. You can also add Outlook contacts to your Windows Live Messenger contact list from within Windows Live Messenger. In this activity, you will add the IM address of Hector Guzman at El Cuero to your Windows Messenger contact list.

1 In the **Windows Live Messenger** window, click the **Add a Contact** button 🔲, located immediately to the right of the **Find a contact...** box. Alternatively, from the Contacts menu, click Add a Contact.

2 In the displayed **Add a Contact** dialog box, in the **Instant Messaging Address:** box, type **Hector.elcuero@live.com** This is the IM address of El Cuero's *Hector Guzman*. Compare your screen with Figure 5.42.

Figure 5.42

Windows Live Messenger Add a Contact box

Specified IM address of contact

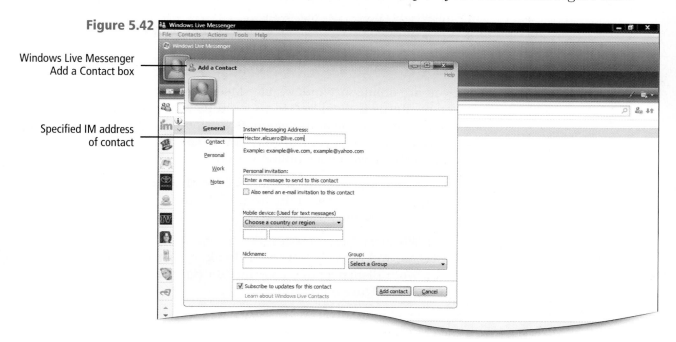

3 In the **Add a Contact** dialog box, click **Add contact**.

The contact is added to Windows Live Messenger contact list; and the Add a Contact dialog box closes. Windows Live Messenger will notify the contact indicating that you have added his name to your list.

The Windows Live Messenger window shows Hector.elcuero@live.com as one of your contacts. He is currently offline. To see his online status in Outlook, you must add his IM address to his entry in your Outlook Contacts list.

4 In the Windows Live Messenger title bar, click the **Minimize** button 🔲. In **Outlook**, in the **Navigation Pane**, click the **Contacts** button 🔲 Contacts , and then open the **Hector Guzman** contact. In the **IM Address** box, type **Hector.elcuero@live.com Save & Close** 🔲 the contact.

The Person Names online presence indicator for Hector Guzman will now show his Windows Live Messenger online status.

More Knowledge

Person Names Online Presence Indicator Colors

The Person Names online presence indicator displays a colored circle based upon a contact's online status in Windows Live Messenger. Green indicates a contact is online. Orange lets you know the person is busy or on a call. Yellow signifies the individual is out to lunch, away, or will be right back. Red means the contact has signed out.

Activity 5.17 Changing Your Online Display Status

When you are online in Windows Live Messenger, you can change how your online status is displayed to your Outlook contacts. You can add messages to your online status such as *Busy* or *Out to Lunch*. In this activity, you will change your display status so that El Cuero employees will see a message with your online status.

1 On the taskbar, click the **Windows Live Messenger** button to bring the Messenger window to the front of the desktop. **Maximize** the Messenger window.

2 In the **Windows Live Messenger** window, from the **File** menu, point to **Status**, and then click **Be right back**. Alternatively, click the **arrow** next to your display name, and click **Be right back**. Compare your screen with Figure 5.43.

To other Windows Live Messenger users with your IM address on their contact list, your online status will now display as *(Be right back)*. On your own screen, you can see that your current status displays next to your display name.

Online status set to *Be right back*

Figure 5.43

Your display name

Contacts list, yours will differ

3 In the Windows Live Messenger title bar, click the **Minimize** button .

4 In the **Contacts** folder, open a new contact form. In the **Full Name** box, type your own first and last names. In the **E-mail** box, type your Windows Live ID.

When the e-mail address is a Windows Live account, you do not need to enter the address in the IM Address box.

5 **Save & Close** the contact.

Your name is added to your Contacts List.

6 In the **Navigation Pane**, click the **Mail** button , and then open a new **Message** form. In the **Message** form, click **To**. In the **Select Names: Contacts** dialog box, click your name, click **To**, and then click **OK**.

Here you can see how your Windows Live Messenger online status displays to others by using your own address in the To box of a message—your Windows Live ID displays in the To box.

7 In the **To** box, point to your name to display the Person Names online presence indicator. Point to the **Person Names online presence indicator** to display the ScreenTip. Compare your screen with Figure 5.44.

The Person Names online presence indicator displays as a yellow circle. Depending on your computer settings, the ScreenTip may include the message *Be right back*, or it may indicate *Available* or *Presence unknown*. This is how your online status displays to other Windows Live Messenger users who have your name on their contact list.

Your name and Windows Live ID will differ

Figure 5.44

Person Names online presence indicator displays in yellow

ScreenTip includes a message regarding online status

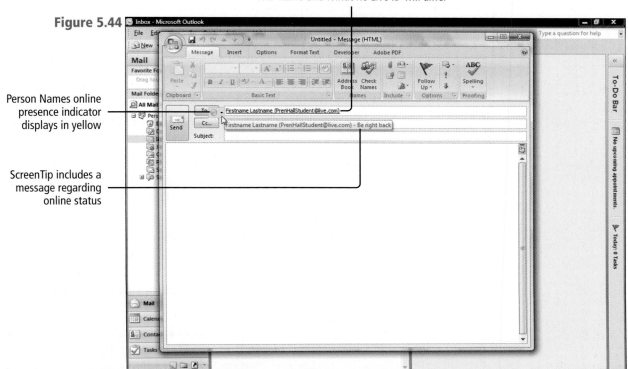

8 On the taskbar, click the **Windows Live Messenger** button to make this the active window.

9 In the **Windows Live Messenger** window, click the **arrow** to the right of your display name, and then click **Online**.

The *Be right back* message next to your display name is removed, and is replaced by *Online*.

10 **Minimize** ☐ the Windows Live Messenger window. In the **Message** form, point to your name, and then point to your **Person Names online presence indicator** to display the ScreenTip.

The Person Names online presence indicator and the ScreenTip indicate that you are online in Windows Messenger.

11 **Close** ☒ the message without saving.

More Knowledge
Making Your Online Status Invisible

When you set your online status to *Appear Offline*, other Windows Live Messenger users will see you as offline. In effect, you are *invisible*; you can see them, but they cannot see you. You might want to do this when you do not want to be contacted but want to see if specific people are online. For example, you might need to discuss something important with one of your contacts, but otherwise, you do not want to be contacted by anyone else.

Activity 5.18 Sending Instant Messages

To open an IM session with someone, the individual's name must display on your Windows Live Messenger contact list, you must have Windows Live Messenger running, and the contact must appear online. In this activity, using your own Windows Live ID, you and a student partner will conduct an IM session between two El Cuero employees, Richard Kelly and Javier Catano.

1 Be sure that **Windows Live Messenger** is still running and that you are signed in. **Minimize** ☐ the **Windows Live Messenger** window. In **Outlook**, display the **Inbox** folder.

2 Determine with your partner who will respond as *Richard Kelly* and who will respond as *Javier Catano*. You and your partner have different steps in this activity, depending on which role you take.

3 *Richard Kelly, Javier Catano*: In the **Navigation Pane**, click the **Inbox**. From the **File** menu, click **Import and Export**. In the **Import and Export Wizard** dialog box, click **Import from another program or file**, and then click **Next**. In the **Import a File** dialog box, under **Select file type to import from**, click **Personal Folder file (.pst)**. Click **Next**.

4 *Richard Kelly*: In the **Import Personal Folders** dialog box, navigate to the student files, select **o05B_Instant_Messaging_Inbox_RK**, and then click **Open**. In the **Import Personal Folders** dialog box, click **Next**.

Javier Catano: In the **Import Personal Folders** dialog box, navigate to the student files, select **o05B_Instant_Messaging_Inbox_JC**, and then click **Open**. In the **Import Personal Folders** dialog box, click **Next**.

5 *Richard Kelly, Javier Catano*: In the **Import Personal Folders** dialog box, under **Select the folder to import from**, click **Inbox**. Click **Import items into the current folder**. Click **Finish**. If a Translation Warning dialog box displays, click OK.

6 *Richard Kelly:* In the **Reading Pane**, right-click on the e-mail address for **Javier Catano**, and then point to **Look up Outlook Contact...** Compare your screen with Figure 5.45a.

Javier Catano: In the **Reading Pane**, right-click on the e-mail address for **Richard Kelly**, and then point to **Look up Outlook Contact...** Compare your screen with Figure 5.45b.

Figure 5.45a

Javier Catano's e-mail address

Richard Kelly Inbox

Look up Outlook Contact... command

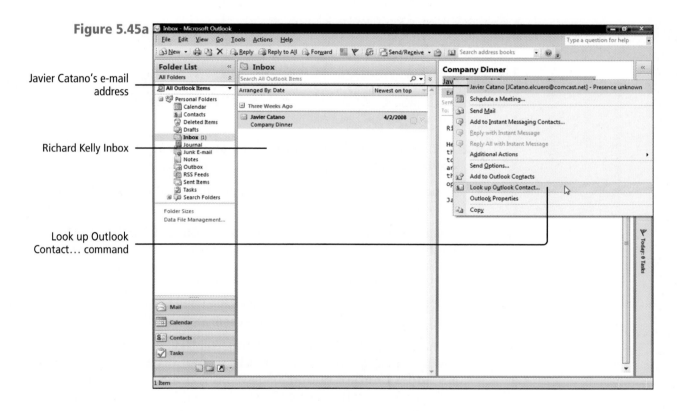

Figure 5.45b

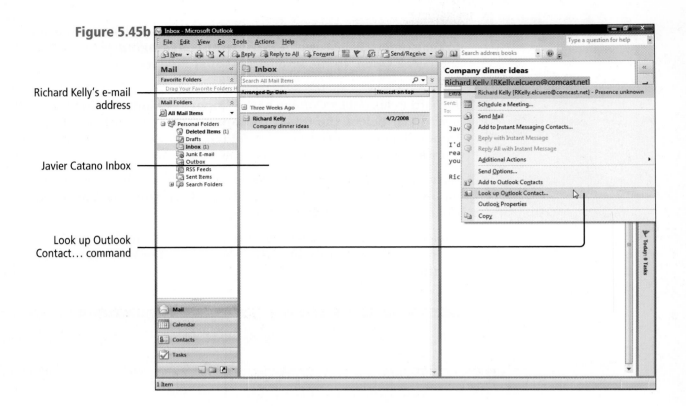

Richard Kelly's e-mail address

Javier Catano Inbox

Look up Outlook Contact… command

7 *Richard Kelly:* Click **Look Up Outlook Contact**. In the displayed **Javier Catano - Contact** form, in the **IM Address** box, type the Windows Live ID of your student partner and then **Save & Close** the contact.

Javier Catano: Click **Look Up Outlook Contact**. In the **Richard Kelly - Contact** form, in the **IM Address** box, type Windows Live ID of your student partner and then **Save & Close** the contact.

You are using your own Windows Live ID accounts for these contacts so that you can conduct a chat session.

8 *Richard Kelly:* In the **Reading Pane**, right-click the e-mail address for **Javier Catano**, and then click **Add to Instant Messaging Contacts**. An **Add a Contact** button displays on your task bar. Click on the **Add a Contact** button to bring the window to the front of the desktop. Click the **Add contact** button, and then compare your screen with Figure 5.46a.

Javier Catano: A **Windows Live Messenger** dialog box notifies you that your partner has added you to his contact list. If this dialog box is not visible, click the appropriate **Windows Live Messenger** button on the taskbar to bring the window to the front of your desktop. Notice the option to add your partner's address to your own contact list. Compare your screen with Figure 5.46b.

Figure 5.46a

Outlook window is displayed ——

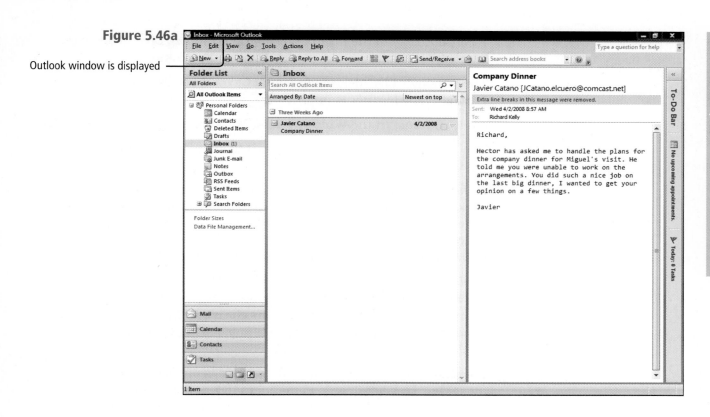

Dialog box indicates your partner has
added your name to the contact list

Figure 5.46b

Student partner's
Windows Live ID—yours
will differ

Selected option adds
your student partner's
address to your
contact list

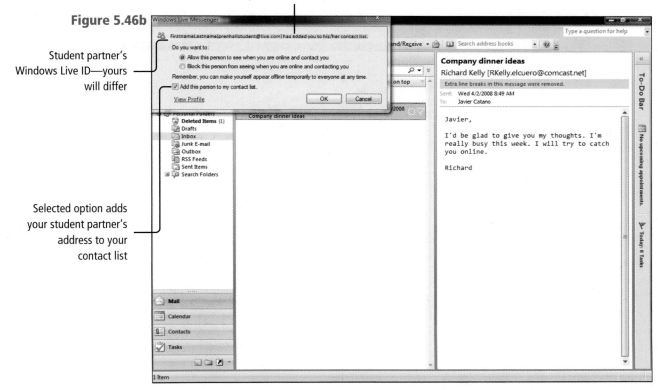

9 *Richard Kelly*: On the task bar, click the **Windows Live Messenger** button to bring the window to the front of the desktop.

The Windows Live Messenger contact icon displays in green, indicating that your partner is online.

Javier Catano: In the **Windows Live Messenger** dialog box, click **OK**.

The Windows Live Messenger contact icon displays in green, indicating that your partner is online.

10 *Richard Kelly*: In the **Windows Live Messenger contact** list, right-click on your partner's name, and then click **Send an instant message** to open a conversation window. Maximize the **Conversation** window, and then type **Hi Javier, is this a good time to chat?** and then click the **Send** button. Compare your screen with Figure 5.47a.

Javier Catano: When the message is received from your partner, click the blinking orange **Windows Live Messenger** button to display the **Conversation** window, and then **maximize** it. In the **Conversation** window, type **Hi Richard. This time is fine. I'm glad you contacted me.** Click **Send**, and compare your screen with Figure 5.47b.

The dialog between you and your partner is opened. When you initiate a chat session, it is good manners to ask the person if this is a good time to chat because instant messages display without notice on someone's screen. The *status area* at the bottom of the Conversation window indicates when the other party is typing or when the last message was received.

Conversation window

Figure 5.47a

Student partner's name —yours will differ

Messages that have been sent and received displayed here

Click Send button to send message

Type message here

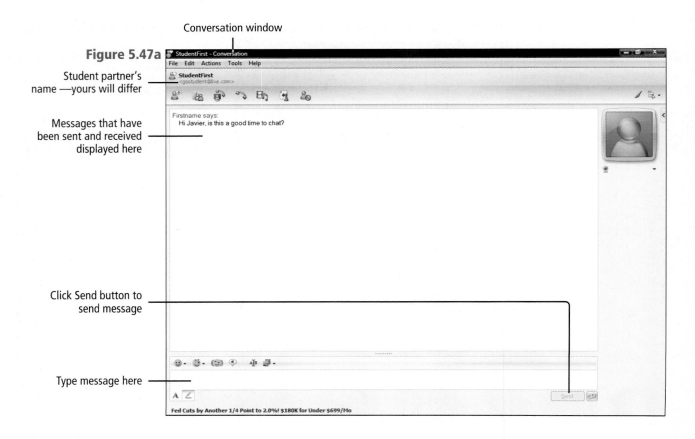

Conversation window

Figure 5.47b

Student partner's name —yours will differ

Messages that have been sent and received displayed here

Click Send button to send message

Status area, indicates current activity in the conversation

Type message here

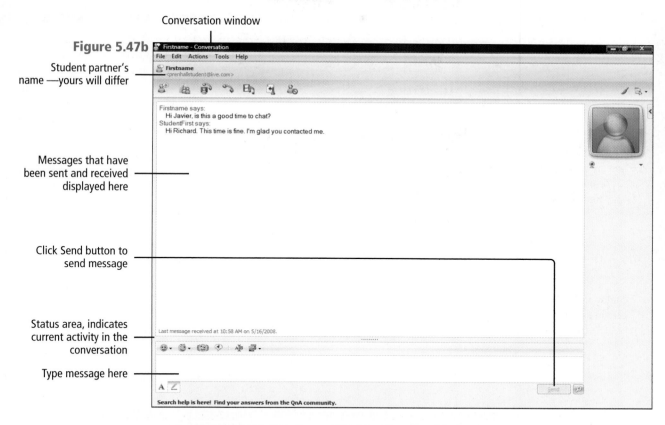

Activity 5.19 Sending a File in an Instant Message

You can send a file during an Instant Message session. This is useful when you want to get information to someone right away. In this activity, acting as El Cuero's Richard Kelly and Javier Catano, you and your student partner will send a Word file during the Instant Message conversation.

1 Be sure the **Conversation** windows for you and your partner are still open.

2 *Javier Catano*: In the **Conversation** window, type **I need your advice on what caterer to use for the company dinner. Any suggestions?** Click **Send**.

3 *Richard Kelly*: In the **Conversation** window, type **Sure, this is easy. I have a list of caterers we've used in the past. I can send it to you right now. Hold on.** Click **Send**.

4 *Richard Kelly*: In the **Conversation** window, click the **Share Files** button , and then click **Send a File or Photo**. In the **Send a File** dialog box, navigate to the student files, and then locate and open **o05B_Instant_Messaging_Caterers**. A message displays indicating that you are waiting for a response to your file transfer request. You cannot transfer a file without permission from the recipient. Compare your screen with Figure 5.48a.

Javier Catano: In the **Conversation** window, notice the message that asks if you want to Accept or Decline the invitation to receive a file. Files cannot be transferred to your computer without your permission. Compare your screen with Figure 5.48b.

Figure 5.48a

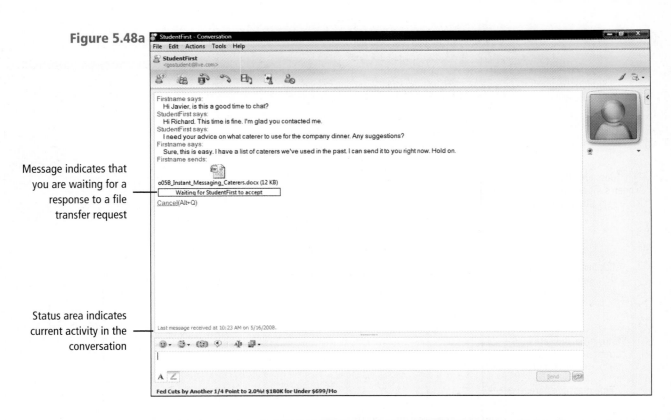

Message indicates that you are waiting for a response to a file transfer request

Status area indicates current activity in the conversation

Figure 5.48b

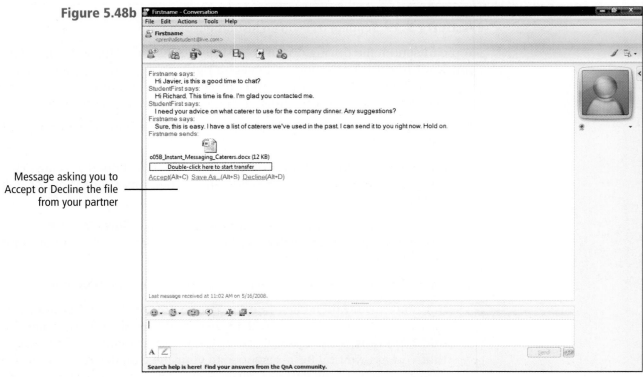

Message asking you to Accept or Decline the file from your partner

5 *Javier Catano:* In the **Conversation** window, click **Accept**. If the Windows Live Messenger box displays a warning about possible viruses, click **OK**. The **Conversation** window shows the location of the received file on your computer. Compare your screen with Figure 5.49a.

Richard Kelly: In the **Conversation** window, notice the messages that display after your partner accepts the file. Compare your screen with Figure 5.49b.

Both Conversation windows display messages when the transfer is complete.

Figure 5.49a

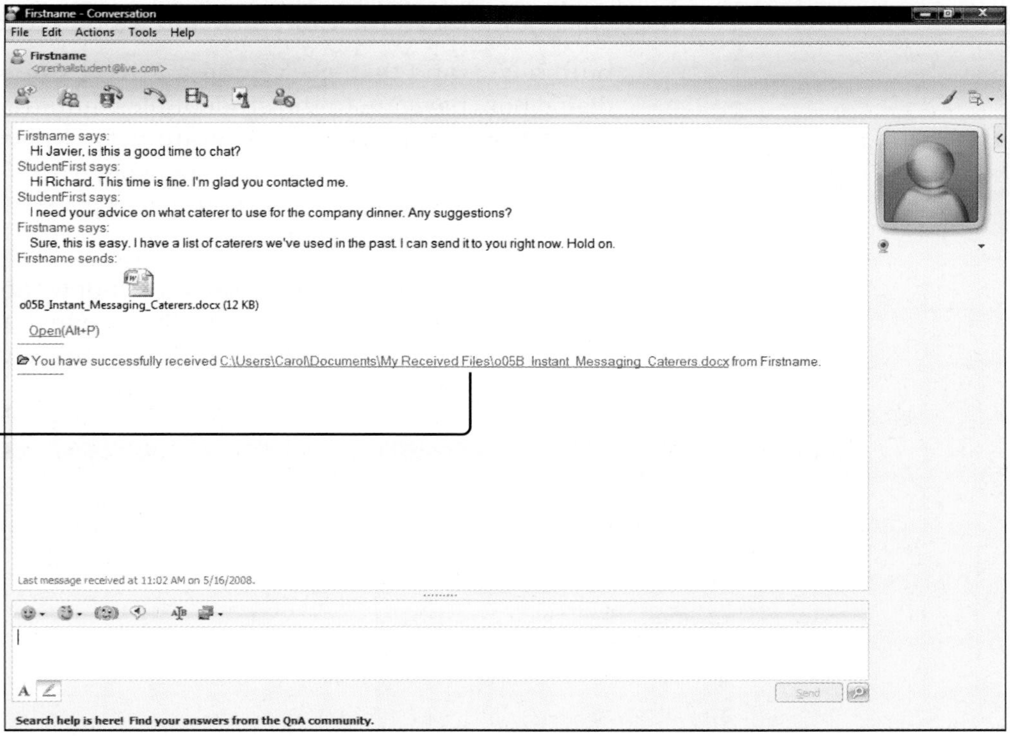

Message indicating the location of received file

Figure 5.49b

Message indicating the transfer of the file to your partner is complete

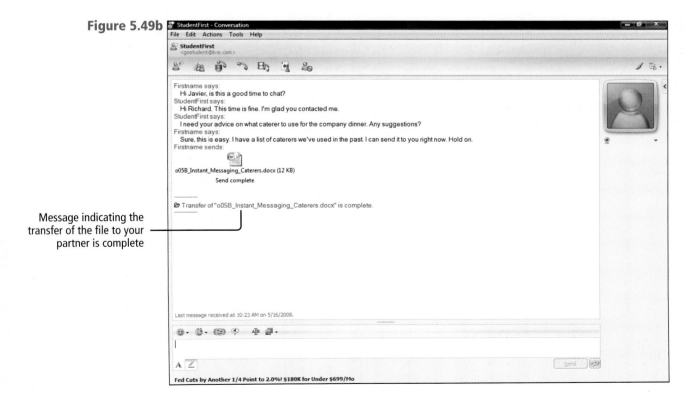

6 *Javier Catano*: In the **Conversation** window, type Thanks. **There's one more thing. Could you look at the list of restaurants we might use instead? Are there any we should avoid? Let me send the list to you.** Click **Send**.

Richard Kelly: In the **Conversation** window, type **OK, send it now.** Click **Send**.

7 *Javier Catano*: In the **Conversation** window, click the **Share Files** button 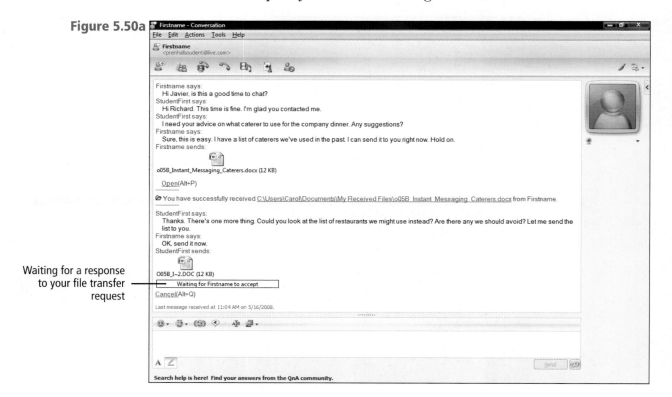, and then click **Send a File or Photo**. In the **Send a File** dialog box, navigate to the student files, and then locate and open **o05B_Instant_Messaging_Restaurants**. A message displays indicating that you are waiting for a response to your file transfer request. You cannot transfer a file without permission from the recipient. Compare your screen with Figure 5.50a.

Richard Kelly: In the **Conversation** window, notice the message that asks if you want to Accept or Decline the invitation to receive a file. Files cannot be transferred to your computer without your permission. Compare your screen with Figure 5.50b.

Figure 5.50a

Waiting for a response to your file transfer request —

Figure 5.50b

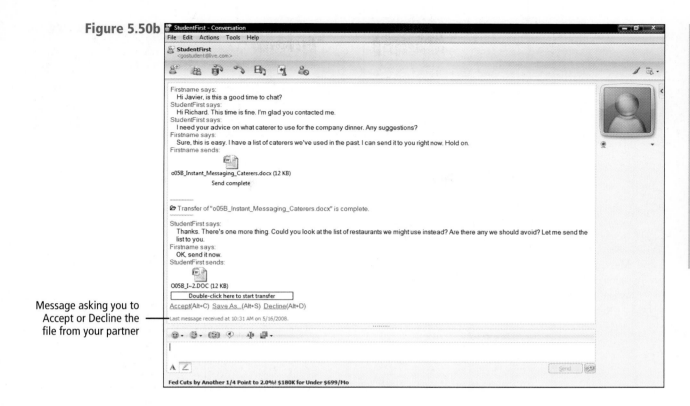

Message asking you to Accept or Decline the file from your partner

8 *Richard Kelly*: In the **Conversation** window, click **Accept**. If the Windows Live Messenger box displays a warning about possible viruses, click **OK**. The **Conversation** window shows the location of the received file on your computer.

Javier Catano: In the **Conversation** window, notice the messages that display after your partner accepts the file.

Both Conversation windows display messages when the transfer is complete.

9 *Javier Catano*: In the **Conversation** window, type **Thanks! That's really all I need.** Click **Send**.

Richard Kelly: In the **Conversation** window, type **No problem. Glad to help.** Click **Send**.

10 *Richard Kelly*: In the **Conversation** window, notice the message indicating the location of the received file, **o05B_Instant_Messaging_Restaurants**. Compare your screen with Figure 5.51a.

Javier Catano: In the **Conversation** window, use the scroll bar to scroll up to the message indicating the location of the received file, **o05B_Instant_Messaging_Caterers**. Compare your screen with Figure 5.51b.

Figure 5.51a

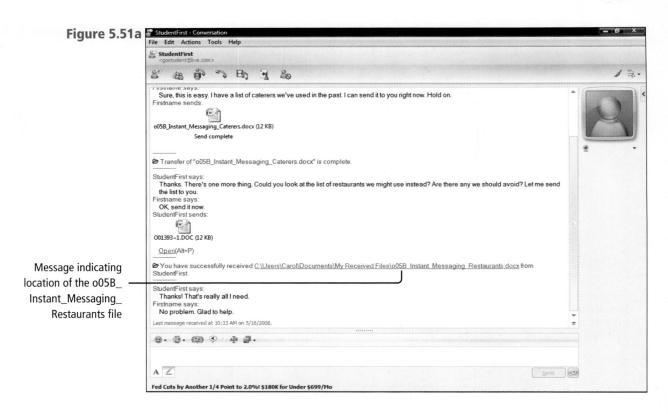

Message indicating location of the o05B_ Instant_Messaging_ Restaurants file

Figure 5.51b

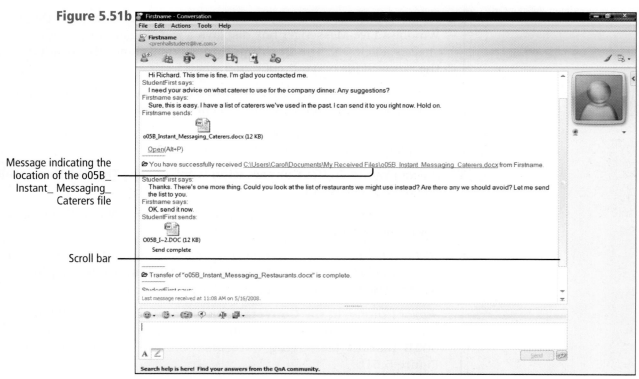

Message indicating the location of the o05B_ Instant_ Messaging_ Caterers file

Scroll bar

11 *Richard Kelly, Javier Catano*: In the **Conversation** window, click the location of your received file. In the **Windows Live Messenger** dialog box, click **Open**.

A Word window opens, displaying your received file. You can save this file to a different location.

12 *Richard Kelly:* Click the **Office** button 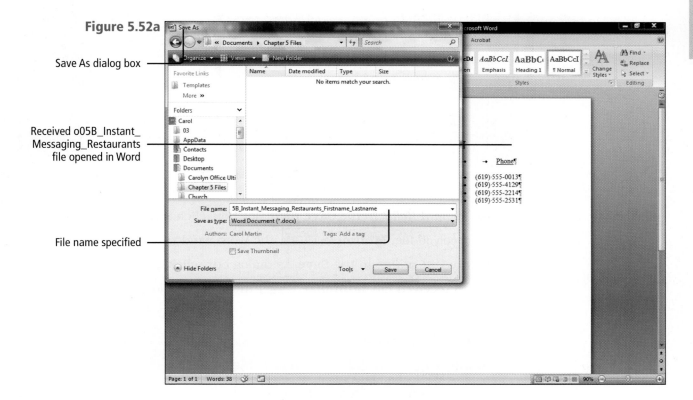, and then click **Save As**. In the **Save As** dialog box, navigate to the location where you are storing your files. In the **File name** box, delete the existing file name, and type **5B_Instant_Messaging_Restaurants_Firstname_Lastname** Compare your screen with Figure 5.52a.

Javier Catano: Click the **Office** button 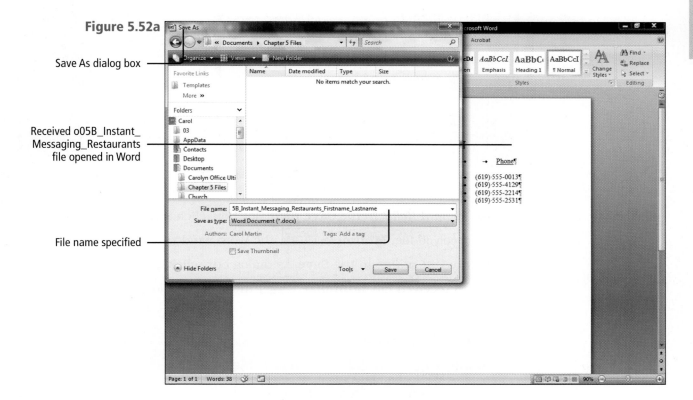, and then click **Save As**. In the **Save As** dialog box, navigate to the location where you are storing your files. In the **File name** box, delete the existing file name, and type **5B_Instant_Messaging_Caterers_Firstname_Lastname** Compare your screen with Figure 5.52b.

Figure 5.52a

Save As dialog box

Received o05B_Instant_
Messaging_Restaurants
file opened in Word

File name specified

Figure 5.52b

Save As dialog box

Received o05B_Instant_
Messaging_Caterers
file opened in Word

File name specified

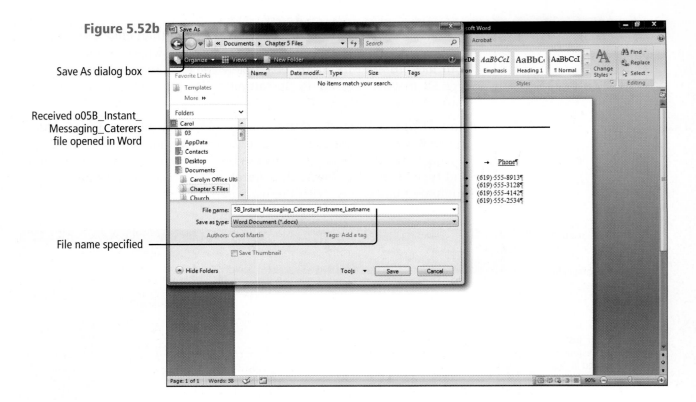

13 *Richard Kelly*, In the **Save As** dialog box, click **Save** to save the received file. **Minimize** [ ] the Word window.

14 *Javier Catano*: In the **Save As** dialog box, click **Save** to save the received file. **Minimize** [ ] the Word window.

More Knowledge

Using Voice and Video in Instant Messages

You can have a voice conversation with an online contact if your computer and your contact's computer are equipped with microphones, speakers, and a full-duplex sound card. To initiate a voice conversation, right-click the name of the contact in the Windows Live Messenger window, and then point to Call and choose an option. If you already have a Conversation window open with the contact, click the Call icon. If you have a camera attached to your computer, you can include a video image of yourself in your contact's Conversation window. To initiate video, right-click the contact name in the Windows Live Messenger contact list, and then point to Video and choose an option. If the Conversation window is already open, click the Video Call icon. You can include both voice and video in the Conversation window.

Activity 5.20 Saving and Printing an Instant Message Conversation

In most situations, you do not need a written record of an IM session. Sometimes, however, you might want to save and print an IM conversation. For example, someone might give you directions that you want to print. In this activity, you will save and print the conversation between Richard Kelly and Javier Catano.

1 With the **Conversation** window still open, click the **Show menu** button 🗐, click **File**, and then click **Save As**. In the **Save As** dialog box, navigate to the location where you are storing your files.

A Windows Live Messenger dialog box displays to indicate that your conversation will be saved in rich text format.

2 In the Microsoft Live Messenger dialog box, click **OK**. In the **File name** box, using your own name, type **5B_Instant_Messaging_ Firstname_Lastname** and compare your screen with Figure 5.53.

The *Save as type* box indicates that the file type is an **RTF** Document; that is, a rich text format file. Recall that **Rich text** is a format that can include character and paragraph formatting and also embedded graphics. You can view and print files saved in this file format in a variety of different programs, including Microsoft Word.

Alert! **Does your instant messaging conversation differ?**

The image shown in Figure 5.53 was taken from Richard Kelly's perspective. If you assumed the role of Javier Catano, your file will vary slightly.

Figure 5.53

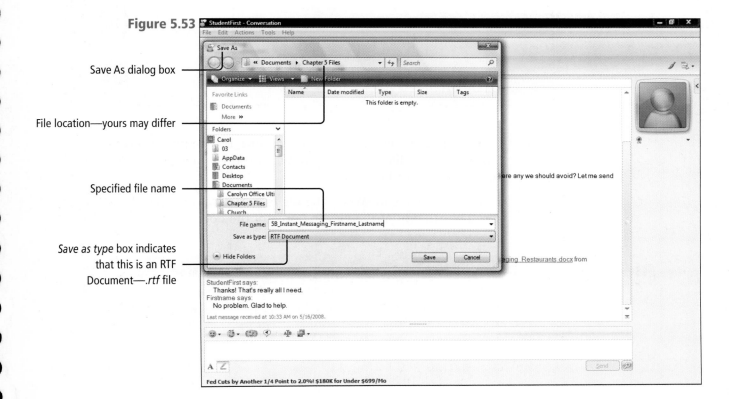

Save As dialog box

File location—yours may differ

Specified file name

Save as type box indicates that this is an RTF Document—*.rtf* file

3 In the **Save As** dialog box, click **Save** to save the IM session as a rich text document.

4 On the taskbar, click the **Word** button. Your received file still displays.

Click the **Office** button [image], and then click **Open**. In the **Open** dialog box, if necessary navigate to the location where you are storing your files. Click the **File type arrow**, click **Rich Text Format (*.rtf)**, and then compare your screen with Figure 5.54.

The Open dialog box lists any Rich Text Format files in the folder, including the file you saved in the previous step.

Open dialog box

Figure 5.54

Location where you are storing your files— yours may differ

File type specifies Rich Text Format

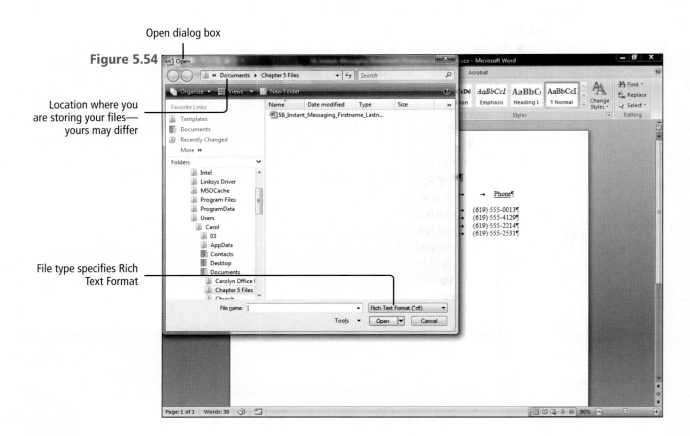

5 In the **Open** dialog box, click **5B_Instant_Messaging_Firstname_Lastname** (the file with your name), and then click **Open**. Compare your screen with Figure 5.55.

Your file displays in Word. The file is in rich text format. Use the scroll bar to adjust the viewing area of the document.

Alert! **Does your instant messaging conversation differ?**
The image shown in Figure 5.55 was taken from Richard Kelly's perspective. If you assumed the role of Javier Catano, your file will vary slightly.

Figure 5.55

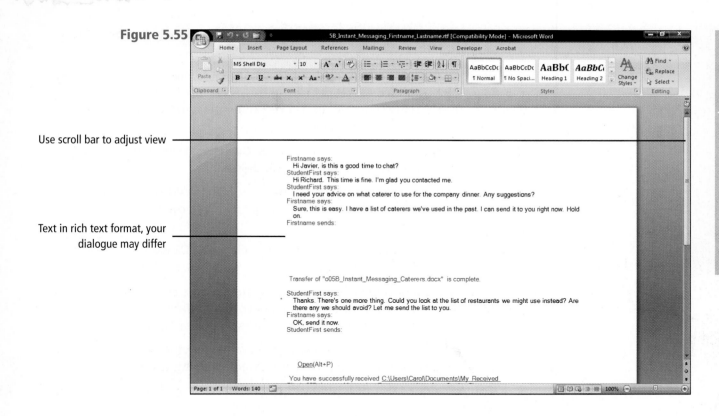

Use scroll bar to adjust view

Text in rich text format, your dialogue may differ

The following appears within the figure:

Firstname says:
    Hi Javier, is this a good time to chat?
StudentFirst says:
    Hi Richard. This time is fine. I'm glad you contacted me.
StudentFirst says:
    I need your advice on what caterer to use for the company dinner. Any suggestions?
Firstname says:
    Sure, this is easy. I have a list of caterers we've used in the past. I can send it to you right now. Hold
    on.
Firstname sends:

Transfer of "o05B_Instant_Messaging_Caterers.docx" is complete.

StudentFirst says:
    Thanks. There's one more thing. Could you look at the list of restaurants we might use instead? Are
    there any we should avoid? Let me send the list to you.
Firstname says:
    OK, send it now.
StudentFirst sends:

Open(Alt+P)
You have successfully received C:\Users\Carol\Documents\My_Received

6 Use the **scroll bar**, and examine the contents of the file. Notice that all the dialogue and system messages have been saved.

7 On the Ribbon, click the **Insert tab**, and then click **Footer**. In the drop-down list, click **Edit Footer**, and then type **5B_Instant_Messaging_Firstname_Lastname** On the Ribbon, at the extreme right, click **Close Header and Footer**.

8 Click the **Office** button , and then click **Print**. In the **Print** dialog box, click **OK** to print the document. Submit the end result to your instructor as directed.

9 **Close** both Word documents, saving any changes, and then **Close** Word.

More Knowledge

Using Other Windows Live Messenger Programs

The Windows Live Messenger window includes other programs that you may find useful in your instant message conversations. If you are having trouble with your computer, the *Remote Assistance* feature enables a contact to help you from his or her computer. To start Remote Assistance, from the Actions menu in Windows Live Messenger, click Request Remote Assistance, and select an online contact. The *Sharing Folders* feature enables both you and a contact to view a file at the same time. To share a file, from the Actions menu in Windows Live Messenger window, click Create or open a sharing folder. The *Whiteboard* feature enables you to draw and type simultaneously with a contact. To start the Whiteboard, from the Actions menu, click Start an activity, and then select Whiteboard. Depending on your computer's configuration, some of these Windows Live Messenger programs may not be available.

Activity 5.21 Closing the Conversation Window and Closing Windows Live Messenger

An instant message conversation ends when you close the Conversation window. Windows Live Messenger remains open until you close the program. In this activity, you will end the conversation between Richard Kelly and Javier Catano and close the program.

1 Display the Windows Live Messenger **Conversation** window with your student partner, if not already displayed.

Although you and your partner have stopped sending messages to each other, the dialog box is still open until you close the Conversation window.

2 In the **Conversation** window title bar, click the **Close** button. If a **Windows Live Messenger** dialog box displays, click **OK**.

The conversation between you and your partner ends. The Windows Live Messenger window still displays you as online. You can go offline by closing the Windows Live Messenger or by signing out.

3 With the **Windows Live Messenger** window displayed, click **File**, and then click **Sign out**. Compare your screen with Figure 5.56.

You are signed out of Windows Live Messenger—not online—but the program is still running. You can leave the program running in case you want to sign in again later. The sign-in ID displayed may be yours or another user's ID.

Figure 5.56

Windows Live Messenger window, after sign out

E-mail address may be your Windows Live ID or another user's ID

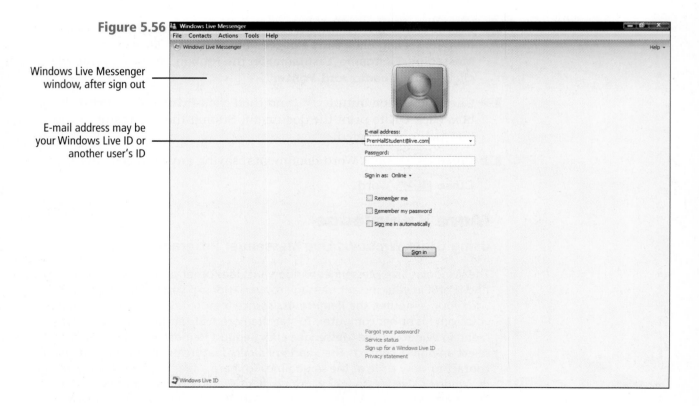

4 In the Windows Live Messenger title bar, click the **Close** button [X].

The Windows Live Messenger window closes and the Outlook window is displayed.

5 Delete the contents of the **Inbox**. Delete the contents of the **Contacts** folder. Delete the contents of the **Deleted Items** folder.

6 From the Outlook **Tools** menu, click **Options**, and then click the **Other tab**. Under **Person Names**, clear the **Display online status next to a person name** and **Display online status in the To and Cc fields only when mouse pointer rests on a person name** check boxes if this is a default setting on your computer. Click **OK**.

7 **Close** Outlook.

More Knowledge

Deleting a Contact in Windows Live Messenger

You can delete contacts from your Windows Live Messenger contact list just as you can delete Outlook contacts. For example, you may want to delete your student partner's name from your Windows Live Messenger contact list. In the Windows Live Messenger window, right-click the contact, click Delete Contact, and then click Yes.

End **You have completed Project 5B** ——————————————

Content-Based Assessments

Summary

In this chapter, you created task requests and assigned them to contacts on your Contacts list. You responded to task requests that you received from others, and accepted and declined task requests. You created a task status report and marked tasks as complete.

In this chapter, you also used instant messaging. You started Windows Live Messenger and created a Windows Live ID. You configured Outlook for Windows Live Messenger and changed your Windows Live Messenger online status. You started an instant message session with your student partner, sent files to each other, saved your instant message dialogue in a file, and printed the dialogue in Word.

Key Terms

Content-Based Assessments

Matching

Match each term in the second column with its correct definition in the first column by writing the letter of the term on the blank line in front of the correct definition.

_____ **1.** A task sent as an e-mail message asking the recipient to complete the activity.

_____ **2.** The individual currently responsible for completing an assigned task.

_____ **3.** An e-mail message sent to the originator of the task request to indicate a task's progress or completion.

_____ **4.** A temporary storage area used by Windows to hold one piece of data, such as text, a file, or a graphic.

_____ **5.** A Windows communication program that is integrated into Outlook, with which you can send instant messages to your online contacts.

_____ **6.** A form of online, real-time communication across the Internet in which users communicate with each other in a private, text-based dialogue.

_____ **7.** Types of commands on a shortcut menu that refer only to the item to which you are pointing.

_____ **8.** The second portion of an e-mail address, which defines the e-mail system or Internet Service Provider.

A Block

B Chat

C Windows Clipboard

D Context-sensitive

E Domain name

F Hotmail

G Instant messaging

H Invisible

I Person Names online presence indicator

J Rich text

K Screen name

L Status report

M Task owner

N Task request

O Windows Live Messenger

_____ **9.** Microsoft's free, Web-based e-mail service that enables users to read and write e-mail messages on any computer with a Web browser that is connected to the Internet.

_____ **10.** IM is an example of this type of real-time conversation on a computer.

_____ **11.** The name other Windows Live Messenger users see when they have your name on their contact list.

_____ **12.** For contacts that have a Windows Live ID, a small button displayed next to the contact's e-mail address that indicates their online status in Windows Live Messenger.

_____ **13.** In Windows Live Messenger, a command that prevents someone from contacting you or seeing when you are online.

_____ **14.** In Windows Live Messenger, a status where you appear to be offline—you can see them but they cannot see you.

_____ **15.** A file format that can include character and paragraph formatting, and also embedded graphics.

Content-Based Assessments

Fill in the Blank

Write the correct answer in the space provided.

1. A personal or work-related activity that you want to track through completion is a(n) _____.

2. An e-mail message showing the changed Task form that is sent to the person who made the task request and also to any prior owners of the task is called a(n) _____.

3. The temporary owner of a task is the _____ _____.

4. The icon for a task you own displays as a(n) _____ clipboard in the Tasks list.

5. IM is an abbreviation for _____ _____.

6. A duplicate of an assigned task that indicates yourself as the owner and to which you can make changes is a(n) _____ _____.

7. You can respond to a task request in the Tasks folder or the _____.

8. The _____ _____ includes the name of the person who originally sent the task request, plus the names of everyone who received the task request, reassigned the task to someone else, or chose to keep a revised copy of the task in their task list.

9. To designate another person as the owner of a task that you have received, you can _____ the task.

10. To refuse a task request, click the _____ button.

11. A set of instructions that causes some items in a folder to display—and others *not* to display—based on conditions you define is a(n) _____.

12. In Windows Live Messenger, the area at the bottom of the Conversation window that indicates when the other party is typing or when the last message was received is the _____ _____.

13. A Windows Live Messenger program with which a contact can help you from his or her computer is called _____ _____.

14. A Windows Live Messenger feature with which both you and a contact can view a file at the same time is called _____ _____.

15. A Windows Live Messenger feature with which you can draw and type simultaneously with a contact is called _____.

Content-Based Assessments

Skills Review

Project 5C — CEO Visit

Objectives: 1. *Assign Tasks;* **3.** *Manage Task Assignments.*

In the following Skills Review, you will assist Richard Kelly, Vice President of Marketing in assigning tasks to his subordinates in preparation for the events surrounding the upcoming visit of El Cuero's CEO. Miguel Hernandez, CEO of El Cuero de Mexico, will be visiting the offices of El Cuero Specialty Wares in San Diego next month. He will attend marketing presentations, review advertising plans, and attend a dinner party for all the San Diego employees. Your completed documents will look similar to the ones shown in Figure 5.57.

For Project 5C, you will need the following file:

o05C_CEO_Visit_Contacts

You will print three files with the following footers:
5C_CEO_Visit_Tasks_Firstname_Lastname
5C_CEO_Visit_Agenda_Firstname_Lastname
5C_CEO_Visit_Message_Firstname_Lastname

Figure 5.57

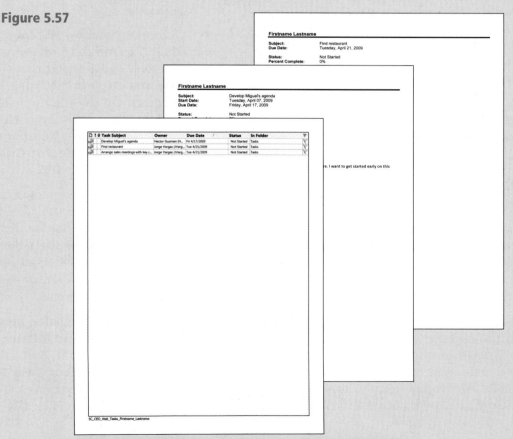

(Project 5C–CEO Visit continues on the next page)

Content-Based Assessments

(Project 5C–CEO Visit continued)

1. **Start** Outlook. Display the **Contacts** folder, and delete any existing contacts. Display the **Tasks** folder, and delete any existing tasks. From the **Tools** menu, click **Options**. In the **Options** dialog box, click the **Mail Setup tab**. Under **Send/Receive**, clear the **Send immediately when connected** check box. Click **Send/Receive**.

2. Under **Setting for group "All Accounts"**, clear both **Include this group in send/receive (F9)** check boxes. If necessary, clear both **Schedule an automatic send/receive** check boxes. Click **Close**, and then click **OK**.

3. In the **Navigation Pane**, click the **Contacts** button. Display the **Import and Export Wizard** dialog box, and under **Choose an action to perform**, click **Import from another program or file**, and then click **Next**. In the **Import a File** dialog box, under **Select file type to import from**, click **Personal Folder File (.pst)**, and then click **Next**.

4. In the **Import Personal Folders** dialog box, click **Browse**. In the **Open Personal Folders** dialog box, navigate to the location where the student files for this textbook are stored. Locate **o05C_CEO_Visit_Contacts**, and click **Open**. In the **Import Personal Folders** dialog box, click **Next**.

5. In the **Import Personal Folders** dialog box, under **Select the folder to import from**, click **Contacts**. Click **Finish**. If a Translation Warning dialog box displays, click OK.

6. In the **Navigation Pane**, click the **Tasks** button. On the Standard toolbar, click the **New Task** button. As the **Subject**, type **Find restaurant** Set the **Due date** as **two weeks from today** Recall that you can use natural language phrases to create dates

and have Outlook convert them to actual dates. Clear the **Reminder** check box. In the comments area of the form, type **Find restaurant with nice banquet facilities for company dinner**

7. On the Ribbon, click the **Assign Task** button, and then click the **To** button. In the **Select Task Recipient: Contacts** dialog box, click **Jorge Vargas**, and then click **To**. Click **OK**, and then **Send** the task request.

8. In the **To-Do List**, click in the **Click here to add a new task** box, and then type **Develop Miguel's agenda** In the **Due Date** box, type **one week from today** and then press Enter. Create another new task with the **Subject Arrange sales meetings with key customers and Miguel** In the **Due Date** box, type **two weeks from today** and then press Enter.

9. Open the **Develop Miguel's agenda** task. Click the **Due date arrow** and advance the due date by three more business days—days that are not Saturday, Sunday, or holidays. On the Ribbon, click the **Assign Task** button, and then click the **To** button. In the **Select Task Recipient: Contacts** dialog box, click **Hector Guzman**, click **To**, and then click **OK**.

10. Using appropriate spacing, create the following message in the comments area: **Hector, Could you handle this for me? We need to manage Miguel's time while he is here. I want to get started early on this because we have a lot for him to do. Richard Send** the task request.

11. Open the **Arrange sales meetings with key customers and Miguel** task. Click the **Assign Task** button, and then click the **To** button. In the **Select Task Recipient: Contacts** dialog box, click **Jorge Vargas**, click **To**, and then click **OK**.

(Project 5C–CEO Visit continues on the next page)

Content-Based Assessments

Skills Review

(Project 5C–CEO Visit continued)

12. Using appropriate spacing, create the following message: **Jorge, This is the principal objective of Miguel's visit. Contact the buyers at our key accounts and set up lunch dates with them. Richard Send** the task request.

13. In the **Navigation Pane**, under **Current View**, click **Assignment**. From the **File** menu, display the **Page Setup: Table Style** dialog box. On the **Header/Footer tab**, delete any existing header or footer information, including dates and page numbers. In the left **Footer** box, type **5C_CEO_Visit_Tasks_Firstname_Lastname Preview** and **Print** the To-Do List. Submit the end result to your instructor as directed.

14. Display the To-Do List in **Simple List** view. In the **To-Do List**, select the **Develop Miguel's agenda** task. From the **File** menu, display the **Page Setup: Memo Style** dialog box. Delete any existing header or footer information, and then, in the left **Footer** box, type **5C_CEO_Visit_Agenda_Firstname_Lastname Preview** and **Print** the task. Submit the end result to your instructor as directed.

15. In the **Navigation Pane**, display the **Outbox** folder. Select the **Task Request: Find restaurant** message. Display the **Page Setup: Memo Style** dialog box,

delete the existing footer information, and type **5C_CEO_Visit_Message_Firstname_Lastname Preview** and **Print** the message. Submit the end result to your instructor as directed.

16. Delete the contents of the **Outbox**. Delete the contents of the **Tasks** folder. Delete the contents of the **Contacts** folder. Empty the **Deleted Items** folder.

17. From the **Tools** menu, click **Options**, and then click the **Mail Setup tab**. Under **Send/Receive**, select the **Send immediately when connected** check box. In the **Options** dialog box, click **Send/Receive**. In the **Send/Receive Groups** dialog box, under **Setting for group "All Accounts"**, select both **Include this group in send/receive (F9)** check boxes. Select both **Schedule an automatic send/receive** check boxes if this is a default setting on your computer. Click **Close**, and then click **OK**.

18. Display the **Inbox** folder. From the **File** menu, point to **Page Setup**, and then click **Define Print Styles**. In the **Define Print Styles** dialog box, click **Table Style**, click **Reset**, and then click **OK**. Click **Memo Style**, click **Reset**, and then click **OK**. **Close** the dialog box. **Close** Outlook.

End You have completed Project 5C

Content-Based Assessments

Skills Review

Project 5D — New Line

Objectives: 2. *Respond to Task Assignments;* **3.** *Manage Task Assignments.*

In the following Skills Review, you will respond to several task requests received by Hector Guzman from his supervisor. Mr. Guzman, an employee of El Cuero Specialty Wares, is responsible for analyzing the sales projections for a new product line the company is developing. Your completed documents will look similar to the ones shown in Figure 5.58.

For Project 5D, you will need the following file:

o05D_New_Line_Tasks

You will print two files with the following footers:
5D_New_Line_Firstname_Lastname
5D_New_Line_Update_Firstname_Lastname

Figure 5.58

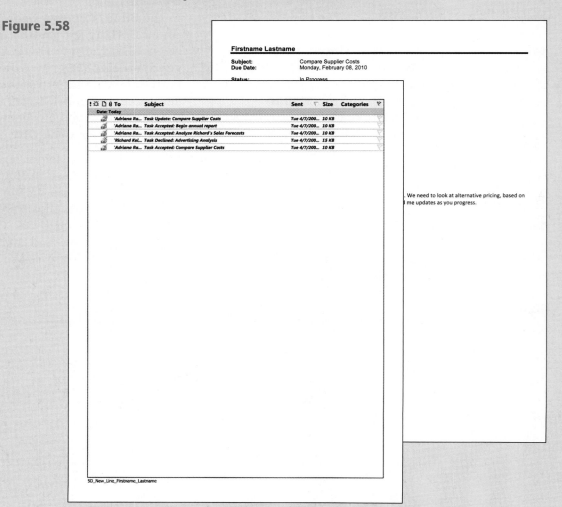

(Project 5D–New Line continues on the next page)

Content-Based Assessments

(Project 5D–New Line continued)

1. **Start** Outlook. From the **Tools** menu, click **Options**. In the **Options** dialog box, click the **Mail Setup tab**. Under **Send/Receive**, clear the **Send immediately when connected** check box. Click **Send/Receive**.

2. Under **Setting for group "All Accounts"**, clear both **Include this group in send/receive (F9)** check boxes. If necessary, clear both **Schedule an automatic send/receive** check boxes. Click **Close**, and then click **OK**.

3. From the **File** menu, point to **Open**, and then click **Outlook Data File**. In the **Open Outlook Data File** dialog box, navigate to the location where the student files for this textbook are stored. Point to **o05D_New_Line_Tasks**, right-click, and then, from the displayed shortcut menu, click **Copy**. Recall that this action copies the file to the Office Clipboard.

4. With the **Open Outlook Data File** dialog box still displayed, navigate to the location where you are storing your files for this chapter, and then right-click any blank area in the **Open Outlook Data File** dialog box. From the displayed shortcut menu, click **Paste**.

5. Still in the **Open Outlook Data File** dialog box, with the file **o05D_New_Line_Tasks** selected, click **OK** to open the file.

6. In the **Navigation Pane**, click the **Tasks** button. Under **My Tasks**, click **Tasks in Personal Folders**. Open the **Compare Supplier Costs** task. On the Ribbon, click the **Accept** button. In the **Accepting Task** dialog box, click **Edit the response before sending**, and then click **OK**. Using appropriate spacing, type **Adriana, I will get started on this right away. Hector** On the Task form, click the **Send** button.

7. Open the **Advertising Analysis** task. On the Ribbon, click the **Decline** button. In the **Declining Task** dialog box, click **Edit the response before sending**, and then click **OK**. Using appropriate spacing, type: **Richard, I think you must have intended this for Javier. I know how easy it is to send these things to the wrong person! Hector Send** the message.

8. Open the **Analyze Richard's Sales Forecasts** task and **Accept** the task. In the **Accepting Task** dialog box, click **OK** to send the response without editing. Open the **Begin annual report** task, and **Accept** the task. In the **Accepting Task** dialog box, click **OK** to send the response without editing.

9. Open the **Compare Supplier Costs** task. In the **% Complete** box, type **25%** and then **Save & Close** the task.

10. In the **Navigation Pane**, click the **Folder List** button. Display the **Outbox**, containing the five messages. If necessary, drag the column divider between the **Subject** and **Sent** column headings so that you can read the subjects of each sent item in the **Outbox**.

11. From the **File** menu, display the **Page Setup: Table Style** dialog box. On the **Header/Footer tab**, delete any existing header and footer information, and then, in the left **Footer** box, type **5D_New_Line_Firstname_Lastname Preview** and **Print** the Outbox. Submit the end result to your instructor as directed.

12. Select the **Task Update: Compare Supplier Costs** message. Display the **Page Setup: Memo Style** dialog box. Delete any existing header and footer information, and then create a left **Footer** by typing

(Project 5D–New Line continues on the next page)

Skills Review

(Project 5D–New Line continued)

5D_New_Line_Update_Firstname_Lastname
Preview and **Print** the message. Submit the end result to your instructor as directed.

13. Delete the contents of the **Outbox**. Empty the **Deleted Items** folder.

14. In the **Navigation Pane**, under **All Folders**, use the **scroll bar** to display the lower portion of the folder list, if necessary. At the bottom of the folder list, locate **Personal Folders**. Right-click **Personal Folders**, and from the displayed shortcut menu, click **Close "Personal Folders"**.

15. From the **Tools** menu, click **Options**, and then click the **Mail Setup tab**. Under **Send/Receive**, select the **Send immediately when connected** check box.

16. In the **Options** dialog box, click **Send/Receive**. In the **Send/Receive Groups** dialog box, under **Setting for group "All Accounts"**, select both **Include this group in send/receive (F9)** check boxes. Select both **Schedule an automatic send/receive** check boxes if this is a default setting on your computer. Click **Close**, and then click **OK**.

17. Display the **Inbox** folder. From the **File** menu, point to **Page Setup**, and then click **Define Print Styles**. In the **Define Print Styles** dialog box, click **Table Style**, click **Reset**, and then click **OK**. Click **Memo Style**, click **Reset**, and then click **OK**. **Close** the dialog box. **Close** Outlook.

End **You have completed Project 5D**

Content-Based Assessments

Skills Review

Project 5E — Customers

Objective: 4. *Use Instant Messaging in Outlook.*

In the following Skills Review, you and a student partner will conduct an instant message dialogue between Michelle Carlton and Richard Kelly, using your own Windows Live accounts. Michelle Carlton works in Sales and Marketing at El Cuero Specialty Wares. Her supervisor, Richard Kelly, needs some information from her about a customer. He has an e-mail in his Inbox from her, and he wants to add her name to his contact list in Windows Live Messenger. You will print the dialogue when you are finished, which will look similar to the one shown in Figure 5.59.

For Project 5E, you will need the following files:

o05E_Customers_Inbox_RK
o05E_Customers_Inbox_MC

You will print one file with the following footer:
5E_Customers_Firstname_Lastname

Figure 5.59

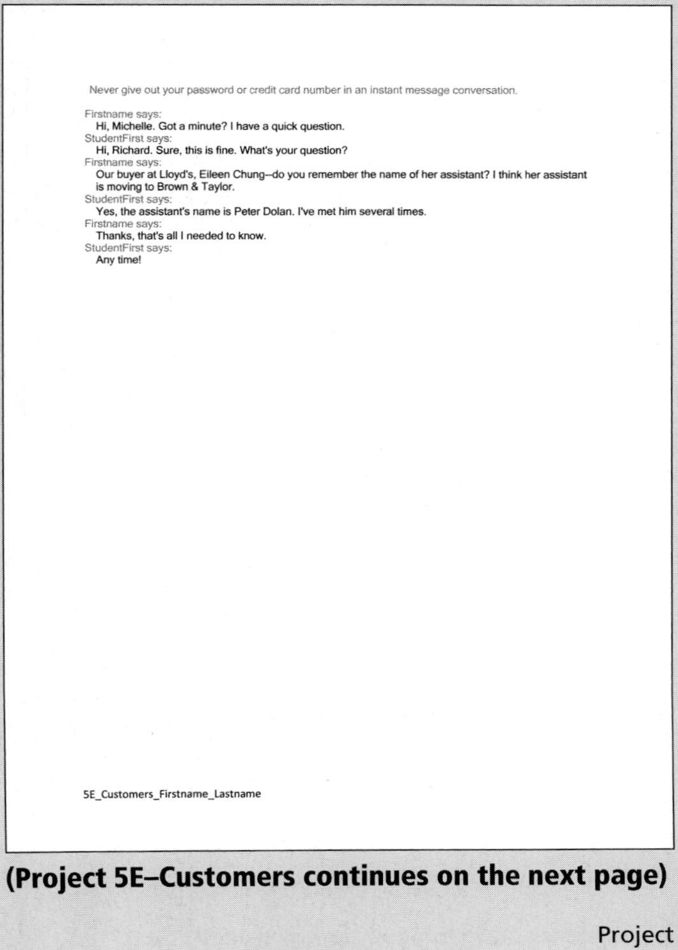

Never give out your password or credit card number in an instant message conversation.

Firstname says:
    Hi, Michelle. Got a minute? I have a quick question.
StudentFirst says:
    Hi, Richard. Sure, this is fine. What's your question?
Firstname says:
    Our buyer at Lloyd's, Eileen Chung--do you remember the name of her assistant? I think her assistant is moving to Brown & Taylor.
StudentFirst says:
    Yes, the assistant's name is Peter Dolan. I've met him several times.
Firstname says:
    Thanks, that's all I needed to know.
StudentFirst says:
    Any time!

5E_Customers_Firstname_Lastname

(Project 5E–Customers continues on the next page)

Content-Based Assessments

(Project 5E–Customers continued)

1. Be sure you are online and connected to the Internet. **Start Windows Live Messenger**, and sign in. On the Windows Live Messenger title bar, click the **Minimize** button. **Start** Outlook. From the Outlook **Tools** menu, click **Options**, and then click the **Other tab**. Under **Person Names**, determine if the **Display online status next to a person name** and **Display online status in the To and Cc fields only when mouse pointer rests on a person name** check boxes are selected; select them if necessary. Click **OK** to close the dialog box.

2. With your student partner, determine who will respond as *Richard Kelly* and who will respond as *Michelle Carlton*.

3. *Richard Kelly, Michelle Carlton*: In the **Navigation Pane**, display the **Inbox**. From the **File** menu, click **Import and Export**. In the **Import and Export Wizard** dialog box, click **Import from another program or file**, and then click **Next**. In the **Import a File** dialog box, under **Select file type to import from**, click **Personal Folder file (.pst)**. Click **Next**.

4. *Richard Kelly*: In the **Import Personal Folders** dialog box, navigate to the student files, locate **o05E_Customers_Inbox_RK**, and click **Open**. In the **Import Personal Folders** dialog box, click **Next**.

   Michelle Carlton: In the **Import Personal Folders** dialog box, navigate to the student files, locate and open **o05E_Customers_Inbox_MC**. In the **Import Personal Folders** dialog box, click **Next**.

5. *Richard Kelly, Michelle Carlton*: In the **Import Personal Folders** dialog box, under **Select the folder to import from**, click **Inbox**. Click **Import items into current folder**. Click **Finish**. If a Translation Warning dialog box displays, click OK.

6. *Richard Kelly*: In the **Reading Pane**, right-click the e-mail address for **Michelle Carlton**. Click **Add to Outlook Contacts**. In the **Michelle Carlton - Contact** form, in the **IM Address** box, type the Windows Live ID of your student partner, and then click the **Save & Close** button.

   Michelle Carlton: In the **Reading Pane**, right-click the e-mail address for **Richard Kelly**. Click **Add to Outlook Contacts**. In the **Richard Kelly - Contact** form, in the **IM Address** box, type the Windows Live ID of your student partner, and then click the **Save & Close** button.

7. *Richard Kelly*: In the **Reading Pane**, right-click the e-mail address for **Michelle Carlton**, and then click **Add to Instant Messaging Contacts**. In the **Add a Contact** dialog box, click **Add contact**.

   Michelle Carlton: On the taskbar, notice that a second **Windows Live Messenger** button displays. On the taskbar, click the rightmost **Windows Live Messenger** button to bring the window to the front of the desktop. In the **Windows Live Messenger** dialog box, click **OK**.

8. *Richard Kelly*: In the **Reading Pane**, right-click the e-mail address for **Michelle Carlton**, and then click **Send Instant Message**. If necessary, to initiate the chat session in Windows Live Messenger display the Windows Live Messenger window, click Actions, and then click Send an Instant Message. In the **Conversation** window, type **Hi, Michelle. Got a minute? I have a quick question.** Click the **Send** button.

   Michelle Carlton: When you receive the message from your partner, in the taskbar, click the orange **Windows Messenger** button to maximize the **Conversation** window.

(Project 5E–Customers continues on the next page)

Content-Based Assessments

(Project 5E—Customers continued)

In the **Conversation** window, type **Hi, Richard. Sure, this is fine. What's your question?** Click **Send**.

9. *Richard Kelly*: In the **Conversation** window, type **Our buyer at Lloyd's, Eileen Chung—do you remember the name of her assistant? I think her assistant is moving to Brown & Taylor.** Click **Send**.

   Michelle Carlton: In the **Conversation** window, type **Yes, the assistant's name is Peter Dolan. I've met him several times.** Click **Send**.

10. *Richard Kelly*: In the **Conversation** window, type **Thanks, that's all I needed to know.** Click **Send**.

    Michelle Carlton: In the **Conversation** window, type **Any time!** Click **Send**.

11. *Richard Kelly*, *Michelle Carlton*: With the **Conversation** window still open, click the **Show menu** button, click **File**, and then click **Save As**. In the **Save As** dialog box, navigate to the location where you are storing your files for this chapter. In the **File name** box, type **5E_Customers_Firstname_Lastname** Click **Save**. Recall that Windows Live Messenger saves the dialogue in rich text format, preserving character and paragraph formatting.

12. On the taskbar, click the **Start** button to display the **Start** menu. On the computer you are using, locate **Microsoft Office Word 2007** and click to open the program.

13. Click the **Office** button, and then click **Open**. In the **Open** dialog box, navigate to the location where you are storing your files. Click the **File type arrow**, and then click **Rich Text Format (*.rtf)**. In the

Open dialog box, click **5E_Customers_Firstname_Lastname** (the file with your name), and then click **Open**.

14. On the Ribbon, click the **Insert tab**, and then click **Footer**. On the drop-down list, click **Edit Footer**. In the **Footer** box, using your own name, type **5E_Customers_Firstname_Lastname** On the Ribbon, in the **Close group**, click **Close Header and Footer**.

15. Click the **Office** button, click **Print**, and then click **OK** to print the document. Submit the end result to your instructor as directed. **Close** the Word document, saving any changes, and then **Close** Word.

16. In the **Conversation** window title bar, click the **Close** button. In the **Windows Live Messenger** window, right-click your student partner's name, click **Delete Contact**, and then click **Yes**. From the **Windows Live Messenger** menu, click **File**, and then click **Sign Out**. In the Windows Live Messenger title bar, click the **Close** button.

17. Delete the contents of the **Inbox**. Delete the contents of the **Contacts** folder. Delete the contents of the **Deleted Items** folder.

18. From the Outlook **Tools** menu, click **Options**, and then click the **Other tab**. Under **Person Names**, clear the **Display online status next to a person name** and **Display online status in the To and Cc fields only when mouse pointer rests on a person name** check boxes if this is a default setting on your computer. Click **OK**. **Close** Outlook.

End   You have completed Project 5E ——————————

Mastering Outlook

Project 5F—Factory Outlet

Objectives: 1. *Assign Tasks;* **3.** *Manage Task Assignments.*

In the following Mastering Outlook, you will assign tasks to Alejandra Domene's subordinates. Ms. Domene, the President of El Cuero Specialty Wares, is considering opening a factory outlet store for the company products. She has assigned several of her subordinates to investigate this as a business opportunity. Your completed documents will look similar to the ones shown in Figure 5.60.

For Project 5F, you will need the following file:

o05F_Factory_Outlet_Contacts

You will print two files with the following footers:
5F_Factory_Outlet_Firstname_Lastname
5F_Factory_Outlet_Message_Firstname_Lastname

Figure 5.60

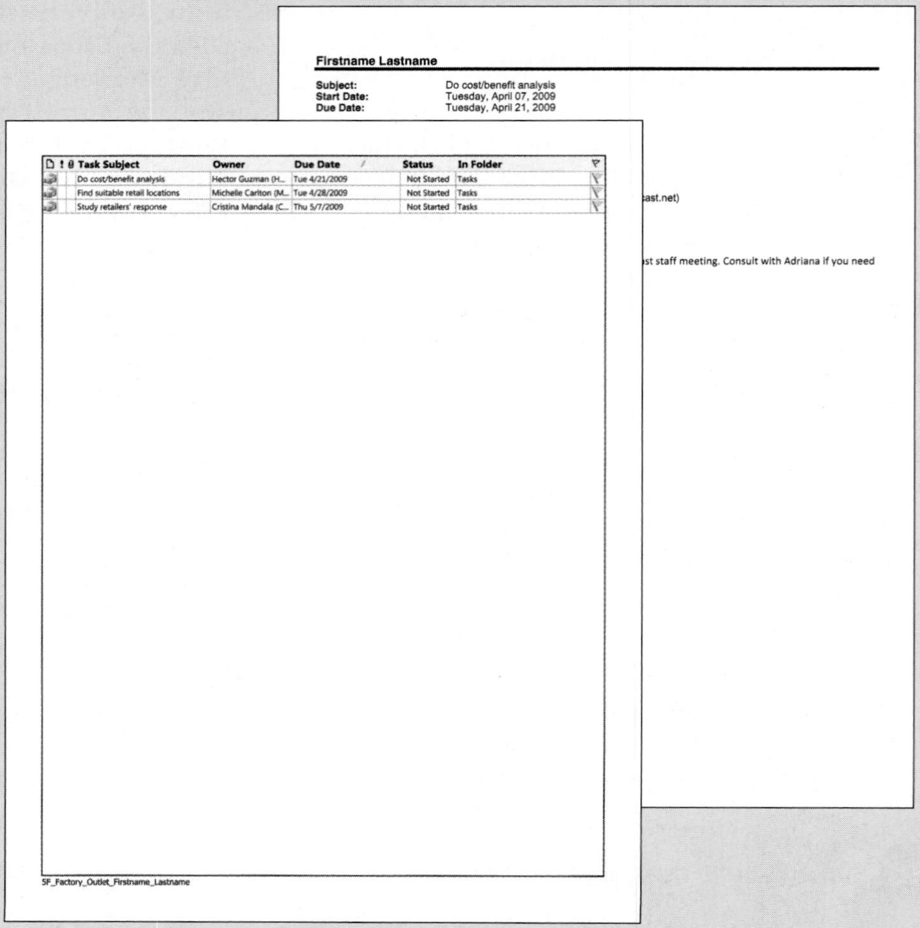

(Project 5F–Factory Outlet continues on the next page)

Content-Based Assessments

(Project 5F–Factory Outlet continued)

1. **Start** Outlook. From the **Tools** menu, display the **Options** dialog box, and then click the **Mail Setup tab**. Under **Send/ Receive**, clear the **Send immediately when connected** check box, if necessary. Click the **Send/Receive** button. In the **Send/Receive Groups** dialog box, under **Setting for group "All Accounts"**, clear both **Include this group in send/receive (F9)** check boxes, if necessary. Clear both **Schedule an automatic send/receive** check boxes, if necessary. Click **Close**, and then click **OK**.

2. Display the **Contacts** folder, and then using the techniques you have practiced, import **o05F_Factory_Outlet_Contacts** into the **Contacts** folder.

3. Create a new task request, and assign the task to **Michelle Carlton**. As the **Subject**, type **Find suitable retail locations** Set the **Due date** as three weeks from the current date. In the comments area, type **I'd like you to look at key mall locations in the San Diego area. Send** the task request.

4. In the **Click here to add a new Task** box, type **Do cost/benefit analysis** In the **Due Date** box, type **two weeks from today** and then press Enter.

5. Create a new task request, and assign the task to **Cristina Mandala**. As the **Subject**, type **Study retailers' response** Set the **Due date** as one month from the current date. In the message area, type **Work with Richard on this. We need to look at the impact this is going to have on our relationships with our key customers. Send** the task request.

6. **Open** the **Do cost/benefit analysis** task, and assign the task to **Hector Guzman**. Type the following message: **Hector, This is**

for our proposed factory outlet store that we discussed at our last staff meeting. Consult with Adriana if you need more input; but I'd like you to get started right away. Alejandra **Send** the task request.

7. Change the **Current View** to **Assignment**. **Print** the **To-Do List** in **Table Style** using the footer **5F_Factory_Outlet_Firstname_ Lastname** Submit the end result to your instructor as directed. Change to **Simple List** view.

8. **Print** the **Task Request: Do cost/benefit analysis** message in **Memo Style** using the footer **5F_Factory_Outlet_Message_ Firstname_Lastname** Submit the end result to your instructor as directed.

9. Delete the contents of the **Outbox**. Delete the contents of the **Tasks** folder. Delete the contents of the **Contacts** folder. Empty the **Deleted Items** folder.

10. From the **Tools** menu, click **Options**, and then click the **Mail Setup tab**. Under **Send/Receive**, select the **Send immediately when connected** check box.

11. In the **Options** dialog box, click **Send/Receive**. In the **Send/Receive Groups** dialog box, under **Setting for group "All Accounts"**, select both **Include this group in send/receive (F9)** check boxes. Select both **Schedule an automatic send/receive** check boxes if this is a default setting on your computer. Click **Close**, and then click **OK**.

12. Display the **Inbox**. From the **File** menu, point to **Page Setup**, and then click **Define Print Styles**. Click **Table Style**, click **Reset**, and then click **OK**. **Reset** the **Memo Style**. **Close** the dialog box, and then **Close** Outlook.

End **You have completed Project 5F**

Content-Based Assessments

Mastering Outlook

Project 5G—Personnel

Objectives: 2. *Respond to Task Assignments;* **3.** *Manage Task Assignments.*

In the following Mastering Outlook project, you will handle Cristina Mandala's replies to task requests. Ms. Mandala's position at El Cuero Specialty Wares includes personnel-related responsibilities—compensation management, performance reviews, and consultant contracts. Alejandra Domene has assigned her several tasks related to these responsibilities. Your completed documents will look similar to the ones shown in Figure 5.61.

> ### For Project 5G, you will need the following file:
>
> o05G_Personnel_Tasks

You will print three files with the following footers:
5G_Personnel_Tasks_Firstname_Lastname
5G_Personnel_Messages_Firstname_Lastname
5G_Personnel_Status_Report_Firstname_Lastname

Figure 5.61

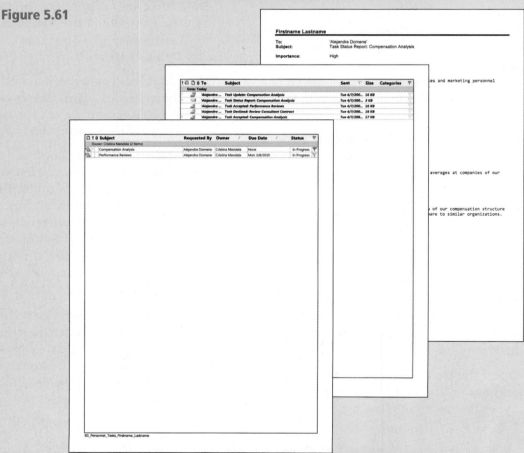

(Project 5G–Personnel continues on the next page)

Content-Based Assessments

(Project 5G–Personnel continued)

1. **Start** Outlook, and display the **Tasks** folder. From the **Tools** menu, display the **Options** dialog box, and then click the **Mail Setup tab**. Under **Send/Receive**, clear the **Send immediately when connected** check box, if necessary. Click the **Send/Receive** button. In the **Send/ Receive Groups** dialog box, under **Setting for group "All Accounts"**, clear both **Include this group in send/receive (F9)** check boxes, if necessary. Clear both **Schedule an automatic send/receive** check boxes, if necessary. Click **Close**, and then click **OK**.

2. From the **File** menu, point to **Open**, and then click **Outlook Data File**. Locate the **o05G_Personnel_Tasks** data file and copy it to the location where you are storing your files for this chapter.

3. With the file **o05G_Personnel_Tasks** selected, click **OK** to open the file.

4. Display the **Tasks** folder, and then, under **My Tasks**, click **Tasks in Personal Folders**. Open the **Compensation analysis** task, **Accept** the task, click **Edit the response before sending**, and then click **OK**.

5. Type the following message: **Alejandra, I plan to research trade publications for recent compensation averages at companies of our size in Southern California. I will update you as I progress. Cristina** Set the **Status** as **In Progress** and the **Priority** to **High**. **Send** the reply.

6. Open the **Review Consultant Contract** task. **Decline** the task and send the following message: **Alejandra, I just spoke with Eduardo. He is putting this project on hold until the beginning of next year. Cristina Send** the reply.

7. Open the **Performance Reviews** task, and **Accept** the task. Edit the response, and

add the comment **Alejandra, I will get going on this right away. I have already received reviews from most of the managers. Cristina** Set the **Status** as **In Progress** and **Start date** as **Today**. **Send** the reply.

8. Open the **Compensation analysis** task. Specify **% Complete** as **50%** and send a status report. Change the **Message format** to **Plain Text**, and in the **Microsoft Office Outlook Compatibility Checker** dialog box, click **Continue**. Type: **Alejandra, So far, my research has shown that we are compensating our sales and marketing personnel along industry lines. I should be done with this by next week. Cristina Send** the status report, and then **Save & Close** the task.

9. Change the **Current View** to **By Person Responsible**. If necessary, click the **expand** button to display all the items in the group. **Print** the **Tasks** list in **Table Style** using the footer **5G_Personnel_ Tasks_Firstname_Lastname** Submit the end result to your instructor as directed.

10. In the **Navigation Pane**, display the **Folder List**. Display the **Outbox**. If necessary, drag the column divider between the **Subject** and **Sent** column headings so that you can read the subjects of each sent item in the **Outbox**. **Print** the **Outbox** in **Table Style** using the footer **5G_Personnel_ Messages_Firstname_Lastname** Submit the end result to your instructor as directed.

11. **Print** the **Task Status Report: Compensation analysis** message in **Memo Style** using the footer **5G_Personnel_Status_ Report_Firstname_Lastname** Submit the end result to your instructor as directed.

12. Delete the contents of the **Outbox**. Delete the contents of the **Deleted Items** folder. At the bottom of the **All Folders** pane, **Close "Personal Folders"**.

(Project 5G–Personnel continues on the next page)

Content-Based Assessments

(Project 5G–Personnel continued)

13. From the **Tools** menu, click **Options**, and then click the **Mail Setup tab**. Under **Send/Receive**, select the **Send immediately when connected** check box.

14. In the **Options** dialog box, click **Send/Receive**. In the **Send/Receive Groups** dialog box, under **Setting for group "All Accounts"**, select both **Include this group in send/receive (F9)** check boxes.

Select both **Schedule an automatic send/receive** check boxes if this is a default setting on your computer. Click **Close**, and then click **OK**.

15. Display the **Define Print Styles** dialog box. **Reset** the **Table Style** and **Memo Style** print styles. **Close** the dialog box, and then **Close** Outlook.

End   You have completed Project 5G _____

chapterfive

Mastering Outlook

Project 5H — Party

Objective: 4. *Use Instant Messaging in Outlook.*

In the following Mastering Outlook project, you and a student partner will conduct an instant message dialogue between Hector Guzman and Cristina Mandala, employees at El Cuero Specialty Wares. Mr. Guzman and Ms. Mandala are planning a birthday surprise party for Michelle Carlton. The party is to take place after work. Hector has an e-mail in his Inbox from Cristina and he wants to add her name to his contacts list in Windows Live Messenger so that he can have a quick chat with her about some last-minute details of the party. You will print the dialogue when you are finished, which will look similar to the one shown in Figure 5.62.

For Project 5H, you will need the following files:

o05H_Party_Inbox_CM
o05H_Party_Inbox_HG

You will print one file with the following footer:
5H_Party_Firstname_Lastname

Figure 5.62

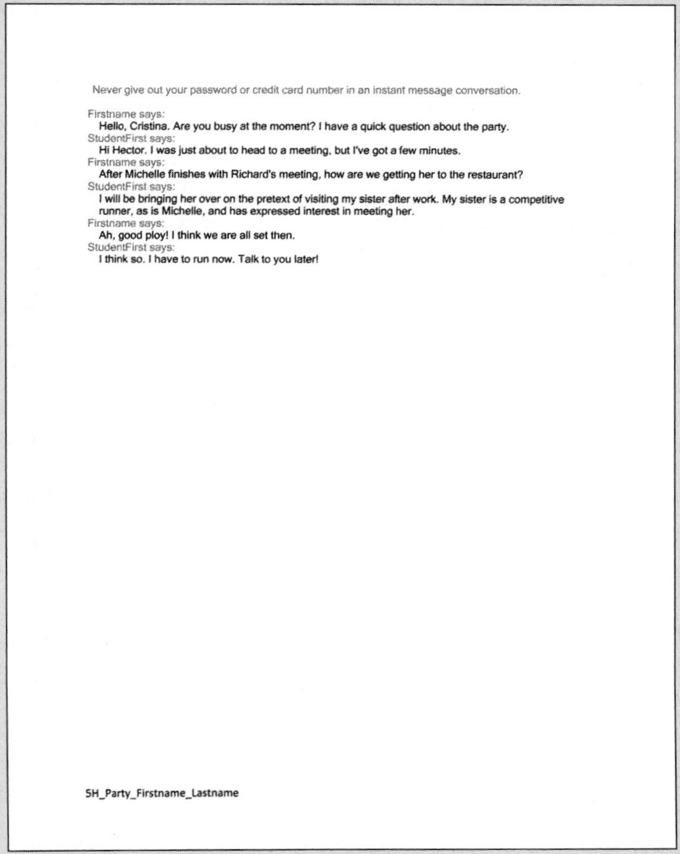

Never give out your password or credit card number in an instant message conversation.

Firstname says:
   Hello, Cristina. Are you busy at the moment? I have a quick question about the party.
StudentFirst says:
   Hi Hector. I was just about to head to a meeting, but I've got a few minutes.
Firstname says:
   After Michelle finishes with Richard's meeting, how are we getting her to the restaurant?
StudentFirst says:
   I will be bringing her over on the pretext of visiting my sister after work. My sister is a competitive runner, as is Michelle, and has expressed interest in meeting her.
Firstname says:
   Ah, good ploy! I think we are all set then.
StudentFirst says:
   I think so. I have to run now. Talk to you later!

5H_Party_Firstname_Lastname

(Project 5H–Party continues on the next page)

Content-Based Assessments

(Project 5H–Party continued)

1. **Start** Windows Live Messenger, and sign in. **Start** Outlook. From the Outlook **Tools** menu, click **Options**, and then click the **Other tab**. Select the options under **Person Names** to enable Outlook to detect your contacts' online status with Windows Live Messenger.

2. Determine with your student partner who will respond as *Hector Guzman* and who will respond as *Cristina Mandala*.

3. *Hector Guzman, Cristina Mandala*: In the **Navigation Pane**, display the **Inbox** folder.

4. *Hector Guzman*: Display the **Import and Export Wizard** dialog box, and then, using the techniques you have practiced, import **o05H_Party_Inbox_HG** into the **Inbox** folder.

   Cristina Mandala: Display the **Import and Export Wizard** dialog box, and then, using the techniques you have practiced, import **o05H_Party_Inbox_CM** into the **Inbox** folder.

5. *Hector Guzman*: Using techniques you have practiced, add **Cristina Mandala** to your Outlook contacts. In the **Cristina Mandala - Contact** form, in the **IM Address box**, type the Windows Live ID of your student partner, and then **Save & Close** the contact.

   Cristina Mandala: Using techniques you have practiced, add **Hector Guzman** to your Outlook contacts. In the **Hector Guzman - Contact** form, in the **IM Address** box, type the Windows Live ID of your student partner, and then **Save & Close** the contact.

6. *Hector Guzman*: In the **Reading Pane**, right-click the e-mail address for **Cristina Mandala**, and then click **Add to Instant Messaging Contacts**. In the **Add a Contact** dialog box, click **Add contact**.

(Project 5H–Party continues on the next page)

Cristina Mandala: On the taskbar, notice that a second **Windows Live Messenger** button displays. On the taskbar, click the rightmost **Windows Live Messenger** button to bring the window to the front of the desktop. In the **Windows Live Messenger** dialog box, click **OK**.

7. *Hector Guzman*: In the **Windows Live Messenger** window, right-click on your student partner's name, and then click **Send an Instant Message**. In the **Conversation** window, type **Hello, Cristina. Are you busy at the moment? I have a quick question about the party. Send** the message.

   Cristina Mandala: On the taskbar, click the blinking orange **Windows Live Messenger** button to maximize the **Conversation** window. In the **Conversation** window, type **Hi Hector. I was just about to head to a meeting, but I've got a few minutes. Send** the message.

8. *Hector Guzman*: In the **Conversation** window, type **After Michelle finishes with Richard's meeting, how are we getting her to the restaurant? Send** the message.

   Cristina Mandala: In the **Conversation** window, type **I will be bringing her over on the pretext of meeting my sister after work. My sister is a competitive runner, as is Michelle, and has expressed interest in meeting her. Send** the message.

9. *Hector Guzman*: In the **Conversation** window, type **Ah, good ploy! I think we're all set then. Send** the message.

   Cristina Mandala: In the **Conversation** window, type **I think so. I have to run now. Talk to you later! and Send**.

10. With the **Conversation** window still open, click the **Show menu** button, click **File**, and then click **Save As**. In the **Save As**

Content-Based Assessments

(Project 5H–Party continued)

dialog box, navigate to the location where you are storing your files. In the **File name** box, type **5H_Party_Firstname_ Lastname** Click **Save**.

11. On the computer you are using, navigate to the location where you are storing your files. Open **5H_Party_Firstname_ Lastname** in Microsoft Word.

12. On the Ribbon, click the **Insert tab**, and then click **Footer**. On the drop-down list, click **Edit Footer**. In the footer, type **5H_Party_Firstname_Lastname** On the Ribbon, click **Close Header and Footer**.

13. Click the **Office** button, click **Print**, and then click **OK** to print the document. Submit the end result to your instructor as directed. **Close** the Word document, saving changes, and then **Close** Word.

14. **Close** the **Conversation** window. In the **Windows Live Messenger** window, right-click your student partner's name, click **Delete contact**, and then click **Yes**. Sign out of Windows Live Messenger, and then **Close** the program window.

15. Delete the contents of the **Inbox**. Delete the contents of the **Contacts** folder. Delete the contents of the **Deleted Items** folder. From the Outlook **Tools** menu, click **Options**, and then click the **Other tab**. Under **Person Names**, clear the **Display online status next to a person name** and **Display online status in the To and Cc fields only when mouse pointer rests on a person name** check boxes if this is a default setting on your computer. Click **OK**. **Close** Outlook.

 You have completed Project 5H ⸻⸻⸻⸻⸻

Mastering Outlook

Project 5I — Sales Calls

Objectives: 1. *Assign Tasks;* **2.** *Respond to Task Assignments;* **3.** *Manage Task Assignments.*

In the following Mastering Outlook project, you will manage the task assignments for Javier Catano. Mr. Catano works in Sales and Marketing at El Cuero Specialty Wares. He reports to Richard Kelly, who is Vice President of Marketing. Richard has assigned Javier a number of tasks related to upcoming sales calls with some of El Cuero's key customers. Javier, in turn, has assigned some tasks to Cristina Mandala and Jorge Vargas, who work with him in Sales and Marketing. Your completed documents will look similar to the ones shown in Figure 5.63.

For Project 5I, you will need the following files:

o05I_Sales_Calls_Contacts
o05I_Sales_Calls_Tasks

You will print four files with the following footers:
5I_Sales_Calls_Assigned_Firstname_Lastname
5I_Sales_Calls_Received_Firstname_Lastname
5I_Sales_Calls_Outbox_Firstname_Lastname
5I_Sales_Calls_Message_Firstname_Lastname

Figure 5.63

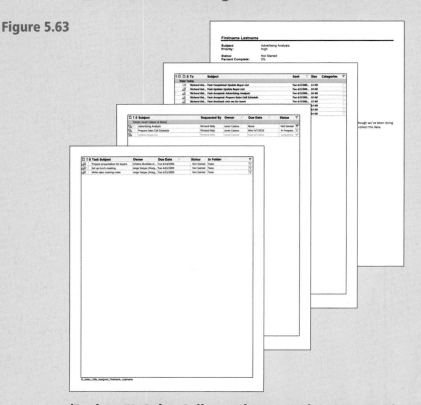

(Project 5I–Sales Calls continues on the next page)

Content-Based Assessments

(Project 5I–Sales Calls continued)

1. **Start** Outlook. From the **Tools** menu, display the **Options** dialog box, and click the **Mail Setup tab**. Under **Send/Receive**, clear the **Send immediately when connected** check box, if necessary. Click the **Send/Receive** button. In the **Send/Receive Groups** dialog box, under **Setting for group "All Accounts"**, clear both **Include this group in send/receive (F9)** check boxes, if necessary. Clear both **Schedule an automatic send/receive** check boxes, if necessary. Click **Close**, and then click **OK**.

2. Display the **Contacts** folder, and then, using the techniques you have practiced, import **o05I_Sales_Calls_Contacts** into the **Contacts** folder.

3. Create a new task request, and assign the task to **Cristina Mandala**. As the **Subject**, type **Prepare presentation for buyers** Set the **Due date** as one week from the current date. In the message area, type **Put together the materials for our Denver sales calls. Send** the request.

4. Create a new task request, assigning the task to **Jorge Vargas**. As the **Subject**, type **Set up lunch meeting** Set the **Due date** as two weeks from the current date. In the comments area, type **Set up lunch meeting with the Rodeo Boulevard buyers.** Set the **Priority** to **High**, and then send the request.

5. Create a new task request, assigning the task to **Jorge Vargas**. As the **Subject**, type **Write sales meeting notes** Set the **Due date** as two weeks from the current date. In the comments area, type **Summarize our meeting with Ted Johnson at Leather Works, Inc.** and then send the request.

6. Change the **Current View** to **Assignment**. **Print** the To-Do List in **Table Style** using the footer **5I_Sales_Calls_Assigned_Firstname_**

Lastname Submit the end result to your instructor as directed.

7. Switch to **Simple List** view. From the **File** menu, point to **Open**, and click **Outlook Data File**. Navigate to your student files, and **Copy** the file **o05I_Sales_Calls_Tasks** to the location where you are storing your files for this chapter, and **Paste** the copied file to that location. Click **OK** to open the file.

8. Click **Tasks in Personal Folders**. Open the **Join me for lunch** task. Decline the task, and edit the response before sending with the message: **Richard, I will be on vacation that day. Javier Send** the reply.

9. **Open** the **Prepare Sales Call Schedule** task, accept the task, and add the following response before sending: **Richard, I can get this to you by the end of the day. Javier** Set the **Status** as **In Progress** and **Start date** as **Today**. **Send** the reply.

10. **Open** and accept the **Advertising Analysis** task, and add the following message: **Richard, I may ask Cristina to help me with this. We will make this a high priority item. Javier** Set the **Priority** as **High**, and send the reply.

11. Accept the **Update Buyer List** task, and then mark it as complete. Display the task list in **By Person Responsible** view. **Print** the Tasks list in **Table Style** using the footer **5I_Sales_Calls_Received_Firstname_Lastname** Submit the end result to your instructor as directed. Display the task list in **Simple List** view.

12. In the **Navigation Pane**, display the **Outbox**. Make certain the subject for each item is completely visible. **Print** the Outbox in **Table Style** using the footer **5I_Sales_Calls_Outbox_Firstname_Lastname**

(Project 5I–Sales Calls continues on the next page)

Content-Based Assessments

(Project 5I–Sales Calls continued)

Submit the end result to your instructor as directed.

13. Select the **Task Accepted: Advertising Analysis** message. **Print** the message in **Memo Style** using the footer 5I_Sales_Calls_Message_Firstname_Lastname Submit the end result to your instructor as directed.

14. Display the **Folder List**. Delete the contents of the **Outbox** and **Contacts** folders. Display the **Tasks** folder, and then, under **My Tasks**, click **Tasks** to display the tasks you assigned to others. Delete the Tasks list. Display **Tasks in Personal Folders**, and delete the tasks without declining or marking any as completed. Delete the contents of the **Deleted Items** folder.

15. Display the **Folder List**. At the bottom of the list, right-click the **Personal Folders**

data file. From the shortcut menu, click **Close "Personal Folders"**.

16. From the **Tools** menu, click **Options**, and then click the **Mail Setup tab**. Under **Send/Receive**, select the **Send immediately when connected** check box.

17. In the **Options** dialog box, click **Send/Receive**. In the **Send/Receive Groups** dialog box, under **Setting for group "All Accounts"**, select both **Include this group in send/receive (F9)** check boxes. Select both **Schedule an automatic send/receive** check boxes if this is a default setting on your computer. Click **Close**, and then click **OK**. Reset the Table Style and Memo Style print styles. **Close** Outlook.

End   You have completed Project 5I

Mastering Outlook

Project 5J — Expenses

Objective: 4. *Use Instant Messaging in Outlook.*

In the following Mastering Outlook project, you and a student partner will conduct an instant message dialogue between Richard Kelly and Javier Catano, using your own Windows Live accounts. Mr. Catano at El Cuero Specialty Wares has begun traveling extensively for the company. He must fill out weekly expense reports, which he submits to his supervisor, Mr. Kelly, who is Vice President of Marketing. He has a question about his report that he needs Richard to answer, and he would like to have a quick dialogue with him about the issue. You will print the dialogue when you are finished. If you are playing the role of Richard Kelly, your solution will look similar to the document shown in Figure 5.64. If you are playing the role of Javier Catano, your solution will differ slightly.

For Project 5J, you will need the following files:

o05J_Expenses_Inbox_JC
o05J_Expenses_Inbox_RK
o05J_Expenses

You will print one file with the following footer:
5J_Expenses_Firstname_Lastname

Figure 5.64

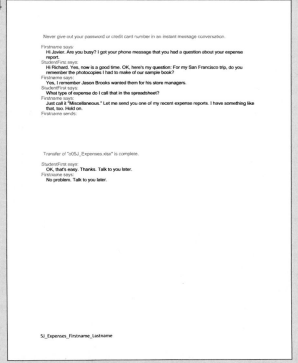

(Project 5J–Expenses continues on the next page)

(Project 5J–Expenses continued)

1. **Start** Windows Live Messenger, and sign in. **Start** Outlook. From the Outlook **Tools** menu, click **Options**, and then click the **Other tab**. Select the options under **Person Names** to enable Outlook to detect your contacts' online status with Windows Live Messenger.

2. Determine with your student partner who will respond as *Richard Kelly* and who will respond as *Javier Catano*.

3. *Richard Kelly*: In the **Navigation Pane**, display the **Inbox** folder. Display the **Import and Export Wizard** dialog box, and then, using the techniques you have practiced, import **o05J_Expenses_Inbox_RK** into the **Inbox** folder.

   Javier Catano: In the **Navigation Pane**, click the **Inbox**. Display the **Import and Export Wizard** dialog box, and then, using the techniques you have practiced, import **o05J_Expenses_Inbox_JC** into the **Inbox** folder.

4. *Richard Kelly*: Using techniques you have practiced, add **Javier Catano** to your Outlook contacts. In the **Javier Catano - Contact** form, in the **IM Address box**, type the Windows Live ID of your student partner, and then **Save & Close** the contact.

   Javier Catano: Using techniques you have practiced, add **Richard Kelly** to your Outlook contacts. In the **Richard Kelly - Contact** form, in the **IM Address** box, type the Windows Live ID of your student partner, and then **Save & Close** the contact.

5. *Richard Kelly*: Right-click the e-mail address for **Javier Catano**, and then click **Add to Instant Messaging Contacts**. In the **Add a Contact** dialog box, click **Add contact**.

   Javier Catano: In the taskbar, click the right-most **Windows Live Messenger**

button to maximize the window. In the **Windows Live Messenger** dialog box, click **OK**.

6. *Richard Kelly*: Display the Windows Live Messenger window and send an instant message to **Javier Catano**. In the **Conversation** window, type **Hi Javier. Are you busy? I got your phone message that you had a question about your expense report. Send** the message.

   Javier Catano: On the Windows taskbar, click the blinking orange **Windows Live Messenger** icon to maximize the **Conversation** window. In the **Conversation** window, type **Hi Richard. Yes, now is a good time. OK, here's my question: For my San Francisco trip, do you remember the photocopies I had to make of our sample book? Send** the message.

7. *Richard Kelly*: In the **Conversation** window, type **Yes, I remember Jason Brooks wanted them for his store managers. Send**.

   Javier Catano: In the **Conversation** window, type **What type of expense do I call that in the spreadsheet? Send**.

8. *Richard Kelly*: Type **Just call it "Miscellaneous." Let me send you one of my recent expense reports. I have something like that, too. Hold on. Send** the message. Locate the file **o05J_Expenses**, and **Send** the file.

   Javier Catano: In the **Conversation** window, **Accept** the received file **o05J_Expenses**, and then type **OK, that's easy. Thanks. Talk to you later. Send**.

9. *Richard Kelly*: Type **No problem. Talk to you later. Send**.

10. With the **Conversation** window still open, click the **Show menu** button, click **File**,

(Project 5J–Expenses continues on the next page)

Content-Based Assessments

(Project 5J–Expenses continued)

and then click **Save As**. Navigate to the location where you are storing your files. In the **File name** box, type **5J_Expenses_Firstname_Lastname** Click **Save**.

11. On the computer you are using, navigate to the location where you are storing your files. Open **5J_Expenses_Firstname_Lastname** in Microsoft Word.

12. On the Ribbon, click the **Insert tab**, and then click **Footer**. In the **Footer** box, type **5J_Expenses_Firstname_Lastname** On the Ribbon, click **Close Header and Footer**.

13. Click the **Office** button, click **Print**, and then click **OK**. Submit the end result to your instructor as directed. **Close** the Word document, saving changes, and then **Close** Word.

14. **Close** the **Conversation** window. In the **Windows Live Messenger** window, right-click your partner's name, and delete the contact. Sign out of Windows Live Messenger, and then **Close** the program.

15. Delete the contents of the **Inbox**. Delete the contents of the **Contacts** folder. Delete the contents of the **Deleted Items** folder. From the Outlook **Tools** menu, click **Options**, and then click the **Other tab**. Under **Person Names**, clear the **Display online status next to a person name** and **Display online status in the To and Cc fields only when mouse pointer rests on a person name** check boxes if this is a default setting on your computer. Click **OK**. **Close** Outlook.

End **You have completed Project 5J** ————————————————————

Outcomes-Based Assessments

Rubric

The following outcomes-based assessments are *open-ended assessments*. That is, there is no specific correct result; your result will depend on your approach to the information provided. Make *Professional Quality* your goal. Use the following scoring rubric to guide you in *how* to approach the problem and then to evaluate *how well* your approach solves the problem.

The *criteria*—Software Mastery, Content, Format and Layout, and Process—represent the knowledge and skills you have gained that you can apply to solving the problem. The *levels of performance*—Professional Quality, Approaching Professional Quality, or Needs Quality Improvement—help you and your instructor evaluate your result.

	Your completed project is of Professional Quality if you:	Your completed project is Approaching Professional Quality if you:	Your completed project Needs Quality Improvements if you:
1-Software Mastery	Choose and apply the most appropriate skills, tools, and features and identify efficient methods to solve the problem.	Choose and apply some appropriate skills, tools, and features, but not in the most efficient manner.	Choose inappropriate skills, tools, or features, or are inefficient in solving the problem.
2-Content	Construct a solution that is clear and well organized, contains content that is accurate, appropriate to the audience and purpose, and is complete. Provide a solution that contains no errors of spelling, grammar, or style.	Construct a solution in which some components are unclear, poorly organized, inconsistent, or incomplete. Misjudge the needs of the audience. Have some errors in spelling, grammar, or style, but the errors do not detract from comprehension.	Construct a solution that is unclear, incomplete, or poorly organized; contains some inaccurate or inappropriate content; or contains many errors of spelling, grammar, or style. Do not solve the problem.
3-Format and Layout	Format and arrange all elements to communicate information and ideas, clarify function, illustrate relationships, and indicate relative importance.	Apply appropriate format and layout features to some elements, but not others. Overuse features, causing minor distraction.	Apply format and layout that does not communicate information or ideas clearly. Do not use format and layout features to clarify function, illustrate relationships, or indicate relative importance. Use available features excessively, causing distraction.
4-Process	Use an organized approach that integrates planning, development, self-assessment, revision, and reflection.	Demonstrate an organized approach in some areas, but not others; or, use an insufficient process of organization throughout.	Do not use an organized approach to solve the problem.

Outlook

chapter five

Problem Solving

Project 5K — Company Picnic

Objectives: 1. *Assign Tasks;* **3.** *Manage Task Assignments.*

For Project 5K, you will need the following file:

o05K_Company_Picnic_Contacts

You will print three files with the following footers:
5K_Company_Picnic_Tasks_Firstname_Lastname
5K_Company_Picnic_Outbox_Firstname_Lastname
5K_Company_Picnic_Message_Firstname_Lastname

The San Diego office of El Cuero Specialty Wares has an annual company picnic. This year, Michelle Carlton has been asked to make the plans, and she has been assigning tasks for the event to her coworkers. In this project, you will handle the task assignments for Ms. Carlton.
Start Outlook, and configure the Send/Receive options to place your sent messages in the Outbox. Import the file **o05K_Company_Picnic_Contacts** to your Contacts folder. Create at least six picnic-related tasks—for example, games, food, park site, and so on. Have Ms. Carlton as the responsible party for a few of the tasks, and assign the rest to different individuals in your Contacts list as task requests. Vary the details and dates of the tasks. From one of the task requests, create an unassigned copy of the task. Display the Tasks list in several different views. Print the Tasks list, using an appropriate view and print style, with the footer **5K_Company_Picnic_Tasks_Firstname_Lastname**. Print your Outbox, using an appropriate print style with the footer **5K_Company_Picnic_Outbox_Firstname_Lastname** Print one of the task request messages using an appropriate print style with the footer **5K_Company_Picnic_Message_Firstname_Lastname**. Submit the end results to your instructor as directed. Restore all the folder views and print styles to their default settings, and empty all the folders you used, including the Deleted Items folder. Restore the Send/Receive options to their default settings.

End **You have completed Project 5K** ———————

Outcomes-Based Assessments

Problem Solving

Project 5L — Off Site Meeting

Objective: 4. *Use Instant Messaging in Outlook.*

For Project 5L, you will need the following files:

o05L_Off_Site_Meeting_Inbox_AD
o05L_Off_Site_Meeting_Inbox_ET

You will print two files with the following footers:
5L_Off_Site_Meeting_Firstname_Lastname
5L_Off_Site_Meeting_Contact_Firstname_Lastname

The President of El Cuero Specialty Wares, Alejandra Domene, would like to have her next senior managers meeting at a location outside the company offices. She has asked Eduardo Terat to organize this for her. He has questions about this event that he needs Alejandra to answer, and he would like to have a quick instant message dialogue with her about these questions. In this project, you and a student partner will conduct an instant message dialogue between Alejandra and Eduardo, using your own Windows Live accounts.

Be sure you are online and connected to the Internet. Start Windows Live Messenger and sign in. Start Outlook. Determine with your student partner who will respond for *Alejandra Domene* and who will respond as *Eduardo Terat*. Import messages into your Inbox—**o05L_Off_Site_Meeting_Inbox_AD** for *Alejandra* and **o05L_Off_Site_Meeting_Inbox_ET** for *Eduardo*. Use the Inbox messages to add each other's names to your Outlook and Windows Live Messenger contact lists, using your own Windows Live IDs as the e-mail addresses of the contacts.

Initiate an instant message dialogue with your partner. Discuss local hotels, conference centers, or other locations that you think might be suitable for a meeting. Mention any that you know personally. Save the dialogue and then print the dialogue using the footer **5L_Off_Site_Meeting_Firstname_Lastname**. Close Windows Live Messenger. Print the contact you added to your Contacts list in an appropriate print style using the footer **5L_Off_Site_Meeting_Contact_Firstname_Lastname**. Submit the end results to your instructor as directed. Empty the folders and reset any print styles you used.

End **You have completed Project 5L** ——————————

Outcomes-Based Assessments

Problem Solving

Project 5M—Volleyball

Objective: 2. Respond to Task Assignments; **3.** Manage Task Assignments.

> ### For Project 5M, you will need the following file:
>
> o05M_Volleyball_Tasks
>
> **You will print three files with the following footers:**
> **5M_Volleyball_Tasks_Firstname_Lastname**
> **5M_Volleyball_Outbox_Firstname_Lastname**
> **5M_Volleyball_Message_Firstname_Lastname**

A group of El Cuero Specialty Wares employees participate in an adult volleyball league for men and women. Adriana Ramos usually organizes the group's practices, but this year she has asked Hector Guzman to help her set up the practice times and location. In this project, you will handle the task assignments Mr. Guzman receives from Ms. Ramos. Start Outlook, and configure the Send/Receive options to place your sent messages in the Outbox. Using the techniques you have practiced in the chapter, create your own copy of the file **o05M_Volleyball_Tasks** in the location you use to store your files, and then open this file. Display the **Tasks in Personal Folders**, and examine the tasks you have been assigned. Respond to the task requests, accepting at least one task. Include messages with your responses that explain Mr. Guzman's reasons for accepting or rejecting the task. In the same folder, create some additional tasks for Mr. Guzman related to volleyball practices for the company team. Vary the details and the dates.

Display the Tasks list in several different views. Print the Tasks list in an appropriate view and print style with the footer **5M_Volleyball_Tasks_Firstname_Lastname**. Print the entire Outbox in an appropriate print style with the footer **5M_Volleyball_Outbox_Firstname_Lastname**. Print one of the sent messages in an appropriate style with the footer **5M_Volleyball_Message_Firstname_Lastname**. Submit the end results to your instructor as directed. Empty all folders, restore all views to their default settings, and reset any print styles you used. Close the Tasks in Personal Folders. Close Personal Folders at the bottom of the All Folders list. Restore the Send/Receive options to their default settings.

End **You have completed Project 5M**——————————

Outcomes-Based Assessments

GO! with Help

Project 5N — *GO!* with Help

Numerous organizations use a firewall with their networks. A firewall is a software system designed to prevent unauthorized access to or from a private network. Normally, you can use Windows Live Messenger from behind a firewall. However, the firewall may cause some limitations in functionality. You may be able to change your Windows Live Messenger settings to increase the functionality of the program. You can use Help in Windows Live Messenger to tell you more.

1. Be sure you are online and connected to the Internet. **Start** Windows Live Messenger. On the Windows Live Messenger menu bar, click **Help**, and then click **Help Topics** to display a list of Windows Live Messenger help topics.

2. In the **Search for** box, type **firewall** and press Enter. Click on the topic related to a firewall and read the information. When you have finished reading, **Close** the Windows Live Help window, and **Close** Windows Live Messenger.

End You have completed Project 5N ——————————

chaptersix

Organizing and Managing Outlook Information

OBJECTIVES

At the end of this chapter you will able to:

1. Manage Mail Folders
2. Modify the Master Category List
3. Use Notes
4. Archive Outlook Information
5. Recover and Export Outlook Information

OUTCOMES

Mastering these objectives will enable you to:

PROJECT 6A
Manage Outlook Information

Southland Gardens

With gardening booming as a hobby, Southland Media, a TV production company headquartered in Irvine, California, saw a need for practical and entertaining information on the subject. *Southland Gardens* was developed especially for the year-round gardener in southern California. The show features experts on vegetable and flower gardening, landscape design, projects for children, and tours of historical and notable gardens. The company also offers a companion Web site where viewers can get more information about show segments, purchase supplies, and e-mail guests of the show.

Managing and Working with Outlook Information

Outlook has several tools that help you keep your information organized. You can create folders for specific types of e-mail and have messages placed in those folders. If you use categories to organize your information, you can create your own category names to add to Outlook's preset list of categories. Outlook's Notes component is also a convenient way to keep track of pieces of information you might need later. For long-term storage, Outlook enables you to store older information either manually or automatically. You can also export and recover Outlook information.

Project 6A **Garden Show**

In Activities 6.1 through 6.20, you will create e-mail folders and use various tools to organize the e-mail received by Elizabeth Robinson, who is cohost of Southland Media's television program, *Southland Gardens*. You will create new categories to assign to Outlook items and use Outlook's Notes feature to store information for a short time. You will print notes and e-mail folders, which will look similar to the ones shown in Figure 6.1.

For Project 6A, you will need the following file:

o06A_Garden_Show_Inbox

You will print three files with the following footers:
6A_Garden_Show_Notes_Firstname_Lastname
6A_Garden_Show_Exported_Firstname_Lastname
6A_Garden_Show_Screens_Firstname_Lastname

Figure 6.1

Objective 1
Manage Mail Folders

To organize e-mail information within Outlook, you can create e-mail folders and rename existing folders and then move messages from one folder to another. You can have Outlook move incoming e-mail into specific folders using *rules*, which are one or more actions taken on e-mail messages that meet certain conditions, along with any exceptions to those conditions. For example, you might have a rule to move all messages you receive from your supervisor into a specific folder.

Outlook also enables you to screen your e-mail messages, sorting legitimate messages from unwanted and junk e-mail. You can also control which messages you want to display in an e-mail folder.

Alert!

Starting Project 6A

It is recommended that you schedule enough time to complete this project in one working session. Allow approximately one and one-half hours.

Activity 6.1 Creating a Mail Folder

When you create a mail folder, the folder is typically a subfolder of the Inbox folder. You can view its contents like any other Outlook folder. In this activity, you will create a mail folder for Elizabeth Robinson's Southland Media messages.

1 Determine the location where you will store your projects for this chapter, for example, on a USB flash drive connected to your computer or another drive location designated by your instructor or lab coordinator.

2 **Start** Outlook. From the **Navigation Pane**, display the **Folder List** , and then display the **Inbox** folder. Delete any existing messages in the **Inbox**.

3 From the **File** menu, point to **New**, and then click **Folder**. In the **Create New Folder** dialog box, in the **Name** box, type **Southland Gardens**

4 Under **Select where to place the folder**, click **Inbox**. Be sure the **Folder contains** box displays *Mail and Post Items*. Compare your screen with Figure 6.2.

You must specify the type of information a new folder will contain. Because the Inbox was selected when you opened the Create New Folder dialog box, Outlook sets the new folder to contain *Mail and Post Items*.

Figure 6.2

New folder name
specified

Create New Folder
dialog box

Outlook sets the
folder to contain *Mail*
and Post Items

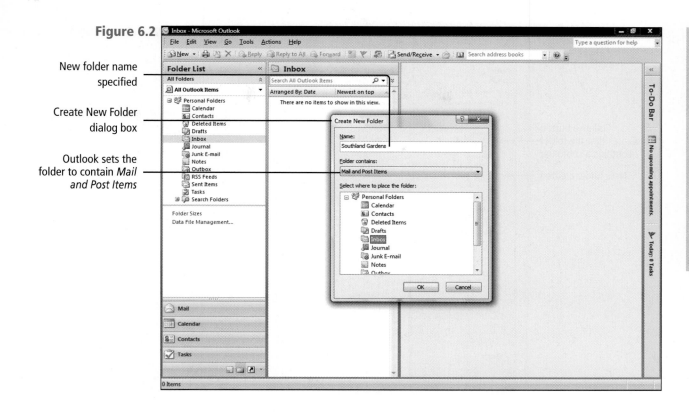

5 In the **Create New Folder** dialog box, click **OK** to create the new folder.

The Southland Gardens folder is a subfolder of the Inbox. An expand (+) or collapse (–) button displays next to the Inbox, indicating that the Inbox folder contains a subfolder. Recall that clicking these buttons shows or hides information in the folder.

Alert!

Does your screen show additional Inbox and Deleted Items folders?

Depending on the configuration of your computer, in addition to the new Southland Gardens subfolder, your Folder List may show additional Inbox, Deleted Items, and other subfolders under your default Inbox folder. Do not confuse these with the default folders of these names under Personal Folders. They will likely contain no data. In this instruction, all references to *Inbox* and *Deleted Items* refer to the default Inbox and Deleted Items folders.

6 Be sure the **Inbox** folder is expanded; if necessary, click the **Expand** button (+) to display the **Southland Gardens** folder. Compare your screen with Figure 6.3.

Activity 6.2 Renaming a Folder and Importing Messages

You can rename a folder in the same manner as you rename a file. Renaming a folder is useful when the contents or purpose of the folder changes and you want the folder name to reflect the kinds of items

Figure 6.3

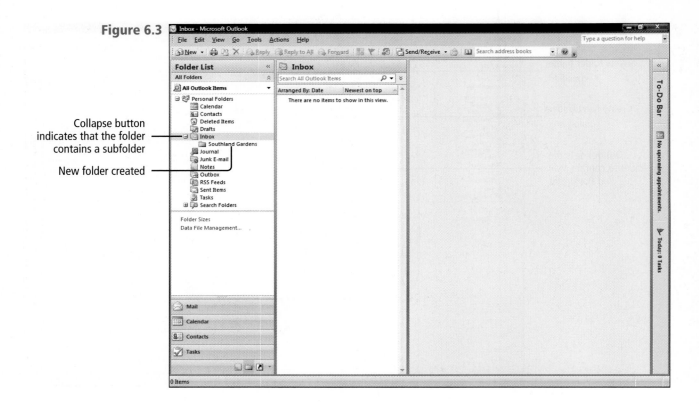

Collapse button indicates that the folder contains a subfolder

New folder created

stored in the folder. In this activity, you will edit the Southland Gardens folder name and then import some messages into your Inbox for Elizabeth Robinson, the cohost of Southland Media's *Southland Gardens* television program.

1 In the **Navigation Pane**, click the **Southland Gardens** folder to select and open it. In the **Folder List**, point to the folder name, right-click to display the shortcut menu, and then click **Rename "Southland Gardens"**. Compare your screen with Figure 6.4.

An outline box surrounds *Southland Gardens*, indicating that the name can be edited.

Figure 6.4

Southland Gardens
folder selected

Outline box indicates
that the folder name
can be edited

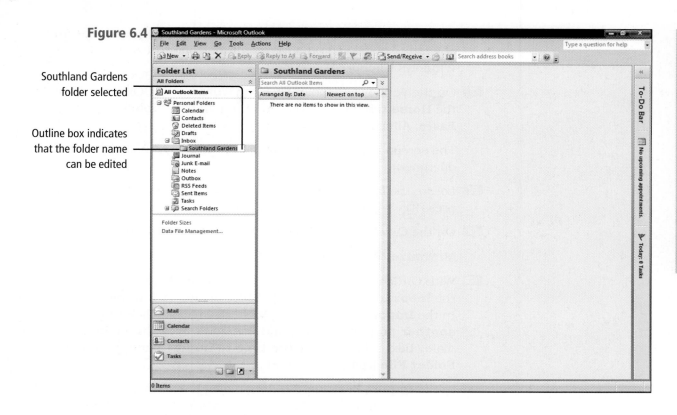

2 Type **Southland** and then press Enter to rename the folder.

3 On the Windows taskbar, click the **Start** button 🌐. In the displayed **Start** menu, locate the **Microsoft Office Word 2007** program. If

necessary, **Maximize** 🔲 the Word window.

The Word program might be located under *All Programs* or *Microsoft Office* or at the top of the Start menu.

4 On the Ribbon, click the **Office** button 🔵, and then click **Save As**. In the **Save As** dialog box, navigate to the location where you are storing your files. In the **File name** box, type **6A_Garden_Show_Screens_ Firstname_Lastname** and then click **Save**.

5 On the Ribbon, click the **Insert tab**, and then click **Footer**. In the drop down list, click **Edit Footer**, and then type **6A_Garden_Show_ Screens_Firstname_Lastname** On the Ribbon, in the **Close group**, click

Close Header and Footer. **Minimize** 🔲 Word.

6 With the **Outlook** window displayed, press PrtScr, located in the upper right area of your keyboard. The key may be labeled in an abbreviated format, such as PrtScr.

Window's **Print Screen** feature creates a **screen capture**—an image of what is displayed on your monitor—and stores that image on the Windows Clipboard.

7 On the Windows taskbar, click the **Word** button. On the Ribbon, click the **Home tab** if necessary, and then, in the **Clipboard group**, click **Paste**. Alternatively press Ctrl PrtScr + V.

The screen capture of your Outlook window is inserted in the document.

8 Locate the insertion point, at the bottom right of the graphic, and press Ctrl + Enter to create a new page.

9 On the Quick Access Toolbar, click the **Save** button 💾, and then **Minimize** ▭ Word.

10 With Outlook displayed, in the **Navigation Pane Folder List**, click the **Inbox** to select it. From the **File** menu, click **Import and Export**. In the **Import and Export Wizard** dialog box, click **Import from another program or file**, and then click **Next**. In the **Import a File** dialog box, under **Select file type to import from**, click **Personal Folder File (.pst)**. Click **Next**.

11 In the **Import Personal Folders** dialog box, navigate to your student files, locate and click **o06A_Garden_Show_Inbox**, and then click **Open**. In the **Import Personal Folders** dialog box, click **Next**.

The Import Personal Folders dialog box displays. The data file contains items in the Inbox and Deleted Items folders. To import all data, the information from both folders, *Personal Folders* is selected.

12 In the **Import Personal Folders** dialog box, with **Personal Folders** selected, click **Finish**. If a Translation Warning dialog box displays, click OK. Compare your screen with Figure 6.5.

Figure 6.5

Group indicates the date of the messages—yours may differ

Six new messages

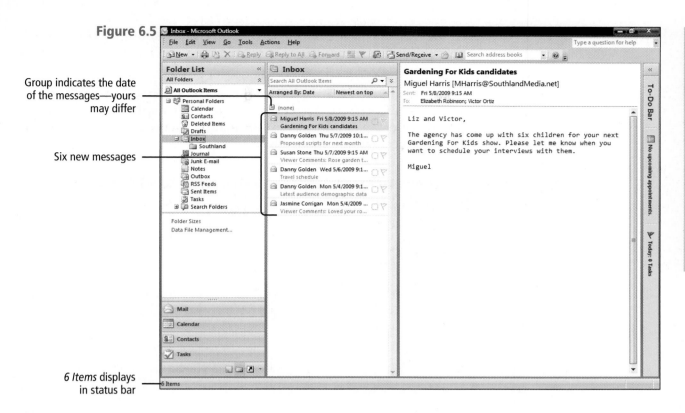

6 Items displays in status bar

Activity 6.3 Creating a POP3 Account

You receive e-mail service in Outlook by configuring an e-mail account using the Add New E-mail Account wizard. You can create several e-mail accounts, and Outlook will retrieve your messages from all of them. Outlook supports several types of e-mail accounts, including Microsoft Exchange Server and POP3 accounts. ***Microsoft Exchange Server*** functions as an e-mail server for a business or organization. When you set up Outlook to receive e-mail for a home account, the most common account type is a POP3 account. ***POP3*** is a common protocol that is used to retrieve e-mail messages from an Internet e-mail server. To set up an e-mail account, you use information provided to you by an administrator or your Internet Service Provider.

Depending on your network and instructional environment, Outlook might not be configured with any e-mail accounts on your computer. Some Outlook features are not available unless Outlook has been configured with an e-mail account. In this activity, to ensure that you have an e-mail account, and to practice setting up Outlook for a home account, you will set up a fictitious POP3 account.

1 From the **Tools** menu, click **Account Settings**.

2 In the **Account Settings** dialog box, with the **E-mail tab** selected, click the **New...** button [New...].

The **Add New E-mail Account** wizard is displayed.

3 In the **Add New E-mail Account** wizard, in the **Choose E-mail Service** screen, click **Microsoft Exchange**, **POP3**, **IMAP**, or **HTTP** to select a service, if necessary. Click **Next**.

4 In the **Auto Account Setup** screen, select the **Manually configure server setting or additional server types** check box, and then compare your screen with Figure 6.6.

Because you are creating a fictitious account for this instruction, you must create your account server settings manually. In a real-life situation, using actual server information, the wizard can configure your connection automatically.

Figure 6.6

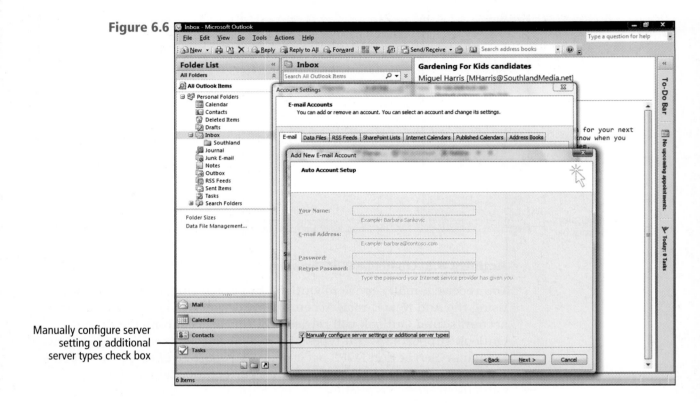

Manually configure server setting or additional server types check box

5 Click **Next**. In the **Choose E-mail Service** screen, click **Internet E-mail** to select it if necessary, and then click **Next**.

The Add New E-mail Account wizard displays the settings for an Internet E-mail (POP3) account. These settings must be completed to create your account. When setting up a home account, your Internet Service Provider supplies you with the Incoming and Outgoing e-mail server information. The name and e-mail address you type in the Your Name and E-mail Address boxes display in the messages you send.

6 With the **Internet E-mail Settings** screen displayed, in the **Your Name** box, using your own name, type **Firstname Lastname** and press [Tab]. In the **E-mail Address** box, type **Firstname_Lastname@GOMAIL.com** and press [Tab] **two** times.

7 In the **Incoming mail server (POP3)** box, type **GOMAIL.com** and press [Tab]. In the **Outgoing mail server (SMTP)** box type **PHMAIL.com** and press [Tab] **two** times.

8 In the **Password** box, type **123456** Your password will display as asterisks. Compare your screen with Figure 6.7.

Add New E-mail Account wizard, Internet
E-mail Settings (POP3)

Figure 6.7

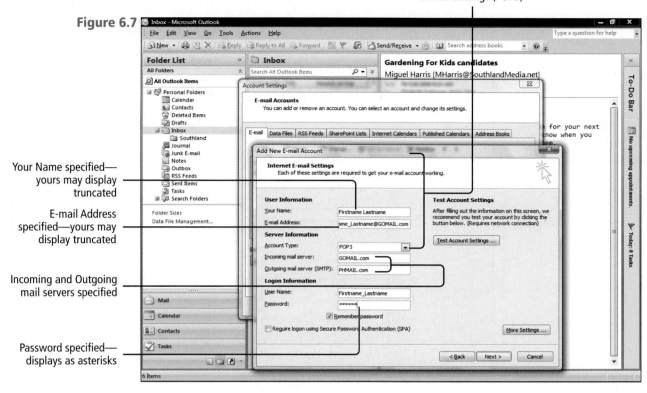

Your Name specified—
yours may display
truncated

E-mail Address
specified—yours may
display truncated

Incoming and Outgoing
mail servers specified

Password specified—
displays as asterisks

Note — Testing Your Account Settings

When setting up a new e-mail account, it is good practice to click the Test Account Settings command button before clicking Next to ensure the specified settings are correct. If the account information is valid, you will receive a sample e-mail message to your Inbox. It is *not* necessary to do this in this instruction because you are using fictitious server information.

9 Click **Next**. In the screen indicating *Congratulations!* click **Finish** to redisplay the **Account Settings** dialog box. Compare your screen with Figure 6.8.

Your newly created account appears in the Account Settings dialog box. There may be additional accounts listed.

Figure 6.8

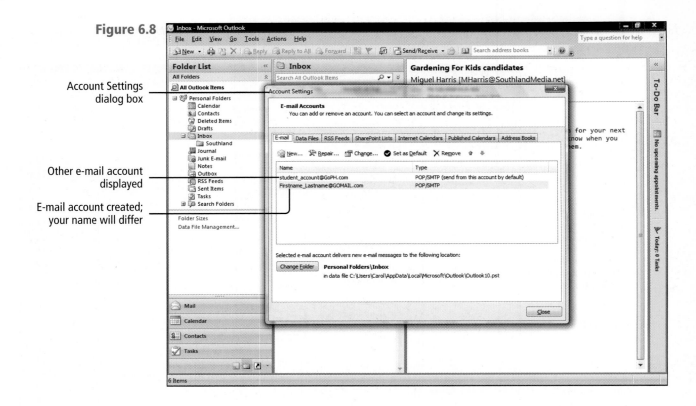

Account Settings dialog box

Other e-mail account displayed

E-mail account created; your name will differ

10 With the **Account Settings** dialog box displayed, press PrtScr.

11 On the Windows taskbar, click the **Word** button. On the Ribbon, click the **Home tab** if necessary, and then, in the **Clipboard group**, click **Paste**. Alternatively press Ctrl + V.

The screen capture of your Outlook window is inserted in the document.

12 Locate the insertion point, at the bottom right of the graphic, and press Ctrl + Enter to create a new page.

13 On the Quick Access Toolbar, click the **Save** button ⊞, and then **Minimize** ▭ Word.

14 With Outlook displayed, **Close** ✕ the **Account Settings** dialog box.

Activity 6.4 Creating Rules to Process Incoming Mail

Receiving a large volume of e-mail messages can be difficult to manage, so Outlook lets you create rules that will organize your messages before you read them. Rules are based on *conditions*—criteria that determine how incoming e-mail messages will be handled. For example, conditions might include the sender's e-mail address, the size of the message, or certain words found in the subject of the message.

You create a rule using Outlook's *Rules Wizard*, which is a program that guides you through the process of creating a message rule. Elizabeth Robinson receives e-mail from viewers of her television program. They send e-mail to the show's hosts using the program's Web site, which adds the phrase *Viewer Comments* to all the subjects of the messages. In this activity, you will create a rule that places all the e-mail messages that Elizabeth Robinson receives from viewers regarding her TV program into her Southland folder.

1 In the **Navigation Pane**, be sure the **Inbox** is the current folder.

In the Folder List, recall that the number in parentheses next to *Inbox* indicates the number of new, unread messages. There are no unread messages in your Inbox, so a number does not display. When you create a rule, that rule applies to the currently selected folder. This rule will apply to *all* Inbox messages.

2 From the **Tools** menu, click **Rules and Alerts**. In the displayed **Rules and Alerts** dialog box, click the **E-mail Rules tab** if necessary, and then click **New Rule**. If a **Rules and Alerts** box containing information about HTTP e-mail accounts displays, click **OK**. Compare your screen with Figure 6.9.

The Rules Wizard dialog box displays. Outlook enables you to create rules from a *template*, which is a set of predefined conditions and actions in rule creation used for common processing tasks. You can also create a rule starting from scratch by using a *blank rule*—that is, you define your rule by specifying your own conditions and actions as you create the rule. Templates are a good way to get started with rules when your processing needs are simple. The default setting is to create the rule using a template.

Figure 6.9

Rules Wizard dialog box

Select a template

Start from a blank rule

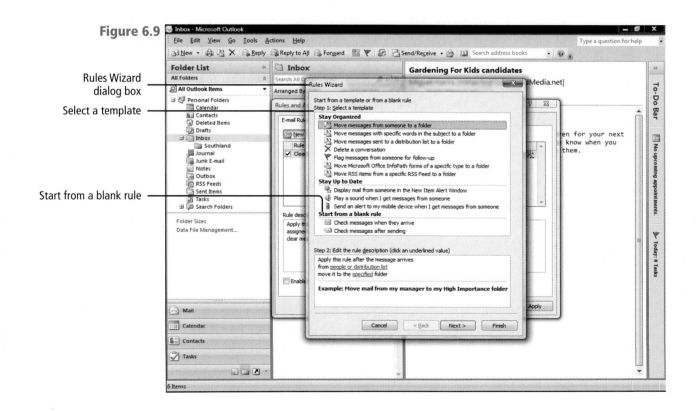

Note — Rules and HTTP E-mail Accounts

Messages sent and received with HTTP e-mail accounts cannot be processed with rules. An example of an HTTP e-mail account would be a Hotmail account. If your Outlook e-mail accounts include an HTTP account, Outlook may display an information box each time you display the Tools menu and click Rules and Alerts. Click OK to bypass the Rules and Alerts box. You can use rules on other types of e-mail accounts.

3 In the **Rules Wizard** dialog box, under **Step 1: Select a template**, click **Move messages with specific words in the subject to a folder**, and then read the information under **Step 2** that describes what the selected template does.

Step 2 in the Rules Wizard contains the ***rule description***—an explanation of the actions a rule performs on a message. The description changes as you add conditions and exceptions to the rule.

At this point in the instruction, the description for this rule is that Outlook will move incoming messages to a designated folder, based on specific words in the subject of the message. Recall that Elizabeth Robinson's goal is to have Outlook automatically move incoming e-mail from viewers of the television show into her Southland folder.

4 In the **Rules Wizard** dialog box, under **Step 2: Edit the rule description (click an underlined value)**, click **specific words**.

A Search Text dialog box displays. Use this dialog box to specify the words Outlook should search for in the Subject field of incoming messages.

5 In the **Search Text** dialog box, in the **Specify words or phrases to search for in the subject** box, type **Viewer Comments** and then click **Add**. Compare your screen with Figure 6.10.

The phrase *"Viewer Comments"* is added to a list of words for which Outlook will search in the Subject field of incoming messages. You can add as many words or phrases as needed.

Figure 6.10

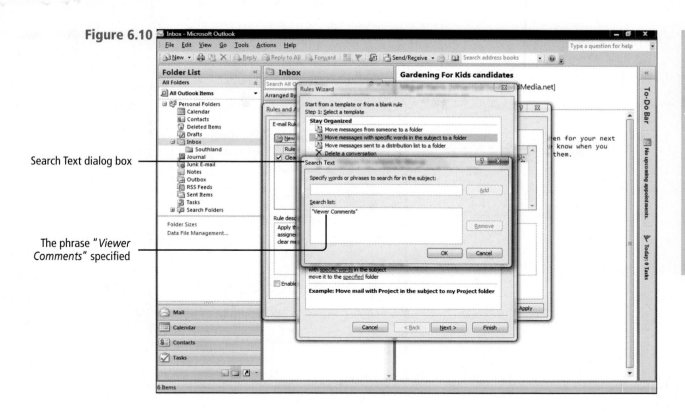

Search Text dialog box

The phrase "*Viewer Comments*" specified

6 In the **Search Text** dialog box, click **OK**.

Under Step 2, the description of the rule indicates that the rule will be applied to messages with *Viewer Comments* in the subject.

7 In the **Rules Wizard** dialog box, under **Step 2: Edit the rule description (click an underlined value)**, click **specified**. Compare your screen with Figure 6.11.

A Rules and Alerts dialog box displays, showing your Folder List. Here you specify the folder where Outlook should move messages that contain the phrase *Viewer Comments* in the subject.

Figure 6.11

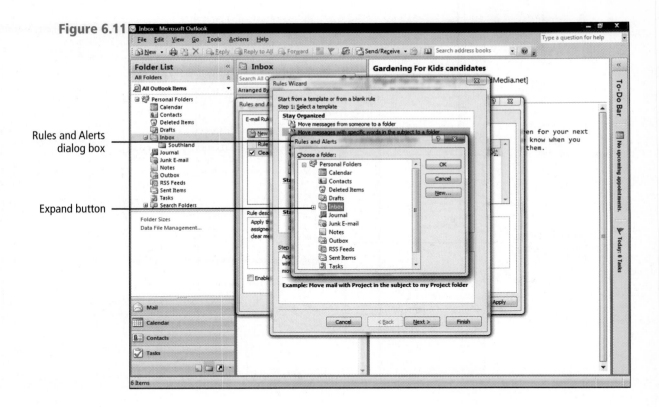

**Rules and Alerts
dialog box**

Expand button

---

8 In the **Rules and Alerts** dialog box, click the **Expand** button (+) next to **Inbox**, and then click **Southland**. Click **OK**.

Under Step 2, the rule description indicates that the message will be moved to the *Southland* folder. If you were done writing the rule, you could click Finish; but, in this instruction, you will continue to modify the rule.

9 In the **Rules Wizard** dialog box, click **Next**, and then compare your screen with Figure 6.12.

Step 1 indicates with check marks the conditions you have already specified. Two conditions are selected—*on this machine only* and *with specific words in the subject*. The condition *on this machine only* is a default condition that means the rule applies only to the computer on which you are creating the rule. Step 2 displays the current description of the rule, which moves messages with *Viewer Comments* in the subject to the *Southland* folder. Under Step 1, you can use the scroll bar to view additional conditions that you can apply.

Figure 6.12

Rules Wizard dialog box, adding more conditions to a rule

Current conditions already specified

Use the scroll bar to view additional conditions you can apply

Current rule description

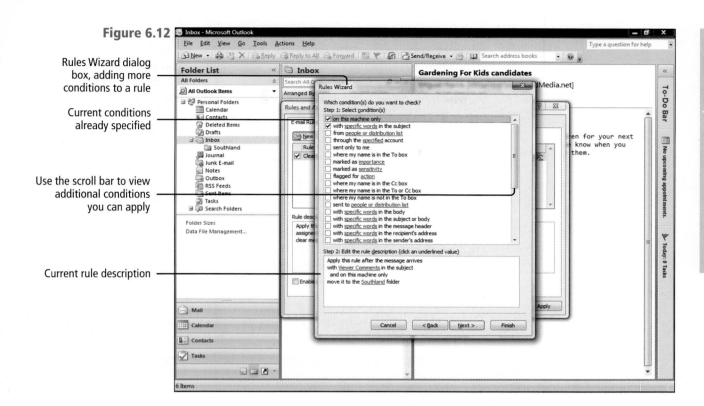

10 In the **Rules Wizard** dialog box, under **Step 1: Select condition(s)**, click the **down scroll arrow** to view the other possible conditions you can add to your rule. Notice that there are numerous conditions you can add.

11 Under **Step 1: Select conditions(s)**, locate **with specific words in the recipient's address**, and click its check box to select this condition.

The new condition is added to the rule description under Step 2.

12 Under **Step 2: Edit the rule description (click an underlined value)**, click **specific words**. In the displayed **Search Text** dialog box, type **SouthlandMedia** click **Add**, and then click **OK**.

The rule description now includes a search for *Viewer Comments* in the subject of a message and *SouthlandMedia* as part of Ms. Robinson's e-mail address.

13 In the **Rules Wizard** dialog box, click **Next**. Under **Step 1: Select actions**, notice that the only currently selected action is to **move it to the specified folder**.

There are numerous actions you can apply to a message if you want to do so. For example, in addition to moving the message to a specific folder, you could also play a sound and move a copy of the message to some other folder. In this rule, the only action you will apply is to move the message to the *Southland* folder.

14 In the **Rules Wizard** dialog box, click **Next** to display the list of exceptions.

When a message meets the conditions you have specified, *exceptions* are instances when you want to exclude the message from the specified action. For example, you could exclude a message that has *Viewer Comments* in the subject and body of the message but is sent from an e-mail account other than the company's Web site. In this rule, there are no exceptions.

15 In the **Rules Wizard** dialog box, click **Next** to finish the rule setup, and then compare your screen with Figure 6.13.

The Rules Wizard dialog box displays a summary of the rule and asks you to name the rule. The wizard uses the phrase you specified in the first condition of the rule as the default name. The default is to turn on the rule. Notice also that you can run a rule on the existing contents of the Inbox. If you decide you want to make changes to the rule, you can use the Back button to return to a previous Rules Wizard page.

Rules Wizard dialog box, finish rule setup

The first specified condition becomes the default rule name

Figure 6.13

Option to turn on the rule selected

Back button to return to previous Rules Wizard page

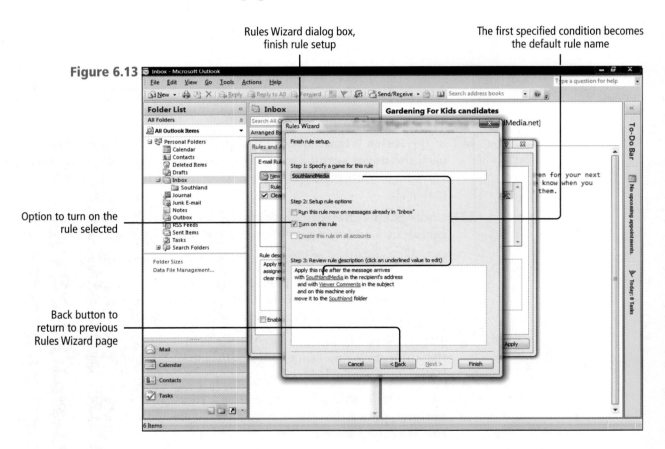

16 In the **Rules Wizard** dialog box, in the **Step 1: Specify a name for this rule** box, delete the existing text, type **Web Mail** and then click **Finish**.

The Rules and Alerts dialog box redisplays and lists the *Web Mail* rule. The check mark next to the rule name indicates that the rule is active and will be applied to all new incoming e-mail. Clearing the check mark gives you the option of turning the rule on and off as needed. For example, you might turn on this rule only when the volume of e-mail from the Web site is particularly heavy.

Are additional rules displayed?

Other rules and alerts may be listed in the Rules and Alerts dialog box. One rule that may be displayed is "Clear categories on mail (recommended)." This is a default rule for Outlook 2007.

17 With the **Web Mail** rule selected, press ⌷PrtScr⌷.

18 On the Windows taskbar, click the **Word** button. On the Ribbon, click the **Home tab**, and then, in the **Clipboard group**, click **Paste**. Alternatively press ⌷Ctrl⌷ + ⌷V⌷.

19 Locate the insertion point, at the bottom right of the graphic, and press ⌷Ctrl⌷ + ⌷Enter⌷ to create a new page.

20 On the Quick Access Toolbar, click the **Save** button 🖫, and then **Minimize** ⬜ Word.

21 In the **Rules and Alerts** dialog box, click **OK** to close the dialog box.

Activity 6.5 Applying a Rule

In this activity, you will apply the rule to Elizabeth Robinson's existing Inbox messages. Recall that viewers of the TV show can visit the show's Web site to send e-mail messages with their comments.

1 In the **Navigation Pane**, be sure the **Inbox** is displayed. Click the first message to display that message in the **Reading Pane**, and then click each subsequent message to read its content. Locate the messages with the phrase **Viewer Comments** in the subject or body of the message. Compare your screen with Figure 6.14.

Two messages contain the phrase *Viewer Comments* in the subject. No message contains the phrase *Viewer Comments* in the body. The rule was not applied to any messages because they were already in your Inbox when you created the rule. However, you can apply a rule to existing Inbox messages.

Figure 6.14

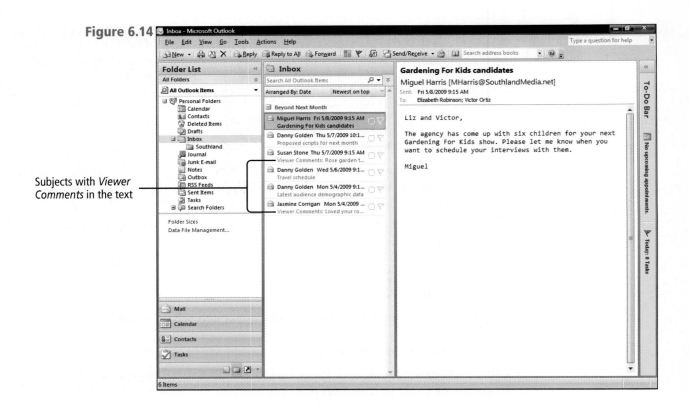

Subjects with *Viewer Comments* in the text

2 From the **Tools** menu, click **Rules and Alerts**. In the displayed **Rules and Alerts** dialog box, click **Run Rules Now**, and then click to select the **Web Mail** check box. Compare your screen with Figure 6.15.

The Run Rules Now dialog box displays. You have created one rule you can run—the Web Mail rule. You can apply the rule to All Messages, Read Messages, or Unread Messages. The default setting is to apply the rule to All Messages.

Figure 6.15

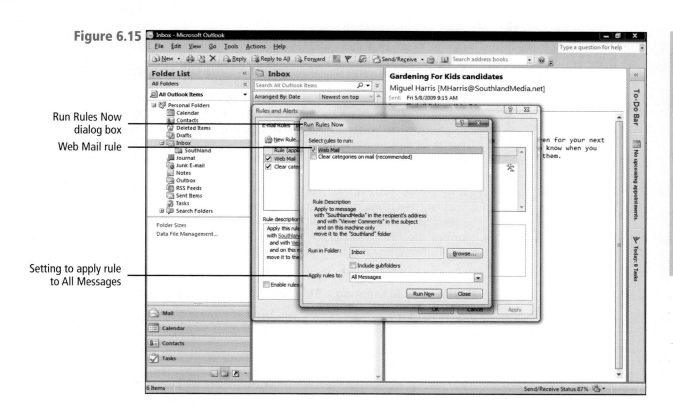

Run Rules Now dialog box

Web Mail rule

Setting to apply rule to All Messages

---

3 In the **Run Rules Now** dialog box, click **Run Now**. Click **Close**. In the **Rules and Alerts** dialog box, click **OK**.

The Inbox redisplays. There are only four messages in the Inbox. The two messages with the phrase *Viewer Comments* in their subjects have been moved to the Southland folder.

4 In the **Navigation Pane**, click the **Deleted Items** folder. Using the scroll bar, locate the e-mail message with the subject **Viewer Comments: Show suggestion**.

You can apply the rules to the Deleted Items folder. Running the Web Mail rule will cause any messages with the specified conditions to be moved to the Southland folder.

5 From the **Tools** menu, click **Rules and Alerts**. In the displayed **Rules and Alerts** dialog box, click **Run Rules Now**.

6 In the **Run Rules Now** dialog box, click to select the **Web Mail** check box; and then, in the lower right corner, click **Run Now**. Click **Close**. In the **Rules and Alerts** dialog box, click **OK**.

7 In the **Navigation Pane**, click the **Southland** folder. To arrange the messages by date, if necessary, click the **Arranged By** column heading, and then click **Date**.

The folder contains the three messages with the phrase *Viewer Comments* in the subject.

More Knowledge

Creating Automatic Responses Using the Out of Office Assistant

If you have an Exchange Server e-mail account, you can use the Out of Office Assistant to create automatic replies to incoming messages when you are not in your office. For example, when you are on vacation, you might want to use this feature to let message senders know that you will respond to their messages when you return. To use the Out of Office Assistant, click the Exchange Server Mailbox in the Navigation Pane, and then click Tools, Out of Office Assistant. In the Out of Office Assistant dialog box, click I am currently Out of the Office, type any additional text you want to include in your reply message, and then click OK. You can also include rules to send the message under specific conditions.

Activity 6.6 Creating a Rule That Uses a Desktop Alert

When new items arrive in your Inbox, by default Outlook plays a sound, briefly changes the mouse pointer, and displays an envelope icon in the *notification area*—the rightmost portion of the Windows taskbar, next to the system time. Outlook can be set to display a New Mail Desktop Alert when new items arrive in your Inbox. A *Desktop Alert* is a notification that displays on your desktop when you receive an e-mail message, meeting request, or task request. This notification presents itself as a small window that displays for a short duration. You can control the duration, location, and appearance of Desktop Alerts. You can also create Desktop Alerts that display for specific messages you receive in your Inbox. In this activity, you will create a Desktop Alert for Elizabeth Robinson's Inbox that notifies her whenever she receives a message from her boss, Danny Golden—the president of Southland Media.

1 In the **Navigation Pane**, display the **Inbox** folder. Click the **Travel schedule** message from *Danny Golden*.

2 Right-click the **Travel schedule** message, and then click **Create Rule**. Alternatively, on the Standard toolbar, click the Create Rule button 🖾. Compare your screen with Figure 6.16.

The Create Rule dialog box displays. This is an alternative method for creating a rule that is especially useful when you are basing the rule on a specific e-mail message. The dialog box contains optional conditions using the name of the sender, the recipient, and the subject of the selected message. The dialog box also has an option to move the message to a specified folder.

Figure 6.16

Create Rule button

Create Rule dialog box

Conditional options based on the selected message

Option to move the message to a specified folder

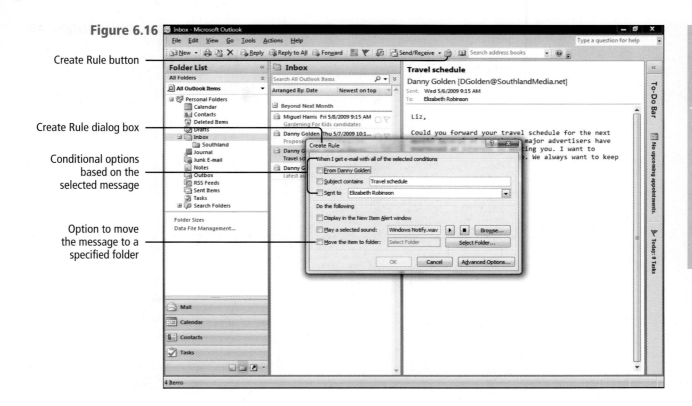

▣ In the **Create Rule** dialog box, click to select the **From Danny Golden** check box, and then click **Advanced Options**.

The Rules Wizard dialog box displays. The condition *from Danny Golden* is already selected.

▣ In the **Rules Wizard** dialog box, using the **scroll bar**, locate and if necessary, click to deselect the **on this machine only** check box. Click **Next** to display the possible actions you can take on messages from Danny Golden.

▣ In the **Rules Wizard** dialog box, under **Step 1**, using the **scroll bar**, locate and click to select the **display a Desktop Alert** check box, and then compare your screen with Figure 6.17.

Under Step 2, the rule description adds the selected action, which is to display a Desktop Alert.

Figure 6.17

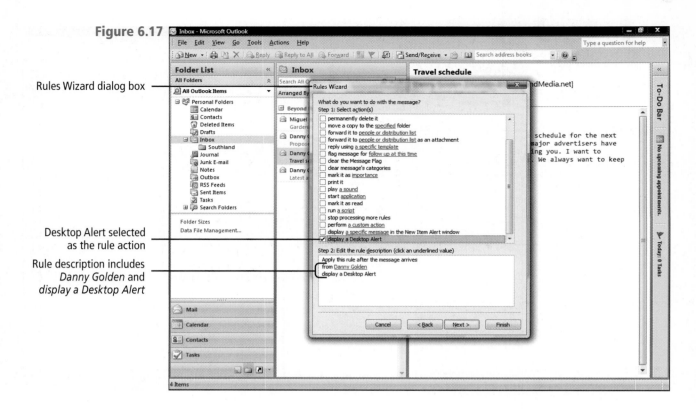

Rules Wizard dialog box

Desktop Alert selected
as the rule action

Rule description includes
Danny Golden and
display a Desktop Alert

6 In the **Rules Wizard** dialog box, click **Next** to display the list of exceptions. Click **Next** to skip the list of exceptions and finish the rule setup.

The Rules Wizard displays the default name for the rule—Danny Golden. This is a good name for this rule, so it does not have to be modified.

7 If any extra characters appear after *Danny Golden*, delete them. In the **Rules Wizard** dialog box, in Step 2, click to select **Turn on this rule** if necessary. Click **Finish** to close the dialog box.

Outlook will display a Desktop Alert for any message arriving in the Inbox from Danny Golden. You can apply the rule to existing Inbox messages.

8 From the **Tools** menu, click **Rules and Alerts**.

The Run Rules Now dialog box lists the two rules you have created—the Web Mail rule and the Danny Golden rule—as well as any other rules that exist.

9 With the **Danny Golden** rule selected, press PrtScr.

10 On the Windows taskbar, click the **Word** button. On the Ribbon, on the **Home tab**, click **Paste**.

11 Locate the insertion point, at the bottom right of the graphic, and press Ctrl + Enter to create a new page.

12 On the Quick Access Toolbar, click the **Save** button 💾 , and then **Minimize** 🔲 Word.

13 With Outlook displayed, in the **Rules and Alerts** dialog box, click **Run Rules Now**.

14 In the **Run Rules Now** dialog box, click to select the **Danny Golden** check box.

15 At the bottom of the **Run Rules Now** dialog box, click **Run Now**. Compare your screen with Figure 6.18.

Outlook displays a Desktop Alert three times, one time for each of the three messages in the Inbox for Danny Golden. Alerts display in the lower right portion of the screen for only a few moments, and the image is transparent. The first two alerts display in quick succession; the third alert remains on the screen the longest. Each alert contains the subject and the first line of the message.

Figure 6.18

Run Rules Now
dialog box

Danny Golden rule
selected to run

First lines of message

Message subject

One of three Desktop
Alerts for Danny Golden
messages — yours
may differ

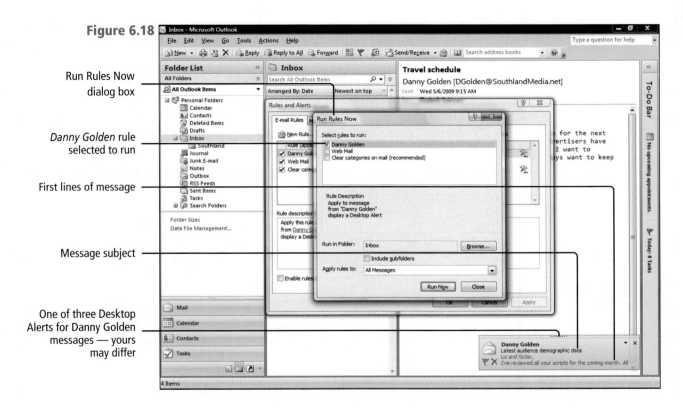

16 In the **Run Rules Now** dialog box, click the **Run Now** button again to watch the three messages display.

More Knowledge

Using New Item Alerts

You can use a New Item Alert instead of a Desktop Alert when you want your alert to remain visible on the screen instead of fading. A **New Item Alert** displays as a button on the Windows taskbar when you receive an e-mail message, meeting request, or task request. When you click the New Item Alert button, a small window opens that is similar to a Reminder window. The New Item Alert window describes the sender of the message, its subject, and the time the message was received, and you can open the message from the window. The alert window remains open until you click the Close button. New Item Alert is an available action in the Create Rule dialog box.

17 Click **Run Now** again, and quickly point to one of the alerts before the alert fades from view. Compare your screen with Figure 6.19.

An alert remains visible as long as the mouse pointer is located in the alert. A ScreenTip indicates that you can open the item by clicking it. Two buttons in the lower left portion of the Alert window enable you to flag or delete the item. A small arrow in the upper right corner of the alert displays an Options menu.

Figure 6.19

ScreenTip indicates that you can open the message by clicking

Click arrow to display Options menu

Desktop Alert remains visible while pointer is located in it

Buttons for flagging or deleting message

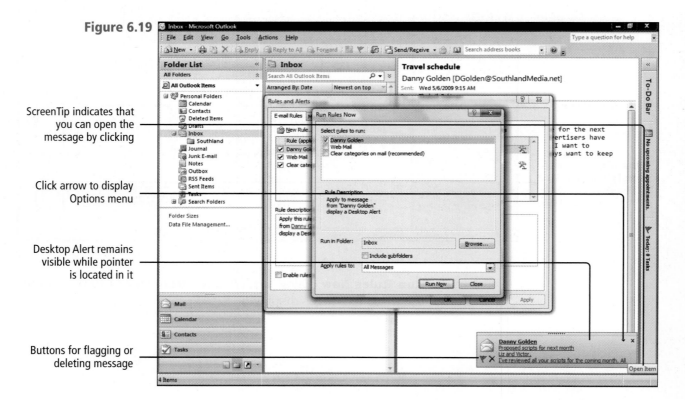

18 In the upper right portion of the displayed **Desktop Alert**, click the **Options arrow**. From the displayed **Desktop Alert Options** menu, click **Desktop Alert Settings**.

The Desktop Alert Settings dialog box displays. You can use this dialog box to control the duration and transparency of the alert. The Preview button enables you to see the effects of your changes.

19 In the **Desktop Alert Settings** dialog box, drag the **Transparency slider** toward *Solid*, to **0% transparent**, and then click **Preview** to view the results.

20 Click **Cancel** to close the **Desktop Alert Settings** dialog box without saving any changes to the alert. In the **Run Rules Now** dialog box, click **Close**. In the **Rules and Alerts** dialog box, click **Cancel**.

More Knowledge

Changing the Location of a Desktop Alert Rule

Desktop Alerts normally display in the lower right corner of the screen. You can change the screen location of the alert. When a Desktop Alert displays, move the pointer to the alert before the alert fades from view. Drag the alert to the desired screen location, and move the pointer away from the alert. All subsequent alerts will display in the new screen location.

Activity 6.7 Disabling and Removing Rules

You might want to apply rules only at certain times. For example, you might have rules that perform cleanup operations on your e-mail folders, but you do not necessarily want these rules to run every time you receive e-mail. For example, you might want to periodically run a rule that deletes all messages from a specific sender. You might also have rules that are no longer needed. You can disable rules and delete rules. In this activity, you will disable and remove the rules you created for Elizabeth Robinson's messages.

1 From the **Tools** menu, display the **Rules and Alerts** dialog box. Click the **Danny Golden** rule, and then click the **Delete** button

X Delete . Compare your screen with Figure 6.20.

Figure 6.20

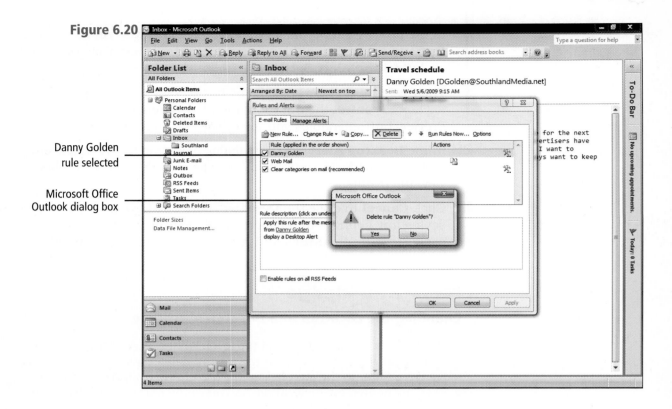

Danny Golden rule selected

Microsoft Office Outlook dialog box

2 In the **Microsoft Office Outlook** dialog box, click **Yes**. Use the same technique to delete the **Web Mail** rule. Click **OK** to close the **Rules and Alerts** dialog box.

More Knowledge

Changing a Rule

You can add and delete conditions, actions, and exceptions to any existing rule. From the Tools menu, click Rules and Alerts. In the Rules and Alerts dialog box, click the rule you want to edit, click Change Rule, and then click Edit Rule Settings. Use the Rules Wizard to edit the rule. In the Rules and Alerts dialog box, you can also click the arrow next to the Change Rule command button to display a menu of other changes you can make to a rule, including changing the name of the rule or applying the rule to a different folder.

Activity 6.8 Moving Messages to Another Folder

When you have a large volume of e-mail, another way to organize your messages is to manually move them to different e-mail folders. There are several ways to move messages. You can drag them from one folder to another. Dragging is the action of pointing to an object, holding down the left mouse button, moving the object to another location on the screen, and then releasing the left mouse button. You can use commands on the menu bar or the shortcut menu. You can also use a toolbar button. In this activity, you will move several of Elizabeth Robinson's messages from her Inbox to her Southland folder.

1 In the **Navigation Pane**, click the **Folder List** button to display the Folder List. If necessary, expand the **Inbox** to display the **Southland** folder in the Folder List. Display the **Inbox**, and then click the **Travel schedule** message from *Danny Golden*.

2 Point to the **Travel schedule** message, hold down the left mouse button, and then drag the message to the **Southland** folder, as shown in Figure 6.21. Release the mouse button.

As you drag the message into the Folder List, a small rectangle is attached to the pointer, and the Southland folder is highlighted when you point to the folder. The *Travel schedule* message moves to the *Southland* folder.

Figure 6.21

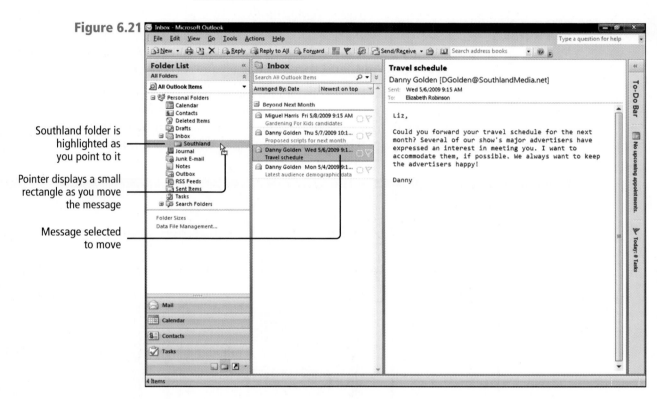

Southland folder is highlighted as you point to it

Pointer displays a small rectangle as you move the message

Message selected to move

3 In the **Inbox**, click the **Gardening For Kids candidates** message. Right-click the selected message, and then click **Move to Folder**. In the displayed **Move Items** dialog box, click the **Southland** folder, if necessary, and then click **OK**.

The Move Items dialog box closes. The message is moved to the Southland folder. Only two messages remain in the Inbox folder.

Another Way

To Move Messages

There are numerous ways to move messages in addition to dragging and using the shortcut menu. You can click a message and press [Ctrl] + [⇧ Shift] + [V] to display the Move Items dialog box. You can click Edit on the menu bar and then click Move to Folder. You can also move a message by clicking the message and then clicking the Move to Folder button on the Standard toolbar.

Activity 6.9 Using Outlook's Junk Mail Filter

Almost everyone with an active e-mail account receives unsolicited junk e-mail. You can use Outlook's junk e-mail filter to screen out a number of these unwanted messages. Recall that a *filter* is a set of instructions to screen a folder, based on conditions you define. In this activity, you will modify Elizabeth Robinson's junk e-mail filter to screen out messages from specific sources.

1 From the **Tools** menu, display the **Options** dialog box. On the **Preferences tab**, under **E-mail**, click **Junk E-mail**.

The Junk E-mail Options dialog box displays. Outlook's default setting for junk e-mail is the Low setting, which filters out most obvious junk e-mail. You can set the filter to High, but doing so risks filtering out some of your regular e-mail.

2 In the **Junk E-mail Options** dialog box, click the **Blocked Senders tab**. Click **Add**, and then compare your screen with Figure 6.22.

In the Add address or domain dialog box, you can enter specific e-mail addresses you always want treated as junk e-mail. The addresses you specify do not have to be junk e-mail. You can block the messages of anyone from whom you do not want to receive e-mail.

Figure 6.22

Add address or domain dialog box

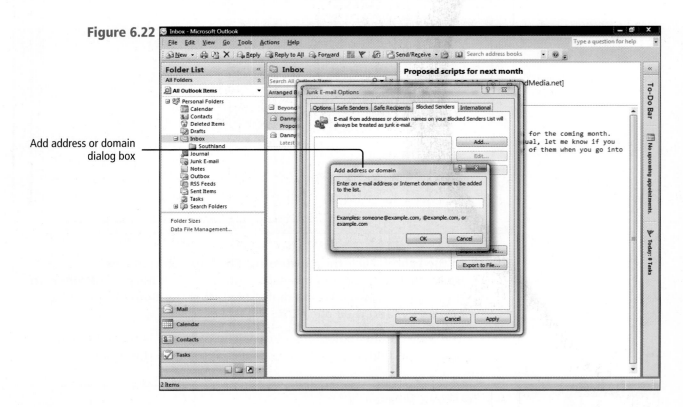

3 In the **Add address or domain** dialog box, type **joespam@annoyingviewer. com** and then click **OK**.

The address is added to your list of blocked senders. You can also block an entire domain name. Recall that a *domain name* is the portion of an e-mail address that defines the e-mail system or Internet Service Provider. Use this option only when you are certain all messages from the domain name are unwanted, because blocking a domain means that messages from anyone with that domain name will be blocked.

4 In the **Junk E-mail Options** dialog box, click **Add**. In the **Add address or domain** dialog box, type **@junkmail.com** and then click **OK**. Compare your screen with Figure 6.23.

Two sources of unwanted e-mail are added to the list. All mail received from these senders will be placed in the Junk E-mail folder.

Figure 6.23

Junk E-mail Options dialog box, Blocked Senders tab selected

Two sources of unwanted e-mail specified

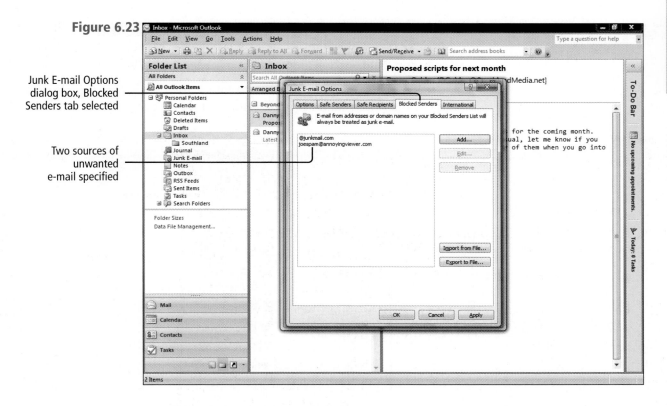

5 With the **Junk E-mail Options** dialog box displayed, press PrtScr.

6 Using the techniques you have practiced, paste the screen capture into your **Word** document.

7 **Save** 🖫 the document, and then **Minimize** 🗖 Word.

8 With Outlook displayed, in the **Junk E-mail Options** dialog box, click **OK**, and then click **OK** to close the **Options** dialog box.

Activity 6.10 Organizing Mail Folders Using View Filters

Another way to organize a large e-mail folder is to create a filter that screens the folder view. A *view filter* leaves all the messages in the folder but displays only those you want to see—based on instructions you define. For example, you might want to see only those messages from a specific individual. In this activity, you will create a view of Elizabeth Robinson's Southland folder that displays only the *Viewer Comments* messages.

1 In the **Navigation Pane**, click to select and display the contents of the **Southland** folder. From the **View** menu, point to **Arrange By**, and then click **Custom**.

2 In the displayed **Customize View: Messages** dialog box, click **Filter**.

The Filter dialog box displays. Here you can create filters with different conditions. You can filter messages based on the sender or on the content of the Subject field. The More Choices tab enables you to filter for additional message characteristics, such as message importance, flags, or attachments.

3 In the **Filter** dialog box, in the **Search for the word(s)** box, type **Viewer Comments** If necessary, click the **In arrow**, and then click **subject field only**. Compare your screen with Figure 6.24.

Outlook will filter the Southland folder messages, displaying only messages with *Viewer Comments* in the subject.

Figure 6.24

Viewer Comments specified as the text to search

Filter dialog box

Search in subject field only

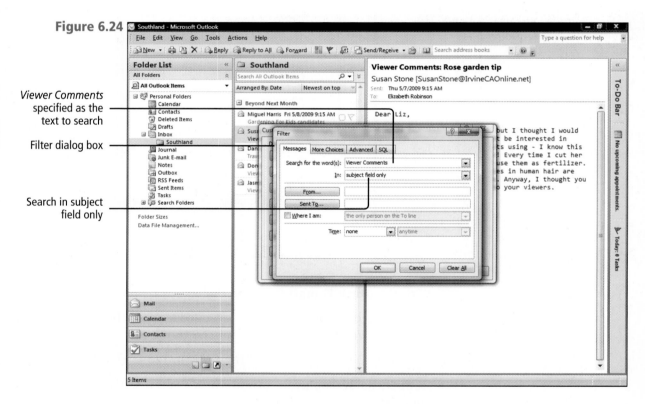

4 Using the techniques you have practiced, press [PrtScr], and then paste the screen capture into your **Word** document. **Minimize** Word.

5 With Outlook displayed, click **OK** to close the **Filter** dialog box. In the **Customize View: Messages** dialog box, notice the text to the right of the **Filter** button—*Messages: Containing Viewer Comments*.

6 Click **OK** to close the **Customize View: Messages** dialog box, and then compare your screen with Figure 6.25.

The *Southland* folder displays only three messages, all containing the phrase *Viewer Comments* in their subjects. The status bar and the folder name show the message *Filter Applied*. Although only three messages display, the status bar indicates that the folder actually contains *5* items.

Message indicates that a view filter has been applied

Figure 6.25

Filtered Southland folder with three messages displayed

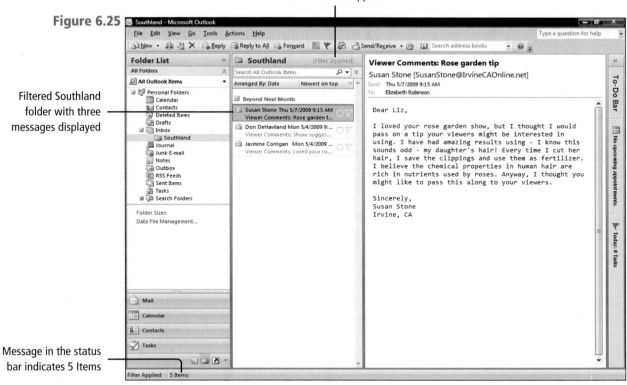

Message in the status bar indicates 5 Items

7 From the **View** menu, point to **Arrange By**, and then click **Custom**. In the **Customize View: Messages** dialog box, click **Filter**.

The Filter dialog box displays. A view filter remains applied to a folder until you clear the filter.

8 In the **Filter** dialog box, click **Clear All**, and then click **OK**. Notice that the text to the right of the **Filter** command indicates that filtering is **Off**.

9 In the **Customize View: Messages** dialog box, click **OK**.

With the filter removed, all five messages in the Southland folder display.

More Knowledge
Managing Mailbox Size by Using Mailbox Cleanup

Another way to manage mailbox information is by using Outlook's Mailbox Cleanup feature. You can use this tool to view total mailbox size and the size of individual folders within the mailbox. You can also locate and delete messages larger than a certain size. This is a useful feature when you have storage limitations on your e-mail server. To use the Mail Cleanup tool, from the Tools menu, click Mailbox Cleanup.

Objective 2
Modify the Master Category List

When you assign Outlook items to categories, you select from the **Master Category List**, which is the Outlook-supplied list of color categories used for grouping, filtering, and sorting Outlook information. You have used categories to organize your calendar items, tasks, and messages. In addition, you have renamed the categories used in the Master Category List to include descriptive terms such as *VIP*, *Personal*, and *Supplier*.

Outlook enables you to create your own categories, which you can add to the Master Category List. The advantage of creating your own categories is that you can organize your Outlook information in a way that is most meaningful to you. For example, you might be assigned to a special project that will last for several months. You can create a category named specifically for that project. As the project progresses, you can assign all the relevant tasks, calendar entries, and messages to the category.

Activity 6.11 Adding New Categories to the Master Category List

In this activity, you will create new categories in the Master Category List that Southland Media's Elizabeth Robinson will use to assign all her company-related messages.

1 In the **Navigation Pane**, be sure the **Southland** folder is selected and its contents displayed. Click the **Travel schedule** message to select it. Right-click the selected message, point to **Categorize**, and then click **All Categories**.

The Color Categories dialog box displays. Here you can add and delete categories in the Master Category List.

2 In the **Color Categories** dialog box, click the **New...** button. In the **Add New Category** dialog box, type **Danny** Click the **Color arrow**, and then click **None**. Click **OK** and then compare your screen with Figure 6.26.

The new category displays at the bottom of the Master Category List, and is selected.

Figure 6.26

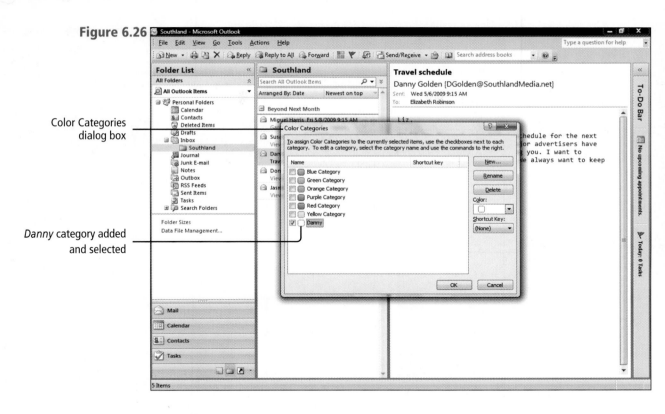

Color Categories dialog box

Danny category added and selected

3 Click **OK** to close the **Color Categories** dialog box.

The *Danny* category is applied to the Danny Golden message, although this is not apparent in the current view.

4 Click one of the messages with the phrase **Viewer Comments** in the subject. Then, hold down Ctrl and click each of the other two messages whose subject begins with the phrase **Viewer Comments**. Right-click one of the selected messages to display the shortcut menu, point to **Categorize**, and then click **All Categories**.

In the Color Categories dialog box, notice that the *Danny* category now appears in alphabetical order.

Note — Viewing New Categories

Immediately after a new category is created, that category will display at the bottom of the Master Category List—before closing the Color Category dialog box. Whenever the Color Category dialog box is reopened, all categories will display in alphabetical order.

---

5 In the **Color Categories** dialog box, click the **New...** button. In the **Add New Category** dialog box, type **Viewers** Click the **Color arrow**, and click **None**. Click **OK**, and then compare your screen with Figure 6.27.

The new category is added to the bottom of the Master Category List, and is selected.

Figure 6.27

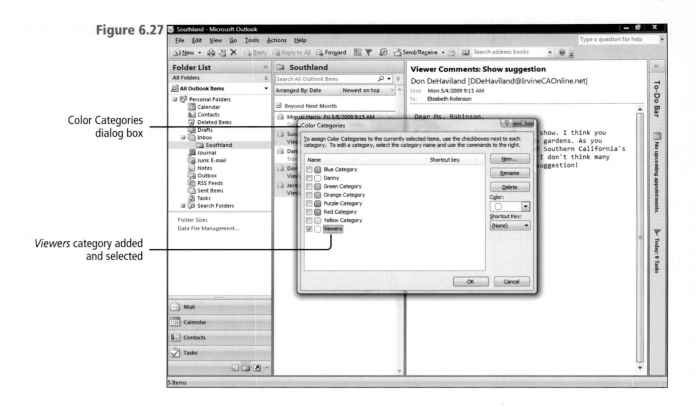

Color Categories dialog box

Viewers category added and selected

---

6. In the Color **Categories** dialog box, click **OK**.

Although not apparent in the current view, the three selected messages are assigned to the *Viewers* category. You can view the contents of the folder by category. In a folder with a large volume of mail, this can be a useful way to organize your messages.

7. From the **View** menu, point to **Arrange By**, and then click **Categories**. If necessary, click the **Expand** button (+) for each category to display all the folder items. Compare your screen with Figure 6.28.

Three groups display: the two new categories—*Danny* and *Viewers*—and one group for unassigned messages—*(none)*.

Figure 6.28

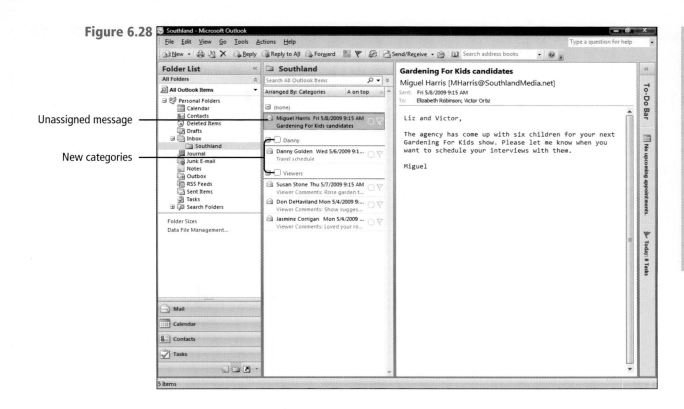

Unassigned message

New categories

8 From the **View** menu, point to **Arrange By**, and then click **Date** to redisplay the folder in its default arrangement—arranged by date.

Activity 6.12 Deleting Categories and Restoring the Master Category List

You can delete categories from the Master Category List as easily as you can add them. In this activity, you will delete categories in Elizabeth Robinson's Master Category List and then restore the list to the Outlook default.

1 With the **Southland** folder still displayed, from the **Edit** menu, point to **Categorize**, and then click **All Categories**.

2 In the **Color Categories** dialog box, click **Danny**, and then click **Delete**. In the **Microsoft Office Outlook** dialog box, click **Yes** to confirm deleting *Danny*.

When you delete a category that is currently assigned to existing messages, the category is removed from the *Master Category List*, but remains assigned to those messages.

3 In the **Color Categories** dialog box, click **Viewers**, and then click **Delete**. In the **Microsoft Office Outlook** dialog box, click **Yes** to confirm deleting *Viewers*.

4 Click **Red Category**, and then click **Delete**. In the **Microsoft Office Outlook** dialog box, click **Yes** to confirm deleting *Red Category*. Compare your screen with Figure 6.29.

All three categories are removed from the *Master Category List*. You can delete any category on the list, including Outlook's preset categories.

Figure 6.29

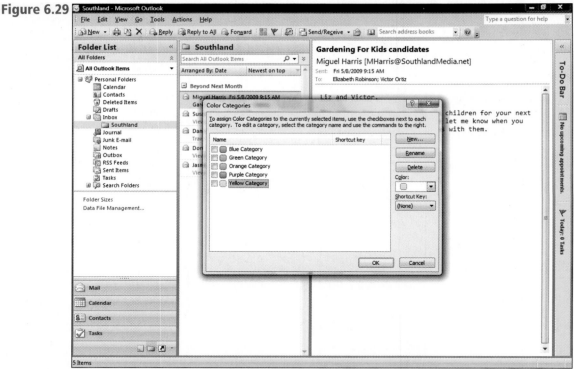

5 Click **OK** to close the **Color Categories** dialog box. From the **View** menu, point to **Arrange By**, and then click **Categories**.

The *Danny* and *Viewers* categories still display. An item retains its category assignment even if the category is deleted from the Master Category List. This enables you to create a custom category, assign items to the category, and then delete the category when you no longer need it. If you display the Color Categories dialog box for an unassigned item, the deleted categories will not be listed.

6 From the **Edit** menu, point to **Categorize**, and then click **All Categories**.

Because the Master Category List is stored in your Personal Folders (.pst) file, if you delete a preset category it cannot be recovered. You must create a new category to replace any deleted category.

7 In the **Color Categories** dialog box, click **New**. In the **Add New Category** dialog box, type **Red Category** Click the **Color arrow** and then make certain **Red** is selected. If necessary, click Red—the first color in the first row. Click **OK**, and then compare your screen with Figure 6.30.

Red Category is restored to the Master Category List.

Figure 6.30

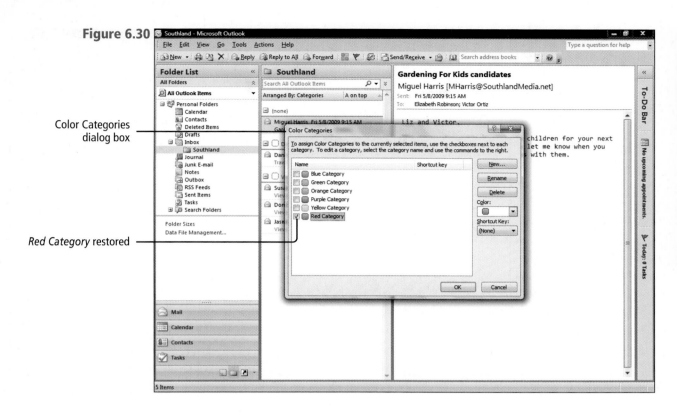

Color Categories dialog box

Red Category restored

8 Click to remove the check mark from the **Red Category** check box. Click **OK** to close the **Color Categories** dialog box.

The Southland folder displays. The contents are still displayed in Category view.

Objective 3
Use Notes

Outlook's **Notes** are the electronic equivalent of sticky paper notes. Notes are a convenient way to organize and keep track of bits of information you want to use later. You might use notes to write down directions, phone numbers, reminders, or ideas—anything you might write on a paper note. You can leave notes open on the screen while you work. Any change you make to a note is saved. You can print notes and display them in different ways.

Activity 6.13 Creating and Editing Notes

You can access the Notes component of Outlook using the Navigation Pane. In this activity, you will create some notes for Elizabeth Robinson.

1 In the **Navigation Pane**, at the bottom of the pane, click the **Notes** button ⬜. **Delete** any existing notes. Compare your screen with Figure 6.31.

The Notes folder displays. As with other Outlook components, the Notes folder has its own commands on the Standard toolbar.

Figure 6.31

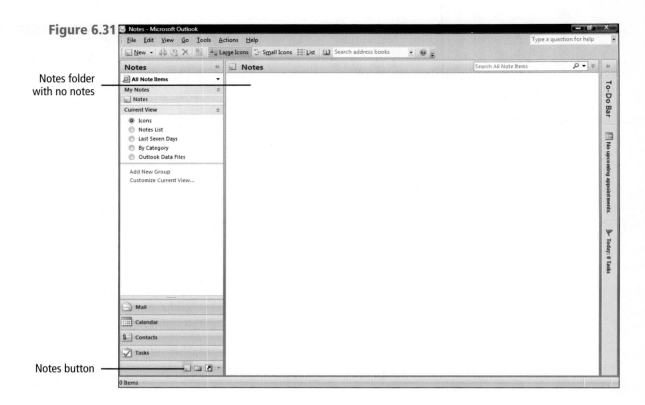

Notes folder with no notes

Notes button

2 On the Standard toolbar, click the **New Note** button ⟨🗒 New ▾⟩.

A blank Note window displays. The blinking insertion point in the Note window indicates that you can begin entering the text of the note.

3 In the **Note** window, type **Get car serviced!** and then compare your screen with Figure 6.32.

Figure 6.32

Note icon

Note window with
new text

Close button

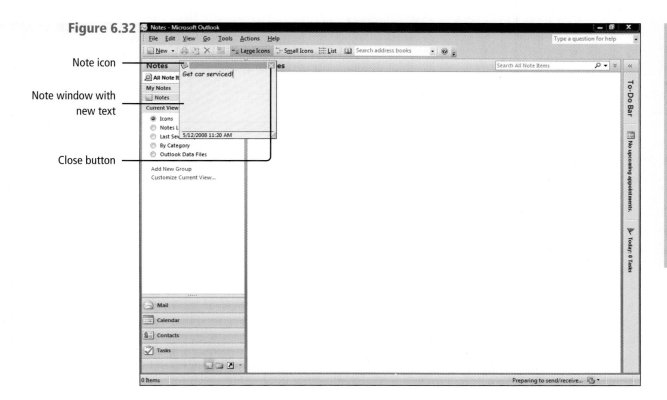

4 In the **Note** window, click the **Note** icon [icon] in the upper left corner of the note, and then click **Close**. Alternatively, in the **Note** window, click the **Close** button [icon].

The note closes, and a new note icon displays in the Notes folder.

5 Right-click any blank area of the **Notes** folder, and then click **New Note**. Type **Show idea: Vacation home gardens?** and then close the note.

Another Way ── **To Open New Notes**

An easy way to open a new note is to double-click a blank area of the Notes folder.

6 From the **File** menu, point to **New**, and then click **Note**. Type **Pick up Bryan's revised script** and then close the note. Create another new note with the text **Get Danny's new cell number** and then close the note.

7 Create a new note with the text **Make dinner reservations** and then close the note. Create another new note with the text **Don't forget to feed Tina** and then close the note. Compare your screen with Figure 6.33.

The Notes folder displays six notes, all of which can be edited.

Figure 6.33

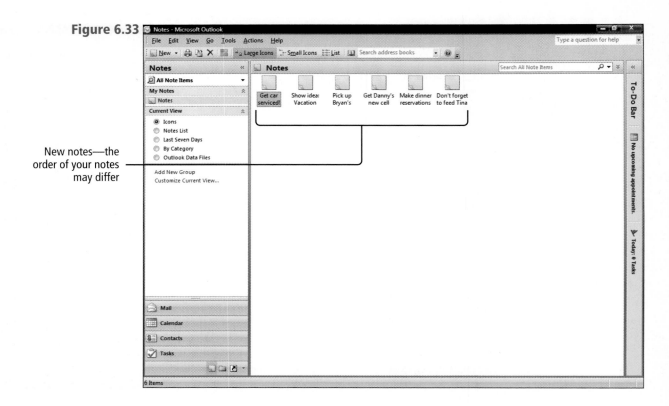

New notes—the
order of your notes
may differ

8 Right-click the **Get car serviced!** note and click **Open**. Alternatively, double-click the note to open it. In the **Note** window, click to place the insertion point at the end of the existing text, press ⏎, type **Dealer phone: 619-555-0400** and then close the note.

Activity 6.14 Viewing, Organizing, and Printing Notes

Outlook has several viewing options for notes, just as it does for messages, contacts, calendar items, and tasks. You can also organize your notes by assigning them to categories. Printing notes is similar to printing other Outlook items. In this activity, you will work with the notes you created for Elizabeth Robinson.

1 Display the **Notes** folder, if necessary. On the Standard toolbar, click the **List** button ⊞ List .

The notes are reduced in size and arranged in a list.

2 From the **View** menu, point to **Reading Pane**, and then click **Bottom**. Click to select the **Get car serviced!** note. Compare your screen with Figure 6.34.

The full content of the selected note displays in the Reading Pane.

Figure 6.34

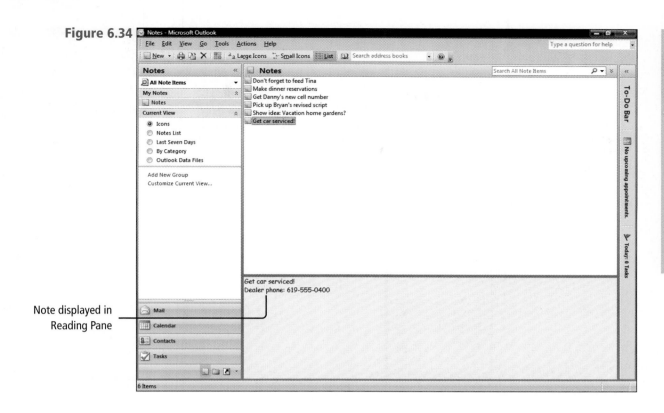

Note displayed in
Reading Pane

3 On the Standard toolbar, click the **Large Icons** button . From the **View** menu, point to **Reading Pane**, and then click **Off** to display the **Notes** folder in its default view.

4 Right-click the **Get car serviced!** note, point to **Categorize**, and then click **All Categories**.

5 In the **Color Categories** dialog box, click to select **Blue Category** and then click **Rename**. With **Blue Category** selected, type **Personal** and then press Enter. Click the **Personal** check box, and then click **OK** to close the **Color Categories** dialog box.

6 Right-click the **Make dinner reservations** note, point to **Categorize**, and then click **Personal**.

7 Click the **Get Danny's new cell number** note to select it. Hold down Ctrl, and then click the **Pick up Bryan's revised script** and **Show idea** notes. Right-click any of the selected notes, point to **Categorize**, and then click **All Categories**.

8 Using the technique you just practiced, rename the **Green Category** as **Southland** Click the **Southland** check box, and then click **OK** to close the **Color Categories** dialog box.

The three notes are assigned to the new *Southland* category.

9 In the **Navigation Pane**, under **Current View**, click **By Category**. If necessary, click the **Expand** button (+) to display the items in each group, and then compare your screen with Figure 6.35.

The Notes folder shows three groups: the *Personal* and *Southland* categories, and one unassigned note.

Figure 6.35

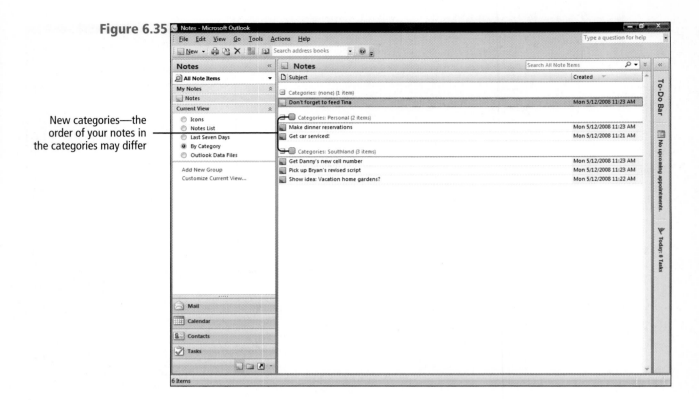

New categories—the order of your notes in the categories may differ

10 Under **Current View**, click **Notes List** to display the folder in a table view. Notice that this view also includes the text of each note and its category but does not *group* the notes by category.

11 From the **File** menu, display the **Page Setup: Table Style** dialog box. On the **Header/Footer tab**, delete any existing header or footer information, including page numbers and dates. In the left **Footer** box, type **6A_Garden_Show_Notes_Firstname_Lastname Preview**, and then **Print** the notes list. Submit the end result to your instructor as directed.

As in other components of Outlook, use the Table Style to print the entire contents of the folder. Use the Memo Style to print individual notes.

12 In the **Navigation Pane**, under **Current View** pane, click **Icons** to display the **Notes** folder in its default view.

Objective 4
Archive Outlook Information

As you accumulate information in your Outlook folders, you will find it helpful to **archive** information you want to keep. When you archive an item, you move that item to a location for storage and future access. Outlook has a feature called **AutoArchive** that performs this task. AutoArchive automates the process of moving Outlook items to a storage location for possible future access. AutoArchive also discards expired items that are no longer valid, such as a meeting request that occurred months in the past but still displays in your Inbox. You can also archive older information manually. Archived information can be stored in a separate folder on your computer or in an external location, such as a network drive.

Activity 6.15 Configuring AutoArchive

Outlook is configured to perform an AutoArchive on all Outlook folders except the Contacts folder. In this activity, you will change the default settings.

1 Display the **Folder List** 📁, and then display the contents of the **Southland** folder. From the **Tools** menu, display the **Options** dialog box, click the **Other tab**, and then click **AutoArchive**. Compare your screen with Figure 6.36.

The AutoArchive dialog box displays. The first option determines how frequently AutoArchive runs. AutoArchive checks for expired items such as old meeting requests and deletes them. AutoArchive checks for the age of items, copies older items to an archive folder, and deletes them from their original location.

The default setting is for AutoArchive to run every 14 days, but you can run AutoArchive more frequently. This can be useful when you have a large volume of daily e-mail. Notice also the second option, in which Outlook prompts before AutoArchive runs. This prompt displays a Microsoft Office Outlook dialog box, similar to a Reminder window, asking you whether you would like to archive your older items.

Figure 6.36

AutoArchive dialog box

Option displays a prompt before AutoArchive runs

Option to set the aging period for archived items

Default setting is for AutoArchive to run every 14 days

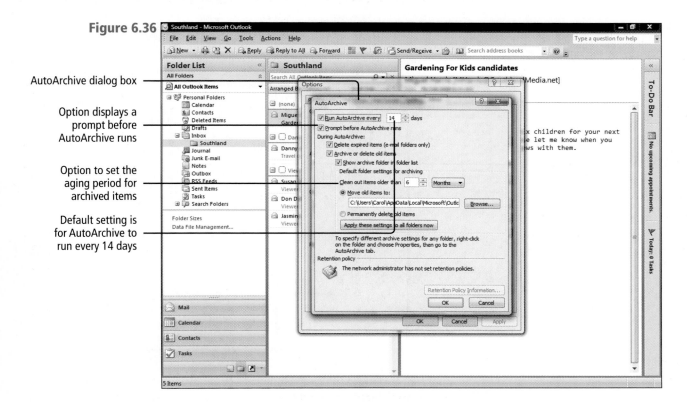

2 In the **AutoArchive** dialog box, in the **Run AutoArchive every** box, click the **spin box down arrow** until **7** displays. Alternatively, delete the existing text and type **7**

AutoArchive is set to run every seven days. You can also change the age of items Outlook archives. Outlook has different aging periods for different folders. The Inbox, Calendar, Notes, Journal, and Drafts folders have a default period of six months. The Outbox default is three months, and the Sent Items and Deleted Items folders defaults are two months. The aging period you set in this dialog box is a *global* setting—that is, the setting applies to all of Outlook's folders. If you prefer, you can apply aging periods to individual folders.

3 In the **AutoArchive** dialog box, click **OK**, and then click **OK** to close the **Options** dialog box. In the **Navigation Pane**, right-click the **Southland** folder, and then click **Properties** to display the **Southland Properties** dialog box.

4 In the **Southland Properties** dialog box, click the **AutoArchive tab**. Click **Archive this folder using these settings**. Use the arrows to set **Clean out items older than** to **2 Weeks**, and then compare your screen with Figure 6.37.

Messages in this folder are set to be archived when they are older than two weeks.

Figure 6.37

Southland Properties dialog box, AutoArchive tab selected

Setting indicates that folder items older than 2 weeks are archived

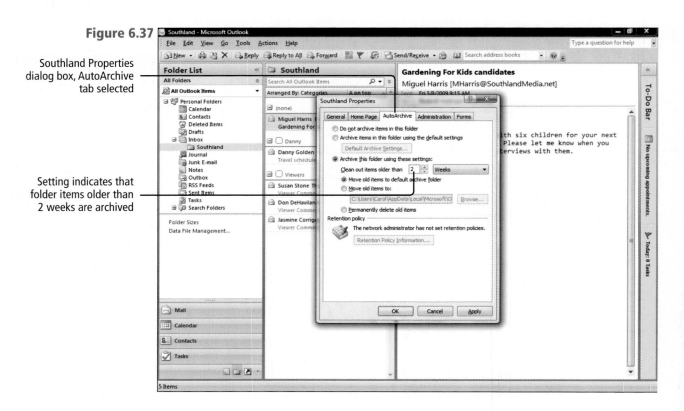

5 In the **Southland Properties** dialog box, click **OK**.

AutoArchive is set to run every seven days, and messages in the Southland folder that are more than two weeks old will be archived.

Alert! Does an AutoArchive prompt display?

When you change the AutoArchive settings to archive your folders, during this instruction Outlook may display the Microsoft Office Outlook dialog box that asks you if you want to AutoArchive your old items now. Recall that this prompt is an option in the AutoArchive dialog box, and this option is selected by default. Normally you would allow Outlook to archive your older items. If this dialog box displays during this instruction, click No.

Activity 6.16 Manually Archiving Mail Messages

Outlook also enables you to archive your data manually. This can be useful when you want to archive a specific folder that is not currently scheduled for archiving with AutoArchive. For example, you might want to archive your Inbox before you go on vacation. In this activity, you will manually archive Elizabeth Robinson's Southland folder.

1 In the **Navigation Pane**, be sure the **Southland** folder displays. From the **File** menu, click **Archive** to display the **Archive** dialog box, and then, under **Archive this folder and all subfolders**, click **Southland**, if necessary.

The Southland folder is selected as the folder that will be archived.

2 In the **Archive items older than:** box, type **05/10/09** and then compare your screen with Figure 6.38.

This specifies the date for Outlook to use in determining which items in the Southland folder to archive. All the items in the Southland folder are older than the date you typed, so all messages in the folder will be archived.

Figure 6.38

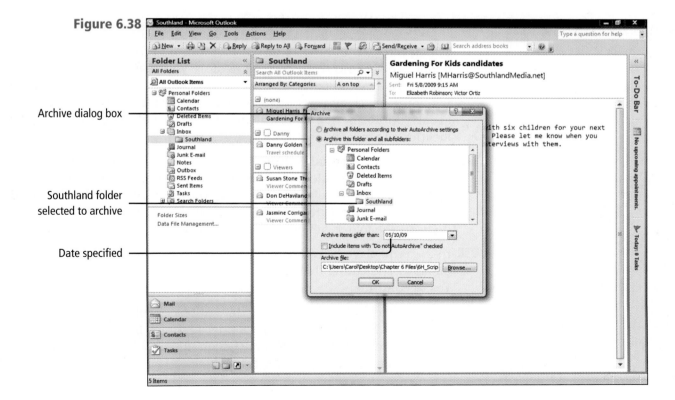

Archive dialog box

Southland folder selected to archive

Date specified

3 In the **Archive** dialog box, click **Browse**, navigate to the location where you are storing your folders and projects, and then click the

New Folder button [New Folder]. In the displayed new folder, with **New Folder** selected, type **Chapter 6** and then compare your screen with Figure 6.39.

Figure 6.39

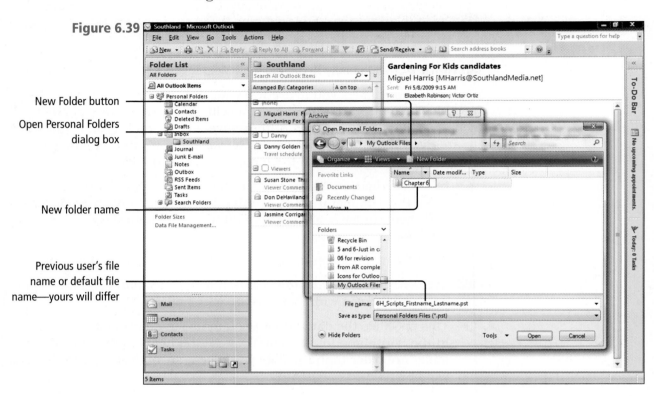

New Folder button

Open Personal Folders dialog box

New folder name

Previous user's file name or default file name—yours will differ

4 With the insertion point located to the right of **Chapter 6**, press [Enter].

The new folder name displays in the Address box, indicating that the folder is open and ready for you to store your files. The File name box may show the name of a previous user's file name or the default file name. Outlook uses *archive* as the default file name for all archived information. You will specify a different file name using the location of your stored files.

5 In the **Open Personal Folders** dialog box, in the **File name** box, delete any existing file name, and then type **6A_Garden_Show_ Southland_Firstname_Lastname** using your own name. Click **OK**. If a **Microsoft Office Outlook** dialog box displays a warning that all items in the folder will be archived, click **Yes** to continue.

6 In the redisplayed **Archive** dialog box, click **OK**. If a warning displays, indicating that the date you entered is in the future, click Yes to continue.

The Archive dialog box closes, and Outlook archives the Southland folder. The folder is empty. The Folder List now includes a set of file folders named **Archive Folders**, which is Outlook's default name for the location of files stored for future use.

7 In the **Navigation Pane**, if necessary, use the **scroll bar** to display

Archive Folders in the **Folder List**, and notice the icon 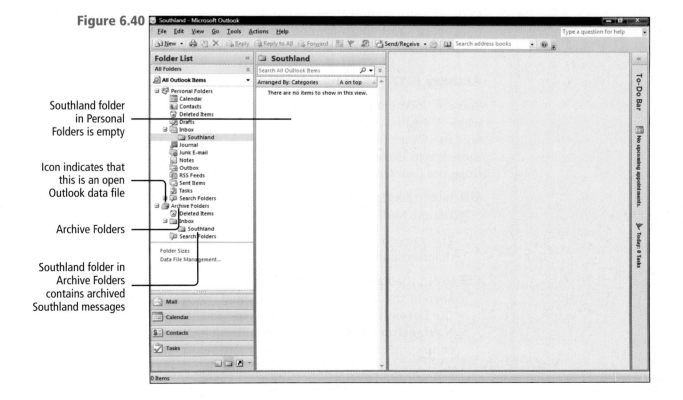 next to **Archive Folders**, which indicates that this is an Outlook data file that can be opened and closed. Archiving Outlook folders opens *Archive Folders*, and the folder remains open every time you start Outlook unless you close it.

Note — Do you have more than one folder labeled Archive Folders?

Your Folder List may show more than one Archive Folders. When Outlook performs an AutoArchive of your Outlook folders, Outlook normally adds Archive Folders to the Folder List. This folder remains open and displayed in your Folder List. Outlook identifies all archive folders in the Folder List as Archive Folders, even if the additional archive files have different file names. If you have more than one Archive Folders displayed in your Folder List, the Archive Folders at the bottom of the Folder List will contain your Southland folder archive data. You should open this Archive Folders.

---

8 In the **Folder List**, click the **Expand** button (+) next to **Archive Folders** to display the Archive subfolders. Click the **Expand** button (+) next to the **Inbox** subfolder. Compare your screen with Figure 6.40.

The Inbox subfolder contains another subfolder—the Southland folder. This is the folder that contains your archived messages.

Figure 6.40

Southland folder in Personal Folders is empty

Icon indicates that this is an open Outlook data file

Archive Folders

Southland folder in Archive Folders contains archived Southland messages

9 In the **Folder List**, under **Archive Folders**, click the **Southland** folder. To arrange messages by category, if necessary, on the **View** menu, point to **Arrange By** and click **Categories**.

The archived messages from the Southland folder display. Notice that Outlook archives the folder contents using the current view of the folder when it was archived.

10 Using the techniques you have practiced, press PrtScr, and then paste the screen capture into your **Word** document. **Minimize** ⬜ Word.

11 With Outlook displayed, in the **Folder List**, right-click **Archive Folders**, and then click **Close "Archive Folders"** to close the Archive Folders. Close any additional **Archive Folders** that may display in the Folder List.

Recall that you saved your archived file earlier in this activity with the file name 6A_Garden_Show_Southland_Firstname_Lastname. Closing the Archive Folders removes the Archive Folders from Outlook, but does not delete the data file.

Objective 5
Recover and Export Outlook Information

There will be times when you must recover information you have deleted or archived. Deleted items can be recovered as long as they still reside in the Deleted Items folder. Archived items can be restored to their original locations by accessing the Archive Folders.

You can also export Outlook information. You might want to export Outlook information to provide folder information to someone else or to place your Outlook information on a different computer, for example, when you acquire a new computer.

Activity 6.17 Retrieving Items from the Deleted Items Folder

You can locate and retrieve items from the Deleted Items folder in several ways. If you have a large number of items in the folder, you might want to sort the folder to locate the specific item. In this activity, you will delete a message in Elizabeth Robinson's Inbox and then retrieve the message from the Deleted Items folder, which already contains many deleted items.

1 In the **Navigation Pane**, display the **Inbox** folder. Right-click the **Latest audience demographic data** message, and then click **Delete**.

The message is sent to the Deleted Items folder. You can undo a deletion as long as the folder is still displayed.

2 From the **Edit** menu, click **Undo Delete** to restore the deleted message to the Inbox. Alternatively, hold down Ctrl and press Z. **Delete** the **Latest audience demographic data** message again. In the **Navigation Pane**, display any other folder, and then display the **Inbox** folder again. Display the **Edit** menu.

The Undo Delete command is not present on the Edit menu. If you delete an item and then display a different folder, you must use the Deleted Items folder to recover the item you deleted.

3 In the **Navigation Pane**, click the **Deleted Items** folder, and then compare your screen with Figure 6.41.

This folder contains a number of deleted items. If your Deleted Items folder contains many items, sometimes the first task is to locate the item you want to retrieve. By default, items are sorted by the date. Note that the date refers to the item's creation date, not the date on which the item was deleted. Sometimes it is easier to locate an item by sorting the folder contents by type. The icons next to each item indicate whether the item is a calendar, task, note, contact, or mail item.

Figure 6.41

Dates refer to an item's creation date, not its deletion date

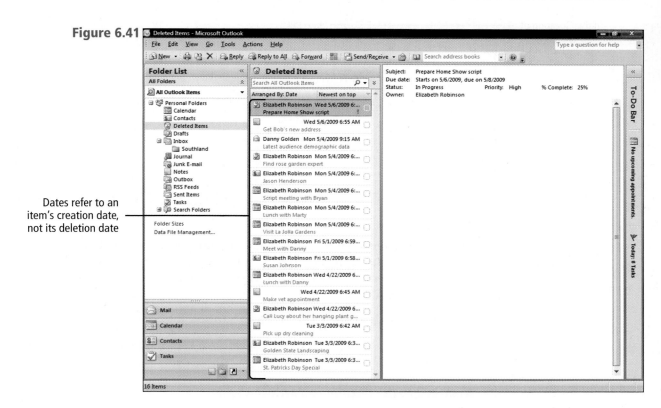

4 In the **Deleted Items** folder, click the **Arranged By** column heading, and then click **Type** to sort the folder by type.

5 Locate and select the **Latest audience demographic data** e-mail message from *Danny Golden*. Right-click the message, and then click **Move to Folder**. Alternatively, click Edit, and then click Move to Folder. Compare your screen with Figure 6.42.

The Move Items dialog box displays. The Inbox folder is already selected—the original location of the message.

Figure 6.42

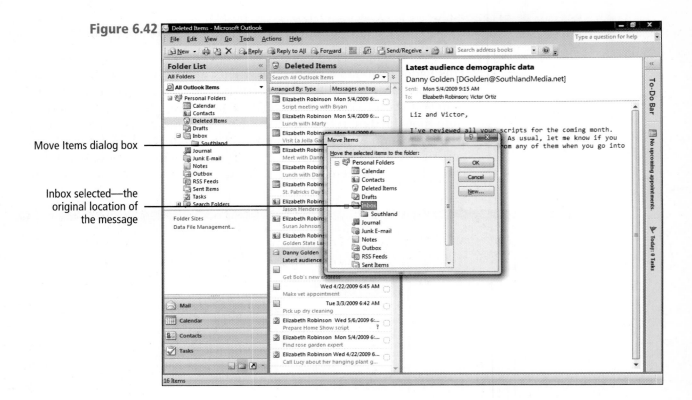

Move Items dialog box

Inbox selected—the original location of the message

6 In the **Move Items** dialog box, click **OK** to move the message to the Inbox. In the **Deleted Items** folder, right-click the **Arranged By** column heading, and then click **Date** to restore the Deleted Items folder to its default sort order.

7 In the **Navigation Pane**, click the **Inbox** folder.

The *Latest audience demographic data* message is restored to the Inbox.

Activity 6.18 Restoring an Archived Item

If you must access archived items, you can display the Archive Folders and return the item to its original location. In this activity, you will restore all the items in Elizabeth Robinson's archived Southland folder to the original Southland folder.

1 Display the **Folder List** if necessary. Use the **scroll bar**, if necessary, to display the lower portion of the Folder List. From the **File** menu, point to **Open**, and then click **Outlook Data File**.

The Open Outlook Data File dialog box displays. Archive Folders is an Outlook data file. When information has been archived, Outlook normally leaves the Archive Folders open. You closed the data file in a previous activity.

Note — Accessing Archived Data

The default location for archived information is an Outlook data file called *archive*. When Outlook archives information, this data file normally remains open and displays in the Folder List. In a previous activity, you created your own data file when you manually archived the Southland folder data. Unless you have created a separate data file for your archived information, you will find the information in the *archive* data file.

2 Navigate to the location where you are storing your folders and projects for this chapter, and then double-click your **6A_Garden_Show_Southland_Firstname_Lastname** file to open it.

Archive Folders displays in the Folder List. Outlook uses this folder name for all archive folders regardless of the name used to store the information.

3 In the **Navigation Pane**, click the **Expand** button (+) next to **Archive Folders**, and then click the **Expand** button (+) next to the **Inbox** folder. Click the archived **Southland** folder to display its contents. In the archived **Southland** folder, right-click the **Arranged By** column heading, and then click **Categories**.

4 In the archived **Southland** folder, hold down ⇧ Shift and then click the first and last item in the folder to select all the items in the folder. Right-click any of the selected items, and then click **Move to Folder**. Compare your screen with Figure 6.43.

The Move Items dialog box displays. The Inbox is already selected as the folder to which the selected messages will be moved.

Figure 6.43

Move Items dialog box

Inbox selected

Archive Folders, Southland folder selected

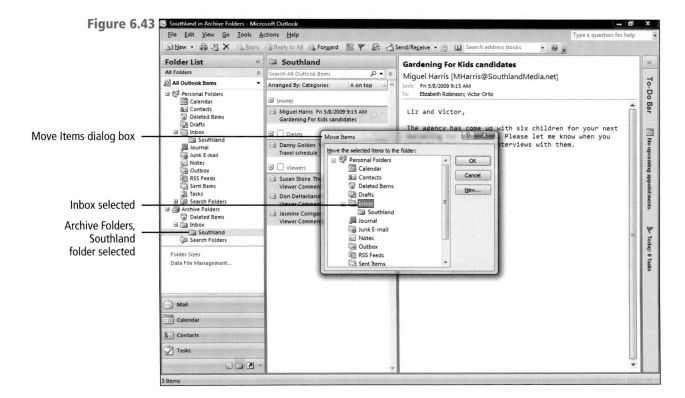

5 In the **Move Items** dialog box, if the Southland folder is not displayed, click the **Expand** button (+) next to **Inbox**. Click **Southland** to select that folder. Click **OK**.

The items in the archived Southland folder are moved to their original location. The archived Southland folder is now empty.

6 Using the techniques you have practiced, press PrtScr, and then paste the screen capture into your **Word** document. **Minimize** ▭ Word.

7 With Outlook displayed, in the **Navigation Pane**, right-click **Archive Folders**, and then click **Close "Archive Folders"** to close the Archive Folders. In the **Navigation Pane**, click the **Southland** folder. From the **View** menu, point to **Arrange By**, and then click **Date**.

The messages have been restored to their original location and are displayed in the default view.

Activity 6.19 Exporting Outlook Information

From Outlook, you can export data to other programs. When you *export* information, you copy data into a file that can be used by another program. You can export Outlook information to Microsoft Access, Microsoft Word, Microsoft Excel, and Microsoft PowerPoint, among other programs.

Exporting Outlook information can be very useful. For example, you may want to use the names and addresses in your Contacts list in an Excel spreadsheet. By exporting the information from Outlook, you do not have to retype the information. You can also export Outlook information to a Personal Folders file, which can then be copied to a different computer. In this activity, you will export and print Elizabeth Robinson's Southland folder.

1 In the **Navigation Pane**, be sure the **Southland** folder is displayed.

2 From the **File** menu, click **Import and Export**. In the **Import and Export Wizard** dialog box, under **Choose an action to perform**, click **Export to a file**, and then click **Next**.

3 In the **Export to a File** dialog box, under **Create a file of type**, click **Personal Folder File (.pst)**, and then click **Next**. Compare your screen with Figure 6.44.

The Export Personal Folders dialog box displays.

Figure 6.44

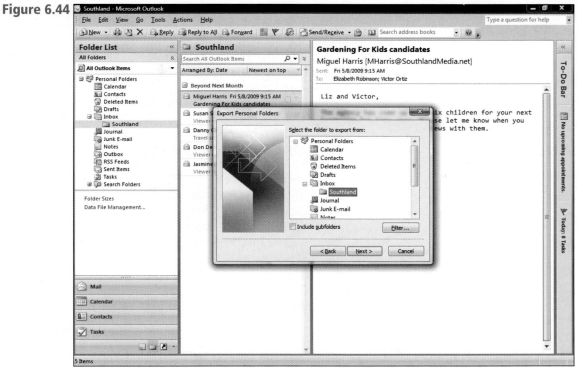

4 In the **Export Personal Folders** dialog box, click the **Southland** folder if necessary, and then click **Next**.

5 In the **Export Personal Folders** dialog box, click **Browse**, and then navigate to the location where you are storing your folders and projects for this chapter. In the **Open Personal Folders** dialog box, in the **File name** box, delete any existing file name, and type **6A_Garden_Show_Exported_Firstname_Lastname** Click **OK**.

The Export Personal Folders dialog box redisplays.

6 In the **Export Personal Folders** dialog box, click **Finish**.

The Create Microsoft Personal Folders dialog box displays.

7 In the **Create Microsoft Personal Folders** dialog box, click **OK**.

The Southland folder is exported to the location of your stored files.

8 From the **File** menu, display the **Page Setup: Table Style** dialog box. Delete any existing header or footer information, and then create a left **Footer** as **6A_Garden_Show_Exported_Firstname_Lastname Preview** and **Print** the document. Submit your end result to your instructor as directed.

9 On the Windows taskbar, click the **Word** button. With **6A_Garden_Show_Screens_Firstname_Lastname** displayed, **Print** the document. Submit the end result to your instructor as directed. **Save** your file and **Close** Word.

More Knowledge

Resending and Recalling Messages

You might want to resend or recall a sent message for any number of reasons. Perhaps someone to whom you sent a message reported that the message was not received or that it was inadvertently deleted. Or perhaps you sent a message to someone and realized that the message contained an error you would like to correct. You can resend any sent message. If you use an Exchange Server e-mail account, you can recall any sent message as long as the message recipient is logged on and has not read the message. (Messages sent to other mail servers cannot be recalled.) To resend or recall a message, display the Sent Items folder, and open the message you want to resend or recall. From the Actions menu, click Resend This Message or Recall This Message. When you recall a message, Outlook will optionally tell you whether the recall succeeds or fails. You can also replace a recalled message with a new one.

Activity 6.20 Restoring Outlook's Default Settings

In this activity, you will restore Outlook to its default settings.

1 In the **Navigation Pane**, right-click the **Southland** folder, click **Delete "Southland"**, and then click **Yes**. Delete the contents of the **Inbox**.

2 In the **Navigation Pane**, click the **Notes** folder. Right-click the **Make dinner reservations** note, point to **Categorize**, and then click **All Categories**.

Recall that you modified the Master Category List. To restore the default categories, you must do so before permanently deleting all items—messages, notes, tasks, contacts, or calendar items.

3 In the **Color Categories** dialog box, click the **Personal** category, and then click **Rename**. With **Personal** selected, type **Blue Category** and then press Enter. Using the technique you just practiced, rename the **Southland** category as **Green Category** Click **OK** to close the **Color Categories** dialog box.

4 In the **Notes** folder, select and delete all the notes. Empty the contents of the **Deleted Items** folder, including the **Southland** subfolder.

5 From the **Tools** menu, click **Options**. Click the **Other tab**, and then click **AutoArchive**. In the **AutoArchive** dialog box, in the **Run AutoArchive every** box, set the number to **14** Be sure that **Clean out items older than** displays **6 Months**. Click **OK**.

6 In the **Options** dialog box, click the **Preferences tab**. Under **E-mail**, click **Junk E-mail**. Click the **Blocked Senders tab**.

7 In the **Junk E-mail Options** dialog box, click **@junkmail.com**, and then click **Remove**. Click **joespam@annoyingviewer.com**, and then click **Remove**. Click **OK**, and then click **OK** to close the Options dialog box.

8 From the **Tools** menu, click **Account Settings**.

The **Account Settings** dialog box displays a list of Outlook's currently configured e-mail accounts. You created the GOMAIL.com account. Your list of accounts may include other accounts.

9 In the **Account Settings** dialog box, under **E-mail Accounts**, click the **GOMAIL.com** account, and then compare your screen with Figure 6.45.

Figure 6.45

Account Settings dialog box

Additional e-mail accounts may display

GOMAIL.com account selected

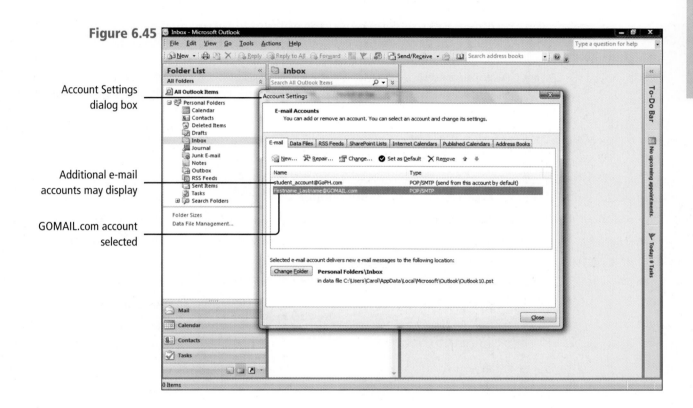

10 With the **GOMAIL.com** account selected, click **Remove**. In the displayed **Account Settings** dialog box, click **Yes**. and then click **Close** to close the **Account Settings** dialog box.

11 From the **File** menu, point to **Page Setup**, and then click **Define Print Styles**. Click **Table Style**, click **Reset**, and then click **OK**.

Close the dialog box. **Close** Outlook.

End **You have completed Project 6A**────────

Content-Based Assessments

Summary

Outlook has a number of tools that help you organize and manage information. In this chapter, you created and renamed e-mail folders. You created rules to have Outlook place incoming e-mail messages into specific e-mail folders. You organized your e-mail messages by moving messages from one folder to another. You worked with Outlook's junk e-mail filter to screen out unwanted and unsolicited e-mail. You organized your e-mail messages by using different view filters. You modified the Master Category List by adding new categories and deleting existing ones. You created, edited, and printed various notes and viewed them in different ways. You also archived Outlook information. Finally, you recovered and exported Outlook information.

Key Terms

Outlook

chapter six

Matching

Match each term in the second column with its correct definition in the first column by writing the letter of the term on the blank line in front of the correct definition.

_____ **1.** Actions taken on messages to organize a folder, based on certain conditions, along with any exceptions to those conditions.

_____ **2.** In a rule, the criteria a message must meet in order for the specified action to be applied.

_____ **3.** A program that guides you through the process of creating a message rule.

_____ **4.** A set of predefined conditions and actions in rule creation used for common processing tasks.

_____ **5.** In a message rule, the criteria that exclude a message from the specified action when all other conditions of the rule are satisfied.

_____ **6.** The rightmost portion of the Windows taskbar, next to the system time, in which Outlook displays information such as alerts.

_____ **7.** A notification that displays on your desktop briefly when you receive an e-mail message, meeting request, or task request.

_____ **8.** A set of instructions to screen a folder, based on conditions you define.

_____ **9.** The portion of an e-mail address that defines the mail system or Internet Service Provider.

_____ **10.** A notification button that displays on the Windows taskbar when you receive an e-mail message, meeting request, or task request.

_____ **11.** To move Outlook information that you want to keep to a location for storage and future access.

_____ **12.** The term used to refer to Outlook settings that apply to all, not just some, of Outlook's folders.

_____ **13.** Outlook's default name in the Folder List for the location of files stored for future access.

_____ **14.** To copy Outlook data into a file that can be used by another program.

_____ **15.** The Outlook feature that automatically moves information that you want to keep to a location for storage and future access.

A Archive

B Archive Folders

C AutoArchive

D Conditions

E Desktop Alert

F Domain name

G Exceptions

H Export

I Filter

J Global

K New Item Alert

L Notification area

M Rules

N Rules Wizard

O Template

Content-Based Assessments

Fill in the Blank

Write the correct answer in the space provided.

1. When you create a new mail folder, the folder typically is a subfolder of the _____ folder.

2. An explanation of the actions a rule performs on a message is called the _____ _____.

3. When a Desktop Alert displays, you can keep the alert displaying by moving the _____ _____ onto the alert while it is still visible.

4. By default, Desktop Alerts display in the lower _____ corner of the screen.

5. A message rule that you define by specifying your own conditions and actions as you create it is called a(n) _____ rule.

6. You can have Outlook screen your incoming e-mail for unwanted, unsolicited e-mail by using the _____ _____ filter.

7. If you want to display only specific messages in an e-mail folder, you can use a(n) _____ filter to define the types of messages that you want to display.

8. A Windows feature that creates a screen capture and stores the image on the Windows Clipboard is called _____ _____.

9. The _____ component of Outlook is the electronic equivalent of sticky paper notes.

10. In the Notes folder, the _____ _____ view displays notes in a table and shows the text of the notes but does not group the notes by category.

11. You can organize your Outlook notes by assigning them to _____.

12. For home accounts, a common protocol used to retrieve e-mail messages from an Internet e-mail server is _____.

13. To immediately recover a deleted item when the folder is still displayed, you can use the Undo Delete command on the _____ menu.

14. In the Deleted Items folder, an item's date refers not to the date the item was deleted, but instead to the date the item was _____.

15. When locating a deleted item in the Deleted Items folder, it is sometimes easier to find an item by sorting the folder contents by _____ and then using the icons to locate the item.

Content-Based Assessments

Skills Review

Project 6B — Advertising

Objectives: 1. *Manage Mail Folders;* **2.** *Modify the Master Category List.*

In the following Skills Review, you will handle the e-mail messages for Elizabeth Robinson, cohost of Southland Media's *Southland Gardens* television program. Ms. Robinson has been asked by Danny Golden, the president of Southland Media, to consider ways to use products marketed by a major new advertiser on Southland Gardens. Subtle product placement has been one of the keys to the program's success with advertisers. Ms. Robinson receives numerous e-mail messages regarding this project. Your completed document will look similar to the one shown in Figure 6.46.

For Project 6B, you will need the following file:

o06B_Advertising_Inbox

You will print two files with the following footers:
6B_Advertising_Firstname_Lastname
6B_Advertising_Screens_Firstname_Lastname

Figure 6.46

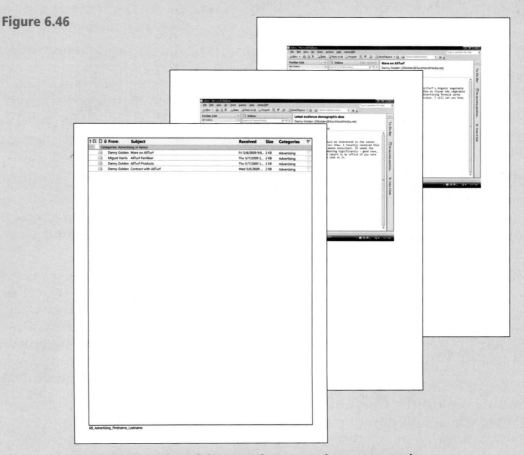

(Project 6B–Advertising continues on the next page)

Content-Based Assessments

(Project 6B–Advertising continued)

1. **Start** Outlook. In the **Navigation Pane**, display the **Inbox**. Delete any existing messages. Display the **Import and Export Wizard** dialog box. Under **Choose an action to perform**, click **Import from another program or file**, and then click **Next**. In the **Import a File** dialog box, under **Select file type to import from**, click **Personal Folder File (.pst)**, and then click **Next**.

2. In the **Import Personal Folders** dialog box, click **Browse**. In the **Open Personal Folders** dialog box, navigate to the location where the student files for this textbook are stored. Select **o06B_Advertising_Inbox** and click **Open**. In the **Import Personal Folders** dialog box, click **Next**. The data file contains items in the **Inbox** and **Deleted Items** folders.

3. In the **Import Personal Folders** dialog box, with **Personal Folders** selected, click **Finish**. If a Translation Warning dialog box displays, click OK.

4. With the **Inbox** folder displayed, from the **File** menu, point to **New**, and then click **Folder**. In the **Create New Folder** dialog box, in the **Name** box, type **Advertising** Under **Select where to place the folder**, click **Inbox**. Be sure the **Folder contains** box displays *Mail and Post Items*. Click **OK**. If necessary, click the Expand button next to Inbox to see the **Advertising** folder.

5. On the Windows taskbar, click the **Start** button. From the displayed **Start** menu, locate the **Microsoft Office Word 2007** program. **Maximize** the Word window.

6. On the Ribbon, click the **Office** button, and then click **Save As**. In the **Save As** dialog box, navigate to the location where you are storing your files. In the **File name** box, type **6B_Advertising_Screens_Firstname_Lastname** and then click **Save**.

7. On the Ribbon, click the **Insert tab**, and then click **Footer**. In the drop down list, click **Edit Footer**, and then type **6B_Advertising_Screens_Firstname_Lastname** On the Ribbon, in the **Close group**, click **Close Header and Footer**. **Minimize** Word.

8. With the **Outlook** window displayed, press PrtScr, located in the upper right area of your keyboard.

9. On the Windows taskbar, click the **Word** button. On the Ribbon, click the **Home tab**, and then, in the **Clipboard group**, click **Paste**. Alternatively press Ctrl + V.

10. Locate the insertion point, at the bottom right of the graphic, and press Ctrl + Enter to create a new page.

11. On the Quick Access Toolbar, click the **Save** button, and then **Minimize** Word.

12. With Outlook's **Inbox** folder displayed, from the **View** menu, point to **Arrange By**, and then click **Custom**. In the **Customize View: Messages** dialog box, click **Filter**.

13. In the **Filter** dialog box, in the **Search for the word(s)** box, type **AllTurf** and then click **OK**. Click **OK** to close the **Customize View: Messages** dialog box.

14. Using the techniques you have practiced, press PrtScr, and then paste the screen capture into your **Word** document. **Minimize** Word.

15. In the **Inbox**, click the first item, hold down ⇧Shift, and then click the last item to select all the items in the folder. Right-click a selected message, and then click **Move to Folder**. In the **Move Items** dialog box, click the **Advertising** folder, and then click **OK**. If a **Microsoft Office Outlook** dialog box displays, click **OK**.

16. From the **View** menu, point to **Arrange By**, and then click **Custom**. In the

(Project 6B–Advertising continues on the next page)

Content-Based Assessments

Skills Review

(Project 6B–Advertising continued)

Customize View: Messages dialog box, click **Filter**. In the **Filter** dialog box, click **Clear All**, and then click **OK** two times to turn off the filter and close the dialog boxes.

17. In the **Navigation Pane**, display the **Advertising** folder. If the **Arranged By: Date** column heading is not displayed, click the column heading, and click **Date**. Select all the messages in the folder. From the **Edit** menu, point to **Categorize**, and then click **All Categories** to display the **Color Categories** dialog box.

18. In the **Color Categories** dialog box, click **New**. In the **Add New Category** dialog box, in the **Name** box, type **Advertising** Click the **Color arrow**, click **None**, and then click **OK**. Click **OK** to close the dialog box.

19. In the **Advertising** folder, click the **Arranged By** column heading, and then click **Categories**. If necessary, click the **Expand** button to display category items. From the **File** menu, display the **Page Setup: Table Style** dialog box. On the **Header/Footer tab**, delete any existing header or footer information, including dates and page numbers. In the left **Footer** box, type **6B_Advertising_ Firstname_Lastname Preview** and **Print** the document. Submit the end result to your instructor as directed.

20. On the Windows taskbar, click the **Word** button. With **6B_Advertising_Screens_ Firstname_Lastname** displayed, **Print** the document. Submit the end result to your instructor as directed. **Save** your file and **Close** Word.

21. In the **Advertising** folder, click the **Arranged By** column heading, and then click **Date** to restore the default arrangement.

22. Right-click any message, point to **Categorize**, and then click **All Categories** to display the **Color Categories** dialog box. Select the **Advertising** category, and then click **Delete** to delete the category from the Master Category List. If a **Microsoft Office Outlook** dialog box displays, click **Yes. Close** the **Color Categories** dialog box.

23. In the **Navigation Pane**, click the **Advertising** folder. On the Standard toolbar, click the **Delete** button, and then click **Yes**.

24. Delete the contents of the **Inbox**. Empty the contents of the **Deleted Items** folder, including the **Advertising** folder. From the **File** menu, point to **Page Setup**, and then click **Define Print Styles**. Click **Table Style**, click **Reset**, and then click **OK. Close** the dialog box, and **Close** Outlook.

End You have completed Project 6B ————————————————

chaptersix

Skills Review

Project 6C — Commercial

Objectives: 3. *Use Notes;* **5.** *Recover and Export Outlook Information.*

In the following Skills Review, you will create notes for Elizabeth Robinson related to an upcoming project. Southland Media is preparing a series of television commercials promoting its gardening show, *Southland Gardens.* These commercials will be broadcast on the cable channel that carries its show and other cable channels serving the San Diego market. The show's cohosts, Ms. Robinson and Victor Ortiz, will be featured in the 15-second spots. Your completed document will look similar to the one shown in Figure 6.47.

For Project 6C, you will need the following file:

o06C_Commercial_Deleted

You will print one file with the following footer:
6C_Commercial_Notes_Firstname_Lastname

Figure 6.47

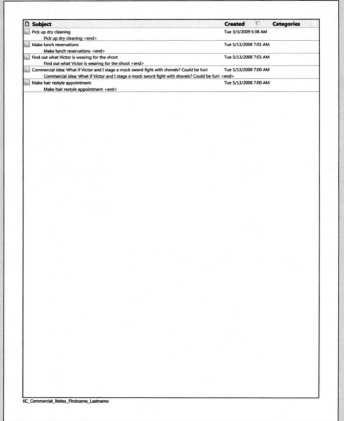

(Project 6C–Commercial continues on the next page)

Content-Based Assessments

Skills Review

(Project 6C–Commercial continued)

1. **Start** Outlook. From the **Navigation Pane**, display the **Inbox**. Delete any existing messages. Display the **Import and Export Wizard** dialog box, and under **Choose an action to perform**, click **Import from another program or file**, and then click **Next**. In the **Import a File** dialog box, under **Select file type to import from**, click **Personal Folder File (.pst)**, and then click **Next**.

2. In the **Import Personal Folders** dialog box, click **Browse**. In the **Open Personal Folders** dialog box, navigate to the location where the student files for this textbook are stored. Select **o06C_Commercial_Deleted** and click **Open**. In the **Import Personal Folders** dialog box, click **Next**.

3. In the **Import Personal Folders** dialog box, with **Personal Folders** selected, click **Finish**. If a Translation Warning dialog box displays, click OK.

4. In the **Navigation Pane**, at the bottom of the pane, click the **Notes** button. Delete any existing notes. On the Standard toolbar, click the **New Note** button.

5. In the **Note** window, type **Make hair restyle appointment** In the upper left corner of the note, click the **Note** icon, and then, from the displayed menu, click **Close**.

6. Right-click any blank area of the **Notes** folder, and then click **New Note**. Type **Commercial idea: What if Victor and I stage a mock sword fight with shovels? Could be fun!** In the **Note** window, click the **Close** button.

7. Open a new note, type **Find out what Victor is wearing for the shoot** and then close the note. Open a new note, type **Make lunch reservations** and then close the note.

8. In the **Navigation Pane**, click the **Folder List** button, and then click the **Deleted Items** folder. In the **Deleted Items** folder, click the **Arranged By** column heading, and then click **Type**.

9. Locate and click the **Pick up dry cleaning** note. Right-click the note, and then click **Move to Folder**. In the **Move Items** dialog box, click the **Notes** folder, and then click **OK**.

10. Display the **Notes** folder. At the bottom of the **Navigation Pane**, click the **Notes** button to display **Current View**. In the **Navigation Pane**, under **Current View**, click **Notes List**. From the **File** menu, display the **Page Setup: Table Style** dialog box. On the **Header/Footer tab**, delete any existing header or footer information, and then, in the left **Footer** box, type **6C_Commercial_Notes_Firstname_Lastname** **Preview** and **Print** the notes list. Submit the end result to your instructor as directed.

11. In the **Navigation Pane**, under **Current View**, click **Icons**. Delete all the notes.

12. In the **Navigation Pane**, click the **Folder List** button, and then click the **Deleted Items** folder. In the **Deleted Items** folder, click the **Arranged By** column heading, and then click **Date**. Empty the contents of the **Deleted Items** folder. From the **File** menu, point to **Page Setup**, and then display the **Define Print Styles** dialog box. Click **Table Style**, click **Reset**, and then click **OK**. **Close** the dialog box, and then **Close** Outlook.

End **You have completed Project 6C**

Project 6D — Vegetable Tips

Objectives: 1. *Manage Mail Folders;* **4.** *Archive Outlook Information.*

In the following Skills Review, you will manage and organize Victor Ortiz's Inbox. Mr. Ortiz is the cohost of Southland Media's *Southland Gardens* gardening show. His expertise is vegetable gardens; and he gets new ideas and tips from viewers, which he often receives as e-mail messages. He likes to keep these messages for future reference. When he uses an idea or a tip in his show, he gives on-air credit to the person who sent the idea to him and sends the person a *Southland Gardens* T-shirt. Your completed document will look similar to the one shown in Figure 6.48.

For Project 6D, you will need the following file:

o06D_Vegetable_Tips_Inbox

You will print two files with the following footers:
6D_Vegetable_Tips_Firstname_Lastname
6D_Vegetable_Tips_Screens_Firstname_Lastname

Figure 6.48

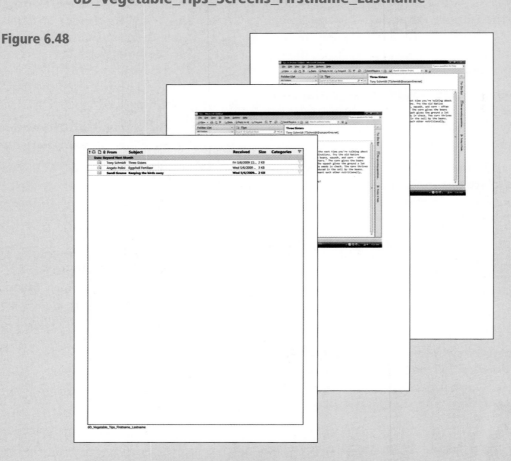

(Project 6D–Vegetable Tips continues on the next page)

Content-Based Assessments

(Project 6D–Vegetable Tips continued)

1. **Start** Outlook, and display the **Inbox**. Delete any existing messages. Display the **Import and Export Wizard** dialog box, under **Choose an action to perform**, click **Import from another program or file**, and then click **Next**. In the **Import a File** dialog box, under **Select file type to import from**, click **Personal Folder File (.pst)**, and then click **Next**.

2. In the **Import Personal Folders** dialog box, click **Browse**. In the **Open Personal Folders** dialog box, navigate to the location where the student files for this textbook are stored. Select **o06D_Vegetable_Tips_Inbox** and click **Open**. In the **Import Personal Folders** dialog box, click **Next**.

3. In the **Import Personal Folders** dialog box, with **Personal Folders** selected, click **Finish**. If a Translation Warning dialog box displays, click OK.

4. Be sure the **Inbox** folder is displayed. From the **File** menu, point to **New**, and then click **Folder**. In the **Create New Folder** dialog box, in the **Name** box, type Tips Under **Select where to place the folder**, click **Inbox**. Be sure the **Folder contains** box displays *Mail and Post Items*. Click **OK**. If necessary, click the Expand button next to Inbox to see the Tips folder.

5. In the **Inbox**, drag the **Tony Schmidt** message to the **Tips** folder. Drag the **Angelo Polini** and **Sandi Greene** messages to the **Tips** folder. Display the **Tips** folder.

6. On the Windows taskbar, click the **Start** button. In the displayed **Start** menu, locate the **Microsoft Office Word 2007** program. If necessary, **Maximize** the Word window.

7. On the Ribbon, click the **Office** button, and then click **Save As**. In the **Save As** dialog box, navigate to the location where you are storing your files. In the **File name** box, type **6D_Vegetable_Tips_Screens_Firstname_Lastname** and then click **Save**.

8. On the Ribbon, click the **Insert tab**, and then click **Footer**. In the drop down list, click **Edit Footer**, and then type 6D_Vegetable_Tips_Screens_Firstname_Lastname On the Ribbon, in the **Close group**, click **Close Header and Footer**. **Minimize** Word.

9. With the **Outlook** window displayed, press PrtScr, located in the upper right area of your keyboard.

10. On the Windows taskbar, click the **Word** button. On the Ribbon, click the **Home tab**, and then, in the Clipboard **group**, click **Paste**.

11. Deselect the graphic, if necessary. Locate the insertion point, at the bottom right of the graphic, and press Ctrl + Enter to create a new page.

12. On the Quick Access Toolbar, click **Save**, and then **Minimize** Word.

13. In the displayed **Tips** folder, if necessary, click the **Arranged By** column heading, and then click **Date**. From the **File** menu, click **Archive**. In the **Archive** dialog box, under **Archive this folder and all sub-folders**, click **Tips**. In the **Archive items older than** box, type 05/10/09

14. In the **Archive** dialog box, click **Browse**, and then navigate to the location where you are storing your folder and projects for this chapter. In the **Open Personal Folders** dialog box, in the **File name** box, delete any existing file name, and type 6D_Vegetable_Tips_Firstname_Lastname Click **OK**. In the **Archive** dialog box, click **OK**. If a warning displays, indicating that the date you entered is in the future, click **Yes** to continue.

(Project 6D–Vegetable Tips continues on the next page)

Content-Based Assessments

(Project 6D–Vegetable Tips continued)

15. In the **Navigation Pane**, click the **Folder List** button. Under **All Folders**, scroll down to view **Archive Folders** in the list. Click the **Expand** button next to **Archive Folders** to display the subfolders. Click the **Expand** button next to the **Inbox** sub-folder, and then click the archived **Tips** folder to display its contents. In the **Arranged By** column heading, be sure the messages in the **Tips** folder are arranged by **Date**; if not, click the **Arranged By** column heading and click **Date**.

16. Using the techniques you have practiced, press PrtScr, and then paste the screen capture into your **Word** document. **Minimize** Word.

17. From the **File** menu, display the **Page Setup: Table Style** dialog box. On the **Header/Footer tab**, delete any existing header or footer information, and in the left **Footer** box, type **6D_Vegetable_Tips_ Firstname_Lastname Preview** and **Print** the document. Submit the end result to your instructor as directed.

18. On the Windows taskbar, click the **Word** button. With **6D_Vegetable_Tips_Screens_ Firstname_Lastname** displayed, **Print** the document. Submit the end result to your instructor as directed. **Save** your file and **Close** Word.

19. With Outlook displayed, in the **Folder List**, right-click **Archive Folders**, and then click **Close "Archive Folders"**. Delete the **Tips** folder. Delete the contents of the **Inbox**. Empty the contents of the **Deleted Items** folder, including the **Tips** folder. From the **File** menu, point to **Page Setup**, display the **Define Print Styles** dialog box, and then **Reset** the **Table Style** print style. **Close** the dialog box, and **Close** Outlook.

End **You have completed Project 6D**

Content-Based Assessments

Mastering Outlook

Project 6E — Supervisor

Objective: 1. *Manage Mail Folders.*

In the following Mastering Outlook project, you will organize Victor Ortiz's Inbox. Mr. Ortiz, the cohost of Southland Media's *Southland Gardens* TV show, receives daily e-mail messages from his boss, Danny Golden, who is president of Southland Media. Victor would like to have Outlook process incoming mail from Danny automatically. Your completed document will look similar to the one shown in Figure 6.49.

For Project 6E, you will need the following file:

o06E_Supervisor_Inbox

You will print two files with the following footers:
6E_Supervisor_Firstname_Lastname
6E_Supervisor_Screens_Firstname_Lastname

Figure 6.49

(Project 6E–Supervisor continues on the next page)

Content-Based Assessments

(Project 6E–Supervisor continued)

1. **Start** Outlook, and display the **Inbox**. From the **Tools** menu, click **Account Settings** to display the Account Settings dialog box. Under **E-mail**, click the **New** button.

2. In the **Add New E-mail Account** wizard, using the techniques you have practiced, set up a **POP3** account with the following information:

   Your Name: Firstname Lastname
   E-mail Address:
   Firstname_Lastname@GOPrenHall.com
   Incoming mail server (POP3):
   GOPrenHall.com
   Outgoing mail server (SMTP): PHGO.com
   User Name: Firstname_Lastname
   Password: 123456

3. With the **Account Settings** dialog box still displayed, press (PrtScr).

4. Using the techniques you have practiced, in Word, **Save** a new document with the file name 6E_Supervisor_Screens_Firstname_ Lastname Add the file name as a footer. **Paste** the screen capture, and then **Minimize** Word.

5. In the **Account Settings** dialog box, click **Close**. From the **Tools** menu, click **Rules and Alerts**. Delete any existing rules, and then close the **Rules and Alerts** dialog box. Display the **Inbox** and delete any existing messages.

6. Using the techniques you have practiced, import **o06E_Supervisor_Inbox** into **Personal Folders**.

7. With the **Inbox** folder selected, from the **File** menu, display the **Create New Folder** dialog box. As the folder name, type **Danny** and then place the folder within the Inbox folder. Be sure the **Folder contains** box displays *Mail and Post Items*. **Expand** the

Inbox, if necessary, to view the *Danny* folder.

8. Using the techniques you have practiced, press (PrtScr), and then **Paste** the screen capture into your **Word** document. **Minimize** Word.

9. Display the **Inbox** folder. Click the **Tractors, etc.** message from *Danny Golden*, and then, on the Standard toolbar, click the **Create Rule** button.

10. In the **Create Rule** dialog box, select the **From Danny Golden** check box, and then click **Advanced Options**. In the **Rules Wizard** dialog box, under **Step 1: Select condition(s)**, select the first check box— **from Danny Golden**—and, if necessary, scroll to the end of the list, and select the **on this machine only** check box.

11. In the **Rules Wizard** dialog box, click **Next**. In the **Rules Wizard** dialog box, under **What do you want to do with the message?** select the **move it to the specified folder** check box. Under **Step 2: Edit the rule description (click an underlined value)**, click **specified**. In the **Rules and Alerts** dialog box, **Expand** the **Inbox** if necessary, and then click the **Danny** folder. Click **OK**.

12. In the **Rules Wizard** dialog box, click **Next** to display the list of exceptions. Click **Next** again to skip the exceptions. In the **Rules Wizard** dialog box, under **Step 1: Specify a name for this rule**, type Danny Under **Step 2: Setup rule options**, select the **Run this rule now on messages already in "Inbox"** check box.

13. Using the techniques you have practiced, press (PrtScr), and then **Paste** the screen capture into your **Word** document. **Minimize** Word.

(Project 6E–Supervisor continues on the next page)

Content-Based Assessments

(Project 6E–Supervisor continued)

14. With the **Rules Wizard** dialog box displayed, click **Finish**.

15. Display the contents of the **Danny** folder. In the **Arranged By** column heading, be sure the messages in the Danny folder are arranged by **Date**; if not, click the **Arranged By** column heading, and then click **Date**.

16. **Print** the messages in **Table Style** using the footer **6E_Supervisor_Firstname_ Lastname** Submit the end result to your instructor as directed.

17. On the Windows taskbar, click the **Word** button. With **6E_Supervisor_Screens_ Firstname_Lastname** displayed, **Print** the document. Submit the end result to your instructor as directed. **Save** your file and **Close** Word.

18. From the **Tools** menu, display the **Rules and Alerts** dialog box, click to highlight the **Danny** rule, and then click **Delete**. Click **Yes** to confirm the deletion, and then close the dialog box. In the **Folder List**, delete the **Danny** folder. Delete the contents of the **Inbox**. Empty the **Deleted Items** folder, including the **Danny** subfolder. Display the **Define Print Styles** dialog box, and **Reset** the **Table Style** print style.

19. From the **Tools** menu, click **Account Settings**. In the **E-mail Accounts** dialog box, under **Name**, click **GOPrenHall.com**, click **Remove**, and then click **Yes**. Click **Finish**, and then **Close** Outlook.

End **You have completed Project 6E** —————————

Content-Based Assessments

Mastering Outlook

Project 6F — Roses

Objectives: 1. *Manage Mail Folders;* **2.** *Modify the Master Category List;* **3.** *Use Notes;* **5.** *Recover and Export Outlook Information.*

In the following Mastering Outlook project, you will organize Elizabeth Robinson's e-mail folders and create notes for her about an upcoming show on roses. Ms. Robinson's *Southland Gardens* program is planning a show devoted exclusively to rose gardening. She has received several messages related to the show. Your completed documents will look similar to the ones shown in Figure 6.50.

For Project 6F, you will need the following file:

o06F_Roses_Inbox

You will print three files with the following footers:
6F_Roses_Firstname_Lastname
6F_Roses_Notes_Firstname_Lastname
6F_Roses_Screens_Firstname_Lastname

Figure 6.50

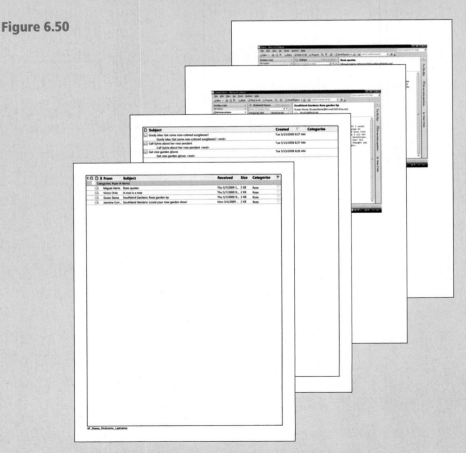

(Project 6F–Roses continues on the next page)

Content-Based Assessments

(Project 6F–Roses continued)

1. **Start** Outlook, and display the **Inbox**. Delete any existing messages.

2. Using the techniques you have practiced, import **o06F_Roses_Inbox** into **Personal Folders**.

3. Display the **Deleted Items** folder. From the **View** menu, display the **Customize View: Messages** dialog box, and then click **Filter**. In the **Search for the word(s)** box, type **rose** Click the **In arrow**, click **subject field and message body**, and then click **OK**. Click **OK** to close the **Customize View: Messages** dialog box.

4. With the **Deleted Items** folder displayed, press [PrtScr].

5. Using the techniques you have practiced, in Word, **Save** a new document with the file name **6F_Roses_Screens_Firstname_Lastname** Add the file name as a footer. **Paste** the screen capture, and then **Minimize** Word.

6. With the **Deleted Items** folder displayed, move the two **Southland Gardens** messages to the **Inbox** folder in the **Folder List**.

7. With the **Deleted Items** folder still displayed, from the **View** menu, display the **Customize View: Messages** dialog box, and click **Filter**. In the **Filter** dialog box, click **Clear All**, and then close the dialog boxes.

8. Display the **Inbox**, and display the **Customize View: Messages** dialog box. Click **Filter**, and create a filter, searching for the word **rose** in the **subject field and message body**. **Close** the dialog boxes.

9. With the **Inbox** displayed, press [PrtScr]. Using the techniques you have practiced, in Word, **Paste** the screen capture, and then **Minimize** Word.

10. In the filtered **Inbox**, select all the messages, right-click any of the selected messages, point to **Categorize**, and then click **All Categories**. In the **Color Categories** dialog box, create a new category with the name **Rose** and color **None**. **Close** the **Color Categories** dialog box.

11. In the **Inbox**, click the **Arranged By** column heading, and then click **Categories**. Turn off the **Reading Pane**. **Print** the messages in **Table Style** using the footer **6F_Roses_Firstname_Lastname** Submit the end result to your instructor as directed.

12. With any message selected, from the **Edit** menu, point to **Categorize**, and then click **All Categories**. In the **Color Categories** dialog box, delete the **Rose** category. **Close** the **Color Categories** dialog box.

13. Display the **Customize View: Messages** dialog box. Click **Filter**, and clear the filter. Click **OK** to close the dialog boxes. From the **View** menu, point to **Arranged By**, and then click **Date**. Redisplay the **Reading Pane** on the **Right**.

14. Display the **Notes** folder. Open a new note, type **Get new garden gloves** and then close the note. Using the same techniques, create two new notes with the following text: **Call Sylvia about her rose pendant** **Goofy idea: Get some rose-colored sunglasses?**

15. Change the **Current View** to **Notes List**. **Print** the notes list in **Table Style** using the footer **6F_Roses_Notes_Firstname_Lastname** Submit the end result to your instructor as directed.

16. On the Windows taskbar, click the **Word** button. With **6F_Roses_Screens_Firstname_Lastname** displayed, **Print** the document. Submit the end result to your instructor as directed. **Save** your file and **Close** Word.

17. With the Notes list displayed, change the **Current View** to **Icons**. Delete the contents of the **Notes** folder. Delete the contents of the **Inbox**. Empty the **Deleted Items** folder. Display the **Define Print Styles** dialog box, and **Reset** the **Table Style** print style. **Close** Outlook.

End **You have completed Project 6F**

Mastering Outlook

Project 6G—Colleague

Objectives: 1. *Manage Mail Folders;* **4.** *Archive Outlook Information.*

In the following Mastering Outlook project, you will organize Elizabeth Robinson's e-mail messages. Ms. Robinson of Southland Media organizes her e-mail messages by sorting e-mail she frequently receives from some of her colleagues into separate folders. Miguel Harris, her colleague, is responsible for much of the production work for their *Southland Gardens* television program, and she likes to keep his messages for future reference. Your printed document will look similar to the one shown in Figure 6.51.

For Project 6G, you will need the following file:

o06G_Colleague_Inbox

You will print two files with the following footers:
6G_Colleague_Firstname_Lastname
6G_Colleague_Screens_Firstname_Lastname

Figure 6.51

(**Project 6G–Colleague continues on the next page**)

Content-Based Assessments

Mastering Outlook

(Project 6G–Colleague continued)

1. **Start** Outlook and display the **Inbox** folder. From the **Tools** menu, click **Account Settings** to display the Account Settings dialog box. Under **E-mail**, click the **New** button.

2. In the **New E-mail Account** wizard, using the techniques you have practiced, create a new **POP3** account with the following information.

   Your Name: Firstname Lastname
   E-mail Address:
   Firstname_Lastname@PrenHall.com
   Incoming mail server (POP3):
   PrenHall.com
   Outgoing mail server (SMTP): GOPH.com
   User Name: Firstname_Lastname
   Password: 123456

3. With the **Account Settings** dialog box still displayed, press PrtScr.

4. Using the techniques you have practiced, in Word, **Save** a new document with the file name **6G_Colleague_Screens_Firstname_Lastname** Add the file name as a footer. **Paste** the screen capture, and then **Minimize** Word.

5. In the **Account Settings** dialog box, click **Close**. With the **Inbox** displayed, delete any existing messages. Display the **Rules and Alerts** dialog box, delete any existing rules, and then close the dialog box.

6. Using the techniques you have practiced, import **o06G_Colleague_Inbox** file into **Personal Folders**.

7. With the **Inbox** folder displayed, display the **Create New Folder** dialog box, and then create a new folder with the **Name Miguel** Under **Select where to place the folder**, click **Inbox**. Be sure the **Folder contains** box displays *Mail and Post Items*. Display the **Miguel** folder.

8. Using the techniques you have practiced, press PrtScr, and then paste the screen capture into your **Word** document. **Minimize** Word.

9. Display the **Inbox** folder, and click the **Garden Tools show** message from *Miguel Harris*. Click the **Create Rule** button. In the **Create Rule** dialog box, select the **From Miguel Harris** check box. Click **Advanced Options**.

10. In the **Rules Wizard** dialog box, under **Step 1: Select condition(s)**, be sure the **from Miguel Harris** check box is selected, and then scroll to the bottom of the list and select the **on this machine only** check box. Click **Next**.

11. In the **Rules Wizard** dialog box, under **What do you want to do with the message?** select the **move it to the specified folder** check box. In the lower portion of the dialog box, under **Step 2: Edit the rule description (click an underlined value)**, click **specified**. In the **Rules and Alerts** dialog box, click the **Expand** button next to **Inbox**, and then click the **Miguel** folder. Click **OK**.

12. In the **Rules Wizard** dialog box, click **Next** to display the list of exceptions. Click **Next** to finish the rule setup. Under **Step 1: Specify a name for this rule**, type **Miguel** Under **Step 2: Setup rule options**, select the **Run this rule now on messages already in "Inbox"** check box.

13. Using the techniques you have practiced, press PrtScr, and then paste the screen capture into your **Word** document. **Minimize** Word.

14. In the displayed **Rules Wizard** dialog box, click **Finish**. Display the **Miguel** folder. Look at the **Arranged By** column heading,

(Project 6G–Colleague continues on the next page)

(Project 6G–Colleague continued)

and be sure the messages are arranged by **Date**. Change the arrangement if necessary by clicking the **Arranged By** column heading.

15. Display the **Archive** dialog box. Under **Archive this folder and all subfolders**, click **Miguel** if the folder is not already selected. In the **Archive items older than** box, type **05/10/09**

16. In the **Archive** dialog box, click **Browse**, and then navigate to the location where you are storing your folders and projects. In the **Open Personal Folders** dialog box, in the **File name** box, delete any existing file name, and type **6G_Colleague_Firstname_Lastname** Click **OK** two times to close the dialog boxes and archive the messages in the **Miguel** folder. If a warning displays, indicating that the date you entered is in the future, click **Yes** to continue.

17. Display the **Folder List**, scroll down to view **Archive Folders**, and then click the **Expand** button next to **Archive Folders**. Click the **Expand** button next to the **Inbox** subfolder. Click the archived **Miguel** folder to display its contents, which are the messages you just archived.

18. Using the techniques you have practiced, press [PrtScr], and then paste the screen capture into your **Word** document. **Minimize** Word.

19. In the archived **Miguel** folder, be sure the messages are arranged by **Date**. **Print** the messages in **Table Style** using the footer **6G_Colleague_Firstname_Lastname** Submit the end result to your instructor as directed.

20. On the Windows taskbar, click the **Word** button. With **6G_Colleague_Screens_ Firstname_Lastname** displayed, **Print** the document. Submit the end result to your instructor as directed. **Save** your file and **Close** Word.

21. Display the **Rules and Alerts** dialog box, and delete the **Miguel** rule. In the **Navigation Pane**, right-click **Archive Folders**, and then click **Close "Archive Folders"**. Delete the **Miguel** folder. Delete the contents of the **Inbox**. Empty the **Deleted Items** folder, including the **Miguel** folder. **Reset** the **Table Style** print style.

22. From the **Tools** menu, click **Account Settings**. Under **Name**, click **PrenHall.com**, click **Remove**, and then click **Yes**. Click **Close**, and then **Close** Outlook.

End **You have completed Project 6G**

chaptersix

Outlook

Mastering Outlook

Project 6H — Scripts

Objectives: 1. *Manage Mail Folders;* **2.** *Modify the Master Category List;*
4. *Archive Outlook Information;* **5.** *Recover and Export Outlook Information.*

In the following Mastering Outlook project, you will organize Elizabeth Robinson's Inbox. Victor Ortiz and Ms. Robinson, cohosts of Southland Media's *Southland Gardens* television show, work closely with the company president, Danny Golden, in preparing scripts for the upcoming shows. Mr. Golden often gives feedback on scripts in e-mail exchanges. Ms. Robinson would like to separate and save for future reference all messages about their script discussions. Your completed document will look similar to the one shown in Figure 6.52.

For Project 6H, you will need the following file:

o06H_Scripts_Inbox

You will print two files with the following footers:
6H_Scripts_Firstname_Lastname
6H_Scripts_Screens_Firstname_Lastname

Figure 6.52

(Project 6H–Scripts continues on the next page)

Content-Based Assessments

(Project 6H–Scripts continued)

1. **Start** Outlook. Start the **New E-mail Accounts** wizard. Using the techniques you have practiced, create a new **POP3** account with the following information:

    Your Name: Firstname Lastname
    E-mail Address:
    Firstname_Lastname@PHMAIL.com
    Incoming mail server (POP3):
    PHMAIL.com
    Outgoing mail server (SMTP):
    GOMAIL.com
    User Name: Firstname_Lastname
    Password: 123456

2. With the **Account Settings** dialog box still displayed, press [PrtScr].

3. Using the techniques you have practiced, in Word, **Save** a new document with the file name **6H_Scripts_Screens_Firstname_Lastname** Add the file name as a footer. **Paste** the screen capture, and then **Minimize** Word.

4. In the **Account Settings** dialog box, click **Close**. Display the **Inbox** folder, and delete any existing messages. Display the **Rules and Alerts** dialog box, and delete any existing rules. Import **o06H_Scripts_Inbox** into **Personal Folders**. Create a subfolder in the **Inbox**, typing **Scripts** as the folder name; be sure the folder contains *Mail and Post Items*. Display the **Scripts** folder.

5. Using the techniques you have practiced, press [PrtScr], and then **Paste** the screen capture into your **Word** document. **Minimize** Word.

6. Display the **Deleted Items** folder. From the **Arranged By** column heading, rearrange the items by **Type**. Locate the **Proposed scripts for next month** message from *Danny Golden*, and then drag

the message to the **Inbox** folder. Rearrange the items by **Date**.

7. Display the **Inbox** folder, and select the **Script for Flower Box show** message from *Danny Golden*. Open the **Create Rule** dialog box, and select the **From Danny Golden** check box. In the **Subject contains** box, delete the existing text, and type **Script** Click **Advanced Options**.

8. Under **Step 1: Select conditions(s)**, be sure the first two check boxes are selected, and then scroll to the bottom of the list and select the **on this machine only** check box. In the lower portion of the dialog box, under **Step 2: Edit the rule description (click an underlined value)**, click **Script**, and add the word **Scripts** in the **Search Text** dialog box so that the search in the subject is for both *Script* and *Scripts*. Click **OK**, and then click **Next**.

9. In the **Rules Wizard** dialog box, under **What do you want to do with the message?**, click the option to move the message to the specified folder—the **Scripts** folder. Click **Next**. There are no exceptions; click **Next**. Name the rule **Scripts from Danny** and select the **Run this rule on the messages already in "Inbox"** check box.

10. Using the techniques you have practiced, press [PrtScr], and then **Paste** the screen capture into your **Word** document. **Minimize** Word.

11. With the **Rules Wizard** dialog box displayed, click **Finish**.

12. Display the **Scripts** folder, ensure that the messages are arranged by **Date**, and then select all the messages in the folder. Create a new category in the **Master Category List** named **Danny** with the

(Project 6H–Scripts continues on the next page)

(Project 6H–Scripts continued)

color **None** selected. Close the **Color Categories** dialog box. Change the **Arranged By** column heading to **Categories**, and notice that the **Danny** category has been applied to selected messages. Reopen the **Color Categories** dialog box, and then delete the **Danny** category from the **Master Category List**. Change the **Arranged By** column heading to **Date**.

13. With the **Scripts** folder still displayed, archive the folder. In the **Archive** dialog box, in the **Archive items older than** box, type **05/10/09** Click **Browse**, and navigate to the location where you are storing your folders and projects. In the **Open Personal Folders** dialog box, in the **File name** box, delete any existing file name, and type **6H_Scripts_Firstname_Lastname** Click **OK** two times to close the dialog boxes and archive the messages. If a warning displays, indicating that the date you entered is in the future, click Yes to continue.

14. In the **Folder List**, display the **Archive Folders**, and then display the archived **Scripts** folder. Display the messages by

Categories. **Print** the messages in **Table Style** using the footer **6H_Scripts_Firstname_ Lastname** Submit the end result to your instructor as directed. Arrange the folder by **Date**.

15. Using the techniques you have practiced, press PrtScr, and then paste the screen capture into your **Word** document. With **6H_ Scripts_Screens_Firstname_Lastname** displayed, print the document. Submit the end result to your instructor as directed. **Save** your file and **Close** Word.

16. Display the **Rules and Alerts** dialog box, and delete all rules. In the **Navigation Pane**, close the **Archive Folders**. Expand the **Inbox** folder if necessary and delete the **Scripts** folder, delete the contents of the **Inbox** folder, and empty the **Deleted Items** folder, including the **Scripts** folder. **Reset** the **Table Style** print style.

17. Display the **Account Settings** dialog box, and **Remove** the **PHMAIL.com** account. **Close** Outlook.

End **You have completed Project 6H**

Mastering Outlook

Project 6I — Expenses

Objectives: 1. *Mange Mail Folders;* **3.** *Use Notes.*

In the following Mastering Outlook project, you will create notes and a Desktop Alert for Victor Ortiz's messages. Mr. Ortiz, the cohost of Southland Media's *Southland Gardens*, travels extensively to promote the company's television show. He generates expenses during his travels, and his busy schedule makes it difficult for him to remember to file expense reports. He finds that reminders help him stay organized. Your completed documents will look similar to the one shown in Figure 6.53.

For Project 6I, you will need the following file:

o06I_Expenses_Inbox

You will print three files with the following footers:
6I_Expenses_Notes_Firstname_Lastname
6I_Expenses_Messages_Firstname_Lastname
6I_Expenses_Screens_Firstname_Lastname

Figure 6.53

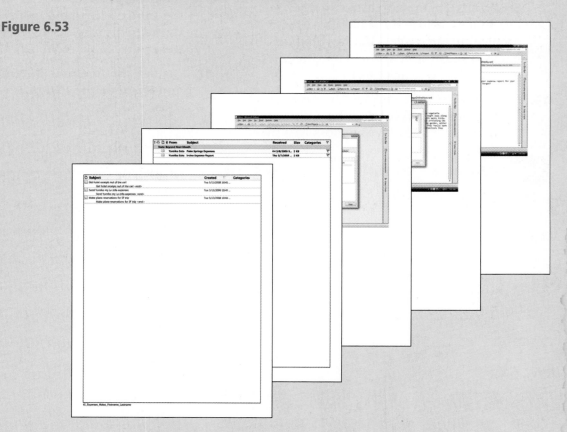

(Project 6I–Expenses continues on the next page)

Content-Based Assessments

(Project 6I–Expenses continued)

1. **Start** Outlook. Start the **New E-mail Accounts** wizard. Using the techniques you have practiced, create a new **POP3** account with the following information.

   Your Name: Firstname Lastname
   E-mail Address:
   Firstname_Lastname@GO.com
   Incoming mail server (POP3): GO.com
   Outgoing mail server (SMTP): PH.com
   User Name: Firstname_Lastname
   Password: 123456

2. With the **Account Settings** dialog box still displayed, press [PrtScr].

3. Using the techniques you have practiced, in Word, **Save** a new document with the file name **6I_Expenses_Screens_Firstname_Lastname** Add the file name as a footer. **Paste** the screen capture, and then **Minimize** Word.

4. In the **Account Settings** dialog box, click **Close**. Display the **Inbox** folder, and delete any existing messages. Check for and delete any existing rules. Using the techniques you have practiced, import **o06I_Expenses_Inbox** into **Personal Folders**.

5. Display the **Notes** folder. Create a new note, typing **Make plane reservations for SF trip** Create another note, typing **Send Yumiko my La Jolla expenses** Create another note, typing **Get hotel receipts out of the car!**

6. Change the **Current View** to **Notes List** view. **Print** the notes list in **Table Style** using the footer **6I_Expenses_Notes_Firstname_Lastname** Submit the end result to your instructor as directed. Change the **Current View** to **Icons**, and then delete the contents of the **Notes** folder.

7. Display the **Inbox** folder, and select the **Irvine Expense Report** message from *Yumiko Sato.* Create a rule for messages **From Yumiko Sato**. The action for the message should **display a Desktop Alert**. Name the rule **Yumiko Sato** and click **Finish**.

8. Display the **Rules and Alerts** dialog box, and select the **Yumiko Sato** rule.

9. Using the techniques you have practiced, press [PrtScr], and then paste the screen capture into your **Word** document. **Minimize** Word.

10. In the displayed **Rules and Alerts** dialog box, click **Run Rules Now**, and select the **Yumiko Sato** rule. Run the **Yumiko Sato** rule. When the Desktop Alerts for the **Palm Springs Expenses** message and **Irvine Expense Report** message display, place the pointer in the alerts to keep the alerts visible. Click the **Flag Item** button on each alert so that flags are assigned to both messages. Click **Run Now** again if you miss the alerts. **Close** all dialog boxes.

11. Display the **Customize View: Messages** dialog box, click **Filter**, and then click the **More Choices tab**. Select the **Only items which** check box, and be sure that the adjacent box displays *are flagged by me.* Display the filtered **Inbox**.

12. Using the techniques you have practiced, press [PrtScr], and then paste the screen capture into your **Word** document. **Minimize** Word.

13. **Print** the messages in **Table Style** using the footer **6I_Expenses_Messages_Firstname_Lastname** Submit the end result to your instructor as directed.

(Project 6I–Expenses continued)

14. On the Windows taskbar, click the **Word** button. With **6I_Expenses_Screens_ Firstname_Lastname** displayed, print the document. Submit the end result to your instructor as directed. **Save** your file and **Close** Word.

15. Clear the **Inbox** filter. Delete the **Yumiko Sato** rule. Delete the contents of the

Inbox. Empty the **Deleted Items** folder. Reset the **Table Style** print style. Display the **Account Settings** dialog box, and **Remove** the **GO.com** account. **Close** Outlook.

End **You have completed Project 6I** ⎯⎯⎯⎯⎯⎯⎯⎯⎯⎯⎯⎯

Outcomes-Based Assessments

Rubric

The following outcomes-based assessments are *open-ended assessments*. That is, there is no specific correct result; your result will depend on your approach to the information provided. Make *Professional Quality* your goal. Use the following scoring rubric to guide you in *how* to approach the problem and then to evaluate *how well* your approach solves the problem.

The *criteria*—Software Mastery, Content, Format and Layout, and Process—represent the knowledge and skills you have gained that you can apply to solving the problem. The *levels of performance*—Professional Quality, Approaching Professional Quality, or Needs Quality Improvement—help you and your instructor evaluate your result.

	Your completed project is of Professional Quality if you:	Your completed project is Approaching Professional Quality if you:	Your completed project Needs Quality Improvements if you:
1-Software Mastery	Choose and apply the most appropriate skills, tools, and features and identify efficient methods to solve the problem.	Choose and apply some appropriate skills, tools, and features, but not in the most efficient manner.	Choose inappropriate skills, tools, or features, or are inefficient in solving the problem.
2-Content	Construct a solution that is clear and well organized, contains content that is accurate, appropriate to the audience and purpose, and is complete. Provide a solution that contains no errors of spelling, grammar, or style.	Construct a solution in which some components are unclear, poorly organized, inconsistent, or incomplete. Misjudge the needs of the audience. Have some errors in spelling, grammar, or style, but the errors do not detract from comprehension.	Construct a solution that is unclear, incomplete, or poorly organized; contains some inaccurate or inappropriate content; or contains many errors of spelling, grammar, or style. Do not solve the problem.
3-Format and Layout	Format and arrange all elements to communicate information and ideas, clarify function, illustrate relationships, and indicate relative importance.	Apply appropriate format and layout features to some elements, but not others. Overuse features, causing minor distraction.	Apply format and layout that does not communicate information or ideas clearly. Do not use format and layout features to clarify function, illustrate relationships, or indicate relative importance. Use available features excessively, causing distraction.
4-Process	Use an organized approach that integrates planning, development, self-assessment, revision, and reflection.	Demonstrate an organized approach in some areas, but not others; or, use an insufficient process of organization throughout.	Do not use an organized approach to solve the problem.

Problem Solving

Project 6J — Fan Mail

Objectives: 1. *Manage Mail Folders;* **4.** *Archive Outlook Information;*
5. *Recover and Export Outlook Information.*

Elizabeth Robinson and Victor Ortiz, the cohosts of the television show
Southland Gardens, receive a significant amount of postal and electronic
mail from viewers. The show's management has begun sending thank-
you notes to all individuals who comment on the show. Ms. Robinson
has received several e-mail messages from viewers, some of which she
inadvertently deleted. In this project, you will organize Ms. Robinson's
viewer e-mail.

For Project 6J, you will need the following file:

o06J_Fan_Mail_Inbox

You will print two files with the following footers:
6J_Fan_Mail_Firstname_Lastname
6J_Fan_Mail_Screens_Firstname_Lastname

Start Outlook, and import **o06J_Fan_Mail_Inbox** into Personal Folders.
Create a new e-mail folder that is a subfolder of the Inbox. Create a Word
document with the file name **6J_Fan_Mail_Screens_Firstname_Lastname**
and add the file name in the footer. Paste a screen capture of your subfolder into the Word document. In the Deleted Items folder, use a view filter to locate all the messages with *Southland Gardens* in the subject, and
paste a screen capture of the filter into the Word document. Move the
messages to the new folder you created. Be sure to turn off the view filter
in the Deleted Items folder.

In the Inbox folder, locate a message from Brent Einhorn, and move the
message to the folder you created. Display the folder you created, and
archive the folder, archiving any message older than 05/10/09. The location of the archive file should be the drive or folder you are using to store
your files; and you should use an archive file name of **6J_Fan_Mail_
Firstname_Lastname**

After you have archived the folder you created, open the Archive Folders in
the Folder List, and locate your archived folder. Paste a screen capture of
your archived folder into the Word document. Print the contents of the
archived folder using an appropriate print style and the footer **6J_Fan_Mail_
Firstname_Lastname** Print the *6J_Fan_Mail_Screens_Firstname_Lastname*
document. Submit the end results to your instructor as directed.

Close the Archive Folders, delete the folder you created and the contents
of the Inbox. Empty the Deleted Items folder. Delete any rules you
created, and reset the printer style you used.

End **You have completed Project 6J**

chapter six	**Problem Solving**

Project 6K — Soil

Objectives: 1. *Manage Mail Folders;* **2.** *Modify the Master Category List;* **3.** *Use Notes.*

Elizabeth Robinson is preparing a show for Southland Media's *Southland Gardens* television show on soil preparation, composting, and other soil-related gardening topics. She has received various messages on the topic and wants to organize her Inbox, separating messages from Danny Golden, her supervisor, from other show-related messages. She also needs to remind herself of several tasks related to the project. In this project, you will organize Ms. Robinson's Inbox.

For Project 6K, you will need the following file:

o06K_Soil_Inbox

You will print four files with the following footers:
6K_Soil_Inbox_Firstname_Lastname
6K_Soil_Folder_Firstname_Lastname
6K_Soil_Notes_Firstname_Lastname
6K_Soil_Screens_Firstname_Lastname

Start Outlook, and import **o06K_Soil_Inbox** into Personal Folders. Create a Word document with the file name **6K_Soil_Screens_Firstname_ Lastname** and add the file name in the footer. Create a view filter in the Inbox for all the messages from Danny Golden, and paste a screen capture of the filtered Inbox into your Word document. Create a category in the Master Category List, and assign these messages to that category. Create another view filter for the Inbox, and locate all the messages with *AllTurf* or *soil* in their subject or message body. Paste a screen capture of the filtered Inbox into your Word document. Create another category, and assign these messages to that category.

In the unfiltered Inbox, display the messages in a view that shows the category assignments. Print the folder in an appropriate print style using the footer **6K_Soil_Inbox_Firstname_Lastname** Submit the end result to your instructor as directed.

Create a new mail folder for the *AllTurf* and *soil* messages, and move the messages into the new folder. Paste a screen capture showing your sub-folder into your Word document. Print the new folder using an appropriate print style and the footer **6K_Soil_Folder_Firstname_Lastname** Submit the end result to your instructor as directed. Delete the folder you created.

Display the Notes folder, and create at least three notes. Choose any subject for the notes that relates to gardening. Display the Notes folder in a view that shows the text of the notes, and print the folder in an

(Project 6K–Soil continues on the next page)

Outcomes-Based Assessments

Problem Solving

(Project 6K–Soil continued)

appropriate print style using the footer **6K_Soil_Notes_Firstname_Lastname** Print the *6K_Soil_Screens_Firstname_Lastname* document. Submit the end results to your instructor as directed. Restore the folder to its default view, and delete the notes you created. Restore the Master Category List to its default categories, delete the contents of the Inbox and the Deleted Items folder, and reset any print style you used. Close Outlook.

End **You have completed Project 6K** ⎯⎯⎯⎯⎯⎯

Problem Solving

Project 6L — Fertilizer

Objectives: 1. *Manage Mail Folders;* **2.** *Modify the Master Category List;* **3.** *Use Notes.*

Elizabeth Robinson has contracted with one of *Southland Gardens'* principal sponsors to be its spokesperson. She would like to organize all her e-mail relating to the company. She also wants to start using the product in her personal gardening activities and wants to ask the company to provide her with some of its products. In this project, you will organize Ms. Robinson's mail and create some notes for her.

For Project 6L, you will need the following file:

o06L_Fertilizer_Inbox

You will print three files with the following footers:
6L_Fertilizer_Folder_Firstname_Lastname
6L_Fertilizer_Screens_Firstname_Lastname
6L_Fertilizer_Garden_Firstname_Lastname

Start Outlook, and import **o06L_Fertilizer_Inbox** into your Inbox folder. Create a Word document with the file name **6L_Fertilizer_Screens_Firstname_Lastname** and add the file name in the footer. Create a view filter in the Inbox to display all messages with the words *AllTurf* in the subject or body of the message. Paste a screen capture of the filtered Inbox into your Word document. Create a new folder as an Inbox subfolder, and move these messages into the new folder. Paste a screen capture of the Inbox subfolder into your Word document. Display the new folder, create a new category, and assign the messages to the category. Display the folder in a view that shows the category assignment. Print the folder in an appropriate print style using the footer **6L_Fertilizer_Folder_Firstname_Lastname** Print the *6L_Fertilizer_Screens_Firstname_Lastname* document. Submit the end results to your instructor as directed. Clear the view filter of the Inbox.

Display the Notes folder, and create four notes that relate to gardening and garden products. Assign the notes to the same category you created for your messages. Display the folder in a view that shows the text of your notes and the category assignments. Print the folder in an appropriate print style using the footer **6L_Fertilizer_Garden_Firstname_Lastname** Submit the end result to your instructor as directed.

Restore the Master Category List to its default categories. Delete the notes you created, and display the folder in its default view. Delete the folder you created, the contents of the Inbox and the Deleted Items folder, including your folder. Reset any print styles you used. Close Outlook.

End **You have completed Project 6L** ⎯⎯⎯⎯⎯⎯

GO! with Help

Project 6M — *GO!* with Help

If you have an Exchange Server e-mail account, you can use the Out of Office feature to respond to received messages while you are out of the office. You might want to do this to alert senders that you are on vacation or otherwise unavailable to respond to their messages. Your automated reply can include the date of your return. You can enhance the Out of Office feature by applying rules to the incoming messages. For example, you might want to give one type of reply to your coworkers and a different reply to customers. Your customers could be given a message suggesting someone else they might contact in your absence.

1. **Start** Outlook. From the **Help** menu, click **Microsoft Office Outlook Help**.

2. In the **Outlook Help** window, click the **Search arrow**, and then under **Content from this computer**, make certain **Outlook Help** is selected to view offline help.

3. In the **Search** box, type **Automatic replies** and press Enter. Click **Automatically reply to incoming messages while out of the office**.

4. In the **Outlook Help** window, read the displayed information.

5. In the **Outlook Help** window, if necessary, click the **Show Table of Contents** button to display the **Table of Contents** task pane. In the **Table of Contents** task pane, scroll down if necessary, and click **Edit the Out of Office Assistant Rules**.

6. Read the information, and click the displayed links. When finished, **Close** the **Outlook Help** window, and **Close** Outlook.

End **You have completed Project 6M** ——————————

Glossary

Accept A meeting invitation response in which you agree to attend a meeting and that notifies the meeting organizer, by sending an e-mail message, that you will attend.

Adaptive An item, such as a menu, that can adapt to the way you work by displaying the commands you use most frequently.

Annual event A recurring event that happens once a year.

Appointment A calendar activity occurring at a specific time and day that does not require inviting other people or reserving a room or equipment.

Appointment area A one-day view of the day's calendar entries.

Archive To move Outlook information that you want to keep to a location for storage and future access.

Archive Folders Outlook's default name for the location of files stored for future access.

At sign (@) A symbol used to separate the two parts of an e-mail address.

Attachment A separate file included with an e-mail message, such as a Word file, a spreadsheet file, or an image file.

Attendees The name Outlook uses to refer to people who are participating in a meeting.

AutoArchive The Outlook feature that automatically moves information that you want to keep to a location for storage and future access.

AutoComplete The Outlook feature that assists you in typing addresses by suggesting previously typed addresses based on the first character you type.

Banner area A location at the top of the calendar that displays important information, including the Day, Week, and Month view buttons.

Bcc An abbreviation for *blind courtesy cop* or *blind carbon copy.*

Black border An outline around an appointment, which is an indication that the appointment is selected.

Blank form A lined page added to the printout of the Card Style print style that you can use to manually list new contacts.

Blank rule A message rule that you define by specifying your own conditions and actions as you create it.

Blind carbon copy (Bcc) Another name for blind courtesy copy.

Blind courtesy copy (Bcc) A type of e-mail message in which the recipient receives a copy of the message, but the Bcc recipient's name is not visible to other recipients of the message.

Block In Windows Live Messenger, the action of preventing someone from contacting you or seeing when you are online.

Business days Days of the week that are not a Saturday, Sunday, or a holiday.

Busy The default free/busy setting that Outlook assigns to all new appointments and that is indicated by an appointment with a blue border.

Calendar The Outlook component that stores your schedule and calendar-related information.

Carbon copy (Cc) The term, formerly referring to a paper copy made with carbon paper, used to denote an electronic copy of an e-mail communication. Another name for courtesy copy.

Categories Colors, words, or phrases assigned to Outlook items for the purpose of finding, sorting, filtering, or grouping them.

Cc An abbreviation for *courtesy copy* or *carbon copy.*

Chat A real-time conversation on a computer whereby one participant types and presses the Enter key, and the typing displays on the other participant's computer.

Client A program that runs on a computer and that relies on the server to perform some of its operations.

Collapse The action of hiding information by clicking a minus symbol (−).

Column headings Text that identifies message fields.

Comments area The lower half of a form where you may enter information not otherwise specified in the form.

Conditions In a rule, the criteria that determine how incoming e-mail messages will be handled.

Contact A person or organization, inside or outside your own organization, about whom you can save information, such as street and e-mail addresses, telephone and fax numbers, Web page addresses, birthdays, and pictures.

Contact Index A set of buttons used to quickly display a specific section of the Contacts list when the list is displayed in the default Business Cards view, as well as other views.

Contacts The component of Outlook that serves as your e-mail address book for storing information about people, organizations, and businesses with whom you communicate.

Contacts folder The default location in which Outlook stores information about your contacts.

Context-sensitive A term applied to commands on a shortcut menu because they refer only to the item to which you are pointing.

Courtesy copy (Cc) Represented by the letters *Cc*, a copy of an e-mail message that is sent to a recipient who needs to view the message.

Date Navigator A one-month, or multiple-month, view of the calendar you can use to display specific days in the month.

Decline A meeting invitation response in which you do not agree to attend a meeting and that notifies the meeting organizer, by sending an e-mail message, that you will not attend.

Desktop Alert A notification that displays on your desktop briefly when you receive an e-mail message, meeting request, or task request.

Distribution list A collection of contacts to whom you send e-mail messages.

Domain name The second portion of an e-mail address, which defines the host name of the recipient's mail server.

Editors Programs with which you can create or make changes to existing files.

Event A calendar activity that lasts 24 hours or longer.

Exceptions In a message rule, the criteria that exclude a message from the specified action to be taken, when all other conditions of the rule are satisfied.

Exchange Server Special Server software that provides a system for sharing Outlook information among members on a network.

Exchange Server environment A shared environment for Outlook that requires a special server and that is set up by your system administrator.

Expand The action of showing information by clicking a plus symbol.

Export To copy Outlook data into a file that can be used by another program.

Field An element of information within an Outlook item, such as the company name in a contact or the subject of a message.

Filter A set of instructions that causes some items in a folder to display—and others *not* to display—based on conditions you define.

Flagging Marking a message with a flag to draw attention to the message.

Form A window in Outlook used to collect and display information.

Formatting text The process of setting the appearance of message text by changing the color, shading, or font size of the text.

Forwarding Sending an e-mail message you have received to someone who did not originally receive the message.

Free/busy information A group of four indicators displayed by Outlook that can be viewed by others who have the ability to view your calendar that indicate your availability for a date and time in your calendar.

Full week view The calendar is arranged in frames displaying a complete seven-day week.

Global The term used to refer to Outlook settings that apply to all, not just some, of Outlook's folders.

Hotmail Microsoft's free, Web-based e-mail service with which you can read and write e-mail messages on any computer that has a Web browser and an Internet connection.

HTML A format for text that can include numbering, bullets, lines, backgrounds, and multimedia features that can be viewed in a Web browser.

Icons Graphic representations of objects you can select and open. In a task list, a graphic object that indicates an item type.

IM The abbreviation for *Instant Messaging*.

Import The action of bringing a file from another program or location into Outlook.

Importance Marks that are applied to messages based on the urgency of the message—for example, information that should be read immediately or information that can be read later.

Inbox The Outlook folder that stores the Mail component.

Instant Messaging A form of online, real-time communication over the Internet in which users communicate with each other in a private, text-based dialogue.

Invisible In Windows Live Messenger, when you select *appear offline* as your status, other users will not be able to see that you are online, but you will be able to see them.

Items Elements of information in Outlook, such as a message, a contact, an appointment, or a task.

Journal A folder that provides a location to record and track all your activities and interactions if you want to do so, and that is a record of your day-to-day events.

Keyboard shortcut A combination of keys on the keyboard that performs a command.

Local Calendar The Outlook calendar stored on the hard drive of your computer.

Master Category List The Outlook-supported list of colors and keywords used for grouping, filtering, and sorting Outlook information.

Meeting A calendar activity that requires inviting other people and/or scheduling a room or equipment.

Meeting form Similar to an Appointment form, this form includes a To: box, a Send button, and a Cancel Invitation button.

Meeting organizer The individual who issues a meeting invitation.

Memo Style This style prints the text of selected items one at a time, for example the contents of an e-mail message.

Menus Lists of commands within categories.

Message delivery options Optional settings for an e-mail message that can include the time a message should be sent or the address that should be used for replies.

Message header The basic information about an e-mail message, such as the sender's name, the date sent, and the subject.

Microsoft Exchange Server An e-mail server in a shared environment for Outlook used by businesses or organizations.

Microsoft Outlook Express A basic, no-cost e-mail service with some of the features of Microsoft Outlook that is included in Microsoft Internet Explorer.

Minus symbol The symbol − that, when clicked, collapses (hides) groups of information such as categories or folder lists.

Natural language   Language spoken or written by humans, as opposed to a computer programming language.

Navigate   The term used to describe moving around within Outlook or other software applications.

Navigation Pane   A column on the left side of the Outlook screen that contains panes, shortcuts, and buttons for quick access to Outlook's components and folders.

New Item Alert   A notification button that displays on your Windows taskbar when you receive an e-mail message, meeting request, or task request.

Notes   The Outlook component that is the electronic equivalent of sticky paper notes, used to keep track of bits of information you want to use later.

Notes area   A blank area of a form that can be used to type information about a contact that is not otherwise specified in the form.

Notification area   The rightmost portion of the Windows taskbar, next to the system time, in which Outlook displays information such as alerts.

Office Clipboard   A memory area in which you can collect text and graphics from any Office program and then place them in another area of the same program or in a different program.

Offline   A computer connection status in which you are not connected to a network or to the public Internet.

Online   A computer connection status in which you are connected to a network or to the public Internet.

Optional attendee   A person whose attendance at a meeting is not required and without whom the meeting can still take place.

Out of Office   A free/busy setting that indicates that you are away from your office and not available for other meetings or appointments and is indicated by an appointment with a purple border.

Outlook Today   A summary view of your schedule, tasks, and e-mail for the current day.

Overlay mode   A view that displays multiple calendars in an overlapping arrangement.

Pathname   The sequence of the drive letter and folder names that identifies the location of a file.

Person Names online presence indicator   For contacts that have a Windows Live ID, a button displayed next to the contact's e-mail address that indicates the contact's online status in Windows Messenger.

Personal Folders   The name of the file, which uses the *.pst* file name extension, that contains data stored in Outlook folders.

Personal information manager   A program that enables you to store information about your contacts and tasks you need to complete as well as keep track of your daily schedule.

Plain text   A format for text that allows no special formatting.

Plus symbol   The symbol + that, when clicked, expands (shows) the display of information such as categories or folder lists.

POP3   A common protocol that is used to retrieve e-mail messages from an Internet e-mail server.

Print screen   A Windows feature that creates a screen capture and stores that image on the Windows Clipboard.

Print styles   A combination of paper and page settings applied to printed Outlook items.

Profile   The Outlook feature that identifies which e-mail account you use and where related data is stored.

Propose New Time   A meeting invitation response in which you request that the meeting organizer change the meeting to a time at which you can attend.

Range of recurrence   The date of the final occurrence of an appointment based on its end date or the number of times an appointment occurs.

RE: A prefix added to a reply to an e-mail message; commonly used to mean *in regard to.*

Read/write access   A type of access to a server that provides you with the ability to both view and store information on that server.

Reading Pane   An Outlook window in which you can preview a message without opening it.

Reassign   The action of assigning a received task to someone else.

Recurrence pattern   The frequency of an appointment, which may be daily, weekly, monthly, or yearly.

Recurring appointments   Appointments that occur regularly on specific dates and times and at specific intervals and have associated reminders.

Recurring task   Any activity that occurs repeatedly on a regular basis.

Reminder   An Outlook window, accompanied by a tone, that displays automatically at a designated date and time before appointments or tasks.

Remote Assistance   A Windows Live Messenger application with which a contact can help you from his or her computer.

Required attendees   A term used to refer to meeting attendees without whom, because of their special knowledge or input, a meeting cannot take place.

Resource   A facility or piece of equipment whose availability and use can be scheduled by Outlook.

Ribbon   An area above an Outlook form that displays commands, organized by groups and tabs.

Rich text   A format for text that can include character and paragraph formatting and embedded graphics.

Right-click   The action of clicking the right mouse button; frequently this action displays a shortcut menu.

RTF   A type of file using rich text format.

Rule description   An explanation of any actions a rule performs on a message.

Rules   One or more actions taken on messages to organize a folder, based on certain conditions, along with any exceptions to those conditions.

Rules Wizard   A program that guides you through the process of creating a message rule.

Scheduling button The button that reveals a Meeting form view that displays a list of all meeting attendees and their available free/busy information.

Screen capture An image of what is displayed on your monitor.

Screen name The name other Windows Live Messenger users see when they have your name on their Windows Live Messenger Contacts list.

ScreenTip A small box that displays the name of a screen element.

Scrolling The action of moving a pane or window vertically (up or down) or horizontally (side to side) to bring unseen areas into view.

Selecting text Highlighting text by dragging with the mouse.

Sensitivity A security label that is applied to messages that should not be read by others because of the message content.

Server A computer or device on a network that handles shared network resources.

Sharing Folders A Windows Live Message feature that enables both you and your contact to use a file at the same time.

Shortcut menu A list of context-related commands that displays when you right-click a screen element.

Signature A block of text that is added at the end of a message and that commonly includes a name, title, address, and phone number.

Status area In Windows Live Messenger, an area at the bottom of the Conversation window that indicates when the other party is typing or when the last message was received.

Status report An e-mail message sent to the originator of the task request to indicate a task's progress or completion.

Submenu A second-level menu activated by selecting a main menu option.

Syntax When referring to e-mail, the way in which the parts of an e-mail message are put together.

Table An arrangement of information with a separate row for each item and a separate column for each field.

Table Style This style can print multiple items in a list with the visible columns displayed, for example the contents of the Inbox.

Tabs Part of the user interface in Outlook 2007 that provide access to different commands based on particular activities, such as setting message options or formatting text.

Task A personal or work-related activity that you want to track to completion.

Task assignee The person to whom a task has been assigned.

Task owner The individual currently responsible for completing an assigned task.

Task request A task sent in an e-mail message asking the recipient to complete the activity.

TBA A common abbreviation for *To Be Arranged* or *To Be Announced*.

Template In rule creation, a set of predefined conditions and actions used for common processing tasks.

Tentative A free/busy setting indicating that you have scheduled an appointment but that it is not confirmed; also, a meeting response in which the meeting organizer is notified that you might attend the meeting.

Third party Someone not included in the original e-mail message exchange to whom you forward a message.

Time Bar The times next to the appointment area of the calendar, displayed in one-hour intervals.

To-Do Bar An Outlook feature that provides a consolidated view of tasks, appointments, and flagged messages.

Today button A button on the Standard toolbar used to change the calendar to display the date, based on your computer system's clock.

Toolbars Rows of buttons, usually located below the menu bar, from which you can perform commands with a single click of the mouse.

Tracking button The button that reveals a Meeting form view that displays a list of the name of each meeting attendee, the attendee's status as required or optional, and the attendee's response status.

Tri-fold Style A calendar print style that includes the daily calendar, the Daily Task List, and the weekly calendar.

Unassigned copy A duplicate of an assigned task that lists you as the owner and to which you can make changes.

Update An e-mail message showing the changed task form that is sent to the person who made the task request and also to any prior owners of the task.

Update list A list that includes the name of the person who originally sent the task request plus the names of everyone who received the task request, reassigned the task to someone else, or chose to keep an updated copy of the task in his or her task list.

vCard An Internet standard file format for creating and sharing virtual business cards.

.vfb The abbreviation for *virtual free/busy*, and the file extension for the Outlook file that stores an individual's calendar information.

View filter A feature that leaves all the messages in a folder, but just displays selected messages based upon user-defined instructions.

Views Ways to look at similar information in different arrangements and formats.

VIP An abbreviation for *Very Important Person*.

Virtual free/busy A type of file that stores an individual's Outlook calendar information.

Ways to Organize Inbox pane An Outlook pane used to manage messages with colors, folders, and views.

Weekly Style A calendar print style that arranges the appointments in frames for each day of the week.

Whiteboard A Windows Live Messenger feature with which you can draw and type simultaneously with a contact.

Windows Clipboard   A temporary storage area used by Windows to hold one piece of data, such as text, a graphic, or a file.

Windows Live   A free Microsoft service that enables you to sign into several different Web sites for services such as instant messaging and e-mail, using a single user name.

Windows Live Messenger   A Windows communication program that is integrated into Outlook, with which you can send instant messages to your online contacts.

Wizard   A tool that walks you through a process in a step-by-step manner.

Wordwrap   The Outlook feature in which text typed in the Message form is moved automatically from the end of one line to the beginning of the next line to fit within the established margins.

Work week view   The calendar is arranged in frames displaying weekdays—Monday through Friday.

Working hours   The weekday hours between 8:00 a.m. and 5:00 p.m.

Index

SINGLE PC LICENSE AGREEMENT AND LIMITED WARRANTY

READ THIS LICENSE CAREFULLY BEFORE OPENING THIS PACKAGE. BY OPENING THIS PACKAGE, YOU ARE AGREEING TO THE TERMS AND CONDITIONS OF THIS LICENSE. IF YOU DO NOT AGREE, DO NOT OPEN THE PACKAGE. PROMPTLY RETURN THE UNOPENED PACKAGE AND ALL ACCOMPANYING ITEMS TO THE PLACE YOU OBTAINED THEM. *THESE TERMS APPLY TO ALL LICENSED SOFTWARE ON THE DISK EXCEPT THAT THE TERMS FOR USE OF ANY SHAREWARE OR FREEWARE ON TH E DISKETTES ARE AS SET FORTH IN THE ELECTRONIC LICENSE LOCATED ON THE DISK:*

1. GRANT OF LICENSE and OWNERSHIP: The enclosed computer programs ("Software") are licensed, not sold, to you by Prentice-Hall, Inc. ("We" or the "Company") and in consideration of your purchase or adoption of the accompanying Company textbooks and/or other materials, and your agreement to these terms. We reserve any rights not granted to you. You own only the disk(s) but we and/or our licensors own the Software itself. This license allows you to use and display your copy of the Software on a single computer (i.e., with a single CPU) at a single location for academic use only, so long as you comply with the terms of this Agreement. You may make one copy for back up, or transfer your copy to another CPU, provided that the Software is usable on only one computer.

2. RESTRICTIONS: You may not transfer or distribute the Software or documentation to anyone else. Except for backup, you may not copy the documentation or the Software. You may not network the Software or otherwise use it on more than one computer or computer terminal at the same time. You may not reverse engineer, disassemble, decompile, modify, adapt, translate, or create derivative works based on the Software or the Documentation. You may be held legally responsible for any copying or copyright infringement which is caused by your failure to abide by the terms of these restrictions.

3. TERMINATION: This license is effective until terminated. This license will terminate automatically without notice from the Company if you fail to comply with any provisions or limitations of this license. Upon termination, you shall destroy the Documentation and all copies of the Software. All provisions of this Agreement as to limitation and disclaimer of warranties, limitation of liability, remedies or damages, and our ownership rights shall survive termination.

4. DISCLAIMER OF WARRANTY: THE COMPANY AND ITS LICENSORS MAKE NO WARRANTIES ABOUT THE SOFTWARE, WHICH IS PROVIDED "AS-IS." IF THE DISK IS DEFECTIVE IN MATERIALS OR WORKMANSHIP, YOUR ONLY REMEDY IS TO RETURN IT TO THE COMPANY WITHIN 30 DAYS FOR REPLACEMENT UNLESS THE COMPANY DETERMINES IN GOOD FAITH THAT THE DISK HAS BEEN MISUSED OR IMPROPERLY INSTALLED, REPAIRED, ALTERED OR DAMAGED. THE COMPANY DISCLAIMS ALL WARRANTIES, EXPRESS OR IMPLIED, INCLUDING WITHOUT LIMITATION, THE IMPLIED WARRANTIES OF MERCHANTABILITY AND FITNESS FOR A PARTICULAR PURPOSE. THE COMPANY DOES NOT WARRANT, GUARANTEE OR MAKE ANY REPRESENTATION REGARDING THE ACCURACY, RELIABILITY, CURRENTNESS, USE, OR RESULTS OF USE, OF THE SOFTWARE.

5. LIMITATION OF REMEDIES AND DAMAGES: IN NO EVENT, SHALL THE COMPANY OR ITS EMPLOYEES, AGENTS, LICENSORS OR CONTRACTORS BE LIABLE FOR ANY INCIDENTAL, INDIRECT, SPECIAL OR CONSEQUENTIAL DAMAGES ARISING OUT OF OR IN CONNECTION WITH THIS LICENSE OR THE SOFTWARE, INCLUDING, WITHOUT LIMITATION, LOSS OF USE, LOSS OF DATA, LOSS OF INCOME OR PROFIT, OR OTHER LOSSES SUSTAINED AS A RESULT OF INJURY TO ANY PERSON, OR LOSS OF OR DAMAGE TO PROPERTY, OR CLAIMS OF THIRD PARTIES, EVEN IF THE COMPANY OR AN AUTHORIZED REPRESENTATIVE OF THE COMPANY HAS BEEN ADVISED OF THE POSSIBILITY OF SUCH DAMAGES. SOME JURISDICTIONS DO NOT ALLOW THE LIMITATION OF DAMAGES IN CERTAIN CIRCUMSTANCES, SO THE ABOVE LIMITATIONS MAY NOT ALWAYS APPLY.

6. GENERAL: THIS AGREEMENT SHALL BE CONSTRUED IN ACCORDANCE WITH THE LAWS OF THE UNITED STATES OF AMERICA AND THE STATE OF NEW YORK, APPLICABLE TO CONTRACTS MADE IN NEW YORK, AND SHALL BENEFIT THE COMPANY, ITS AFFILIATES AND ASSIGNEES. This Agreement is the complete and exclusive statement of the agreement between you and the Company and supersedes all proposals, prior agreements, oral or written, and any other communications between you and the company or any of its representatives relating to the subject matter. If you are a U.S. Government user, this Software is licensed with "restricted rights" as set forth in subparagraphs (a)-(d) of the Commercial Computer-Restricted Rights clause at FAR 52.227-19 or in subparagraphs (c)(1)(ii) of the Rights in Technical Data and Computer Software clause at DFARS 252.227-7013, and similar clauses, as applicable.

Should you have any questions concerning this agreement or if you wish to contact the Company for any reason, please contact in writing:

Multimedia Production
Higher Education Division
Prentice-Hall, Inc.
1 Lake Street
Upper Saddle River NJ 07458